A Vision Unfulfilled

A Vision Unfulfilled

Russia and the Soviet Union in the Twentieth Century

JOHN M. THOMPSON

With Historiographic Essays by

WILLIAM GLEASON

Doane College

D. C. Heath and Company
Lexington, Massachusetts   Toronto

Address editorial correspondence to:

D. C. Heath and Company
125 Spring Street
Lexington, MA 02173

Acquisitions Editor: *James Miller*
Developmental Editor: *Lauren Johnson*
Production Editor: *Andrea Cava*
Photo Researcher: *Mark Corsey*
Production Coordinator: *Michael O'Dea*
Permissions Editor: *Margaret Roll*

International Standard Book Number: 0–669–28291–X

Library of Congress Catalog Number: 94–73265

10 9 8 7 6 5 4 3

PREFACE

Why This Text?

Most histories of modern Russia written before 1991 underscore the stability and durability of the Soviet system that emerged from the Russian Revolution of 1917. The fallacy of this premise, however, became obvious with the Soviet state's disintegration between 1989 and 1991. In addition, the U.S.S.R.'s collapse revealed the powerful impact on Soviet society of escalating urbanization, nearly universal secondary education, and growing access to information. The confluence of these forces catalyzed antisystem attitudes and values among the Soviet populace. The Soviet empire's implosion also highlighted the role of non-Russian nationalism, long smoldering under the cloak of Soviet patriotism.

Writing a book that interprets twentieth-century Russian history in the aftermath of the revolution of 1989 to 1991 requires a thorough recasting of the subject; it is not enough to refurbish a pre-1991 interpretation "around the edges." The conviction that modern Russian history demands a fresh, new analysis underlies this volume. *A Vision Unfulfilled* reinterprets late tsarist and Soviet history in light of recent insights and events. It also seeks to balance treatment of domestic events with explanations of foreign policy and to show the interaction between these two aspects of modern Russian history. Equally important, the book strives to redress most texts' neglect of the non-Russian peoples living in the Russian and Soviet empires. Without slighting developments among the Russians or at the state's center, the narrative delineates the position of the minority groups, from Balts and Ukrainians to Central Asians, under tsarist and Soviet rule; the stirring of nationalism among them; and the grievances that finally led in 1987 through 1991 to non-Russians' rejection of Soviet and Russian tutelage. Further, the book includes as much social and cultural history as space permitted without losing sight of the central role of politics and economics.

Approach and Features

In preparing *A Vision Unfulfilled*, I weighed conservative, liberal, radical, and neo-Marxist interpretations while striving to maintain my own strongly held centrist viewpoint. Although I did not hesitate to present personal judgments concerning key issues and personalities, I labeled these assessments as my opinion. It is my belief that texts ought not to "tell students what to think"; thus I have endeavored to preserve an even-handed presentation. I also built my analyses on the most important recent scholarship, including findings based on access to newly opened archives.

To enhance students' appreciation of crucial issues of historical research and interpretation, Heath's editors and I commissioned Professor William Gleason of Doane College, a specialist in late tsarist history, to prepare a historiographical addendum—the "New Light on the Issues" essay—for each chapter. These brief essays introduce students to key challenges of historical study and judgment in modern Russian and Soviet history. In each essay, Professor Gleason summarizes conflicting views on significant topics, assesses recent scholarship, poses provocative questions, and encourages students to develop their own conclusions.

Drawing on my experience teaching twentieth-century Russian history at Indiana University and other institutions, I have aimed the book primarily at students, striving for clarity, logical organization, and liveliness. At the same time, I hope that the book's presentation and analysis will interest lay readers curious about the drama and mystery of Russia's stormy evolution since 1900. With this goal in mind, I open each chapter with a concise historical vignette of a dramatic episode from the relevant period. A selective Further Reading list is also available at the end of each chapter for readers who wish additional information. Finally, the appendixes—an abbreviations key, a list of prominent leaders in the late tsarist and Soviet periods, and a selective chronology—and a glossary of terms should serve as convenient reference tools.

How to Use This Text

A Vision Unfulfilled is designed for the one-semester, upper-division course in modern Russian history. Such courses sometimes begin with the year 1855 or 1861, sometimes with 1894 or 1900, often with 1914 or 1917. Moreover, in some courses a survey of Russian history is a prerequisite; in others, it is not. To encourage flexible use of the text and to make it accessible to the widest number of advanced undergraduate students, I focused the narrative on the century between 1894 and 1994. However, I included an introductory chapter on key developments from the mid-1850s to 1900 for students without a background in Russian history or whose earlier study of tsarist times ended with 1861. Students already familiar with late nineteenth-century Russia can skip this introductory chapter and plunge immediately into Chapter 2, perhaps replacing Chapter 1 with supplementary reading in Russian and Soviet fiction or with additional historical accounts.

The book's twelve chapters are roughly equal in length; if all are assigned, students need to read approximately one chapter a week during a semester. Such a schedule would still leave two weeks for extra projects, supplemental readings, or other activities.

Because students are accustomed to the Western calendar, all dates in the book are given according to the modern calendar used in Western Europe since the eighteenth century. Until 1917 Russia continued to employ the Julian calendar, which ran twelve days behind the Western calendar in the nineteenth century and thirteen days behind in the twentieth century. In a few cases where old calendar dates are significant (for example, during the 1917 revolution), the text explains the two dates. Except for Anglicized names, customary transliteration of names has been followed, although *ii* is rendered as *y*.

Acknowledgments

Originally, I had hoped to coauthor this text with Professor Donald Raleigh of the University of North Carolina. To my great regret, he proved too busy with his evolving research on postrevolutionary Saratov to participate. Nevertheless, he warmly encouraged my efforts and provided wise counsel concerning both new materials that I should consult and clashing interpretations that I needed to consider. Professor Raleigh also meticulously critiqued outlines and first drafts of each chapter. His support and assistance proved crucial throughout this book's preparation, but naturally he is not responsible for any errors or interpretations.

The following reviewers offered helpful advice:

John T. Alexander, *University of Kansas;* John Barber, *Ball State University;* John Bushnell, *Northwestern University;* William Chase, *University of Pittsburgh;* Barbara Clements, *University of Akron;* Wallace Daniel, *Baylor University;* Richard Debo, *Simon Fraser University;* Eric Duskin, *Northern Illinois University;* David Edwards, *University of Arkansas;* Daniel Field, *Syracuse University;* Cathy Frierson, *University of New Hampshire;* Joseph T. Fuhrmann, *Murray State University;* Frederick Giffin, *Arizona State University;* R. Edward Glatfelter, *Utah State University;* Abbott Gleason, *Brown University;* Steven Hoch, *Iowa University;* Heather Hogan, *Oberlin University;* Larry Holmes, *University of South Alabama;* Charles Holt, *Morehead State University;* David McDonald, *University of Wisconsin;* Michael Melancon, *Auburn University;* J. Gregory Oswald, *University of Arizona;* Peter Petschauer, *Appalachian State University;* Hugh Ragsdale, *University of Alabama;* Elmo Roach, *Bradley University;* Marian Jean Rubchak, *Valparaiso University;* Rochelle Ruthschild, *Norwich University;* Alfred Senn, *University of Wisconsin-Madison;* John Steinberg, *Georgia Southern University;* Ted Uldricks, *University of North Carolina;* Mark von Hagan, *Columbia*

University; Joseph Wieczynski, *Virginia Polytechnic Institute;* John Windhausen, *Saint Anselm College.*

James Miller, senior acquisitions editor for history at D. C. Heath, saw the need for a new text with a post-Soviet perspective and asked me to write such a book. His advice and support improved the work at every stage. I am also deeply grateful to Lauren Johnson, developmental editor, who patiently coordinated reviewers' and her own comments and made many valuable suggestions. In addition, her careful editing greatly enhanced the clarity and readability of the text. Finally, she played a key role in selecting illustrations; recommending tables, charts, and maps; and preparing the reference aids. Many thanks as well to Margaret Roll, permissions editor at Heath; Andrea Cava, production editor; Alwyn Velásquez, designer; and Mark Corsey, photo researcher. I wish also to express my gratitude to the reference and circulation librarians of Bowdoin College, who assisted me cheerfully in finding the books and articles that I needed. Most important, I want to thank my wife, Anne, for her constant encouragement and support.

J.M.T.

CONTENTS

MAPS

GRAPHS, CHARTS, AND TABLES

A Vision Unfulfilled

INTRODUCTION

~

Soviet Socialism: A Bold Alternative

"It makes your head swim," Lenin marveled to his revolutionary comrade, Leon Trotsky.[1] It was early November 1917, and Lenin's radical socialist party, the Bolsheviks, was about to seize power in Russia. Lenin was right to be astounded. The Bolsheviks had been a tiny fringe party when the tsarist regime collapsed seven months earlier. Now they were taking charge of a vast country and dared to challenge the well-established capitalist system in Europe with a program based on the radical and visionary ideas of nineteenth-century German philosopher Karl Marx. Few in Russia, and almost no one outside the country, believed that they could hold power for long or that their proposals for a new socialist order could possibly succeed. Yet Soviet socialism, the system that the Bolsheviks created, would endure for seventy years, and the struggle between revolutionary socialists and their fascist and capitalist opponents would dominate world history for most of the twentieth century.

The overriding importance of the Russian Revolution can best be understood in the context of two other decisive events of modern history: the Industrial Revolution that emerged in England in the eighteenth century, and the French Revolution of 1789. The leaders of the French Revolution, drawing on the ideas of the eighteenth-century Enlightenment, aimed at reordering traditional society in Western Europe. Confident that they could reshape the sociopolitical environment, the revolutionaries established radical principles of representative government, social equality, and civil liberty that spread through Western Europe and North

---

[1]Leon Trotsky, *My Life* (New York: Pathfinder Press, 1970), p. 337.

America in the nineteenth century. Indeed, these principles continue today to spark change in Eastern Europe, Asia, Africa, and Latin America. The French Revolution also helped to create the doctrine of nationalism, which drove so many events of the nineteenth and twentieth centuries and which remains a powerful and disruptive force throughout the contemporary world. The French Revolution failed, however, to resolve the social and economic problems that the advent of industry spawned.

Bolshevik leaders, acting some 130 years after their French forerunners, also determined to eradicate what they saw as a repressive and unjust system. They wanted to replace it with a society of equality and abundance based on Marx's critique of nineteenth-century Western European society and his vision of the future under socialism. Working in a unique environment, the Bolsheviks nevertheless hoped to capitalize on the benefits of industrialization while curing its ills. Moreover, they sought to make good on the French Revolution's promises by combining economic security and justice with the social and political rights espoused by the earlier revolutionaries. For several important reasons that this book explores, the socialist society that the Bolsheviks set up in Russia failed. Soviet socialism—as an alternative to the capitalism that emerged from the Industrial and French revolutions and that has spread worldwide since—reached a dead end.

Some may rejoice at the collapse of Soviet socialism and dismiss the whole endeavor, but in fact we can learn much from what the Bolsheviks attempted. The search for the best way to combine freedom with economic sufficiency and equity continues throughout the world, and new efforts to create a just society should draw on the lessons of the Soviet failure. Consequently, as one focus of this book, we explore how and why the Russian revolutionaries developed their vision of a fair and good society, what permitted them to come to power and to try to put their ideas into practice, how that experiment fared over seven decades, and why their dream remained unfulfilled. We examine carefully the factors—historical, cultural, and international—that impeded the Bolsheviks' efforts. It is at times a heroic tale, marked by great courage, harrowing sacrifice, and remarkable persistence. Other scenes though reveal remorseless cruelty, astounding stupidity, and grinding tyranny. The story of the Russian and Soviet peoples' struggle with the terrible circumstances of their lives in this century is full of excitement, tragedy, and fascination.

As a second focus, we probe the relations among the predominant Russian ethnic group and the wide variety of non-Russian peoples living in the tsarist empire and the Soviet Union. In particular, we look at the rise of nationalist sentiment among Russians and non-Russians and its impact on the evolution of overall society. Although nationalism burgeoned among the tsar's Polish, Finnish, and Ukrainian subjects earlier in the nineteenth century, it developed most rapidly during 1880 to 1914. Lacking a consistent ethnic policy, the tsarist government most often attempted to counter nationalist feelings by imposing strict Russification in education, religion, the legal system, and governance. The resulting opposition helped to spur the first Russian revolution in 1905 and the upheavals of 1917.

As a radical, antitsarist party, the Bolsheviks wanted to harness nationalistic unrest to their cause. Yet they had to take into account the prescription of Marxist theory that the workers' solidarity as a class would outweigh nationalism. So they followed a somewhat contradictory policy of encouraging nationalist opposition to tsarism under the banner of self-determination of peoples while urging the non-Russian peoples to channel their dissent through the Russian revolutionary movement. Once in power, the Bolsheviks acknowledged the independence of Poland and Finland but fought non-Bolshevik nationalist movements in Ukraine, the Caucasus, and Central Asia, all of which proclaimed independence or autonomy during the civil war that followed the 1917 revolution. The Baltic states of Lithuania, Latvia, and Estonia, strongly supported by Britain, managed to assert their independence by 1920 and 1921 (although they were annexed by Stalin in 1940). Between 1918 and 1922, however, the Bolsheviks succeeded, with some difficulty, in establishing their dominion over almost all the remaining non-Russian lands of the former tsarist empire.

Guided by the slogan "national in form, socialist in content," Soviet leaders, predominantly Russian in outlook, strove over the next seventy years to integrate non-Russian peoples into a harmonious system that combined economic and political centralization with some cultural and social autonomy. The Soviet government did its best to promote a new "Soviet nationalism" that would foster a sense of common purpose and facilitate cooperation among the disparate groups. Although the regime made some progress, deep-seated anti-Russian sentiment and centrifugal forces persisted and even strengthened, as we shall see. Under the stimulus to self-expression permitted by Mikhail Gorbachev's policies of *glasnost'*, or openness, and of democratization, nationalist feelings surged to the fore after 1985. In 1991 the federation known as the Soviet Union collapsed. The former Soviet republics gained their independence, although most of the new states joined a loose association, the Commonwealth of Independent States (CIS), whose future remains nebulous.

As a third theme, we explore the rapid and radical transformation of a far-flung, populous society from an agrarian to an industrialized, urbanized way of life. In little more than a hundred years, the Russian and non-Russian peoples of the tsarist empire, sometimes willingly, sometimes under duress, converted a backward agricultural economy based on serfdom into a modern economy grounded in technology, science, and skilled labor. At the same time, they scrapped a social order built on hereditary privilege and autocratic rule and tried to erect a classless society of merit and equality. As these changes unfolded, the population grew urbanized, educated, and increasingly open-minded. Yet although the revolutionaries intended to replace the oppression and caprice that marked tsarist rule with democratic governance, they ultimately imposed new repression and arbitrariness. Today the peoples of the former Soviet Union are again struggling to create a representative political system and a productive economy to support their social and cultural advances.

The significance of Russian and Soviet modernization lies in part in the scope and complexity of the transformation. In building an industrial, urban-based society, Soviet leaders burdened 200 million people with wrenching and sweeping changes. Until the Chinese revolution of 1949, the modernization of Russia stood as the most far-reaching social upheaval in history. Often marred by violence, this transformation radically altered the Soviet peoples' destiny.

In modernizing, Russian and Soviet citizens possessed several clear advantages. They occupied a country rich in the natural resources needed for rapid economic development. Moreover, they could draw useful lessons from the example of Western European industrialization as well as adapt advanced technology from the West. They lived under a centralized political system, first tsarism, then Stalinism, that set ambitious goals and mobilized resources and people behind them. Finally, although the bulk of the population was illiterate and lacked technical skills, an elite culture and science provided the intellectual foundation for quick progress.

But Russia also confronted numerous obstacles. Climate, soil, and other natural factors set limits to agricultural growth. Natural resources and the centers of population often lay far from each other. Two world wars, revolution, and civil war devastated the country several times during the height of modernization. Last, the strategy that Stalin adopted for rapid industrialization, although it achieved certain goals, also exacted staggering costs.

This history focuses chiefly on the internal development of Russian and Soviet society, but we pay considerable attention to foreign relations and events. Consequently, as a fourth and final theme, we examine the ongoing effort of the Soviet rulers and people to protect their new order against external opponents and to extend Soviet power and revolutionary socialism throughout the world. Lenin and subsequent Soviet leaders saw their endeavor as part of the international proletarian revolution forecast by Marx. They believed that the revolution in Russia was only the opening salvo in a global struggle for socialism. To that end, they promoted and supported socialist revolutionaries in all parts of the globe. Although they assigned primary importance to the survival and development of the Soviet socialist state, they never lost sight of their ultimate goal—a world revolution that would give birth to a worldwide system of Soviet-type societies. Further, they saw the building of a powerful socialist structure in the Soviet Union as a way to inspire other countries, especially in Asia, Africa, and Latin America, to adopt socialism.

To be sure, Soviet leaders pursued nationalistic and self-interested as well as universal goals. Like their tsarist predecessors, they strove to enhance the security of their lands, to take advantage of the country's size and strength to extend Soviet influence and control in neighboring territories, and to participate fully in European and world affairs, especially after World War II. Much of the history of the past half-century revolves around the expansion of Soviet influence across the globe and the efforts of the United States and its allies to counter Soviet power. Whether the national interest of the Soviet people was well served by the imperialistic and universalistic aspects of Soviet foreign policy is another question that this book tries to answer.

About Terminology

Two problems of word usage confront those studying twentieth-century Russian history. One is the meaning of the terms *Russian* and *Soviet*. Unfortunately, the two words are often used interchangeably, but to be correct, *Russian* should refer only to a particular Slavic group, the Great Russians, the area that they have traditionally inhabited or colonized, and events and institutions associated with them. This usage distinguishes these people and their territory from the other Eastern Slavic groups, the Belarusans (formerly called Byelorussians) and the Ukrainians, and from the many non-Slavic nationalities living within the former tsarist empire and later the Soviet Union.

Soviet, by contrast, refers to the federated state and society that the Bolsheviks created between 1917 and 1924, plus later annexations. It encompasses all the people of that union, including Russians, other Slavs, and non-Slavs. Thus *Soviet* is a multicultural, multinational term, whereas *Russian* refers to a single group. It is not just inaccurate, but also offensive to non-Russians, to call the Soviet Union Russia or to speak of everyone and everything there as Russian.

The rules of usage for the period since the Bolshevik Revolution in 1917 are therefore fairly clear; the difficulty comes in applying precise terminology to the pre-1917 period. The post-Mongol state of Muscovy, centered in the Great Russian city of Moscow, came to be known as Russia, and this label stuck even after Ukrainians, Tatars, and other non-Russians were incorporated into the Moscow tsar's realm. By the middle of the nineteenth century, the tsar ruled a vast multinational empire, including several nationalities, such as Finns and Poles, who did not become significant components of the later Soviet Union. Nevertheless, at the time and in most historical usage, this state, society, and territory were called Russian. This book does not try to correct this error and uses the term *Russian* to apply to the late tsarist empire. Earlier in this introduction, for example, we refer to the upheaval of 1917 as the Russian Revolution, when in fact many non-Russians participated in that decisive event. As often as feasible, however, we remind readers of what *Russian* really meant by referring to "the multinational Russian empire" or "the multicultural tsarist society." After the break-up of the Soviet Union in 1991, the terms *Russia* and *Russians* apply to the largest successor state of that union and its people, even though the new Russian Republic includes territories inhabited by many non-Russian minorities such as Tatars, Bashkirs, and Yakuts.

As a minor but related misusage, journalists and others often employ the term *Soviets* to refer to people who lived in the former Soviet Union. No such group or set of persons exists because there is no Soviet nationality. Thus the correct usage is to be specific: Soviet leaders, Soviet thinkers, Soviet military officials, or Soviet workers.

A second terminological confusion arises over the words *socialism* and *communism* and their adjectives *socialist* and *communist*. Again, people often use the two sets of terms interchangeably. *Socialism*, however, is the more general term. It encompasses but is not equal to *communism*. In its generic sense, socialism is the belief that all members of a society (or their instrument, the state) should own the productive forces of that society, its economy. Socialism has many varieties, including Utopian and Christian socialism. Another type is Marxian socialism, which consists of Marx's analysis of the capitalist system and his "scientific" laws of history predicting that socialism inevitably succeeds capitalism as the basis for human social organization. Marx also postulated, however, that the final stage of history, socialism, would have two phases: a first and lower level also called socialism and a later and higher level called communism.

Lenin, who believed in Marxian socialism and adapted it to Russian conditions, emphasized the revolutionary aspects of Marx's theories. Thus in 1918, when Lenin sought to distance himself and his Bolshevik party from other, more moderate socialists, he changed the official name of the party to Communist. The new name had another advantage: it linked the party to the ultimate utopian future that Marx had predicted. Lenin's supporters in the Soviet Union and outside therefore came to be called communists and the type of socialism introduced in the Soviet Union, communism. Although the latter is incorrect, because neither Lenin nor his successors claimed that the U.S.S.R. had yet achieved communism, the labels *communism* and *communist* have often been applied to Lenin's theories and to the Soviet practice of socialism. At times we refer to the Communist Party, its official name, but we use the terms *revolutionary socialism* or *Marxism-Leninism* for Lenin's theories, and *Soviet so-*

Leaders of the Russian Revolution Lenin expounding the virtues of socialism to a crowd during the revolution and civil war. Trotsky is standing at right of podium.

cialism for the system established in the Soviet Union after 1917. Readers nevertheless should know that confusion among these terms persists in popular literature and the media.

A Vast and Varied Stage

The history of twentieth-century Russia and the Soviet Union was played out on a vast and variegated geographic stage. Although the setting did not determine the course of events, it strongly influenced the evolution of Russian and Soviet society in this period.

Most Americans, albeit vaguely aware of the broad sweep of their own country, find it difficult to grasp the immense size of the former Soviet Union, which stretched from the Baltic and Black seas to the Pacific Ocean. Soviet citizens living in the western extremity of their nation went to bed as their compatriots on the eastern edge of the union were just waking up. Indeed, anyone contemplating a train trip across Russia on the justly famous Trans-Siberian Railroad should consider that the journey involves seven days and nights of traveling!

The Soviet Union in 1990 was by far the largest country on earth and the third most populous, after China and India. More than twice the size of the United States, bigger than all of South America, the Soviet Union extended almost 6,800 miles and eleven time zones from east to west and about 3,500 miles from north to south. Its land border with twelve countries was the longest in the world, and it occupied the eastern half of Europe and the northern half of Asia. This huge territory encompassed every kind of terrain: desert, semitropical beaches and fruit groves, inland seas, sweeping semiarid plains, towering mountains, fertile treeless agricultural fields (the famous steppe), thick forests, long rivers, and the icy tundra of the far north. (See the map, The U.S.S.R. in Eurasia to 1991.)

How did the enormous size of the Russian Empire and the Soviet Union influence the historical development of these societies? First, in modern times it yielded a large population and an abundance of natural resources. Russia and the Soviet Union possessed extensive supplies of petroleum (oil and natural gas), coal, iron, gold, diamonds, and other minerals. This wealth facilitated industrialization and made the U.S.S.R. more nearly self-sufficient economically than any other nation.

At the same time, the huge expanse of the land and the extent and diversity of its population made the country difficult to control and govern. Both the autocratic rule of the tsars and the centralized authoritarianism of the Soviet system grappled with localism, indifference, and outright resistance to directives from the center. Beginning in 1987 and accelerating rapidly through 1990 and 1991, Soviet national governance disintegrated, and the union fragmented.

Size also spawned economic problems. Natural resources lay far from population centers, so raw materials and finished goods often had to be transported over daunting distances. For much of the twentieth century, the transportation system, particularly the railroads, operated under enormous strain, especially during both world wars. Moreover, the country never developed an adequate network of highways.

To be sure, the country's vastness provided both strategic benefits and defensive liabilities. Confronting enemies on as many as five frontiers over the past five centuries, Russian and Soviet leaders, when pressed, could withdraw into the interior of their realm, eventually to regroup and expel invaders. They proved themselves in this way when the Poles occupied Moscow in 1610, when Napoleon captured the city in 1812, and when Hitler approached the gates of Moscow in 1941.

Yet the strategic coin has a reverse side. Because of its size, its location in the heart of Eurasia, and its lack of natural defenses in all directions (except in the Arctic north and in the southeast, where the massive Tien-Shan Mountains shield it), Russia and the Soviet Union regularly suffered invasions. First, nomads from eastern Asia periodically galloped across the great plains of Eurasia, including southern Russia, from the early centuries of the Christian era down to the seventeenth century. Following the Mongol conquest of the first state, Kievan Rus', in the thirteenth century, Russia and the Soviet Union battled Teutonic Knights, Swedes, Poles, Turks, Tatars, French, British, Japanese, Americans, and Germans at various times over the next seven hundred years. Poor in agricultural resources and trade for most of this period, a centralized government imposed harsh rule and heavy taxes on its subjects to ensure defense of its large territories.

Another important geographic factor derives from the location of Russia and the Soviet Union on the globe. As a northerly country, the bulk of the Soviet Union was situated in latitudes north of the forty-eight lower states of the United States; its position compared with that of Canada or Alaska. Over a third of the land is frozen much or all of the year; icy temperatures make farming impossible and mere survival difficult. The climate is also continental, with extremes of brief hot summers and long frigid winters. The resulting short growing season imposes severe limits on agriculture. Finally, because rainfall peters out as it passes across European Russia from the Atlantic Ocean eastward, large areas in the center of the country must rely on irrigation for farming. Because of these and other factors, a tiny one-eighth of the U.S.S.R. was suitable for cultivation, and only part of that portion was actually farmed. The need to improve agriculture has presented a constant problem for tsarist, Soviet, and now post-Soviet leaders.

Russia and the Soviet Union's location in the center of the great Eurasian land mass carries both historical and contemporary significance. It facilitated regular contact with other civilizations in Europe and Asia in the past, and today the country is again open to technological, cultural, economic, and political influences from East and West. Once at the interface between the Christian and Islamic worlds and now positioned between the West and the Third World, Russia and the Soviet Union have always served as an important crossroads of world history. These connections to differing cultures both stimulated and stymied Russian and Soviet development. Should the country orient itself primarily toward Europe, as Peter the Great urged, or should it combine European ways with its strong Asian heritage to develop a unique civilization

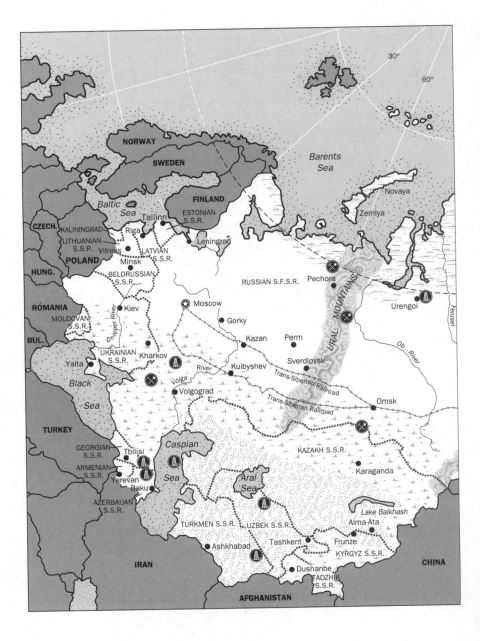

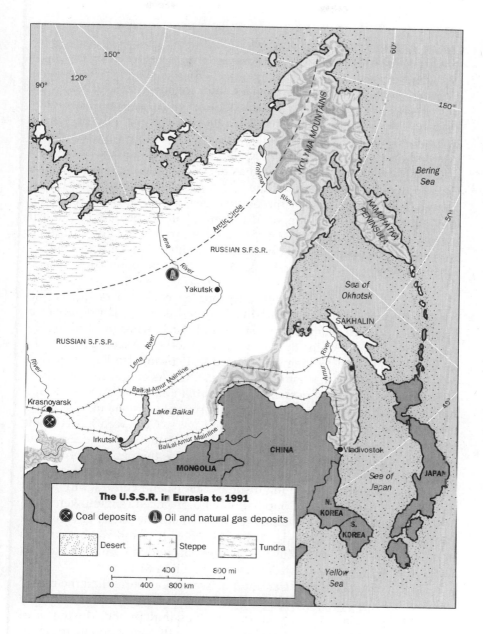

The U.S.S.R. in Eurasia to 1991

Coal deposits   Oil and natural gas deposits

Desert   Steppe   Tundra

0   400   800 mi

0   400   800 km

that would incorporate only the most desirable elements from East and West? Today, as Russia attempts to build a new order, this question again confronts the peoples of the area.

The Peoples

At the last census in 1989, the Soviet Union contained 286.7 million persons. The most striking characteristic of this population was its diversity, with approximately one hundred separate ethnic groups, twenty-one of whom embodied more than a million people. The largest related grouping were the Eastern Slavs, who together made up 69 percent of the population. The Great Russians ranked as the overwhelming majority in the Russian Republic, the largest of the fifteen republics of the Soviet Union. Substantially represented in the populations of several other republics, they numbered 145.1 million, or 51 percent of all the people. To put it in more significant terms, *almost half* of the country's population were *not Russian*. The remaining Eastern Slavs—the Ukrainians and the Belarusans—made up 15 percent and 3 percent of the total population, respectively.

The next largest and significant grouping consisted of the Turkic-speaking peoples, most of whom lived in the Central Asian republics of Uzbekistan, Kazakhstan, Kyrgyzstan, and Turkmenistan, and in the Azerbaijan Republic in the Caucasus. Another Asian people, the Tadzhiks, who speak a language related to Persian, also had their own republic, Tadzhikistan. Islamic in heritage, these Asian groups numbered 41 million people, or 14 percent of the population. Other substantial minorities included the Caucasian peoples, primarily Armenians and Georgians (3 percent), Finns (1.1 percent), and Jews (1.1 percent). The Baltic peoples (Lithuanians, Latvians, and Estonians) composed some 2 percent of the total but became independent in 1991. (See the figure, Ethnic composition of the U.S.S.R.)

Ethnic diversity created linguistic, religious, and cultural differences as well. The majority of the population who practiced religion were Russian Orthodox Christians. Neither that church nor the Soviet government provided figures, but Orthodox believers probably numbered between 50 and 75 million people. Muslims totaled around 40 million; Roman Catholic and Protestant Christians, several million each.

The Muslim peoples of Central Asia were more rural than the rest of the country. An average of 40 percent lived in cities, compared with 74 percent urban residents in the enormous Russian Republic. Muslims also reproduced more rapidly than other groups, with population increases of 15 to 40 percent from 1979 to 1989 for the Central Asian peoples. For the nation as a whole, the growth rate was 9 percent. As a result, between

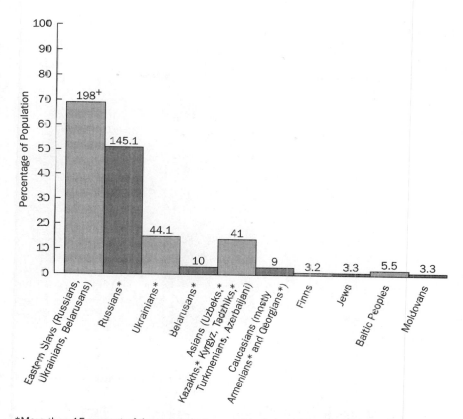

*More than 15 percent of these groups live outside their nationality's union republic.
Ethnic Composition of the U.S.S.R. (in millions) (Total population: 286.7 million, 1989 census)

1979 and 1989, 70 percent of the country's rise in working-age population derived from Central Asian Muslims.

The increase in the number of older people provides another key demographic trend. Individuals beyond working age (sixty and above for men, fifty-five and above for women) grew by 21 percent in the decade 1979–1989 and totaled 49 million persons by the latter year. A growing burden for future governments, these people rely on pensions and on the working sector for support.

Because of the huge losses suffered by the Soviet army during World War II, women significantly outnumbered men in the first decades after the war. Many women could not find husbands. By 1989 that imbalance had evened out markedly. That year, women made up 52.9 percent of the population, and there were 1,116 women for 1,000 men; in 1959 women had constituted 54.9 percent of the total, with 1,220 women for 1,000 men. The remaining disparity stemmed from a higher mortality rate for males,

A Non-Russian Visits Moscow A typical non-Russian citizen of the Soviet Union: A Kazakh from Central Asia in Red Square.

which most demographers attributed to alcoholism, heart disease, and cancer.

In our study of twentieth-century Russia, three long-term demographic trends hold particular significance. First, the population has expanded rapidly despite the terrible losses of World Wars I and II, the civil war of 1918–1921, and the forcible collectivization and Stalinist purges of the 1930s. In 1897 the population in the Soviet Union's 1989 borders stood at about 124 million. By 1914 it had swelled to more than 170 million, and by 1959 it totaled 209 million. The 1989 census showed that growth among the Slavic and Baltic peoples had slowed to almost zero, but, as we have seen, the Central Asian and Caucasian populations were still proliferating.

Second, an overwhelmingly agricultural and rural country has become industrialized and urban, partly as a result of calculated government policies. Less than 20 percent of the population reportedly were city dwellers in 1900, up to only 33 percent in the 1930s. By 1959, in part because of wartime dislocation, postwar reconstruction, and continuing industrialization, the urban population grew to 48 percent. In 1989 it climbed to 66 percent, ranging considerably higher in the non-Asian areas. That same year, twenty-three cities boasted a population of more than 1 million.

Finally, the peoples whom this book studies have become not only far more numerous and urban but much better educated than their nineteenth-century forebears. Again, state policy accelerated this trend. Literacy supposedly stood at around 25 percent in 1900; today it is almost universal. In 1989 almost every Soviet youth completed at least eight years of education, and many finished ten years. Moreover, at the turn of the century, less than 1 percent of college-age youth entered postsecondary education; in 1989 almost 30 percent did so. In that year, the Soviet Union ranked second only to the United States in percentage of people participating in postsecondary schooling. This surge in education produced a demanding and sophisticated population that helped to transform Soviet society after 1985.

Russia's Relationship to the West: The Historical Legacy

Before we examine the development of modern Russia and the Soviet Union, several aspects of its complex history deserve mention. One dimension, often overlooked in American discussions about the Soviet Union, is the Christian and European cultural tradition of the majority of the population. The Slavs of the area converted to Greek Orthodox Christianity a little over one thousand years ago. Russia remained predominantly Christian (even after absorbing Muslims from the sixteenth through the nineteenth centuries) down to the Russian Revolution, when the Bolsheviks proclaimed an atheistic state. In the past few centuries, the Russian Orthodox Church provided little intellectual leadership, discouraged social action, and remained thoroughly conservative politically and economically. Nevertheless, its cultural tradition persisted even during the seventy-plus years of Soviet rule.

With Christianity came Byzantine influence. It is important to remember that Byzantium, the eastern half of the old Roman Empire, built a highly developed civilization that endured for a thousand years. Thus, to some extent, both the Soviet peoples and Americans have descended from the same ancient Mediterranean civilization and share a Christian heritage. On the other hand, our religious and cultural traditions reflect notable differences. Latin or Catholic Christianity in Western Europe developed institutional and intellectual forms that diverged markedly from those of Russian Orthodox Christianity. Western Europeans also drew heavily on the legacy of Roman law and administration, both little known in Russia.

In the mid-thirteenth century, the state of Kievan Rus' was overrun by the Mongols, who dominated the area for over two centuries. Although the Orthodox Church preserved the old traditions, the Mongol conquest introduced a steppe or nomadic culture that altered Russian administrative and economic life. The so-called Mongol Yoke largely cut off

Russian society from its previous close ties with Byzantium and with Western Europe. The Russian people therefore participated only marginally in the artistic and intellectual ferment of the Renaissance and in the flourishing of the European economy in this period. In addition, Mongol devastation and taxes impoverished Russian society. Thus when Russian leaders reestablished an independent state in the fifteenth and sixteenth centuries, they battled various external enemies with scarce resources and from a position of semi-isolation.

This dilemma—how to defend and later expand state borders with a weak economy—troubled Russian rulers for the next five hundred years. It led to the people's dependence on a centralized authority to husband resources and to protect the nation; it contributed to the development of serfdom in Russia in the late sixteenth century, just when the institution was disappearing in Europe; and it reinforced the dominant role of the state. The authority of the tsars, based in part on Byzantine and Mongol models, burgeoned in the sixteenth and seventeenth centuries, as Russia's rulers gained control over the church and the nobility, institutions that in Western Europe had tempered royal power. The tsars broke the resistance of the old noble families, or boyars, and established a new service gentry who furnished military and administrative support in return for grants of land. Also, unlike Western Europe, where merchants and urban dwellers asserted their rights against the monarch, Russian towns developed primarily as administrative centers, and no influential middle class arose to challenge the tsar's autocratic power.

Beginning with their acquisition of Siberian and Tatar lands in the 1500s, Russian tsars spent much of the nation's treasure and their own efforts on expanding into neighboring lands, including the Caucasus and Central Asia in the nineteenth century. The Russian Empire therefore developed as an imperial power, dominating and heavily taxing subject peoples and often trying to Russify them. At the same time, from the era of Peter the Great in the early eighteenth century, Russia immersed itself in European affairs, protecting Russian interests and winning territory during wars with Sweden, Poland, Prussia, and France. Russian trade with Europe broadened, and Western European ideas and science infiltrated the educated elite of Russian society. As Western Europe industrialized, Russian tsars, strapped by an inefficient agricultural economy, found it increasingly difficult to keep up with the power and influence of the West and at the same time defend their far-flung empire. This stretching of resources imposed hardships on much of the population; finally, after Russia's defeat in the Crimean War, the pressure led to the abolition of serfdom, limited reform, and the first stirrings of industrialization.

The intercourse with Europe that developed after Mongol domination ended in the fifteenth century forced Russian society to confront the question of its relationship to Western civilization. Some leaders favored importing and adopting both Western technology and ways; others preferred a selective drawing on the West. Still others argued that Russian society should instead concentrate on developing its own Slavic culture and institutions. Peter the Great forcibly Europeanized the society in many ways, but even he did not favor slavish imitation of the West. Much of the older Slavic values and culture survived his reforms.

As relations with the West intensified, the educated nobility developed an ambivalence toward Western civilization that persists among the former Soviet peoples today. In 1900, when we pick up the story, Russian society clearly reflected this long-time equivocation: It possessed a Westernized elite, and industrialization was proceeding apace. Yet the majority peasant population remained parochial and uneducated, and much of the country's social, economic, and political structure reflected traditional and anti-Western ideals. As one example, whereas Western liberalism emphasized individualism, Russian doctrine stressed collectivist ethic and communal institutions such as the Orthodox Church and the village assembly.

Russia's pre-twentieth-century past clearly had not set the society on any predetermined course. The country might have developed, although belatedly, along the lines of Western European society, or it might have found some middle way and combined elements of Slavic and Western civilization in a unique mix. As we shall see, the revolutionary vision of a small group of intellectuals, determined to found a modern society while avoiding the evils of capitalism as Marx described them, shaped much of twentieth-century Russian history.

Soviet leaders strove to revolutionize and modernize traditional society and to extend their influence around the globe. They also attempted to integrate the country's non-Russian minorities into the new order. Yet the Soviet position in the world faltered, and the union itself flew apart in 1991 Moreover, the emergence of an educated citizenry determined to establish civic norms and the growing inefficiency and stagnation of a mismanaged economy led to the dismantling of the socialist system itself. The vision of the Marxist revolutionaries remained unfulfilled. This book explores that tragic failure and considers whether a foundation for a reformed, just, and humane society can be built amid the rubble of the collapsed Bolshevik dream.

1

TRADITION AND CHANGE IN IMPERIAL RUSSIA

~

On May 27, 1896, dawn broke early across Khodynka Meadow outside Moscow. As the light strengthened, it revealed a milling mass of several hundred thousand people—old people and children, women and men, a number of whom were drunk. A murmur rippled through the throng as those on the outer edge caught sight of what they had been waiting for through the night: wagons from Moscow loaded with special cups decorated with the tsar's emblem, and large carts carrying barrels of beer. In accordance with tradition, the cups and the beer were coronation gifts to the people of his realm from the new tsar, Nicholas II. Nicholas had inherited the throne late in 1894, but his solemn crowning by the patriarch of the Russian Orthodox Church had taken place only the day before in the Uspensky Cathedral of the Moscow Kremlin. The imperial couple themselves were scheduled to make a customary appearance before the crowd around noon.

As the wagons arrived, people edged toward them. Suddenly a rumor flashed through the throng that the free beer would soon run dry. Individuals at the front rushed forward, and before the few soldiers stationed near the carts could react, the crowd stampeded. People tripped or were knocked down, and many were trampled by those behind them. Crushed by onrushing feet, more than one thousand were killed and thousands wounded before the soldiers could stop the panic. Afterward a peasant-worker reported meeting "military wagons [on the road to Moscow] piled with corpses covered with bast mats; arms, legs, and heads could be seen dangling out from under the mats. . . . It was terrifying."

The tragedy stunned the twenty-eight-year-old tsar. At first he and his wife, Alexandra, refused to go to the coronation ball that the French ambassador was hosting that evening. But overbearing imperial uncles argued that the royal couple's absence would disappoint and offend foreign guests as well as the tsar's most important subjects: high state and church officials and members of the nobility. Reluctantly, Nicholas and Alexandra agreed to attend. The tsar's appearance at the ball made him seem callous, even though he was doing his best to ease the pain of the bereaved. Indeed, he arranged separate burials for the victims and paid each suffering family one thousand rubles, a huge sum at the time. Many superstitious citizens saw the disaster at Khodynka Meadow as an ill omen for the reign of Tsar Nicholas II. And perhaps it was.

Autocrats and Bureaucrats: The Tsarist System

Nicholas inherited from his father, Alexander III (reigned 1881–1894), a realm full of contradictions and in considerable ferment. As background to the complexity of twentieth-century Russian and Soviet history, this chapter focuses on the transitional and fragmenting society to which Nicholas II fell heir. On the one hand, Russia in the late 1800s reflected its agrarian, traditional, and authoritarian past and appeared little changed from earlier centuries. Its governance, based on the tsar's autocratic rule and a burgeoning bureaucracy, remained outmoded, arbitrary, and inefficient. Its social structure, legally based on customary groupings, masked the rise of new classes and the extensive ethnic diversity of the Russian Empire's population. Conservative values, patriarchal attitudes, Orthodox Christian beliefs, and nationalist ideology dominated public discourse and official culture.

On the other hand, change exploded in many aspects of Russian life at the end of the 1800s. Rapid industrialization altered the country's socio-economic structure, creating new classes and radical outlooks. Western culture and political thought undermined the tenets of the old order, sparking innovations in the arts and antigovernment parties and doctrines. Old social relationships broke down, and customary behavior lost ground against an onslaught of new activities, ideas, and challenges. Torn between the trusted past and the enveloping wave of modernization, the Russian peoples struggled to find a stable and peaceful path to modernity.

The government itself had initiated an era of change when in 1861 Nicholas's grandfather, Alexander II (1855–1881), abolished serfdom. This institution, which dated back to the late sixteenth century, defined the country's social system and dominated its economy. Further reforms (discussed below) had followed in the 1860s and early 1870s.

Despite these profound changes, the autocracy remained largely unaltered. How completely the tsar and his administrators controlled the vast Russian Empire remains a matter of dispute. In theory, the tsar wielded unlimited power. His personal and patriarchal dominance over all elements in society meant that he alone had responsibility for the welfare of the state and its citizens. In practice, however, his rule had limits. First, the reforms of Alexander II in the 1860s had circumscribed tsarist authority over certain aspects of local government and the judiciary.

Second, no single individual could possibly command enough information and wisdom to formulate all the policies and to make all the decisions needed to govern the vast, multinational, and increasingly complex Russian Empire of 1850–1900. Thus the tsar had to depend on personal advisers, often members of the royal family, and on ministers, civil servants, and various regional and local institutions of governance. Although all of these resources were beholden to the tsar, they shaped the nature and quality of government simply by making day-to-day decisions.

Third, in the last decades of the tsardom, senior bureaucratic officials managed to exert some direct influence, even if fitfully, on the governing process. Many top civil servants had absorbed the German concept of a "regulated" state run according to fixed rules and based on established laws. This developing legal consciousness led them to serve not just as personal agents of the tsar as they had in Muscovite times, but also as guardians of an orderly administration dedicated to efficient governance and the welfare of the people. They thus sometimes acted independently, although the tsar could still intervene and dismiss any official.

Finally, to maintain the system, the tsar needed the support of the country's top two social orders, or estates: the nobility and the clergy. Indeed, the last two tsars, Alexander III and Nicholas II (1894–1917), often yielded to pressure from relatives, friends, and personal advisers, the so-called "court circles," a coterie who generally represented conservative and noble interests.

Despite all these limitations, the autocracy retained its full power at the national level and remained the predominant political force in Russia. Indeed, as his official title proclaimed, the tsar stood at the head of his people as "Emperor and Autocrat of all the Russias."

One inevitable effect of autocracy was that Russian governance and politics came to depend heavily on the outlook, capabilities, and personality of the tsar. A farseeing, talented individual could initiate and manage bold policies and new departures, as Alexander II did. Stubborn and conservative tsars like Alexander III and Nicholas II could impose reactionary programs and block reform. In fact, the institution of autocracy impeded change within the whole tsarist system: only the autocrat could initiate or approve new policies, and he could likewise block or weaken reform if he so desired. This defect made the old order rigid and capricious.

Autocracy also reinforced the state's dominant position in society. People at all levels had traditionally looked to the tsar for protection, guidance, and assistance. This customary attitude led to the state's prominent role in the economy, in social life, and, after it had established full control over the Orthodox Church in the seventeenth and eighteenth centuries, in religion and culture. Values of self-reliance failed to take root, and institutions independent of the autocracy remained weak. Conservatives and reformers alike expected the government to initiate change, and even revolutionaries conceived a utopian future primarily in terms of eliminating the tsar and the existing state system. The autocracy and the society were thus locked in a death grip that made evolutionary change virtually impossible and the overthrow of the tsar almost certainly fatal for the political system.

A huge bureaucracy ran the state for the tsar. Its agents acted throughout the empire, but its policies received central direction from the capital at St. Petersburg. Although Russia had fewer officials per citizen than the states of Western Europe, its civil servants had greater control over society because of the state's sway and the lack of alternative power centers. Russian bureaucrats failed to master some areas of peasant life, and many non-Russians managed to preserve local customs and cultural traditions. Nevertheless, the bureaucracy's reach extended to most institutions and citizens.

At the same time, serious problems plagued the Russian civil service. For example, the system depended entirely on the tsar, who often interfered in its workings. Bureaucrats could propose, but only the tsar could dispose. Further, the administration's upper levels were still staffed largely by nobles, who until 1906 had preference in entering and being promoted in the civil service. In the 1850s, 43 percent of all civil servants were nobles, a proportion that fell to 30 percent in 1897. Yet the preponderance of top officials remained nobles; in 1903 all the ministers and provincial governors came from the nobility, as well as 84 percent of all deputy ministers and department heads. Although half of these men still had landed estates, they increasingly identified themselves with state service and sometimes differed sharply over policy with those nobles who were preoccupied with their landholdings. Overall, however, senior civil servants reflected an elite and conservative point of view.

The bureaucracy, too, operated clumsily and lacked any effective mechanism to coordinate the disparate ministries at the top of the system. To slow things further, important issues at lower levels had to be referred to St. Petersburg for decision. Arbitrariness also plagued the Russian bureaucratic system. Sudden changes in the tsar's policies or whims often produced unexpected rules and decisions. Moreover, the governors of the seventy-eight provinces and twenty-two administrative areas of the empire often ruled as "little tsars" in their own right, against whom citizens had scant recourse. Finally, because lower civil servants earned paltry wages, local extortion and corruption flourished. As a peasant proverb put it, "Go before God with a pure heart, go before the court with rubles."

Carrying out the state's will in every town and village of the vast empire was difficult enough. Add to size the bewildering array of ethnic groups, whose traditions, institutions, and values differed substantially from those of the dominant Russian culture. Such handicaps severely complicated and strained the bureaucracy's task. In ruling the Caucasus, parts of Poland, Finnish areas, and the former khanates in Central Asia, for example, the state faced special challenges, such as accommodating Islamic law and nomadic customs.

The Faces of Tsarist Society

Although the autocracy and bureaucracy dominated the political structure of imperial Russia, they governed a complex and multicultural society. The legal hierarchy for the Slavic majority of the population consisted of broad categories known as *sosloviia* (sing., *soslovie*). Comparable in some respects to the estates of premodern Europe, four basic *sosloviia* existed in late tsarist Russia: upper and provincial nobles, clergy, townspeople, and peasants. Subcategories within each group further complicated the social structure.

Social Contrasts in Russia Two faces of Russian society: The mistress of a noble estate seeks to interact with local peasant women.

As education and industrialization forged ahead in the last quarter of the nineteenth century, new social groups cropped up, particularly industrialists, professionals, and workers. Although all social distinctions were growing hazy, and liberal and revolutionary reformers alike demanded full equality and an end to privilege based on birth and status, many aspects of the *soslovie* system persisted down to 1917. For census, tax, and administrative purposes, citizens of the empire continued to be divided among at least a dozen categories within the four basic *sosloviia*. Nevertheless, we focus on the five broad social groups germane to understanding late tsarist society.

The **upper nobility** comprised society's dominant and privileged elite. These "first families," including some eight hundred princes, counts, and barons plus the largest landowners and highest state officials, totaled about a hundred thousand persons in 1897. These men filled the top jobs in the civil service and the army and were closest to the tsar. Many of them owned elaborate mansions in St. Petersburg and Moscow as well as landed estates in rural Russia.

The **provincial nobility,** totaling about 750,000 individuals, lived in regional towns or in the countryside, predominantly in central and southwest European Russia. Prominent members of this group participated in local government and sometimes provided intellectual and cultural leadership in their region or district capital. Some lower nobles, however, took no part in public life and remained isolated in rural areas. A very few lived in poverty on small holdings.

Emancipation of the serfs in 1861 removed the nobility's single greatest privilege—the sole right to own serfs—and over the next fifty years, other juridical prerogatives disappeared as well. Historians dispute how well the Russian aristocracy adjusted to their new circumstances.[1] Some nobles prospered, expanding their holdings into profitable commercial farms, but most aristocratic landowners suffered economically in the last two decades of the nineteenth century. Many chose to sell their land, or were forced to do so to pay off debts. A large number moved to towns and cities and entered government service, business, or the professions. Thus between 1862 and 1914, noble landholding in European Russia declined by 53 percent, whereas the proportion of nobles living in towns and cities rose from some 20 percent to an estimated 70 percent. By 1914 only about one in three noble families still held land.

---

[1]For a conclusion that the nobility adjusted well, see Seymour Becker, *Nobility and Privilege in Late Imperial Russia* (Dekalb, Ill.: Northern Illinois Univ. Press, 1985); for an opposing view, see Roberta T. Manning, *The Crisis of the Old Order in Russia* (Princeton, N.J.: Princeton Univ. Press, 1983).

The aristocracy retained preeminent social status, however, and dominated political, military, and administrative institutions. The landowners among them strove to protect their socioeconomic position and succeeded in blocking reforms between 1906 and 1914. They won backing from the official ideology of the court and from conservative circles. Yet divided in their economic interests and fragmented socially and ethnically, the nobility never formed a true class or an effective political force. Because their privileged position hinged on the tsarist regime, the revolutions of 1917 swept the nobles away together with the outmoded political system.

The **clergy of the Orthodox church** consisted of hierarchs such as bishops and archbishops, regular priests administering parishes, and monks. Often well-educated and worldly, the prelates exercised unquestioned authority within the church. With close ties to the tsar and the upper nobility, they held essentially conservative theological, political, and social views. They accepted the church's dependence on the state and rejected social activism. The parish priests were required to marry and lived as part of the local community. Poorly educated and poorly paid, many subsisted at the same level as the peasants whom they served, yet only a few supported radical ideas for change.

Townspeople were subdivided into distinguished citizens, merchant guilds, artisans, and laborers. In 1897 these categories totaled about 11 million persons, or a little over 10 percent of the population. This figure included factory workers (discussed on p. 44), as well as other new subgroups of urban citizens that emerged as social and economic change accelerated.

Industrialists, bankers, and businessmen enrolled in the merchant guilds, but some also earned noble status through state service. Many urbanites served as administrative and military employees of the government, although they were listed officially as artisans. Lowest on the social scale were household servants, apprentices, and laborers. Because Russian towns lacked the independent status of those in Western Europe, their inhabitants did not wield the same political influence that their European counterparts enjoyed.

The **peasantry** composed 84 percent of the population in the 1897 census, or about 100 million persons. Before 1861 peasants had fallen into two roughly equal groups: private serfs owned by the nobility; and state peasants owned by the tsar, various branches of the government, and monasteries. Instead of living on individual farmsteads as American farmers did, peasants dwelled together in villages as in most of Europe, setting out daily from their small huts to tend the surrounding fields. They farmed with primitive tools, in some cases still using wooden plows. Consequently, they produced meager crops, and most of them struggled close to dire poverty. Nevertheless, according to some historians, as many as one-fifth of these peasants began to prosper in the early twentieth century through buying or leasing land given up by nobles and through hiring labor. Conversely, another fifth of the peasants lost their land and became agricultural laborers. Although most peasants lacked schooling and could not read, a growing number benefited from government and church sponsorship of elementary education during the last years of the nineteenth century. Literacy training that male peasants received as part of their required military service under reformed conscription laws adopted in 1874 also proved a boon. Until 1906 peasants had their own courts, administration, and judicial system, all of which defined their separate social and legal status.

Peasant social organization centered on the village commune or *mir*, composed of the male heads of all village households. Each family or household held strips of land in different open fields, and in "repartitional" communes these holdings were reallotted periodically to account for changes in the size and needs of the household. The *mir* collectively

Rural Decision Makers A meeting of village elders in a Russian peasant *mir* (commune).

scheduled major agricultural tasks, such as plowing, sowing, and reaping; apportioned state and local taxes among households; and selected village youth for military conscription. Each household had one vote, and *mir* decisions were usually unanimous, reflecting a community consensus. Minority or unorthodox views were suppressed, and the *mir* enforced a numbing conformity on the drudgery of village life. According to some historians, by imposing collective decisions and by periodically redistributing the land, the *mir* served to discourage the village's more ambitious and progressive farmers. Other analysts see social welfare and community support benefits in the *mir*. In their view, the system provided every household with a subsistence niche and reduced and dispersed the risks inherent in agriculture.

During the nineteenth century, several groups emerged that did not fit the categories described above. Russia never developed a distinct, cohesive middle class as arose in Western Europe. Instead, the late 1800s saw the rise of nontraditional strata with differing outlooks and beliefs: professionals such as lawyers, doctors, and educators; businessmen, including bankers, engineers, and factory owners; and the so-called "third element" of technicians, agronomists, construction specialists, teachers, and health-care workers employed by the *zemstvos*, organs of local self-government set up in the 1860s. As industrialization accelerated, these groups occupied key positions in the economy and gained prominence in urban society and cultural activities. They also developed political aspirations, as we shall see.

The intelligentsia, primarily intellectuals such as writers, composers, professors, and other university-educated individuals, formed another important nontraditional category. Its members grew conscience-stricken over the injustices of tsarist society and determined to change the system. The intelligentsia had begun to develop as a special social entity in the late eighteenth century, and their ranks expanded in the nineteenth century. Their class origins were mixed: some were educated nobles who had developed intellectual interests and a critical outlook; others were sons and daughters of lower-level bureaucrats or married clergy. The intelligentsia assimilated a wide range of both Western and traditional ideas, and many became harsh critics of the tsarist regime.

Both moderate and radical opponents of tsardom felt alienated from the existing order. Yet although they championed the people's interests, their education and higher social status separated them from the bulk of the population, especially the peasants. These rural people mistrusted all outsiders, including intellectuals, reformers, and revolutionaries, as well as government officials. As a result, a three-way split developed in Russian society during the eighteenth and nineteenth centuries. "Privileged" Russia, one branch of the split, comprised the official, hereditary order backed by the Orthodox Church, the army, and the tsarist government and police. Opponents of the establishment, a second branch, encompassed a range of moderate and radical critics from various socioeconomic strata. The **narod,** the people as a whole, stood apart as a third branch. Predominantly peasants, they had suffered over the centuries, for the most part stoically and silently. On several memorable occasions, however, they had risen violently against their landlords and the government, and both tsarist officials and the intelligentsia worried about what "the masses" might do in the future.

An Empire at Risk: Non-Russians and the Rise of Nationalism

In addition to the widening fissures among social groups in late nineteenth-century Russia, national and ethnic divisions increasingly upset the empire's stability. The first census, taken in 1897, classified people by their dominant language and revealed the multicultural nature of the realm (see the map, The Russian Empire, 1900). Although Great Russians dominated society and government, non-Russians made up a majority of the population—55 percent of the total 124 million. Great Russians, concentrated in the northwest and center of the state, composed a little more than 44 percent. Other Slavs—Ukrainians, Belarusans, and Poles—made up another 29 percent; and non-Slavs, about 27 percent of the population. The latter group included 13 million Muslims, mostly Turkic-speaking; 5 million Jews; 3.5 million Finns; and more than 1 million each of Georgians, Armenians, Latvians, and Lithuanians, along with many other smaller groups.

Up to the mid-seventeenth century, the Russian state had been fairly homogeneous, comprising mostly Great Russians and a few Finns and Tatars. But in the following two hundred years, the state expanded continuously, swallowing up Ukrainians, Balts, Belarusans, Poles, Jews, Moldavians, Central Asians, and peoples of the Caucasus, eastern Siberia, and the Pacific coast of Eurasia. With minor deviations, the tsars treated newly acquired territories and peoples as an integral part of the empire. Almost everyone was considered a servant of the state and a subject of the tsar. Significant exceptions were nomadic groups and the Finns, who enjoyed special rights up to the late nineteenth century, and Jews, who faced unique limitations. The tsarist government sporadically pursued a program of Russification, imposing administrative and legal uniformity and urging subject peoples to convert to the Orthodox faith and to adopt Russian culture and language. Not until the last quarter of the nineteenth century, however, did the regime pursue this policy vigorously. In the

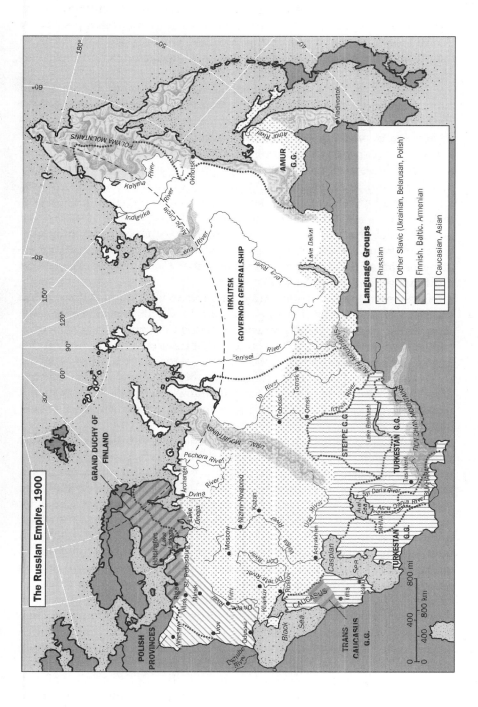

first half of the century, the non-Russian groups displayed little overt opposition to their subject status. Exceptions included mountain peoples of the Caucasus, who fought a guerrilla war against Russian annexation of their lands during the 1830s and 1840s, and the Poles, who rebelled in 1830 and in 1863.

Around 1850 two developments coalesced to end the generally placid relations between the tsarist government and the non-Russians. First, as the revolutionary movement spread among the intelligentsia, accompanied by some peasant disorders and later by workers' protests, the regime grew concerned that unrest would spread to the non-Russian borderlands. These regions played a crucial role in Russia's defense and secured its standing as an imperial power in Europe. The regime's anxiety, together with a rising tide of Russian nationalist feeling, inspired government attempts to bind the non-Russians more closely to the state. Yet the policies it selected to accomplish this goal—Russification and the persecution of non-Orthodox religions—backfired, spurring instead intense anti-Russian and antigovernment sentiment just as nationalism raised its head in most of the non-Russian areas.

This second factor, local nationalist emotion, blossomed during the last part of the nineteenth century and profoundly influenced the revolutions of 1905 and 1917. The sense of belonging to a coherent group with a common history, language, and culture that developed from the Enlightenment and the French Revolution spread across central Europe in the 1800s and reached the Russian Empire by the second half of the century. Once sown among the non-Russians, this new concept of allegiance to a nation often spawned local anti-Russian and antigovernment movements.

Nationalism appeared first, and proved strongest, among the Poles, who were Catholic and oriented toward Western Europe. Because Polish-speaking nobles had dominated the vast Polish-Lithuanian Commonwealth, which had stretched almost as far east as Kiev until the 1700s, their nineteenth-century descendants deeply resented rule by Russian tsars, whom they regarded as half-Asiatic tyrants. Although the Russian government tried various formulas for ruling its Polish lands, none worked well, and the authorities had to resort to force to quell the 1830 and 1863 Polish uprisings. After the latter revolt, tsarist policies at first favored the Polish peasants, many of whom practiced the Orthodox religion, over their Catholic noble landlords. But in 1869, the tsarist administration launched its Russification campaign by closing the Polish-speaking University of Warsaw. In the 1880s, public schools were thoroughly Russified, private Polish schools forbidden, and Catholic religious education much restricted. Russian replaced Polish as the language of the courts, the administration, and the railway system. These policies catalyzed a resurgence of militant Polish nationalism and the first stirrings of Polish socialism. In the 1890s, two important Polish political parties were founded, the National Democrats led by Roman Dmowski and the Polish Socialist party led by Józef Piłsudski, who would become the dictator of an independent Poland after World War I.

By the mid-1800s, nationalism simmered in the Ukraine as well. The first Eastern Slavic state had been founded in this area in the ninth century, but during and after the Mongol conquest, the Slavs living there had gradually fallen under the control of Poland. They were called Little Russians to distinguish them from the Belarusans to the north and the Great Russians of Muscovy to the northeast. The term *Ukraine*, by which the region came to be known, meant "on the border." This name reflected Ukraine's frontier position between the Great Russians in the center of European Russia and their diverse enemies to the south and west— Tatars (descendants of the Mongols), Ottoman Turks, and Poles. Ukraine was notorious as home to the Cossacks. Originally adventurers, outlaws, and runaway serfs, by the seventeenth century the Cossacks had developed well-organized communities on the lower Dnieper River and had won renown for their military prowess.

In the 1640s, a Cossack *hetman* (chieftain), Bogdan Hmelnitsky, led a revolt against Polish rule in Ukraine. During the upheaval, the Ukrainians, seeking help from the Great Russians, made a treaty with the Muscovite state. This cooperation led gradually to establishment of Russian influence on and eventually governance over eastern Ukraine. A century later, Catherine the Great (reigned 1762–1796) added western Ukraine and territories along the northern shore of the Black Sea to the Russian Empire. The St. Petersburg government treated the whole region and its people as an integral part of Russia.

In the first half of the nineteenth century, interest among educated Ukrainians in their own language and literature sparked nationalist fever. Ukrainians began to view their language, closely related to the Russian spoken in Moscow, as an independent tongue, and the author Ivan Kotliarevsky published the first widely circulated works in Ukrainian. Taras Shevchenko, a talented poet writing in the mid-nineteenth century, further stimulated nationalist feeling. In the 1870s, the tsarist government forbade all publication in Ukrainian except for historical documents and precensored literary works. It also suppressed the Uniate Church, a Catholic body with Slavic rites founded in 1595 that had gained strength particularly in southeastern Poland and western Ukraine. Under this harassment, the Ukrainian nationalist movement shifted its center of activity to the city of Lvov (Ukrainian: Lviv) in Galicia, then part of Austrian Poland. In 1899 the historian Mihailo Hrushevskyj founded the National Democratic party, and in the early 1900s, several socialist Ukrainian parties arose. Radical Ukrainian nationalists helped to stir peasant unrest in 1902 and 1903.

Finland, which Russia had annexed from Sweden in 1809, provided a special case within the multinational tsarist empire. Ruled as a grand duchy with the tsar at its head, Finland nevertheless had its own postal service, university, state church, and law courts. This degree of autonomy, however, did little to stem a surge of Finnish nationalism that crested in the mid-nineteenth century, reflected in publication of the powerful national folk epic *Kalevala*, introduction of Finnish-language schools, and finally establishment of a national representative assembly. In 1899 Nicholas II sharply curtailed the assembly's powers, and when the Finns resisted a 1901 decree requiring them to serve in the Russian army, the tsarist government established a virtual military dictatorship over the country in 1903.

The first signs of nationalism among the Baltic peoples appeared in the third quarter of the nineteenth century. However, this sentiment grew fitfully, because Baltic Germans, descendants of the crusading Teutonic Knights who had settled in the area in the thirteenth and fourteenth centuries, dominated the Baltic lands. These Germans were major landowners and merchants and held important administrative positions not only in the Baltic provinces but throughout the Russian Empire. Estonians, Latvians, and Lithuanians—the indigenous peoples—were for the most part peasants, artisans, and workers. Consequently, the first Baltic nationalist societies aimed to establish the local population's rights against not only their Russian imperial masters but their German overlords as well. In the 1880s, the tsarist government directed its Russification policies against both the Baltic Germans and the indigenous groups, closing German schools and a German university and forbidding teaching in the local languages. Tsarist bureaucrats also harassed the Lutheran churches of the Germans, Estonians, and Latvians, and the Roman Catholic faith of the Lithuanians. Marxist ideas spread in the 1890s among Latvian workers in Riga, who would soon join in the Revolution of 1905.

In the Caucasus, the earliest nationalist organization was founded in 1890 in Armenia. Called the Armenian Revolutionary Federation (known as *Dashnaktsutiun*), it strove to liberate Armenians living in Ottoman Turkey. By 1903, anti-Russian sentiment and parties developed, particularly in furious reaction to the tsarist government's seizure of the funds of the independent Armenian Christian Church. In Georgia Marxism took root, and revolutionary and anti-Russian protests broke out in 1902–1903.

Among the empire's Muslims, interest in Turkic languages and literature and a desire to spread Islam impelled the first self-awareness movement in the 1890s. Centered in the ancient Tatar capital of Kazan and in the Crimea, this resurgence promoted Muslim education and at first was not particularly directed against Russians or the tsardom.

The non-Russians who suffered most in the late nineteenth century were the Jews. This people, the one minority who did not live together on their own territory, were scattered through the western provinces of the empire. A few Jews had resided in Russia since medieval times, but their numbers burgeoned during the late eighteenth century, when Catherine the Great annexed Polish-Lithuanian lands (modern Belarus and Ukraine west of Kiev) in which extensive Jewish minorities resided. In the first half of the nineteenth century, Jews suffered under several restrictions: they were required, with some exceptions, to live in an arc of cities and towns in western and southwestern Russia known as the Pale of Settlement; they were forbidden to enter certain professions; and they often had to pay special taxes or levies. Nevertheless, although many Jews were poor, some prospered as merchants, artisans, and moneylenders. They retained their local communities, and they adhered to their cultural and religious identity. The tsarist government did not at first persecute either Judaism or secular Jewish culture, which flourished particularly in the Black Sea city of Odessa.

Because the Jews kept apart; because the Orthodox religion made clear its distaste for the "murderers of Christ"; and because those Jews involved in trade, the sale of spirits, and banking became objects of envy and resentment, primitive anti-Semitism took root among Slavic peasants and workers in the 1800s, and irrational anti-Jewish attitudes permeated many upper-class and bureaucratic circles. As a result, a series of vicious, anti-Semitic riots, or pogroms, broke out in 1881. Mobs beat and killed Jews and looted their stores and homes. Central government officials neither instigated nor encouraged these pogroms or those that erupted during the next twenty-five years. In fact, some bureaucrats saw the pogroms as symptoms of dangerous revolutionary activity. Nevertheless, many tsarist leaders, including Nicholas II, harbored anti-Semitic prejudices and believed that the Jews had brought the pogroms on themselves by exploiting Christian Slavs. Moreover, conservatives sometimes made the Jews the scapegoats for the country's growing unrest, blaming them for fomenting protests and disorders. Finally, local officials were not above indirectly fostering anti-Semitism. Only reluctantly did they provide protection for Jews and seek punishment of pogrom instigators.

In the 1880s, the regime stepped up legal discrimination against Jews, forbidding them to live on or acquire rural property, putting restrictions on Jewish lawyers and doctors, and establishing quotas for Jews admitted to secondary schools and universities (3 percent in St. Petersburg and Moscow). In 1890 Jews were prohibited from voting to elect local government bodies, and in 1903 new pogroms erupted.

In the face of this intensifying persecution, more than 2 million Jews fled the empire. Many emigrated to the United States, where they and their descendants enriched the American economy, society, and culture. Some Jewish intellectuals and workers in Russia turned to socialism and in 1897 formed the *Bund*, which after 1901 supported Jewish autonomy in a proletarian socialist Russian state. Others became active in Zionism, the Europewide movement to establish a Jewish homeland in Palestine.

Russia and the West:
An Ambivalent Relationship

Nationalism was only one of many forces that penetrated Russian society from Western Europe. Like many Western concepts, the notion of national identity at first influenced primarily the empire's better educated citizens and widened the gap in values and outlook between the small Europeanized elite and the peasant masses. The latter had little knowledge of Western ideas, science, and culture and were only marginally touched by the nationalist fervor. Instead, peasant popular culture centered on traditional songs and tales, small prints called *liubki* depicting folk or religious themes, ancient Slavic rituals associated with the seasons or agricultural tasks, and religious ceremonies of the Orthodox Church. These rites included mass, the sacraments of baptism, marriage, and death, and numerous saints' days usually celebrated with feasting and heavy drinking. Few peasants had any schooling, and they comprehended almost nothing of the Western European ideas and lifestyles of their noble owners and of the urban bureaucrats and intelligentsia.

By contrast, upper-crust groups had a lengthy history of contact with Western Europe. Before the Mongol conquest (1240–1480) temporarily isolated the Russians, Kievan society had close links to the rest of Europe by trade and intermarriage of princely families and through the eastern Mediterranean culture of Byzantium. As Mongol domination ebbed in the fifteenth and sixteenth centuries, intercourse with other European states, never totally cut off, revived, and Western ideas and technology began to seep into tsarist society. Tsars, clerics, and nobles displayed an ambivalence toward the influx of Western European culture. They coveted the science, inventions, and efficient practices of the West but feared the subversive impact of these ideas on traditional Slavic culture and religion. This mixed reaction remained a striking characteristic of Russian society throughout the next four centuries and persists in the post-Soviet states.

Despite Peter the Great's efforts in the early eighteenth century to force-feed Western European culture to Russians, many nobles as well as peasants clung to the old ways. Nevertheless, throughout the eighteenth century, European education, science, art, music, and literature much enriched Russian society, a process that Catherine the Great strongly encouraged in the last third of the century. In the 1830s and 1840s, educated Russians, thoroughly cosmopolitan and well versed in European philosophy and science, initiated a new debate over the merits of Westernization.

One group, the Slavophiles, argued that the tsarist system had lost its true bearings and that foreign ideas and values had corrupted Russian society. They further contended that Western institutions, particularly the bureaucratic state, had distorted the pure relationship between the wise, patriarchal tsar and his simple, good people. The Slavophiles espoused a return to traditional virtues of communality, concern for the people's welfare, and moral probity that derived, in their view, from the Orthodox faith and Slavic culture. Sometimes unfairly labeled as reactionaries, the Slavophiles in fact advocated far-reaching reform of the existing system.

A second group, the Westernizers, drew particularly on the Enlightenment ideas of the eighteenth century and after. They opposed the Slavophiles, calling for modern, secular education and culture and a complete transformation of the social and political system along Western lines. They castigated tsarism's inefficiency and oppressiveness, urged the abolition of serfdom, and pressed for social equality and freedom of expression. Westernizers and Slavophiles alike, along with their descendants, sought to change society by gradual reform, but both movements grew increasingly frustrated at the intransigence of the tsars and their advisers. In the last four decades of the nineteenth century, some of their numbers became radical opponents of the regime and joined the ranks of revolutionary parties determined to overthrow the tsar by force.

The Slavophile-Westernizer debates were only part of the lively and productive cultural flowering of the mid-1800s. Russian writers, critics, philosophers, and historians all felt duty-bound to describe and evaluate contemporary society, believing that art and culture must serve socially useful purposes. Despite government efforts to stifle criticism by censoring and punishing its opponents, creativity and originality flourished in this Golden Age of Russian culture. Paradoxically, some of the greatest works of modern literature were produced at the height of tsarist repression, including the poems and stories of Alexander Pushkin, the powerful novels of Leo Tolstoy, Ivan Turgenev, and Feodor Dostoevsky, and, near the end of the century, the brilliant stories and plays of Anton Chekhov. Concurrently, Russian music was enriched by the masterful works of such composers as Modest Moussorgsky, Peter Tchaikovsky, and Alexander Borodin. The world-renowned Russian writers and musicians of this era admirably blended folk and traditional themes and approaches with modern styles, ideas, and techniques. Their masterpieces are still read, performed, and enjoyed throughout the world.

This burst of Russian high culture coincided with the country's prominence as an international power. When Tsar Alexander I rode his handsome white charger into Paris in 1814 at the head of the Russian and allied armies who had defeated Napoleon, no one doubted that Russia had emerged from the Napoleonic Wars the strongest state on the European continent. This triumph crowned just over a hundred years of Russia's close participation in European international affairs that began with Peter the Great's dragging the country headlong into central Europe's territorial and dynastic struggles early in the eighteenth century.

Yet during the nineteenth century, Russia's position on the continent weakened as the empire became deeply embroiled in the so-called Eastern Question: the competition among European states to exert influence over the extensive but ailing and disintegrating Ottoman Empire. In this rivalry, Russia had to contend with the large Austro-Hungarian Empire and, after its unification in 1870–1871, a powerful Germany, as well as with France and Britain. Moreover, the Western European states' rapid industrialization in the nineteenth century and subsequent gains in economic and military strength overwhelmed agricultural and underdeveloped Russia's ability to compete. Although during the European revolutions of 1848 and 1849, Tsar Nicholas I (1825–1855) displayed Russian power by dispatching troops to suppress a liberal revolt in Hungary, only five years later, in a dispute related to the Eastern Question, France and Britain invaded Russian territory on the Crimean peninsula and handily crushed the tsarist armies.

This humiliating defeat stimulated the reforms of Alexander II but did not persuade Russian leaders to revamp their foreign policy. Tsarist diplomats persisted in trying to expand Russian influence in the Balkans, especially among fellow Slavic groups such as the Serbs and the Bulgarians. Russia also pressed the Ottoman government for access to the Turkish Straits, the waters that connect the Black and Mediterranean seas, and for other concessions. These issues, along with a Slavic rebellion in the Turkish Balkan province of Bosnia, spawned the Russo-Turkish War of 1877–1878, a bloody struggle that the tsarist empire finally won, although the Europewide Congress of Berlin in 1878 forced Russia to give up some of its gains.

Russia's rivalry with the European Great Powers temporarily abated in the 1880s when, under the guidance of the shrewd German statesman Otto von Bismarck, Germany's Kaiser Wilhelm II, Austria-Hungary's emperor Franz Joseph, and tsars Alexander II and Alexander III joined forces in the Three Emperors' League. As we shall see in Chapter 3, however, this association fell apart in the 1890s. The subsequent diplomatic realignment set Europe on the road to World War I.

Tsarist diplomats and leaders, although presiding over an autocratic and repressive state, felt themselves very much a part of Europe. Some of them recognized the urgency of modernizing their country if Russia were to stay competitive with the European Great Powers. Nevertheless, at the end of the nineteenth century, they still considered their nation an equal player in the game of European politics. At the same time, well aware that the Russian Empire covered much of the Eurasian land mass, they tried to expand their control and influence into Asia (see the map, Expansion of Russian Empire, 1853–1905). In Persia and Afghanistan, Russian

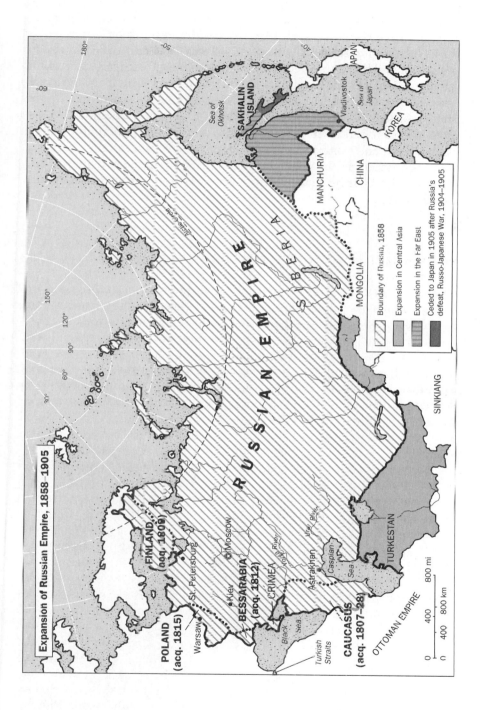

Expansion of Russian Empire, 1858–1905

Legend:
- Boundary of Russia, 1858
- Expansion in Central Asia
- Expansion in the Far East
- Ceded to Japan in 1905 after Russia's defeat, Russo-Japanese War, 1904–1905

RUSSIAN EMPIRE

SIBERIA

SAKHALIN ISLAND

Sea of Okhotsk

MANCHURIA

CHINA

Vladivostok

Sea of Japan

JAPAN

KOREA

MONGOLIA

SINKIANG

TURKESTAN

OTTOMAN EMPIRE

POLAND (acq. 1815)

FINLAND (acq. 1809)

BESSARABIA (acq. 1812)

CAUCASUS (acq. 1807–28)

CRIMEA

Warsaw

St. Petersburg

Kiev

Moscow

Astrakhan

Caspian Sea

Black Sea

Turkish Straits

Volga River

Ural River

Arctic Circle

0   400   800 mi

0   400   800 km

penetration met with resolute resistance from the British, who wanted above all to protect the outer defenses of their lucrative position in India.

The Russians succeeded, however, in extending their control over Turkestan in Central Asia between 1864 and 1895 and over the Pacific coast along the Amur River valley. There they founded Vladivostok (meaning "ruler of the east") as a major commercial, administrative, military, and naval center in 1860. After Russia sold Alaska to the United States in 1869, tsarist officials and imperialist adventurers moved to expand Russian influence in Manchuria and Korea, where they soon clashed with an emerging, aggressive Japan, as we shall see in Chapter 2. Although interested in Asia, the late tsarist state remained thoroughly committed to Europe, and indeed that is where the empire's fate would soon be settled.

Alexander II Reforms Russia

Convinced that a weakly industrialized economy and an archaic serf-based social system had propelled Russia's defeat in the Crimean War, many educated Russians favored thorough revamping of the country's institutions and policies after 1856. They found a receptive ear in the successor to the reactionary Nicholas I: Tsar Alexander II. With his close advisers, the new ruler soon initiated a series of far-reaching measures designed to improve the system but not replace it. He sought to strengthen the autocracy by making it efficient, productive, and rule-

Ripe for Revolution Peasants in their village, probably a few years after their emancipation by Tsar Alexander II.

based. These Great Reforms, undertaken between the late 1850s and 1874, inducted an era of change that would transform Russia over the next fifty years.

As Alexander's most important reform, he liberated privately owned serfs in 1861 and state peasants in 1866. This emancipation affected some fifteen million families, making it the most sweeping state-directed social upheaval in history up to that time. Whatever its defects, it marked the first step in freeing the great majority of the population from three centuries of bondage. Because serfs had no rights and could be bought and sold as chattel (although in practice this happened infrequently), serfdom in Russia closely resembled outright slavery. Whereas in the United States slavery was confined to one region of the country and slaves were of a different ethnic origin and color, in Russia serfdom spread throughout the central regions of the empire and Russians enslaved Russians. Moreover, Russian serfs substantially outnumbered American slaves.

Under serfdom, peasants generally worked both the noble's land and their own allotted fields. The emancipation transferred to the peasantry a significant portion of the noble land that they had cultivated for themselves, for which they had to pay "redemption dues" spread over forty-nine years. Although the reform freed peasants from the juridical, fiscal, and economic control of the nobles, they still struggled under the thumb of the *mir*, to which the government gave the burden of collecting redemption dues.

It is hard to judge the utility and fairness of such a complex development, but on balance the emancipation had several serious drawbacks. Because of a concurrent fiscal crisis, the government failed to provide credit to peasants to help them with redemption payments and to spur improved farming techniques. In addition, peasants received about one-fifth less land than they had previously worked. Even though they now had the right to lease or purchase land, this reduction wrought havoc when the peasant population mushroomed at the end of the century. The jump in their numbers led to a land shortage while peasants' land hunger escalated. Many peasants felt that the emancipation had cheated them, especially those who believed the peasant proverb, "O *barin* (noble serf-owner), we are yours, but the land is ours."

Industrious peasants, now bound more closely than ever to the *mir*, also had few incentives to expand production or to improve farming efficiency. The *mir* discouraged peasants from leaving the commune as well, for departures deprived the village of taxpayers and increased the burden on those who stayed behind. Finally, after the emancipation, the government set up special peasant courts and local administrations to replace the supervisory and juridical functions of nobles. Thus while they gained economic rights, peasants hardly received full social and political rights. No longer enserfed, they nevertheless remained second-class citizens.

For many years, historians vigorously debated whether Russia in the early twentieth century was a frozen, xenophobic society or a westernizing one on the road to constitutional democracy. Sometime in the 1970s, scholars stopped asking this question as they came to assume, first, that the Bolshevik Revolution had sprung from deeply rooted social forces and, second, that the Soviet Union was here to stay. Now, however, the collapse of communism in 1991 has forced some historians to rethink the "place" of 1917 in Russian history; in other words, to what degree did 1917 serve as a pivotal moment in the fate of modern Russia?

If Russia in the early twentieth century indeed had started (however fitfully) down the path toward constitutional democracy, then the reformist agenda of the current Russian regime in the 1990s represents a movement back to what is normal for that country. If, on the other hand, Western patterns had left only a faint stamp on Russia, and Bolshevism did grow inexorably out of the country's earlier development, then attempts today to forge a democracy may again run aground, as they did in 1917.

Which way was Russia tending before the Great War? This question continues to fascinate Western scholars. A central piece of the puzzle remains the peasants, for they made up the great majority of Russia's inhabitants at the time, and they would hold enormous significance for the Soviet regime. Recent scholarship challenges the established orthodoxy of a hungry, overpopulated village. The traditional view, best articulated by Geroid Robinson (*Rural Russia Under the Old Regime,* 1949), held that the explosive pressure of population stymied economic progress in late-nineteenth-century rural Russia. "For every new worker in the field there had also to be found a new place at the table, but too often the new place could not be found."

Writing in the *Slavic Review* (Vol. 53, No. 1, 1994), Stephen Hoch takes issue with Robinson, noting that the population increase, an undeniable fact, reflected a lowering death rate, which is "hard to square with the overall thesis of declining rural standards." Hoch attributes lower mortality to substantially improved rural nutritional levels from the 1880s onward, along with larger crop yields. Indeed, over a three-decade span (1885–1913), the increase in retained food grains far outpaced the growth in population. "The picture is one of an agricultural population that was experiencing rising per capita income and living standards." Perhaps Hoch's most intriguing postulate is that the 1861 emancipation of the serfs may have bettered the peasant's lot because the redemption dues required in the emancipation were less burdensome than the pre-1861 fixed rents. "Reductions in the peasant's obligations were real and helped explain the [downward] mortality trends."

But there are many ways in which to evaluate quality of life. What about facets such as peasant education and urban influences on the village? Richard Pipes (*Russia Under the Bolshevik Regime,* 1994) surveys the rural landscape and finds scant evidence of modern patterns. Disrespect for private property, a poorly developed sense of law, the prevalence of communal landowning—all made the peasants a kind of cannon fodder for the passions of the revolutionary intelligentsia. "He [the peasant] felt no patriotism and no attachment to the government save for a vague devotion to the distant tsar from whom he expected to receive the land he coveted."

Pipes's view of the peasantry as a nation apart is challenged by two superb studies of rural schools and literacy. In *Russian Peasant Schools: Officialdom, Village Culture and Popular Pedagogy, 1861–1914* (1986), Ben Eklof writes that primary schooling became widespread in the late nineteenth and early twentieth centuries. By World War I, the majority of peasant children most likely attended school, although the state never required it. Despite a significant expansion of basic literacy, Eklof also finds that many peasant parents were suspicious of schools because teachers sometimes encouraged children to abandon rural habits and trek off to the city. As a result, some parents pulled their offspring from the classroom as soon as they could read and master the basic skills.

By examining what peasants read in these years, Jeffrey Brooks throws valuable light on the issue of peasant values. In *When Russia Learned to Read* (1986), Brooks asserts that rural dwellers primarily consumed popular commercial literature, including serialized novels published in cheap editions, short detectives stories, and tales of adventure and female heroism. These books and pamphlets "spun dreams of material success which won over many peasant readers." Notions of personal achievement and of individualism permeated the newly literate village. The idea of freedom—of individual ability to control one's destiny—"eventually came to resemble that expressed in Western Europe and American popular fiction." Brooks concludes that the "social structure of Russia in the last half century of the old regime was rapidly becoming more like the West and so was its popular culture."

Ordinary people's response to tales of heroism and opportunity brings us back to the issue, "whither prerevolutionary Russia." At the very least, the growth of individualism and the pursuit of literacy in rural society invalidates previously held views of peasant isolation from mainstream political, economic, and cultural life. Less clear, but increasingly problematic, is whether collectivist values and patterns had deep roots in the countryside before 1917, as many historians have previously asserted. Might Stolypin's reforms and the expansion of private agriculture have taken on even greater dimensions without the setbacks of the Great War? Apparently, more and more peasants resisted appeals from both the right and left—from the right with its insistence on obedience to authority and to the existing social order, from the left with its call for a collectivist repartition of all land. More research on peasant life is necessary, but the findings to date suggest that, in the absence of the catastrophe of World War I, the dynamics of village life might have served as a springboard for a slow but steady transition to a more open society. If so, the big question—"whither Russia in 1996'—remains open.

In another important reform, Alexander II established local self-governing councils called *zemstvos* charged with tasks such as road building, education, and public health. Although dominated by the nobility, *zemstvo* assemblies were elected by all social groups, including peasants, and could hire technical specialists (the "third element" discussed earlier). A related urban reform permitted propertied citizens to elect a municipal *duma*, or council, that took over management of certain aspects of city government. Those involved in running the *zemstvos* and the *dumas* acquired valuable experience in self-government and in public administration, which many of them later put to use as liberal opponents of the autocracy.

Other Alexandrian reforms relaxed censorship and encouraged publishing, granted the universities greater autonomy, created an independent judiciary, introduced universal military service, and modernized the military establishment. Taken together, these changes improved public life and governance at the local level, but they stopped well short of providing full civil liberties or a national representative government. This failure disappointed many people who had hoped for introduction of a constitutional system. Some frustrated radical reformers became revolutionaries and turned to terrorist attacks on the government. Nevertheless, the reform era served as a first step toward modernization and pointed the way to future change. Although Alexander's new policies strengthened Russia, the country remained economically, socially, and politically weaker than its Great Power rivals. They, too, grew stronger in this period and made it harder than ever for Russia to catch up.

Factories and Cities:
The Wave of Industrialization

It is difficult to imagine life before industrialization, when almost everyone eked out a living in the countryside. For Russian and Soviet citizens, as for all those who experienced the coming of industrialization, the process sparked profound changes in their way of life, in their attitudes, and before long, in their social and political system.

Russian manufacturing, especially of weapons and other implements, dated back to the sixteenth century. Peter the Great had promoted industry, and at the end of the 1700s, Russia stood as a leading producer of iron. But by the mid–nineteenth century, the country lagged behind Western Europe. Only in the last quarter of the nineteenth century did Russian industrialization take off, encouraged by government policies and an influx of foreign capital. Between 1861 and 1905, the number of Russian factories multiplied from about 10,000 to 40,000, and the value of their output rose from about 200 million to more than 4 billion rubles.

During the 1890s, economic growth reached 8 to 9 percent a year, roughly comparable to the rates concurrently achieved in the United States and Japan.

Several special features marked Russian industrialization. For one thing, the state acted forcefully to promote and finance economic development. The most important advocate of industrial growth was Sergei Witte, a self-made man who became minister of finance in the 1890s and served as an adviser to both Alexander III and Nicholas II. Able, diligent, and farseeing, Witte recognized that, to compete with Europe, Russia had to build up its economy rapidly. He introduced an array of government policies, known as the Witte system, that included subsidizing railroad building and key industries, putting Russia on the gold standard, raising tariffs while promoting exports, and encouraging foreign investment in Russia. To finance industrialization, Witte levied heavy indirect taxes on the peasants and borrowed extensively from Germany and France. Witte's policies succeeded, but at some cost. They neglected agriculture, overburdened the peasants, and left Russia dependent on foreign support.

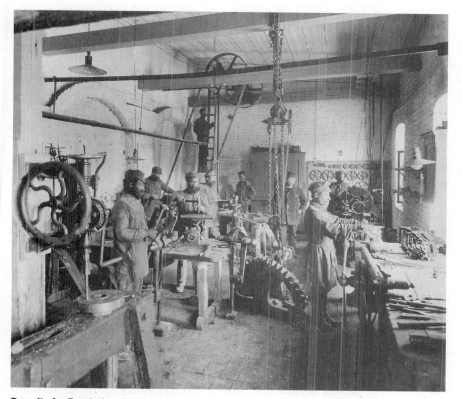

Recruits for Revolution Russian workers in a munitions factory, 1900s.

Because foreign capital and state investment and production orders played such a large role in industrialization, no strong commercial middle class developed in Russia. Unlike their European and American counterparts, Russian businessmen were unable to force changes in the country's political and social structure, even when they teamed up with the growing professional class.

Russian industrialization also concentrated itself in a few large cities and regions and in huge factories employing thousands of workers. Because of deplorable working and living conditions and the large-scale clustering of laborers, workers soon formed mutual-aid societies and other organizations to defend their rights. The density of the work force also facilitated the spread of revolutionary ideas among this new proletariat.

Indeed, the flourishing of cities became the most visible sign of industrialization in Russia as country people swarmed to the new urban factories in search of work. As in Western Europe, urbanization brought overcrowded housing, inadequate sanitation, and menacing crime rates. At the same time, new technology demanded new skills, and education expanded while illiteracy declined. With more people able to read, printing and publishing grew. Improved communications systems, like the telegraph and railroad, also served to spread ideas, including revolutionary ones.

Industrialization changed peasants' lives in both direct and indirect ways. Numbers of peasants flocked to the cities, although they often retained ties to the village. The proliferation of railroads and commerce supplied manufactured household goods and agricultural tools far superior to the home-made products to which peasants were accustomed. Although evidence about the overall economic plight and tax burden of the peasantry is mixed, the high indirect taxes imposed on items of daily use under the Witte system likely forced peasants either to pay more or to consume less.

The main cause of peasant distress, however, stemmed not from industrialization but from the shrinking of land per family as a result of a population explosion among the peasantry. Between Emancipation in 1861 and 1900, their numbers increased 70 percent, while their landholding rose only about 30 percent. Historians attribute this population boom in part to regular food supplies and a reduction in the death rate resulting from improved public health, but a complete explanation remains a mystery. In any case, with less land per family and the price of land doubling, many peasants struggled to survive. In 1891 a severe famine struck, and by the early 1900s, peasant unrest and violence were spreading throughout central Russia.

Of all segments of the population, factory workers felt the impact of industrialization most directly. Although estimates of their numbers vary, clearly the industrial labor force mushroomed in the last half of the nineteenth century and the beginning of the twentieth, from a few hundred thousand around 1850 to about 2 million in 1900 and some 3.5 million by 1914. In the 1890s, most workers came directly from the villages and still owed taxes and other obligations there. Some labored for only part of the year in the factory, mine, or railroad yard, and returned to the farm seasonally, especially for plowing and harvesting. Because they came home regularly and the cities offered limited housing, workers customarily left their families behind in the village. Later, second- and third-generation workers composed a plurality if not majority of the labor force.

Although a few skilled workers managed to live comfortably, most laborers suffered appalling working and living conditions, including dormitory or crowded housing, long hours, low pay, and no safety standards. In 1882 the government created the Factory Inspectorate, charged with enforcing existing regulations and improving workers' circumstances. One inspector graphically described laborers' plight in the 1880s.

> The majority of the workers lived in . . . low, ugly mud huts. The roofs are made of earth and rubbish. . . . The walls are covered with wood planks or overlaid with stones which easily let in the dampness. The floors are made of earth. These huts are entered by going deep down into the ground along earthen stairs. The interiors are dark and close, and the air is damp, still, and foul-smelling. . . .
>
> The very worst, most unhealthy conditions I saw were in tobacco factories. . . . [They] are so filled with caustic dust and nicotine fumes that each time I entered one of these rooms I had spasms in my throat and my eyes watered. . . . Yet even women sometimes work in this atmosphere . . . [and] even children under twelve. . . .[2]

In addition to the squalor and health hazards, bosses often proved demanding and fined or fired workers capriciously. Unionizing and striking were illegal, and management often called in the police to repress workers' protests.

Many workers, recently peasants, had difficulty adjusting to factory and city life. Uprooted from family and village and disoriented by the alien urban culture, workers fell prey to loneliness, crime, and despair. Searching for purpose and community, some entered clubs or discussion circles, where they encountered socialist and revolutionary ideas.

Industrialization also gradually affected the position of women in Russia. Traditionally, women had been considered impure—an attitude

---

[2]Report in Thomas Riha, ed., *Readings in Russian Civilization*, Vol. 2, *Imperial Russia*, 2nd ed. (Chicago: Chicago Univ. Press, 1969), pp. 410, 413.

fostered in Russian Orthodoxy—and inferior to men. Until the eighteenth century, upper-class women had been segregated in special living quarters known as the *terem*. Even in the nineteenth century, a woman was treated as the sexual chattel of her husband. In the village, as in most peasant societies, the patriarchal social structure relegated women to a submissive and servile role. Occasionally, if a family's adult males were absent, women served as heads of households and participated in the *mir*, but a peasant proverb summed up the prevalent attitude: "The hair is long but the mind is short." Women not only performed arduous agricultural work and shared other burdens of village life with men, but they also had responsibility for childbearing, child rearing, cooking, sewing, and care of the house.

Urban women fared little better. Many worked as domestic servants or apprentices in artisan shops, and they had no economic security or social rights. Even women in the merchant and noble classes were in a subservient position. Better off economically, however, they enjoyed more social opportunities and sometimes a chance at education, either by private tutors or in a few select schools for girls. A handful traveled abroad to study in European universities. Unlike most Western European women of the time, upper-class women also had property and partial inheritance rights. Yet they were expected to comply with a provision of the legal code that stated, "The woman must obey her husband, reside with him in love, respect, and unlimited obedience, and offer him every pleasantness and affection as the ruler of the household." In 1863 women were exempted from legal corporal punishment, but a husband's right to impose physical discipline at home remained.[3]

Finally, all women lacked a clear legal identity, being registered after marriage only on the internal passports of their spouses. A woman thus could not travel, take employment, or study without permission from her husband.

The reform atmosphere of the 1860s sparked the first women's rights movement in Russia, which focused primarily on access to education and to employment opportunities. These apolitical early feminists struggled by peaceful means to obtain secondary and university courses for women. They also set up committees to provide assistance to needy and disadvantaged women. As part of a general expansion of education, the government instituted public secondary schools for women from all classes during the 1860s, and 27,000 women were enrolled by 1870. In 1872 a special course for women was finally established at Moscow Uni-

---

[3]Richard Stites, *The Women's Liberation Movement in Russia* (Princeton, N.J.: Princeton Univ. Press, 1978), pp. 6–7; Laura Engelstein, "Gender and the Juridical Subject: Prostitution and Rape in 19th Century Russian Criminal Codes," *Journal of Modern History*, 60 (Sept. 1988): 462–463.

versity, and a women's medical school opened in St. Petersburg. In 1876 all universities were permitted to offer courses for women, primarily because the tsarist authorities feared that women who went abroad to study became radicalized. As we shall see, women indeed took part in revolutionary agitation of the 1870s.

Industrialization opened opportunities for women but created new burdens as well. Women's participation in the labor force rose steadily in the 1880s, reaching 27 percent in 1901. In textile, paper, and tobacco manufacturing, female laborers made up nearly half the employees at the turn of the century. Yet their wages amounted to only one-half to two-thirds of men's pay. Moreover, bosses and foremen were more apt to fine women workers. Single women in particular struggled to find housing and to subsist on their meager incomes, and married women were forced to work through pregnancy and to return to the job almost immediately after giving birth. Child care, it goes without saying, proved a daunting problem. Finally, laboring women had limited chances to gain an education and to learn to read. Neither government authorities nor most feminists expressed much concern about the plight of working women, although a few Marxist groups sought to attract them.

The Roots of Russian Opposition

The changes in Russian society instigated by Alexander II's reforms and industrialization strained the tsarist system and emboldened its foes. Indeed, government critics in the late nineteenth century could draw on a long tradition of opposition to tsarism. As far back as the seventeenth and eighteenth centuries, large-scale peasant uprisings had broken out occasionally, climaxing in the massive rebellion led by Emelian Pugachev in 1773 and 1774, during the reign of Catherine the Great. In the nineteenth century, local peasant violence and unrest erupted sporadically, and fear of a peasant mutiny persuaded some nobles to accept emancipation of the serfs. Nevertheless, in these years the main source of resistance to tsarism shifted from the peasantry to the intelligentsia.

In the last half of the eighteenth century, subversive Enlightenment ideas spread among the upper classes, seeded by books, journals, and scholars imported from Western Europe and watered by the education of some Russian nobles abroad. These notions prompted a few writers to deplore serfdom and other aspects of the tsarist system. This criticism was reinforced when, during the Napoleonic Wars, precepts of the French Revolution such as liberty and equality gained currency in Russia, particularly among officers and administrators who had served in Europe.

Beginning in the 1810s, young officers and nobles formed semisecret societies to discuss ways to improve the system. In December 1825, during confusion over which of his brothers would succeed Alexander I, leaders of two loosely affiliated groups staged a revolt to install a constitutional regime in Russia. Unfortunately for the revolutionaries, the attempt was poorly organized. Because the liberal ideas then spreading across Western Europe meant little to the Russian masses, the coup attempt also received minimum support from the ranks of the army or the population at large. The ringleaders, known as Decembrists, were brought to trial; some were executed and others exiled to Siberia. Yet despite their lack of wide appeal, the Decembrists came to symbolize revolutionary resistance to tsarism. Their memory would be invoked by later reformers and revolutionaries, including the Bolsheviks as well as the democrats who renounced Soviet socialism in the late 1980s.

During the 1840s and again in the 1860s, criticism of the tsarist system intensified among the intelligentsia. Slavophiles and Westernizers censured the regime for opposite reasons. Foes of tsarism in the 1860s included a younger generation, the sons and daughters in Ivan Turgenev's fine novel *Fathers and Children*, who rejected the past entirely and placed their faith in science and reason. These youthful rebels argued that the first step toward creating a just society was to transform the Russian people through education.

From this strand of thought arose the antigovernment movement known as populism. Led by members of the intelligentsia and appealing primarily to educated youth, populism postulated a vague socialism that combined some elements of traditional Slavic culture with ideals of the liberal West. Populists argued that once the masses were informed of the necessity for change, they would cooperate to remove the tsar and establish a new communal order based on the *mir* but also guaranteeing civil liberties and the rule of law.

In 1873 and 1874, populism spawned the *v narod*, or going-to-the-people, movement. Hundreds of students and other idealistic urban youth traveled to the villages of Russia to enlighten the peasants with the doctrines of populism and to prepare them for the coming revolution. Although a few peasants listened sympathetically, most looked on these intruders with suspicion. Bewildered by the new ideas, they either ignored the propagandists or pressured them to depart the village.

Many opponents of the tsarist regime, frustrated by the failure of populist methods and disappointed by Alexander II's unwillingness to grant national political reforms, began to consider other solutions to Russia's problems and alternative means of disposing of the tsarist system. For some, deeds, not words, seemed the answer. Even in the 1860s, a few people had urged direct action as the best way to transform Russian society. The most influential was Nicholas Chernyshevsky, whose utopian novel *What Is To Be Done?* became the bible of young radicals. Chernyshevsky, like the populists, argued for a vaguely socialist society graced by cooperative harmony and plenty. But achieving this materialist utopia, he insisted, required dedicated revolutionaries willing to take action.

By the mid-1870s, a radical group called the People's Will had split from the populist movement and began to practice terrorism. Although today we see terrorism used as a political weapon in the Middle East and elsewhere, it is still hard to comprehend what terrorists hope to achieve. Adherents of the People's Will movement expressed their goals as follows:

> The purpose of terroristic activities . . . is to break the spell of governmental power, to give constant proof of the possibility of fighting against the government, to strengthen in this way the revolutionary spirit of the people and its faith in the success of its cause, and, finally, to create cadres suited to and accustomed to combat.[4]

As we saw earlier, a movement for equal rights for women, particularly for access to education and jobs, had developed in the 1860s and scored some success by the 1870s. Women also participated in the populist movement, and a few became radical revolutionaries. According to one estimate, they numbered some 65 of 2,000 radicals in the 1860s and about 15 to 20 percent of the revolutionaries of the 1870s.[5] Most women joined the revolutionary movement not primarily to advance the cause of women's rights but because of generalized idealism. They believed in the need to replace repressive government with a fair and humane system. In such a system, women would be fully emancipated, as Chernyshevsky had predicted in *What Is To Be Done?* Most female revolutionaries hailed from upper-class backgrounds and were well educated; a number had become radicals while studying in Switzerland. Women participated at all levels of antigovernment activity, from terrorism to propaganda to underground operations, and their male revolutionary colleagues generally accepted them as equals.

Several women played outstanding roles in the radical and terrorist activity of this period, notably Vera Zasulich, who was acquitted of attempted assassination after a much-publicized trial; Vera Figner, who became well known in radical circles in Europe; Sofia Bardina, who at her trial delivered a powerful and widely read speech defending women's rights and radicalism; and Sofia Perovskaya, the daughter of a high tsarist official who has hanged for masterminding the assassination of Tsar Alexander II. A number of radical women of the 1870s later became Marxian or peasant socialists, including Catherine Breshko-Breshkovskaya, known in the West as "the little grandmother

---

[4]In George Vernadsky, *et al*, eds., *A Source Book for Russian History from Early Times to 1917*, Vol. 3, *Alexander II to the February Revolution* (New Haven, Conn.: Yale Univ., 1972), p. 664.

[5]Stites, op. cit., pp. 116, 149.

of the Russian revolution." Russian socialists included equal rights for women as a goal but failed to give it high priority. Because most women revolutionaries at the time concerned themselves primarily with the larger battle—the overthrow of the tsar and the victory of socialism—they accepted this hierarchy of aims.

Terrorist groups, in which women participated, succeeded in the 1870s in assassinating several dozen officials and finally Tsar Alexander II in 1881. Instead of "strengthen[ing] the revolutionary spirit of the people," however, one of the terrorists' goals, their actions alienated much of society and provoked a strong conservative reaction. The reign of Alexander III in the 1880s would be, in retaliation, an era of repression.

The Government Strikes Back

After terrorists assassinated Alexander II, his son and heir, Alexander III, hesitated briefly but soon announced his firm intention to defend and reinforce the autocracy. Indeed, he had little reason to continue the reforms associated with his predecessor. He and his father had differed personally and politically for some time, and the new tsar recoiled from any seeming threat to the old order. After taking office, Alexander III de-

Terrorists at Work An engraving showing a bomb exploding under Alexander II's carriage during his assassination by terrorists, 1881.

clared, "The voice of God commands us to stand resolutely by the task of governing, relying on Divine Providence, with faith in the strength and truth of the autocratic power that we have been called to confirm and protect for the good of the people against all encroachment."[6]

Taking advantage of public revulsion after the assassination of Alexander II, the new tsar and his advisers pursued a policy of counterreform. This reaction prevented the system from responding to changing conditions and stimulated long-term antigovernment sentiment. Although senior bureaucrats often blocked his turn-back-the-clock efforts, Alexander III managed to institute new repressive regulations. He staunchly defended autocratic prerogatives, for example, and vigorously espoused Russian nationalism and Orthodox Christianity. In the 1880s, he curtailed the ability of the *zemstvos* to raise money for their programs and narrowed their jurisdiction. Indeed, because conservatives in the bureaucracy and among court circles clearly feared the liberal ideas and growing criticism expressed by noble leaders and "third element" specialists of the *zemstvos*, they did all they could to muzzle these self-governing bodies. From the 1880s on, the government also increasingly relied on special administrative rules and edicts outside the regular codes of civil and criminal law. As a particularly repressive example, decrees placed certain cities, districts, or even regions under martial law or restrictive regulations of "strengthened security." This policy amounted to extralegal governance of a highly authoritarian kind.

To combat criticism and opposition, the government intensified censorship, reduced university autonomy, closed special courses for women at all the universities except St. Petersburg, and used the special or secret police, the *Okhrana*, to keep tabs on antigovernment and dissident activity. By means of administrative procedures quite outside the judicial process, the government sentenced hundreds of social critics and political opponents to exile in Siberia, an infringement of civil rights widely condemned in Western Europe and the United States. The government, as we saw earlier, also tried to stanch non-Russian nationalism with policies of repression and Russification.

In the countryside, Alexander III and his advisers expanded government control over the peasants. Post-1861 mandates had given peasants their own courts of customary law and a local administrative unit (the *volost*). Some officials grew concerned that this special status as well as peasant participation in the *zemstvos* had given the rural population too much autonomy. Consequently, in 1889 the government established a new rural position, *zemsky nachalnik*, or land captain, to oversee peasant affairs at the district level. This additional bureaucratic layer augmented

---

[6]Quoted in Heide W. Whelan, *Alexander III and the State Council* (New Brunswick, N.J.: Rutgers Univ. Press, 1982), p. 27.

state interference in village life while doing nothing to ameliorate the increasingly desperate straits of many peasants.

Alexander III and his successor, Nicholas II, also faced growing worker unrest. Although both tsars endorsed their advisers' policies of industrialization, they failed to respond to the new class of workers' demands that those policies stimulated. Accumulating resentment against factory bosses and the government, laborers at times expressed their frustration in individual or group protests. As early as 1879, a few workers resorted to strikes, which were illegal. Sporadic walkouts, assaults on supervisors, work stoppages, and demonstrations continued over the next two decades.

At first the government ignored signs of trouble among workers. Beginning in the 1880s, however, authorities established a system of factory inspection to improve safety and sanitary conditions in the workplace. But the rules did not apply to all factories, and the government rarely enforced them. The regime soon forbade night work for women and children and limited the workday to eight hours for children. An 1897 decree introduced a maximum workday of eleven and one-half hours for men and women, but it was widely disregarded and many employees still routinely worked twelve-to-fourteen-hour days, six days a week. The government also permitted formation of mutual-aid societies designed to help workers in emergencies, but it largely ignored such issues as old-age pensions, accident and disability insurance, protection against arbitrary treatment by supervisors, and the right of workers to bargain collectively. Unions and strikes were still outlawed, and wages remained low.

Nicholas II: The Reluctant Tsar

Most of the government's reactionary policies began or were intensified during the reign of Alexander III. Almost all received backing from his son, Nicholas II, who added a few of his own. Because Nicholas reigned during a time of rapid change and because he survived one revolution and was overthrown by a second, it is important to examine his conservative views and to assess his abilities and outlook.

Nicholas had no desire to serve as tsar and would gladly have avoided the responsibility. A slightly built, rather serious youth, he was nevertheless handsome and soon sported a stylish beard. Because his bluff, austere father appeared hale and hearty, there seemed no urgency about training Nicholas for the throne, even though as the eldest son he was heir apparent. Nicholas was allowed to indulge his interests in sports and military training, but he gained almost no experience in public affairs and administration. When Alexander III died unexpectedly in 1894, Nicholas succeeded to the throne at the age of twenty-six. The bewildered new tsar plaintively asked his brother-in-law, "Sandro, what am I going to do? What is going to happen to me, to you, to all of Russia? I am not prepared to be a tsar. I never wanted to become one. I know nothing of the business of ruling. I have no idea of even how to talk to the ministers."[7]

In view of Nicholas's domineering father and mediocre education, it is no surprise that he proved insecure and at times narrow-minded. Coming of age in reactionary court circles, tutored by one of Alexander III's most conservative advisers, Konstantin Pobedonostsev, and too cowed to challenge his father's legacy, the young tsar ascended the throne imbued with the credo that autocracy was the most important institution in the empire and that it was his God-given duty to defend it. Early in his reign, he labeled as "senseless dreams" proposals from liberal nobles to set up limited representative institutions. His other social and political views were ill-formed but decidedly conservative. He knew

A Devoted Father Nicholas II and his family, 1913.

---

[7]Quoted in Robert K. Massie, *Nicholas and Alexandra* (New York: Atheneum, 1967), p. 41.

little about the social and economic changes that industrialization and modernization were igniting in Russian society and, sheltered in the narrow and artificial court environment, he had no chance to learn about and appreciate important developments in his vast empire.

Nicholas's intellectual limitations and restricted social outlook might not have mattered so much had he relied on some of the talented and farsighted nobles and bureaucrats who gained prominence during the last decades of the Russian Empire. But as so often happens with weak leaders, Nicholas distrusted individuals brighter and abler than himself. Instead, he depended on relatively incompetent advisers and officials who mirrored his own conservative opinions.

Although occasionally charming and by nature gentle and kindly, Nicholas was both weak-willed and stubborn. He often acted from instinct or intuition and then stuck to his position even when proven wrong, a trait that resulted in erratic decision making. Moreover, he hated confrontation and often would outwardly agree with a minister or adviser during personal discussion, only later to reverse his opinion.

A dedicated family man, deeply in love with his wife Alexandra and devoted to his five children, Nicholas was also genuinely patriotic. He truly cared for his country and his people, albeit remotely. But these qualities failed to compensate for the tsar's limited vision, stubborn incompetence, and outdated conservatism. His blindness to the needs and desires of his subjects, his steadfast opposition to fundamental social or political reform, and his rooted determination to defend autocratic prerogatives wrought deprivation and suffering for many in the empire. Nicholas II led Russia poorly in two wars that cost millions of Russian lives, and his weakness and indifference precipitated a social revolution that swept away everything that he believed in and sought to preserve.

Marxism and Liberalism: The New Opposition

Nicholas's attitudes and policies ran absolutely counter to the social and economic changes sweeping his realm and rendered the tsar blind to the new opposition movements that arose in Russia at the end of the nineteenth century. As the most significant portent for the future, although hardly noticeable at first, members of the Russian intelligentsia adopted the ideas of German political philosopher and revolutionary Karl Marx. Tsarist censors, deeming Marx's writings too abstract and incomprehensible to be dangerous, had allowed publication of his works in Russia. Indeed, some who read Marx could not see how his theories about industrial society in Western Europe applied to tsarist Russia. A few intellectuals, however, found Marx's ideas attractive. Among them was

George Plekhanov, a radical critic of tsarism living in exile in Europe, who converted to Marxism from populism. Plekhanov is now remembered as "the father of Russian Marxism."

To understand why Marxism appealed so strongly to some radicals, we need briefly to review the main points of Marx's ideology. Marx sought to describe what he saw as the unjust nature of capitalism, to demonstrate the inevitable collapse of that system, and to point the way to a future society that would combine economic security and equity based on large-scale industrial production with the legal and social equality and the personal and political freedom proclaimed by the French Revolution. In essence Marx tried to set up a system that would make good on the promise of that revolution to provide "liberty, equality, and fraternity." Although vague about how this somewhat utopian society would come into being and how it would operate, Marx was definite about the steps leading up to its formation.

Marx believed in materialism and concluded that the economic base provided the most important determinant of any social system. Politics, culture, education, and social structure all derived from that base. Society changed because the economic base contained elements constantly in conflict. In particular, better methods of surviving and making a living kept challenging old ways. The class of those who controlled or owned the new methods competed with older economic groups or classes. Change through conflict between old and new classes is known in Marxism as the dialectic process.

This process was embodied in laws of history that Marx firmly believed he had scientifically discovered. Moreover, these laws were predetermined and inevitable; nothing could stop or alter them. Marx and his collaborator, Friedrich Engels, argued that history is divided into five great stages: *gentilism*, whereby human beings live in clans and hold property in common; *slavery*, in which a society's economy is based on slave labor, and slave owners dominate; *feudalism*, in which society depends on serf labor and the rule of lords and nobles; *capitalism*, whereby entrepreneurs or capitalists pay workers, or *the* proletariat, wages to produce goods for the market; and *socialism*, in which private ownership is abolished and replaced by public ownership of the means of production, and only one class exists, thus ending inequality and oppression. These theories of Marx are known as dialectical and historical materialism. (See the figure, Marx's stages of history.)

Most of Marx's research and writing focused on the stages of feudalism and capitalism. Through a lengthy analysis that few endorse today, Marx concluded that inherent contradictions characterized capitalism. The most serious of these derived from the theoretically unlimited potential of capitalism to increase production, versus the reality that capitalists, driven to maximize profits, instead strove to limit production. As a result, Marx predicted, an increasingly violent struggle would emerge between the capitalist factory owners and their wage slaves, the proletariat, who represented socialist or common ownership. In most of his writings, Marx foresaw the outcome of this class struggle as a bloody revolution that would bring the workers to power and establish the foundation of the new socialist society. Occasionally, Marx implied that this change-over could take place peacefully.

After the proletarian or socialist revolution, the workers, already an overwhelming majority of the population, would establish a "dictator-ship of the proletariat," or firm rule by the workers to demolish remnants of the capitalist order. This dictatorship would be brief, serving as a tran-sition to a one-class society in which the state as a coercive mechanism would disappear. In the new socialist society, production, freed from capitalist restraints, would increase multifold, yielding a superabun-dance of goods. This plenitude would provide enough to meet every-one's basic needs. At the same time, common ownership of the economy would end greed and acquisitiveness and lead citizens to become socially oriented. These "new-type socialist individuals" would eagerly seek to help the whole society and would contribute to the full extent of their tal-ents in work. Socialism would serve as the final stage of history because

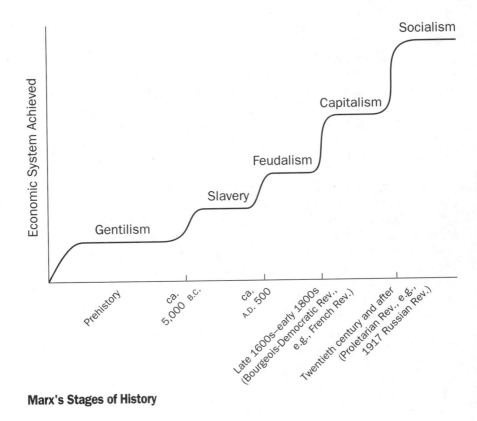

Marx's Stages of History

it would abolish the economic and class contradictions that drive the dialectic process.

For several reasons, this theory, although focused on industrialism in Western Europe, appealed powerfully to Russian radicals. Mindful of the setbacks and uncertainties that had characterized the Russian revolutionary movement from the 1360s through the 1880s, when both education and terrorism had failed to produce change, the radicals were inspired and emboldened by Marxism's scientific certainty. It was not a question of *whether* the old tsarist system could be overthrown and replaced with a benevolent socialist society, but simply *when*. The revolution's inevitability gave its proponents a confidence that no other ideology could provide. Marxism appealed also because it focused on the most beleaguered and powerless group in Russia, the workers. Dialectical materialism promised them a key historic role and a dramatic victory.

Through illegal pamphlets, study circles, and personal contacts, the tenets of Marxism spread among the Russian intelligentsia and reached some workers during the 1880s and 1890s. Although Marx himself formulated conflicting analyses of Russian society, Russian radicals easily adapted his theories to their own predilections. Because of the country's very backwardness and communal traditions, they argued, Russia would pass from its present feudal stage quickly through capitalism and on to the utopian ideal of socialism, and hence avoid the drawn-out evils of capitalism that Marx had described in Western Europe.

Vladimir Ulianov, who later adopted the pseudonym Lenin (perhaps based on a childhood nickname), was only in his early twenties when he became a prominent Marxist revolutionary in the 1890s. Ulanov had grown up in an intellectual atmosphere. His father, a middle-rank civil servant, was an inspector of state schools, and his mother, who encouraged her children's academic interests and critical attitudes, was the daughter of a doctor. An outstanding student in secondary school, Ulianov was expelled from Kazan University during his first year for participating in radical activities. He later acquired a law degree but practiced only briefly. From the beginning, he made revolution his profession. An idealist in many respects, Ulianov believed that the suffering and injustice he observed in the tsarist system could be cured only by the forcible overthrow of that system, and he devoted his life to this goal.

Arrested in 1895 for leading Marxist study circles for workers in St. Petersburg, Ulianov was exiled to a village in Siberia. When his exile ended, the young revolutionary, now calling himself Lenin, left for Europe. He would not return to Russia until the first revolution broke out in 1905. While in Siberia, Lenin had married Nadezhda Krupskaya, who became his revolutionary companion. She supported his plans to overturn the tsar and after the Bolshevik Revolution, took an active role in promoting socialist education. Following Lenin's death in 1924, Krupskaya remained a loyal Party member until her death in 1936, although she became increasingly disillusioned with Stalin's policies.

In 1898 the first Marxist party, the Russian Social Democratic Labor party (RSDLP), held its founding meeting; most of the attendees were quickly arrested. In those early years, Russian Marxists coped not only with police surveillance and harassment but also with heretical ideas within the revolutionary movement. Lenin and his supporters railed particularly against "economism," an emphasis by some radicals on concrete and immediate benefits for workers, such as shorter hours, higher wages, and improved working and living conditions. Lenin argued that these aims were entirely wrong for the Russian labor movement. Even if these concessions were won, he argued, the system would remain unchanged. In Lenin's view, economism only diverted workers from their true goal—revolution—and played into the hands of the government and the capitalist exploiters of the proletariat. Lenin urged that workers be educated to concentrate instead on overthrowing tsarism and establishing a socialist order.

His arguments against economism strengthened Lenin's inherent sense that the proletariat, left to its own devices, would fall into the trap of "trade union consciousness," that is, the seeking of specific workplace benefits. He became convinced that workers needed strong leadership to educate them, to raise their "revolutionary consciousness," and to guide them in organizing and carrying out the revolution. Lenin believed that the revolutionary party should provide that leadership, and to do so, it had to be a small, close-knit, disciplined band of professional revolutionaries. A paternalistic concept, this view of the party as a vanguard was set forth in Lenin's 1902 pamphlet, *What Is To Be Done?* Lenin's ideas, some critics argue, amounted to a case of "party knows best" and contributed to the authoritarian nature of the Soviet socialist system that emerged after the 1917 revolutions. Lenin defended his concept of an elite, centralized party by insisting that only such a tightly knit organization could withstand police attempts to infiltrate (although the police later did so) and liberals' efforts to water down its doctrine with fuzzy-minded reform ideas.

Lenin's outspoken views on the structure of a revolutionary Marxist party in Russia soon brought him into conflict with other prominent Marxists, including Plekhanov, the movement's first prominent leader, Iuli Martov, and Pavel Akselrod. They argued for a broad-based party open to anyone who accepted its goals, even those who could not work for it full time, and they urged a focus on education and agitation rather than on revolution. These opposing views of the nature of the party led to a serious division in the Russian Marxist party (RSDLP) at its second congress, which met in 1903 in Europe to avoid surveillance. On one crucial vote, Lenin and his followers won a majority, even though on most issues they proved a minority at the congress and within the overall movement. Lenin's faction thus acquired the name "Majorityites," or Bolsheviks, whereas his opponents were labeled "Minority-ites," or Mensheviks. Despite repeated attempts to heal this rift over the next few years and the indifference of many active revolutionaries inside Russia to the factional quarrels of party leaders, most of whom lived in Western Europe, the party formally split in 1912. After the collapse of tsardom in 1917, important new differences between the Mensheviks and Bolsheviks came to light, as we shall see in Chapter 3.

The chief rival of the Russian Marxist party at the turn of the century was the Socialist Revolutionary (SR) party, based on peasant socialism. This group, an outgrowth of populism, stressed the role of the masses in overthrowing the tsar and building a new communal order. But unlike populism, the peasant socialism that emerged in the 1890s supported violent revolution and foresaw a socialist society based on industrialism as well as the peasant *mir*. Thus, although it recruited heavily among the peasantry, the SR party also sought to propagandize and win over workers. As part of its attraction, the party promised that Russian society would pass directly to the elysian stage of socialism without experiencing capitalism's brutal exploitation of the masses. The SRs were vague as to just how this leaping transition would be accomplished, but the idea of a direct road to socialism held more appeal for many workers than did the Marxists' premise that Russia would have to suffer through capitalism first albeit briefly.

Just as populism had spun off a terrorist strand in the People's Will movement, the Socialist Revolutionary party contained a minority faction who urged the use of terror to undermine the government's will and to rouse the masses to action. SR terrorist units succeeded in assassinating hundreds of tsarist officials in the early years of the twentieth century.

The SRs and Marxists, led by members of the intelligentsia, won over a few thousand workers and some peasants in the first years of the twentieth century, but most Russians considered both parties radical fringe groups. The growing numbers of liberals in various walks of Russian life proved more influential. Eschewing the socialists' revolutionary methods, liberals urged peaceful change while strongly opposing the existing tsarist government. Some liberals wanted to see Russia become a constitutional monarchy; others favored replacing tsarism with a republic. All heartily endorsed civil liberties, rule of law, and some form of representative government at the national level. Many also supported free-market forces and wanted to curtail government intervention in the economy. Proponents of liberal ideas existed among the leaders and technical specialists of the *zemstvo* system, throughout the professions, in the ranks of educated nobility, and increasingly in the emerging class of Russian businessmen and industrialists. A prominent historian, Paul Miliukov, who had lectured at the University of Chicago, helped to found the first liberal party in 1905, the Constitutional Democratic party (known as the Kadets from its Russian initials, K.D.).

Conclusion

By the first years of the twentieth century, ferment roiled the Russian Empire. On the surface, the old order persisted. The political system of autocracy stood largely unchanged, despite earlier reforms of local government and the judicial system. The nobility still dominated. The government continued to glorify conservative values of Russian nationalism, Orthodox religion, and Slavic virtue and to repress other ideas.

Yet underneath, change percolated. Industrialization and urbanization were transforming the economic and social structure of Russia. A new class of factory workers was taking shape, and the old merchant class was rapidly expanding into a new social stratum of bankers, businessmen, engineers, and persons trained in the professions. Both groups demanded an overhaul of the system. Staggering under a heavy tax burden and the pressures of a population boom, peasants, too, felt the first impact of modernization as new ideas and technology reached them. Driven by a desperate need for more land and economic betterment, they turned more and more to violence and direct action. National minorities in almost every corner of the empire resisted Russification policies. They demanded fairer treatment and greater autonomy, and their nationalistic sentiment grew.

Ignoring signs of an imminent eruption, Tsar Nicholas II and his advisers sat atop this volcano and pursued standpat or regressive policies. A few farsighted officials, like Sergei Witte, urged modest and controlled reform, but the autocrat and most nobles ignored such advice. They persisted in their belief that the Russian government could continue to manage its problems at home while advancing its national interests abroad in competition with the European Great Powers and with the rising threat from Japan. They would soon be proved tragically wrong on both counts.

Spurred in part by a deep resentment of the injustice and oppression of the old order and in part by the problems that arose as Russia industrialized, opposition to tsarism mushroomed in the last third of the nineteenth century. United in their determination to change the old order, critics of the government advanced two main alternatives: liberalism and socialism. Liberals argued for constitutional government, individual rights, and the rule of law, and enjoyed growing support at many levels of society. Socialists strove to replace tsarism with a communally owned economy and an egalitarian system. One group of socialists, the Marxists, emphasized the scientific inevitability of revolution, the need for Russia to develop a capitalist economy, and the dominant role of industrial workers in both the revolution and the future good society. A second group, the Socialist Revolutionaries, believed that Russia could establish socialism by building on the collective institutions of peasant life and thereby avoid the evils of capitalism. The SRs did not neglect the workers but emphasized the potential of the peasantry for revolutionary action and socialist reconstruction.

As the twentieth century dawned, tsarist leaders had largely forgotten the dark omen of the Khodynka Meadow coronation tragedy. Yet in fact the imperial system showed severe strains and the prognosis appeared grim. Fundamental socioeconomic changes were deepening, and anger, dissent, and unrest intensified. The government, however, staunchly resisted reform. This volatile brew needed little to touch off an explosion. Two events between 1900 and 1904—a crisis in the agricultural economy and an unpopular war with Japan—would spark Russia's first modern upheaval, the Revolution of 1905, which is the focus of the next chapter.

FURTHER READING

For a brief, general introduction to Russia's earlier history, consult John M. Thompson, *Russia and the Soviet Union*, 3rd ed., (Boulder, Co., 1994). On the nineteenth century, see Hugh Seton Watson, *The Russian Empire, 1801–1917* (Oxford, Eng., 1967). The best analytical overview of the last years of tsardom is Hans Rogger, *Russia in the Age of Modernisation and Revolution, 1831–1917* (London and New York, 1983).

A few selected works from the vast literature on late nineteenth century Russia include, on economic history: William Blackwell, *The Industrialization of Russia*, 2nd ed. (Arlington Heights, Ill., 1982); Peter Gatrell, *The Tsarist Economy, 1850–1917* (New York, 1986); Paul Gregory, *Before Command: An Economic History of Russia from Emancipation to the First Five Year Plan* (Princeton, N.J., 1994); and Alexander Gerschenkron, "Russian Economic History Before 1917," in Gerschenkron, *Continuity in History and Other Essays* (Cambridge, Mass., 1968).

On urban issues: Joseph C. Bradley, *Muzhik and Muscovite. Urbanization in Late Imperial Russia* (Berkeley, 1985); Daniel Brower, *The Russian City Between Tradition and Modernity, 1850–1900* (Berkeley, 1990); and Michael Hamm, ed., *The City in Late Imperial Russia* (Bloomington, Ind., 1986).

On workers: Theodore H. Friedgut, *Iuzovka and Revolution.* Vol. 1: *Life and Work in Russia's Donbass, 1869–1924* (Princeton, N.J., 1989); Rose Glickman, *Russian Factory Women: Workplace and Society, 1800–1914* (Berkeley, 1984); and Victoria E. Bonnell, *Roots of Rebellion: Workers' Politics and Organizations in St. Petersburg and Moscow, 1900–1914* (Berkeley, 1983).

On reform, change, and the government's reaction: C. E. Black, ed., *The Transformation of Russian Society: Aspects of Social Change Since 1861* (Cambridge, Mass., 1960); Dominic Lieven, *Russia's Rulers Under the Old Regime* (New Haven, 1989); Terence Emmons and Wayne S. Vucinich, eds., *The Zemstvo in Russia: An Experiment in Local Self-Government* (New York, 1982); W. Bruce Lincoln, *The Great Reforms: Autocracy, Bureaucracy, and the Politics of Change in Imperial Russia* (Dekalb, Ill., 1990); David A. J. Macey, *Government and Peasant in Russia, 1861–1906* (Dekalb, Ill., 1987); W. E. Mosse,

Alexander II and the Modernization of Russia (New York, 1962, 1992); T. Von Laue, *Sergei Witte and the Industrialization of Russia* (New York, 1963); Heide W. Whelan, *Alexander III and the State Council: Bureaucracy and Counter-Reform in Late Imperial Russia* (New Brunswick, N.J., 1982); Peter A. Zaionchkovsky, *The Russian Autocracy in Crisis, 1867–1882*, ed. and trans. Gary M. Hamburg (Gulf Breeze, Fla., 1979); and Edward Judge, *Easter in Kishinev: Anatomy of a Pogrom* (New York, 1993).

On various social strata: Seymour Becker, *Nobility and Privilege in Late Imperial Russia* (Dekalb, Ill., 1985); Gary Hamburg, *Politics of the Russian Nobility, 1881–1905* (New Brunswick, N.J., 1984); Roberta T. Manning, *The Crisis of the Old Order in Russia* (Princeton, N.J., 1983); George Fischer, *Russian Liberalism: From Gentry to Intelligentsia* (Cambridge, Mass., 1958); Gregory L. Freeze, *The Parish Clergy in Nineteenth Century Russia: Crisis, Reform, Counter-Reform* (Princeton, N.J., 1983); Geroid T. Robinson, *Rural Russia Under the Old Regime* (repr. New York, 1949); E. Kingston-Mann and T. Mixter, eds., *Peasant Economy, Culture, and Politics of European Russia, 1800–1921* (Princeton, N.J., 1991); R. Bartlett, ed., *Land Commune and Peasant Community in Russia* (London, 1990); Barbara Alpern Engel, *Mothers and Daughters: Women of the Intelligentsia in Nineteenth-Century Russia* (Cambridge, 1983); Christine D. Worobec, *Peasant Russia: Family and Community in the Post-Emancipation Period* (Princeton, N.J., 1991); Richard Stites, *The Women's Liberation Movement in Russia* (Princeton, N.J., 1978); Barbara Evans Clements, Barbara Alpern Engle, and Christine D. Worobec, eds., *Russia's Women: Accommodation, Resistance, Transformation* (Berkeley, 1991); Thomas C. Owen, *Capitalism and Politics in Russia: A Social History of the Moscow Merchants, 1855–1905* (Cambridge, Mass., 1981); Bruce W. Menning, *Bayonets Before Bullets: The Imperial Russian Army, 1861–1914* (Bloomington, Ind., 1992).

On the revolutionary movement, many monographs exist. Overviews include Franco Venturi, *Roots of Revolution: A History of the Populist and Socialist Movements in Nineteenth-Century Russia* (New York, 1960); John H. L. Keep, *The Rise of Russian Social Democracy* (Oxford, 1963); Philip Pomper, *The Russian Revolutionary Intelligentsia*, 2nd ed. (New York, 1993); and Avraham Yarmolinsky, *Road to Revolution: A Century of Russian Radicalism* (London, 1957, 1986).

On foreign affairs: Dietrich Geyer, *Russian Imperialism: The Interaction of Domestic and Foreign Policy, 1860–1914*, trans. Bruce Little (New Haven, 1987); Steven G. Marks, *Road to Power: The Trans-Siberian Railroad and the Colonization of Asian Russia, 1850–1917* (Ithaca, N.Y., 1991); and B. H. Sumner, *Tsardom and Imperialism in the Far East and Middle East, 1880–1914* (London, 1968).

On culture: Jeffrey Brooks, *When Russia Learned to Read: Literacy and Popular Literature, 1861–1914* (Princeton, N.J., 1985); Ben Eklof, *Russian Peasant Schools: Officialdom, Village Culture, and Popular Pedagogy, 1861–1914* (Berkeley, 1986); and Louise McReynolds, *The News Under Russia's Old Regime* (Princeton, N.J., 1991).

2

REVOLUTION AND REFORM

In St. Petersburg, the beautiful capital of the Russian Empire, the bright sun, although low in the sky, sparkled on the golden domes of Orthodox churches and reflected glaringly from the snow piled up along the streets. It was Sunday, January 22, 1905. In the outlying quarters of the city, workers and their families gathered for a procession to the Winter Palace, the city residence of Tsar Nicholas II. From the southwestern suburbs, a substantial crowd moved slowly toward the Narva Gate, a major entrance to the central city. The marchers, several thousand strong now, carried icons, portraits of tsars, and a large cross. With bared heads, they sang hymns as they proceeded.

At their head walked Father Georgy Gapon, an enigmatic priest turned savior of the poor, who with the blessing and support of the police and the tsarist government had organized a dozen workers' assemblies in various parts of the city over the previous two years. These local associations largely promoted cultural and charitable activities among the working poor, but as they gained popularity, Gapon's assemblies began to defend workers' rights more broadly. In response to a recent labor dispute at the huge Putilov metallurgical factory, Father Gapon and his followers had helped to instigate a widespread strike that crippled not only the plant but many other industrial enterprises in the city. Apparently convinced that the tsar would intercede, Gapon and his supporters determined to present the workers' most urgent needs and long-range demands directly to the sovereign.

Their petition to Nicholas II urged him to redress the people's grievances and to ease their miserable living and working conditions. The workers also requested bold political reforms, including an elected legislative assembly, a move that directly challenged the traditional autocratic rule of the tsar. Although these radical demands frightened

Nicholas II's conservative advisers, the tone of the petition was respectful and supplicatory.

> We, the workers and inhabitants of St. Petersburg, . . . our wives, our children, and our aged, helpless parents, come to Thee, O Sire, to seek justice and protection. We are impoverished; we are oppressed, overburdened with excessive toil, contemptuously treated. We are not even recognized as human beings, but are treated like slaves who must suffer their bitter fate in silence and without complaint. . . . We are suffocating in despotism and lawlessness, O Sire, we have no strength left, and our endurance is at an end. We have reached that frightful moment when death is better than the prolongation of our sufferings. . . .
>
> Issue Thy orders and swear to fulfill them, and Thou wilt make Russia happy and glorious, and Thy name will forever be engraved in our hearts . . . But if Thou . . . failest to respond to our supplications, we will die here on this square before Thy palace.

And in one of the senseless tragedies that mar twentieth-century Russian history, die they did. For as the procession drew close to the Narva Gate, the front ranks met a squadron of cavalry and a line of riflemen drawn up across the road to block their path. Linking arms, the crowd sang more loudly and advanced resolutely. The bugler sounded "fire" three times, and the troops shot twice into the air. Undeterred, the march leaders hastened onward, pressed by the rear ranks who could not see what was happening. Suddenly the riflemen lowered their guns and fired point-blank into the crowd. Amazingly, Gapon was not killed. Standing amid the bodies and the groans of the wounded, he reportedly cried, "There is no God any longer! There is no tsar!" Indeed, the tsar was not even in the Winter Palace but at his country residence, and his officials' callous and panic-stricken shooting of several hundred unarmed workers throughout the city on that Bloody Sunday marked a turning point in the Revolution of 1905. Traditionally, the masses had looked to the "Father-Tsar" as their benevolent protector and ultimate solace. The debacle shattered that trust and reverence, and the people's demands for change would ring repeatedly in the years to come.[1]

---

[1]This account of Bloody Sunday is based on the description in Walter Sablinsky, *The Road to Blood Sunday* (Princeton, N.J.: Princeton Univ. Press, 1976), pp. 239–244; the full petition is translated on pp. 344–349.

A Blood Bath Tsarist troops firing on demonstrators during Bloody Sunday, 1905.

On the Brink

Bloody Sunday ushered in a year of upheaval that saw much of the populace mount a broad revolutionary challenge to the autocracy and the whole tsarist system. Galvanized by an unpopular, losing war against Japan and by a severe recession in the countryside, Russians, as well as many non-Russians, resorted to strikes, mutinies, rural violence, and a workers' rebellion in Moscow to express their displeasure. By a mix of concession and repression, Nicholas II survived and managed to preserve much of the old order. For the next eight years, apparent calm reigned as the country progressed economically, and conservative governments cooperated uneasily with a new semilegislative body, the Duma. Public education spread, popular and high culture flourished, and the authorities pushed through a major reform of peasant landholding and society. Yet the ongoing industrialization and concomitant social changes heightened cleavages within the system, and resentment sharpened toward the largely unresponsive governing structure and the continuing privileges and arrogance of the elite. By 1914 Russia again hovered on the brink of chaos. Its disastrous involvement in World War I sufficed to push the nation over the edge.

The underlying tensions in Russian society outlined in Chapter 1 heightened as the twentieth century dawned. Bloody Sunday highlighted workers' complaints and governmental callousness, but other groups expressed similar outrage. The bitterness of those working the land was summed up in the rural adage, "The shortage will be divided among the peasants." Liberals and non-Russians felt no happier. Spreading literacy and education facilitated the exchange of increasingly critical and reformist ideas.

Specific grievances in the first years of the twentieth century built on this restive foundation. In late 1899, the Russian economy staggered under a depression that wore on until 1903 and into 1904. Workers suffered layoffs, wage reductions, and efforts by industrialists and the government to cut costs at their expense. To defend themselves, workers hit back with protests, demonstrations, and strikes. In 1903 alone, 138,877 workers participated in 550 work stoppages. Their efforts were to little avail, however: management customarily responded by firing the strikers.

In 1902, faced with steadily worsening land shortages and falling grain prices, peasants began to take violent action, seizing landlords' tools and seed, occupying woodlots and pasture, and occasionally taking over state or private lands. Kharkov and Poltava provinces experienced the worst uprisings. The alarmed government commissioned a national study of "The Needs of Rural Society" but failed to act quickly enough to dampen the growing unrest.

Liberals, who advocated mainly civil liberties and representative government, fumed at the government's continued refusal to expand even the limited self-governing *zemstvo* system. In the mid-1890s, some *zemstvo* leaders had talked of convening a national congress of their representatives as an advisory body to the tsar. Nicholas II and his officials resolutely opposed the idea and began to harass the more active *zemstvo* leaders. This policy only radicalized many liberals, who organized private meetings and pursued their political goals in publications and by word of mouth. Opposition to the tsarist system intensified, and some liberals debated joining forces with angry workers and disgruntled peasants against the government.

Among the empire's non-Russian minorities, socioeconomic complaints often combined with local nationalism to ferment a dangerous revolutionary brew. In Gurya, for example, a district in the Caucasus, government authority broke down completely during 1903 in the face of peasant demands for land and their refusal to pay taxes. Local Georgian Marxists managed in part to capture and guide this minirebellion, which in 1905 blended with a broader anti-Russian revolutionary movement. In Armenia, nationalist agitation forced the government to rescind its earlier sequestration of funds of the Armenian church. In Azerbaijan, a deplorable side effect of nationalism surfaced in 1905 when Armenians and Muslims living in the city of Baku battled in ethnic riots that left almost a thousand people dead, an ominous harbinger of the fighting between Armenians and Azerbaijanis that would break out in 1987.

In Poland, where nationalist feeling accelerated at the end of the nineteenth century, opposition to the tsarist system was split. Those who benefited from Poland's rapid industrialization or who feared German annexation of the area urged only cultural autonomy within the Russian Empire, not independence. Others favored political autonomy achieved by negotiation. More radical leaders demanded the overthrow of the autocracy and formation of a separate Polish state. Militant Polish workers, prepared to crusade for not only economic demands but also political rights, ranked among the most unruly revolutionaries in 1905.

In Ukraine, nationalist groups demanded a local assembly and cultural and political autonomy. Peasant unrest in the area also had nationalistic overtones. In the Baltic provinces and Finland, workers joined strikes, while intellectuals continued to protest Russification.

By 1903 dissent and unrest rent the vast Russian Empire. The detachments of a broad revolutionary army—peasants, workers, liberals, and national minorities—marshaled their forces against the unyielding tsarist system. At this pivotal juncture, the government blundered into an unpopular conflict with Japan that it soon lost. The Russo-Japanese War of 1904–1905 did not cause the Revolution of 1905, whose origins, as we have seen, had far deeper roots. But clearly the conflict helped to trigger that upheaval.

The tsarist government became embroiled with Japan as a direct consequence of Russia's policy of imperialist expansion. During the mid-nineteenth century, Russia had acquired Central Asia and founded the city of Vladivostok as a naval and commercial outpost on the Pacific Ocean. When the Russian government's efforts to extend its influence into the Balkans were checked by the other European powers following the Russo-Turkish War of 1877–1878 and Bulgaria's independence victory in 1885, tsarist officials focused their attention on opportunities for expansion in East Asia, particularly at the expense of the declining Chinese Empire. Tsarist bureaucrats became convinced that Russia's economic interest and its "manifest destiny" as a civilizing power compelled it to extend its control over Manchuria and possibly Korea. The Japanese, who had launched a radical modernization of their society, grumbled at the prospect of Russian encroachments into territory, particularly Korea, that they regarded as within their sphere of influence.

In 1896 the Russian government acquired the right to build a railroad line across Manchuria, and in 1898 it obtained a long-term lease to Port Arthur on the Liaotung Peninsula between China and Korea. Two years later, Russian forces joined troops from several European powers to suppress the Boxer Rebellion, an antiforeign uprising by the Chinese of northern China. As a result, the tsarist government increased its military presence in Manchuria, stationing armed units along the Chinese Eastern Railway there. Imperial activists also obtained a timber concession along the Korean border as a first step toward establishing Russian domination of Korea. Thoroughly alarmed, the Japanese offered a tentative diplomatic settlement under which they would retain control over Korea while leaving Manchuria to the Russians. Tsarist officials ignored these conciliatory feelers.

How could the tsar and his advisers have failed to see the danger in snubbing Japan? The answer sheds light on some of the system's faults. First, Nicholas II, unrealistic and still relatively inexperienced, convinced himself despite warning signals that war would not break out simply because he did not want it. Second, the most adventurous of the tsar's ministers and advisers gained the upper hand over the cautionaries and captured the autocrat's ear. Third, owing to racist attitudes about the Japanese, most Russian officials felt sure that if war came, Russia would easily prevail. Finally, almost no one saw any link between Russia's imperialistic foreign policy and its internal affairs. Those who did perceive a connection believed, as Minister of the Interior Viacheslav Plehve allegedly concluded, that a "short victorious war" might even help to quell popular unrest. Consequently, although tsarist officials were surprised and annoyed when in January 1904 the Japanese launched a sudden attack on Russian military and naval units in the Far East, they remained unperturbed. According to one senior bureaucrat, Japan's military blow was ". . . a mere episode; no one attached any importance to it. . . . Everyone was supremely confident that there would be a speedy termination of the 'adventure.'"[2]

At first most Russians greeted news of the conflict with patriotic enthusiasm. Speeches, demonstrations, and press articles proclaimed loyalty to the tsar and urged the nation to rally around the armed forces. But from the start, the Russian army and navy fared badly, as the Japanese racked up land and sea victories and Russian losses mounted. Moreover, although the war benefited factories that produced military goods, it placed enormous burdens on the textile and other consumer industries, on artisan production, and on agriculture, from which conscripts and work animals were taken. As early as April 1904, criticism that the government was mismanaging the war and complaints about worsening economic conditions began to proliferate. Within eighteen months, this grumbling would turn into a full-fledged, nationwide revolution that nearly toppled Nicholas II from his throne and that spread aftershocks for months to come.

1905

The customary appellation in English for the first modern popular uprising against the Russian autocratic system, the Revolution of 1905, implies

---

[2]Quoted in Abraham Ascher, *The Revolution of 1905* (Stanford, Calif.: Stanford Univ. Press, 1988), p. 46.

a precision that the event itself lacked. Active opposition to the tsarist government evolved over many months and gradually engaged a wide variety of classes and groups. The tsar's determination to concede as little as possible only stoked the insurrectionary fire. Although inchoate and untidy, the uprisings nevertheless climaxed in a revolution, for some participants indeed nearly overturned the system. Yet it is impossible to say exactly when the Revolution of 1905 began or ended. No single event triggered it, but by mid-to-late 1904, discontent with the government had reached a fever pitch. Soldiers and peasants continued to rebel well into 1906 and a few even into 1907. Thus this upheaval could more accurately be called the Revolution of 1904–1907.

A defining event early in the revolution's unfolding was the terrorist assassination of Minister of the Interior Plehve in July 1904. After his appointment in 1902 and the subsequent resignation of Minister of Finance Witte in 1903, Plehve dominated the government and unabashedly advocated a policy of repression and intransigence. So when the assassins struck him down, no public outcry followed. Instead liberals stepped up their criticism of the system, implying that with Plehve gone, the moment for fundamental change had arrived. In the fall of 1904, the liberals broadened their campaign. Defying the tsar, they called a national meeting of *zemstvo* representatives. Although the central authorities refused to sanction the congress, they allowed it to meet unofficially and agreed to receive a report on its recommendations. Everyone at the congress favored the rule of law and civil liberties. The attendees also put forth several resolutions on governance, one of which suggested an elected advisory body to the tsar. In a more radical and widely backed statement, some delegates proposed establishing a representative parliament.

At about the same time a liberal group that had formed among exiles abroad, the Union of Liberation, promoted a series of banquet meetings throughout Russia. Modeled on agitational dinners held on the eve of the French revolution of 1848, these occasions allowed educated opponents of the government to gather, exchange views, and articulate demands for reform. From mid-November 1904 to mid-January 1905, thirty-eight such banquets were held in a number of major cities and large provincial towns. Although usually organized by liberals, the meetings also attracted revolutionaries. Consequently, the banquet campaign broadened and consolidated opposition to the tsarist system and put the government under increasing pressure to act. The agitation of newly formed associations of professionals, such as doctors and engineers, and of their umbrella organization, the Union of Unions, supported the campaign.

Two women's organizations, the Russian Women's Mutual Philanthropic Society, founded in 1895, and the recently established All-Russian Union for Women's Equality, also backed the liberals. During the decade of repression under Alexander III, the women's movement had been quiescent. When several female activists revived it as the Mutual Philanthropic Society, its methods proved moderate and its goals modest—broadening intellectual opportunities for women and improving conditions for needy and working women. During the Revolution of 1905, the society took up the cause of political rights for women. The Union for Women's Equality, which demanded that women be allowed to vote for deputies to city *dumas* and *zemstvos*, stepped up its efforts in the political arena.

Although fully cognizant of the liberals' mounting demands for political reform, Nicholas II and his advisers waffled. Prince Peter Sviatopolk-Mirsky, a moderate who had replaced Plehve as minister of the interior, suggested limited reform. But the tsar, stiffened by conservatives at court, finally decided to strike a key point from the reform decree prepared by Mirsky and others: no elected representatives would advise this tsar on legislation. Nicholas declared in relief, "Under no circumstance will I ever agree to a representative form of government, for I consider it harmful to the trust God gave me over the people. . . ." Hearing of the tsar's decision, Mirsky lamented, "Everything has failed. Let us build jails."[3]

Whether marginal concessions could have blunted the liberal attack on the autocracy in late 1904 and early 1905 is doubtful. The majority of the autocracy's educated opponents had determined to achieve at least a constitutional monarchy. Moreover, the liberals were being pushed from below by other malcontents: workers, peasants, and non-Russians, most of whom would have scorned mere parliamentary concessions. The government's hesitant gestures toward reform whetted liberal appetites and encouraged the radical aspirations of other imperial subjects. Only sweeping changes could have dampened the building conflagration, changes that Nicholas II had determined not to grant.

Workers took the next step on the road to outright revolution. Their dissatisfaction with the war and the economy had mounted throughout 1904, and after Bloody Sunday, strikes and protest meetings erupted across the empire. In January 1905, almost 500,000 workers went on strike, dealing a severe blow to the economy. Some strikes centered on local issues; most embraced a range of economic demands such as shorter hours and higher wages. Although the majority of strikes broke out spontaneously, Social Democratic (Marxist) and Socialist Revolutionary agitators often helped to articulate workers' economic demands and encouraged them to add political goals, such as the right to unionize. These activists also called for a constituent assembly, to be elected by the "four-tailed formula" (secret, direct, universal, and equal elections), and for instituting a republic. Although most of the revolutionary parties' chief ideologists were in exile abroad, some, like Lenin, returned to Russia at the height of the Revolution of 1905.

---

[3]Both quoted in ibid., p. 71.

"Down with Autocracy!" So proclaims a banner carried by Moscow workers demonstrating during the Revolution of 1905. Other standards demand a constituent assembly and emblazon the Marxist slogan "Proletarians of All Countries, Unite!"

Women workers and socialists played a pivotal part in the 1905 revolution. Women had entered the labor force in droves during the 1890s, and by 1905 about 400,000 women held jobs, mainly in textile mills, small garment factories, and light consumer industries. Like women in other industrializing countries, they received less pay than men and were considered inferior to male workers. In 1895 women organized a major strike at a cigarette factory in St. Petersburg, and in 1905 they furthered the expanding strike movement. Nadezhda Krupskaya, Lenin's wife, and Alexandra Kollontai proved active Marxist socialists in the early 1900s, and after 1917 gained prominence in the Soviet government. The two activists believed that the proletarian revolution would bring female emancipation and equal rights, and urged women to back the cause. After agitating among women workers, however, Kollontai became convinced that a special program and organization were necessary to educate women and to lead them to revolution. Some male socialists criticized her separatist stance as diverting resources and energy away from the larger effort.

Women liberals like Ariadna Tyrkova, a prominent Kadet, also embraced the revolutionary movement in 1905. They primarily demanded female suffrage, and many joined the Union for Women's Equality. The union's first congress in May 1905 counted some eight thousand members in twenty-six chapters, still only a small fraction of women in Russia who possessed secondary or higher education. Although the liberal movement's male leaders endorsed the vote for women in principle, they maintained that now was an inopportune time to press this demand. Nevertheless, they reluctantly accepted the women's union as a member association of the Union of Unions in July 1905.

Later that year, after the tsar had agreed to a limited representative assembly, the national Duma, Russian women campaigned for the right to vote in elections to this body. Their efforts came to naught, despite the government's granting Finnish women suffrage for Finland's regional assembly. This defeat prompted the formation of a more militant Russian organization, the Women's Progressive party, which not only lobbied vigorously for female suffrage but also demanded an end to licensed prostitution. The party failed to achieve either goal and eventually dissolved. In December 1908, the government permitted the convening of the First All-Russian Women's Congress. When its working-class delegates could not agree with the conservative majority on a common program, they walked out, and the congress ultimately had little impact.

As the revolutionary movement gained momentum in 1905, peasants joined women, workers, and liberals in opposition to the old order. Rebellion in the countryside, which broke out in late February 1905, coincided with peaks of worker unrest only late in the year, when both the workers' and peasants' movements reached a crescendo. The peasants' revolt, however, had no direct ties to the liberal opposition or worker protests, although some peasants may have been emboldened by news of other groups' demanding their rights. Most peasant violence initially targeted landlords, not officials or government institutions. Nevertheless, by August 1905, an embryonic national organization, the Peasants' Union, had formed and began advancing political demands. A petition sent to the government in late May 1905 poignantly reflects the peasants' point of view: "Our needs are great, Your Majesty! . . . For two and a half centuries we endured servitude and thereby made it possible for the privileged classes to live in clover; we alone carried the burden of harsh military service. . . . For our unfailing centuries-old service to the state we received a wretched allotment of land with high redemption dues [and] we were deprived of all rights. . . ."[4] Peasants primarily demanded more land and equal rights, but their pleas revealed a broad spectrum of local variations. Although it is impossible to estimate the number of peasants involved in direct action, their movement touched most provinces of European Russia.

The actions of sailors and soldiers, the last group to join the expanding revolution in 1905, thoroughly frightened the government. If the armed forces could not be trusted, the administration concluded, the autocracy surely faced mortal danger. Army and navy mutinies stemmed

---

[4]Quoted in ibid., p. 165.

Cooked to Perfection In Eisenstein's 1925 film, *Battleship Potemkin*, sailors inspect rotten meat crawling with maggots.

mainly from anger over the humiliating conditions of enlisted men in both services. Indeed, a classic 1920s film by the great Soviet director Sergei Eisenstein depicts a sailors' uprising on the cruiser *Potemkin* in June 1905; in one scene, the camera zooms in on worms slithering across the meat served to the sailors. So graphic is the sight that the viewer wants immediately to take up arms with the rebellious crewmen. The *Potemkin* mutiny supported a general strike in the port of Odessa, but radicals tried in vain to incite a mass uprising and to spread the mutiny to other ships of the Black Sea fleet.

At the same time, Japan continued to hammer at Russia, crushing its armies on land and destroying most of a prime Russian naval squadron at the Battle of Tsushima Straits in May 1905. Although Russia made peace with Japan in early September 1905, the war's end did not immediately release troops that the tsar could then turn against the revolutionaries. A crippling, nationwide railroad strike that October temporarily blocked the return of reliable units from the Far Eastern armies. Moreover, mutinies erupted among army regiments in various parts of European Russia. Thus at the moment when the rebellion peaked among the civilian population, the tsarist authorities' trust in the armed forces as allies evaporated.

The October Manifesto

As 1905 ground on and the revolutionary movement in the country widened and deepened, the government continued to vacillate between minor concessions and suppression, by turns frustrating and enraging the populace. The public furor worsened, and the government seemed increasingly powerless to contain it. As an appalling by-product of the virtual anarchy, crime and vigilantism mushroomed in towns and cities across Russia. The incidence of murder and robbery soared, and citizens formed self-defense associations when the police failed to maintain order. In some cases, pogroms against Jews resumed, organized by a right-wing, protofascist group, the Union of Russian People, often associated with strong-arm squads known as Black Hundreds. Because the union proclaimed nationalist and monarchist slogans and implied that it had the backing of the Orthodox Church, many tsarist officials turned a blind eye to its atrocities.

In August 1905, the tsar finally approved plans for a limited representative body with advisory power, the Bulygin **Duma.** By now, however, this move hardly satisfied the bulk of the regime's opponents. In September 1905, the Russo-Japanese War ended as representatives of the two countries met in New Hampshire to sign the Treaty of Portsmouth. Although U.S. president Theodore Roosevelt, eager to burnish his reputation as a world leader, brokered the accord, in fact both sides had exhausted themselves financially and eagerly sought peace. As the loser, Russia acknowledged Japanese hegemony over Korea and southern Manchuria and gave up half of Sakhalin Island, which lay between Japan and the Russian Far East (see the map in Chapter 1, Expansion of the Russian Empire, 1853–1905, page 37). Russia might have incurred worse losses but for the skillful negotiating and public relations work of Sergei Witte, Russia's chief delegate at the peace talks.

Neither the war's conclusion nor the offer of the Bulygin Duma checked the revolutionary movement. In late summer and early fall, the number and length of strikes rose sharply, and for the first time, workers set up a militant organization—a *soviet,* or council of elected representatives—to defend their interests. Although the precise origins of the soviet are unclear, it probably arose as a committee of workers that directed and managed strike actions against foremen and owners. The soviet seems to have been modeled on the *mir*, in which each peasant household was represented. Workers' delegates to the soviet were elected democratically, often on the basis of one deputy for every several hundred workers in large factories and proportionally in smaller plants. The first soviet-type council was set up in the textile city of Ivanovo-Voznesensk, north of Moscow, but the idea soon spread to other industrial cities.

In October, workers struck a number of railways, hamstringing communications and transportation. With support from the liberals and revolutionaries, this and other strikes soon coalesced into a general strike. In St. Petersburg, the work stoppage brought life to a standstill, as factories, trolleys, stores, newspapers, schools, and universities ceased to operate. Even some of the tsar's officials walked off the job.

The government appeared paralyzed, and the end of the autocracy seemed at hand. Overwhelmed, Nicholas II finally turned to Witte, now a count as a reward for his success in negotiating the Treaty of Portsmouth. Witte bluntly informed the tsar that he must either appoint a dictator to crush the revolution by force or make concessions. Nicholas II reluctantly chose the latter strategy, confiding in a letter to his mother, "There was no other way out than to cross myself and give what everyone was asking for."[5]

On October 30, the tsar issued an imperial decree, drawn up by Witte and two colleagues, that was soon known as the October Manifesto. In it Nicholas promised a representative assembly that would be elected indirectly but that would have legislative powers. He also granted full civil liberties, that is, freedom of press, speech, and assembly. Subsequent decrees allowed for some concessions to national minorities, the right to unionize, and abolition of the peasants' redemption payments. Taken together, these measures went far toward establishing a constitutional and free society in Russia. Nicholas, who had yielded only because the alternative would bring a bloody war against his own subjects, expected that with one stroke the October Manifesto would sweep away the dissent and unrest that had brought the country to near chaos. When disorders and violent opposition, including programs against Jews, persisted, the frustrated tsar tried to whittle down his concessions. Nicholas also turned against Witte, now prime minister, who he felt had misled him into sacrificing his sacred authority.

Despite the tsar's disappointment and the continuing tumult, the October Manifesto did weaken the revolutionary movement by splitting the motley army of government opponents. Nicholas's concessions satisfied

---

[5] Quoted in Howard D. Mehlinger and John M. Thompson, *Count Witte and the Tsarist Government in the 1905 Revolution* (Bloomington, Ind.: Indiana Univ. Press, 1972), p. 46.

some liberals, who before long broke away from the recently founded liberal party, the Kadets. Together with other moderates, they formed a group called the Octobrists, who opposed further reform and pressed for an end to violence. In addition, many Kadets, though favoring a full parliamentary system, grew alarmed as disorders continued, especially when revolutionaries trampled the rights of landholders and factory owners. They agreed to accept the October Manifesto and to work within its provisions for further reform. In Saratov province, a scene of widespread peasant unrest, several nationally prominent *zemstvo* leaders turned against the revolution when rampagers attacked and pillaged their own estates or those of neighbors.

As respected liberals began to call for law and order, the workers' revolution crested in November and December 1905. With its advantageous location in the capital, the St. Petersburg Soviet of Workers' Deputies played a leading role in pushing the workers' cause. Although Social Democratic and Socialist Revolutionary leaders, including Lenin, had returned to Russia in 1905 and exerted some influence on the workers' movement, many delegates to the St. Petersburg soviet were not affiliated with any revolutionary party. They thus acted on their own as the soviet began to exercise a number of welfare, administrative, economic, and semipolitical functions. In this respect, the soviets of 1905, despite their disappearance after the revolution, foreshadowed the soviets that would become basic institutions of the new order after 1917.

In a tactical mistake, the St. Petersburg soviet decided in early December to press for an eight-hour workday, finally calling a general strike to back up this demand. But the workers were exhausted after weeks of strikes and demonstrations, and the government, enjoying greater public support than in October, resolved not to yield this time. The strike fizzled, and Prime Minister Witte had the soviet's leaders arrested. In protest, Moscow workers launched a series of strikes and demonstrations. With the encouragement of some Social Democrats in the Moscow Soviet, their actions led to an armed uprising against the government in December. Regular troops loyal to the tsar were dispatched to Moscow and brutally suppressed the rebellion.

In late fall, the government also sent detachments of loyal troops to the Baltic provinces and the Caucasus, along strike-bound railway lines, and into districts struck by the worst peasant violence. These punitive expeditions restored order by force and brought hundreds of revolutionaries to summary justice. Such measures, combined with the easing of Russification policies, eventually stifled the rebellions in non-Russian areas of the empire, but many of these regions remained under martial law or in a special state of "strengthened security" for some time. Thus by early 1906, the worst of the disorders had either died out or had been suppressed. Sporadic peasant violence, occasional strikes, and scattered mutinies in the armed forces continued for another eighteen months but posed no threat to the autocracy.

The tsar survived the Revolution of 1905, but barely. Because so many groups in the empire opposed the regime, the autocracy nearly collapsed by popular demand. Yet the revolutionaries' major strength also proved their chief weakness. Because of its breadth and spontaneity, the movement lacked unity and leadership. Neither the Kadet Miliukov nor the Bolshevik Lenin could control events or the public. Nor could the disparate antigovernment groups agree on goals and tactics. Instead, the revolution unfolded as a set of parallel mass demonstrations against the government, each faction clamoring for its own timetable, methods, and purposes. Moreover, the concessions to liberals in the October Manifesto and fears of the violence and threat to property that the workers' and peasants' rebellions represented divided the revolutionary movement and allowed the government to right itself. The regime might still have foundered but for the army, which despite continuing mutinies in 1906 retained loyal units that carried out repression.

Lenin called 1905 a "dress rehearsal" for the bigger revolution in 1917. Indeed, in 1917 Russia once more would find itself losing a war, and the same groups would again rebel, still divided in many ways. But the two revolutions had crucial differences. By 1917 the tsarist government would be more thoroughly discredited, and World War I would sicken and anger the Russian people far more than the Russo-Japanese War had. The workers' movement would prove bigger, more sophisticated, and with more solid leadership, and the non-Russian minorities stronger and more nationalistic than in 1905.

Nevertheless, the Revolution of 1905 exerted a tremendous impact on Russia. Although it failed to overthrow the tsar, it transformed the structure, psychology, and political culture of Russian society. Despite Nicholas II's determination not to give up one iota of the holy autocratic authority entrusted to him by his father Alexander III, he in fact yielded on the most crucial point. He conceded that representatives of the people should have some say in passing laws and, by implication, in governing themselves. No matter how the reactionaries tried to circumscribe this concession, the October Manifesto marked the end of absolutism in Russia and opened the door to popular sovereignty. After 1905 the regime also proposed measures to make even peasants equal citizens.

The 1905 upheaval thoroughly refuted the view of some contemporary observers that the Russian people were inherently subservient, if not servile, and were incapable of social and political consciousness and action. Not only educated liberals but simple peasants, oppressed national minorities, and barely literate workers, sailors, and soldiers articulated their grievances in that turbulent year. Organizing protests, demonstrations, strikes, and mutinies, they even fought on occasion to defend their rights and persons. No longer objects of class and governmental manipulation, they strove to control their own destiny.

Finally, almost all revolutionary groups, although they sought different goals, attained some of their objectives. Liberals did not see a full parliamentary system nor the complete rule of law, but they won a limited legislature, considerable civil freedom, and some expansion of legal constraints on the arbitrariness of the old regime. Workers did not achieve either a fully democratic or a socialist society nor gain all their economic demands, but they received some improvements in hours and working conditions, as well as the right to unionize and to join parties and associations. The peasants commanded the attention of the government and inspired a number of agricultural reforms. They also saw their redemption payments canceled and, because many frightened landowners sold their holdings, had the opportunity to lease or purchase land. Courses for women were opened or reestablished at every university, and women were allowed to enroll in men's programs at St. Petersburg and Moscow universities. Women gained little else, however. Non-Russian groups benefited unevenly: the Finns reacquired their autonomous status, but life for other groups remained largely unaltered. Nonetheless, for almost all non-Russians, the revolution temporarily moderated Russification policies and eased discrimination.

The Revolution of 1905 left several important legacies. Because the government offered some reform measures and a few groups benefited substantially, almost everyone's expectations for the future rose. Yet people had little faith in a regime that had yielded so reluctantly and that had then tried to retract some of its concessions. Whether Russian society could stave off future upheaval depended in part on the realization of the new social and political order promised in 1905.

The Duma Experiment

Reformed Russia lasted only eight years before the cataclysm of World War I engulfed it—too short a period to determine the restructured system's effectiveness and where Russian society was headed. Yet eight years was long enough for the nation to chalk up considerable progress in political participation, important changes in the lives of peasants and others, further industrialization, and a burst of cultural creativity. At the same time, the Duma period brought to light once again the deep-seated strains and fundamental anachronisms in the tsarist system. Would Russian society grow more modern and stable, or would it slide inexorably toward violent resolution of its persistent problems? The Duma years provide conflicting answers to this question.

The political system saw progress between 1905 and the eve of war in

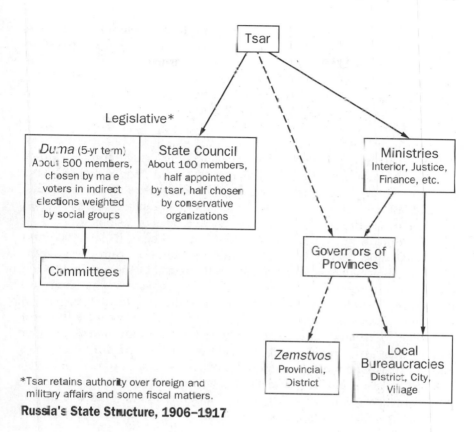

Legislative*

Duma (5-yr term)
About 500 members,
chosen by male
voters in indirect
elections weighted
by social groups

State Council
About 100 members,
half appointed
by tsar, half chosen
by conservative
organizations

Ministries
Interior, Justice,
Finance, etc.

Committees

Governors of
Provinces

*Tsar retains authority over foreign and
military affairs and some fiscal matters.

Russia's State Structure, 1906–1917

Zemstvos
Provincial,
District

Local
Bureaucracies
District, City,
Village

1913, but intrinsic and perhaps insurmountable contradictions remained. In the October Manifesto, the tsar had promised a legislative system and even hinted at instituting universal suffrage (male, of course). But once the revolt was brought under control, Nicholas and his conservative advisers bent every effort to restricting the concessions made in the manifesto. Thus when the "constitution" implied in the October decree finally won approval as the Fundamental Laws of the Russian Empire in early May 1906, it contained several important limitations on the Duma, or national legislative assembly. The most crippling of these reconstituted the old State Council, a weak advisory body, as an upper house of the Russian legislature. Its members, half elected by conservative organizations and half appointed by the tsar, had to approve all legislation. As the tsar and the conservatives intended, the State Council provided a powerful reactionary block to progressive lawmaking. Its expanded role signaled the government's innate unwillingness to cooperate with the new political order.

The Duma itself was to be elected by virtually all male citizens over the age of twenty-five but in a complex, indirect system and by classes. Individuals voted in five or six socioeconomic categories for deputies to electoral assemblies, which in turn selected Duma representatives. The proportional system at first heavily favored the nobility and the peasantry over other groups. Later changes shrank the peasantry's electoral influence. (See the figure, Russia's State Structure.)

In addition, the tsar retained full authority over certain key policy areas, including foreign and military affairs and some financial matters. Article I of the Fundamental Laws restated the principle of autocracy (even though the rest of the document breached it), and Article 87 gave the tsar the power to dissolve the Duma and to issue decrees with the force of law when it was not in session. This emergency clause permitted reactionaries to bypass the Duma on several crucial occasions.

Electoral campaigning for the First Duma began in late 1905 and continued until March 1906, with little interference from the government. The Socialist Revolutionaries and the Social Democrats boycotted the electoral process and castigated the Duma system as a sham, although in the final weeks a number of Mensheviks decided to participate and a few eventually won seats. The Kadets proved the best organized party and, not surprisingly, obtained a plurality. A number of non-Russian deputies were also elected, including fifty-one Poles and thirty Muslims. Surprisingly, the peasants, whom the tsar's advisers and most bureaucrats and nobles hoped would be a conservative political force, chose deputies who, although not belonging to a liberal or radical party, adopted thoroughly antigovernment and reformist positions.

By the time the Duma opened in May 1906, the government had recovered some of its former strength. The Russo-Japanese War had almost bankrupted the regime, but through the diligence and skill of Count Witte, Russia in early 1906 obtained a huge loan from France. As a consequence of this transaction, the empire tied itself ever more closely to France in European power politics, but the government gained some financial independence from the Duma, at least for a year or so. In addition, by spring 1906, the government had retrieved most of the extra troops sent to Manchuria to fight the Japanese; the majority of these proved loyal to the tsar.

Finally, the tsar and his advisers determined to treat the Duma with appropriate disdain. Vladimir Gurko, an attending senior bureaucrat, graphically described the opening session, at which Nicholas II read his address from the throne.

> The court had decided that this reception was to be particularly solemn and brilliant. The Imperial regalia . . . ranged on both sides of the throne. The throne was draped in the Imperial ermine mantle; it was said that the Tsarina herself had draped

The Duma Experiment Begins Prelates blessing the opening of the First Duma in May 1906.

the mantle so that it would hang in artistic folds. . . . The court and the government, flourishing gold-laced uniforms and numerous decorations, was set opposite the gray, almost rustic group representing the people of Russia. Naively believing that the people's representatives, many of whom were peasants, would be awed by the splendor of the Imperial court, the ladies of the Imperial family had worn nearly all their jewels; they were literally covered with pearls and diamonds. But the effect was altogether different . . . setting in juxtaposition the boundless Imperial luxury and the poverty of the people. The demagogues did not fail to comment upon this ominous contrast. Nor did the Tsar's address improve matters.[6]

Many other observers shared Gurko's evaluation of Nicholas's speech, for it contained no program or charge to the Duma. In fact, Count Witte had prepared a comprehensive and sensible set of proposals for the government to place before the Duma, but he had been forced out of office shortly before the assembly opened. The tsar, irrationally but stubbornly, still held Witte responsible for the weakening of autocratic authority in October and accused him of inconsistency and deceit. Witte, although he kept a seat on the State Council, never again played a major role in Russian politics, a regrettable loss of talent. Ivan Goremykin, the toady bureaucrat and political nonentity who replaced Witte, failed to introduce Witte's program in the Duma. As a result, the Kadets seized the initiative and demanded that the tsar's ministers be responsible to the assembly, that the Duma have greater control over the budget, and that a radical land reform be enacted at once. The government rejected all these requests, and after three months the tsar took advantage of his authority to dissolve the Duma.

Elections to the Second Duma in the fall of 1906 worsened the political impasse. Although the Kadets lost ground, radical parties participated fully and elected several deputies, and the peasants again returned oppositionist representatives. Openly hostile to the government, the Second Duma, like the first, proved unable to find a compromise program, and it too was dissolved after several months.

At this juncture, Peter Stolypin, Goremykin's successor as prime minister, decided on a bold step to restore political life to the system. Taking advantage of Article 87 of the Fundamental Laws, he issued new electoral rules that increased the representation of the nobility in selecting deputies from 32 to 50 percent and decreased that of the peasantry from 42 to 22 percent. One elector now represented 250 landowners, 1,000 large property holders in cities, 15,000 small property holders, 60,000 peasants, and

---

[6]Vernadsky, et al., Vol. III, p. 775.

125,000 workers. The new law also reduced the number of non-Russian deputies in the Duma by about two-thirds. From Stolypin's point of view, the changes, although carried out extraconstitutionally, worked. Under the new law, elections returned 270 conservative deputies, 114 Kadets, 30 leftists, and 17 nonparty deputies to the Third Duma, giving the government a comfortable working majority. Consequently, the Third Duma lasted out its full term of five years, from 1907 to 1912.

Even before he distorted the Duma system into conformity with the government's outlook, Stolypin had emerged as the outstanding political figure in postrevolutionary Russia. A wealthy landowner, he had entered the civil service and from 1904–1906 served as governor of the revolution-torn province of Saratov and then briefly in mid-1906 as minister of the interior. Prime Minister Stolypin was a conservative reformer. Like Witte, he had no use for radicalism and sought not to replace the autocracy but instead to make it more rational, effective, and fair. Personally courageous, he declared after an attempt on his life that injured his son and daughter, "This shall not alter our program. We shall continue to carry out our reforms. They are Russia's salvation."[7]

Stolypin favored law and order as well as reform. While altering the Duma system and proposing a sweeping set of peasant reforms, he also ruthlessly suppressed remaining pockets of violent opposition to the government. He permitted the use of field courts-martial to try and to punish those accused of inciting disorder. Individuals sentenced to death were hanged, a form of execution soon dubbed "Stolypin's neckties." Even official figures acknowledged that more than a thousand people were put to death in 1906–1907. Tens of thousands were imprisoned or exiled to Siberia.

A staunch Russian nationalist, Stolypin reinstituted Russification policies that had lapsed during the revolution. In Poland a 1905 decree permitting private Polish schools was rescinded, while in Ukraine political parties were suppressed and the major Ukrainian cultural organization closed down in 1910. That same year, the Finnish Diet was curtailed and then dissolved. This assembly had been restored in 1906 in elections that for the first time in Europe enfranchised women. In 1911 Stolypin imposed new restrictions on Jews and introduced measures to halt the spread of Islam.

As a provincial governor, Stolypin had grappled with peasant unrest. He also heeded the peasantry's revolutionary outbursts in 1905 and peasant intractability in the Duma politics of 1906. The prime minister therefore aimed his major reform effort at agriculture. Fortunately for him, he had access to government data on the peasants, collected in 1902, and a comprehensive reform package for agriculture prepared by Count Witte

---

[7]Ibid., p. 782.

Conservative Reformer Peter Stolypin, chairman of the Council of Ministers, 1906–1911, and sponsor of agricultural reforms.

and his colleagues in the winter of 1905–1906. Thus although the shifts in peasant life undertaken after 1906 are usually referred to as the Stolypin reforms, they could just as correctly be called the Witte reforms. Stolypin followed the plans of the earlier prime minister in seeking three major changes for the peasants: to make them equal citizens by removing all remaining legal and social restrictions, a task substantially accomplished by 1914; to enable them to acquire more land through credit and other forms of assistance, a program that increased peasant landholding but that could not match the demands for land prompted by the skyrocketing of the peasant population; and finally and most important, to encourage peasants to become individual private farmers, a plan that the authorities hoped would make them more productive and more politically conservative than before.

This last objective entailed a second major social revolution in the Russian countryside, almost as sweeping and significant as the emancipation of 1861. To give peasants incentives to grow crops, to work efficiently, and to protect their property, the government planned to dissolve the *mir*. This massive undertaking affected some 100 million people and had extraordinarily complex legal and social ramifications. Peasants were permitted to withdraw from the commune and its system of collective landholding and to establish their private, individual ownership over the scattered strips of *mir* land that they and their household had worked in 1906. They could then consolidate these strips in a single unified holding, which they would own and could farm as individuals. Not surprisingly, these changes raised mind-boggling surveying, tax, deed, and equity problems

Some evidence suggests that the peasants welcomed the breakup of the commune and eagerly established themselves as private farmers. Other information indicates that they responded lethargically if not reluctantly and that only sustained pressure by the government kept the program moving. Certainly the peasants had mixed reactions. Better-off and more energetic peasants welcomed independence, whereas poorer and landless peasants dragged their feet or sold their strips and moved to the cities. In any case, by 1915 more than 1 million peasant households, or about 10 percent of those who had belonged to communes, had participated in the program and owned consolidated farmsteads. Another 6 million had left the commune and owned their land, which nevertheless remained in scattered strips. The remaining 7 million households were still in transition.

If completed on Stolypin's timetable of twenty years, would these reforms have made the peasants productive and conservative? A clear answer eludes us, but some evidence suggests that peasant productivity and exports were rising by 1914. On the other hand, tremendous land hunger persisted, and many marginal or landless peasants benefited little from the reforms. To some degree, the changes sharpened economic differentiation in the villages and heightened the resentment of the poorest peasants toward their more comfortable neighbors and the privileged classes. Yet perhaps we should heed Lenin, a shrewd judge of revolutionary conditions. The Bolshevik leader feared that in the long run land reform would dampen the peasants' rebellious ardor.

Stolypin also tried to introduce reforms in local government and to extend the system of *zemstvos* to western provinces of the empire in Ukraine and Belarus. But here he met sustained conservative opposition, primarily from the landed nobility who desperately clung to the remnants of their former social, economic, and political domination of rural life. In 1911, in the midst of his efforts to push further reform, Stolypin was assassinated by an undercover police agent whose motives and sponsorship for the deed remain obscure.

Despite Stolypin's increasing difficulties and the fact that the Third Duma majority represented only the conservative wing of the political spectrum in Russia, the government and the Duma managed to work together to pass much useful legislation in addition to the agricultural reforms. They approved laws that provided for establishing universal primary education by 1922 and upgraded secondary and higher education. In addition, a program of accident and disability insurance provided some protection to workers. Supply to and administration of the armed forces improved. Migration to Siberia was encouraged, and in 1912 the Duma restored the system of elected justices of the peace for rural courts.

On the Eve of World War I

From the Revolution of 1905 to the outbreak of World War I in 1914, the biggest social transformation in Russia came when peasants, still some 75 percent of the population, moved toward full equality as citizens and left the commune to become independent farmers. In addition, railroads and telegraph lines, spreading like a giant spider's web, dispersed new products, people, and ideas across the empire. Peasants could now buy the latest manufactured goods: tools, housewares, and factory-made, Western-style clothing. They also gained exposure to new information, passed on first by telegraph operators, clerks, and schoolteachers. By the early 1900s, newspapers, magazines, pamphlets, and popular books reached all classes of citizens, providing news, data, and a range of diverse opinions as well as entertainment.

The period also witnessed a steady rise in literacy, a change that had begun after the 1860s. Although we cannot measure its impact precisely, the spread of literacy undoubtedly helped to fuel the revolutions of 1905 and 1917. Once peasants and other lower-class citizens could read even simple materials, they encountered radical ideas and new values that challenged their old loyalties, expectations, and self-perceptions. These new perspectives inexorably eroded support for the twin pillars of the old order: Orthodoxy and the tsardom. No figures exist for literacy in 1861, but some scholars estimate that only 10 to 15 percent of the overall population could read. The 1897 census reported 21 percent literate, and this figure grew to 40 percent by 1914. Rates, however, ranged higher in European Russia and in cities, and higher for men than women. As early as 1897, male literacy in the province of Moscow reached 70 percent; other provinces of central European Russia boasted levels almost as high.[8] Thus we can reasonably conclude that during the revolutions of 1905 and 1917, most workers could read simple revolutionary pamphlets and newspaper articles.

The drive for literacy was impelled from both above and below. As part of the post-emancipation reforms and the industrializing process, and in light of the new document-regulated administration of peasant and local affairs, the regime decided that the lower classes should learn to read. Literacy would also benefit those who went to work on the railroads or in factories. The government and enlightened sectors of society joined to establish *zemstvo* primary schools, chiefly for peasants. Later, the Orthodox Church and the Ministry of Education, concerned that *zemstvo* schools were not imparting "correct" information and values to stu-

---

[8]Cited in Jeffrey Brooks, *When Russia Learned To Read: Literacy and Popular Culture* (Princeton, N.J.: Princeton Univ. Press, 1985), p. 4.

dents. each set up its own system of schools. The number of primary schools multiplied from some 20,000 in 1870 to 108,280 in 1914, and as we have seen, the Third Duma approved plans to institute universal primary education by the mid-1920s.

The peasants themselves also began to take an interest in literacy. They left little evidence of their motivations, but we can surmise that they wanted to read the mass of regulations and documents connected with their emancipation and their governance and taxation. Some also undoubtedly recognized the advantage of literacy in commercial transactions— keeping records, selling and buying agricultural and handicraft products, and obtaining off-farm and city jobs. In addition, peasants saw literacy as a tool to shape a better life, perhaps an opportunity to become a clerk or townsman. The determination of many peasants to make sure that their children, primarily sons, became literate comes to light in their willingness to organize and pay for their own schools. In the 1880s, these institutions numbered 15,000 to 20,000 and boasted 300,000 to 400,000 pupils. By 1914, however, *zemstvo*, state, and church schools predominated in primary education, and the number of peasant-run schools dwindled.[9]

As another indication of peasant interest in literacy, in 1911 three-quarters of all children aged seven to eleven entered primary school, and one-half continued for a second year. Yet because school attendance was never mandatory, only 12 percent completed all four years of primary education. These figures suggest that peasants sent their children to school not for general education but chiefly to learn to read. But to maintain even the primitive reading skill acquired in one or two years of schooling, students had to practice. A considerable body of people's literature thus arose, a phenomenon examined below.

As literacy climbed between 1906 and 1914, so too did the cooperative movement. Despite its importance in parts of Europe, few Americans have any experience with cooperatives, although many people now belong to credit unions, a form of cooperative. In Russian cities during the 1860s and 1870s, populists and other social reformers founded consumer cooperatives, in which individuals banded together to purchase goods for distribution among themselves and sometimes for retail sales. The cooperative movement spread to the countryside when wealthy, progressive landowners established credit cooperatives in the last two decades of the nineteenth century. Seeking to spur agricultural productivity and assist the recently emancipated peasants, the government and *zemstvos* also fostered the growth of cooperatives in the years just before the Revolution of 1905.

Producer cooperatives, in which members pool tools and other capital, acquire raw materials, and combine their labor to make a product,

---

[9]Ibid., pp. 36–38.

developed sporadically in Russia. The largest producers' co-op, the Union of Siberian Dairy Associations, prospered, however, by supplying milk and especially cheese throughout the empire and to Europe. Many Russians favored consumer cooperatives, which expanded in the early twentieth century. In 1905, 950 consumer cooperatives, three-quarters of them in towns and cities, totaled 350,000 members. The movement then spread rapidly to the countryside. On the eve of World War I, the number had risen to 10,080, of which three-quarters were in villages, and totaled 1.4 million members. Credit cooperatives and savings-and-loan associations also saw phenomenal growth after the Revolution of 1905: by 1915, 11,412 credit cooperatives boasted 7.8 million members, and 4,042 savings-and-loan associations had 2.3 million members.

This spreading cooperative movement enlivened the expanding and diversifying rural economy before 1914. Moreover, during World War I, co-ops would play an important role in distributing goods and financing agriculture. The new Soviet government took over most cooperatives in 1918 but permitted the revival of independent cooperative organizations after 1921. Placed under tight government control in 1929, the cooperative movement nonetheless survived the Soviet era and would revive after 1987.

After the depression of 1899–1903 and the disruption of the Revolution of 1905, the Russian economy rebounded between 1907 and 1914, achieving an average annual rate of growth of 6 to 7 percent. By World War I, Russia ranked fifth among industrial powers, after Great Britain, Germany, France, and the United States. But three problems blurred this rosy economic picture. The population continued to explode, reaching an estimated 165 million by 1914. Per capita income thus increased only marginally. In addition, despite ongoing industrialization, Russia continued to lose ground to Germany, Britain, and France, especially in quality and efficiency of production. Finally, the Russian economy remained heavily dependent on the state for orders, subsidies, and protection, and on foreign countries, especially France, for government and private loans. Almost one-third of the economy was foreign-owned, with outside investment concentrated in several key industries. This dependence on foreign capital retarded the growth of a strong indigenous business class in Russia and permitted radical socialists to trumpet the xenophobic charge that outside capitalists were exploiting Russian workers.

As the economy expanded, more and more women entered the work force, their numbers approaching 35 percent of laborers as World War I neared. Women usually held more menial jobs than men and received less pay. Low wages and terrible working conditions persisted for domestic servants and for women in clothing workshops and other small enterprises, and women still had less access to education and a lower literacy rate than men. After its first national congress in 1908, the feminist movement continued to press the Duma on women's rights but with little success. An exception came with a 1914 law that gave women the right to hold internal passports separate from their husbands'. Some liberal and radical political leaders supported female suffrage, but the movement failed to obtain the vote for women.

The workers' movement subsided after the Revolution of 1905. Although unions were legal, employers did their best to prevent their formation and to harass them once organized. Marginal gains in working conditions and the government's new social insurance program failed to satisfy workers, and the number of strikes began to rise again in 1911. In the following year, authorities brutally suppressed a strike in the Lena gold mines. Police killed more than a hundred workers and injured several hundred others, provoking nationwide public criticism and a Duma investigation. During 1913, out of a total labor force of about 3.5 million, 900,000 workers went on strike. The number surpassed a million in 1914.

The socialist parties, although represented by a few deputies in the Duma, were unable to expand their activities and membership in the face of continuing government surveillance and Stolypin's repressive policies. Police agents infiltrated both the Socialist Revolutionary and Social Democratic organizations, and the most prominent leaders of both parties remained in exile, either in Siberia or abroad. Some Bolsheviks participated in extortions and robberies to raise funds, and a wing of the SRs continued its terrorist activities, murdering several thousand government officials. But the majority of socialists condemned these activities. As the strike movement grew, SRs, Bolsheviks, and Mensheviks accelerated their agitational efforts and established links with more radical workers. Nevertheless, how much influence each group wielded among the Russian proletariat on the eve of World War I remains controversial.

The Silver Age: Culture and Science Before the War

Along with education and literacy, popular culture flourished in Russia in the last years of tsarism, primarily through publications. High culture showed vitality as well, mainly in the performing and fine arts and in *belles lettres*. The spreading popular culture tried to meet the needs and interests of those who could now read simple publications. Two groups issued materials for "readers from the people," as the newly literate were called: commercial publishers, who strove to make money; and leaders of private and government organizations, who wanted to instill "correct" ideas and attitudes among ordinary people. The latter group included reformers, who aimed to "improve" the way of life and outlook of the lower classes; politicians, especially socialists, who sought to convert

Did the collapse of tsarism in 1917 stem more from deeply rooted conflicts in Russian society or from the chaos that Russia's involvement in World War I engendered? Western scholarship on the final decade of imperial Russia almost unanimously condemns the shortcomings of the autocracy, especially as tsarist leaders dug in their heels against further change following Stolypin's assassination in 1911. But beyond that conclusion, little consensus exists on dominant trends in the prewar years. Scholars disagree on where Russia was headed—toward a socialist or moderate democratic system, or perhaps toward an authoritarian right-wing regime resembling Franco's Spain in the 1930s? Put another way, did liberalism or radicalism (either of the left or right) hold the promise of Russia's future before the Great War?

Debates about the fate of prerevolutionary Russia have a rich pedigree and often center on the relationship between educated elements and the masses, mostly those living in the cities. Many historians argue that here, in the sprawling urban centers, local leaders faced their greatest challenge as runaway population growth forced them to confront overwhelming health, crime, and housing problems. Thirty years ago, Leopold Haimson and Arthur Mendel, two eminent scholars of Russia's heritage, sparred over the essential features of the urban landscape ("The Problem of Social Stability in Urban Russia, 1905–1917," *Slavic Review,* December 1964, March 1965). Haimson argued that two polarities, one between state and society, the other between workers and the bourgeoisie, characterized Russia. The latter split reflected middle-class fears of worker violence, which overrode liberals' distaste for the monarchy and doomed any chance of their combining with the masses against the state to force political and social reform. By implication, then, the Bolshevik Revolution flowed naturally from the crucible of Russia's smoldering social caldron.

Mendel countered that many educated Russians sympathized with the plight of the workers, especially when labor unrest intensified after the Lena Goldfield Massacre of 1912. In the end, Mendel goes on to say, the Bolshevik Revolution (and possibly the February Revolution against the crown) would have failed if World War I had not fatally weakened the *ancien régime* institutions, including the army.

Who was right—Haimson or Mendel? Until a few years ago, Haimson seemed to carry the day. In *Why Lenin? Why Stalin?* (1964), itself a classic, Theodore Von Laue backed Haimson's argument, seeing almost no chance for liberal constitutionalism because of Russia's frantic tempo of industrialization. That tempo "cracked society . . . separating educated elements from the dark masses, the villages from the towns . . . and the intelligentsia from everyone else, including themselves." Von Laue's doubts concerning Russia's peaceful evolution were echoed in a fine study of working-class life by Victoria Bonnell (*Roots of Rebellion,* 1983). Bonnell portrays government harassment of the newly independent trade unions after 1906, a policy that infuriated labor and led to a Bolshevik upsurge in many union elections in 1913.

Recent research, much of it focused on municipal politics in prerevolutionary Russia, paints a more nuanced picture. Granted, as Michael Hamm, a leading historian of urban Russia, notes, municipal administrations rested on an infinitesimally small electoral base that disfranchised almost everyone except wealthy property owners. And municipal conservatives fought a rear-guard defense of their economic well-being. Often this self-interest took the form of denying basic services to city inhabitants. In Kiev, for example, the city council refused to raise taxes because it preferred cheap water to clean water (see Hamm's *Kiev: A Portrait, 1800–1917,* 1994).

But these factors, Hamm continues, should not obscure the surge of reformism that swept through many cities during the same period and that inspired improvements in public-health facilities and social services. By 1913 progressives had won elections in Moscow, Odessa, Kursk, Smolensk, Saratov, and Kostroma. And in Kharkov the city fathers' legacy was "stunning by any standard," as they opened schools and built a hospital and power plant ("Kaharkov's Progressive Duma, 1910–1914: A Study in Russian Municipal Reform," *Slavic Review,* Spring 1981). The evidence therefore suggests that urban leaders often did not ignore the problems of the poor: to the contrary, they moved aggressively to address some of the root causes of social unrest.

But why stop here? Russia s future hinged not only on the policies of particular local leaders but on the actions of the overall urban middle c ass. Adele Lindenmeyer chronicles the explosion after 1905 of literally thousands of grass-roots associations that attacked social blight ranging from homelessness to prostitution to alcoholism (*The Carl Beck Papers,* 1990). One organization, the Societies of Residents and Voters, which first appeared in 1908 in St. Petersburg but spread rapidly to other cities, embraced a gamut of welfare measures. including food dispensaries for the unemployed and soup kitchens for the poor. Lindenmeyer concludes that by World War I, the impetus for social-reform programs had shifted from the autocracy to the private sector. A civic society was in the making.

In *Liberal City, Conservative State: Moscow and Russia's Urban Crisis* (1987), Robert Thurston offers additional evidence of a leftward shift of liberal sentiment by 1914. In Moscow, long considered Russia's most active municipal government, progressives unseated conservatives in 1912 in the city and national elections, the latter to the Fourth State Duma. Similarly, William Gleason concludes that a growing number of businessmen became convinced that the monarchy could no longer ensure their survival, let alone their progress (*Alexander Guchkov and the End of the Russian Empire,* 1983). Businessmen's uneasiness sprang from the growing labor militancy that spawned widespread strikes and demonstrations in 1913 in Moscow and in 1914 in St. Petersburg. Reflecting the change in middle-class thinking, Alexander Konovalov, a spirited liberal industrialist from Moscow, in March 1914 urged an alliance of "progressive forces," including Marxists of the radical left. Once fashioned, Konovalov hoped, the new bloc's program would call for coordinated strikes against the regime to achieve a constitutional order. Six months earlier, Alexander Guchkov, another scion of the Muscovite business elite and leader of the Octobrists in the Third Duma (1907–1912), appeared before the largest gathering of municipal representatives in Russian history to denounce the autocracy for its hostility to "the very idea of local governments which threatens the country with ruinous consequences." These episodes illustrate how far libera business circles were prepared to go in their search for an alternative political order. They also suggest that "fear of revolution" drove some businessmen in the direction of the workers rather than into the repressive arms of the state.

Was Mendel right, then, when he posited a regrouping of progressive forces for another run at the autocracy, as in 1905? Some evidence indeed indicates that educated urban Russia was less isolated from the lower classes than earlier studies had asserted. Moreover, research has uncovered clear instances of a civic commitment to urban renewal and social reform, notwithstanding the central government's heavy-handed control of local authorities. Undoubtedly, the central question—did the war or class struggle weaken liberalism as a force for stability and progress in Russia?—merits continuing scrutiny.

poor readers to a liberal or revolutionary stance; and officials of the state and Orthodox Church, who tried to inculcate piety, obedience, and loyalty to the tsar and government. Not surprisingly, commercial publications enjoyed the most success and far outnumbered works with a "message." Between 1887 and 1912, the number of popular titles issued grew ninefold, in the latter year composing one-fifth of the 34,630 books published.

The earliest popular literature of the period, which emerged shortly after the 1861 emancipation, took the form of booklets that peddlers carried throughout the countryside. These short works were called *lubochnaia* literature, taking their name from *lubok*, a print or illustration usually depicting a folk tale or a religious episode. Peasants traditionally had bought *lubki* to decorate their homes from the peddlers who hawked them in the villages. At first the new booklets also focused on familiar religious or folk themes, but before long, romance and adventure began cropping up in the genre. A typical title was *The Tale of Ivan the Knight, His Fair Spouse Svetlana, and the Evil Wizard Karachun*.[10]

From the 1880s on, popular fiction appeared in new forms: serialized novels in cheap newspapers, adventure stories and detective novels sold in installments, and women's novels of romance or life in upper-class society. Detective stories were sometimes based on Western heroes like Sherlock Holmes and Nat Pinkerton. All these works won a wide readership throughout Russia, although city dwellers had more opportunity to keep up with the serialized and installment novels.

Because commercial publishers wanted profits, we can assume that the contents of the books they produced directly reflected their readers' interests. If so, the newly literate Russian citizen clearly was absorbing a set of values and ideals directly antithetical to the old order. Indeed, special-interest groups, politicians, reformers, and bureaucrats scorned the commercial publications and redoubled their efforts to transmit a different, more acceptable message.

The values and ideals expressed in the popular literature reveal reader interest in becoming more secular, rational, and independent. Abandoning beliefs based on the Orthodox faith and the tsarist patriarchy, the stories advanced tenets associated with an industrializing and modernizing society. The novels portrayed individuals not passively accepting their lot but acting to change and control their lives. Many authors ridiculed superstition and argued for reasoned explanations of events. These publications also indirectly attacked traditional Russian xenophobia by providing positive characterizations of foreigners and sometimes setting the action in other countries. Finally, the stories emphasized individuality, choice, and social and economic rewards for talented, ambitious, and moral people. One would expect values of this sort in an industrializing society, but the

---

[10]Ibid., p. 70.

hybrid Duma system did not fully reflect them. If newly literate Russians indeed aspired to these ideals, they had placed themselves on a collision course with the old culture and regime. More significant, what they desired stood just as patently at odds with the collectivist, egalitarian, and class-conscious goals of the Bolsheviks, perhaps one of the cruelest ironies of the 1917 Bolshevik victory.

Paralleling the rise in literacy, opportunities in secondary and higher education expanded in the Duma period. Such opportunities inspired initiative among lower- and middle-class Russians and were a prerequisite for membership in high culture. By 1913 some 600,000 pupils were enrolled in high school and 127,000 students in university. University autonomy, abolished in 1884 during the counterreforms of Alexander III, was partially restored during the Revolution of 1905. Although student participation in the revolution closed most universities in 1905 and 1906, the following several years marked the high point of university freedom and vitality before 1917. Student disorders and government crackdowns marred university autonomy in the years preceding the war, but by the time it revived in 1915, conscription of students and young faculty, along with wartime exigencies, curtailed university life.

Russian scientific achievements, begun in the eighteenth century and peaking in the last decades of the nineteenth century, continued to win worldwide recognition in the Duma years. Government policies and attitudes toward science revealed an ambivalence, however. Tsarist officials recognized the essential contribution of science and technology to the country's economic, industrial, and military strength, but they also feared that the rationalism, inquiring spirit, and individualism of science undercut traditional authority and fostered liberalism. Nevertheless, government funds supported wide-ranging research conducted in universities and at special institutes.

Several Russian scientists of this period achieved world renown. Ivan Pavlov, a pioneering physiologist, won the Nobel Prize in 1904 and continued his work on conditioned reflexes and the process of digestion into the Soviet era before his death in 1936. The strong Russian tradition in mathematics was carried on by Andrei Markov, a specialist in probability theory, and Sofia Kovalevsky, one of the first women to achieve international recognition in this field. Kovalevsky wrote poetry and fiction as well. Leading chemist Dmitry Mendeleev developed the periodic table of the elements, and Russian scientists advanced such fields as comparative embryology, non-Euclidean geometry, geography, ethnography, and descriptive sociology.

Paralleling the achievements of Russian scientists, a talented and innovative group of writers and artists enriched world culture in the years before World War I, a period of creativity labeled the Silver Age of the arts. The Silver Age differed from the earlier Golden Age in that now Russian and European writers and artists enjoyed a close and mutually stimulating relationship. The symbolist poetry, daring ballet and stage productions, and avant-garde music and painting that sprang from their cooperation left a lasting legacy.

Besides its cosmopolitanism, Russian high culture of this period was noteworthy for artists' willingness to experiment and for the interweaving of various cultural fields. In many ways, the early Russian modernists became the first multimedia artists, crossing and embracing diverse fields from graphics and typography to costume design and music. Named for its journal, *Mir iskusstva* (*The World of Art*), the dominant cultural movement in Russia from 1898 to 1910 illustrated this principle of melding artistic interests. The World of Art group published essays, poems, stories, criticism, and artwork, and made an esthetic statement with their journal's innovative typography, graphics, and illustrations. Articles in the journal encouraged a keen appreciation of Russia's artistic heritage but kept readers up to date on contemporary currents in European and Russian culture as well.

To some extent, leaders of the World of Art movement built on the artistic freedom established in the 1870s and 1880s by a group of painters known as the Wanderers. These artists had rebelled against the dominant academic classicism of the time and showed their works in traveling exhibitions around the country. The most famous Wanderer was Ilia Repin, who painted realistic scenes of Russian life that often excoriated contemporary hardship. His well-known *Volga Boatmen* depicted the exploitation of barge haulers along the Volga River.

In the early 1900s, several participants in the World of Art movement formed the Ballet Russe, a unique collaboration that brilliantly combined several artistic fields. Its organizer and inspired director, Sergei Diagilev, assembled a team of outstanding creative personalities to produce integrated performances that stunned audiences and the art world. Alexander Benois and Leon Bakst colorfully designed settings, costumes, lighting, and scenery; Igor Stravinsky wrote wildly original scores; Mikhail Fokine developed intricate and still performed choreography; and Anna Pavlova and Vaslav Nijinsky, perhaps the finest dancers ever to perform, breathed vibrant life and powerful emotion into the ballets. At the debut of Stravinsky's *Rite of Spring* in Paris in 1911, the ballet's raw exoticism, repressed violence, and amazing exuberance so shocked the audience that the onlookers, accustomed to lyrical and romantic ballets, rioted. After World War I and the Russian Revolution of 1917, Diagilev and Stravinsky would pursue their careers in Europe. Although neither ever returned to his homeland, each left a deep imprint on Russian culture.

In the theater, talented actors, the brilliant director Konstantin Stanislavsky, and the great playwright Anton Chekhov combined their skills to produce such unforgettable dramas as *The Seagull, Uncle Vanya, The Three Sisters,* and *The Cherry Orchard.* Chekhov also wrote wry and poignant short stories, and it was a profound tragedy for world literature

Dazzling Dancers Ballet stars Tamara Karsavina and Adolph Bolm brilliantly costumed for performances in Serge Diagilev's Ballet Russe company.

when in 1904 tuberculosis ended his life at the age of forty-four. Trained as a physician, Chekhov espoused no particular political or philosophic point of view, but his writing reflected a diagnostic and bemused analysis of human nature. His sharply delineated characters speculate, theorize, and most of the time fail to understand or communicate with one another. Aware of the changes transforming educated Russian society, Chekhov's characters feel bewildered and powerless to control their lives. They nevertheless harbor a vague and tentative optimism, as expressed by Olga, the melancholy schoolteacher and oldest of *The Three Sisters*.

> Listen to the band. What a splendid, rousing tune. It puts new heart into you, doesn't it? Oh, my God! In time we shall pass on for ever and be forgotten. . . . But our sufferings will bring happiness to those who come after us, peace and joy will reign on earth, and there will be kind words and kind thoughts for us and our times. We still have our lives ahead of us, my dears, so let's make the most of them. . . .[11]

---

[11]*Five Major Plays by Anton Chekhov*, trans. Ronald Hingley (New York: Oxford Univ. Press, 1982), p. 265.

In some ways, Chekhov's work bridged the realism of older authors and the more abstract style of the Silver Age. Another transitional author, Maxim Gorky (born Alexei Peshkov), grew up in harsh circumstances in the city of Nizhnii-Novgorod (renamed Gorky in the Soviet era, but in 1990 returned to its older name). Gorky traveled widely throughout southern Russia as a young man, working at various menial jobs. His first stories contained stark accounts of life among the lower classes and opened a window on the dark side of Russian society. Gorky's most successful play, *The Lower Depths*, pursued a similar theme, whereas a later work, *Mother*, offered an idealized description of a female worker and revolutionary. Gorky became a radical, eventually joining the Bolshevik party, and after 1917 advanced to elder statesman among Soviet writers. Asked to leave Russia in 1905 because of his revolutionary activities, Gorky spent some time in the United States. Stung by public criticism and some social ostracism when the press reported that he was traveling with his mistress, Gorky later wrote a highly critical account of American life.

Symbolism, an important literary movement of the 1890s and early 1900s, attracted such innovative poets and authors as Valery Briusov, Konstantin Balmont, Andrei Bely, and Alexander Blok. More interested in words and form than in content, these writers tried to express the essence of individual experience and insights in novel ways. Opposed to conformity and established rules and approaches, they exalted estheticism, beauty, and individual lyricism, and explored and expanded language through fresh structures and usages. They vaguely endorsed radical ideas and revolutionary activity, but those like Blok who supported the Bolsheviks in 1917 soon grew discomfited by proletarian Marxist orthodoxy.

A bit arrogant, and determined to flaunt their unique approach, the symbolists reveled in word play, as Konstantin Balmont's exuberant poem, "I Am the Exquisite Voice," illustrates.

> *I'm the exquisite voice of the broad Russian tongue*
> *Other poets before were precursors who'd sung.*
> *I was first to discover the speech-cadence bounds,*
> *In which vary the angry, melodious sounds.*
> *I am that—sudden break.*
> *I am that—thunder shake.*
> *I am that—limpid lake.*
> *I am for all and no one. . . .*
> *I'm the exquisite poem.*[12]

---

[12]Vladimir Markov and Merrill Sparks, eds. and trans., *Modern Russian Poetry* (Indianapolis: Bobbs-Merrill, 1967), pp. 5–7.

Other modernist writers followed the symbolists after 1910. One group, the Acmeists, sought direct, pure expression of subjective experience and included the esteemed poets Anna Akhmatova and Osip Mandelshtam, later silenced under Stalin. Another school, the Futurists, boasted the brash young poet Vladimir Mayakovsky, the poet laureate of the Bolshevik Revolution. (Disillusioned and frustrated, he would commit suicide in 1930.) Futurists enjoyed shocking society and occasionally appeared with painted faces and wooden spoons in their buttonholes. Tellingly, they titled a 1915 manifesto "A Slap in the Face of Public Taste."

In music, new composers emerged, notably Alexander Skriabin, a founder of modern music. Expressing a mystical, eerie emotionalism, Skriabin developed experimental harmonies and approaches, including the use of colored lights and exotic odors to enhance musical performance. A talented group of modernist painters appeared as well. A few drew inspiration from the French impressionists but brought distinctive Russian skills and themes to their works. Valentin Serov painted soft, glowing colors and produced *Girl with a Peach*, a masterpiece from this period. Mikhail Vrubel used dark, powerful shades to depict an almost illusionary reality. His various versions of *The Demon* are moving and disturbing reflections of his own deepening obsessions and madness.

By 1910 modernist artists in Russia associated closely with the leaders of avant-garde painting in Europe, and after World War I they made important contributions to Western contemporary art. As one example, Vladimir Tatlin, a leader in the constructivist movement, designed not only buildings but furniture, housewares, and clothing. Mikhail Larionov and Natalia Goncharova developed rayonism, a new approach stressing the interplay of light, color and geometric planes. Kazimir Malevich initiated suprematism and became a forerunner of minimal art. Marc Chagall and Vasily Kandinsky earned renown as abstract artists, although both painters worked mainly in Western Europe after the Bolshevik Revolution.

Several other intellectual fields flourished during the Silver Age. Sparked by the World of Art movement, the study of icon painting and traditional arts attracted interest in both academic and popular spheres. Philosophy and historical writing flowered in this period, as did architecture. In 1909 a group of Christian philosophers, liberals, and former Marxists published a collection of articles, *Vekhi (Signposts)*, that stingingly refuted the political and ideological assumptions of the radical intelligentsia. One author argued that "the individual's inner life is the sole creative force of human existence," whereas others heaped scorn on the ineffectualness, utilitarian narrow-mindedness, and messianism of the socialists and other leftist opponents of the old regime. One contributor ridiculed student rebels and budding intellectuals as sexually licentious, often drunk, lazy, and swathed in "spiritual arrogance and intellectual intolerance." The publication of *Vekhi* aroused a storm of protest and stirred heated debate in academic and intellectual circles.

Finally, the popular lecturer and eminent historian Vasily Kliuchevsky stimulated broad curiosity about Russia's past as book publishing and general reading flourished. During this era, passionate interest and participation in cultural life and artistic developments grew among educated Russians. Concerts, art exhibits, lectures, plays, and ballet performances drew huge audiences, and journals, newspapers, and books both contained and catalyzed lively discussion of the latest trends and issues in the arts.

The remarkable creativity of artists and writers and the high level of Russian cultural life in the two decades before the Russian Revolution arose in part from a strong folk tradition in music, tales, and popular art and from the powerful base of Russian achievements of the nineteenth century. At the same time, indigenous trends in Russian culture drew strength from the close interaction between Russian artists and their counterparts in the West. The innovative quality of the Silver Age reflected the new strivings for freedom and self-expression in late tsarist society and presaged the revolutionary upheavals yet to come.

Conclusion

In 1914 was Russia hurtling inevitably toward a new revolutionary crisis? Or did the civic reforms and socioeconomic changes of the Duma period presage a gradual and peaceful transition to an industrialized and stable democracy? Historians still vigorously debate these questions, and the dialogue takes on added meaning in the 1990s as the successor states of the former Soviet Union struggle to establish a new order and a viable system. Some reformers in Russia and the other post-Soviet republics look back nostalgically to the prerevolutionary era. In their view, that period provides a model for the free society they wish to build. In romanticizing the late tsarist period, however, they fail to acknowledge that although Russia, progressed economically, socially, and politically in the first years of the twentieth century, it also grappled with a hydra of deep-rooted problems and a repressive regime.

In the decade after the Revolution of 1905, Russia continued to industrialize rapidly. Yet its economic strength declined relative to other industrialized nations as the economies of the United States and Western European countries spurted ahead. It is not even clear that Russia's growth benefited the majority of its citizenry. Because the rural population kept expanding, land hunger still consumed many peasants. Overall, their lives probably improved only marginally, whereas the gap between rich peasants and poor peasants widened. Under the Stolypin reforms, some peasants might eventually have prospered, but World War I cut short this prospect. Moreover, because new and unskilled workers flooded the labor force, real wages for workers probably did not rise much, if at all. Working and living conditions may have improved slightly, but workers' expectations had far outrun the anguished but simple pleas of the Bloody Sunday marchers.

The Revolution of 1905 forced unprecedented changes in the Russian political system. The newly created Duma chalked up important accomplishments, despite the restrictions under which it labored, and some public issues sparked wide discussion in the press. In addition, numerous citizens gained political experience in parties or as members of the Duma and government. Yet on the eve of the war, the system showed no signs of evolving further, and conservatives fought to prevent broadening of its political base. An obstinate and shortsighted Nicholas II continued to defend autocracy as well and presented a formidable barrier to additional reform. Finally, non-Russians had little role in either national or local governance. Indeed, just before 1914, the government's Russification policies intensified, hardly a promising sign for a future multicultural system that would respect the rights of minorities.

The Duma period witnessed transformations in Russia's social structure as well. Peasants slowly gained equal status, and employment opportunities for everyone improved. But the old elite strongly opposed change, and the nobility bitterly fought diminution of their privileged status and dominant role in national and local government. New professional and middle classes took shape but had not yet attained decisive economic and political power.

However, Russia's future development depended not only on economic, political, and social progress but on popular attitudes and ideals as well. If the old verities of tsar and church were fading, what would replace them in a time of overwhelming change? Did improvement satisfy most people, or did it only raise their expectations faster than any progress that the Duma era registered?

The empire seemed pregnant with revolution, primarily because the heightening popular demand for justice, dignity, political participation, and economic rights outstripped the governing system's capacity for change. The tsar and his supporters, obstinate in opposing reform, virtually guaranteed that an explosion would occur. And the exhausting war into which they blundered in 1914 lit the fuse.

FURTHER READING

The best introduction to the 1900–1914 period is chapters 7–11 of Hans Rogger, *Russia in the Age of Modernisation and Revolution, 1881–1917* (London, 1983). Other important general accounts include Sidney Harcave, *The*

Revolution of 1905 (London, 1970); Abraham Ascher, *The Revolution of 1905*, 2 vols. (Stanford, 1988, 1993); Geoffrey Hosking, *The Russian Constitutional Experiment: Government and Duma, 1907–1914* (Cambridge, 1973); W. Bruce Lincoln, *In War's Dark Shadow: The Russians Before the Great War* (New York, 1983); D. M. Wallace, *Russia on the Eve of War and Revolution* (New York, 1962); and Theofanis Stavrou, ed., *Russia Under the Last Tsar* (Minneapolis, 1969).

Useful monographs on the 1905 revolution are John Bushnell, *Mutiny and Repression: Russian Soldiers in the Revolution of 1905–1906* (Bloomington, Ind., 1985); Andrew Verner, *The Crisis of Russian Autocracy: Nicholas II and the 1905 Revolution* (Princeton, N.J., 1990); Walter Sablinsky, *The Road to Bloody Sunday* (Princeton, N.J., 1976); Terence Emmons, *The Formation of Political Parties and the First National Elections in Russia* (Cambridge, Mass., 1983); and Howard Mehlinger and John M. Thompson, *Count Witte and the Tsarist Government in the Revolution of 1905* (Bloomington, Ind., 1972).

A firsthand analysis appears in liberal leader Paul N. Miliukov's *Russia and Its Crisis* (1905, repr. New York, 1962). A colorful account of Russia's naval disaster in the Russo-Japanese War is Richard Hough, *The Fleet That Had to Die* (New York, 1961).

On the diplomatic background to that war, consult Barbara Jelavich, *A Century of Russian Foreign Policy, 1814–1914* (New York, 1964); George Lensen, *The Russian Push Toward Japan* (Princeton, N.J., 1959); John A. White, *The Diplomacy of the Russo-Japanese War* (Princeton, 1964); and Raymond A. Esthus, *Double Eagle and Rising Sun: The Russians and Japanese at Portsmouth in 1905* (Durham, N.C., 1988). Excellent treatment of foreign policy for the whole period is David M. McDonald, *United Government and Foreign Policy in Russia, 1900–1914* (Cambridge, Mass., 1992).

A thorough biography of the key figure of the Duma period is Mary S. Conroy, *P. A. Stolypin: Practical Politics in Late Tsarist Russia* (Boulder, Co., 1976). For one aspect of the revolutionary movement, see Anna Geifman, *Thou Shalt Not Kill: Revolutionary Terrorism in Russia, 1894–1917* (Princeton, N.J., 1993).

Helpful on cultural life is Camilla Gray, *The Great Experiment: Russian Art, 1863–1922* (London, 1962). On science, see Loren Graham, *Science in Russia and the Soviet Union* (Cambridge, Mass. 1992).

Selected works on social developments include Victoria E. Bonnell, *Roots of Rebellion: Worker Parties and Organizations in St. Petersburg and Moscow, 1900–1914* (Berkeley, 1983); Laura Engelstein, *Moscow 1905: Working-Class Organization and Political Conflict* (Stanford, 1982); Robert B. McKean, *St. Petersburg Between the Revolutions: Workers and Revolutionaries, June 1907–February 1917* (New Haven, 1990); Laura Engelstein, *The Keys to Happiness: Sex and the Search for Modernity in Fin-de-Siècle Russia* (Ithaca, N.Y., 1992); Barbara Alpern Engel, *Between the Fields and the City: Women, Work, and Family in Russia, 1861–1914* (Cambridge, 1993); and Linda Edmondson, *Feminism in Russia, 1900–1917* (Stanford, 1984).

The key arguments on whether Russia was headed for revolution appear in Leopold Haimson, "The Problem of Social Stability in Urban Russia, 1905–1917," *Slavic Review* 23 (Dec. 1964): 619–642; and 24 (March 1965): 1–22, with comments by Arthur Mendel and Theodore von Laue on pp. 23–33 and 34–46.

3

A VISION LAUNCHED
War and Revolution

~

It was the morning of March 15, 1917. Nicholas II, the last of the Romanov emperors, received senior army commander General Nikolai Ruzsky in the tsar's private train in Pskov, headquarters of the Northern Front. Alarmed by news of riots in Petrograd (formerly St. Petersburg), Nicholas had left general staff headquarters, where he personally commanded Russian forces fighting Germany, intending to join his family in the imperial palace of Tsarskoe Selo near the capital. But military traffic and rebellious soldiers blocking the railroad lines north from the front had forced the tsar to turn west to Pskov.

General Ruzsky brought with him a sheaf of telegrams; after reading them and hearing Ruzsky's report, the tsar sat in stunned silence, then rose and stared out the train window. The telegrams contained the unanimous opinion of Russia's highest generals that Nicholas must give up his throne if the monarchy were to survive the political upheaval rocking the capital. Nicholas's fellow officers and trusted military subordinates maintained that only the tsar's abdication would rally public support for the war effort and save the country from the German onslaught. Their argument appealed strongly to Nicholas's patriotism. After a few moments, he turned from the window and announced, "I have decided that I shall give up the throne in favor of my son, Alexis." He crossed himself and thanked his staff for their faithful service.

Later that day, after the family doctor had reminded the tsar of the frail condition of Alexis, who suffered from hemophilia, Nicholas resolved to transfer the throne instead to his brother, Grand Duke Michael. That evening, two representatives of the temporary government forming in Petrograd arrived in Pskov to obtain the tsar's formal document of abdication. Waving aside their long explanation of why he must abandon the throne, Nicholas explained that he had "changed my decision in favor of my brother Michael. I trust you will understand the feelings of a father." He then helped to prepare and signed the proclamation of abdication. Several hours later, he returned by train to the front to bid his staff there good-bye.

Although calm and dignified while making the decision to abdicate, that night Nicholas wrote bitterly in his diary: "For the sake of Russia, and to keep the armies in the field, I decided to take this step. . . . All around me I see treason, cowardice and deceit." Grand Duke Michael refused to accept the throne, heeding liberal politicians' warnings that the Petrograd crowds vehemently opposed any continuation of the monarchy. The three-hundred-year-old Romanov dynasty thus ceased to exist.[1]

At no time did Nicholas regret Russia's involvement in the war that brought incalculable suffering to his people and spurred his own downfall. This chapter explores the complex reasons for Russian participation in World War I, the burdens that conflict imposed on the nation, and the mounting conviction of citizens of all classes that the tsarist system had to go. The autocracy's collapse left turbulent aftershocks. Despite the liberals' desperate struggle both to craft a new order and to continue the war, public sentiment swung leftward as workers, peasants, soldiers, and non-Russian minorities escalated their demands for concrete rewards from the demise of the old regime. Taking advantage of the masses' radicalization, the Bolsheviks swept to power on promises of "peace, land, and bread." Yet they too soon faced the crushing problems of disorder, a ravaged economy, and restive populations.

Pulled into the Fray

In light of the war's costs, it is natural to wonder how Nicholas could have led his fragile nation into a world struggle. Yet neither the man nor the institution of autocracy deserves the entire blame. External forces, unrealistic expectations, and the pressure of chauvinistic public opinion also propelled Russia into the conflict. The tsar and his advisers did not seek war, but like other European statesmen, they believed that their country's national honor and great-power standing were at risk. They also assumed that a Europewide conflict would prove short and affordable. Thus Russia slid tragically into what became the most frightful conflagration in human history to that point, a senseless struggle that cost almost 8 million Russian casualties and sparked a profound social upheaval. The Russian Revolution in turn led to three more years of civil war and ruinous internal destruction.

---

[1]This account is based on Robert K. Massie, *Nicholas and Alexandra* (New York: Atheneum, 1976), pp. 391–397.

Two developments led Russia most directly down the path to war. For one thing, the country's leaders wanted to protect fellow Slavs in the Balkans while counterbalancing German and Austro-Hungarian influence there. To pursue these goals, they embroiled the empire in a web of diplomatic and military alliances with Serbia, France, and Britain. These entanglements eroded Russia's control of its own destiny.

After Russia's defeat by Japan in 1904–1905, its position in the Far East had stabilized. The government could afford to resume an active diplomatic interest in the Balkans and the Near East. As the power of the Ottoman Empire, "the sick man of Europe," waned during the nineteenth century, nationalist movements against Ottoman rule had flourished. Greece, Serbia, Romania, and Bulgaria had gained independence by the end of the century. Russia and the other European powers moved to extend their influence in the new nations and with the Turkish government. As the largest Slavic nation and the upholder of Orthodox faith, Russia particularly desired recognition as protector of the Slavic states of Serbia, Montenegro, and Bulgaria, and of Orthodox Christian sites under Ottoman rule. For trade and security purposes, tsarist statesmen also wanted unhampered passage through the Turkish Straits. Yet Russo-Bulgarian relations were strained over Bulgaria's allegations that Russia had failed to support it in its struggles with its neighbors. Thus Russia gave priority to solidifying its links with Serbia and to defending the rights of Slavs within the Austro-Hungarian Empire.

These strategic and diplomatic concerns to the southwest might have reached peaceful resolution over time, and any conflict might have remained limited to Russia and Turkey, as in the 1870s, or to Russia and the Austro-Hungarian Empire. But Russia's membership in the so-called Triple Entente (Russia, France, and Britain) and the growing power of recently unified Germany complicated matters.

Russian involvement in the entente had begun between 1891 and 1894, when France and Russia agreed to a diplomatic and military alliance. Autocratic Russia and democratic France seemed unlikely partners, but each hoped to draw strength from the other. Russia, for its part, resented the fact that in the late 1880s the German kaiser had abandoned the Three Emperors' League linking Russia, Germany, and Austria-Hungary. Feeling isolated, it hoped that France would help to check the Germans' and Austrians' deepening diplomatic and economic penetration of the Balkans and Turkey. Russian diplomats also looked to France for loans and investment. French leaders, intent on avenging France's defeat in the Franco-Prussian War of 1870–1871, counted on the military counterweight of the Russian army on Germany's eastern border. In 1907 Russia and Britain, long imperialist rivals in China, Afghanistan, and Persia, also settled their differences and reached an understanding. The resulting Triple Entente was now pitted against the Triple Alliance of Germany, Austria-Hungary, and Italy (see the map, European Alliances

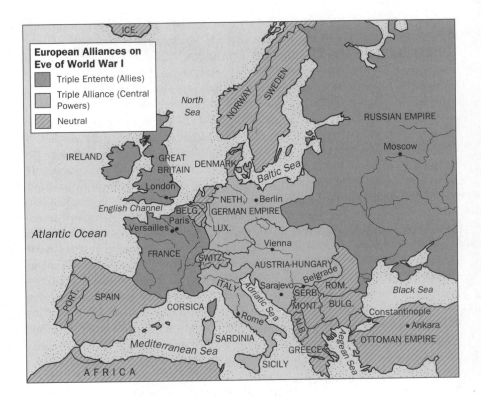

European Alliances on Eve of World War I

- Triple Entente (Allies)
- Triple Alliance (Central Powers)
- Neutral

on Eve of World War I). (After war broke out in 1914, Italy switched sides and joined the entente in 1915. Bulgaria and the Turkish Empire entered the conflict on the side of the Central Powers. Serbia, Montenegro, Albania, Greece, and Portugal, as well as France's colonies in north Africa, fought with the Allied powers, as did Japan, China, and the United States.) Because the two systems were fairly evenly matched, their balanced rivalry might have precluded hostilities indefinitely.

However, both sides continued to arm. Germany in particular gathered strength quickly, frightening the British, the French, and the Russians and emboldening the Austrians. Nevertheless, the Great Powers had resolved several crises early in the twentieth century, and European leaders had come to trust the alliance system. The most important conflict for Russia arose in 1908 over Bosnia and Herzegovina. These two small Balkan enclaves of mixed population (Croats, Slavic Muslims, and Serbs) had belonged to Turkey, but Austria-Hungary had occupied them since 1878. Serbia also coveted Bosnia-Herzegovina, as it would again in the 1990s. Most Bosnian Serbs wanted to join the kingdom of Serbia, but the remaining Bosnians rejected this option. In diplomatic talks with the Austrians, the Russian foreign minister, Alexander Izvolsky, believed that he had worked out a deal: Austria-Hungary would support Russia's demand for free use of the Straits in return for Russia's recognition of Austrian acquisition of Bosnia-Herzegovina. But while Izvolsky tried to secure the assent of the other Great Powers to this arrangement, Austria-Hungary acted unilaterally to annex the area. Furious Russian leaders could do nothing.

This humiliation strengthened Russia's resolve to act forcefully in the next crisis, which was not long in coming. In June 1914, a Bosnian Serb nationalist who belonged to a Serbian-backed revolutionary organization assassinated the heir to the Austrian throne. Austria-Hungary's leaders, tired of Serbian encouragement of nationalist agitation among Slavs under their rule, determined to exact revenge. They presented an ultimatum with outrageous demands to the Serbian government and then quickly obtained support from Germany. Although the Serbs were eager to negotiate, Austria pressed its claims and declared war on Serbia on July 28. The Serbs appealed to Russia for assistance. Fearing that another embarrassing setback in the Balkans would lead to German and Austrian domination of the area and might end Russia's role as a Great Power, the tsar and his advisers decided to pressure Austria to back down. They mobilized the army, well aware that their military reserves took longer to organize than those of the other European nations.

Because the armies of Europe depended on complicated mobilization procedures based on rail transport, and any delay handed an enemy a key advantage, Russia's action forced Germany to follow suit. This move pulled France into the fray. When Germany, following a long-established plan, attacked France across neutral Belgium, Britain, too, jumped in. Within a few weeks, the major European nations were embroiled in a conflict that no one had expected or wanted. Nicholas II and his advisers, although cognizant of the price of war, chose to protect Russian prestige and led the country into battle.

At first the Russian press and public, as in the other belligerent countries, welcomed the hostilities in a burst of emotional patriotism. A spreading strike wave in the spring and summer of 1914 that reflected renewed unrest among urban workers and threatened a repetition of 1905 collapsed. Speeches and rallies trumpeted support for the war and reviled the enemy. The name of the capital was changed from St. Petersburg (which had a Germanic sound in Russian) to Petrograd. In the Duma, even liberal critics of the regime voted for war credits, except for twenty-one leftists who abstained.

The war posed a dilemma for socialists, who had predicted before 1914 that European workers' solidarity would prevail over national loyalties and thus ensure peace. But when the conflict erupted, patriotic sentiment proved so fierce that most socialist leaders soon dropped their opposition to the war. One leader who disagreed was Lenin, then in exile in Switzerland. From the beginning, he denounced the conflict as a struggle among capitalists at the expense of workers. He urged the European proletariat to turn the war into revolutions against their own governments. A few socialists supported the war without equivocation, but most adopted the stance of "defensism," that is, defense of their country but not an aggressive drive for conquest or profit.

World War I Abroad and at Home

In accordance with long-established war plans, the Russians launched an attack on Austria-Hungary from Russian Poland. The armies met with considerable success and seized most of Galicia (see the map, World

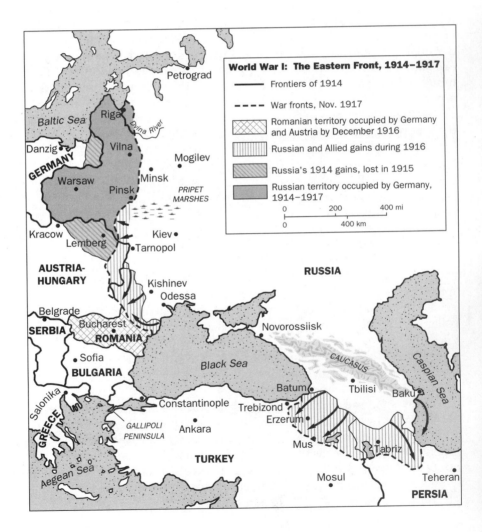

World War I: The Eastern Front, 1914–1917

— Frontiers of 1914

--- War fronts, Nov. 1917

Romanian territory occupied by Germany and Austria by December 1916

Russian and Allied gains during 1916

Russia's 1914 gains, lost in 1915

Russian territory occupied by Germany, 1914–1917

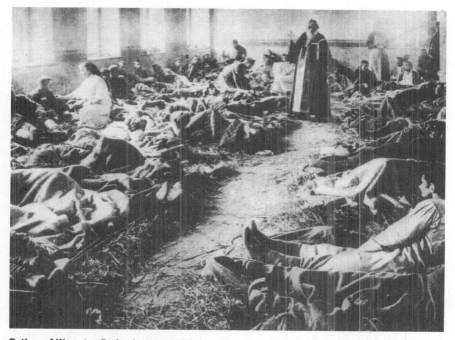

Pathos of War An Orthodox priest blesses the wounded in the primitive conditions of a Russian field hospital in World War I.

War I: The Eastern Front, 1914–1917). But the German attack on France also earned impressive initial victories, and within a few weeks Paris itself was in danger. Responding to frantic French calls for help, Russian armies invaded East Prussia, the northeastern corner of Germany. This strategy drew off a number of German divisions from the Western Front and may have saved Paris. Nonetheless, the Russian forces, hampered by poor generalship, shoddy training, and inadequate supplies, soon suffered massive defeats and more than 300,000 casualties. *August 1914*, a novel by renowned Russian author Alexander Solzhenitsyn, graphically captures the mood of the fighting.

After dividing, the two masses of men flowed on through the forest, groping blindly, stopping now and then. The troops, who had not eaten for two days, were staggering; their water bottles empty, their mouths were dry as dust; having lost all faith in their generals, they refused to believe there was any reason for this forced march. Some began covering up their company numbers, so they could not be recognized and pulled into line;

others simply dropped by the wayside and fell asleep on the ground.[2]

By mid-fall, when it became clear that the war would drag on and as news of defeats and casualties sank in, public enthusiasm dissipated. Liberals and conservatives alike privately voiced their concern for the viability of the tsardom. The authoritarian former minister of the interior, Peter Durnovo, had predicted even before the war that "social revolution in its most extreme form" and "hopeless anarchy, the issue of which cannot be foreseen," would ensue from an unsuccessful war. Yet Nicholas continued to appoint aged or incompetent ministers and to cling to a benign optimism about the future. In a November 1914 letter to his wife, he reported on his tour of the Caucasus.

> [The people] are beginning to be wealthy, and above all they
> have an inconceivably high number of small infants. All future
> subjects. This all fills me with joy and faith in God's mercy. I
> look forward in peace and confidence to what lies in store for
> Russia.[3]

At the war's start, Russia's leaders had sought only to aid the Serbs, to fulfill their treaty obligations to the French, and to check Austrian and German ambitions. Their war aims changed, however, after Turkey entered the melée in late 1914 on the side of the Central Powers (Germany and Austria-Hungary) and after the British failed to capture the Straits in the spring of 1915. Now the Russians pressed for postwar control of the Straits and Constantinople, which the French and British promised them in the secret three-way Treaty of London of May 1915.

Although the leadership took heart at this diplomatic success, the military campaign in 1915 brought disaster. The Russians were forced to relinquish to the Austrians all the territory that they had seized the year before, and to the Germans they yielded Poland and Lithuania, as well as parts of Belarus. (See the map, p. 108.) They lost 1 million dead and wounded and almost as many as prisoners. German superiority in artillery and machine gun firepower took its toll especially as the Russians ran out of ammunition, rifles, uniforms, and basic supplies. The loss of trained line officers and noncommissioned officers during the first year of fighting also weakened the Russian effort. Inexperienced replacements often commanded raw conscripts, a recipe for chaos in the ranks.

As the Russian armies retreated, up to 4 million people living in

---

[2]Alexander Solzhenitsyn, *August 1914* (New York: Farrar, Strauss, Giroux, 1971), p. 445.

[3]*The Letters of the Tsar to the Tsaritsa, 1914–1917,* trans. A. L. Hynes (London and New York: The Bodley Head, 1929), p. 16.

western Russia fled eastward before them, worsening supply and transport problems behind the military front. Many refugees settled in Russia's central and provincial cities, exacerbating fuel, food, and housing shortages. This displaced group fueled the growing criticism of the war.

The bureaucratic and inefficient tsarist government proved ill-equipped to fight the total war that unfolded in 1914 and 1915. Officials only slowly involved the empire's private sector, which they distrusted. The ministries also lacked the capability to galvanize the country's full resources and to channel them into the war effort. In the first two years of fighting, industrial production plummeted as a result of shortages of raw materials, thoughtless drafting of highly skilled workers, and lack of organization. Alarmed at supply deficiencies and discouraged by the government's mismanagement of the economy, public-spirited citizens and organizations volunteered to assist. In 1915 War Industries Committees of industrialists, joined later by workers, formed to boost production in key economic sectors. The Union of Towns and the Union of *Zemstvos*, national associations of municipal and *zemstvo* officials, took primary responsibility for health and welfare services. By 1916 military production picked up, and the army was better equipped than at any time since the war started.

Women played a significant role in this brief economic resurgence and in the war effort. At the outbreak of the conflict, many women had lost their jobs because garment factories, artisan and handicraft workshops, and restaurants—enterprises employing mostly women—reduced output or closed down. But in agriculture, women as well as boys and old men filled in for the 10 million peasants mobilized during the war, and village agricultural production temporarily sustained prewar levels. Women also began to supplant men in other jobs, on the railways, as trolley conductors, and increasingly in major industries. By 1917 the percentage of women in the factory work force had grown to 43 percent, from about 29 percent in 1914. Women were also active in nursing and caring for refugees, and in the Unions of Towns and *Zemstvos*.

Russian women, alone among women of the countries embroiled in World War I, fought as soldiers. At first they disguised themselves as men to enlist, but soon women's combat battalions were authorized. The most famous was commanded by Maria Bochkaryova, a talented leader and strict disciplinarian. A few socialist women, such as Alexandra Kollontai, opposed the war, and many women suffered either as refugees or as soldiers' wives receiving paltry financial allotments. Housewives felt the pinch most directly from food, fuel, and housing shortages. Indeed, disgruntled female shoppers and working women would help to ignite the 1917 revolution.

By the end of 1916, as the Germans sustained their advance into the Baltic region and Russia proper in the northwest, morale in the army and on the home front sank. The nation faced several formidable problems,

Women to Arms Officers inspect troops of a women's battalion accompanied by the unit's commander, Maria Bochkaryova.

among them a dire food shortage. That year the bread ration for each soldier fell from a scant three to two pounds and finally, in early 1917, to one pound per day. Scarcity of grain stemmed in part from peasants' reaction to what is called a "scissors crisis": while the cost of manufactured goods soared (the upper blade of the scissors), procurement prices for grain and other agricultural products rose only slightly (the other blade of the now opened scissors). Because of this gap between the cost of goods to buy and the income received for crops, peasants sent little food to market. Instead they consumed more food themselves, fed more to their livestock, or hoarded it.

To worsen matters, the rail transport system gradually broke down as military and war-production traffic clogged the routes and as railway personnel struggled to replace locomotives and rolling stock. Such troubles exacerbated the shrinking of food supplies from the countryside and reduced fuel stocks for the cities. These shortages, plus ongoing inadequacies in housing and high inflation, fostered intense resentment among urban dwellers by the winter of 1916–1917. Moreover, the conscript army chafed under the burdens of defeat, incompetent leadership, news of their families' suffering at home, and tales of profiteering and treachery among the "privileged." The sentiment of garrison soldiers in the cities reached volatile levels as disabled veterans, socialist agitators, and the soldiers' own fears of being sent to the front heightened their anxiety.

Most ominous of all, the Russian people lost what little faith they had had in their government and its elite supporters. At a time of national traval and hardship, their leaders responded weakly and ineptly. Committed to the war and fatalistically convinced that God would save the nation, Nicholas II decided in September 1915, against the advice of his ministers, to take personal command of the Russian armies. Militarily, this change made no difference, for the chief of staff continued to oversee operations, but symbolically the tsar thus linked himself with Russia's military destiny.

With Nicholas away at front headquarters, the government's credibility withered further. Rumors circulated that the German-born tsarina sympathized with the enemy and was meddling in government affairs. Many people also became aware that Alexandra had fallen under the influence of enigmatic Grigory Rasputin. This self-proclaimed holy man had won Alexandra's confidence when on several critical occasions he had stopped the bleeding of her young hemophiliac son, Alexis. How Rasputin accomplished this medical feat is unclear, but Alexandra, a mystically religious woman, grew convinced that Rasputin possessed "holy powers," and she refused to countenance well-founded charges of his drunkenness and sexual licentiousness. Instead she consulted Our Friend, as she called Rasputin, about appointments of ministers and other high officials and then pressured Nicholas to implement these recommendations.

Alexandra and Rasputin espoused no policy except staunch conservatism, but they championed incompetent and poorly regarded people. Their meddling, the frequent changes of ministers, and the complete lack of effective leadership prompted the tsar's cousin to comment, "The government itself is the organ that is preparing the revolution." The leader of the Kadet party, Paul Miliukov, deplored the government's conduct in the fall of 1916 with a major speech entitled "Is This Stupidity or Treason?" Aware that the growing scandal surrounding Alexandra discredited the entire tsarist system, several conservative conspirators, including a prince and a grand duke, fed Rasputin cakes laced with cyanide. When, to their horror, he kept eating them instead of keeling over, they shot him. He survived even this assault, however, and the desperate assassins finally clubbed him and dumped him into the icy waters of Petrograd's Neva River, where at last he perished.

The tsar and his reactionary circle rejected advice to inspirit the people by promising reforms after the war. Nicholas also spurned offers of cooperation from liberal groups in the Fourth Duma, who suggested formation of a "ministry of public confidence" to rally the population behind the war effort. The liberals, motivated by patriotism and fears that the combination of defeat and governmental bungling would lead to anarchic revolution, formed a coalition within the Duma. This Progressive Bloc pressed urgently for reform and effective prosecution of the war. The bloc attracted deputies from all parties except the extreme left and right but accomplished little in the face of governmental intransigence and ineptitude. By late 1916 and early 1917, spiraling inflation and short-ages in the cities, an outbreak of strikes, and declining morale in the army foreshadowed a major crisis. A few politicians contemplated a coup d'état, and foreign ambassadors reported the growing popular dissatisfaction with the tsarist regime to their governments. But the revolution, when it came nine weeks into 1917, surprised everyone with its timing, sweep, and thoroughness.

The February Revolution: Tsarism Laid Low

Several forces brought on the sudden breakdown of the tsarist system in 1917. Perhaps the most important was Russia's long history of social injustice and oppression. The political, socioeconomic, and cultural gap between the privileged elite and struggling masses undermined the stability of Russian society in the twentieth century. Perhaps the reforms after 1861 and 1905 and the changes associated with industrialization and the spread of education were closing that gap before 1914. But Russia's involvement in World War I markedly heightened social tensions and augmented popular disenchantment with the monarchy and the upper classes, virtually ensuring an upheaval. With defeats, huge human and material losses, and desperate living conditions in the cities, bitterness and resentment mounted, and the government floundered. The sacrifices of everyone, especially the soldiers at the front, seemed maddeningly pointless. According to an American historian of the Russian army, "The soldiers felt they were being used and recklessly expended by the rich and powerful, of whom their officers were the most visible, immediate representatives."[4] With hopes of victory dimming, radical change seemed the only way out.

Tension also was heightening between Russia's rulers and the large non-Russian element of the population. Only after the Central Powers had occupied most of Russian Poland did Nicholas II reluctantly promise substantial autonomy to the Poles after the war. To the other nationalities he yielded nothing. Consequently, when the tsar's authority disintegrated in 1917, the empire fell apart, with most non-Russian groups struggling for autonomy or independence.

Further, the war's disruption of daily life hastened the disintegration of the old order. The conflict displaced tens of millions of Russian citizens through conscription, the flight of refugees, and the movement of people undertaking war work in factories and in war-related organiza-

---

[4]Allan K. Wildman, *The End of the Russian Imperial Army: The Old Army and the Soldiers' Revolt, March–April 1917* (Princeton, N.J.: Princeton Univ. Press, 1979), p. 89.

tions. Traditional loyalties, customs, and attitudes hence came into question, and people gained exposure to new ideas and experiences. They began to question the old order.

At the same time, the war brought dishonor to the tsar and, through him, to the system that he symbolized. Traditionally, the people had looked to the tsar as their benevolent protector. Bloody Sunday had weakened this ideal. Nicholas's personal role in the war, particularly after he assumed command of the armies, and the rumors swirling around Alexandra destroyed any remaining popular reverence for the tsardom. Peasants, workers, and soldiers wondered why Nicholas did nothing to stem the flood of sacrifice and suffering. When the revolution came, almost no one stepped forward to defend the monarchy.

Finally, the war brought the Russian economy to near collapse. The high cost of living, food and fuel shortages, and soldiers' fears for their families spurred urban unrest and troop mutinies. People blamed the government for their misery, and soon they decided to act.

Tsarist rule toppled on February 23–27, 1917, according to the Julian calendar used in prerevolutionary Russia, and on March 8–12 by the Gregorian calendar then employed in Europe and adopted in Russia beginning in 1918. Sometimes authors refer to the regime's collapse as the March Revolution. In Soviet historiography and in much Western writing, however, the events are known as the February Revolution, the term we use here (although we cite Gregorian calendar dates).

Under whatever name, the revolution brought surprise and drama. By the end of 1916, almost everyone, from conservatives to radicals, believed that important change lay just ahead. Yet when the February Revolution broke out in the form of strikes, protests over bread shortages, and a few street demonstrations in Petrograd, no one suspected that within five days the entire tsarist system would collapse. The revolution was above all a genuinely populist movement: ordinary people, with workers and soldiers in the forefront, took to the streets and rejected the old order. Radical and anarchist agitators coaxed the uprising along but neither group precipitated or controlled it. Liberal and socialist politicians hastened to take advantage of it but did not create it. The February Revolution, in short, stemmed from spontaneous action.

It also garnered huge popular support. Almost 500,000 citizens directly participated in Petrograd alone. Only high tsarist officials opposed it, although some intellectuals worried that it might spawn anarchy and violence. As a warmly welcomed people's uprising, the revolution would have few parallels in the rest of the twentieth century until the overthrow of the Filipino dictator Ferdinand Marcos in 1986 and the "velvet revolutions" of 1990 in East Germany and Czechoslovakia.

The revolution clearly reflected the Russian people's ardent desire for a better life. The rebels set their sights on removing the tsarist government, which they blamed for their woes. Beyond that aim, the revolutionaries nurtured the inchoate vision of somehow creating a just, free, and secure society. Few knew exactly how to reach that goal, but almost everyone shared the dream. On specific issues, viewpoints diverged. Some opposed the war; many supported it. Large numbers favored a republic; some had no idea what the word meant. Although party leaders soon sought to articulate aims for the revolutionaries, over the next few months the people began to formulate their own interpretation of the revolution's significance. Peasants, workers, non-Russians, and liberals each had their own agendas, which sometimes conflicted. In the pursuit of selfish interests, few remembered the needs of the larger society.

The February Revolution erupted in one city and was compressed into a few days. Although strikes, food lines, and a few demonstrations had broken out in Petrograd and other cities off and on during the winter of 1916–1917, on March 8, 1917, several forces combined to unleash a larger-than-usual outpouring of popular unrest. Most of the commotion centered in the Vyborg district of Petrograd, the location of many factories and workers' apartments.

March 8 was International Women's Day, a socialist holiday. To mark it, activists met during lunch hour in some factories. A number of striking textile workers, many of them women, also ranged through the streets, along with laborers from the giant Putilov factory whom management had locked out a few days earlier. As one worker described the situation,

> . . . women's voices were heard in the alley . . . shouting, "Down with the war! . . . Down with hunger! Bread for the workers!" Myself and a few other comrades immediately went to the windows. . . . Those [women strikers in the alley] who spotted us began waving their arms and yelling, "Come out! Stop work!" Snowballs pelted the windows. We decided to join the demonstration.

Women's Day rallies at several dozen factories ended with employees deciding to quit work. Some headed home; many others organized or joined gatherings in the streets. Holiday celebrants, workers, and citizens standing in long lines for bread soon mingled, and the police labored to disperse the crowds that spontaneously gathered. Between 75,000 and 100,000 people participated in the bread protests, strikes, and demonstrations of that day.

Over the next two days, the movement swelled into a general strike that shut down trolleys, schools, stores, and newspapers and virtually paralyzed the city. Crowds burgeoned to several hundred thousand, and the demonstrators infiltrated the center of the city, crossing the Neva on the ice when police blocked bridges. Mostly cheerful and expectant, although unsure of what they were waiting for, the protesters chatted and joked with soldiers and Cossacks.

On to Revolution Revolutionary soldiers with red flags on their bayonets ride a commandeered car during the February Revolution.

Two events served as major turning points. First, troops in the capital mutinied and joined the milling crowds, and then top army generals decided not to use loyal troops from the front to quell the Petrograd uprising. Initially, officials in Petrograd sent police and Cossacks to control the unruly throngs. On March 11, when this tactic clearly had failed, the tsar ordered deployment of garrison soldiers against the rebels. Several times that day, troops opened fire on demonstrators, and several hundred people were killed or wounded. (Casualties in the February Revolution ultimately totaled about 1,500.)

Authorities also arrested a number of radicals, and the government dismissed the Duma, which happened to be in session. Some mutinous soldiers from the Pavlovsky regiment were rounded up, and by nightfall the city seemed secure. Officials made plans to use additional troops the next day to subdue any remaining outbursts. That evening, however, soldiers from the Volynsky regiment who had fired on the crowds discussed the event and decided that tomorrow they would not shoot at their fellow citizens. Before morning these troops managed to win over the main training unit of the regiment, which agreed to disobey orders to patrol the streets. The best Soviet account of the February Revolution describes what happened next.

> At 6:00 A.M. . . . the training unit, in full battle array, lined up in parade formation. Officers began arriving, the soldiers greeted them as always. . . . Yet, as agreed, when greeting the chief of the unit, Capt. Lashkevich, the soldiers unanimously responded, with a yell, "Hurrah!" Lashkevich asked noncommissioned officers . . . what this meant but they did not answer. Lashkevich . . . took out a paper, declared it contained an order from the tsar, and was about to read it. He didn't get a chance. A rousing "Hurrah" again rang through the ranks, and cries were heard. . . . "We won't kill any more. Enough blood!" . . . and the entire unit banged rifle butts against the floor. At this threatening sound the officers fled. . . . Crossing the yard, the officers drew level with the barracks window; shots rang out. . . . Capt. Lashkevich fell dead.[5]

The training unit in turn soon gained the confidence of the rest of the regiment, whose rank and file encouraged nearby detachments to mutiny. By that afternoon, soldiers and even a few officers mingled with the revolutionary crowds on the streets. The tsarist regime had lost control of the capital.

The only reliable forces left to the government were loyal front-line troops, and on March 12, Nicholas II ordered General Nikolai Ivanov to take eight regiments to the capital and restore order. Fearing that the Petrograd riots would undermine the home front and spread to combat units, the army's high command initially supported this decision. Soon they reversed themselves, however, and ordered General Ivanov to suspend his plans. With the capital already in the hands of the revolutionaries, they argued, and a new temporary government apparently in control, sending troops would only prolong the civil strife and impede Russia's efforts to resist Germany. In fact, the officers had also had enough of the ineffectual tsarist government and hoped that the new authorities in Petrograd would rally the people and prosecute the war effectively. Their decision left the tsar powerless and spelled the end of the old regime.

The Question of Power

The revolutionaries' success in Petrograd and the military authorities' failure to squelch the uprising did not solve the urgent question of who would take command of the country. On March 13, a revolutionary com-

---

[5]E. N. Burdzhalov, *Russia's Second Revolution: The February 1917 Uprising in Petrograd,* trans. and ed. Donald J. Raleigh (Bloomington, Ind.: Indiana Univ. Press, 1987), p. 107.

mittee arrested the tsarist ministers, and two days later, the tsar pliantly abdicated. No one came to the defense of the discredited monarchy, and the tsarist system collapsed almost overnight. (After fifteen months of lenient "house arrest" in Siberia, Nicholas and his family were executed by local Bolsheviks, apparently on orders from Lenin, who feared that the tsar might fall into the hands of advancing anti-Bolshevik armies. Despite allegations ever since that Nicholas's daughter Anastasia or other members of the family survived, forensic and DNA examination of recently disinterred bones provided convincing evidence that the entire royal family perished.)

The February Revolution soon rippled throughout the country. In most cities, towns, and villages, Russians and non-Russians alike greeted news of the tsar's downfall with enthusiasm. Tsarist authorities willingly relinquished their posts. Only scattered violence erupted, nothing to approach the casualties in Petrograd. Local committees of public figures soon formed to keep order, and soviets sprang up in most areas. In Moscow, workers went on strike and disarmed the police while revolutionaries established the Committee of Public Organizations to administer city affairs and maintain order. In Saratov, an important provincial city, despite the efforts of the tsarist governor to withhold news of the Petrograd uprising, a public executive committee and a soviet formed within days. As elsewhere, Saratov socialists participated from the beginning in the public executive committee.

Outside Russia, the Central Powers and the Allies welcomed the February Revolution. Germany and Austria-Hungary deemed that it would weaken Russia's ability to fight. The Allies, relieved to see the end of the anomaly in which an absolutist state fought alongside democracies, hoped the revolution would rejuvenate Russia's war effort. U.S. president Woodrow Wilson, about to enter the war on the Allied side, grandiloquently declared that "the great, generous Russian people have been added in all their native majesty and might to the forces that are fighting for freedom in the world, for justice. and for peace."

As the Russian crowds, now joined by soldiers, roamed through the streets of Petrograd on March 12, moderate leaders of the Duma, which had been prorogued the preceding day, met unofficially at the Tauride Palace, the seat of the assembly. They formed a temporary committee, which that evening named a Provisional Government. Headed by a respected nonparty figure, Prince Georgy Lvov, the new body included Kadet leader Paul Miliukov as minister of foreign affairs and Alexander Guchkov of the centrist Octobrist party as minister of war. One leftist, Alexander Kerensky, a prominent Duma deputy during the war, was appointed.

From its inception, the Provisional Government labored under severe handicaps. As its name implied, its leaders considered themselves only a transitional authority until election of a constitutional convention. Soon known as the Constituent Assembly, this latter body, everyone expected, would democratically express the population's wishes on fundamental issues such as the political structure of the country, land reform, and the position of the non-Russian nationalities. The Provisional Government hence refused to act on some of the very questions to which people most craved answers. This temporizing, along with the masses' conviction that the new administration was merely a puppet of "privileged Russia," severely damaged the Provisional Government's legitimacy and undercut its popularity.

Further, the new leaders desired not only to continue the war but in fact to step up Russia's participation in it. As liberals and democrats, they ideologically embraced the Allied cause; as men of honor, they would not betray their alliance with Britain and France; as patriots, they resolved to evict Germany from Russian soil and defeat what they labeled "German militarism." Their views were principled and admirable, but it is hard not to agree with the distinguished American historian George Kennan. According to Kennan, the Russian leaders' decision to enter and stay in the war proved a tragic blunder that saddled the Russian people with an authoritarian system for the next seventy years.

Nevertheless, the Provisional Government's stance on the war was at first not out of step with public opinion overall. Although leftist agitators and some workers had advanced antiwar slogans during the revolution, the bulk of the population, while war-weary, continued patriotically to support the fight against the German invaders. Later, when majority opinion switched to opposing the war, the Provisional Government nevertheless stuck to its prowar views.

In addition, because the tsarist system collapsed so rapidly, and confusion reigned afterward, the Provisional Government's leaders failed to establish their authority in the far-flung territories of the former Russian Empire. As we shall see, most non-Russian areas swiftly passed out of their control, but even in Russia their writ ran only weakly in many provincial towns and districts in the first weeks and virtually disappeared after a few months. In the villages, the new government had practically no authority. Peasants immediately began forming their own committees and soviets and next turned to seizing land.

As a final structural weakness, the Provisional Government faced competitors for power. After the revolution, public executive committees representing a broad spectrum of the population sprang up in many cities, towns, and districts. The committees acted as stop-gap administrations at the local level, and they resisted the new regime's efforts to extend its authority from the center to the regions. More important, from the beginning the Provisional Government had to share power with another institution, the Petrograd Soviet, and before long with soviets throughout the country. On the same evening during which the Provisional Government formed, and in another part of the same building,

workers and socialist leaders met and decided to reconstitute the proletarian arm of the 1905 revolution, the Soviet of Workers' Deputies. Soon
soldiers clamored for representation, and the group was renamed the
Petrograd Soviet of Workers' and Soldiers' Deputies. At first the Soviet,
although led by moderate Mensheviks and SRs, was attuned to the demands and interests of the revolutionaries. As the year advanced,
though, its leaders lost touch with mass sentiments. Sensitive to democratic pressures, the Soviet initially concerned itself with practical issues
such as food supply, public security, housing, and the status of the garrison troops in Petrograd. Because railway and telegraph workers looked
to the Soviet for guidance, it controlled transportation and communication. Thus, whether it wanted to or not, the Soviet in fact exercised
considerable authority in the city and its environs, an anomalous
arrangement that led to a case of "dual power."

The relationship of the Soviet to the Provisional Government was
shaped in part by the ideological tenets of the Soviet's moderate socialist
leaders. These men believed that the February Revolution represented
the transition from feudalism (that is, tsarism) to capitalism, or the
"bourgeois-democratic" revolution that Marxian theory called for. Only
after an unspecified period of time under capitalism would Russian society be ready to advance to socialism be means of the proletarian revolution. The Soviet leaders, and at first local Bolsheviks, therefore decided to
support the liberal Provisional Government as long as it defended the
revolution and acted democratically. Moreover, the Menshevik and SR
politicians remained convinced that, no matter how strongly the masses
urged it, a Soviet assumption of power would be premature, according to
the historical laws of socialism. They also feared that socialist rule might
provoke the propertied classes to armed resistance and counterrevolution. Most socialists persisted in their aversion to taking over the government as late as the Bolshevik Revolution in the fall, even when this stance
foreshadowed political suicide. They saw the Soviet as a watchdog instead, charged with keeping a careful eye on the "bourgeois-democratic"
revolution, guarding the interests of the workers in the new order, and
asserting the workers' rights to civil and political freedom. Mentors of
the proletariat, they believed, should use the new liberties to educate the
masses and to prepare for the ultimate socialist revolution.

On some issues the Soviet and the Provisional Government saw eye
to eye. The Soviet endorsed governmental decisions to guarantee full
civil and political liberties, to amnesty religious and political prisoners, to
organize elections to a Constituent Assembly, and to protect the rights to
strike and to form trade unions. On socioeconomic issues, however, the
two bodies clashed. The Provisional Government rejected Soviet demands for an eight-hour workday, higher wages, the prohibition of lock-
outs, and improved welfare and insurance benefits.

The most difficult, and ultimately the decisive, issue confronting the

Soviet and the Provisional Government was the war. Immediately after the February Revolution, the problem arose indirectly when soldiers who had participated in the revolution pressed their demands on the Soviet. Alarmed by an abortive government directive requiring Petrograd garrison soldiers to return to their barracks and obey their officers, several of these men dictated a list of soldiers' rights to a member of the Soviet Executive Committee during the night of March 14–15. Although never adopted by the Executive Committee or a Soviet plenary meeting, this list was issued the next day as Order No. 1 of the Petrograd Soviet. Intended only for the local garrison, the declaration was soon telegraphed nationwide and applied in many other localities. Its provisions included abolition of military regulations that abased enlisted men, guarantees of full civil and political rights for soldiers, and election of soldiers' committees in units down to the company level. Order No. 1 also forbade transfer of troops out of Petrograd without approval of the Soviet.

Although the soldiers' committees were not to interfere in strictly military matters, many officers considered the units an infringement of the command structure. The high command and the Provisional Government, after trying to block Order No. 1, eventually accepted the committee principle in a nationally promulgated declaration of soldiers' rights.

Soviet control over the Petrograd garrison clearly weakened the Provisional Government. Contemporary critics of Order No. 1 and a few historians also have blamed it for the subsequent dissolution of the Russian Army. In fact the order simply instituted long-overdue reforms and reflected widespread longing in the ranks for a responsive and democratic military structure. The later collapse of the army stemmed rather from widespread disgust with the war, hatred of the upper classes, and the desire of peasant and worker soldiers to share the fruits of the revolution.

At heart everyone was sick of the war, but inertia, the lingering effects of patriotism, and fear of the Germans led most people initially to support continued fighting. Even the Petrograd Soviet, and for a time Stalin and other second-rank Bolshevik leaders heading the party in Petrograd, backed the war effort. In an April 9 manifesto, the Soviet hedged its position by calling for a redefinition of Allied war aims to eliminate territorial annexations and indemnities against the losers.

By early April, the Provisional Government and the Petrograd Soviet had built an uneasy working relationship. The war against the Central Powers ground on, and most people enjoyed the taste of their new freedoms. In some outlying areas, however, the moderate public executive committees had already lost influence, and radical views were gaining ground. The return of Lenin accelerated this drift to the left. Immediately after the February Revolution, which he had not foreseen, Lenin eagerly sought a way back to Russia from his exile in Switzerland. The German government, believing (correctly) that radicals might further disrupt the Russian war effort, gladly allowed Russian leftists to cross Germany en route home in a "sealed" train. (The revolutionaries were forbidden to make speeches or hand out radical literature while they passed through Germany.) Later, the Germans furnished funds to the Bolsheviks and other radical groups, provoking charges by the Bolsheviks' political foes that Lenin was a German agent. This allegation missed the mark: Lenin's purpose in taking German money was not to support the German cause but to aid the Bolsheviks in fomenting revolution in Russia. In fact, Lenin believed that the Russian revolution would then spark a similar upheaval in Germany.

Shortly after arriving in Russia on April 16, Lenin issued policy guidelines known as the April Theses. Far more radical than anything that the Bolsheviks in Russia had put forth, Lenin's demands called for rejecting the "bourgeois" Provisional Government, ending the war, and preparing for a transfer of all power to the soviets. Local Bolsheviks gasped at this extreme program; other politicians thought Lenin deluded, out of touch with the real Russia, or suffering from revolutionary romanticism. With his usual doggedness and with support from rank-and-file workers and radical lower-level party officials, Lenin set about winning over his comrades. A Bolshevik party conference in early May duly adopted most of his ideas.

Patron of Revolution A striking photo of Lenin, reflecting his intelligence and determination.

Lenin had reached these views partly by evaluating the development of capitalism since Marx's time. In a pamphlet published in 1916, *Imperialism: The Highest Stage of Capitalism,* Lenin argued that, to prop up the capitalist system, bankers and financiers (such as J. P. Morgan) had taken over the economy, established monopolies and cartels, and expanded their operations into Asia, Africa, and Latin America. In these regions, cheap labor and raw materials, new markets, and profitable investment opportunities made it possible for this new breed of capitalists, whom Lenin called imperialists, to stave off the collapse of capitalism temporarily. To enforce their rights overseas, the imperialists had to take over the governments of their own countries and use military force to establish colonies, to subjugate the native peoples, and to keep out other nations. But once the world was divided among the imperialists, Lenin claimed, they would start quarreling among themselves, and war would break out. Thus for Lenin, World War I was an imperialist war. Workers everywhere, he believed, should try to turn the conflict into a civil war between the proletariat and imperialist governments and between factory workers and business owners. This transformation would precipitate a proletarian revolution.

According to Lenin, Russian workers had just such an opportunity before them. They also had several special advantages deriving from their unique circumstances inside Russia. Specifically, the Russian proletariat, although small in numbers because of Russia's backwardness, still had more strength than the Russian bourgeoisie, whose development tsarism had stunted. Russian workers could therefore take the lead in pushing the country to revolution. In addition, the Russian peasantry, with its intolerance for the war and fervent desire for land reform, constituted a valuable revolutionary ally. Finally, because Russia lagged behind other imperialist countries, the international workers' revolution could break through at this "weak link" in the chain of capitalist states. Touched off in Russia, socialist revolution would soon radiate to the advanced capitalist countries of Western Europe.

Dissolution of Authority

Lenin's return and the Bolsheviks' shift to active opposition against the Provisional Government had little immediate impact. The gradual erosion of authority in many institutions and at various levels throughout the country counted for more. In the long run, this disintegration left a power vacuum that Lenin and the Bolsheviks willingly filled in the fall of 1917.

Neither the Provisional Government nor the Soviet fully controlled the political situation, as a crisis in early May revealed. The Soviet wanted to clarify Russia's war aims and to ensure that the nation's goals precluded territorial gains from the war. But Provisional Government supporters insisted that Russia endorse the Allies' war aims, which included territorial acquisitions. Misunderstandings on this issue provoked street demonstrations in Petrograd. These protests forced the resignation of Miliukov, the foreign minister, who favored maintaining the secret treaty that promised Constantinople and the Straits to Russia. The Provisional Government was forced to appeal to the Soviet for help in calming the crowds. When the cabinet of the Provisional Government was reconstituted, several Menshevik and SR leaders agreed to take portfolios in it. Their participation, they believed, was necessary to unify the country and to bolster the war effort. They could also foster progressive policies on the part of the government, they felt. From then until the collapse of the Provisional Government in November 1917, the moderate socialists continued to take seats in the cabinet. Their involvement proved a fatal mistake, however. It linked the moderates inextricably with the government's unpopular policies, and it isolated them from the masses, who adopted increasingly radical views.

Two events in July further weakened the Provisional Government. First, Russia undertook a military offensive against the Central Powers to assist the Allies, to restore confidence in victory among the public, and to invigorate army discipline and morale. Although these may have seemed reasonable goals at the time, the government's decision proved an ill-considered gamble that further eroded the regime's position. The attack failed, and, predictably, Russia's war-weariness turned to antipathy. The army nearly dissolved as hundreds of thousands of disgusted soldiers deserted and headed home.

Second, a series of street demonstrations and protests, known as the July Days, broke out in Petrograd in July 1917. Although touched off by a regiment's refusal to go to the front and fueled by agitation among anarchists, radical workers, and sailors, the upheaval reflected growing popular objection to the war, as well as anger at the ongoing deterioration of the economy and frustration over the government's bumbling. Judging circumstances premature for socialist revolution, the Bolsheviks hesitated, then finally decided to lead the demonstrations. With help from moderate socialists, however, the government eventually regained control of the city. Leon Trotsky, the fiery leader of the St. Petersburg Soviet in the Revolution of 1905 and a recent recruit to the Bolsheviks, was arrested; Lenin escaped into hiding; and the Bolsheviks suffered a temporary setback.

Yet conditions continued to develop in the Bolsheviks' favor, as the positions that Lenin outlined in his April Theses more and more paralleled the mood of the people. The fabric of governance began unraveling, and popular grievances, starting at the grass roots, mounted. Indeed, peasants had begun to occupy state, church, and noble-held land from the first days after the February Revolution. The wave of land seizures crested between June and September, with peasants completing their own version of land reform—taking land and dividing it among themselves. Like other groups, peasants formed their own self-governing and direct-action organs, such as expanded *mir* assemblies and district (*volost*) committees. Later they turned the government's land committees into peasant-run institutions, and in late 1917 and early 1918, they set up village soviets.

In towns and cities as well, the Provisional Government's ability to execute its policies and to exact compliance from the population steadily eroded. In many areas, power passed from public executive committees or city *dumas* to district, town, and city soviets, in which Bolsheviks and radical workers' and soldiers' deputies gained the upper hand. In one provincial city, Tsaritsyn (later Stalingrad, today Volgograd), a radical soviet temporarily seized power as early as September 1917.

In part this leftward sweep of opinion reflected the deterioration of the economy. As long as they were committed to continuing the war, the Provisional Government's leaders, including the Mensheviks and SRs, had to control the grain supply by fixing prices, which drove the peasants from the market. They also had to maintain war production, which blocked reforms that workers sought. Moreover, although employers regularly raised wages, inflation overmatched these increases, and workers' real income fell during the summer by an estimated 50 percent. Most troubling to workers, relations with management turned bitter as factory owners closed plants, blaming fuel and raw material shortages. Workers had been forming trade unions and setting up factory or shop committees ever since the February Revolution. During the summer, several committees abandoned their advisory and watchdog role and took over factories. The drive for enhanced worker participation in factory operations was known as workers' control.

Soldiers, many of whom were conscripted peasants, turned against the authority structure of the army, especially after the failure of the July offensive. Desperate to escape the war and eager to share in the division of land at home, soldiers grew increasingly radical. *Frontoviki,* soldiers who had returned from the front lines to retrain, recuperate from wounds, or rest, pushed soviets leftward in provincial towns that housed garrisons.

Failed promises also eroded the Provisional Government's credibility. Many supporters of the February Revolution looked to the pledged Constituent Assembly to implement reforms. In addition, the regime's leaders shifted responsibility to the Constituent Assembly for such urgent issues as land reform, the future shape of governance, and relations among Russians and non-Russians. Yet, because of the press of other business and the difficulties of compiling voter lists and organizing universal and fair elections in a divided and war-torn country, the government kept postponing the balloting for delegates to the assembly.

Scheduled finally for November 1917, the elections were overtaken by events, although Lenin allowed the voting to proceed even after the Bolsheviks came to power.

Besides institutional and policy flaws, a psychology of liberation eroded the system that had replaced tsarism. After centuries of obedience to landlords, officers, bureaucrats, church officials, factory overseers, and other members of the privileged elite, the Russian people were in no mood to follow any institution that they themselves had not created, nor to obey leaders who ignored their immediate needs. Transfixed by the promise of freedom and intoxicated with the idea of rejecting all old authority, they favored local control of daily affairs. Almost everyone believed that in some magical way "the Revolution" would deliver the good life. When their dreams were not realized, amiability and optimism turned to bitterness and frustration. People sought a scapegoat and instant solutions. In the fall of 1917, the Provisional Government and the privileged upper classes of Russia made a handy scapegoat, and the Bolsheviks supplied the solutions.

An Empire Shattered

As authority slipped from the central bodies and turned volatile in most Great Russian areas, powerful centrifugal forces burst forth in other regions of the tsarist state. During 1917 and 1918, these energies led to the complete breakup of the old empire. The complex developments that accompanied this process took place under varying circumstances and at a different pace in each region, but the local cases shared several common characteristics. Each non-Russian group began by seeking not independence but some degree of autonomy within a democratic Russian state. Only later did separatist sentiments come to the fore.

Also, the dominant political coloration of each national movement was initially liberal-moderate or center-left, not radical. Socialists played a leading role in the Caucasus, for example, but they were moderate Mensheviks, not Bolsheviks. Class, ethnic, and nascent nationalist loyalties intermingled in a bewildering admixture of change. In addition, the capacity of the new regime to control non-Russian areas steadily dissipated over the summer, and by fall 1917, diverse local parties and movements competed for authority in these regions. Finally, in every instance, regional leaders bristled when centrists in the Provisional Government or local Russian inhabitants of the minority region failed to support the non-Russians' claims. The nationalities escalated their demands, and frequently launched armed attacks on supporters of the old empire or the Bolsheviks, who favored a unitary, centralized state.

Shortly after its formation, the Provisional Government rescinded tsarist restrictions on minorities and promised all citizens full equality regardless of religion, race, or national origin. It also pledged independence to Poland, then under German occupation, and full autonomy to Finland. In other regions, the new regime tried to replace tsarist officials with local leaders, or with representative committees, as in the Caucasus and Turkestan.

These interim authorities possessed little power. Moreover, although the government's proclamation of equal rights pleased non-Russian groups, its temporizing on nationality issues enraged them. Government leaders, across the spectrum from liberals to socialists, believed that only the upcoming Constituent Assembly could determine final constitutional and juridical relations within the new state. Although morally and legally correct, this policy of postponement confounded relations between the Provisional Government and the non-Russians and weakened the new regime. Aware that Russians made up the single largest group in the country and would elect half the deputies to the Constituent Assembly, non-Russian leaders worried about Russian domination of that body. In addition, fervent nationalists seized on the constitutional delay to step up their separatist demands, arguing that the longer a nationality waited, the less chance it had of asserting its claims. As the Provisional Government hedged on minority rights and as elections to the Constituent Assembly kept being postponed, many non-Russians began to castigate the Petrograd government as Russocentric and uninterested in their needs.

The biggest nationality problem facing the Provisional Government arose in Ukraine. Immediately after the revolution, a local executive committee formed in Kiev, the region's main city, to replace tsarist authorities. The committee represented a wide range of social and political groups and the main nationalities in Ukraine; by late March, the Soviet of Kiev joined it. Before long, however, a competing center of power emerged, the Ukrainian Central Council, or *Rada*. Formed in early March and composed of Ukrainians only, it originally focused on cultural and educational issues under moderate leadership that pledged to cooperate with the Provisional Government. By early April, ardent nationalists led by the historian Mihaile Hrushevskyj took over the *Rada* and began to advance a political agenda: complete self-rule and territorial autonomy. This radical stance was buttressed by pressure from Ukrainian soldiers in the army, who demanded formation of national Ukrainian regiments that would report to the *Rada*. Ukrainian peasants, who feared that an all-Russian land reform would transfer Ukrainian acreage to land-hungry Russian peasants, also rallied to the *Rada*, demanding that it administer an autonomous Ukrainian nationalization and division of the land. (In Ukraine, unlike Great Russia, peasants tended to own individual farmsteads, and the collective *mir* was not customary.)

In June the *Rada* asked the Provisional Government to administer Ukraine as a separate region under an appointed commissar for Ukrainian affairs, to recognize the principle of Ukrainian autonomy, and to permit formation of a national Ukrainian army. Although not opposed to Ukraine autonomy, government leaders believed that only the projected Constituent Assembly could resolve the issue. They also feared that separating out Ukrainian military units would weaken the army just as it braced itself to launch an offensive against the Central Powers. They therefore returned a vague and unsatisfactory reply to the *Rada*, which soon struck back by unilaterally declaring Ukrainian autonomy and the *Rada*'s right to tax citizens of the region.

After protracted negotiations with the Provisional Government, a compromise announced on July 16 provided for a special administration for Ukraine appointed jointly by the Provisional Government, the *Rada*, and other nationalities in the region (the largest were Russians and Jews). At the same time, the Provisional Government negotiators urged the Ukrainians to draft proposals for the Constituent Assembly on land reform and on future constitutional arrangements. This move went too far, according to the Kadets, and their cabinet ministers resigned in protest. The *Rada* was left as the dominant political force in Ukraine for the next few months. Its leaders fell to quarreling among themselves, however, and the tension provoked a new crisis in the fall.

The most distinctive national movement in 1917 emerged as an effort to create an all-Muslim body to assert and guard religious, cultural, and educational rights for followers of Islam throughout Russia. Led by westernized intellectuals, this organization initially sought the secularization and democratization of Muslim society and lacked clear nationalist goals. At its first congress in May 1917, after a bitter struggle over women's rights, the delegates approved full equality for women, formed a new separate administration for Islamic affairs, and appointed their own religious leader, or Mufti.

By fall, however, regional Muslim groups began to lose interest in the movement and to concentrate instead on satisfying local needs. In the Crimea, the Tatar National Party had formed in July 1917 and now vied for control of the region with a local Kadet-oriented administration. The latter body represented Russian and Ukrainian elements, who made up about half the population on the Crimean peninsula. Originally the Crimean Tatars did not seek independence, but after the Bolshevik Revolution, they temporarily set up their own government. Muslims in southeastern Russia and what is today Kazakhstan and Kyrgyzstan primarily sought to undo Russian colonial seizure of much of the region's land in the preceding decade. In 1916, when the tsarist government had repealed the Muslims' traditional exemption from military service and tried to draft them for noncombat duty, they had rebelled, killing several thousand Cossacks, Russian colonists, and administrators. The government had bloodily suppressed the revolt, but in July 1917 local Muslims met to organize an indigenous party and to seek local autonomy. Their actions soon led to further tension with the local Russians, and civil war between the two groups broke out in September 1917. The ensuing cruel struggle dragged on intermittently for two and a half years.

In the remainder of Central Asia, or Turkestan, an analogous split developed between the Muslim inhabitants and Russian immigrants and administrators. The former were represented by the Turkestan Muslim Central Council; the latter by the soviet of Tashkent, the area's capital city. An abortive uprising by the soviet in September 1917 was suppressed. During the Bolshevik Revolution, however, the area split: the soviet established power in Tashkent and several other towns, and the Muslims controlled the countryside.

In the Caucasus, because political parties had formed well before World War I, the Provisional Government had little success in establishing a commission to rule the area. In 1915, after Turkey entered the war on the side of the Central Powers, Armenian nationalists, or *Dashnaks*, had made the fateful decision to side with Russia. This move ignited a frightful Turkish campaign of genocide against the Armenians living in Turkey and worsened the long-standing suspicion between the Armenians and the chief Muslim group in the Caucasus, the Turkic-speaking Azerbaijanis. In September 1917, the Armenians formed a national council and their own military forces, but because the Turkish army still operated just across the border, they supported the Provisional Government and did not insist on autonomy.

In both Georgia and Azerbaijan, socialists controlled soviets in Tbilisi and Baku that wielded considerable local authority. Although the second-echelon Bolshevik leader, Joseph Stalin, was Georgian, Mensheviks dominated the political scene there. Several of them played an important role in the national party and in national politics, and one of them, Irakli Tsereteli, served as a minister in the Provisional Government. In 1917, content to run things in Georgia through the Tbilisi Soviet, these Georgian Mensheviks had no interest in separatism. In Azerbaijan, the Baku Soviet, which included workers from the Russian and Armenian minorities in the city, coexisted with a strong national movement, *Mussavat*, which favored federalism. During 1917, although the Caucasus exercised self-rule, few urged independence or secession.

The rise of nationalism in the empire had attracted Lenin's attention well before 1917. In fact, he possessed an unusual ability to blend pragmatic politics and Marxist theory, even if he warped the theory a bit in the process. Eager to instigate revolution in Russia, Lenin had begun before the war to ponder how he could use the growing antitsarist sentiment among non-Russians in his campaign to overthrow the monarchy. Until 1913 the Bolshevik leader had adhered to the classic Marxist position that under socialism, class solidarity would prevail over national loyalties, and he opposed federalism within the Bolshevik party. Between 1913 and 1917, he worked out a theoretical position that he hoped would harness the national minorities to Bolshevik purposes. He argued that each group should have the right of self-determination, but he assumed that this right would be exercised only in class terms—that is, the proletariat of each nationality would determine what was in its group's best interests. By adding the slogan of self-determination to his propaganda arsenal, Lenin enhanced Bolshevism's appeal among non-Russians. Ultimately, however, his strategy failed to prevent friction among the nationalities once the Bolsheviks came to power.

The Path to Bolshevism

In mid-1917, Lenin's main focus remained Russia proper. The radical program that he espoused in the April Theses stood as the most significant harbinger of his and the Bolshevik party's plans. Nevertheless, the first concrete event leading to a Bolshevik triumph in the fall came with the so-called Kornilov affair in early September 1917. Conservative elements, terrified by the masses' show of strength in the July Days, attempted a right-wing putsch designed to restore order. A confused, almost comic-opera tangle of cross purposes, the incident involved Kerensky, a Petrograd Soviet member who had entered the Provisional Government on its formation and now served as its prime minister; General Lavr Kornilov, recently appointed supreme commander of the army by Kerensky; and several meddling conservative politicians. After the July offensive failed, Kerensky and others in the Provisional Government labored to restore discipline in the army and to shore up the entire military effort against Germany. Kornilov, a war hero because of his capture by the Austrians and subsequent escape, was brought in with the support of other senior army officers. His purpose was to initiate military reforms, including reinstitution of the death penalty at the front and in the rear. Kornilov, whom a fellow general described as having "the heart of a lion, but the brains of a sheep," was patriotic and well meaning but possessed no political sense. He completely misread the mood of both the army and the Petrograd public.

Urged on by intriguers and inept conservative politicians, convinced that leftist leaders in the capital were German agents, and puffed up by his enthusiastic reception at a recent national conference, Kornilov became convinced that he could simply arrive in the capital with a few loyal troops and arrest leaders of the Petrograd Soviet. Unrest would end, military reforms could proceed, and the fighting will of the country would revive. Whether Kornilov had any political program beyond these aims is uncertain. Clearly, however, he believed that by becoming a temporary military dictator he could save Mother Russia.

Apparently, Kerensky intended to use Kornilov to spearhead needed reforms in the army and to placate the right-wing elements who increasingly criticized his predominantly socialist cabinet and his government's wishy-washy performance. But he had no intention of substituting Kornilov's military dictatorship for the Provisional Government. Through miscommunication, Kornilov thought that Kerensky had fallen in with his plans, and on September 9 he ordered detachments to move on Petrograd. Outraged, Kerensky fired Kornilov as army commander and appealed to the populace to protect the capital and the revolution. Under direction of the Petrograd Soviet, defenses were thrown up, rail and telegraph workers disrupted Kornilov's communications and train movements, and agitators sent to meet Kornilov's units soon won over his troops. Within forty-eight hours, the clumsy coup attempt collapsed, and Kornilov and his colleagues were arrested. Whether a better planned effort led by an intelligent and politically astute general might have succeeded remains a moot question. If it had, civil war would certainly have ensued.

The Kornilov affair had three decisive consequences that helped to seal the fate of the Kerensky government and to sweep the Bolsheviks to power. First, the blunder thoroughly discredited senior military leaders (even those not implicated). It also damaged the reputations of conservative political circles, now widely seen as dangerous counterrevolutionaries. Second, it isolated and besmirched the Provisional Government and the liberals and moderate socialists associated with it. Tainted by press reports that the government had originally supported Kornilov's hardline plans, the centrist leadership earned mistrust from a public already dissatisfied with its failure to end the war and to improve living conditions. Moreover, to save itself, the government had had to rely on the Soviet's ability to mobilize the masses, including workers' detachments known as Red Guards. This dependence revealed the government as essentially powerless, cut off from the right and the army and distrusted by the left. If, as soon happened, moderate socialists lost control of the Soviet, the government's days were surely numbered. Third, the Kornilov affair furnished the Bolsheviks with a powerful psychological weapon. Ever since Lenin's return, they had encouraged suspicion of the Provisional Government and warned that enemies of social democracy lurked in the wings. Now a whiff of counterrevolution dramatically proved their point. From September on, the Bolsheviks insisted stridently that only they qualified as the genuine defenders of "the Revolution." They soon captured the support of soldiers in rear garrisons and won majority control of soviets in the capitals and in many provincial cities.

In March the Bolshevik party numbered somewhere between 25,000 and 40,000 supporters in a population of 165 million; seven months later their ranks had swollen to 260,000, and they were running the country. The reason for this remarkable surge to power lies partly in the closeness with which the Bolshevik political program corresponded to the aspirations of the masses. Their slogan of "peace, land, and bread" plus their encouragement of workers' control of industry and the promise of national self-determination coincided with the public's fervent desires. Indeed, some writers have concluded that Lenin and the Bolsheviks cynically tailored their program to mass demands solely to ensure their rise to power. To be sure, the Bolsheviks wanted to make and lead a revolution. At the same time, their platform accurately reflected what many people most wanted. Lower-level Bolshevik party workers were in a particularly favorable position to hear and articulate the sentiments of the population. They and the people for whom they spoke undoubtedly sought a democratic, peaceful, and just society in which privilege and oppression had no place. For a few trained in Marxism, socialism embodied this hope, but for many, the vision was more compelling than the ideology. Most people followed the Bolsheviks not as socialists but because they longed for a better life, and the Bolsheviks promised to lead them to it.

In their rise to power, the Bolsheviks also benefited from the weakness and disunity of the government and other political groups. Particularly after the Kornilov affair, right-wing forces had little support among the populace and could not organize themselves to oppose the Bolsheviks until some time after the latter had come to power. The moderate socialists, who should have been the chief rivals of the Bolsheviks, instead fatally compromised themselves. Although Menshevik and SR leaders insisted that it was premature for socialists to take power, they nevertheless joined the government. They thereby became associated in the public mind with unpopular policies such as continuing the war and delaying decisions on land reform and non-Russian autonomy. The Mensheviks and the SRs steadily lost support among the urban masses, although the SRs retained some influence in the army and among the peasantry. The SRs' more radical elements, however, split off in the fall of 1917 to form the separate Left SR party.

As we saw earlier, the government also failed to control the non-Russian regions and most local districts in Russia proper. In addition, as a coalition, the Provisional Government struggled with divergent views among its socialist and nonsocialist members and could seldom agree on decisive measures.

Finally, Kerensky proved a weak leader. Probably no one could have saved the centrist position of the Provisional Government as conditions worsened during the summer of 1917, but Kerensky's combination of bombast, indecision, and shortsightedness dealt a damaging blow at a time when the nation needed forcefulness, clarity, and practicality. Vain and ambitious, the well-meaning Kerensky lacked a clear program. Trying to please all sides, he veered between capricious action and bouts of apathy. At the end, he had no political capital or mass support on which to draw. In fact, the Bolsheviks did not really need to make a revolution. They simply tapped the government, and it toppled over.

A Deficient Democratic Leader
Alexander Kerensky, last head
of the Provisional Government,
brooding over a military map.

The Bolsheviks Ascendant

Under the Julian calendar, the Bolsheviks came to power on October
25–26, 1917; under the post-1918 calendar, on November 7–8, 1917. Although sometimes called the November Revolution, the events of those
days are widely known as the October or Bolshevik Revolution, terms
that we employ here (although, again, we use new calendar dates).

Lenin played a key role in the takeover, providing one of those rare
moments when a single individual demonstrably alters the course of history. Without Lenin's single-minded insistence on seizing power in the
fall, the Bolsheviks would not have acted at that time. Had they delayed,
they might not have succeeded. Yet in late summer and early fall, even
after the Kornilov affair, Lenin had not favored revolution. At the Sixth
Party Congress in early August, he had joined the majority to urge continued agitation among the masses rather than direct action. And for the
first three weeks of September, his writings espoused a moderate, cautious line. Between September 25 and 27, he changed his mind and advocated immediate insurrection. Lenin never explained why he reversed
course. However, news of peasant land seizures and military mutinies
throughout the country; reports (unfounded as it turned out) that revolution was brewing in Germany; and the Bolsheviks' winning a majority in
the Petrograd and Moscow Soviets and in several important provincial
soviets undoubtedly encouraged him to seize the moment.

We may well ask, as his moderate socialist opponents and even some Bolsheviks did, how a proletarian revolution following so soon after the bourgeois-democratic revolution in the spring of 1917 could be justified according to Marxism. Earlier, Lenin had decided that special circumstances made Russia ripe for revolution. Now, as he assured doubting Bolsheviks, the time for action had come. As Lenin explained, the party heading the Russian proletariat had backing from the mass of the peasantry. It could oversee the uninterrupted "growing over," or passage, from the bourgeois-democratic revolution to a nascent socialist revolution that would establish a "democratic dictatorship of the proletariat and the poorest peasantry." During this process, the capitalist stage of history in Russia would be fulfilled "in passing." The party could guide the workers in appropriating factories and other productive forces of capitalist-imperialist Russia to build the new socialist society. Lenin acknowledged that because of Russia's economic backwardness, its transition to socialism could reach completion only with assistance from the advanced societies of Western Europe. In these regions, workers inspired by proletarian revolution in Russia would overthrow their imperialist states and set up socialist systems. Lenin's explanation of the rapid passage from the bourgeois-democratic to the socialist revolution and of Russia's role in touching off the world proletarian revolution in Europe strongly resembled views advanced earlier by Trotsky, in his concept of permanent or uninterrupted revolution.

In practice as well as in theory, Lenin and Trotsky collaborated to bring about the Bolshevik Revolution. Lenin, who in October had moved to Petrograd from his hiding place in Finland, now lobbied his reluctant Bolshevik colleagues to act at once. Meanwhile, Trotsky, released from prison after his July Days arrest, took over leadership of the Petrograd Soviet and began to organize the insurrection. By good fortune, on October 22 Soviet Mensheviks proposed formation of a Military Revolutionary Committee (MRC). This body was charged with organizing the defense of the city in case of German attack or of government efforts to undermine the position of the Petrograd garrison or the Soviet itself. Trotsky skillfully used the MRC as an instrument to plan and prepare the seizure of power.

Lenin's persistent campaign finally bore fruit on October 23, when a meeting of leading Bolsheviks voted 10 to 2 to make insurrection "the order of the day," although they did not specify which day. Two influential Bolsheviks, Lev Kamenev and Grigory Zinoviev, dissented. Afterward, they continued to argue against the decision in the party press, their complaints alerting others to the plan.

Lenin particularly wanted the rebellion to take place before the forthcoming Second All-Russian Congress of Soviets. Election of delegates to the congress had revealed widespread disaffection with the Provisional Government. Most voters expressed a desire to replace Kerensky with a soviet government in which all socialist parties would be represented. Although Lenin calculated that the Bolsheviks and their Left SR allies might control a majority in the congress, he preferred that the Bolsheviks seize power before that body convened. He could then present the delegates with a fait accompli but still claim to rule in the name of the Soviet.

On November 4 and 5, two days before the actual uprising, Trotsky took a bold step that largely decided the outcome of the October Revolution. He issued a manifesto asserting the right of the MRC to control the Petrograd garrison. MRC commissars were posted to each major detachment, and no unit was to act without written authorization from the committee. Kerensky thus lost authority over the readily available forces, some of whom might otherwise have come to his defense. Although few troops actually fought for the Bolsheviks, the MRC veto neutralized the 200,000-man garrison. With fewer than thirty thousand armed men and only a few hundred casualties, the Bolsheviks easily seized control of the city several days later.

News in the press of the Bolsheviks' plans and the MRC's monitoring of the garrison prompted a last-ditch flurry of activity among the Provisional Government's defenders. Moderate socialists tried in vain to persuade Kerensky to proclaim immediate peace negotiations and far-reaching land reform, but the prime minister foolishly vowed that he would welcome a test of strength with the Bolsheviks. Kerensky played right into Trotsky's hands. For several weeks, Trotsky had urged that the uprising be cast as a defense of the democratic revolution, not a takeover by the Bolshevik Party. On November 5, Kerensky ordered the closing of the Bolshevik printing plant and the arrest of a number of Bolshevik leaders. Trotsky immediately cried that the revolution was in danger of rightist repression and activated the forces he had organized. The next day, the Bolsheviks retook the printing plant and secured the central telegraph office and several bridges over the Neva River. In the early morning darkness of November 7, Bolshevik units seized other key points in the city and by noon had besieged the cabinet of the Provisional Government inside the Winter Palace. Kerensky, however, had slipped out of the city that morning to seek reinforcements among front-line troops.

During the afternoon of November 7, Trotsky reported the overthrow of the government to the Petrograd Soviet, and a proclamation announcing its demise was distributed throughout the city. Meanwhile, Lenin contrived to delay the opening of the Congress of Soviets, scheduled for early evening, insisting that the ministers of the Provisional Government be arrested first. After midnight, the few government loyalists defending the Winter Palace, including some officers in training and a detachment of the Women's Battalion, finally deserted or surrendered, and the Bolsheviks peacefully apprehended the cabinet.

At the congress, which had perforce started deliberations a few hours earlier, the Bolsheviks and the Left SRs enjoyed a comfortable majority of

A Call to Revolutionary Arms A dazzling poster entitled, "To Horse, Proletarians!," designed to attract recruits for the newly forming Bolshevik cavalry.

about two-thirds of the delegates. After acrimonious debate about the propriety of the Bolsheviks' actions, most Menshevik and other SR deputies walked out. Although their opposition to the illegality and ideological incorrectness of the Bolshevik insurrection is understandable, and although they believed the Bolsheviks would not hold power for long, their withdrawal proved costly. The Bolsheviks now could freely organize the new government and proclaim it in the name of the Congress of Soviets. At about 5 A.M. on November 8, the rump congress approved a manifesto drafted by Lenin announcing the transfer of power. A new epoch in modern history had opened.

The next day, Lenin had the congress endorse resolutions on world peace and on land reform. To end the war, he proposed to all combatants a three-month armistice and the immediate opening of negotiations for an "honest and democratic" peace with no annexations or indemnities. Both the Allies and the Central Powers ignored Lenin's appeal, forcing him to open armistice negotiations directly with the Austrians and Germans. The separate peace that followed held dire consequences for the Bolsheviks, as we shall see in Chapter 4.

The land decree ratified the peasant seizures of the preceding summer, in an outright contradiction of Bolshevik ideology, which called for the socialization of agriculture. It also drew unabashedly on the land program of the SRs, who were closest to the peasantry. Hoping to salvage a bit of socialism, Lenin hedged on the issue of land ownership; the decree stated that all land belonged to the state but that peasants and communes had an unrestricted right to use it. This arrangement satisfied the peasants, most of whom then expressed either support for the new government or indifference toward it. Peasant control of the land would create problems later, when the Bolsheviks tried to squeeze grain from the peasantry during the civil war of 1918–1920.

On November 8, Lenin also announced a new government to act on behalf of the soviet congress with a cabinet called the Council of People's Commissars, *Sovnarkom,* which he headed. All its members were Bolsheviks, a fact that catalyzed a political crisis. Most delegates to the Second Congress of Soviets, regardless of party, were elected on a platform that included the slogan "All Power to the Soviets." Bolshevik leaders had downplayed this idea after the July Days, only to reinstitute it in September, when they gained a majority in many soviets. For most workers, soldiers, and peasants who voted for delegates to the congress, the slogan meant formation of a soviet government to replace the despised Provisional Government. Almost everyone, including rank-and-file Bolsheviks, assumed that a soviet government would reflect the range of political forces in the soviet movement; that is, it would comprise other socialist parties as well as the Bolsheviks. Support for an all-socialist government was strong, and the executive committee of the powerful railway workers' trade union, *Vikzhel,* soon demanded that the Leninist government announced on November 8 be transformed into an all-socialist one. Despite backing for this demand from five prominent moderate Bolsheviks, Lenin resolutely opposed the idea. He managed to drag out negotiations with the moderate socialists on the issue for several weeks, and then finessed the idea by appointing several Left SRs to the Council of People's Commissars.

Although the Bolsheviks controlled Petrograd and formed a "Soviet" government, they did not yet rule the nation. Loyal troops from the front had the potential to move against them; indeed, on November 9–10, Kerensky returned to the outskirts of Petrograd with a small force of Cossacks commanded by General Peter Krasnov. Faulty communications and misunderstandings led to a premature uprising of anti-Bolshevik groups in the city, and on November 12, Bolshevik units blocked Krasnov's advance in a bloody but indecisive battle. His troops lost heart and melted away, while Kerensky escaped to Britain. (Eventually he moved to the United States and died there in 1970. He never admitted to making mistakes that contributed to the Bolshevik victory.) In addition, the supreme commander of the army refused to recognize the new government or to accept orders from Lenin. However, he also refused to organize military opposition to the Bolsheviks, and in early December, radical soldiers arrested and murdered him. The killing presaged the brutal civil war that would soon break out.

In Moscow severe fighting between Bolshevik forces and moderates organized around the Committee of Public Safety lasted a week and cost more than a thousand casualties before the Bolsheviks triumphed. Elsewhere the October Revolution spread sporadically from provincial capitals to districts, towns, and villages. In several areas, radical peasant soldiers and Left SRs played a crucial role in expanding Soviet power. The Bolsheviks often used local soviets to mask and legitimize the transfer of power. By late December, pro-Bolshevik local bodies were installed everywhere, with some notable exceptions. In Ukraine an uneasy balance of power developed; the *Rada* held power in Kiev and some rural western districts, whereas mostly Bolshevik-dominated soviets ruled the remaining cities and towns. In Georgia the Mensheviks controlled the Tbilisi Soviet, and in Azerbaijan and Central Asia, power split between indigenous groups and pro-Bolshevik city soviets. Anti-Bolshevik forces triumphed in the homeland of the Don and Kuban Cossacks in southeastern Russia, and the area soon became the base for a national effort to unseat the Soviet government.

Conclusion

The abdication of Nicholas II initiated a train of events that profoundly shaped twentieth-century world history. The upheavals of 1917 saw the

The Bolshevik Revolution stands as a key event of the twentieth century and has always attracted scholarly attention. Precisely because of its global impact—for millions the Bolsheviks' seizure of power promised a paradise on earth, while for other millions it struck fear and terror—few other historical topics have proved as charged as this one. Politics and scholarship intertwined, a circumstance that, according to Martin Malia, "made Soviet Studies the most impassioned social science" (*The Soviet Tragedy*, 1994). Richard Pipes and Stephen Cohen, two prominent historians of the Revolution, epitomized that fact. For Pipes, President Reagan's choice as adviser to the National Security Council in 1981, the Soviet Union truly was an "evil empire." For Stephen Cohen, friend of Gorbachev and consultant to CBS during the Gorbachev years, the Revolution contained many seeds, including those of socialism's regeneration and rebirth.

For a quarter century after World War II, most Western interpretations of 1917 reflected an ideological stance. The seminal work was Leonard Schapiro's *The Origins of the Communist Autocracy* (1955), which depicted the Bolshevik overthrow as a coup d'état by a conspiratorial elite dedicated to destroying all rival political groups and concentrating power in its hands. According to Schapiro, the Bolsheviks hoodwinked the masses behind the mask of a socialist democracy that they never intended to implement. Only a handful of figures around Lenin, Schapiro argues, knew his true intention: a one-party dictatorship disguised by the slogan "All Power to the Soviets" and by calls for a Constituent Assembly. Schapiro's view of the Soviet Union as totalitarian—a monolith drawing its energy from Lenin's deception—prevailed throughout the heights of the Cold War.

Only in the 1970s, as Soviet-American antagonisms cooled in the face of arms-control talks and summits, did a breakthrough occur in Western scholarly sentiments. In 1976 two influential books appeared to recast the story of 1917: *The Bolsheviks Come to Power* by Alexander Rabinowitch, and *The Russian Revolution* by John Keep. Both studies plumbed the lower depths of Russia, in contrast to previous works on high-level party politics in that fateful year. Both authors scrutinized the critical role played by mass organizations—factory committees, trade unions, and the Soviets of Workers, Peasants, and Soldiers—in ensuring the Bolshevik triumph. And both agreed that conditions in 1917—war-weariness and civilian demands for economic security—spurred the "bolshevization" of the masses.

But except for their focus on society, Rabinowitch and Keep differed sharply in their characterization of Bolshevism. Rabinowitch contended that the October Revolution was neither a historical anomaly nor a stealth operation orchestrated by Lenin. Rather, it grew out of a dynamic relationship between the Party and the people, one that reflected the Bolsheviks' "relatively tolerant, democratic, and decentralized method of operation." That openness in turn attuned the leadership to the popular mood in Petrograd. In effect, Rabinowitch turned the totalitarian paradigm of Bolshevism on its head: instead of an elite coup, the Revolution represented the triumph of a decentralized Party fulfilling popular demands.

Keep countered that the peasants, not the workers, were the true revolutionary force. He also saw much less "democracy" in Lenin's apparatus than Rabinowitch did, insisting that the Bolsheviks "alone were schooled in techniques of organizational manipulation that permitted them to channel mass discontent to the party's purpose." Moreover, after February 1917, the passion for politics among the workers fell off considerably, and radical intellectuals subverted the mass organizations to gain the upper hand. Real decisions took place behind closed doors, and a Bolshevik core bent on power maneuvered these organizations toward the overthrow of the Kerensky regime.

The 1980s witnessed a deluge of monographs that questioned Keep's conclusion that professional intelligentsia bent on glory manhandled the workers. Both David Mandel (*The Petrograd Workers and the Seizure of Power*, 1984) and Diane Koenker (*The Moscow Workers and the 1917 Revolution*, 1981) pictured an energetic proletariat fired by economic misery and active in its own defense through political organization. Although these studies did not romanticize these bodies—even effective groups sometimes fell sway to bureaucratic gamesmanship on the part of worker activists—the idea that the workers were passive or dominated by a scheming elite was put to rest.

Or so it seemed until the end of the Soviet Union. For what is remarkable since 1991 is a full-circle return by several historians to earlier notions of totalitarianism and a coup d'état. Nowhere is this revision of the revisionists more forcefully presented than in Martin Malia's sweeping history of the Soviet Union. Malia made four major points. First, worker radicalism plummeted during 1917; by October it was largely spent. Second, Lenin's party, while "democratic" within, was dictatorial without. Democracy, such as it was existed only for one class and for one party. Third, and following from the first point, in the actual seizure of power in October the masses acted as spectators who even ignored Bolshevik appeals to storm the Winter Palace. Finally, the October Revolution became a nationwide upheaval only when the peasants turned against all authority several months later.

What are we to make of this seeming *déjà-vu*? Malia's conclusions, in truth a recasting of Schapiro's classic scheme, are remarkable because of the avalanche of research over the previous two decades. Even before Malia's book appeared, British historian Edward Acton had detected the staying power of the traditional totalitarian approach as "one of the most striking features of recent trends" (*Society and Politics in the Russian Revolution*, Robert Service, ed., 1992).

Several explanations for the resurgence of older historiographic views come to mind. Perhaps the end of communism in the midst of the conservative intellectual climate in the West of the late 1980s reinforced the traditional view of the October Revolution as little more than a palace overthrow by a club of *intelligenty*. In other words, if communism could vanish so suddenly and totally, then maybe the system had been built on a rotten foundation.

Second, the return to a totalitarian interpretation may reflect some observers' growing skepticism that politics mirrors popular aspirations or class struggle. Again, the traditional interpretation of the Revolution depicted political leadership as an independent force, whereas the revisionist one saw October 1917 as the product of a broad-based revolutionary movement of social malcontents. Perhaps the Gorbachev era, with its theatrics and dynamism, stirred a renewed respect for the autonomy of politics.

Last, no sweeping masterwork of revisionist scholarship has yet appeared to rout the traditionalists. The task is a daunting one, to be sure, and probably beyond the capacity of a single author. Such an integrated history of the Revolution would be welcome, and the archives are open. Whether those archives will confirm either view of the Russian Revolution remains to be seen.

collapse of the old regime in Russia and the coming to power of an ideology and political system that would challenge the existing global capitalist and colonial order over the next seventy years. The Russian Revolution also spawned what would become a powerful state. Twenty-five years later, this state crushed Nazi Germany and then competed with the United States for world leadership during the next forty years. Finally, the events of 1917 remolded the course of Russian development itself, leaving a legacy that the peoples of the region today are struggling to transform.

In broadest terms, two powerful strands dominated 1917 in Russia and what evolved afterward: the populist, almost anarchic character of the revolution; and the contradictions inherent in the Bolshevik ascendancy. Almost every citizen of the Russian Empire participated in the turmoil of that year. Because of the breadth and intensity of the people's grievances, the movement initially carried unstoppable momentum, despite the vagueness of its goals. Popular disgust swept away the old order in March. A mystique of "the Revolution" soon followed, wherein people looked to the new order to solve the country's and their own problems. The February Revolution provided a heady draft of freedom, and people eagerly anticipated the bright, fast-approaching future. When "the Revolution" not only failed to right all wrongs but in fact seemed to have worsened conditions, bewilderment, resentment, and finally burning anger set in.

As another expression of the revolution's populist nature, people spontaneously formed organs of self-government and direct democracy: soviets, factory committees, soldiers' committees, peasant organizations, and, in non-Russian areas, nationalist institutions like the Ukrainian *Rada*. These bodies, instruments for mobilizing the masses and channeling their energy into social and political action, also gave individuals a sense of participation and control. As the summer wore into fall, the people's revolt also manifested itself in mounting distrust of the remaining privileged elite: officers, landlords (and sometimes rich peasants), factory owners and shop supervisors, priests, politicians, and, not infrequently, educated professionals. This suspicion often blended with frustration over unrelenting hardship, for which the miserable blamed the rich and the powerful. Finally, even though "the Revolution" had not fulfilled its promises, people still cherished it and agonized lest the upper classes snatch it from them. The threat of conservative counterrevolution provided a lethal weapon for the Bolsheviks.

This great popular revolution failed, not, as some would have it, because the Bolsheviks captured and distorted it, but for more fundamental reasons. The Russian people strove to assert their rights and to craft a democratic society in a country horribly entangled in a world war that had all but destroyed its social and economic fabric. It would be hard to imagine less propitious circumstances in which to build a new order. The population's limited social and political experience and relative lack of culture and education presented other formidable hurdles. Representative government and the compromises that make democracy work require a degree of sophistication and group cooperation, neither of which graced the Russian people in 1917. Finally, the organs of self-government that the people created proved more effective at expressing desires, tearing down old institutions, and opposing authority than at building new, complex systems, especially above the local level. On the one hand, the soviets and other bodies became vehicles for expressing selfish and group interests without regard for others or for the common welfare. On the other hand, politicians of various stripes, but especially the Bolsheviks, captured the soviets and used them for their own ends. In the process, the institutions thrown up by the people grew centralized and hierarchical, run not by and for the many, but by and for the few.

The second major strand of 1917 was the rise of Lenin and Bolshevism. As we saw, the party came to reflect popular aspirations and to harness those hopes to its own political agenda. As the revolution evolved in 1917, it was far from ideal, in the Bolsheviks' view, for they had to work through the soviets. With their own party in disunity, they also had to cooperate with a wavering and unreliable ally, the Left SRs. Last, they were forced to rely on a peasantry neutralized by distinctly unsocialist promises of dividing the land into small individual plots, and they had to base their newly won power on a backward and war-ravaged economy. Under these circumstances and because of Lenin's concept of the party's role, the Bolsheviks never believed in popular decision making, either in the October uprising itself or in the Soviet government that followed, although they endorsed popular goals. Lenin scoffed at the idea of an all-socialist government, even though that was exactly what most people wanted. Sure that he and the party elite knew best, he seized authority as it slipped from the hands of the moribund Provisional Government, but he had no intention of sharing power with others. He thereby laid the foundation for the one-party dictatorship that would rule Soviet society down to 1989.

Bolshevism nevertheless offered a bold vision that conformed to the goals of the populist revolution. As we shall see, the reality of the Soviet system as it evolved proved quite different from the dream. However, this original vision is what made the October Revolution and Soviet socialism such a powerful force. We also must remember that Lenin and the early Bolsheviks took power not for power's sake but because they deeply believed that theirs was the first step on the road to a glorious future. By initiating the proletarian revolution in Russia, they expected to fuel its expansion to the advanced countries of Europe, whose workers would then help the valiant Russian people bring their dreams to fruition. Lenin and his comrades were wrong, and events dashed their expectations; but their vision remains a beacon for many still striving to balance freedom with security.

FURTHER READING

No comprehensive, scholarly account of Russia during World War I exists. Military developments are covered in W. Rutherford, *The Russian Army in World War I* (London, 1975) and Norman Stone, *The Eastern Front, 1914–1917* (New York, 1974). W. Bruce Lincoln, *Passage through Armageddon: The Russians in War and Revolution, 1914–1918* (New York, 1986) offers a popular treatment of the whole period.

Useful monographs on the wartime era include Joseph T. Fuhrmann, *Rasputin: A Life* (New York, 1990); R. Pearson, *The Russian Moderates and the Crisis of Tsarism, 1914–1917* (New York, 1977); Michael Florinsky, *The End of the Russian Empire* (New York, 1931, repr. 1979); and C. Jay Smith, *The Russian Struggle for Power, 1914–1917: A Study of Russian Foreign Policy During the First World War* (New York, 1956).

A short introduction to the revolutionary period is John M. Thompson, *Revolutionary Russia, 1917*, 2nd ed. (New York, 1988). A standard, still useful history that covers the civil war as well is William H. Chamberlin, *The Russian Revolution, 1917–1921*, 2 vols. (New York, 1935, repr. 1965).

Important studies of the February Revolution include Tsuyoshi Hasegawa, *The February Revolution* (Seattle, 1981); E. N. Burdzhalov, *Russia's Second Revolution: The February 1917 Uprising in Petrograd*, trans. and ed. Donald J. Raleigh (Bloomington, Ind., 1987); M. Ferro, *The Russian Revolution of February 1917* (Englewood Cliffs, N.J., 1972); and George Katkov, *Russia 1917: The February Revolution* (New York, 1967).

Donald J. Raleigh, *Revolution on the Volga: 1917 in Saratov* (Ithaca, N.Y., 1986), and Ronald G. Suny, *The Baku Commune, 1917–1918: Class and Nationality in the Russian Revolution* (Princeton, N.J., 1972), provide valuable insights to the revolutionary process as a whole by examining developments outside the two capitals.

Parties in the revolution are carefully examined in Alexander Rabinowitch, *Prelude to Revolution: The Petrograd Bolsheviks and the July 1917 Uprising* (Bloomington, Ind., 1968, repr. 1990), and *The Bolsheviks Come To Power: The Revolution of 1917 in Petrograd* (New York, 1976); Oliver Radkey, *The Agrarian Foes of Bolshevism: Promise and Default of the Russian Social Revolutionaries, February–October 1917* (New York, 1958); William Rosenberg, *Liberals in the Russian Revolution: The Constitutional Democratic Party, 1917–1921* (Princeton, N.J., 1974); Paul Avrich, *The Russian Anarchists* (Princeton, N.J., 1976); and Z. Galili y Garcia, *The Menshevik Leaders in the Russian Revolution* (Princeton, N.J., 1989).

Helpful studies of social groups in the revolution include Allan Wildman, *The End of the Russian Imperial Army*, 2 vols. (Princeton, 1980, 1987); Evan Mawdsley, *The Russian Revolution and the Baltic Fleet* (London, 1978), and Norman Saul, *Sailors in Revolt: The Russian Baltic Fleet in 1917* (Lawrence, Kan., 1978); Graeme Gill, *Peasants and Government in the Russian Revolution* (London, 1979); Diane Koenker, *Moscow Workers and the 1917 Revolution* (Princeton, N.J., 1981); David Mandel, *Petrograd Workers and the Fall of the Old*

Regime (New York, 1983), and *Petrograd Workers and the Soviet Seizure of Power* (New York, 1984); and S. A. Smith, *Red Petrograd: Revolution in the Factories, 1917–1918* (New York, 1983); Rex Wade, *Red Guards and Workers' Militias in the Russian Revolution* (Stanford, 1984).

Important biographies for the period include Isaac Deustscher, *The Prophet Armed: Trotsky, 1879–1921* (Oxford, 1954), and Irving Howe, *Leon Trotsky* (New York, 1978); H. Shukman, *Lenin and the Russian Revolution* (New York, 1981), and Robert Service, *Lenin: A Political Life*, vol. 2, *Worlds in Collision* (London, 1991); Bertram D. Wolfe, *Three Who Made a Revolution* (Boston, 1958); Thomas Riha, *A Russian European: Paul Miliukov in Russian Politics* (Notre Dame, Ind., 1969); and Richard Abraham, *Alexander Kerensky: The First Love of the Revolution* (New York, 1987).

Analyses of the October Revolution include Rabinowitch's *The Bolsheviks Come to Power* cited above; Robert V. Daniels, *Red October* (New York, 1967), which ascribes the Bolshevik victory largely to chance; M. Ferro, *October 1917: A Social History of the Russian Revolution* (London, 1980); and the classic eyewitness account by a sympathetic American journalist, John Reed, *Ten Days That Shook the World* (New York, 1919, repr. 1967).

Studies of foreign policy include Rex Wade, *The Russian Search for Peace: February–October 1917* (Stanford, 1969), George Kennan, *The Fateful Alliance: France, Russia, and the Coming of the First World War* (New York, 1984) and *Soviet-American Relations, 1917–1920*, 2 vols. (New York, 1967).

Excellent monographs on special topics are John H. L. Keep, *The Russian Revolution: A Study in Mass Mobilization* (New York and Toronto, 1976); Richard Pipes, *The Formation of the Soviet Union*, (Cambridge, Mass., 1964), the first part of which deals with the revolution in the non-Russian borderlands; Tim McDaniel, *Autocracy, Capitalism, and Revolution in Russia* (Berkeley, 1988); Louise E. Heena, *Russian Democracy's Fatal Blunder: The Summer Offensive of 1917* (New York, 1987); and Richard Stites, *Revolutionary Dreams: Utopian Vision and Experimental Life in the Russian Revolution* (New York, 1989).

Kerensky presents his own defense of the failure of the Provisional Government in various works but most fully in Alexander Kerensky, *Russian and History's Turning Point* (New York, 1965). A still valuable memoir from a Menshevik perspective is N. N. Sukhanov, *The Russian Revolution: A Personal Record*, 2 vols. (London, 1955). Novels that capture the atmosphere of the times are Mikhail Sholokov, *The Quiet Don*, 2 vols. (New York, 1960), and Boris Pasternak, *Doctor Zhivago* (New York, 1965).

4

A VISION BESIEGED
The Bolsheviks Cling to Power
~

January 18, 1918: For almost a year, people had eagerly anticipated this day, the meeting in Petrograd of the Constituent Assembly, the democratic body charged with settling the revolution's urgent issues—peace, land, government, and freedom. Yet when the assembly finally convened in the Tauride Palace, the expected celebration fizzled, and only a few demonstrators showed up in support. Moreover, the prelude to the meeting had struck an ominous note: armed detachments of the Soviet government had cordoned off the palace early that morning. Twice they had fired on and wounded small groups of anti-Bolshevik protesters who had come to back the assembly.

Inside the palace the people's representatives, freely elected throughout the nation in late November 1917, gathered slowly. Lenin would have preferred to have canceled the Constituent Assembly elections, but the Bolsheviks, like the other parties in 1917, had stressed the importance of the assembly in their popular appeals. Lenin finally agreed to hold the balloting and to decide afterward how to deal with the assembly. But the SRs and their allies, running strongly among the peasant majority of the electorate, won more than 50 percent of the deputy seats. The Bolsheviks polled majorities or pluralities in the cities and in the army but earned only 22 percent backing overall. A concerned Lenin made clear, well before the Constituent Assembly met, that its only acceptable role was to support the Soviet government unconditionally.

As the meeting hall filled on January 18, the SR deputies found themselves confronted by a phalanx of Bolshevik and Left SR deputies ranged behind the speaker's podium. In addition, several hundred boisterous workers and sailors, many of them toting rifles, packed the gallery overlooking the hall. The representative of the Soviet government, Yakov

Sverdlov—bearded, tall, and imposing despite his youth—took his time opening the session. When the senior SR deputy tried to speed proceedings, booing from the gallery and the din of Bolshevik deputies banging the tops of their desks drowned him out. Finally, Sverdlov officially convened the assembly.

Turning to the election of a chairman, the deputies chose Viktor Chernov, the stolid SR leader, over Maria Spiridonova, a fiery Left SR. Chernov, tactfully eschewing direct criticism of the Bolsheviks, delivered a conciliatory speech. Nevertheless, Nikolai Bukharin, a young Bolshevik ideologist, derisively demanded that the SRs choose between the Soviet government's program and "a wretched little bourgeois republic." The gallery crowd rewarded Bukharin with shouts of "Hurrah!" and copious applause. Debate raged for hours before Chernov granted the leftist deputies' request for a recess.

When the meeting resumed, the Bolshevik deputies and their allies, the Left SRs, promptly walked out. The remaining majority stayed well beyond midnight to discuss proposals for land reform, a general democratic peace, and creation of a federal republic for the Russian state. Around 4 A.M., the gallery crowd finally howled, "That's enough!" The captain of the exhausted guard implored Chernov to let everyone go home. Amid a rising chorus of protests from the onlookers, the deputies quickly passed the measures before them and agreed to reconvene the following afternoon. By noon that day, however, the Bolsheviks had announced dissolution of the Constituent Assembly. The body, they charged, "could only serve as a screen for the struggle of the counterrevolutionaries to overthrow Soviet power." That afternoon armed guards blocked the return of the deputies. Thus ended the most resolute attempt to establish a democratic order in Russia before 1989. Lenin had decreed that the Soviet regime was not to be a democracy but a leftist dictatorship.[1]

Leadership in the Making

Terminating the Constituent Assembly proved only a minor irritant among the array of pressing problems that confronted Lenin and the Bolsheviks after they came to power. In trying to build a new order, they knew broadly where they wanted to go. They counted on their revolution to inspire workers' uprisings throughout the economically advanced

---

[1]This account is based on Sergei Mstislavsky, *Five Days Which Transformed Russia*, trans. E. K. Zelensky (Bloomington, Ind.: Indiana Univ. Press, 1988), pp. 131–155, and W. Bruce Lincoln, *Red Victory: A History of the Russian Civil War* (New York: Simon & Schuster, 1989), pp. 120–123.

countries of Europe. These revolutions would then provide the assistance essential for constructing socialism in relatively backward Russia. Under socialism, freedom, economic security, and social equality would replace oppression, deprivation, and privilege. To most exhilarated Bolsheviks, this vision appeared clear and feasible.

To be sure, the details of how to proceed once in power—how to facilitate the European revolutions, how to begin building socialism in Russia, and how to manage internal and external opponents—eluded Lenin and his cohorts. Marx had not provided a blueprint for the transition to socialism that would follow a workers' revolution, and Lenin's musings on this subject in a 1917 pamphlet, *State and Revolution*, reached vague, naive, and sometimes contradictory conclusions. As with shutting down the Constituent Assembly, the Bolsheviks often improvised their policies and actions, tailoring responses to the unique circumstances of each case.

In struggling to defend the revolution and to construct the bases of a socialist society, the Bolsheviks soon offended domestic critics—not only political liberals, property owners, church officials, and army officers but moderate socialists and radical democrats as well. This wide-ranging resistance to Bolshevik policies would soon escalate into a fierce civil war that devastated Russia from 1918 to 1920. The effort of non-Russian minorities to gain autonomy or independence complicated this internecine struggle.

Lenin's decision to make a separate peace with the Central Powers in March 1918 further complicated the early development of Soviet society. The Bolsheviks' only political allies, the Left SRs, rejected this arbitrary settlement and mounted an abortive rebellion against Lenin's government. More telling, the Allied leaders, furious that Russia's withdrawal from World War I permitted Germany to concentrate its forces on the Western Front and alarmed at the Bolsheviks' avowed goal of overthrowing capitalist governments in the West, sent troops to Russia in the summer of 1918. They sought to reopen an eastern front against the Central Powers and to support those Russians and non-Russians who favored sustaining the struggle with Germany and who opposed the Bolsheviks. After World War I ended in November 1918, Western and Japanese intervention in Russia continued, now with an openly anti-Bolshevik purpose. The combined impact of widespread civil war, ethnic strife, and foreign invasion battered the Bolsheviks, yet the upstart revolutionary government narrowly survived and emerged in 1921 as a viable state and society. How much this birth trauma affected and perhaps distorted the nascent Soviet regime remains controversial among historians.

Throughout this time of turmoil, the Bolsheviks focused on one overriding concern—survival. If the revolution were to fail and Soviet rule to collapse, the crucial base for the forthcoming world revolution would disappear. The proletarian cause would flounder. This need to stay in power drove most of Lenin's policies during the first few years after the October Revolution. In his view, the Bolsheviks had to hold on until help from Western European workers could reach them.

> . . . [W]e must remain at our post until our ally, the international proletariat, comes to our aid. . . . We must stick to our tactics of waiting and taking advantage of the conflicts and antagonisms among the imperialists, and of slowly accumulating strength— the tactics of maintaining the island of Soviet power intact amidst the raging sea of imperialism . . . that island to which the eyes of the working people of all countries are even now turned.[2]

Lenin repeated this rhetoric often during the civil war and foreign intervention of 1918 through 1921.

The goal of retaining power dictated pragmatic policies that sometimes contradicted ideological precepts. Often, expediency forced the Bolsheviks to appease or compromise with class enemies, such as the militaristic Germans, the imperialistic Allies, and the petty-bourgeois peasants. Nevertheless, in defending their government, the Bolshevik leaders possessed several advantages. They spoke and acted in the name of "Soviet power," which the majority of the population supported in late 1917 and early 1918. Thus, understandably, no great outcry followed the demise of the Constituent Assembly, which during its brief existence had rejected unconditional submission to Soviet power. Indeed, the elections to the assembly revealed that *four out of five* voters chose socialist candidates, who came from and stood for the system of soviets. Although Lenin finessed the issue of an all-socialist government by adding Left SRs to his cabinet, he made certain to call the new regime "soviet" and to espouse a soviet-style platform: all power to the soviets, peace, land, and economic betterment. Because almost everyone strongly supported these goals, the Bolsheviks, reflecting mass aspirations, set aside their ideological credos on two of these points. They accepted dividing the land among individual peasants instead of socializing it, and they decided to make a separate peace with Germany rather than launch a revolutionary war against the European imperialist powers.

The pattern of voting for the Constituent Assembly reflected another advantage that the Bolsheviks enjoyed during their first months in power. The party scored a plurality of votes (36 percent) in the largest cities and towns, almost equal success in the armed forces as a whole (40 percent Bolshevik, 41 percent SR), and a clear majority in the centrally located front armies and in the rear garrisons. By giving the peasants land and hence neutralizing the rural majority who voted SR, the Bolsheviks

---

[2]V. I. Lenin, *Sochineniia* (*Collected Works*), 2nd ed., vol. 23 (Moscow, 1928–1929), p. 16.

could build their political base on city dwellers and soldiers in the central core of European Russia. Although this support shrank during the strife of the next three years, it guaranteed the survival of the new Soviet state.

Finally, in the first few years of Soviet control, the Bolsheviks benefited from the ruthless determination and political sagacity of Lenin, the drive and organizational skills of Trotsky, and the talent and energy of other seasoned revolutionary leaders. Owing to the rapid expansion of party membership in 1917, the rank and file had less experience and discipline by comparison. Yet at the top, and to a growing extent at lower levels, the Bolsheviks cultivated a zeal and dedication that helped to ensure their success.

Just as in their rise to power, the Bolsheviks also profited from their opponents' vulnerability in the months after the October Revolution. The political right, weakly developed under the tsarist autocracy, had been severely compromised by the Kornilov affair and at first offered no serious challenge to the Bolsheviks. The center, represented by the liberal Kadet party, proved largely impotent. Teetering on a limited political base, the Kadets' 7 percent showing in the Constituent Assembly elections probably stood not far below their actual strength, although Kadet candidates and electioneering suffered some harassment during the campaign. The middle classes, to whom the Kadets appealed, probably comprised only about 5 or 6 million individuals in a total 1918 population of some 140 to 150 million, and many of them were socialists. In addition, after the February Revolution the party had diverged politically from the popular mainstream. Ineligible to participate in the soviets, the Kadets increasingly became identified with the failing Provisional Government and with "privileged Russia." Finally, the Kornilov affair fatally isolated them. Conservatives charged that the party had withheld necessary support from the rightist putsch, and the left lumped them in with reactionaries and counterrevolutionaries.

The most effective opponents of the Bolsheviks should have been the Mensheviks and SRs, who commanded considerable support among workers, soldiers, and peasants up to September 1917 and who together won the majority of votes in the Constituent Assembly elections. Yet the moderate socialists' electoral tally did not reflect their actual political strength. The candidate lists for the elections had been drawn up in September, when Menshevik and SR support had run much stronger. By the November voting, both parties had lost ground. Divisions among the leadership further weakened the Mensheviks. Even on the issue of the Bolsheviks' usurpation of power, many Mensheviks hesitated to follow their leaders in opposing a workers' government, no matter how flagrantly Lenin's action violated ideology. In 1918 and after, a number of Mensheviks harbored doubts about other party members' willingness to associate with "bourgeois" forces in battling the Bolsheviks.

The SRs, too, suffered from timid policies and deep fractures within the party. In the fall of 1917, their radical wing, the Left SRs, split off altogether. Moreover, the SRs had remained essentially a peasant party, and positive political force in 1917 and 1918 rested in the cities, not the countryside. In sum, the SR leaders failed in manifold ways: they could not hold the party together; they did not foresee the disastrous political results of delaying a solution to the land question and of joining the Provisional Government; and they held back from setting up a political and armed organization to oppose the Bolsheviks until it was too late.

Putting Slogans into Effect: Peace, Power, and Plenty

Attuned to the popular mood, the Bolsheviks had overturned the Provisional Government partly on the strength of their slogans of peace, land, bread, and power to the soviets. Once in office, Lenin and his colleagues struggled to implement this platform. On each plank they had to compromise between Marxian principle and the stark reality of conditions in 1918 Russia.

World War I posed the most immediate threat to the newly successful Bolsheviks. If they could not achieve peace, Bolshevik supremacy would sink. The Central Powers, already occupying a large part of western Russia, clearly intended to dominate, if not conquer, the fledgling state. As we saw in Chapter 3, Lenin's first act was to issue an appeal for peace addressed to all combatants. When this offer elicited no response, Lenin opened negotiations with the Germans and Austrians in December 1917. But the Central Powers demanded a high price for peace, a problem that ballooned into a major crisis within the Bolshevik Party. Radical, ideologically orthodox Bolsheviks proposed a plan. Rather than dealing with the Prussian militarists and imperialists, they argued, Soviet Russia should instigate a "revolutionary war" among its enemies by fraternizing with their troops, sending calls for revolution to their workers, and encouraging agitation inside their countries. Lenin judged this tactic unrealistic and strongly opposed it. To stay in power and save the revolution, he believed, the Soviet government had no choice but to strike a bargain with these capitalist foes. Besides, he reasoned, the coming proletarian revolution in Europe would soon nullify any agreement with the Central Powers. For a time Trotsky pressed for a middle position, advocating that the Soviet government stop fighting and unilaterally declare a cessation of hostilities, a formulation often labeled "no peace, no war."

In heated debates throughout January 1918, the Central Committee of the Bolshevik Party first supported the "revolutionary war" policy but finally adopted Trotsky's plan, which Soviet negotiators presented to the Central Powers on February 10. Initially taken aback, German General

Max von Hoffman soon responded by ordering German forces to advance farther into Russia. Even faced with imminent conquest by Central Powers armies, many leading Bolsheviks hesitated to act. Lenin's insistence on making peace regardless of the price finally passed in the Central Committee by only one vote. In early March the Soviet government agreed to harsher terms than the Central Powers had offered in January. Under the Treaty of Brest-Litovsk, Germany and Austria forced the revolutionary regime in Moscow to give up regions on its western border that constituted one-quarter of its territory and population. These areas contained one-third of Russian industry and valuable mineral and agricultural resources

Despite these huge losses and the humiliation of having to make a separate peace with the German and Austrian imperialists, Lenin maintained that the agreement provided an essential "breathing space" in which Soviet Russia could consolidate its position while awaiting the socialist revolution in Europe. That upheaval, he promised, would overturn all the concessions that the Bolsheviks had been forced to make. Although Allied victory, not proletarian revolution, would cancel the Brest treaty, Lenin undoubtedly calculated correctly that peace permitted the Bolsheviks to hold on to power for the moment.

At the same time, his policy spawned long-term complications. The separate peace alienated many patriotic Russian citizens, even some who had felt sympathetic or neutral toward the Bolsheviks. These people saw the signing of the treaty as a cruel betrayal of the nation, as surrendering Russian lands to the enemy and negating all the sacrifices of the war. Indeed, this resentment of a Bolshevik sell-out fueled the spread of civil war in the summer of 1918. Moreover, the Left SRs, who sided with radical Bolsheviks in their desire to launch a revolutionary war against Germany, found the Brest agreements repellent. They withdrew from the government and soon actively opposed the Bolsheviks.

Last, Brest-Litovsk outraged the Allies. The deal permitted Germany to transfer forces to the Western Front, where they proceeded to launch a major offensive that, as in 1914, threatened Paris. Irked by the subversive rhetoric of the Soviet government after the Bolshevik Revolution, the Allies nevertheless had kept unofficial lines of communication open with the new leaders, in hopes that they might be persuaded to sustain the fight against Germany. These contacts fizzled as the Bolsheviks moved toward peace with the Central Powers and as local Allied agents realized that the Soviet government had neither the resources nor the will to stay in the war. The Brest peace strengthened the French and British leaders' impulse to intervene against the Soviet government and to assist anti-Bolshevik Russians. The first Allied landings in Russia soon followed. Thus, Lenin's Brest policy helped to ignite three years of civil conflict and to invite foreign intervention in Russian affairs. Yet without the treaty, the Germans would likely have crushed Russia and its new government.

In addition to seeking peace, the Bolsheviks had to anchor their political authority quickly. One factor worked in their favor: many of their opponents—socialist, liberal, and conservative alike—believed that Bolshevik rule was transitory. The Bolsheviks could stay in power only a few weeks or months, they thought, before people tired of their extremist, impractical ideas and turned them out. This misreading of popular attitudes and underestimating the Bolsheviks' determination and ruthlessness rendered their opposition ineffectual during the regime's first eight months in power.

The Bolsheviks succeeded in abolishing some political institutions, such as city *dumas*, provincial and district *zemstvos*, the regular army, and the police. They took over others, including ministries of the central government, renamed *commissariats*. Still other organizations—for example, trade unions, factory committees, and soviets—kept their autonomy for a time but gradually came under Bolshevik control. The soviets provided a particularly interesting case. These bodies had arisen as genuinely representative organs of the people and provided the mechanism for the transfer of power in the October Revolution. Well into the summer of 1918, many soviets continued to operate fairly independently, serving primarily as instruments of local government and administration. Although Bolshevik leaders on occasion discussed the Party's role in the soviets, they did not set out to make these councils pliant executors of the Party's will. Yet beginning with Lenin's conception of the Party's function—to guide the workers to class consciousness and revolution—it followed naturally that the Party should also lead the institutions of the workers' state.

Too, the exigencies of the civil war that broke out in mid-1918 eroded the soviets' independence. When plenary deputies' meetings proved cumbersome, legislative and executive power in many soviets fell to their executive committees and then sometimes to their secretariats. These smaller bodies increasingly consisted of full-time officials, usually party politicians. After the October Revolution, more and more Bolsheviks stepped in. Although the whole soviet was supposed to review and ratify decisions of the executive committees and secretariats, under time pressure members gradually relinquished this responsibility. Moreover, as the demands of waging war against domestic and foreign enemies pressed on the Bolsheviks, the Party faced a desperate shortage of qualified personnel. Some of the most loyal and able comrades departed to join the new Red Army. These losses cut into the pool available to serve at the lower levels and encouraged higher officials and Party leaders to make decisions and to impose them on local soviets. Last, chaotic economic conditions undermined the fiscal independence of local soviets. Unable to raise funds locally, they had to turn to the central government for assistance. In sum, owing to the Party's traditional Leninist role and to the force of circumstances, political authority ultimately coalesced in the Bolsheviks while most soviets lost their democratic, representative, and independent character.

The Red Army and the secret police, supplanting existing organizations with the same functions, formed in the first few months after the revolution. Both proved important instruments for maintaining Soviet power. In the initial euphoria after October, the Bolsheviks tried to replace the regular army with a people's militia, which had no ranks and which elected officers. The force lacked discipline and effectiveness, however. In April 1918, as the threat of outside intervention and stepped-up internecine war loomed, Trotsky undertook to create a new armed force, composed first of volunteers and, by June, of conscripts. He restored discipline, as well as ranks, and required all units to undergo rigorous training. Yet few revolutionaries qualified as military leaders, and Trotsky instituted a controversial policy of recruiting former tsarist officers. He also dismantled soldiers' committees and introduced political commissars, almost always Bolsheviks, to act as watchdogs over the officers and to raise the fighting morale and ideological consciousness of the troops. Beginning with about 350,000 men in midsummer 1918, the Red Army rose to 5.5 million strong by the end of 1920.

In assembling the Soviet secret police only two months after seizing power, the Bolsheviks did not initially intend to use the force as an instrument of repression. Known as the *Cheka*, the Russian acronym for the Extraordinary Commission to Combat Counterrevolution, Sabotage, and Speculation, the secret police at first strove to eradicate lawlessness, cor-

Terror Boss Feliks Dzerzhinsky, head of the *Cheka*, who supervised the hunt for alleged enemies of the revolution in the early years of Soviet rule.

ruption, black marketeering, and active opposition to the new government. But by late January 1918, its purview broadened. Lenin and the head of the Cheka, Feliks Dzerzhinsky, extended the definition of opposition to include "class enemies"—that is, individuals not necessarily openly fighting the Soviet regime but who allegedly belonged to former "oppressing" social strata. By midsummer 1918, the Cheka was running its own program of summary justice, including charging, trying, and executing individuals outside the revolutionary judicial system of people's courts. The Cheka also established the first concentration camps for "enemies of the people." Following an attempt on Lenin's life in August 1918, the Bolsheviks officially instituted the Red Terror, a policy of indiscriminate arrest and often execution of suspected foes, a campaign that further enhanced the power of the secret police. Founded as a separate institution not directly responsible to the Soviet government nor to Bolshevik party organs, the Cheka, under different names, would serve as an extralegal arm of repression for over seventy years.

As another urgent task, the Bolsheviks strove to make good on their promise of a better life for the masses by addressing the economic chaos that tormented the country by the end of 1917. Their failure fanned the flames of anti-Bolshevism and would lead in 1921 to a marked, although temporary, reversal of course: the New Economic Policy (NEP). Initially party leaders managed to appease the peasants by acquiescing in their 1917 land seizures. Yet this land "reform" did not improve the food supply. Like earlier governments, the Bolsheviks proved unable to reverse the breakdown of transport, the decline of agricultural production, and the refusal of the peasants to exchange crops for high-priced town goods, all factors that diminished produce. By mid-1918, shortages in the cities reached such a critical point that popular suffering threatened the political stability of the regime. Pushed to the wall, the new government reacted with draconian measures: in June 1918 authorities moved to seize grain from the peasants. First, the Bolsheviks sent detachments of workers and unemployed into the countryside to take peasant stocks by force. Then they organized committees of poor peasants to compel allegedly richer peasants to hand over produce to the state. These efforts only marginally enhanced the food supply and naturally alienated many peasants. By late 1918, the Bolsheviks abandoned "class war" in the villages and resigned themselves to a vast illegal trade in agricultural goods carried out by "bagmen," who traveled between town and country linking peasant producers and urban consumers. Despite the government's official monopoly on commerce, many peasants as well as city dwellers became perforce part-time private traders in order to survive.

In the industrial sector, Bolshevik economic policy passed through two distinct stages. From the October Revolution until June 1918, Lenin pursued a strategy of state capitalism. The Bolsheviks seized control of major industries and banks but did not restructure them. Most enterprises operated as before but under government supervision. Lenin adopted this policy for practical as well as theoretical reasons. He wanted to ensure the continued functioning of the economy in the desperate circumstances of revolutionary upheaval and ongoing war with the Central Powers. Yet he also admired the productive achievements of the imperialist powers during World War I; they had succeeded in centralizing their economies and in creating a form of state capitalism to support their war efforts. The Bolshevik leader became convinced that state control of industry could serve as an effective transition to a socialized economy.

Yet by late spring 1918, this interim policy had clearly failed. On one hand, factors over which the Bolsheviks had little control undermined output and aggravated burgeoning unemployment. These hindrances included hyperinflation; a flight of capital, managers, and technicians; the economic losses under the Brest treaty; and the difficulties of converting wartime industry to peacetime production. Political pressures also made state capitalism unworkable. Workers demanded a say in operating the enterprises, and in some cases their "factory committees" seized plants. Urban dwellers, too, clamored for more goods and lower prices than the economy could muster.

After June 1918, Bolshevik economic strategy evolved unevenly but generally in the direction of highly centralized and invasive control over all aspects of economic activity, national planning of the industrial sector, socialization of ownership and elimination of private property, and a shift from money exchanges to rationing, goods allocation, and barter. Lenin and his comrades improvised these policies, later dubbed "war communism," in part to parry economic crises and the exigencies of a war of survival. But they also believed that such prerogative policies would implement socialist and egalitarian principles.

During their first weeks in power, the Bolsheviks annulled all debts of the tsarist and provisional governments (stoking the fires of intervention among such creditors as France and England) and nationalized banks and financial institutions. Yet not until June 1918 did they decree state ownership of most industrial enterprises. At that time they also authorized the Supreme Council of the National Economy, established in December 1917, to expand its coordinating role to overall planning and central administration of the economy. Numerous obstacles challenged the council, however. Staffed and led by inexperienced visionaries, the body never received control of such key sectors as finance and food supply. It could not run economic life in the breakaway border regions of the former tsarist empire nor overcome even local economic autonomy. Hyperinflation and economic collapse impeded its efforts, and after 1918 the council no longer supervised the war industry, which came under direct control of the powerful Council of Workers' and Peasants' Defense. Thus, despite the council's "supreme" authority, it never fulfilled its intended role.

Popular pressure to implement the catchy 1917 slogan, "workers' control," raised further ongoing problems for the new leaders. Efforts to decentralize and democratize the economy provoked disputes within the Bolshevik Party and strained relations between the Party and workers' groups. During the first few months of Soviet power, some Bolsheviks encouraged workers to operate the factories themselves. Their urgings gave substance to a favorite postrevolutionary demand—"Loot the looters"—and carried out Lenin's utopian vision in *State and Revolution*. Inexperienced and disorganized worker-managers could not sustain production, however, and "workers' control" plants often degenerated into chaos. By January 1918, Lenin began to abandon the concept. In the spring of 1918, he urged "one-man management" of the factories and the use of "bourgeois" specialists—former engineers, technicians, and managers—to run industrial enterprises.

As an important example of the balance between necessity and ideology in "war communism," runaway inflation and the breakdown of rural-urban and intrastate commercial exchanges reduced the utility of money and encouraged rationing and barter. Yet Bolshevik theory was also clearly prejudiced against the market, particularly money transactions and private trade. Direct exchanges of products were encouraged, in the hope that barter and more equitable distribution would develop. In mid-1918 the Bolsheviks nationalized housing and instructed local soviets to allocate the best units to supporters of the proletarian revolution. They nationalized commerce as well, introducing state shops and markets. Finally, as shortages of food and goods persisted, the government introduced extensive rationing and distribution of commodities to individuals at their workplaces.

Despite these efforts, sporadic grain requisitioning, and tight state controls, the economic collapse that had begun during World War I continued and even accelerated under "war communism." The Bolshevik leaders failed to overcome the peasants' traditional subsistence mentality or to channel the workers' anarchic tendencies into disciplined production. They also struggled to replace dispossessed managers and trained specialists. To be sure, some factors were beyond their control: the loss of non-Russian areas and the devastation caused by the civil war. As the Soviet leaders coped *ad hoc* with recurring emergencies, production and productivity steadily declined. Nevertheless, the Bolsheviks accomplished some goals during their first year in power. They made peace with Germany; accepted the peasant-initiated solution to land reform; established the Party's authority over central institutions, the soviets, and many regions of the country; and abolished private property. Their economic policies, however, and growing opposition to their rule would eventually require a change of course.

Civil Strife and Foreign Meddling

Some historians assert that the civil war between Bolsheviks and anti-Bolsheviks that swept across Russia from 1918 to 1920 began in the early hours of the October Revolution, when Red Guards and armed sailors battled officer trainees for control of the Winter Palace. Others believe that the struggle between the Reds and their Russian opponents, known as Whites, began in early summer 1918, when anti-Bolshevik governments seized control of Siberia and north Russia and sparked the first major military engagements. Both arguments have merit. Sporadic armed opposition to the Bolsheviks commenced as they gained power, and skirmishes continued in Ukraine, south Russia, and other scattered locales through the rest of 1917 and early 1918. Yet none of this fighting posed a serious danger to the new regime. Substantial threats to the Bolsheviks' hold on power and major armed conflict date from May–June 1918. At that point, incipient civil war flared into a conflagration that eventually reached into almost every corner of the country and that nearly consumed the revolutionary government.

An interesting question remains: Why did internal strife intensify as late as seven or eight months after the Bolsheviks came to power? We may find some clues in conservatives' expectation that the Soviet government would not last, and in the disarray among the Bolsheviks' opponents—rightists, army officers, Kadets, industrialists, moderate socialists, and nationalists. In addition, evidence of the damage to some social strata from the Bolsheviks' policies emerged only gradually. As the new government seized property, attacked religion, discriminated against privileged classes, and curtailed civil and political freedom, individuals and groups belatedly began to defend their interests.

Yet two highly unpopular Bolshevik actions of early spring 1918 did the most to foment widespread hostility. As we saw earlier, the peace agreement with the Germans angered a broad array of patriotic citizens as well as the Bolsheviks' radical allies, the Left SRs. Many turned against Bolshevism as a way of saving the nation from German militarism. Second, requisitioning grain from the countryside alienated the bulk of the peasantry, whose benevolent neutrality toward the Bolsheviks suddenly soured to suspicion and defensiveness.

Then and later, peasant attitudes helped to shape the course of the civil war. By angering the peasant majority in 1918, the Bolsheviks handed their opponents a chance to win the rural population to the anti-Bolshevik cause. But the Whites also enraged peasants by trying to restore the land that the villagers had acquired in 1917 to former private, state, and church owners. Yet many peasants, immersed in parochial concerns, ignored both Reds and Whites. Some rural inhabitants favored soviet power, albeit not in the hands of the Bolsheviks, and many peasant soldiers, under the spell of the Left SRs, had grown thoroughly radicalized. Other peasants simply wanted all outsiders to leave them alone. Conscripted as a Red or White, a village soldier would fight briefly and sullenly and then desert at the first opportunity. The peasants' primary concern lay in taking advantage of the recent land divisions. One villager's retort to a Soviet official sums up how sharply peasant attitudes differed from the outlook of urban revolutionaries: "Power may belong to you workers, but the potatoes are ours." Thus neither Bolsheviks nor anti-Bolsheviks could count on the support of the peasantry; rather, each side had to maneuver around the obstacle of rural isolationism. In 1921 the Bolsheviks finally were forced to appease massive resistance to requisitioning with conciliatory policies. This grudging decision only postponed a showdown with the peasantry.

Given the peasantry's sentiment of "a plague on both your houses," the civil war unfolded largely among urban dwellers and along Russia's extensive railway lines. Non-Russian minorities jumped into the fray, and involvement by foreign powers muddied the picture and prolonged the war. Yet neither the nationalities' opposition to Soviet authority nor outside meddling decided the outcome of the struggle. Instead, the decisive battles hinged on small forces consisting mainly of Great Russians. Reds and Whites alike fought savagely and on occasion committed sickening atrocities. The civilian population suffered not as much from the clash of arms or political persecution as from rampant destruction of property, starvation, and disease. The civil war became a searing crucible from which the new Soviet state and society arose.

Senior army officers, including General Kornilov and several colleagues who had walked away from prison, formed the first anti-Bolshevik army in December 1917, based in south Russia. The new force, christened the Volunteer Army (although it later resorted to conscription in areas that it controlled), earned some encouragement and limited financial support from the Allies. Nevertheless, hastily assembled Bolshevik units put the Whites to flight by February 1918.

A few months later, another threat to the fledgling Soviet state emerged in western Siberia. During World War I, the Russian government had formed a Czechoslovak Corps, consisting of Czech workers in Russia and Czech and Slovak prisoners captured from the Austro-Hungarian armies. These brother Slavs were eager to fight the Central Powers in hopes of returning to an independent Czechoslovak state after the war. Disappointed by the Bolsheviks' separate peace with the Central Powers, the leaders of the Czechoslovak Corps crafted a plan. With the Soviet government's compliance, they arranged with the Allies to have the corps evacuated from the Eastern Front across the five-thousand-mile Trans-Siberian Railroad and then shipped from the Russian Far East to fight with the Allies in France.

In mid-May 1918, with units of the corps strung out along the railway, a riot broke out in the town of Chelyabinsk between eastbound Czechoslovak troops and westbound Hungarian prisoners of war being repatriated according to the terms of the Brest-Litovsk Treaty. When the Czechoslovaks seized the town, Bolshevik leaders rashly ordered local soviets to disarm all corps units. The Czechoslovaks resisted and, possessing stronger forces than local authorities, they soon controlled most of Siberia. In effect they removed up to two-thirds of Russian territory from Soviet control.

Nevertheless, the corps might have resumed its evacuation but for several coincidental developments. The Czechoslovaks' deposing of local soviet officials allowed a group of SRs, most of them deputies to the defunct Constituent Assembly, to organize an embryonic anti-Bolshevik government along the Volga River. Concurrently, the British and French, who originally had advised the Czechoslovaks to fight their way eastward, changed their minds. They now saw the corps as a heaven-sent instrument for restoring a fighting front in the east against Germany and for eliminating the reviled Soviet government. As we shall see shortly, the Allies also used the Czechoslovaks as a device to draw the United States into their interventionist designs.

As the Bolshevik leaders grappled with the Czechoslovak problem and the pending Western intervention, an additional challenge materialized from within. The Left SRs had resigned from the Council of People's Commissars in the spring over internal policy disagreements with the Bolsheviks and to protest the separate peace with Germany. The party grew increasingly disgruntled at Bolshevik requisitioning of peasant grain and at the government's failure to block Germany's expansion of its occupation zone in south Russia. On July 6, 1918, two radical SR members assassinated the German ambassador to Soviet Russia, and Left SR uprisings flared in Moscow, the provincial town of Yaroslavl', and several other locales. Within a week, the Red Army bloodily suppressed these rebellions, and the Cheka executed fifty-seven SRs.

In August a Left SR assassin severely wounded Lenin and provoked the retaliatory Red Terror. Lenin had earlier called for "war to the death against the rich and their hangers-on" and demanded that "enemy agents, profiteers, marauders hooligans, counterrevolutionary agitators, and German spies" be shot on sight. During the next two years, the Cheka seized hostages, often randomly, shot them, and dumped the bodies into mass graves. Red Army units also executed alleged Whites and enemy prisoners, as this passage from Soviet author Mikhail Sholokhov's epic civil war novel, *The Quiet Don*, reflects:

Civil War Atrocity Villagers stare as Whites hang two Bolsheviks. The bodies of two earlier victims appear in the foreground.

... [The Red Army detachment commander] tore his sword from its scabbard, flung himself violently forward, and struck Chornetsov [a White officer] with terrible force across the head.

Gregor saw the officer shudder and raise his left hand to ward off the blow; he saw the sword cut through the wrist as though it were paper and come down on Chornetsov's defenceless head. First the fur cap fell; then, like grain broken at the stalk, Chornetsov slowly dropped, his mouth twisted wryly, his eyes agonizingly screwed up and frowning as if before lightning.

As the officer lay, Podtielkov sabred him again, then turned and walked away with an aged, heavy gait, wiping his bloodstained sword. Stumbling against the cart, he turned to the escort and shouted in a choking, howling voice: "Cut them down. . . . Damn them! All of them! We take no prisoners!"[3]

The anti-Bolsheviks also sometimes resorted to White Terror, arbitrarily slaughtering alleged radicals and Red Army prisoners. Although it is im-

---

[3]Mikhail Sholokhov, *The Silent Don:* Vol. I, *And Quiet Flows the Don* (New York: Alfred A. Knopf, 1946), p. 456.

possible to know the number of victims of repression in the civil war, cautious estimates gauge the bloodbath at several hundred thousand individuals.

Besides combating real and imagined domestic foes, the Bolsheviks had to fend off Allied intervention in Russian affairs after July 1918. From then until the defeat of Germany in November 1918, the Western powers sought primarily to restore a fighting front against Germany in the east, either by persuading the Soviet government to scrap the Brest peace or, more often, by aiding anti-German Russians (who were also anti-Bolshevik). In retrospect the idea seems far-fetched, given the exhaustion of Russian forces and resources and the vast distances required to reposition troops against the German armies. Yet the strain of years of war and the fears of a German victory on the Western Front in late spring 1918 warped the Allied leaders' judgment and drove them to desperate measures. Western statesmen's secondary motives—fear of the Bolsheviks' socialist radicalism and imperialistic hopes for carving out spheres of influence in a weakened Russia—gained prominence only after Germany's defeat. Nevertheless, as early as December 1917, the French and British governments had agreed that France should dominate in postwar Ukraine and Great Britain in the Caucasus and Transcaspia. Meanwhile, Japan had designs on the Russian Far East and Siberia.

In March 1918, French and British leaders, fuming over Brest-Litovsk, had resolved to salvage a front in Russia against the Germans. Only the United States balked. Intervention depended on American ships, men, and money; however, and the French, British, and Japanese governments exerted strong pressure on Woodrow Wilson to cooperate. The U.S. president, in his own words, "sweat blood" over the Russian question. Two of his fundamental beliefs—democracy and self-determination—directly conflicted here: he opposed the Bolsheviks because of their antidemocratic practices and socialist ideology, yet he firmly believed that the Russians should decide their own fate. The Czechoslovak Corps suddenly provided a handy solution to this dilemma. Convincing himself that the Czechoslovak units needed assistance, Wilson justified intervening in Russian affairs. He salved his Calvinist conscience while admitting to his advisers that he had yielded to the importuning of the French, British, and Japanese primarily to preserve Allied unity for the final assault on Germany.

In accord with a joint Allied declaration, the United States and Japan disembarked troops at Vladivostok in July 1918. Wilson's instructions limited the Americans to safeguarding the Trans-Siberian Railroad and to preserving order against local warlords and bandits. The Japanese sent units partway into Siberia but did not directly join the civil war. Under the pressure of postwar isolationist sentiments at home, the Americans would withdraw in January 1920; the Japanese would remain until 1922.

The British, with the compliance of the Soviet government, had

Americans Intervene in Russia U.S. soldiers and sailors on parade after they landed in Vladivostok in July 1918. An ad for Nestle products appears on the building wall to the right.

landed small units in the north Russian ports of Archangel and Murmansk as early as March 1918 to prevent wartime supplies shipped to Russia from falling into the hands of pro-German Finns. American troops and British reinforcements arrived in June and August 1918, and British representatives assisted in building an anti-Bolshevik government in north Russia. In February 1919, Wilson, opposed to further intervention in Russia and responding to congressional criticism of the north Russian expedition, called back U.S. forces. That summer the British government also removed its troops. Although American intervention in Russia had little effect on the civil war, during the four decades of Cold War tensions, the Soviet government would ensure that every Soviet citizen learned in school and through the media that American troops had occupied Russian soil in 1918–1919 (see the map, Civil War and Foreign Intervention, 1918–1921). Even today, however, few U.S. citizens are aware of this fact.

Because the Allies' victory over Germany eliminated the chief argument for their presence in Russia, logically the Western powers should have withdrawn their forces and ended the blockade that they had imposed on Soviet Russia. Indeed, Woodrow Wilson and British prime minister David Lloyd George wanted to pull out so as to end the civil war in Russia and hoped to establish trade relations with the area. Both heads of

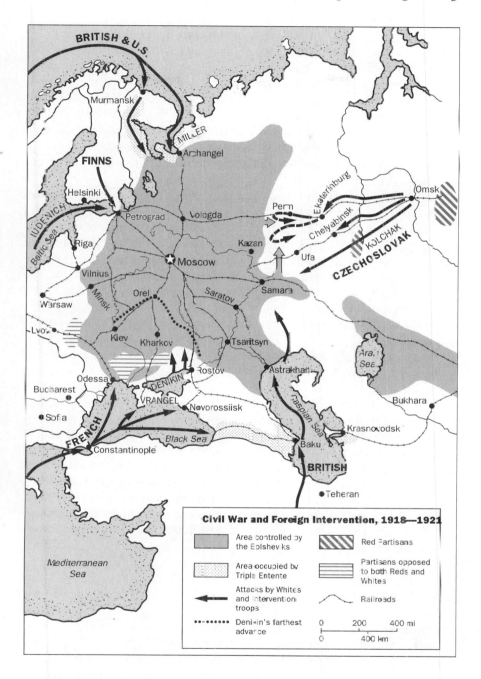

Civil War and Foreign Intervention, 1918—1921

Area controlled by the Bolsheviks

Red Partisans

Area occupied by Triple Entente

Partisans opposed to both Reds and Whites

Attacks by Whites and intervention troops

Railroads

Denikin's farthest advance

0   200   400 mi

0   400 km

state sponsored several peacemaking efforts. The first came in January 1919, a proposal for the combatants to meet on the Prinkipo Islands in Turkey to negotiate terms. The Bolsheviks accepted the plan, but the Whites, encouraged by the French, rejected it. American and British leaders then launched a "secret" mission headed by William Bullitt, later America's first ambassador to the Soviet Union in 1933, to sound out Lenin on conditions for accommodation between Soviet Russia and the West. Preoccupied by pressure to complete peace terms for Germany, Wilson and Lloyd George never fully considered Lenin's proposals. Instead, they settled on a relief plan for Russia, which they subsequently dropped when it seemed that the anti-Bolsheviks might win the civil war. The French government and Winston Churchill, Lloyd George's war minister, opposed all three ideas and urged the Allies to mount an all-out anti-Bolshevik crusade.

In the end, all peacemaking efforts collapsed, and the Allies continued to support the anti-Bolsheviks in Russia with advisers, matériel, and funds. They still hoped to eradicate Bolshevism and to dominate the region politically and economically. The British leaders also felt a sense of obligation to the anti-Bolsheviks, whom they had encouraged originally as instruments for reestablishing an eastern front against Germany. The French actively sought to assert control over south Russia. In March 1919, they sent an expeditionary force of French, Romanian, and Greek troops to Odessa in Ukraine but had to abandon the enterprise when some units mutinied.

Divided counsels among Western statesmen led to damaging policies toward Russia in 1919. Woodrow Wilson ignored the new Soviet state, while European leaders' efforts to mount a Churchillian crusade against Bolshevism ran afoul of universal war-weariness and leftist opposition. Western politicians lacked the force and the backing to crush what they perceived as a dire threat to capitalist society. Ironically, their indirect aid to the anti-Bolsheviks, insufficient to secure a White victory, permitted the Bolsheviks to cast themselves as staunch defenders of Russia's patrimony and to paint their foes as lackeys of foreign imperialists. Further, Allied support for the anti-Bolshevik cause prolonged the civil war and thereby worsened the country's devastation and loss of life. The intervention thus left a legacy of suspicion and hostility that would poison Soviet-Western relations for years to come.

The Bolsheviks Besieged

Domestic enemies, not foreign schemes, posed the most serious initial danger for the Soviet regime. During the summer of 1918, combined anti-Bolshevik civilian governments along the Volga and in Siberia chalked up military successes. In early fall 1918, however, Trotsky's recently formed Red Army recaptured Kazan on the Volga River and advanced toward the Ural Mountains. In November the anti-Bolshevik coalition of SR and Kadet politicians succumbed to a right-wing coup supported by White officers and tacitly approved by local British representatives. This putsch ended civilian anti-Bolshevik governance in Russia and revealed the disunity of the Soviet regime's political foes. Military leaders would fight the rest of the civil war.

The coup plotters installed war hero Admiral Alexander Kolchak as leader of the new Siberian government and a virtual dictator. Politically inexperienced and often moody and indecisive, Kolchak proved unable to restore the economy, to develop an appealing political program, or to administer the region effectively. He and his supporters turned to military prowess to maintain their grip on power. In the spring of 1919, their armies moved west to the Volga River, garnering victories along the way. On the strength of these conquests, Kolchak won tentative recognition from other White forces and from the Allies as Supreme Ruler of Russia. Alarmed, the Soviet leaders poured men and supplies into the battle against Kolchak. By June the Red Army had checked the Whites' impetus, and in the fall of 1919 and early 1920, Trotsky crushed Kolchak's forces and recaptured most of Siberia. The Bolsheviks executed Kolchak in January–February 1920.

The next challenge to the Bolsheviks originated in the Don and Kuban regions southeast of Moscow. In the summer of 1918, the Cossacks, led by popular *ataman* General Peter Krasnov, had overturned Soviet rule and besieged the important Volga River city of Tsaritsyn. The Reds prevailed in defending the city, but in the process Trotsky and Stalin quarreled over the use of former tsarist officers and over centralized versus local control of operations. Lenin supported Trotsky, undoubtedly contributing to Stalin's later resentment of the Red Army leader.

To the south of the Don Cossacks, the Volunteer Army, now strengthened by the enlistment of thousands of trained Kuban Cossack veterans, enjoyed a string of victories over Red forces through the summer of 1918. At the end of the year, the talented General Anaton Denikin emerged as the dictator of an anti-Bolshevik army and government just as threatening as Kolchak's. By October 1919, Denikin's White armies had conquered most of southern Russia, including eastern and central Ukraine. Twice they advanced perilously close to Moscow, once penetrating to within 240 miles of the city. Luckily for the Bolsheviks, distance and poor planning prevented Denikin from coordinating his attacks with those of Kolchak to the east. The Red Army thus overcame each crisis *seriatim*, with Trotsky skillfully shuttling troops and supplies between fronts.

Denikin, too, proved his own worst enemy in many respects. Extremely nationalistic and politically narrow, his conservative program alienated workers and peasants. His insistence on "Russia, One and Undivided," blocked cooperation with non-Russian groups, even Ukrainians, Baltic peoples, Finns, and Poles, whose military cooperation might have helped him to overcome the Reds. After Denikin's defeat in late

1919, his able successor as leader of White forces in the south, General Piotr Vrangel, organized a new government with an appealing program, and in the summer of 1920 launched one last attack on the Bolsheviks from a base in the Crimea. By then, however, the Soviet state had grown strong enough to withstand this final White assault.

Finally, anti-Bolshevik threats arose in northwestern Russia, where with the acquiescence of the German occupiers, a small rebel force under General Nikolai Iudenich assembled in the latter part of 1918. After Germany's defeat, the British encouraged and helped finance Iudenich's army, which advanced to the outskirts of Petrograd[4] in the fall of 1919. But Trotsky mounted an effective defense of the city, and Iudenich's effort collapsed when he lost Estonian and Finnish support over his refusal to promise them unconditional independence.

The Borderlands: The Fight for Self-Determination

From 1918 to 1920, the Soviet government also had to battle partisan bands in the Caucasus and Central Asia, bandits and warlords in eastern Siberia, and several anarchist peasant movements, notably the Greens led by Nestor Makhno, in Ukraine. Repeated political and military struggles by non-Russians to establish independence or autonomy further challenged Soviet rule and complicated the prosecuting of the war and the entangling foreign interventions. During 1917 the Provisional Government had increasingly lost control over the non-Russian areas of the former empire. Nevertheless, after the October Revolution, Lenin felt sanguine that the slogan of national self-determination would draw the minorities to the Soviet cause. He even anticipated that non-Russian Bolsheviks would help set up Soviet rule in the country's periphery. At first, many regions acceded to Soviet authority, but a combination of growing separatist sentiment among the nationalities; military intervention by German, Austro-Hungarian, and Turkish forces; and the weakness of the Soviet government stripped away almost all the non-Russian areas by the end of 1918. The Soviet regime was confined to a core of the old state inhabited predominantly by Great Russians (see the map on page 165).

The new government initially focused on Ukraine, with its substantial population, bountiful harvests, and mineral and industrial wealth. In the first weeks after the collapse of the Provisional Government, the Ukrainian *Rada* and Bolshevik-dominated soviets in key cities and towns in Ukraine shared authority uneasily. The Soviet government in Moscow and *Rada* leaders wrangled over control of Ukrainian units in the army

---

[4]Petrograd was no longer the capital; Lenin had moved Soviet headquarters to Moscow in March 1918.

and demobilization procedures. While blandly professing peaceful intentions and continuing to negotiate with the *Rada*, Lenin and his colleagues installed a separate Ukrainian government run by Bolsheviks in Kharkov, the chief city of eastern Ukraine, an area home to a large Great Russian minority. The *Rada*, disorganized and lethargic, declared the independence of Ukraine but failed to stop the advance of armed Bolshevik units, who captured Kiev on February 8, 1918.

Fortunately for Ukraine nationalists, *Rada* spokesmen had opened separate peace talks with the Germans and Austro-Hungarians several weeks earlier. Happy to weaken their Russian adversary further and eager to obtain supplies from Ukraine for blockaded Germany, the Central Powers recognized the *Rada* as an independent government and soon ousted the Bolsheviks and reinstalled the *Rada*. Toward the end of April 1918, the Germans extended their occupation to eastern Ukraine, extinguishing the Soviet government in Kharkov. At the same time, the invaders replaced the quarrelsome and ineffectual *Rada* leaders with a German puppet government that lasted until Germany's defeat in November 1918.

Anarchy plagued Ukraine during most of 1919. A nationalist Ukrainian government known as the Directory took power in Kiev after the German withdrawal. In less than two months, however, the Directory fell to Bolshevik political and military attacks. During its six-month rule, the replacement Soviet government managed to alienate the Ukrainian peasantry by socializing the land and the Ukrainian intelligentsia by trying to reimpose the Russian language. The new regime also failed to control the Greens and other peasant anarchist bands. Turned out of office briefly by the advance of General Denikin's armies in August 1919, Ukrainian Bolsheviks regained power in early 1920, only to face Polish incursions. By the time the region recovered stability in the fall of 1920, it had endured almost three years of continuous civil warfare and the misrule of nine different governments. Limited support among the peasantry, strong Bolshevik opposition in the cities and among workers, and consistent blunders and factionalism had doomed the Ukrainian nationalists' bid for independence. By the close of 1920, the Ukrainian Bolshevik group that favored submission to the Russian party and close ties with Moscow took charge, and Lenin soon integrated Ukraine into the new Soviet Union.

In the Crimea, Bolsheviks supported by Russian workers and sailors from the naval base at Sebastopol supplanted the local Tatar government in January 1918. Three months later, the Germans deposed them as part of the German occupation of Ukraine. In 1919 and 1920, Whites, Ukrainian nationalists, and Reds fought over the area, with the last finally winning out.

Between 1918 and 1920, the Bolsheviks lost control of the northwestern borderlands of the former tsarist empire. While recognizing the independence of Finland on one hand, they also encouraged and gave limited logistical support to Finnish Bolsheviks, who wrestled to seize power in the country during the first half of 1918. Finally, conservative Finns led by General Gustav Mannerheim gained the upper hand, with aid from the Germans. Finland has remained independent ever since despite two wars with the Soviet Union in the period 1939–1945.

After the October Revolution, local Bolsheviks raised the Soviet flag briefly in Belarus and in Estonia and part of Latvia (German forces occupied Poland and Lithuania). Within four months the Brest treaty gave control of these territories to the Germans, who replaced the local Bolsheviks with their own figureheads. In 1918 and 1919, following German withdrawal from the Baltic region, Lenin and his colleagues supported local Bolsheviks who sought to establish Soviet governments in Lithuania, Latvia, and Estonia. Although Bolshevik forces almost won control of Latvia, by the end of 1919 all three areas had become independent states anchored in strong nationalist sentiment, a landowning peasantry, and a growing middle class. Russian inhabitants and indigenous Bolshevik workers and intelligentsia proved too small a minority to bring the region under Soviet hegemony. In addition, the British backed the new independent governments with military, political, and economic assistance. Lenin soon signed peace accords with each government that would last until 1940.

In southeastern Russia, three important Cossack groups, or "hosts," who enjoyed special privileges and exercised local self-rule, rejected Soviet authority in November 1917. This decision touched off a bitter, three-year civil war in the region. At first the rule of the well-off and conservative Cossack *atamans* wavered under the hostility and radicalism of poor and landless Cossacks and the frustration of returning front-line Cossack troops. Red Guards and detachments of revolutionary soldiers, sailors, and workers from Soviet Russia overthrew the Cossack government in Orenburg in late January 1918. The Don Cossack leadership fell in February 1918; the Kuban host, a month later. Bolsheviks ruled the Don region for only a few months until local forces supported by the Germans ousted them. In 1919 the Whites dominated the area until Denikin's defeat that fall.

In the north Caucasus, a three-way struggle among local Cossacks, Russian settlers, and indigenous mountain groups complicated matters for the Bolsheviks. Siding at first with the Russians and Cossacks, the Bolsheviks established Soviet rule in March 1918. Nevertheless, by midsummer civil war had erupted in the area. The Bolsheviks managed to retain power in part of the north Caucasus only by allying with the Chechen-Ingush, the strongest of the mountain peoples.

South of the mountains in Transcaucasia lived a volatile mix of large and small nationalities, some Christian and some Turkic-speaking Muslims. With entrenched cultures and an ancient history of independence, most of them rebuffed Bolshevik rule during 1917 to 1919. Only in 1920 did Soviet power begin to spread over this region. After the Bolshevik Revolution, the Armenian *Dashnaks* set up an autonomous government, but they soon found themselves surrounded by enemies and burdened by crushing economic problems. During 1918 the Turks occupied over half of Russian Armenia, and refugees from the invaders doubled the population in Armenian-controlled areas. Of all the Transcaucasus peoples, the Armenians suffered the most from ethnic tensions, boundary disputes, and economic rivalries with their neighbors. Nevertheless, they managed to maintain a precarious separate existence until 1920. Turkey's defeat, Western, particularly American, support; and their remoteness from Moscow all helped them to remain independent.

The Bolsheviks scored early success in Transcaucasia only in Baku, the chief city on the Caspian Sea. After the October Revolution, the Red-dominated Baku Soviet shared power with the local nationalist party, *Mussavat*. This strained alliance faltered in late March 1918, when an esti-mated three thousand Muslims perished in ethnic riots. In April the Bol-sheviks, led by the charismatic Stephan Shaumian, established their own local government known as the Baku Commune. The commune followed a radical socialist program, but economic difficulties and political in-trigue soon weakened it. In July Shaumian and his lieutenants fled the city. After anti-Bolshevik forces captured and executed them, Bolshevik propagandists enshrined them as revolutionary martyrs, known as "The Twenty-six Baku Commissars."

After a brief British occupation of Baku, Turkish units seized the city in mid-September 1918 and retaliated for the April massacres by execut-ing some four thousand Armenians. Memories of such atrocities would poison relations between Armenia and Azerbaijan in the late 1980s and early 1990s. At the end of November 1918, the Turks withdrew from Baku under the armistice arrangements that ended World War I, and British contingents replaced them. The area was soon drawn into the larger civil war between the Bolsheviks and the Whites.

In contrast to the Armenians and Azerbaijanis, the Georgians, the best organized minority in the Transcaucasus during 1918, possessed ex-perienced leaders, a relatively robust economy, and links to the outside world. Although the Bolsheviks of the Georgian capital, Tbilisi, had gained some following among the city's workers, the Mensheviks domi-nated Georgia's government and foreign policy. In early 1918, partly to thwart the threat of Turkish conquest, the Georgians took the lead in forming the independent Transcaucasian Democratic Federative Repub-lic, which included Armenia and Azerbaijan. However, after a few months, when it became clear that the Turks did not intend to annex the whole region, the federation fell apart and each state declared its separate independence. The Georgians sought security by allying with the Ger-mans, whom they invited to occupy key ports and rail centers in June

1918. Unlike their brutal conduct in Ukraine and the Crimea, the Germans behaved civilly in Georgia, and trade with Germany boosted the Georgian economy. After the British replaced the defeated Germans in November 1918, the Georgian Mensheviks remained in power. Persisting in their efforts to create a viable, moderate socialist society, they enacted a radical land reform and nationalized most industry and communications. Nevertheless, their harsh treatment of other minorities in Georgia, particularly the Ossetians, Abkhazis, and Adzhars, created a legacy of mistrust that would plague independent Georgia in the 1990s.

Although numerous, small non-Russian groups peopled eastern and southeastern regions of the old tsarist empire, the various Muslim nationalities held the most significance for the Bolsheviks. Lenin sought to use Soviet Muslims as a channel to encourage Muslim uprisings in Asia and Africa against the European powers. This effort, he believed, would hasten the advent of the world socialist revolution by weakening the imperialist nations' colonial economies. He proffered some form of autonomy to the Muslim movement in Russia. When his overtures were rebuffed, Stalin, then serving as head of the Commissariat for Nationalities, formed a special section of the commissariat to handle Muslim affairs in January 1918. This move engendered some Muslim support for the Soviet government, but White advances into the Volga region ended local efforts to establish an autonomous Muslim government there.

In southeastern Russia, conflict between Muslim groups and Russian settlers and townspeople that had erupted in 1917 persisted throughout the following year. The Bolsheviks backed the Muslims in most cases, but control over the region fluctuated until the whole area became caught up in the spreading civil war. In Central Asia, Russian workers and administrators with a Bolshevik orientation controlled the soviets in Tashkent, the region's largest city, and other towns along the railway lines. Various Muslim groups ruled the countryside. Muslim leaders, however, divided politically between conservative and reforming factions. Their dependence on a scattered and nomadic population hampered efforts to raise effective forces. Bolshevik troops from Tashkent overran an autonomous Muslim government based in Kokand in February 1918. Much Muslim resistance to Soviet rule from that time on came from armed bands known as *Basmachi*, who waged guerrilla warfare from 1918 into the mid-1920s.

The revolution and civil war also raised fresh challenges for the Jews, the only substantial non-Russian minority who did not reside primarily in the borderlands but were scattered throughout the country. The Soviet government ended all forms of discrimination from the tsarist era and accorded Jews full equality. Moreover, Trotsky, Zinoviev, Kamenev, and other important Bolshevik leaders were Jewish. Yet among much of the population, particularly the peasantry, anti-Semitism persisted. Further, some White propagandists did not hesitate to appeal to longstanding anti-Jewish sentiment by depicting the Bolshevik government as part of a worldwide Jewish conspiracy. Thus occasional pogroms broke out in White-controlled areas in Ukraine.

The campaign of various non-Russian groups for autonomy or independence between 1918 and 1920 produced important long-term consequences. For those minorities who succeeded in establishing separate governments, even temporarily, the experience provided a taste of self-rule that stimulated nationalist sentiment and would serve as a beacon during the non-Russians' resurgence in the late 1980s. The struggle also aggravated class tensions, pitting Bolshevik workers and intellectuals against other social strata. In addition, disputes in the borderlands revealed the complexity of multicultural regions such as Ukraine and the Caucasus, the dilemmas of which continue to haunt the development of post-Soviet states. Finally, outside support for certain non-Russian groups, such as Finns, Balts, and Caucasians, heightened Soviet suspicions of Western imperialistic ambitions in the former Russian Empire and helped to set the stage for the Cold War conflict that would come decades later.

Just as the prolonged conflict with the Whites wound down, the Soviet government faced its final military challenge from the periphery, a Polish invasion from the west. When the Germans and Austrians withdrew from Belarus and Ukraine at the end of 1918, the leaders of the newly recreated Polish state decided to expand eastward in the hope of reestablishing a "Greater Poland" that would include lands belonging to Poland-Lithuania at the height of that state's power in the sixteenth century. They moved their forces into Russia until they ran up against Soviet units. Throughout 1919 a shifting boundary thus divided Poland and Soviet Russia. In the spring of 1920, the Poles attacked, interested less in destroying the Soviet state than in ensuring a favorable determination of the border. At first they achieved considerable success, but by midsummer the Red defense stiffened and the Bolsheviks launched a counteroffensive that soon threatened Warsaw.

Lenin briefly abandoned his usual military realism and dreamed of carrying the socialist revolution into central Europe on the bayonets of the Red Army. With French backing, however, and thanks to tactical mistakes by the Bolshevik forces, the Poles recovered, answering with their own counterattack. The two sides finally concluded peace in the Treaty of Riga of March 1921. The Poles acquired territory inhabited by some four million Ukrainians and one million Belarusans. The Riga settlement would endure until 1939, when Stalin and Hitler carved up Poland as the prelude to World War II. In 1945, the victorious Soviet Union would redraw the border substantially in its favor.

Why did the Bolsheviks triumph? We have seen that they benefited from their opponents' weaknesses. Domestic foes, from rightists to Kadets through Mensheviks and SRs, proved fractured and ineffective and stood for programs that held little appeal for most of the population. Moreover, White generals and politicians could not bring themselves to concede enough to the non-Russian minorities to win their cooperation against the Bolsheviks, which in the case of the Ukrainians, Estonians, and Finns might have brought the White armies victory. Finally, Western intervention—divided, uncertain, and ultimately impotent—failed to bring down the Soviet regime.

The Bolsheviks, on the other hand, capitalized on several important advantages. They held the center of the country, where not only their greatest political strength but also the majority of the population and the most economic resources lay. Once their war effort took shape in 1918, the Bolsheviks always commanded more troops and armaments than the Whites. They also benefited militarily from interior lines of communication that enabled them to rush supplies and troops by rail from front to front.

Yet Bolshevik determination and leadership may primarily have tipped the scales in their favor. Although he made mistakes, Lenin managed to hold the Bolshevik party together, to motivate his subordinates, and to organize and direct the mobilization and centralization needed for victory. He and the other Bolshevik bosses also skillfully combined agitational and propaganda efforts aimed at the former lower classes with a ruthless and efficient repression carried out through the Cheka and local Party officials. The crackdown silenced or eliminated domestic opponents. The Party, to be sure, contained its share of careerists, opportunists, sadists, and thugs. But many dedicated and skilled individuals, including "shock" detachments of revolutionary sailors and workers who were thrown into crucial battles, also served in the lower echelons. These contributors added a significant ingredient to the Bolsheviks' triumph.

Mastering a Ravaged Country

During the conflict with Denikin's Volunteer Army, Lenin pithily described the civil war's impact on Soviet society: "The Soviet republic is besieged by the enemy. It must be a *single armed camp* not in words but in deeds."[5] To ensure the revolution's survival, Bolshevik leaders sought to centralize and militarize the Soviet system, concentrating all resources—human and material—on defeating the Whites and the outsiders. They did not always succeed; individuals, local groups, and regions often

---

[5]Quoted in Evan Mawdsley, *The Russian Civil War* (Boston: Allen and Unwin, 1987), p. 178. Italics in original.

managed to evade Bolshevik *diktat*. Confusion and near anarchy, rather than order and Soviet rule, sometimes reigned. At the same time, the exigencies of the struggle and the regime's harsh measures frequently reduced daily life to a primitive hand-to-mouth existence marked by shortages, random violence, and the arbitrary orders of local Bolshevik authorities or the Red Army. Struggling to survive, tyrannized civilians faced mobilization for public works projects, conscription into the Red Army, random seizures of property by local officials, and repeated humiliations if they were tagged as part of the old propertied classes.

The decline and shift in population from 1917 to 1921 provides one measurable impact of the civil war. Though data are scanty, conservative estimates place loss of life at a staggering 7 to 8 million people, more than *four times* the deaths in World War I. Of this number, civilians comprised some 5 million, the majority of whom succumbed to starvation and disease. An estimated 2 million people fled the country. Further, if we combine the effects of World War I, the revolution and civil war, and the famine of 1921–1922, the Russian population shrank from about 160 million to 135 million in eight years—the worst catastrophe in human history to that time.

People who survived moved in huge numbers from cities to villages to escape urban shortages of food, fuel, and jobs. In the countryside, they could at least share in the division of land and live on locally produced food. Between 1917 and 1920, the twenty-three cities of Russia boasting populations of over 50,000 lost one-quarter of their inhabitants. The two capitals suffered the most, Moscow losing 40 to 50 percent and Petrograd 50 to 60 percent of its citizens.

This flight from the cities had important social and political repercussions. Workers left jobless when factories closed for lack of raw materials or loss of markets returned to their recent roots in the villages. Thus a large proportion of those leaving the towns embodied the very proletariat on whom Soviet power depended. In addition, many of the best workers were drafted, either into the Red Army or as officials of the Bolshevik Party and Soviet government. As the proportion of workers among city inhabitants dwindled, a process that Bukharin called "the disintegration of the proletariat," the significance of "petty-bourgeois" elements, in Bolshevik terms, increased. To keep the economy functioning, even at a rudimentary level, the Bolsheviks had to rely more and more on "bourgeois specialists," that is, engineers, technicians, and former managers who knew how to run things. In addition, former bureaucrats, small shopkeepers, artisans, and white-collar workers began to dominate the administrative system and the service sector of the economy. Although most of these groups ultimately supported Soviet power, partly because they had no other choice, the petty-bourgeois hardly constituted the proletarian base on which Marxist theory predicated the new society would arise. Indeed, these shifts only

For many years, interpreting the events of the Russian civil war in the early Soviet system divided Western scholars along two fault lines. First, how important was this internecine struggle in determining Stalin's revolution at the end of the 1920s? Scholars of the totalitarian school such as Leonard Schapiro downplayed the civil war era. While noting the significance of the Bolshevik victory over the Whites, they viewed Marxist-Leninist ideology before 1917 and the establishment of one-party rule in 1917 as the crucial determinants of Stalin's monolithic system. Stalinism was encoded in these long-standing blueprints (*The Origins of the Communist Autocracy*, 1955). Revisionist historians, who abandoned the totalitarian model, saw striking similarities between the civil war years and the 1930s: class conflict in the village, full nationalization of production, utopian dreams of a new world, and fear of counterrevolution. For scholars like Robert Tucker, the civil war experience militarized Bolshevik political culture, leaving behind a solid residue of administrative fiat and coercion that Stalin capitalized upon after 1929 (*Stalin as Revolutionary, 1879–1929: A Study in History and Personality*, 1973).

The second controversy turned on the role of ideology in early Soviet politics. War communism, as historians labeled Bolshevik economic policies of nationalization and centralization, generated massive historiographical heat. Scholarly sparring matches usually erupted over what Soviet leaders had in mind in starting war communism in 1918. Was it, as some argued, an improvised scheme designed to ensure the regime's survival amid deepening economic chaos or, as others rejoined, a conscious effort to go straight to communism? Richard Stites chose expediency over ideology, noting that Lenin's writings before 1917 and his actions during the eight months after the Bolshevik Revolution showed no signs of "leaping over Marxian stages into a state of communism" (*Revolutionary Dreams*, 1989). On the other hand, Reginald Zelnik, another historian, was less sure. Focusing on a specific issue, Zelnik questioned whether the 1919 militarization of the transportation system derived exclusively from fears of economic collapse. Although he conceded that conditions were bad, with nationwide food shortages threatening widespread hunger and famine, Zelnik wondered how much the "circumstances" stemmed primarily from a "preconceived [Bolshevik] bias against private labor and against independent railroad workers in particular." What at first appeared to be the dictate of objective reality—economic chaos necessitating the establishment of a transportation dictatorship—on closer inspection resembled a subjective condition created by the "pressures of political action." From this perspective, the transport crisis dovetailed with worker apathy, a perfectly predictable outcome of Bolshevik assaults on labor autonomy from the first days of the revolutionary state ("Circumstance and Political Will in the Russian Civil War," *Party, State and Society in the Russian Civil War*, Diane Koenker, William Rosenberg, and Ronald Suny, eds., 1989).

In the 1980s, a third historiographical debate flared up as social historians entered Soviet studies, almost invariably rejecting the totalitarian model in which people were muted objects of manipulation by politicians. Questions now revolved around the role of society in Soviet politics. Did war communism, they asked, represent only actions from above, from top Party circles, whether motivated by doctrine or by circumstances? Or did it reflect pressures from below? More generally, this fresh approach sought to discover how ordinary people adjusted to, circumvented, or even profited from government decrees and their slipshod application.

Three recent studies offer intriguing suggestions about society's influence on the state. Orlando Figes examined social forces underlying the consolidation of Bolshevik rule among the peasants of the Volga region. He concluded that the prerevolutionary village commune retained its identity through the civil war years and decisively influenced Bolshevik policies toward the peasantry. As one example, Bolshevik attempts to organize class war through committees of the rural poor (*kombedy*) failed miserably because the "natural-patriarchal bonds of the village were stronger than the socio-economic division" among its inhabitants. A year later, this pattern repeated itself when "passive resistance" in the village stymied food-requisitioning campaigns organized by the Volost Soviet Executive Committees (*VIKs*), the Bolsheviks' instrument of rural administration. By 1921 the Bolsheviks exercised less control over the Volga peasantry than had their tsarist predecessors (*Peasant Russia, Civil War: Volga Countryside 1917–1921*, 1989).

Policies to nationalize the food supply system and to regiment railroad workers proved equally problematic, as Robert Argenbright shows. In 1918 Moscow created the Food Supply Committee (*Narkomprod*) to manage all food provisioning for the country. Yet supplies depended on the transport system, and like the peasants, railroad workers asserted their authority, "helping themselves on the sly, trading stolen goods on the back market, and requisitioning food freight." Throughout 1919 and 1920, the regime faced pressure from below to permit self-requisitioning on the railroads. In 1921 soberminded Bolshevik commissars finally gave railroaders four days a month to search for food on their own. All attempts to "impose centralism on the railroads" collapsed a year later. By the end of the civil war, Lenin was compelled to admit that popular resistance, especially in the countryside and on the railroads, had derailed his plans for a socialized economy ("Bolsheviks, Baggers, and Railroaders: Political Power and Social Space 1917–1921," *Russian Review,* October, 1993).

Like peasants and railroad workers, scientists also forced the Bolsheviks to make compromises. Kendall Bailes focused on the prestigious Academy of Sciences, home to scientific luminaries from the *ancien régime*. Beginning right after the Bolshevik Revolution, several thousand Academy members battled the Commissariat of Enlightenment over issues of professional independence and control of research. The strategic importance of this group was obvious—the scientific community held the keys to the industrial kingdom that the Bolsheviks hoped to build. For the new leadership, science opened the door to material prosperity, technological progress, advanced education, and national power. Lenin recognized the importance of enlisting scientists and scholars in the Bolshevik cause. In 1919 he told Commissar of Enlightenment Anatoli Lunacharsky not to let the Academy "be devoured by a few Communist fanatics." As a result, war communism did not lead to a centralized scientific establishment. To the contrary, as prominent geochemist V. I. Vernadsky confided in 1923, "the Russian Academy of Science [was] the single institution in which nothing has been touched." Vernadsky attributed the Academy's independence to the resistance of the scientific intelligentsia. But, as Bailes concluded, Lenin and Lunacharsky—two pragmatic Soviet leaders—also "deserve credit" for this reprieve ("Natural Scientists and the Soviet System," in *Party, State and Society in the Russian Civil War*, 1989).

These studies by Figes, Argenbright, and Bailes pose tantalizing questions for students of twentieth-century Russia. Perhaps wellsprings of autonomy among scientists, railroad workers, and communal peasants, as well as elsewhere in Soviet society, help to explain why Stalin felt compelled to apply massive violence against the Soviet people to carry through his revolution a decade later. Even in the peak years of Stalin's rule, S. Frederick Starr argues, pockets of civil society persisted. In the 1930s, to take one instance, classics of Russian literature were reissued, thus reacquainting younger readers with such "champions of civil society as Chekhov, Turgenev and Radishchev" (*Prospects for Stable Democracy,* 1991). The interplay of state and society, a dynamic that reopened with considerable force under Gorbachev in the 1980s and continues to this day, may prove to be the Russian civil war's lasting legacy.

reinforced the bureaucratization of the system that socialist measures had initiated.

The early years of Soviet rule also profoundly altered Russia's spiritual and social life. In early 1918, the Bolsheviks separated church and state, ended religious education, and nationalized church lands. Because Lenin recognized that persecution of the church would antagonize the faithful, particularly among the peasants, the Bolsheviks at first expressed their ideological detestation of religion primarily through verbal and press criticism of the church. But as the internecine conflict intensified and most Orthodox prelates and priests sided with the Whites, the Party stepped up its repression of the clergy and encouraged mobs to loot church possessions and burn church buildings.

In early 1918 the revolutionary government replaced church marriages with civil ceremonies and sanctioned divorce. Abortion was legalized, and administrators worked to improve the care of orphans and illegitimate children. The Party proclaimed equal rights for women, and Soviet social policy aimed to create a new "socialist" family. Women had played an important role in the revolutionary year 1917, and after strenuous campaigning they received the right to vote in the elections to the Constituent Assembly. The Bolsheviks had benefited from the revival of their special publication for women, *Rabotnitsa (Woman Worker)*, and from the successful organizing and agitational work of the Women's Bureau, headed by Alexandra Kollontai.

During the civil war, women suffered particularly, as wives of soldiers on both sides, as workers in industries especially hard hit by the near collapse of the economy, and as mothers and consumers struggling to survive and care for their families. Several million peasant women, widowed or abandoned, had to run their family's farm alone. Although the Bolsheviks encouraged rural women to overcome the traditional patriarchal structure of the village, these exhortations fell on deaf ears. Most village women were neither inclined nor positioned to challenge centuries-old custom. In the cities, a prewar trend toward nuclear families continued, and marriage rates increased. Radical feminism, such as Kollontai's espousal of complete freedom in sexual relations and the rearing of children in common public nurseries, gained little support among urban women, who, like peasant women, sought stability and security instead in these catastrophic times.

During the civil war, the economy veered dangerously close to ruin. Industrial production plummeted to about one-quarter of its prewar level; agricultural production, to about 60 percent of 1914 output. Railway transport virtually ceased to function except for military purposes, and overall rail traffic declined to 20 percent of its prewar volume. As a result, city and village inhabitants grew increasingly isolated from one another, and urban centers began to run out of food, fuel, and raw materials. The Bolsheviks soon introduced rationing, at first according to an elaborate, four-step hierarchy of consumers. Red Army personnel, workers, and state officials received the most. Before long, however, this system degenerated into a two-tier arrangement, with four out of five people squeezing into the top category. In some places during 1919 and 1920, the bread ration sank to a scanty half- or even quarter-pound a day. Despite Bolshevik prohibitions, the black market flourished. Almost everyone was forced to become a petty trader, bartering clothes, family heirlooms, items stolen from state enterprises, and homemade goods for basic provisions. To stay warm, citizens burned every scrap of wood in the cities, even stripping their houses and apartments of moldings, doors, window frames, and furniture.

The privation and the regimentation of society degraded the Russian population, as testified in the following excerpts from the diary of Alexis Babine, an American-educated Russian librarian and historian who taught at Saratov University in 1917 to 1920

> *Dec. 28, 1917:* . . . three robbers got into a house nearly opposite ours. The inmates managed to raise the alarm, one of the robbers was killed outright, one ran away, and one was caught by soldiers. The crowd that had assembled . . . roared for the last named—and our maid hastened there to see the execution. . . . When she got to the scene, soldiers were killing the second man with their bayonets.
> *Jan. 2, 1918:* A crowd of only about five hundred persons marched down Moscow Street. Shouts were heard of "Down with the Bolsheviks." At that a post office guard rushed out of the building and began to shoot. A young woman carrying one of the flags was wounded. A student ran to her support when she tottered down. "Ah, you too are with her," shouted a soldier and shot him dead.
> *Feb. 17, 1918:* As I was dozing on a sofa at our vigilance league . . . one of our members came in and told those present that just a few minutes before the Bolsheviks, by force of bayonets, had taken possession of his drugstore in the name of the government and generously offered him a clerk's job in his own store. Everybody was duly indignant and duly acknowledged the convincing power of the bayonet argument.
> *Oct. 18, 1918:* The local official organ contains an order to those evicted from their lodgings on twenty-four hours' notice not to trouble the authorities with petitions for leniency, but immediately to move to the outskirts of the city, where basements stand ready to receive the evicted bourgeoisie.
> *Oct. 21, 1918:* In order to save wood we have abandoned the use of our regular kitchen oven and cook our food, almost exclusively potato soup and grits, in our big brick Dutch heating

A Desperate Search for Fuel Citizens tearing down a house in Petrograd for firewood during the austere days of the civil war.

stoves, not at all built for that purpose. Our entire evenings are spent at this task. . . . Both our, and everybody else's, pervading problem is to keep alive and to outlast the Bolsheviks.

May 4, 1919: A general muster of citizens from 18 to 45 years of age was called yesterday, to report at 6 A.M. this morning . . . to be taken to an unknown place to dig trenches.

Feb. 20, 1920: During the last two weeks the temperature in my room never went above 35 degrees Farenheit. Today it is 33 degrees. This phenomenon is common everywhere. . . . To keep warm at night, one of my neighbors piles on himself four blankets, a quilted overcoat, and a fur coat. I cannot take more than half this dose—which is all I have, anyway.[6]

Power Versus Democracy: Conflict Divides the Party

As the civil war intensified, the militarization required to prosecute that conflict sharpened Lenin's penchant for firm central control and strict

---

[6]Donald J. Raleigh, ed., *A Russian Civil War Diary: Alexis Babine in Saratov, 1917–1922* (Durham, N.C.: Duke Univ. Press, 1988), *passim.*

party discipline. Beginning with his rejection of an all-socialist government at the time of the October Revolution, Lenin had revealed his intention not to share power with other political groups. Yet although the Kadets were banned after the Constituent Assembly elections, along with the Left SRs following their abortive uprisings in July 1918, the Bolsheviks pursued an erratic policy toward the Mensheviks and other SRs during the first years of Soviet rule. They sporadically tolerated opposition socialist journals and newspapers, permitted Mensheviks and SRs to contest local elections, and even allowed them to send delegates to the Congress of Soviets in December 1920. In 1921, however, the Soviet government pressured remaining Menshevik leaders to emigrate; most of them complied by 1922. In that year, in Soviet Russia's first publicized political trials, the government convicted a number of SR leaders of anti-Soviet activity, imprisoned them briefly, and then sent them into exile. This elimination of all non-Communist parties officially confirmed what in practice had existed since the October Revolution: a one-party dictatorship by the Bolsheviks.

Within the Party, Lenin faced recurring policy disputes during the first years of Soviet rule. At the Seventh Party Congress in March 1918, debate had centered on whether to ratify the oppressive Treaty of Brest-Litovsk, a battle that the Left Communists lost. During the Eighth Party Congress in March 1919, members approved a restructuring of the party. Because the Central Committee, which had traditionally served as the directing core of the party, had grown too unwieldly to respond quickly to the exigencies of the civil war, the Congress created three top-level organizations. The first, the Political Bureau (Politburo), originally had five members—Lenin, Trotsky, Kamenev. Stalin, and Nikolai M. Krestinsky—who set and oversaw policy. The Organization Bureau (Orgburo) administered Party affairs and checked on the execution of Party directives. Finally, the Secretariat staffed the other two institutions and kept track of Party personnel. (See the figure, Structure of the Communist Party.) The Ninth Party Congress in March 1920 endorsed the compilation of lists of key positions in the Party, government, and other institutions of Soviet society in order to match qualified Party members to appropriate jobs. This system, eventually known as *nomenklatura,* enhanced the Party's ability to control all aspects of life in Soviet Russia.

At the same congress, an articulate group opposed to the leadership emerged. Dubbed Democratic Centralists, they took their name from the basic Leninist principle of Party life. Under this formula, Party members at each organizational level, from the lowest unit, the Party cell, to the highest, the congress and Central Committee, were to elect their own officials, such as chairmen and secretaries, as well as delegates to the next highest Party body. Members also had the right to discuss and debate freely any Party policies and actions under consideration. These elective and deliberative prerogatives provided the democratic side of democratic

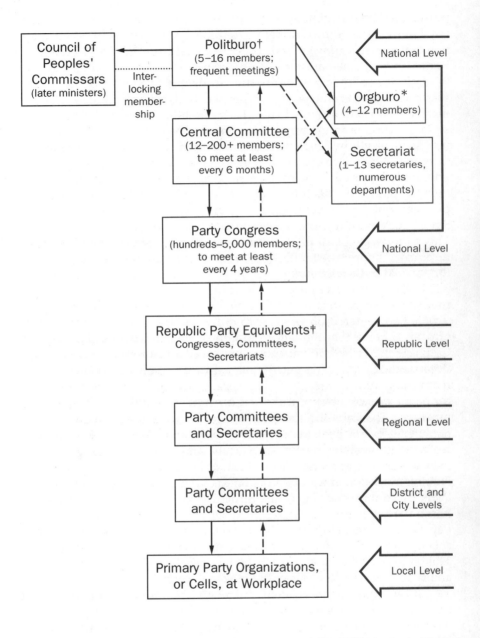

Structure of the Communist Party

centralism. The centralist aspect required that once a Party body reached a decision, all Party members had to cease discussion, accept the ruling, and bend every effort toward implementation. Moreover, actions of higher Party bodies were binding on lower ones.

The Democratic Centralists criticized current Party operations, deriding the lack of open elections and free debate. True, because of a shortage of qualified personnel and the pressure of civil war emergencies, Party leaders had often bypassed the elective process to appoint or co-opt officials and frequently had set policies and made decisions without prior Party discussion. The opposition attacked the growing bureaucratization of the Party and condemned the use of bourgeois specialists in administrative and military positions. Despite the pertinence of their criticisms, the Democratic Centralists won only minority backing at the congress and failed to reform Party procedures.

During the remainder of 1920, a second dissenting group, known as the Workers' Opposition, emerged within the Party. This bloc had first appeared at the Ninth Congress in March and persisted in another line of attack against the leadership. Alexandra Kollontai and other members of the Workers' Opposition rejected the concept of "labor armies," an idea that Trotsky had broached in early 1920. According to his plan, Red Army soldiers scheduled for demobilization would work under military discipline on major public works and industrial projects. Arguing that the proletariat had lost control of its own revolution and its pivotal role in building the new society, Workers' Opposition leaders urged that trade unions, not labor armies, take primary responsibility for reconstructing the economy. This strategy would also grant them a larger political role. By 1921 the idea of labor armies had been dropped, but the Workers' Opposition continued to resist the Party's domination of the trade unions and the lack of proletarian control over basic Party and state policies. Sporadic strikes and labor disputes gave force to these criticisms, but the Workers' Opposition remained only an annoying minority within the Party.

Despite internal criticism and friction, Lenin and his supporters maintained tight control over the Party and the government. With battlefield threats and economic crises incessantly pressing on the Bolshevik leaders, they had neither the time nor the personnel for deliberate consideration and careful execution of policy. Conditions demanded that they act immediately, cut corners, and produce results, or the whole enterprise would come crashing down. Increasingly, the Soviet government ruled by decree, bypassing the Soviet congresses and their executive committees. The center decided more and more, while in regions and localities, higher bodies began to preempt lower ones. For their part, local soviets and Party committees, overwhelmed by the demands on them, increasingly turned to Moscow for help and quick solutions to their predicaments. In the capital, because the Politburo set policy for the government and because Party personnel staffed the Council of People's Commissars as well as most other governmental institutions, the political system settled into a dictatorship of the Bolshevik Party.

Yet the Party itself was changing. Its numbers skyrocketed, from some 350,000 members in the fall of 1917 to almost 800,000 at the end of 1920. As a result of this expansion, "revolutionary Bolsheviks"—that is, individuals who had gained their formative experience in the October struggle—now ranked in the minority. Under the new configuration, six out of ten Party members had matured during the sacrifice, expediency, discipline, and militarization associated with the civil war. These recruits proved less ideological and idealistic, and more pragmatic and goal-oriented, than the revolutionary Bolsheviks. Consequently, the Party leadership found them easier to control and bureaucratize. Further, over half of all Party members served in the Red Army, which became an important ladder of upward social mobility for many workers and some peasants. With their disciplined and rigid outlook, civil war veterans grew accustomed to taking orders and cared little about inner-party democracy and debating policy alternatives. Stalin soon would take advantage of this state of mind.

Red Dawn and New Buttons: Revolutionary Culture

The Bolshevik Revolution and early years of Soviet rule profoundly changed not only the Party, the political system, and Russian society but cultural and artistic life as well. To many intellectuals, the October Revolution spawned a new era of purity and of human creativity and understanding. This pristine, mechanistic world would reflect in its order, color, and form the confidence, equality, and promise of the good society envisioned under socialism. Everything would change for the better—art, film, prose, poetry, drama, behavior, learning, forms of speech, rituals, architecture, furniture, even clothing. As Vladimir Mayakovsky, the poet laureate of the revolution, proclaimed, "We will remake life anew, right down to the last button on your vest."

The avant-garde artists and modernist writers who had gained Russian and Europewide fame before and during World War I evinced the most enthusiasm about a sweeping cultural revolution. Still, some more significant leaders in the arts left Russia, either because they disliked, or came to dislike, the Bolsheviks or because they found it impossible to work in the chaos and hardship that characterized daily life in the postrevolutionary years. The abstract painter Vasily Kandinsky, the composer Sergei Rachmaninoff, the author Ivan Bunin, and almost everyone in the budding Russian movie industry, among others, never returned to their homeland. This exodus opened the door especially to young, innovative directors and cinematographers, who would make brilliant films in the 1920s. Many scientists and university professors also departed during the first years of Bolshevik rule. The painter Marc Chagall played an important role in launching the unrestrained revolutionary art but left Russia permanently after a few years. Some, like the writers Maxim Gorky, Ilya Ehrenburg, and Alexei Tolstoy, lived in Europe for a time but returned later.

Artists who supported the Bolshevik Revolution saw their task as twofold: to get rid of the traditional and the old and to create the new and the bold. The poet Alexander Blok summed up their purpose as "to *remake* everything . . . so that our false, filthy, boring, hideous life should become a just, pure, merry, and beautiful life."[7] The iconoclastic attack on bourgeois and aristocratic forms and rituals ranged from replacing the double-eagle emblem of tsardom with the hammer and sickle, to addressing everyone as "comrade," to orchestras playing without that symbol of authority, the conductor. Sympathizers destroyed some statues, as would recur following the overthrow of Soviet communism in 1991; burned a few important buildings and churches; and looted several art collections, primarily in mob attacks on the private homes of landlords and industrialists.

Fortunately for the cultural heritage of Russia, both Lenin and the man whom he appointed as commissar of education and culture, Anatoly Lunacharsky, adamantly opposed the destruction of artistic treasures and historic buildings. A highly educated and cosmopolitan Bolshevik, Lunacharsky managed to save almost all this heritage and to make available to the public both the cultural achievements of the past and the revolutionary artistic works of the times. He nationalized and subsidized theaters, setting ticket prices low enough so that almost anyone could attend. In addition, he increased the number of museums, most of them offering free entry, and encouraged concerts, poetry readings, and street performances. Lunacharsky also nationalized publishing and sought to use books, journals, and newspapers as purveyors of the Bolsheviks' revolutionary message. Lacking paper, ink, and presses, however, the number of publications dropped drastically between 1917 and 1920, with a rampant rumor mill replacing printed communication.

In education, Lunacharsky oversaw a broad campaign against illiteracy. He strove to introduce universal, coeducational, and compulsory education up to age seventeen through an expansion of primary and secondary education. Shortages of books, teachers, and school buildings crippled this campaign, however. In two important pedagogical innova-

---

[7]Quoted in Richard Stites, *Revolutionary Dreams* (New York: Oxford Univ. Press, 1989), p. 38.

tions, the commissar of education started schools for workers in or near factories and changed school curricula to relate classroom learning more closely to life, particularly to work. In higher education, new universities opened and existing academies were required to admit anyone and to abolish examinations and degrees. These changes, although populist and democratic, made it difficult to maintain the quality of instruction or to measure students' progress, and were abandoned after a few years.

As Marxists, Bolshevik leaders saw the arts as a reflection of the economic base of society. Thus, while the revolutionaries strove to build socialism, they alleged that artists existed to support that effort. Toilers in the cultural vineyard should communicate the goals and policies of the Soviet government to the masses and inculcate in them the values and attitudes essential for socialism. At first, writers and artists enjoyed fairly free rein in selecting the forms and media for this task. Many chose imaginative and exciting ways to reach the public. Because so many comrades were barely literate or could not read at all, cultural leaders, including Mayakovsky, elevated the poster to a fine art, utilizing brilliant colors

Taking the Revolutionary Message to the People Citizens listening to a gramophone recording in front of a modernistically decorated "agit-train."

and eye-catching designs. In fact, graphic arts soon became, and would remain, one of the most admired aspects of Soviet culture.

As another original device, performers organized traveling troupes of actors and musicians to carry the Bolshevik message to the people through playlets and concerts performed on multimedia trains and boats. These mobile instruments of propaganda sported festive decorations and painted slogans. At each stop Party cultural activists organized lectures, showed films, and distributed posters and pamphlets trumpeting the Bolsheviks' message. Street festivals and performances also sprang up, the most spectacular being the commemoration of the third anniversary of the revolution in Petrograd on November 7, 1920. During this extravaganza, 6,000 performers, including a Red Army battalion, reenacted in front of the Winter Palace the fall of the old regime before an audience of 45,000.

Among several innovative artistic schools that developed in the revolutionary period, **constructivism** generated the broadest range and the most penetrating influence on modern art and architecture. Believing that form should follow function and that works should serve a utilitarian purpose as well as reflect the machine age, constructivist artists designed workers' clothing, furniture, household utensils, and books, as well as public buildings and futuristic cities. One architect, Vladimir Tatlin, drew up plans for a monumental and inspiring headquarters for the new Communist International. His design depicted a tall, canted cylinder that would revolve slowly, while from its top a powerful light

A Building for the Future Vladimir Tatlin's constructivist model for Comintern headquarters. Lack of funds doomed this design and most other avant-garde architectural projects.

would project the latest revolutionary news to reflect from the clouds. Like so many constructivist projects, lack of resources confined the tower to the drawing board.

Supremacism developed as another important school, led by Kazimir Malevich, whose pre–Space Age paintings feature stark geometric forms and brilliant colors, or sharply contrasting black and white. As with the Ballet Russe earlier, many artists worked in the theater, designing sets, costumes, and lighting and sometimes collaborating with the innovative and influential director-producer, Vsevolod Meyerhold.

In literature, poetry dominated the revolutionary epoch. Mayakovsky rushed from one public reading to another, sometimes puzzling and sometimes electrifying his proletarian listeners with his outrageous and dramatic works. Some of the most dazzling poets of the twentieth century graced this place and time: Alexander Blok; Anna Akhmatova; Sergei Yesenin, who committed suicide in 1925 at the age of thirty-two; Osip Mandelshtam; Boris Pasternak, later a Nobel Prize winner; and Marina Tsvetayeva, who soon emigrated. During the 1920s these writers became disenchanted with Bolshevik policies and ran afoul of Soviet censorship, publishing less and less in their own country and writing increasingly for private consumption. Most would be persecuted by the Soviet regime after 1930.

In addition to these poets, other writers and artists, even some who at first had thrown themselves wholeheartedly into the Bolsheviks' propaganda efforts, grew uneasy about Soviet cultural policy. Some disdained the prostitution of culture to political ends, maintaining that the revolution gave them freedom to pursue their own creative bent, that it ensured "art for art's sake." Others increasingly objected to Bolshevik censorship and terror. Government authorities in turn deplored the efforts of some artists to dictate the standards and practices of revolutionary culture. They focused especially on a group called *Proletkult* (the Association for Proletarian Culture and Education), which sponsored workshops for proletarian writers, palaces of culture, and workers' clubs. In 1920 the government ended *Proletkult's* independent functioning, putting it under Lunacharsky's commissariat.

The most significant divergence between the government's cultural views and those of many artists stemmed from the accessibility of their art. Although some realist painters and musicians continued to produce works in representational form, much revolutionary art was abstract and illusional. A modernist musical composition, for example, that represented the noise on the factory floor proved quite incomprehensible to almost every listener. The masses much preferred revolutionary and civil war popular songs, which a few composers produced and which the government encouraged. A ballad about the Bolshevik partisan hero Chapayev captivated millions of Soviet citizens, whereas most avant-garde pieces only baffled workers and peasants and even sophisticated citizens.

Soviet officials worried that the people were not getting the intended message. Although the government permitted and even supported modernist expression well into the late 1920s, its obscure inaccessibility sowed the seeds for the later imposition of strict Party control over the arts.

Conclusion

By late fall 1920, more than six years after the outbreak of World War I, most citizens of the former Russian Empire at last had found peace. But apocalyptic changes had swept the country. Many non-Russians now resided in independent nations such as Finland, Poland, Estonia, Latvia, Lithuania, Armenia, and Georgia. (The Soviet Union, the federal state that would form in 1923–1924, soon reabsorbed the latter two nations.) Most Russians, Ukrainians, Belarusans, and Muslims, as well as many smaller nationalities, now lived in a revolutionary socialist society under strict control of the Bolshevik Party. Beginning with his shutting the Constituent Assembly, Lenin had clamped down on political liberty and free expression. Bolshevik authorities ruthlessly squelched anti-Soviet and antisocialist agitation and activity.

As Lenin had hoped, the Bolsheviks had "held on" to power, and the revolutionary Soviet state had survived the cruel ordeal of internal conflict and outside interference. In the fall of 1918, many Bolshevik leaders had fervently believed that the expected European workers' revolution was at hand, as mutinies, strikes, and riots broke out in defeated Austria, Hungary, and Germany. Lenin had gone so far as to order food stockpiled, when the Bolsheviks had little enough themselves, to assist German workers on the morrow of their revolution. But the crushing of a brief uprising of radical socialists in Germany in January 1919 dashed Soviet hopes for assistance from European revolutionaries.

In 1918 Lenin had dropped "Social Democratic" from the Party's name, retitling it the Russian Communist Party (Bolshevik). He wanted to make clear that his Russian socialists had discarded forever the mistaken, chauvinist views of those European Marxists who had compromised with their own bourgeoisie in 1914 and supported the imperialist war. The Russian Communists, Lenin asserted, stood firmly for immediate revolutionary action against the imperialists and were fully prepared to assist their European comrades in this endeavor. In March 1919 at a meeting in Moscow, Lenin thus founded the Third or Communist International, known subsequently as the Comintern, to replace the Second International, which had collapsed in 1914. Under the direction of Russian Bolshevik Grigory Zinoviev, the Comintern helped to organize pro-Leninist Communist parties in Europe and around the world. The Soviet government also funded and supported revolutionary propaganda and agitation abroad, using its diplomatic missions in countries with which it had established formal relations. In 1919 Bolshevik hopes for world revolution fluttered again briefly when Soviet regimes cropped up in the German state of Bavaria and in Hungary, but before long conservative forces squelched these governments.

Hence, by the end of 1920 the revolution was mired in a stalemate. The Allies had failed to destroy the radical Soviet state, and the Russian Communists had not inspired a workers' revolution anywhere else. Lenin and his colleagues had achieved survival, but not salvation. Moreover, the Bolsheviks' aggressive rhetoric, their aid to radical revolutionaries abroad, and the Western powers' misguided intervention all combined to sour Soviet Russia's relations with the outside world. This unfortunate mix created an aura of mistrust and hostility between Russia and the West that would persist for seventy years and that we are only now gingerly reversing.

To what extent did the civil war and foreign intervention shape the future development of the Soviet system? Because the institutions and molders of the later socialist society were forged in those terrible years of the struggle for survival, the conflict did serve as a powerful formative experience. In particular, Bolshevik leaders were driven to institute highly centralized rule and arbitrary policies to overcome imminent economic and military threats to the fledgling state. They confined major decision making to a small circle of Party elite. They forbade questioning or dissent and treated alleged enemies harshly. Yet did these characteristics of the new system stem primarily from wartime exigencies, or did the demands of survival simply reinforce innate tendencies in Bolshevism? Well before 1918, Leninist doctrine had pointed to a one-party dictatorship and a centralized and regimented system. Attacks on class enemies and the squelching of alternative opinions certainly predated the military struggle. Clearly, both inherent principles and force of circumstances contributed to the rigid, semimilitarized society that emerged from the cauldron of the years 1918 to 1920. Although we can never rewrite the script of history, it is still intriguing to speculate about what would have happened if the Bolsheviks had been permitted to put their ideas into effect without outside meddling or the need to improvise. We can only guess at what sort of socialism might have emerged.

After the October Revolution, Lenin and his comrades fulfilled certain promises that had impelled their rise to power. They made peace; they confirmed the peasants' seizure of the land; they destroyed oppressive aspects of the older order. Nevertheless, in other areas the new regime abandoned or undercut key planks of their revolutionary platform. Instead of providing freedom and justice, they regimented and repressed society. Rather than produce a bountiful economy, they were compelled to reduce daily life to a primitive existence. The price of retaining power proved terribly high. The Bolsheviks lost substantial regions of the former state, and the economy lay in ruins. As the population grew embittered and degraded, unrest spread throughout the country. As assets, the Bolsheviks counted a large army and a core of tested and loyal cadres willing to go to great lengths to restore the nation. Their surprising victory had also generated buoyant self-confidence. Still, they puzzled over what to do next.

FURTHER READING

An essential collection of excellent articles on the social history of the period is Diane P. Koenker, William G. Rosenberg, and Ronald G. Suny, eds., *Party, State, and Society in the Russian Civil War* (Bloomington, Ind., 1989). Useful surveys emphasizing political and military developments are Evan Mawdsley, *The Russian Civil War* (Boston, 1987) and John F. Bradley, *The Civil War in Russia, 1917–1920* (London, 1975).

Works by Chamberlin, Deutscher, Keep, Kennan (*Soviet-American Relations*, vol. 2), Pipes, and Stites cited in Chapter 3's "Further Reading" pertain to the years 1918–1920, as do the novels by Pasternak and Sholokhov in that same list.

Economic policy is succinctly treated in Chapter 3 of Alec Nove's invaluable *An Economic History of the USSR* (London, 1969). See also the monograph by Sylvana Malle, *The Economic Organization of War Communism, 1918–1921* (Cambridge, 1985).

On social issues, see the pertinent chapters of Richard Stites, *The Women's Liberation Movement in Russia . . . 1860–1930* (Princeton, N.J., 1978); Barbara Clements, *Bolshevik Feminist: The Life of Alexandra Kollontai* (Bloomington, Ind., 1979); and Dorothy Atkinson, *The End of the Russian Land Commune, 1905–1930* (Stanford, Calif., 1983).

On education and culture, Abbot Gleason, Peter Kenez, and Richard Stites, eds., *Bolshevik Culture: Experimentation and Order in the Russian Revolution* (Bloomington, Ind., 1985); Robert C. Williams, *Artists in Revolution* (Bloomington, Ind., 1977); Sheila Fitzpatrick, *The Commissariat of Enlightenment* (Cambridge, 1970); Peter Kenez, *The Birth of the Propaganda State: Soviet Methods of Mass Mobilization, 1917–1929* (New York, 1985); and Christina Lodder, *Russian Constructivism* (New Haven, Ct., 1983).

For political history, consult Robert C. Tucker, *Stalin as Revolutionary, 1879–1929* (New York, 1973); Stephen F. Cohen, *Bukharin and the Bolshevik Revolution* (New York, 1974); Vladimir Brovkin, *Behind the Front Lines of the Civil War: Political Parties and Social Movements in Russia, 1918–1922* (Princeton, N.J., 1994); T. H. Rigby, *Lenin's Government: SOVNARKOM, 1917–1922* (Cambridge, 1979); Oliver Radkey, *The Sickle Under the Hammer: The Russian Social Revolutionaries in the Early Months of Soviet Rule* (New York, 1963); Oskar Anweiler, *The Soviets . . . 1905–1921* (New York, 1974); George Leggett, *The Cheka: Lenin's Political Police* (Oxford, 1981); Israel Getzler, *Kronstadt, 1917–1921: The Fate of a Soviet Democracy* (Cambridge, 1983); James Bunyan, *The Origin of Forced Labor in the Soviet State, 1917–1921* (Baltimore,

Md., 1967); Leonard Schapiro, *The Origins of the Communist Autocracy, 1917–1922* (2nd ed., London, 1977); and Robert V. Daniels, *The Conscience of the Revolution: Communist Opposition in Soviet Russia* (Cambridge, Mass., 1960).

Diplomatic and military history are treated in Peter Kenez, *Civil War in South Russia*, 2 vols. (Berkeley, 1971 and 1977); Richard Luckett, *The White Generals* (London, 1971); Peter Fleming, *The Fate of Admiral Kolchak* (London, 1963); John A. White, *The Siberian Intervention* (Princeton, N.J., 1950); Betty Unterberger, *America's Siberian Expedition, 1918–1920* (Durham, N.C., 1956); and John M. Thompson, *Russia, Bolshevism, and the Versailles Peace* (Princeton, N.J., 1966).

Of many memoirs, two are of special interest: Leon Trotsky, *My Life: An Attempt at an Autobiography* (New York, 1972) and P. N. Wrangel, *The Memoirs of General Wrangel* (London, 1930).

5

A VISION DEFERRED
Soviet Society Under NEP

~

At 3 A.M. on March 17, 1921, twenty miles west of Petrograd, Soviet commanders mobilized hardpicked and specially equipped units. Under cover of darkness and thick fog, thousands of soldiers camouflaged in white crept silently across the frozen Gulf of Finland. As the Red columns approached the outer redoubts of the island city and naval fortress of Kronstadt, many men dropped onto all fours. Shivering with cold and fright, they inched forward in the thin layer of frigid water that skimmed the ice. Their targets were not hated Whites or despised imperialists but mutinous sailors, soldiers, and workers inside Kronstadt. Until a few days before, these rebels had been considered comrades and brave heroes of the 1917 revolution and the civil war. Now, bizarrely, Red fought Red.

The difficulty had begun a month earlier, when unrest among Petrograd workers over high prices, short rations, and unemployment stirred up Kronstadt workers and sailors. In addition. rumors of Bolshevik grain requisitioning and suppression of rural resistance alarmed conscript peasant soldiers in the garrison. Food and fuel shortages exacerbated matters. On March 1, speakers at a mass meeting in Kronstadt's main square had upbraided Communist policies, and the crowd had hooted down two Bolshevik leaders. The next day, sailors took the lead in arresting the Bolshevik commissar of the Baltic Fleet and the Kronstadt Soviet chairman and in forming a Provisional Revolutionary Committee to maintain order and to organize elections to a new soviet. Disaffection had flowered into rebellion.

The turn of events in Kronstadt horrified Bolshevik leaders gathering in Moscow for the Tenth Party Congress. Kronstadters had participated actively in the revolutionary events of 1917, particularly the July Days and the October Revolution, most of them as solid Bolshevik supporters. Shock detachments from the city had fought gloriously against the Whites. It was unthinkable that what Trotsky had called "the pride and glory of the revolution" should now turn against Soviet rule. The rebels' demands flagrantly challenged current Bolshevik programs and poignantly harked back to the revolutionary ideals of 1917. Moreover, Lenin feared that the uprising would leapfrog to the mainland, where grumbling rippled through towns and villages. Or White and foreign anti-Bolsheviks might rush aid to Kronstadt, using the city as a springboard for renewed attacks on the shaky Soviet state. Finally, Lenin knew that the Bolsheviks had to act fast to subjugate the rebels; the ice covering the Gulf of Finland would melt during the next few weeks, making an infantry onslaught impossible. The island might hold out indefinitely.

Lenin saw the Kronstadt uprising as a manifestation of the ancient Russian spirit of spontaneous mass rebellion that he had always feared and rejected. For this reason, and because the Kronstadters contravened the Bolsheviks' monopoly of power, Lenin never considered acceding to their demands. The rebels' program combined socialist idealism with anarcho-populism and called for a "third revolution" (following the February and October revolutions) to rid the country of Communist dictatorship. They urged new soviet elections and a coalition government of all left-wing parties, from Mensheviks to anarchists. They castigated "war communism" and sought economic equality and better living conditions. Yet, somewhat contradictorily, the Kronstadt insurgents also endorsed individual small-scale manufacture and the right of peasants "to do as they please with all the land," both functions to be exercised "without the employment of hired labor." The rebels rejected the Communists as a new ruling stratum, condemned Bolshevik repression, demanded the release of nonbourgeois political prisoners, and called for independent trade unions and free speech, assembly, and press for all "toilers."

Ignoring an ultimatum from War Commissar Trotsky, the rebels easily turned back Soviet offensives on March 7 and 8. A week later, the Party Congress repealed grain requisitioning and made other concessions to the peasants. This symbolic break with the draconian policies of "war communism" inspirited the Soviet forces ranged against the fortress, and by March 16, Mikhail Tukhachevsky, the brilliant Red Army general and future marshal, had organized a massive assault spearheaded by battalions of officer trainees and units stiffened with Bolshevik shock troops. At dawn March 17, the Kronstadters spied these forces, bathed them in the glare of flares and searchlights, and opened barrages of artillery and machine-gun fire on them. Caught on the open icefields, swathes of Red Army troops were cut down or plunged to a watery grave when Kronstadt shells blew holes in the ice. Nevertheless, a number of officers and men charged forward, shouting the traditional army "Hoorah!" With a superiority of 45,000 fresh troops to 15,000 exhausted defenders, Red Army forces finally seized control of Kronstadt by midnight, and on March 18, they fully suppressed the uprising. Each side suffered thousands of casualties. The Cheka executed several hundred ringleaders, sent thousands more rebels to concentration camps, and transferred the rest from the Baltic Fleet to other naval units. Eight thousand Kronstadters escaped across the ice to Finland, although some of these later returned to Soviet Russia and were imprisoned.[1]

The Bolsheviks implemented none of the political reforms that the rebels had demanded. Although Soviet propagandists attempted to depict the insurrection as a White Guard and interventionist plot, Lenin understood its populist nature and the threat of spreading anarchy that the outburst represented. No matter the cost to the Bolsheviks' image as standard-bearers of a democratic, socialist revolution, Lenin recognized that he had to extinguish the sparks of Kronstadt to ensure the Soviet regime's survival under Bolshevik control. In his own words, the rebellion "was the flash that lit up reality better than anything else." He and his colleagues had already decided to abandon the socioeconomic policies of their first three years in power, but the Kronstadt mutiny graphically underscored the extent of popular disgruntlement with those programs.

One Step Backward, Two Steps Forward

Long a proponent of swallowing temporary retreats to marshal strength for later advances, Lenin realized at the end of 1920 that to preserve the Bolsheviks' authority, he needed to change course drastically. From 1905 he had maintained that revolution in Russia would lead to a socialist society only with major assistance from expected proletarian uprisings in the West. Three years after the October Revolution, no such help had yet materialized. Moreover, Lenin had anchored his revolutionary strategy to the link (smychka) between the small but well-led Russian proletariat and the majority population of peasants. By the fall of 1920, under the weight of relentless grain requisitioning, that link was snapping. Finally, although in September 1920, fighting had stopped across most of Russia for the first time in over six years, world war, revolution, foreign intervention, and civil war had exhausted and dispirited the survivors. Their country ravaged, the isolated Soviet leaders pondered how to proceed. They had survived, but where had their victory stranded them?

To navigate through these uncertain times, Lenin and his successors

---

[1]This account is based on Paul Avrich, *Kronstadt 1921* (Princeton, N.J.: Princeton Univ., 1970), *passim,* and W. Bruce Lincoln, *Red Victory: A History of the Russian Civil War* (New York: Simon & Schuster, 1989), pp. 489–512.

espoused a modified socioeconomic program known as NEP (New Economic Policy) and simultaneously tightened their political dictatorship over the country. As we shall see, they managed partially to restore the economy but stalled on fundamental decisions on how to construct a genuinely socialist system. Establishing a federal state, the Soviet leaders sought to control their regime's large non-Russian population while permitting some cultural autonomy. Communist efforts to recast society and beliefs became mired in the swamp of traditional mores and social ties. Experimentation in the arts flourished in the early 1920s, but the Party gradually reined in and exploited culture for its own political purposes. Abroad, Soviet statesmen pursued the sometimes contradictory paths of promoting world revolution and establishing normal relations with nonsocialist nations.

The immediate priority in early 1921 was the challenge of restoring Russia's bankrupted economy. Figures alone fail adequately to depict the primitive level to which daily life had sunk, as millions scrounged for food, fuel, and shelter, trading and bartering just to stay alive. By 1921 industrial production crawled at less than 20 percent of its 1914 level. Overall agricultural production had fallen some 40 percent, and grain output, even more, with 30 million tons produced in 1919 as against 74 million tons in 1916. Because of the lack of goods and the government's printing of rubles to meet expenses, inflation had skyrocketed. Prices of basic necessities had tripled or quadrupled, far surpassing wage increases. Factories closed or produced at low levels, and unemployment mushroomed.

As the economic crisis intensified in late 1920, Lenin at first foresaw no clear remedy. Afraid of further disrupting grain supplies and the trickle of goods from the factories, he hesitated to abandon the policies of grain requisitioning and of centralized production that had helped to spawn economic chaos. But Kronstadt and other spontaneous uprisings against Soviet power forced his hand. At harvest time in September 1920, as grain requisitioning teams headed into the villages, peasants in western Siberia, Tambov, and several Volga-area and south central provinces revolted, killing local Party members and Soviet officials. Acting on their own, without links to anti-Bolshevik parties or to disgruntled town workers, the rebels had no chance of overturning the Communist regime. At one point, however, some twenty thousand armed and angry men maurauded across the countryside in southeast Russia. Lenin proclaimed the end of the hated grain requisitioning in the region and sent punitive army expeditions to the disaffected villages, as Count Witte and Tsar Nicholas II had done fifteen years earlier. This combination of concession and repression soon quelled the rural revolt, but the Communists would have to make fundamental policy changes to win back peasant support.

Party leaders were still debating policy alternatives when surprising ideological and political shocks assailed them in the late winter of 1921. It was now the workers' turn to question the core principle of the recently established "dictatorship of the proletariat and poor peasantry." The labor force's resentment of their conscription for emergency projects in 1920 and of the Party's decision to downgrade the role of trade unions as guardians of workers' rights finally exploded. In February 1921, strikes and labor protests broke out in Petrograd, Moscow, and other cities, culminating in March 1921 in the Kronstadt rebellion.

The combined pressure of peasant uprisings and worker discontent prompted the Party to adopt a revised course of action at its Tenth Congress in March 1921. Party leaders had haltingly worked out the plan during the preceding weeks. Soon known as the New Economic Policy (NEP), these measures ended "war communism" and established nonsocialist sectors in the economy. Leftist critics within the Party bemoaned the admission of socialism's failure and retreat to capitalism that NEP implied, whereas anti-Communists gloated. Lenin, however, saw NEP as a "peasant Brest-Litovsk," a much-needed breathing space before a renewed drive to build socialism. As NEP's centerpiece, the government made a direct concession to peasant demands: for forcible requisitioning of grain, it substituted a progressive fixed tax on agricultural output, a measure Trotsky originally proposed a year earlier. At first the policy stipulated that peasants pay the tax in kind; after 1922 they could pay in either money or produce. To stimulate peasants to boost yields, the Party promised that growers could sell whatever they produced above the tax. As further incentives to agricultural productivity, the government later permitted farmers to lease land and to hire labor. The Party also introduced private trade and free prices to facilitate peasant marketing of their surplus and to stimulate the overall economy. To provide goods for villagers to buy, the government encouraged production of consumer items in private industries limited to no more than twenty employees. The state retained control only of the "commanding heights" of industry: large factories, banks, transport, communications, and foreign trade. Most workers could freely enter a competitive labor market.

Finally, NEP attempted to open Russia to outside investors. The Soviet government granted to foreign capitalists timber, mining, and other concessions designed to spur the output of natural resources, a policy that many Party members strongly resented. These concessions induced little economic impact, for few foreign investors wanted to risk operations in a socialist society. By 1928 external investments accounted for less than 1 percent of all Soviet output.

The NEP reforms were barely in place when disaster struck in 1921 and 1922. Before the incentive policies could stimulate agricultural production, crops failed widely in the 1921 harvest. The disaster stemmed in part from a summer drought in southeast Russia and in part from the peasants' reduction of sown acreage to thwart the Bolsheviks' grain requisitioning policies. In the ensuing famine, almost 5 million people died. The toll would have climbed even higher but for the extensive efforts of

Western relief agencies, including the American Relief Administration (ARA) headed by future president Herbert Hoover, a program originally set up for postwar food relief to Europe. Local citizens felt deeply grateful for the aid, although later the Soviet government tried to erase all memory of this Western humanitarianism.

After the famine, economic recovery proceeded apace, bolstered by NEP. Industrial output advanced to its prewar level by 1927, and agricultural production neared 1914 figures the following year. In this sense NEP succeeded, and many Soviet citizens felt themselves (and indeed were) better off than ever. The improved standard of living and the relaxed and comparatively free atmosphere of NEP lent this era a golden aura when measured against the turbulent and sacrificial years preceding it. Later, during Stalin's purges and World War II, many individuals would look back longingly to NEP. In the late 1980s and early 1990s as well, nostalgia for NEP revived, although only the oldest citizens could remember the period.

Yet the surface success of NEP masked deep-seated problems. In the first place, when Lenin and the Party leaders instituted its policies in 1921, they saw NEP as temporary. In articles written in January and February 1923, however, Lenin began to explore the possibility that NEP, if linked to massive expansion of peasant-producer cooperatives, might lead directly to the building of socialism. But a third stroke that led to Lenin's death in 1924 prevented his developing this alternative view of NEP. To do so, he would have had to finesse the serious ideological obstacles implicit in NEP's reinforcement: that NEP encouraged capitalist production in consumer and light industry; private trade, with its profiteers and speculators; and "petty-bourgeois" peasant use of the land. After Lenin's incapacitation, Party leaders would recognize NEP's distortions of socialism but disagreed sharply about how to modify or replace them.

Even in its effectiveness, NEP possessed deficiencies. In industry, the state was too poor to modernize plants and machinery. Economic recovery thus depended on prewar outmoded and outworn capital goods; future progress would require fresh investment. Moreover, meeting peasant demand for household goods and agricultural implements proved tricky. The newly privatized small enterprises incurred high initial costs, which they passed along as price increases. Yet prices for agricultural output rose only slowly and irregularly. Hence, as early as 1923, observers noted a small "scissors crisis," the irreversible gap between prices of manufactured goods and those of marketed crops that had plagued the tsarist and Provisional governments during the war. If the scissors were to widen, peasants would withhold grain from the market, threatening famine in the cities. Under NEP, the government could do little in response.

Agriculture labored under other difficulties as well. Peasants naturally welcomed the end of requisitioning and the restoration of a free market. Yet only a few managed to prosper under NEP. Although Lenin's land decree at the time of the Bolshevik Revolution led to expropriation of private, state, and church holdings, this acreage, once divided among innumerable peasant households, yielded a mere two-to-three-acre increase per family. Even this modest increment soon disappeared with continued population growth and the return to the villages of urban unemployed and demobilized soldiers, who demanded their share of communal land. As a result, the number of peasant family holdings rose from some 17 to 18 million in 1917 to 23 to 24 million in 1922 Moreover, by 1928–1929, although total agricultural output approached prewar levels, grain production per capita fell, as did the percentage of the harvest sent to market. These developments did not augur well for the health of Soviet agriculture nor for Party leaders, who counted on grain supplies to feed workers and to build new industry. Peasants remained distrustful of the government, even under NEP. Few joined the model state and cooperative farms that the government set up. More telling, less than one-quarter of 1 percent of the rural population enrolled in the Communist Party.

Workers also had problems with NEP, with several million out of work and underemployment widespread. The number of industrial workers had plummeted during "war communism," thus weakening the Party's mass base. As the economy recovered and jobs multiplied, private factories as well as some state enterprises that the government no longer fully subsidized tried to keep wages low in order to reduce costs and maximize profits. Moreover, many denationalized plants were run by former owners, managers, and supervisors, who, with government support, drove employees harshly and often introduced piece-rate pay to goad them to produce. Trade unions offered little help, for under government control their activities focused on raising output and productivity, not protecting the work force. Abandoned by the unions, ignored by the "proletarian" state, toiling under old bosses, lacking job security, and paid poorly, workers understandably complained, lamenting the loss of *their* revolution. As labor disputes and worker protests erupted, the Communists increasingly relied for political support not on the proletariat but on state and Party bureaucrats.

Peaceful Coexistence and World Revolution

Just as NEP retained the goal and overall structure of socialism while accommodating socioeconomic realities, so Soviet foreign policy in the early 1920s combined the longstanding Marxist-Leninist aim of worldwide proletarian revolution with traditional diplomatic and commercial intercourse with Soviet Russia's neighbors and other nonsocialist states. These dual objectives sometimes clashed, particularly when Communist

"You Have Nothing to Lose But Your Chains"
Propagandized art on the cover of the
Comintern journal showing a brawny
worker liberating the world from
capitalism's chains.

revolutionary activities undercut efforts to establish or maintain friendly
ties with a capitalist nation. Most of the time, the Soviet leadership
blithely supported subversive agitation in other countries while conducting normal relations with the very governments that it hoped to overturn. The Bolsheviks' ability to pursue this two-faced course improved
when Lenin set up the Comintern in March 1919. As an organization of
national Communist parties around the world, the Comintern claimed to
be independent of all governments. Yet it was based in Moscow and
headed by a Russian, Grigory Zinoviev. The Soviet Communist Party,
which also ran the Soviet government, controlled and largely financed
this body. Through the Comintern and agents attached to Soviet trade
and diplomatic missions, wily Soviet leaders strove to foster revolution
in nonsocialist countries. Their efforts bore little fruit, however, and after
a 1923 leftist uprising in Germany failed, dim prospects for proletarian
revolution in Europe flickered out.

In Asia, Lenin supported anticolonial movements directed against
the British, French, and Dutch empires, in September 1920 convening in
Baku the propagandistic Congress of the Toiling Peoples of the East. At
the same time, he recognized Turkey and established friendly relations
with its nationalist and reformist leader, Kemal Ataturk. In East Asia, Soviet leaders extended Russian influence into Outer Mongolia, installing a
puppet government there. (The Mongolian People's Republic would remain a Soviet ally until 1990, when it rejected socialism and gained full
independence.) Soviet Russia also abrogated tsarist treaties and special
rights regarding China. While maintaining formal relations with the

postwar Chinese government, it encouraged the fledgling Chinese Communist Party to make common cause with the forces of the nationalist revolutionary leader, Sun Yat-sen. This advice would yield disastrous results, as we shall see in Chapter 6.

Lenin justified rapprochement with nonsocialist countries, the other track of Soviet foreign policy, by his theory of peaceful coexistence. He argued that in the transition from the eruption of proletarian revolution in Russia to its inevitable worldwide triumph, the prototype socialist nation had to get along with nonsocialist states. During this era of accommodation, Soviet Russia would monitor the imperialist countries vigilantly, maneuvering among these sworn enemies to disrupt any further effort to crush the embryonic socialist state. Lenin also made clear that *peaceful* coexistence meant only the absence of armed conflict. The first socialist state, and Communists throughout the world, still had a duty to use nonviolent means—political, ideological, and economic strategies—to weaken imperialist nations. Finally, Lenin predicted that peaceful coexistence would not last forever. Ultimately, after socialism had spread and gained strength, the rivalry with imperialism would end in a series of "frightful collisions" between the two systems, from which socialism would emerge victorious.

Lenin had begun to put the concept of coexistence into practice even during the years of foreign intervention in Russia, sending the Allies a series of peace proposals in 1919 and 1920. These overtures hit their mark at the end of 1920, when the Allies lifted their blockade of Russia, Britain entered trade negotiations with the Soviet government, and the Baltic states signed nonaggression and commercial treaties with Moscow. In his effort to establish normal relations with the Western powers, Lenin nevertheless faced several obstacles. His denouncing of capitalist governments and urging of global revolution naturally put the Allies on guard. In October 1924, Soviet-British relations suffered a severe setback when the press published an alleged letter from Zinoviev detailing plans and financing for revolutionary activity in Britain. Here and on numerous other occasions, the Soviet government denied responsibility for Comintern actions and agreed duplicitously not to engage in revolutionary agitation and other subversive operations.

Lenin also had to grapple with a postwar order based on the 1919 Versailles peace settlement and its resulting League of Nations. Indeed, he viewed this organization as a concert of imperialist oppressors determined to block revolution and to sustain exploitation of European workers and colonial peoples. While decrying the Versailles conspiracy, Lenin did not hesitate to enter into normal commercial and diplomatic affiliation with key "imperialist" signatories to that treaty.

One of the Allies' demands, however, presented an obstacle to normalizing relations. France and Britain insisted that Soviet Russia take responsibility for the debts of the tsarist and Provisional governments that it had repudiated in 1917 and 1918. By pressing counterclaims for damages caused by Western intervention, the Soviet government skillfully kept the debt issue in abeyance while developing regular relations with the chief Western governments in 1924. Only the United States declined to cooperate; under the domestic pressure of anticommunism and isolationism, it would refuse to recognize Soviet Russia until 1933.

The Soviet leaders turned their attention particularly to Germany, where they hoped postwar economic hardship and the disillusionment of defeat might spark the anticipated European revolution. When the upheaval failed to materialize, Soviet Russia appealed to Germany as a fellow victim of the hated Versailles peace arrangements. Lenin and his diplomats soon seized an opportunity to establish ties with this potential ally. In April 1922, as part of the gradual thawing in relations between the West and Soviet Russia, the Allies invited a Soviet delegation to attend a conference at Genoa designed to speed the economic reconstruction of Europe. The meeting's atmosphere sharply diverged from the flamboyant revolutionary days of 1917–1918. Trotsky, in those years commissar of foreign affairs, had arrived for the Brest peace negotiations with Germany and Austria-Hungary accompanied by a symbolic people's delegation—a worker, a peasant, a soldier, a sailor, and a woman. By contrast, the Soviet diplomats at Genoa sported conservative dress and demeanor and behaved with professional propriety. Much to the annoyance of the Allies, the Soviet delegates skillfully wooed the German representatives. The two outcast countries went as far as to sign the Treaty of Rapallo, which normalized relations and strengthened trade ties between them. Their agreement would lead to secret Soviet-German cooperation in military training and weapons production, in direct defiance of the restrictions imposed on Germany by the Versailles treaty. By the mid-1920s, the strategy of peaceful coexistence seemed to be working. Soviet Russia had cultivated diplomatic and commercial connections with most countries around the globe.

Centralism Versus Federalism: The Forging of the Soviet Union

Besides adjusting the revolutionary government's relations with the outside world, Lenin had sought since 1918 to forge new links between Soviet Russia and the non-Russian areas of the former tsarist empire. After coming to power, Lenin had attempted to appeal to the minority nationalities, hoping to facilitate the extension of the socialist revolution to the borderlands. In mid-November 1917, he reiterated his promise of self-determination for nationalities, and in January 1918 he approved the Declaration of the Rights of the Toiling and Exploited Peoples. This manifesto described the revolutionary Soviet state as "a federation of Soviet national republics," even though at that time the Bolsheviks controlled only Russia. Lenin simultaneously insisted, as he had from the founding days of Bolshevism, that the Party's structure had to be centralized; there would be no national or regional parties, only territorial branches of the one and indivisible Bolshevik (later Communist) Party.

The first Soviet constitution adopted in July 1918 had largely ignored the place of non-Russians in the new state and included no provisions for a federal structure. The Soviet leaders had still to settle on a consistent policy toward the non-Russians. Yet in an effort to win over the Tatars and the Bashkirs, Stalin with Lenin's support almost immediately proposed an autonomous republic along the middle Volga River. By 1922 the Russian Soviet Republic embraced seventeen autonomous republics and national regions. Although in his commissariat of nationalities Stalin formed a council of representatives from these areas, in practice he ensured that regional authorites lacked genuine economic or political autonomy. He restricted their jurisdiction chiefly to public welfare, educational, and cultural matters.

By 1919 separate Soviet republics existed in Byelorussia (today Belarus) and Ukraine. Lenin pursued a pragmatic policy toward these states. During the strife of foreign intervention and civil war, Russian bodies like the Politburo, the Council of People's Commissars, and the Council of Labor and Defense made and implemented most political and military policy for the neighboring republics. These states were allowed, however, to conduct their own (but Soviet-directed) foreign relations and to manage some economic and local affairs. In treaties signed with these "union republics" in late 1920 and early 1921, the Soviet Russian Republic guaranteed their security and territorial integrity but with the other hand grasped control of their economic development and policies.

At about the same time, the Communists' final defeat of the Whites and the standoff with Poland left some minority groups in limbo. To be sure, the Finns, Poles, and Balts had gained full independence, and the Bessarabians (today Moldovans) had been absorbed by Romania. On the other hand, the status of the peoples of the Caucasus remained uncertain, parts of Central Asia resisted Soviet rule, and the Japanese still occupied the Pacific coast. The Soviet leaders soon found their relationship with the Caucasian states of considerable urgency. Important economically, the area supplied Russia with two-thirds of its oil needs before the war, as well as substantial amounts of manganese, copper, and lead. The Allies recognized the independence of the Caucasian states in January 1920. However, America's isolationist refusal to accept a mandate over Armenia and Lenin's decision to seek friendly relations with nationalist Turkey eliminated potential protectors of the Armenians and the peoples of Azerbaijan, respectively. These circumstances forced Caucasian leaders to strike the best bargain that they could with their looming neighbor to the north. Quarreling among themselves and struggling to build local economic strength and political support, the Caucasian governments, except for the Georgians, offered little resistance to the reimposition of Russian rule. The Soviet government, through a combination of internal subversion and external pressure, established sovereignty over the three states between 1920 and 1922.

Azerbaijan fell first in March–April 1920, as the nationalist *Mussavat* party split in the face of demands from Communist cadres in Baku and threats of invasion by the Eleventh Red Army to the north. The local government capitulated without a fight, although a rebellion later broke out in western Azerbaijan. The new Soviet authorities executed a number of nationalist leaders and installed a Communist-controlled, all-Muslim government to run the Soviet Republic of Azerbaijan.

The Armenians sealed their own fate when they rashly tried to take advantage of Turkey's defeat in World War I to push their boundaries westward into Turkish Armenia. Intermittent fighting flared in May 1919 and ended with Turkish forces defeating Armenia in the fall of 1920. To prevent Turkish occupation, the Armenian government sought aid from the Red Army and cooperated in establishing a joint nationalist-Communist government. By early 1921, the Soviet authorities had ousted and arrested the nationalists and proclaimed the Soviet Republic of Armenia.

The Georgians most staunchly resisted the renewal of Russian control. In late 1919, Georgia's Menshevik-dominated independent government suppressed a Communist uprising in Tbilisi. Undeterred, Soviet leaders began in the spring of 1920 to exert pressure on Georgia as an extension of their successful campaign to incorporate Azerbaijan. Because the Georgians vowed to stand firm, however, and because war with Poland broke out that April, the Soviet government instead signed a treaty of cooperation with the Georgian government in May 1920. Under its terms, imprisoned Georgian Communists were released, and they began preparing an assault against the Georgian government.

As commissar of nationalities, Stalin, although a Georgian by birth, bolstered centralized authority over the non-Russian peoples during the waning days of the civil war. To manage the reincorporation of Georgia, he commissioned one of his trusted aides, Sergo Ordzhonikidze, also a Georgian. Aggressive and overly optimistic, Ordzhonikidze asked the Politburo in December 1920 for permission to spark an uprising in Tbilisi and to support it by dispatching the Red Army. Until the end of the civil war, Lenin had had little time to think about nationality issues and had relinquished them almost entirely to Stalin. Now, for the first time, he began to question the direction of Stalin's policies toward non-Russian peoples. Consequently, he demurred, instructing Ordzhonikidze to work out an accommodation with the Georgians. Stalin and Ordzhonikidze instead kept badgering the Politburo, and on January 26, 1921, Lenin reluctantly agreed to their plans. He stressed, however, that the Red Army must wait for a genuine popular revolt inside Georgia before acting. Lenin perhaps had learned a lesson from the failed invasion of Poland the previous summer, when the advance of Soviet troops had served only to unite Poles in a fiercely patriotic defense of their country.

Nevertheless, Stalin and Ordzhonikidze—making a token obeisance to Lenin's wishes by inciting disorders in only one district of Georgia—called in the Red Army on February 16, 1921. Despite raging Georgian resistance, an anti-Communist outbreak in Armenia, and a Turkish attempt to seize west Georgia, the Communists finally established their rule in Georgia and set up a Soviet republic. Lenin urged that the Georgians receive special concessions, including conciliatory treatment of former Mensheviks and of nonproletarian groups such as merchants. But against bitter Georgian objections, Stalin forced through the melding of the three Caucasian republics into a new Soviet Transcausasian republic. His overall handling of the Georgian case irritated Lenin and marked the widening of a growing rift between the two Soviet leaders.

Soviet leaders soon moved to establish a new state structure known as the Union of Soviet Socialist Republics (U.S.S.R.). Formed in December 1922 and ratified in January 1924, the Union would last until 1989–1991. Its disintegration at that time becomes comprehensible in the light of the conflicting interests that complicated the creation of the Union. At one extreme stood the centralizers, including Stalin and other high-level Communist leaders, who favored a unitary state dominated by a strong central government—much like the tsarist empire. At the other extreme were the non-Communist, non-Russian nationalists in the various regions, including Georgian Mensheviks, supporters of the Ukrainian *Rada*, and others, who had created and ruled separate states during the turmoil of the revolution and civil war. In 1917 and earlier, few nationalist leaders had sought full independence, most envisaging only a degree of autonomy or federal status. But in resisting Bolshevik pressure and foreign occupation, and warming to growing nationalism among their own intelligentsia, they had moved, or had been pushed, toward asserting full sovereignty for their regions. By 1922 the Soviet government had overcome most of these separatists, and they had little say in the formation of the Soviet Union. Their striving for independence left a legacy, however, of the example and memory of freedom. As mediators between the Moscow centralists and the local nationalists, non-Russian Communists tried to blend their commitment to socialism with some protection of their people's identity, religion, and culture. Likewise, Lenin and some Russian Communists sought to balance the efficiency and control provided by centralization with the support and cooperation that some non-Russian autonomy would engender.

Because of his post as commissar of nationalities, Stalin received the Party's mandate in 1921 to draw up a new constitution. Working on a draft during the rest of that year and into 1922, Stalin faced tough opposition to his centralist position from the Georgian, Ukrainian, and some Muslim Communists, including the brilliant Tatar leader Sultan Galiev, whom the Cheka later purged as a Muslim nationalist. The Georgians bristled at Stalin's forcing them into a Transcaucasian federation and at the continuing encroachment on their political autonomy. The Ukrainian Communists resented Moscow's waiving rights promised them under the 1920 treaty with Soviet Russia and abhorred Stalin's heavy-handed treatment of them. In August 1922, Stalin presented a draft constitution that reduced the union republics to autonomous status and that emphasized the authority of the central government. Georgian and Ukrainian Communists objected, and Lenin supported them. Winning Central Committee backing, Lenin insisted on moving toward a less centralized structure, and Stalin submitted a modified draft in December 1922.

Lenin was still not entirely satisfied. As early as the Tenth Party Congress in March 1921, he had warned of the dangers of Russian chauvinism. Struggling to design a new state system, Lenin became alarmed at the incipient conflict between the nationalism evinced by loyal Communists in Georgia, Ukraine, and elsewhere and the strong Russocentric trend among top leaders. He knew that almost 80 percent of Party members were either native Russians or fully Russified minorities and that powerful currents of Russian nationalism ran within the Party. He feared that excessive centralism would not only endanger the cohesion of the new socialist society but weaken the Communist appeal in the colonial world, where nationalist and anti-imperialist sentiments burgeoned. During 1921 and 1922, as we have noted, Lenin grew increasingly disturbed by Stalin's handling of the national question. In the fall of 1922, his concern mounted when he learned that during a meeting among Stalin, Ordzhonikidze, and several leading Georgian Communists, Ordzhonikidze had struck one of the Georgians. The Soviet leader also objected to Stalin's general style of behavior and his growing power within the Party organization. In December 1922, Lenin's qualms moved him to concentrate on two related tasks: drafting the tenets of a revised nationality policy for consideration by the Twelfth Party Congress, scheduled for the spring of 1923; and organizing a documented critique of Stalin and his actions. This latter report, Lenin hoped, would persuade the congress to curtail Stalin's swelling authority and perhaps to oust him from a dominant role in the Party and government.

Pursuing the former goal, Lenin completed a memorandum that warned of the danger of Russian nationalists dominating the new state. His paper also urged linguistic, educational, and cultural autonomy for non-Russians. During January and February 1923, he continued to prepare his brief against Russocentric trends in the Party, asking Trotsky in early March to collaborate with him in presenting the case to the upcoming congress.

Concurrently, Lenin stepped up his campaign against Stalin. He dictated a secret assessment of the strengths and weaknesses of top Party leaders. Although he found fault with everyone, Lenin reserved his sternest criticism for Stalin, accusing him of rude and callous treatment of comrades and of having accumulated too much power. This document, later known as Lenin's Testament, recommended that the party curb Stalin's authority and assign him to another position. The Soviet leader also made clear to confidants that he intended to make Stalin's misbehavior over Georgia the key charge in persuading the Party to demote him. These efforts were cut off when, only three weeks before the congress, Lenin suffered a third, incapacitating stroke. Although he had asked Trotsky personally to support his two initiatives at the congress, Trotsky did nothing when the meeting convened. Neither then nor later did Trotsky satisfactorily explain his failure to act on Lenin's wishes. Perhaps he did not at that time consider Stalin's behavior a serious threat to the Party. Perhaps he believed that asserting his right to speak for the gravely ill Lenin on such sensitive issues would only provoke anger and resentment among the Party rank and file and weaken his own position as a possible successor. Had Trotsky pursued Lenin's anti-Stalin campaign, he undoubtedly would have faced considerable criticism. Yet the congress might also have respected Lenin's wishes, and Stalin's career thus would have suffered serious damage.

The constitution, embodying linguistic and cultural rights for minorities, finally won approval in July 1923, and the Congress of Soviets ratified it in January 1924. The new Union of Soviet Socialist Republics thus formally came into being. Originally, the federation included four republics: Russia, Ukraine, Belarus, and Transcaucasia. In 1922, after the Japanese withdrew from eastern Siberia, Soviet authorities established a separate Far Eastern republic there but soon incorporated it into the Russian Republic. In Central Asia, modified Soviet policies combining repression with concessions to Islam and local culture brought the *Basmachi* revolt under control during 1923 and 1924. The government folded the regions of Bukhara and Khorezm (Khiva) into the new Turkmen and Uzbek republics in 1924–1925. (See the map, U.S.S.R. 1924.) The republics of Kazakhstan, Kyrghyzstan, and Tadzhikistan were added later. In 1936 the Transcaucasian republic dissolved into Armenia, Georgia, and Azerbaijan. Under the 1924 constitution, each union republic possessed the theoretical right to secede from the Union. The Party assumed, however, that the republics would never exercise this right, for secession would not be in the best interest of their workers. The Russian Republic, known formally as the Russian Socialist Federated Soviet Republic (R.S.F.S.R.), remained by far the largest in area and population and dominated the Union politically and economically.

The governmental structure established in 1924 rested on the foundation of the old All-Russian Congress of Soviets. At the apex stood a na-

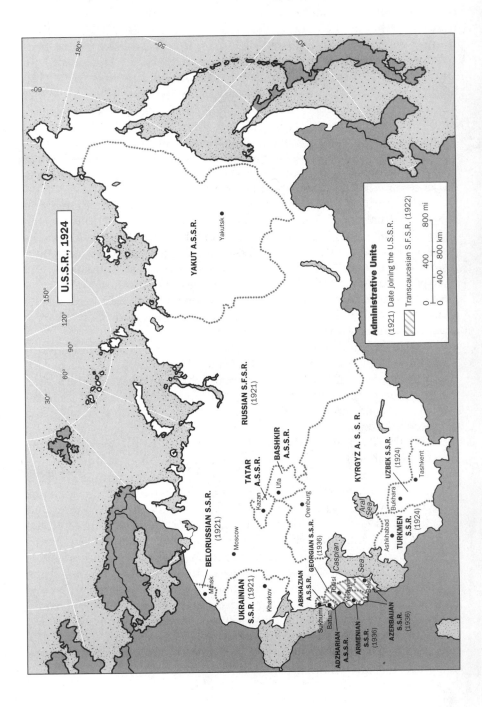

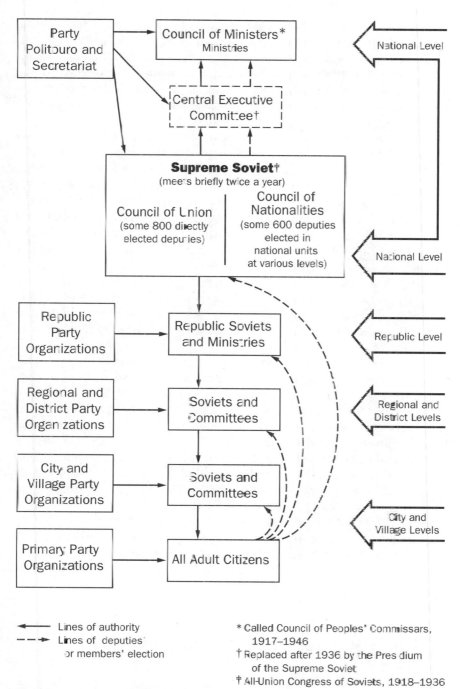

Structure of the Soviet Government

tional legislative body, the All-Union Congress of Soviets. This congress comprised the Council of the Union, representing the whole country, and the Council of Nationalities, with deputies from the constituent union republics and from autonomous republics and national regions within the Russian and other union republics. The congress elected the Central Executive Committee, which in turn chose the Council of People's Commissars, whose chair served as the nation's chief executive. The federal government controlled foreign affairs, defense, foreign trade, and transport and communications. It also set general economic and financial policy. The union republics managed local economic affairs, as well as cultural matters, education, and welfare. Each republic had its own soviet and council of commissars. Moreover, the system of soviets penetrated from the republic level down through provincial, regional, and district soviets to city, town, and village soviets. The clergy, the bourgeoisie, and other undesirables were disfranchised, and voting was indirect and unequal, with urban votes carrying five times the weight of peasant votes. In practice, real power remained in the hands of the Communists, for the pyramid of soviets had parallels at each stage in a corresponding Party heirarchy, whose leaders served in the soviets and controlled their policy and actions. (See the figure, Structure of the Soviet Government.)

Stalin took credit for the new constitution and union, comparing his achievement to that of the Red Army during the civil war. His vainglory might have been muted had he realized that the compromise worked out in 1922 and 1923 contained the seeds of destruction of the Union. By according non-Russians the right to use their own language and to develop local literature, culture, and traditions, the constitution and the official policies that upheld it provided a way for the minorities to maintain and even to enrich their identity and national solidarity, despite decades of political and economic subordination to Communist centralizers in Moscow. In fact, Soviet nationality guidelines fostered a sense of separateness in some ethnic groups who had experienced little national feeling before 1917. As we shall see in Chapter 12, when Mikhail Gorbachev loosened the bonds of censorship and centralist control after 1985, national pride and self-assertion would explode and destroy the structure erected sixty-five years earlier.

A Vision Stymied: Party and Society in the NEP Era

With external relations stabilized, the economy recovering, political opposition eliminated, and the nationality problem papered over in a federal system that masked centralized control by Russian Communists,

1923 might have been an appropriate year for Party leaders to turn to fulfilling the October Revolution's promise of a plentiful, just, and socialist society. Several obstacles, however, stood in the way. Although the Party controlled the Soviet government, its own composition and outlook were changing, and its leadership grew increasingly divided.

Traditionally, Lenin had tolerated, within reason, a considerable range of debate on Party policies. After the October Revolution, for instance, he had blocked efforts to punish Zinoviev and Kamenev or to expel them from the Party for their public opposition to the decision to take power. In March 1921, however, justifying his action with the desperate economic and political crisis confronting the Party, Lenin persuaded the Tenth Party Congress not only to approve NEP but also to condemn the Workers' Opposition. At Lenin's urging, the congress passed a resolution entitled "On Party Unity," which criticized the organization of factions within the Party and ordered "the immediate dissolution, without exception, of all groups that have been formed on the basis of some platform or other." The resolution strongly advised vigilance against factionalism and warned that violation of the unity rule would result in "unconditional and immediate expulsion from the Party." Although disagreements among Party members over policy issues recurred for several more years, the basis for suppressing all dissent within the organization was in place, a tool that Stalin would soon only too enthusiastically employ. Thus, by 1921–1922 the Party had tight control over the country, and the Bolshevik elite had won unassailable authority over the Party. Within a decade, Stalin would complete this pyramid of centralization: one individual would rule supreme over the elite, the Party, and the country.

During the summer of 1921, the leadership purged the Party rolls, slashing membership from 730,000 to 530,000. Aimed at routing careerists, adventurers, and other unworthy types, this housecleaning also strengthened the top leaders' grip on the Party. In April 1922, the Politburo named Stalin general secretary of the Party, making him the only person to serve on all three top Party bodies: the Politburo, Orgburo, and Secretariat. His new role enhanced his control over Party affairs, including personnel matters. In May 1922, Lenin suffered a stroke, perhaps an aftermath of the wounds that he had received in the 1918 attempt on his life. Although partially paralyzed, he recovered sufficiently to engage part-time in state and Party work for the next ten months. By early 1923, though, subsequent strokes had deprived the Party of Lenin's experience, intellect, and zeal. For a time a triumvirate of Stalin, Zinoviev, and Kamenev managed state and Party affairs, but Lenin's absence was keenly felt. Soon uncertainties about who would lead the Party and the country degenerated into bitter rivalries and political infighting that consumed the elite's energies through the years 1925 to 1929. These quarrels would become closely intertwined with a lengthy and crucial debate over economic strategies for moving beyond NEP. As Party leaders saw it, the

U.S.S.R. would need fresh policies to build the industrial foundation necessary for a fully socialist society.

As the Party grew more centralized and opportunities for intra-Party dissent and democracy narrowed, the organization's relationship to Soviet society also began to shift. Many industrial, service, and white-collar workers, a majority of military personnel, and some intellectuals backed the Party wholeheartedly. Yet the Party's waxing authoritarianism and its emergence as a separate ruling elite disillusioned individuals in all social strata. The majority of peasants, especially, remained largely indifferent to socialist values and goals, focusing instead on their own economic welfare and that of their families. The symbiosis between revolutionaries and urban workers that had crested in the fall of 1917 had withered in the crucible of the civil war. During the 1920s, the Party struggled, largely in vain, to overcome widespread resistance to change. A rigid, elite leadership plumped for socialism and modernization, and an intransigent and uninterested populace clung to old ways and institutions. In this silent, mainly nonviolent contest, the Party exhorted and pushed, and the obstinate masses, rarely showing open defiance, gave as little ground as possible.

In its efforts to transform Russian society, the Party also encountered major structural obstacles. The country remained underdeveloped and predominantly rural. Slightly less than 20 percent of the population lived in the cities. The economic collapse and urban depopulation during the civil war had drastically pared the Party's proletarian base. Workers totaled only 1.5 million (out of a population of some 130 million) in 1921 and by 1928 reached a mere 4.5 million. The Party thus headed and spoke for a minority class. The percentage of workers among Party members also fell, from 30 to 40 percent in 1917 to an unimpressive 18 percent in 1924. The Lenin Enrollment, a major recruitment campaign following Lenin's death, doubled Party membership to 1 million in 1926 and raised the number of members of worker origin to 39 percent in 1927. This figure was misleading, however, for a majority of these labor members held administrative or military jobs; factory-floor workers contributed only 8 to 9 percent of the total. Moreover, most new enrollees possessed less education than pre-1917 members. Some non-Party workers no longer looked to the organization to protect their interests. With 1 million unemployed, low wages, crowded housing conditions, and the unions' now cooperating with factory managers, the proletariat felt abandoned.

The Party faced other challenges beyond the dissolving of its worker connections. It struggled in particular with a shortage of skilled people, both within its ranks and throughout society. Several million of the best educated and most talented people in tsarist Russia died, were killed, or emigrated between 1914 and 1921. Even by using "bourgeois specialists," by hurriedly advancing individuals who had proven themselves in the Red Army, and by recruiting promising workers and peasants into the

Party, the leadership could not fill the gap. Despite intensive efforts to train new cadres, in 1926 less than 1 percent of Party members had completed higher education and only 8 percent, secondary education. Rougher, coarser types crowded into the organization beginning in 1924, beneath only a thin layer of the old intelligentsia leadership.

Moreover, the new 1920s Party members often had experience in military or administrative positions in the civil war and immediately after. Although many came from proletarian or peasant backgrounds, they had advanced by getting a tough job done in times of stress. They felt themselves part of a governing elite and knew nothing of revolutionary agitation, underground activity, and factory unrest. Some were careerists, but many felt a deep commitment to socialist ideals. When socialism failed to emerge full-blown and indeed collided with popular resistance, these new Party members reacted with annoyance and frustration. They wanted orders issued and problems solved, with coercion applied if necessary to obtain results. They had little patience for the slow reeducation of the masses and the nurturing of new outlooks that the peaceful building of socialism in a backward and tradition-bound society required.

Lenin, on the other hand, in his last months began to fear that the population's—especially the peasantry's—lack of culture and education threatened to block progress. As he saw it,

> [To advance toward socialism] there must be a veritable
> revolution—the entire people must go through a period of
> cultural development. . . . Without universal literacy, without a
> proper degree of efficiency, without training the population
> sufficiently to acquire the habit of bookreading, and without the
> material basis for this . . . we shall not achieve our object.[2]

Lenin called for broad education of the people, a task that he recognized would take at least a decade, as a prerequisite to creating a socialist society. Five years later, Stalin, energetic and impatient, would abandon NEP and reject a gradualist path to socialism in favor of forcibly imposing a sweeping economic and social transformation.

As the Party struggled to delineate the path to socialism, its leaders and members found much in 1920s urban society to distress them. They wanted social groups to fit neatly into Marx's clear-cut class categories— workers and capitalists. Instead, they confronted paradoxes and uncertainties. For example, workers and Party members obviously deserved priority in such vital matters as university admissions, voting, and access to housing, but should non-Party government officials, administrators,

---

[2]V. I. Lenin. "On Cooperatives" (written January 4 and 6, 1923), in Marx, Engels, Lenin, *On Communist Society: A Collection* (Moscow: Progress Publishers, 1973), p. 138.

and intelligentsia from prerevolutionary days be favored as well, because they performed crucial services? This dilemma proved particularly frustrating in the professions and sciences, where the Party leadership had to tolerate people without the correct class origin because of the desperate need for doctors, teachers, professors, and engineers.

Moreover, the old, privileged elite was gone, but a new one composed of NEP traders and entrepreneurs seemed to have replaced it. Although the number of "NEPmen" probably never rose above 500,000, to Party stalwarts they seemed to be everywhere, wheeling, dealing, and profiting. They did not hesitate to flaunt their wealth, dressing well and dining in the best restaurants. In 1922, 80 percent of retail trade lay in private hands. Through harassing regulations and the promotion of state and cooperative stores, the Soviet government reduced this figure to 40 percent by 1926. The remaining traders nevertheless served as a highly visible and deeply irritating reminder that the system still fell far short of socialism.

In addition to blurred class demarcations, the one-fifth of the population that lived in the cities often displayed markedly unsocialist behavior and attitudes. Most workers, drifting away from the Party, seemed primarily interested in economic issues that directly affected them. They

Orphans on the Loose Homeless waifs, thousands of whom roamed the streets of Soviet cities in the 1920s.

showed little inclination to take up civic responsibility and socialist values. Idle after work, they passed up political lectures and cultural events to gather at beer kiosks and workers' clubs. Alcoholism worsened after the government ended prohibition in 1924 and used its vodka monopoly to augment state revenues. Crime was common. Until the late 1920s, some 6 million orphaned and homeless children from the civil war years roamed the streets, stealing and fighting. Prostitution, which the Bolsheviks had pledged to eradicate, flourished because NEP profiteers had rubles to spend and economic destitution drove some women to whoredom. These problems coalesced to make the urban landscape a far cry from the promise of socialism.

Only the armed forces provided a strong asset for the Party, but this picture hardly reflected Marxist principles or traditional socialist goals. Instead of a people's militia replacing a professional standing army and navy, after the civil war the Red Army and Fleet, although shrinking, became permanent career services. Officers and noncommissioned men emerged in the 1920s as a separate, increasingly urbanized social stratum. Recruits came mainly from peasant backgrounds, yet they were often stationed in or near urban centers. The cities' entertainments and material opportunities enticed them to forsake village life. After basic reforms in 1923 stabilized the institutional structure and role of the armed forces, the military services functioned to socialize young men into the Soviet system and to inculcate literacy and socialist values among untrained peasants and workers. With former tsarist officers reduced to below 20 percent of the officer corps by 1923, the military leadership's prosocialist stance strengthened, and these comrades provided unwavering support of the Party throughout the NEP era.

Peasants constituted the vast majority of the Soviet Union's population: 82 percent of the total of 145 million persons in 1926. From the Bolsheviks' point of view, peasants also formed a monumental roadblock to a new socialist society. Pursuing small-scale farming with primitive, nonmechanized tools under the traditional and inefficient three-field system, they remained largely under the control of the *mir*. Most rural dwellers cared little for the modernized state or socialist agriculture that the Party insisted were necessary to support the advance toward socialism. Although Party ideologists and researchers continually tried to differentiate among rich, middle, and poor peasants, the subjects of this analysis ignored these categories and banded together against all outsiders. To be sure, under NEP a few peasants prospered, leasing land and hiring labor. The Party quickly labeled them *kulaks*, a prerevolutionary epithet for avaricious and affluent villagers. At the other extreme, however, landless and land-poor peasants subsisted by hiring themselves out, by performing artisan work, or by finding temporary jobs in the towns. The remaining bulk of the peasantry eked out a living on the land.

Beyond land reform, the socialist revolution had brought a few additional changes to the villages. Circles to eradicate illiteracy flourished, and by 1926 two-thirds of male and half of all peasants could read and write. Urged on by Lenin, the government also began the electrification of rural Russia. By the end of the 1920s, many villages boasted lights as well as radios, their first continuous link with the outside world. In many respects, however, rural life remained as socialists had always viewed it: brutish and retrograde. Peasants had few modern amenities and clung steadfastly to old traditions. Party attacks on religion and on the Orthodox Church did little to erode the central role of religious observations in the village. Peasants scorned efforts to replace Christmas and other sacred festivals with socialist rites. One Russian writer satirized the so-called Red Wedding, an attempt by Party activists to spruce up civil marriage, by citing the vow exchanged by bride and groom: the officiator asks,

Let There Be Light! Amazed peasants switch on the first light in a village during the Bolsheviks' electrification campaign in the 1920s.

Do you promise to follow the path of Communism as bravely as
you are now opposing the church and the old people's customs?
Are you going to make your children serve as Young Pioneers,
educate them, introduce scientific farming methods, and fight
for the world revolution? Then in the name of our leader,
Comrade Lenin, I declare the Red Marriage completed.[3]

Besides the important ceremonies of baptism, marriage, and burial, peasants eagerly anticipated the many religious holidays, saints' days, and
other Christian observances and seasons that studded the calendar. Each
holiday gave rural dwellers a day off and cause to celebrate by feasting
and drinking, the latter usually to excess and often with violent consequences. Indeed, during the four-day Easter holiday in 1926, the police of
Tver province logged 286 instances of hooliganism; 207 minor brawls
(without weapons); 31 severe and 749 minor injuries; 45 cases of slander;
111 cases of theft, bootlegging, and rape; 46 cases of manslaughter; and
355 arrests.[4] The Party had little success in orienting peasants in a more
socialist, or cultured, direction.

The persistence of religious practices and beliefs among the peasantry reflected one aspect of the failure of the Party's antireligion campaign. Although much weakened, the Orthodox Church and other
organized religious institutions survived. Consistent with the views of
Marx and Engels, Lenin thought religion dangerous because it misled
people and obscured their ability to find the true socialist path: "Religion
teaches those who toil in poverty all their lives to be resigned and patient
in this world and consoles them in the hope of reward in heaven." However, once in power, the pragmatic Lenin moved only cautiously against
religious institutions in Russia. After nationalizing church property, banning religious teaching, and separating church from state in January
1918, he avoided closing churches or abolishing religion by decree. The
1918 constitution included a provision guaranteeing freedom of both religious and antireligious propaganda, and Lenin warned that it was more
politic to educate than to persecute believers. Although the Soviet government and the Cheka took harsh action against church officials and
clergy who supported the Whites in the civil war, Party leaders eschewed
a vendetta against the organized faiths and permitted church worship to
continue as a private, nonsubsidized affair.

During the early 1920s, the Party and government stepped up pro-

---

[3]Quoted in Stites, *The Women's Liberation Movement*, 364.

[4]Cited in Helmut Altrichter, "Insoluble Conflicts: Village Life Between Revolution
and Collectivization," *Russia in the Era of NEP*, eds. Sheila Fitzpatrick, Alexander
Rabinowitch, and Richard Stites (Bloomington, Ind.: Indiana Univ. Press, 1991),
p. 198.

paganda attacks on Orthodoxy in particular, forming an antireligious public organization later called the League of the Godless, which published atheistic tracts. The Party also converted churches it closed or seized into museums of antireligion. In addition, Soviet leaders took advantage of a developing split in the Orthodox Church. Beginning early in the twentieth century, a reform movement had sprung up in the church led by younger clergy and by a few intellectuals, including former Marxists, who became active in church affairs. The war cut short this effort to revitalize Orthodoxy. In 1917, however, when the Provisional Government permitted the calling of the first All-Russian Orthodox Sobor (council) since 1681, representatives of the dissident movement attended and pressed their case for renewal. The Sobor elected Tikhon as patriarch, or head of the church, the first such official since Peter the Great had abolished the position over three hundred years earlier. A controversial figure, Tikhon was conservative but not reactionary and did his best to preserve the church in the gathering firestorm of revolution and civil war.

Opposing the Bolsheviks' religious policy, Tikhon in January 1918 publicly criticized the Soviet government and in March 1918 the Brest-Litovsk treaty. Later in 1918, he charged the Bolsheviks with suppressing basic rights and freedoms and even dared to excommunicate some Communist leaders and active participants in the antireligion movement. The government responded by placing him under house arrest. As the Red Terror spread, twenty-eight bishops were executed and hundreds of clergy killed or imprisoned. In September 1919, Patriarch Tikhon tried to insulate the church from further damage, declaring that clergy would disassociate themselves from all political activity and that parishioners could act in accordance with individual conscience without regard to religious obligations. At the same time, he refused to condone clergy who had joined the ranks of the Whites.

Tikhon's effort to establish an uneasy coexistence with Soviet rule foundered in 1921 and 1922, however, when he resolutely opposed government attempts to confiscate and sell all church treasures, including those used for the sacraments, the proceeds of which would go to famine victims. In May 1922 he was arrested, and the government turned to supporting the reform group inside Orthodoxy. These "renovationists," also known as the Living Church, favored democratization of the church's structure, less authority for bishops and monks, modernization of the services, and use of Russian instead of the old language, Church Slavonic, in the liturgy. Some reformers also had socialist leanings and supported the Soviet government. In 1922 and 1923, the Orthodox Church split, with thirty-six bishops supporting Patriarch Tikhon, thirty-seven the Living Church, and twenty-four undecided. About one-third of the parishes fell under the renovationists' domain.

In 1925 Tikhon died. One of his assistants, Metropolitan Sergei, although lacking ecclesiastical sanction to lead the church, soon became its de facto head. In June 1926 Sergei, supported by a number of bishops, called for reconciliation with the government. A year later, he in essence capitulated to Soviet rule and acknowledged the subservience of the church to the state. Recently published evidence suggests that Sergei acted under heavy pressure from the OGPU, as the secret police was then known. Now in control of the established or Patriarchal Church, the Soviet government withdrew its support for the Living Church, which nevertheless would persist into the late 1940s, to the irritation of the authorities. Although the 1920s witnessed the subordination of the Orthodox Church (and soon thereafter other faiths) to the government and Party, religious belief and practice endured, a distinctly unsocialist feature of the new society.

Unlike the clergy, many women benefited from the new revolutionary order and hence welcomed it. But like religious belief, longstanding attitudes toward women persisted despite Soviet agitation supporting change. Bolshevik policies regarding women frightened many members of both sexes, who feared an erosion of family and traditional values. Women nevertheless made great gains after 1917. New laws and decrees guaranteed them equal rights with men. Legally, Soviet women could no longer be discriminated against in any way. In practice they obtained complete civic equality: women could vote and hold office, express themselves freely, own property, and receive equal treatment in the courts. They also enjoyed full access to education and to social benefits in the Soviet system. Women flooded into secondary schools and universities, soon making up half or more of the students. These major advances occurred well before women won similar rights in Western societies.

The revolution and the early NEP years also saw a raising of women's consciousness in all sectors of society, particularly among young urban women. Encouraged to develop their talents and potential and free to acquire secondary and higher education, many Soviet women embarked on busy and fruitful careers in all fields. The Party stimulated and supported women's independence, not only legally but organizationally through institutions known as *zhenotdels*. These commissions on women's affairs were attached to Party bodies at all levels, from the Secretariat at the top down through republic, district, city, and sometimes even village committees. In accordance with prerevolutionary policy, Party leaders considered the drive for women's rights an ingredient of the larger struggle to build socialism. The *zhenotdel*, therefore, was not to seek separate goals or to act independently but rather to work closely with other Party organizations and to support the common aim of ending all exploitation and injustice in Soviet society.

In fact, the *zhenotdels* were almost entirely staffed by women. Directing their agitational and educational efforts almost exclusively toward women, they worked to improve policies and institutions, such as maternity leave, health services, and day-care facilities, that interested women especially. *Zhenotdels* scored their greatest success in urban areas, but they also strove to arouse peasant women to assert their rights through publications and through direct visits to villages and even to Muslim communities in Central Asia. Apart from certain specific improvements, the impact of the *zhenotdels* remains hard to measure. Memoirs, fiction, and contemporary reports, however, strongly suggest that these bodies inspired many women to take charge of their own lives and to become involved in civic, organizational, and professional activity that they would never have dreamed of before. Despite their useful role, *zhenotdels* were abolished in 1930 as the Party concentrated on industrialization.

Against these achievements for Soviet women, we must balance at least three significant areas of inequality and failure. Although they obtained full political rights, women possessed little real political power. The most prominent women in the Party were Alexandra Kollontai, Inessa Armand, and Nadezhda Krupskaya, Lenin's wife and an active revolutionary in her own right. Lenin considered Armand, who helped to found and who successfully led the central *zhenotdel* in Moscow, exceptionally able, but she died in 1920. Her successor Kollontai became a

Standing Up for Women's Rights Nadezhda Krupskaya, Lenin's widow, with a group of Russian and Central Asian women. The Party's *zhenotdels* strove to improve the lot of such women.

leader in the out-of-favor Workers' Opposition and as punishment was relegated to a minor diplomatic post in Norway in 1922. She later became the Soviet ambassador to Sweden. Subsequent *zhenotdei* directors had less standing in the Party. Krupskaya, who never liked Party politics, continued to play an important policy and organizational role in educational and cultural affairs even after Lenin's death in 1924 but exerted less and less influence as Stalin rose to power. In short, after the first years of Soviet rule, few women would hold important positions in either the Party or the government until the 1950s. Moreover, women were severely underrepresented on most lower Party bodies and in the key position of Party secretary at various levels.

Economic inequality remained another problem for women. Legally, they had access to all professions and jobs and, legally, merited equal wages for equal work. In practice, economic conditions and discrimination by men in the 1920s exacerbated unemployment and low wages for women. These factors also almost entirely shut women out of certain fields. In the NEP era, socialist goals and values and the necessity for women to support themselves or to contribute to the family budget drew increasing numbers into the workplace. But the lack of jobs and the competition of surplus population (including many young females) pouring into the cities from the countryside left many women without work, often grappling with desperate circumstances. Few women rose to top management positions in any fields.

Finally, the effort to inculcate new mores of independence and equality among women frequently failed, especially among older women, peasant women, and women with strong religious or traditional values. These women feared that the modern norms and policies threatened the cohesiveness of the family, as well as the mother's role in child-rearing and the moral tenets they esteemed. They rejected the sexual liberation, public nurseries, and communal living that some radical socialist women espoused. In particular, traditional women pointed out the damage done by the laws legalizing abortion and making divorce easy. These changes, they believed, encouraged sexual licentiousness and cavalier attitudes toward marriage. Equally dire, the laws gave rise to irresponsible husbands who failed to support current or former wives and offspring, and resulted in abandoned and homeless children. In part they were right, although the widely discussed sexual revolution affected primarily young people. The shift also had more to do with some women's rejection of continued patriarchal attitudes among Soviet men and a general relaxation of standards in reaction to the civil war era than with socialist doctrine or changes in family law. On balance, the rights granted to women provided the basis for a radical restructuring of social relations and set an example for nonsocialist countries. Yet traditional attitudes and values persisted, and Soviet leaders in the NEP years could not eliminate economic and political discrimination against women.

The 1920s: The
Transitional Decade?

What is the place of the New Economic Policy (NEP) and the 1920s in Soviet history? Must we understand this era primarily as a transitional period from the early years of Bolshevism to the mature Stalinism of the 1930s? Or is the concept of "transition," of Russia's moving seamlessly from the end of the civil war to the onslaught of forced industrialization and collectivization, too one dimensional, too deterministic? As American scholar Stephen Cohen mused at the start of the Gorbachev years: history studied without reference to lost causes or lapsed alternatives implies that what happened— in this instance, unparalled violence as an instrument of industrial growth—had to happen (*Rethinking the Soviet Experience,* 1985). And even if we accept a certain probability to the turn of events in 1929 and thereafter, Cohen's admonishments notwithstanding, what exactly does the term *transition* mean? Shall it refer only to the transition within the Bolshevik Party in the years between Lenin and Stalin, or more broadly, within Soviet culture as a whole? And if the latter, how did culture and politics interact with one another in this pivotal decade?

That the 1920s proved a critical era in Soviety history seems beyond dispute if we measure the volume of historical research or the intensity of scholarly debate that the decade has stimulated. With the possible exception of the Gorbachev years, no other period of Soviet history has attracted more attention than this one. For years, historians defined the decade as a "breathing space" between the violent upheavals of 1917 to 1921 and the Stalin revolution of the 1930s. Assessments centered on high politics and the degree to which Stalin's rule emerged as either an inevitable by-product of the NEP or a profound perversion of Bolshevik values. Then new voices appeared, led by Stephen Cohen, whose biography of NEP proponent Nikolai Bukharin garnered wide acclaim. Cohen saw the NEP as a workable alternative to the rigors of war communism and the horrors of Stalinism. More pragmatic than Trotsky's final prescription, Bukharin's moderate policies supplied a sensible option for the Soviet Union's development. The NEP was not a "breathing space" but a permanent model for the achievement of socialism by evolutionary means (*Bukharin and the Bolshevik Revolution,* 1973).

In the 1980s, the so-called Bukharin alternative to Stalin appealed to both Western academics and to Moscow politicians. Scholarship spilled over into real life, as Gorbachev's efforts to jump-start the Soviet economy featured measures reminiscent of the NEP, including the privatization of small business ventures. With the demise of the Soviet Union, even Bukharin's moderate socialism was jettisoned. Martin Malia cautioned that lionizing of the NEP came at a cost of ignoring not only the dominance of the Party over the economy "but the communists' ambition to socialize . . . all aspects of life" ("From Under the Rubble, What?" in *Problems of Communism,* January–April, 1992).

As provocative as these discussions were, other writers insisted that more fundamental developments than battles at the top over policy and ideology shaped Soviet society in the 1920s. By the end of the 1980s, a second group of revisionists, so named because they took social (as opposed to political or intellectual) history as the proper object of study, presented another argument. In the words of William Rosenberg, "Political issues [in the 1920s] were remote from day-to-day matters with which millions of ordinary Russians were concerned" ("Understanding NEP Society and Culture in the Light of New Research," in *Russia in the Era of NEP,* 1991).

The social historians concluded that the state's agenda in the 1920s fundamentally contrasted with the values of wide segments of society. For "ordinary Russians," traditional attitudes and relationships remained paramount in their daily lives, with ominous implications for a leadership passionately committed to building a modern polity. The tension between cultural realities and political aspirations surfaced dramatically in education, where the Commissariat of Enlightenment (*Narkompros*) quickly discovered that its dream of making schools the agents of grand social change clashed with the one group on which everything depended—the teachers. Whether out of habit, lack of resources, low pay, or confusion over the "progressive" curriculum rained down from Moscow on their heads, teachers dug in their heels. As Larry Holmes, chronicler of this episode, notes: during the 1920s, teachers "consistently demonstrated the folly of policies that were far in advance of the ability of people to accept them' (*The Kremlin and the Schoolhouse*, 1991)

The issue of NEP as a "transitional" period was not laid to rest, however, even for revisionist scholars. In 1991 a major work appeared that posed the question anew: could social or cultural history really be divorced from the decade's better known political wars? *Russia in the Era of NEP* was the fruit of fresh research into every corner of Soviet life. Two overarching themes emerged from the study: weak or nonexistent mechanisms of control (police, militia) to build a revolutionary order in the countryside, *and* a society still anchored in numerous ways to pre-1917 customs. Neil Weissman, for example, showed that NEP Russia lacked a police force adequate to the tasks at hand in spite of early hopes to construct "a responsible apparatus, capable of winning popular assent through patient work over time." Poorly trained and underpaid, local law enforcers soon lapsed into arbitrary methods that resembled those of their hated tsarist predecessors. The resulting antagonism further isolated the peasantry from a regime already distrustful of Russia's largest class ("Policing the NEP Countryside," in *Russia in the Era of NEP*).

Examining women's issues, Wendy Goldman also discovered the persistence of traditional values. Even among working women, theoretically a key social bastion of the young revolutionary state, socialist ideals—especially the notion of free union between the sexes—ran aground on the rocks of high unemployment, miserable wages, and the persistence of customary attitudes toward marriage and the family. Women quickly realized that "freedom was not an abstract concept," but a function of the "harsh material realities of everyday life." Rejection of the new patterns of male-female relationships soon followed ("Working-Class Women and the 'Withering Away' of the Family: Popular Responses to Family Policy,' in *Russia in the Era of NEP*).

How could these "older" values, as exemplified by teachers and female workers, be made to work in the socialist order? If, as recent research in social history suggests, NEP culture ran backward to traditional behaviors rather than forward to "modern" patterns stipulated by the Bolsheviks as integral to a new society, what did the future hold? From a scholarly perspective, can a cultural survey of the 1920s be left at asking this question, or must it lead inescapably to considerations of politics and the political process? Several contributors to the NEP volume believed that politics should be omitted from the analysis because, in the words of Sheila Fitzpatrick, "political questions had been run into the ground." William Rosenberg dissented. What, he asked, if Russia's transition to socialism necessitated the "inculcation of more or less uniform" beliefs? What, however (we might further add), if the implantation of new beliefs was rendered even less likely by the absence of enforcement mechanisms in the countryside? Perhaps, then, in Rosenberg's words, "the brutal authoritarianism which accompanied Stalin's revolution from above after 1920 was connected to the party's failure under NEP to develop broad support . . . for the 'modernizing' tasks at hand."

Diversity and Control: Culture in the 1920s

Concertgoers, unaware that the performance that they had come to attend was advertised as "revolutionary," were puzzled when they entered Moscow's Hall of Columns one evening in early 1922 to find the musicians sitting in a large semicircle facing each other. Several players even had their backs to the audience. Even more astonishing, the orchestra gave a polished performance—without a conductor. Thus was born Moscow's First Symphonic Orchestra Without a Conductor, which put on concerts regularly until it disbanded in 1932.

This orchestra strikingly exemplified the idealistic projects and utopian dreams that typified Soviet culture during the 1920s. The undertaking reflected the genuine commitment of its organizer, Lev Tseitlin, a talented violinist and concertmaster, and of its seventy players to end oppression in the workplace. The group also sought to share equally in all decisions and activity and to encourage maximum participation of each individual in creative labor. They agreed that "an orchestra was not 'a lifeless machine' that the conductor could play like an instrument, as a pianist plays a piano. Rather, it was a community of players, democratic, socialist, and egalitarian." The musicians hoped to provide a "utopia in miniature and a model workshop for the communist future."

Each orchestra member helped to choose the repertoire, and all received the same pay. Each player learned the whole score, so that together they could decide how the piece should be played and how best to rehearse it. Because the musicians drawn to this experiment possessed exceptional talent, they put on concerts of high quality, performing classical pieces as well as revolutionary works that aimed to reflect the rhythms and sounds of machines and industrial production. The First Symphonic Orchestra Without a Conductor played not only in concert halls but in factories, workers' clubs, and military barracks. By 1928 the Soviet Union boasted eleven conductorless orchestras, and several such ensembles modeled on the original Moscow group had sprung up abroad. This bold experiment in egalitarian and participatory labor would disappear in the 1930s under the harsh conformity of Stalinism, as would most such revolutionary utopias.

Fired by the idealistic enthusiasm of the 1920s, Soviet citizens explored innovative ideas not just at work but in living arrangements as well. Long before hippie communes dotted rural America in the 1960s and 1970s, Russians tried communal residences in their cities and countryside. One of the best known, the Automotive Works of Moscow Commune (the A.M.O. Commune, by its Russian initials), evolved out of a 1928 joint vacation taken by six men and four women workers from the car factory. By 1930 the group, expanded to sixty, had taken over two floors of an apartment building.

All for Reading and Writing A poster equating illiteracy with blindness used in the Bolsheviks' 1920s literacy crusade.

The A.M.O. Commune members strove to develop a true socialist mentality and to rid themselves of selfish and petty interests. Amazingly, they shared their earnings equally, even though individual wages ranged from 25 to 200 rubles a month. They all took turns doing housework, and in an inspired gesture, the musically talented among them formed a string ensemble that played soothing airs while others ironed the wash. As a group, the commune members attended concerts, the theater, and political meetings, or conducted readings and discussions at home. Those who married outside the commune could invite their spouses in, but no accounts of the A.M.O. Commune reveal the pattern of sexual relations within the group. Like conductorless orchestras, the communes would not survive the regimentation that Stalin imposed on Soviet society in the 1930s. They nevertheless reflected the revolutionary spirit of hope and concern for a better life that many Soviet citizens carried into the 1920s.[5]

That dedication took concrete form in the acceleration under NEP of widespread efforts to eradicate illiteracy and to introduce universal compulsory coeducation. Schools for workers attached to universities

---

[5]This account of the First Symphonic Orchestra Without a Conductor and of the A.M.O. Commune is based on Richard Stites, *Revolutionary Dreams: Utopian Vision and Experimental Life in the Russian Revolution* (New York: Oxford Univ. Press, 1989), pp. 135–140 and 216–217, respectively.

(*rabfaks*) and tutorials or circles to spread literacy (*likbezy*) reduced illiteracy from 70 percent in 1897 to less than 35 percent by the end of the 1920s. Elementary education also progressed, with almost all urban children enrolled in the primary grades by 1929, and opportunities in secondary and higher education expanded. Soviet officials continued to emphasize polytechnical and socially oriented education, together with approaches that paralleled American educator John Dewey's focus on "the whole child." Nevertheless, traditional pedagogy also endured. Schools became instruments to instill socialist goals and values in the new generation, although the Party did not impose narrow conformity in education during NEP. In 1922 the Party established two youth organizations—the Octobrists and the Pioneers—to offer extracurricular activities for children and to assist in socializing young people into the Soviet system. From the Pioneers, a youngster could enter the *Komsomol*, or Communist League of Youth, whose members served as adjuncts of the Communist Party from age seventeen into their early thirties. These young people stirred political agitation, undertook socially useful projects such as planting trees along urban thoroughfares, and modeled standards of socialist behavior and work.

In cultural life, too, the NEP era witnessed remarkable diversity of literary and artistic activity, and a range of approaches, forms, and views. The revolutionary modernists so prominent in the arts after the revolution continued to play an important role in the 1920s. Vladimir Mayakovsky, one of their leaders, nevertheless had limited success with his movement and journal *LEF* (*Left Front of Art*). Radical "proletarian" intellectuals assailed his efforts as insufficiently revolutionary, whereas noncommunist writers and critics derided *LEF* as propagandistic pap. A plethora of literary and artistic schools sprouted, assisted in the beginning by government toleration of private and cooperative publishing houses and journals. One of the most influential groups, the Serapion Brotherhood, insisted that it had no common platform or purpose; each writer had the freedom to advocate individualistic literary or political ideals. The Brotherhood supported nonconformist creativity unencumbered by ideology and urged authors to pursue their own artistic visions. Evgeny Zamiatin, a member of the group, published abroad *We*, his satire of a future totalitarian society. The work foreshadowed later nightmares of "utopian" control such as George Orwell's *1984* and Aldous Huxley's *Brave New World*. In Zamiatin's well-ordered paradise, citizens have no names, only numbers, and protagonist D-503, like everyone else, submits to a completely regimented routine. He muses,

> I have had opportunity to read and hear many improbable
> things about those times when human beings still lived in the
> state of freedom, that is, in an unorganized, primitive state. . . .

How could a government, even a primitive government, permit people to live without anything like our Tables—without compulsory walks, without precise regulation of the time to eat, for instance? They would get up and go to bed whenever they liked![6]

During most of the 1920s, fiction gained popularity, although Mayakovsky, Boris Pasternak, Sergei Yesenin, and others continued to publish occasional poems. Well-enacted novels came from the pens of members of the Serapion Brotherhood and from other independent authors. Boris Pilnyak's *The Naked Year* linked revolutionary events with indigenous traditions. Leonid Leonov's *The Thief*, a powerful psychological study of an embittered revolutionary, sharply delineated NEP social conditions. Isaac Babel's at once lyrical and horrifying work *Red Cavalry* offered vignettes of the civil war. The Party tolerated these authors, even though they were not Communist idealists. Trotsky labeled them "fellow-travelers" on the road to socialism (a term originally without the pejorative connotations that U.S. Senator Joseph McCarthy would give it in his witch hunt for Communists in America in the 1950s). The Party also did not object to artistic contacts with the West. Soviet intellectuals remained closely connected with their European counterparts, traveling back and forth, publishing and exhibiting their works in Europe, and importing the latest literature and information from the capitalist countries.

A number of more fervently Communist-oriented groups disapproved of the "fellow-travelers" and avidly backed pure "proletarian" art. Among these organizations, "On Guard" wielded the most influence. The On Guardists denounced petty-bourgeois individualism and modernist techniques and glorified the masses in their works. Yet in their best efforts, they, too, depicted the dilemma of individuals wrestling with the adjustment to the revolutionary order. "Proletarian" writers often focused on recent historical events, as in two graphic and extremely readable novels about the civil war, Dmitri Furmanov's *Chapayev* and Mikhail Sholokhov's *The Quiet Don*. These works are still useful to students of history seeking to understand the atmosphere of the era. Both novels, although underscoring the inevitability and certainty of the revolutionary triumph of the people, revolve around complex individuals. Furmanov offers the controversial partisan leader Chapayev and his political commissar Klychkov. Sholokhov's novel features Grigor Melekhov, an adventurous Don Cossack torn by conflicting loyalties to both Reds and Whites.

Still a delight for readers, satirists Ilia Ilf and Evgeny Petrov poked

---

[6]Eugene Zamiatin, *We*, trans. by Gregory Zilboorg (New York: Penguin, 1991), 13.

fun at contemporary Soviet life through the misadventures of aspiring millionaire and con artist Ostap Bender in *Twelve Chairs* and *The Little Golden Calf*. In 1936 the two writers published an account of a trip to the United States entitled *Little Golden America*, which is full of whimsical insights into American mores and society. Mikhail Zoshchenko wrote biting and pensive short stories about human foibles in the Soviet setting.

Depressed and tired of battling literary opponents and Soviet officials, Mayakovsky committed suicide in 1930, not long after writing *The Bedbug* and *The Bath*, two satirical plays ridiculing the philistinism and bureaucracy that he saw enveloping Soviet society. In *The Bedbug*, Prisypkin, a typical Soviet proletarian of the twenties more interested in tobacco, vodka, petty-bourgeois baubles, and a good time than in production goals and socialist self-sacrifice, is accidentally frozen in a block of ice. Discovered and thawed out fifty years later in the perfect Communist society of the future, he quickly reveals his unsocialist behavior and characteristics. Authorities cage him for the edification of the public, who can study this odd "specimen" at the zoo. At then end of the play, the zookeeper releases Prisypkin, who, bewildered but interested, walks to the front of the stage, peers out at the audience, and expresses his delight at seeing people like himself.

> Citizens! Brothers! My own people! Darlings! How did you get here? So many of you! When were you unfrozen? Why am I

Mayakovsky Pokes Fun at Soviet Society A scene from *The Bedbug*, Vladimir Mayakovsky's play, showing the bourgeois-infected protagonist, Prisypkin, in his cage.

alone in the cage? Darlings, friends, come and join me! Why should I alone suffer? Citizens![7]

Playgoers and readers enjoyed humor and satire, but the public particularly favored so-called Red detective stories, mystery and adventure yarns with a Communist slant. In Marietta Shaginyan's *Mess-Mend, or a Yankee in Petrograd*, serialized during 1923 through 1925 under the pseudonym Jim Dollar, virtuous heroes foil capitalist villains. The chases, escapes, and murder mesmerized Soviet readers. The novel even contained a science-fiction subtheme, as Mick Thingmaster employs technological wizardry to subdue his adversaries. The most popular science-fiction writer, Alex Belyaev, set his *Amphibian* in the tropics, where the hero lives in a technological underwater Eden and outmaneuvers sly imperialist businessmen ashore. Soviet audiences also appreciated American authors Upton Sinclair and Jack London, as well as the Russian classics of the nineteenth century.

In addition to literature, theater and film both catered to popular tastes and showed particular diversity and creativity under NEP. The director/producers Vsevolod Meyerhold and Evgeny Vakhtangov experimented with new forms, staging, and techniques in presenting contemporary dramas, historical plays, and the classics. By discarding the curtain and footlights and by sending actors into the theater itself, they brought the performance more directly to the audience. They also developed acting styles that stressed discipline and mechanical movement, and they explored innovative set and costume designs. In the cinema, Sergei Eisenstein was joined by other experimental directors such as Vsevolod Pudovkin and Alexander Dovzhenko. Brilliantly using the new technique of montage (short, juxtaposed scenes) and employing innovative lighting and camera angles, they made powerful films that glorified the masses and the modern machine. Not as popular with Soviet audiences as Charlie Chaplin's comedies or Western action epics such as *Tarzan, The Mark of Zorro*, and *The Thief of Baghdad*, these films nonetheless influenced modern cinematography.

Although contending artistic groups regularly appealed to the Party for support, often with demands to suppress their opponents, Lenin and for a time his successors refused to impose an artistic orthodoxy. In a Central Committee decree of June 1925, the Party first voiced warm support to the "proletarian" writers but then called for toleration of the old cultural heritage and of "fellow-travelers." The decree concluded that "the Party should, therefore, encourage the free competition of various

---

[7]V. Mayakovsky, *The Bedbug and Selected Poetry*, trans. Max Hayward and George Reavey, ed. Patricia Blake (Bloomington, Ind.: Indiana Univ. Press, 1975), p 302.

groups and tendencies in any given field" and not permit a cultural monopoly by any one group.

In contrast to this license for relative creative freedom, during the 1920s the Party tightened censorship. Gradually closing down private journals and publishers, it placed loyal Communists on the editorial boards of periodicals and literary associations and established a monopoly over radios, films, and newspapers. Concurrently, Soviet leaders increasingly centralized decision making on cultural matters in Moscow. This creeping control of intellectual and artistic life expanded the Soviet state's authority and narrowed individual freedom, a process that the American critic Katerina Clark has perceptively called "a quiet revolution." This trend reflected the preference of some younger Party members and cultural commissars for a more authoritarian organization of Soviet society.

Equally important, younger, more compliant writers, critics, and artists supplanted the prewar and the revolutionary intelligentsia in positions of intellectual prominence and cultural control. Many of these newcomers would dominate Soviet culture until the 1960s or 1970s. By the end of the 1920s, although intellectual life retained some diversity, state control was well advanced. The groundwork had been laid for Stalin's imposition of total Party domination of Soviet culture.

Conclusion

The Kronstadt revolt threw into bold relief the bankruptcy of the Soviet government's early policies of "war communism" and regimentation. In turning a deaf ear to the Kronstadters' demands and forcibly suppressing the uprising, Lenin underscored the Party's determination to retain its monopoly of power and to muffle free expression and participatory democracy in Soviet Russia. Yet the end of the civil war also stirred utopian hopes and revolutionary dreams among many Soviet citizens. The adoption of NEP in 1921 signified that Bolshevik leaders intended to defer, but not to abandon, these aspirations. Ironically, economic changes, although they gave the era its name, proved the least significant aspect of the NEP years. The temporary retreat to partial capitalism restored the ravaged economy but accomplished little in advancing the country toward socialism, creating an ideological and policy dilemma for Lenin's successors. Although the dying Lenin toyed with the idea that NEP plus cooperative farming might pave the way to socialism, most Party leaders feared that the expedient policies were producing a distinctly unsocialist economy and society. They also soon realized that NEP contained limits beyond which Soviet industry and agriculture could not grow without major investment, modern technology, and substantial restructuring. The socialist future they all sought required hard choices.

In most political and some social respects, however, the NEP years were more than a transition period. They firmly established basic characteristics of the Soviet system that would endure for the next sixty years. The duality of foreign policy, simultaneously promoting world revolution and peaceful coexistence with imperialism, clearly emerged in 1920. Although the weight given each objective would shift with changes in external and internal circumstances, the overall framework would persist unaltered in succeeding decades. The bogey of renewed attacks on the nascent socialist state by the encircling imperialist powers also became a recurrent theme justifying Party control and direction of society.

Similarly, the network of soviets and the federal system created in 1924 formed the fundamental structure of the Soviet government and state. This configuration would last into the late 1980s despite minor adjustments made in the Constitution of 1936. Finally, the pattern of political power that gelled at the start of the NEP era—a one-party dictatorship over the country and an elite leadership running both the Party and the country through an ever-expanding bureaucracy—prevailed for over half a century, albeit intensified and extended under Stalin.

But it is the complexity of the social relations of the 1920s that have increasingly intrigued historians in recent years. As with so many other countries in the twentieth century, Soviet society evolved rapidly as it confronted advancing technology, a burst of literacy and education, new ideas and values, and the demands for progress generated by a modernizing elite. NEP neither advantaged nor savaged workers, but the proletariat clearly lost the pride of place that the revolution and civil war had bestowed on them. Women made progress but faced serious obstacles as well. Artists and writers worked in comparative freedom and produced some fine novels, films, and plays, providing in some cases an innovative example to the West. Yet the Party inexorably extended its grip on cultural life. It also completely subjugated the Orthodox Church, although failing to stamp out religion. Peasants, still the bulk of the nation, remained for the most part economically and socially backward, resistant to change, and insulated from the rest of society. They formed a formidable barrier to progress toward either socialism or modernization. By the mid-1920s, Soviet leaders recognized the imperative need to reform and enlarge the economy and to bring the population abreast of the advanced industrial societies of the West and Japan. The instrument to effect this looming revolution—the Communist Party—lay at hand. The ruling elite generally agreed on what the nation required. The burning issue centered on how to proceed, and this question would split the leadership and boost Joseph Stalin to power.

FURTHER READING

No comprehensive history of NEP exists. Helpful introductions are *Russia in the Era of NEP*, eds. Sheila Fitzpatrick, Alexander Rabinowitch, and Richard Stites (Bloomington, Ind., 1991), with articles on class, workers, trade, culture, and social issues; Roger Pethybridge, *One Step Backward, Two Steps Forward: Soviet Society and Politics in the NEP* (New York, 1990); and Lewis Siegelbaum, *Soviet State and Society Between Revolutions, 1918–1929* (New York, 1992).

For Stalin and the political history of the period, the last half of Robert C. Tucker, *Stalin as Revolutionary, 1879–1929* (New York, 1973), provides excellent coverage. Important biographies of Trotsky are Isaac Deutscher, *The Prophet Unarmed: Trotsky, 1921–1929* (Oxford, 1951), and Irving Howe, *Leon Trotsky* (New York, 1978). Bukharin is admirably served by Stephen Cohen, *Bukharin and the Bolshevik Revolution: A Political Biography, 1888–1938* (New York, 1973). Moshe Lewin, *Lenin's Last Struggle* (New York, 1968), chronicles the end of Lenin's career. Richard Pipes, *The Formation of the Soviet Union* (rev. ed., Cambridge, Mass., 1964), treats in detail Moscow's relations with the borderlands and the creation of the Soviet state.

On foreign policy, George Kennan, *Russia and the West Under Lenin and Stalin* (Boston, 1961); Adam Ulam, *Expansion and Coexistence* (New York, 1968); and Franz Borkenau, *World Communism* (Ann Arbor, Mich., 1962), are helpful. For various aspects of cultural life, consult Christopher Read, *Culture and Power in Revolutionary Russia* (New York, 1990); Edward J. Brown, *Russian Literature Since the Revolution* (Cambridge, Mass., 1982); Robert A. Maguire, *Red Virgin Soil: Soviet Literature in the 1920s* (Princeton, N.J., 1968); and John S. Curtiss, *The Russian Church and the Soviet State, 1917–1950* (Boston, 1953).

Significant monographs include Richard Stites, *Revolutionary Dreams: Utopian Vision and Experimental Life in the Russian Revolution* (New York, 1989); Sheila Fitzpatrick, *Education and Social Mobility in the Soviet Union, 1921–1934* (New York, 1979); Larry E. Holmes, *The Kremlin and the Schoolhouse: Reforming Education in Soviet Russia, 1917–1931* (Bloomington, Ind., 1971); Alan Ball, *And How My Soul Is Hardened* (Berkeley, 1993), a fascinating account of homeless child vagabonds; Peter Kenez, *The Birth of the Propaganda State: Soviet Methods of Mass Mobilization, 1917–1929* (Cambridge, 1985); Mark Von Hagen, *Soldiers in the Proletarian Dictatorship: The Red Army and the Soviet Socialist State, 1917–1930* (Ithaca, N.Y., 1990); Nina Tumarkin, *Lenin Lives! The Lenin Cult in Russia* (Cambridge, Mass., 1983); Alan Ball, *Russia's Last Capitalists: The Nepmen, 1921–1929* (Berkeley, 1988); Richard Stites, *The Women's Liberation Movement in Russia: Feminism, Nihilism, and Bolshevism, 1860–1930* (Princeton, N.J., 1978); and Wendy Z. Goldman, *Women, the State, and Revolution: Soviet Family Policy and Social Life, 1917–1936* (New York, 1993).

6

A VISION RENEWED
Stalin's Economic Revolution

~

Classes at Kiev Polytechnical Institute had only recently resumed after the summer vacation. The small group of students standing on the pavement in front of the main classroom building shivered in the cool dusk. A few days before, at the end of October 1929, they had volunteered to assist Stalin's recently announced drive to carry the socialist revolution to the countryside. He and the Party had decided to establish collective farms. The Soviet leaders hoped that poor and middle-income peasants would join these farms voluntarily. Each peasant family would contribute its land, seed, large agricultural tools, and livestock to the collective farm, or *kolkhoz*. Using the pooled resources of all who entered the *kolkhoz*, member families would work the farm together. The government would supply tractors and other machinery and would buy the farm's output at fixed prices. Each collective farmer would receive a share of the farm's income and surplus produce proportionate to the amount and complexity of his or her labor This sort of cooperative farming had been tried during the NEP era, but only on a small scale. Now Stalin wanted to transform almost all agriculture into *kolkhozes*.

All but one of the waiting students belonged to the Komsomol, the youth organization of the Communist Party; a few served as section leaders, or *aktivisti* (activists). Although missing classes for a few days would disrupt their studies, most of the students embraced the new plan. They also knew that special worker volunteers, called the Twenty-five Thousanders after the number that the Party sought to recruit, were assembling to aid the collectivization drive. They felt proud to be part of a national effort.

That evening the students entrained for a small town some two hundred miles from Kiev. There they attended a two-hour briefing by local authorities and then traveled by bus to a village of some eighty-five families a few miles away. The Party officials in charge explained that the peasants had shown little interest in the state's proposal to establish a collective farm. Each student was assigned to visit four or five dwellings, to outline to the residents the advantages of the planned *kolkhoz*, and to persuade the family head to sign, or mark an X, on a copy of the collective's articles of organization.

The oldest female student, Sonya, was dismayed to find most of the peasants she spoke to indifferent or hostile to the proposed change. Around three in the afternoon, when a Party official stopped by to assess her progress, Sonya reported that only one family had tentatively agreed, but they had suspiciously refused to sign the document. Apparently unpertubed at these disappointing results, the official politely asked Sonya to assemble at the village store, whence the bus would take her group back to town. As the students waited for transportation, they saw camouflaged army trucks pull up at both ends of the village's two main streets. Armed men (special troops of the secret police, as she later discovered) clambered down and began ranging through the village, stopping at each cottage. Horrified, Sonya heard one of the officers bluntly informing a resistant family that they had forty minutes to pack their belongings. She learned subsequently that those who refused to join the collective farm were loaded onto the soldiers' trucks with a few personal possessions and driven to town. That night, they were put aboard a cattle car, which later was attached to a deportation train that carried the hapless peasants to exile in the Urals. Many died on the way.[1]

As part of the 1929–1930 collectivization drive, the Party especially targeted *kulaks*, allegedly "rich" peasants. A Soviet novelist, reflecting what actually happened, gives this account of events in a typical village:

> From our village . . . the "kulaks" were driven out on foot. They took what they could carry on their backs: bedding, clothing. The mud was so deep it pulled the boots off their feet. It was terrible to watch them. They marched along in a column and looked back at their huts, and their bodies still held the warmth from their own stoves. What pain they must have suffered! After all, they had been born in those houses; they had given their daughters in marriage in those cabins. They had heated up their stoves, and the cabbage soup they had cooked was left there behind them. The milk had not been drunk, and the smoke was

---

[1]This account is based on the recollections of Sonya, the oldest female student, whom the author knew in the 1960s.

still rising from the chimneys. The women were sobbing—but were afraid to scream. The Party activists didn't give a damn about them. We drove them off like geese.[2]

Collectivization comprised one part of a late–1920s "second revolution," an upheaval perhaps even more momentous and sweeping than that of October 1917. The earlier revolution had brought the Bolsheviks political power and had thoroughly rearranged economic, social, and ethnic relations in Russia. The next revolution, however, transformed the economic basis of the Soviet system. Forcing peasants into collective farms absolutely reordered work and life for the rural majority of the population. The Party also dramatically accelerated the industrialization and urbanization of the nation. Moreover, this mammoth effort resulted in the entrenchment of an authoritarian political system dominated by a small elite who linked state and Party functions in a huge and powerful, albeit inefficient, bureaucracy. This regime, known in recent Soviet parlance as the command-administrative system, would endure with only modest changes for more than half a century until Mikhail Gorbachev's policies of *perestroika* and *glasnost'* undermined it in the late 1980s.

In this and the next chapter, we explore first the economic and then the social, cultural, and political dimensions of this transformation of Soviet life. Sometimes called the revolution from above, this upheaval is also closely associated with Stalin's name. In advance of this transformation, Stalin labored assiduously during the 1920s to broaden his contacts and support in the Party-state apparatus and to enlarge his authority. Adroitly playing rivals to succeed Lenin against each other, he managed to cripple them politically and to emerge at the end of the decade as the dominant figure in the Party and the nation. He at first assumed a moderate position in the raging debate among the Party elite over how best to proceed to socialism. In 1928 and 1929, however, the new leader, appealing to nationalist sentiment and calling for sacrifice and dedication, committed the nation to headlong industrialization and all-out collectivization of agriculture.

Yet historians profoundly disagree over Stalin's intentions and over how much he controlled this second Bolshevik revolution. Some believe that Stalin, motivated by a desire to emulate Lenin and earlier tsar-reformers such as Peter the Great and Ivan the Terrible, carefully planned and manipulated a radical overhaul of Soviet society. At the same time, desperately seeking to eliminate anyone who might challenge his self-image, the Soviet dictator moved from ousting political foes from power

---

[2] Quoted from Vasily Grossman, *Forever Flowing* (New York: Harper & Row, 1972), p. 145, in Robert Conquest, *The Harvest of Sorrow* (New York: Oxford Univ. Press, 1986), p. 137.

in the 1920s to a campaign of terror against former opponents, suspected "enemies of the people," and potential doubters in the shocking purges of 1936 through 1938.

Others argue that Stalin had no blueprint but rather reacted haphazardly to economic, social, and political crises of the late 1920s. As these analysts see it, one emergency measure led to another, building toward an outcome that Stalin had not foreseen. Once he had blundered into a radical restructuring of the economy, in this view, the huge sacrifices that the changes required and the arbitrariness of the Party's action provoked sufficient resentment and resistance among the population to endanger Communist rule. Determined to maintain their authority, Party leaders granted extensive power to regional and local officials but could not control them fully. As tension grew and remedial measures failed, the elite resorted to dismissing officials. This practice, which various Communist leaders, not Stalin alone, initiated, soon got out of hand, sparking indiscriminate denunciations and purging at all levels of the government and Party.

Each of these interpretations contributes to an understanding of Soviet history, for they reflect different facets of the complex social and political reality of the 1930s. Fluidity and instability characterized Soviet society at that time, as occupations, places of residence, family relations, education, and attitudes all rapidly shifted. Bolshevik policies speeded these dislocations and tried to direct them, but despite its lofty pretensions the Party could not dominate every element of the revolution. Moreover, Party leaders disagreed over how fast and how far to push the radical restructuring of society. Nevertheless, to a considerable degree, the Party managed to harness most Soviet citizens to its drive for industrialization and socialism. Those who benefited, including some workers, the new intelligentsia, the officials of the Party-state, and some young people, enthusiastically supported Communist policies. Those who openly resisted were purged or incarcerated in the camps of the *Gulag* (a Soviet acronym for the system of correctional-labor or concentration camps run by the secret police). A large majority retreated into passivity or closed their eyes to the chaos.

Calling this upheaval the Stalin Revolution is apt, because although Stalin was forced to react to events, he also possessed a general sense of where he wished to drive Soviet society—into conformity with his distorted vision of Soviet socialism. Moreover, Stalin dominated the shaping of Party policies, working primarily with pliant colleagues whom he had identified and promoted. Finally, the Soviet dictator initiated and supervised the purges at the highest levels, although the process soon gathered its own momentum and snowballed through the lower ranks of Party and society with little direction and tragic results. To understand Stalin's role in this second revolution of the 1920s and 1930s, we must examine his earlier life and his rise to prominence in the Party.

The Boy and the Party Stalwart

Joseph Djugashvili, who as a young revolutionary adopted the pseudonym Stalin (meaning "man of steel"), was born on December 21, 1879, in Gori, a small town in the Caucasus near the Georgian capital, Tbilisi (then Tiflis). Stalin came from humble origins, one of the few Bolshevik leaders not of the intelligentsia or the middle class. His father, a former serf, was a cobbler and later worked in a shoe factory. A heavy drinker, the father at times beat his wife and son. Stalin's strong-willed, devout mother, an uneducated peasant, determined to see her son trained for the priesthood. She insisted on sending the boy to the local church school, where he proved a capable pupil. At age fourteen, Stalin entered the Orthodox seminary in Tbilisi. By then the youth had lost contact with his father, who had moved away.

In seminary, Stalin found the academic subjects and ideas challenging but he objected to the strict regime. Having learned some Russian in the Gori school, he soon began reading Russian and translated Western writings, including works by Marx and his followers. He gravitated to a coterie of young Georgian intellectuals with radical and anti-Russian ideas. Rebelling against the Russification and authoritarianism imposed by his teachers, Stalin by age sixteen or seventeen delved into clandestine revolutionary activities. In 1899, before he turned twenty, he stopped attending classes and the seminary expelled him.

Because Stalin recorded almost nothing about his private life and

A Future Tyrant Although a young man in this photo, Joseph Stalin's face already suggests the determination and will that he later displayed.

views, it is difficult to gauge the impact of his childhood and youth on his character. However, three significant circumstances from his upbringing clearly influenced his development. First, he was doubtless an insecure young man, doted on by his mother and resentful of his father's behavior and, later, his absence. His family's poverty and lack of status earned Stalin as a student and seminarian the scorn of his schoolmates. This sense of inadequacy plagued him throughout his life. As his preeminent biographer, Robert Tucker, has shown, Stalin continually strove to become the idealized person of his dreams. Woe to those who doubted that image or who stood in the way of his efforts to actualize it.

Moreover, on the basis of scattered recollections of contemporaries, the young Stalin seems to have carried a "chip on his shoulder." He quickly took offense at any behavior that he deemed ridicule or ill treatment. He also seems to have cared deeply about the injustice and deprivation he observed everywhere in contemporary society. His rejection of religion and his embrace of Marxism during his first eighteen months at the seminary appear to have stemmed equally from resentment and from idealism. Marx's call for a class war of the oppressed against the exploiters appealed to Stalin's militancy and to his outrage at the repression that he observed in Georgia.

Finally, as American historian Ronald Suny has argued, Stalin was strongly influenced by the Georgian milieu in which he grew up and worked as a revolutionary during his first thirty-four years. In fact, his rebelliousness first emerged as strong anti-Russian feelings at the seminary, where he protested the banning of the Georgian language and literature and the requirement to speak and study only in Russian. In light of his later conversion to Russian nationalism and his repression of Georgian aspirations in 1921 and 1922, it is ironic that as a youth, Stalin ardently espoused Georgian nationalism. Until around 1912, he used the revolutionary pseudonym Koba, after a romantic and vengeful Georgian hero, and his first writings were lyrical Georgian poems.

Stalin also internalized several key values of the masculine culture of Georgia: trust, loyalty, and the need to exact vengeance. For Georgian men, family ties and friendship, as well as the confidence to depend on these qualities, ranked as the highest priority. To betray that trust, to behave disloyally, constituted a cardinal sin for which a traitor must expect severe retribution. Later in life, as Stalin struggled with Party colleagues over issues of power and policy, he increasingly judged those who opposed him as violating his trust, as betraying him and the Party. Thus as antisocialist "enemies of the people," they deserved punishment. In a rare, personally revealing episode, Stalin and two Party friends were relaxing one summer day in 1923 and began, over a glass of wine, to muse about what they loved most in life. When Stalin's turn came, he asserted, "The greatest delight is to mark one's enemy, prepare everything, avenge oneself thoroughly, and then go to sleep."[3] This "theory of sweet revenge," as it became known among his Communist comrades, chillingly portended the fate of millions of innocent Soviet citizens in the 1930s.

After leaving the seminary, Stalin continued to spread Marxist ideas among the workers of Tbilisi. By the spring of 1901, he had slipped underground as a full-time, professional revolutionary. For a little over ten years, he pursued that career, with brief periods of imprisonment and Siberian exile (from which he escaped at least three times). Apart from his energy and resolve, several aspects of this phase of his life merit attention. He always defined himself as a Bolshevik, despite the preference of most Georgian Social Democrats for Menshevism. He never explained his choice, but the "hard-line" quality of Lenin's views—the emphasis on commitment, on discipline, on a dedicated elite—probably appealed to Stalin, as did Lenin's revolutionary activism and radical program. A man of action, Stalin pursued extreme measures to achieve the cherished goal of socialism. Unlike many other Bolsheviks, he seldom wavered in his devotion to the Leninist cause.

Further, Stalin's zeal and ability brought him to the attention of Lenin, almost ten years his senior. They met in 1905, and Lenin soon supported Stalin's advancement in the Bolsheviks' ranks. In 1912, when Bolshevik leaders in Europe established their own Central Committee, Lenin arranged for Stalin, still operating covertly in Russia, to be co-opted to the committee. Later that year, the Georgian Bolshevik visited Lenin in Kracow, a city in Austrian Poland, where the Bolshevik leader asked for Stalin's assistance. Would he put his experience in minority politics to work formulating Party policy toward the non-Russian nationalities in the tsarist empire? Together they prepared a pamphlet, written by Stalin, entitled "Marxism and the National Question." This work marked the emergence of Stalin as a significant, although still second-rank, Bolshevik leader.

The trip to Kracow also highlights a major difference between Stalin's experience in the prewar years and that of most other Bolshevik leaders. Except for the few months in Kracow and Vienna in 1912 and 1913 and some weeks in London and Stockholm in 1905 and 1906 to attend party congresses, Stalin never left the Russian Empire. Almost all other top Bolsheviks spent considerable time abroad. As a result, they gained familiarity with international currents in Marxism and developed cosmopolitan outlooks. Stalin's only other trip abroad would be a brief sojourn, shrouded in wartime secrecy, to attend the Teheran Conference, where he met Churchill and Roosevelt in 1943.

Last, although Stalin lived and worked primarily in the Caucasus

---

[3]Tucker, *Stalin as Revolutionary*, p. 211.

from 1900 to 1910, these years witnessed his metamorphosis from a Georgian patriot into a thoroughgoing Russian nationalist. Shortly afterward, he began to shed all external signs of his Georgian heritage. He even spoke in a low monotone in an apparent effort to mask his Georgian-accented Russian, and he adopted thoroughly Russian behavior, dress, and attitudes. Why he underwent this transmutation is unclear. Nevertheless, his passion to be treated as an equal by his sophisticated fellow Bolsheviks, most of whom were Russians; his growing desire to emulate the Russian Lenin; and his acceptance of the authoritarian centralism of Lenin's Russocentric party probably all played a role. At this time Stalin also struggled with fellow Georgians who were Mensheviks, and occasionally he displayed flashes of anti-Semitism. In light of this behavior, perhaps he wanted to assuage his own feelings of inadequacy by associating himself with the dominant and winning nationality, the Russians. Thus he could continue to hate Russian tsarism while fervently believing that the Russian proletariat, whom he now represented, would emerge triumphant in the brave new world of socialism.

In February 1913, the authorities again arrested Stalin and in mid-summer sent him into exile in Siberia, where he remained until the 1917 February Revolution. One of the early returnees from Siberia after the Provisional Government amnestied all political prisoners, Stalin became an influential Bolshevik leader in Petrograd in the weeks before Lenin's return in April 1917. Despite his later efforts to portray himself as a pure Leninist, Stalin at that time supported a policy of tolerating the existence of the Provisional Government. He also favored Russia's continuing to defend itself against German aggression in World War I. Lenin strongly criticized both positions in his April Theses, and the Party soon repudiated them.

After some hesitation, Stalin too accepted Lenin's more revolutionary stance. Through 1917, he faithfully supported the Bolshevik leader and served as a useful but not influential, second-tier Party leader. He did not play a prominent role in the October Revolution. Only after his appointment as commissar of nationalities in the new Soviet government did he emerge as a noteworthy figure among the Bolsheviks and in Russia.

Stalin rendered loyal service to Lenin and the Soviet cause during the civil war, undertaking important special assignments to several major battlefronts. However, two of his missions ended in controversy. In 1918, as an adviser in the defense of the Volga River city of Tsaritsyn, he clashed with Trotsky over tactics and control of operations. As we saw in Chapter 4, Trotsky prevailed, fostering Stalin's resentment of him that would culminate in their duel for power in the 1920s. In addition, during the Soviet offensive into Poland in 1920, Stalin, who served as political commissar for the Southwestern Front, ignored GHQ orders to shift troops northward. His decision proved a factor in the collapse of the drive on Warsaw and the subsequent Soviet defeat.

Stalin's wartime service nevertheless furthered his career, as his travels about Soviet Russia permitted him to cultivate political connections and to begin building a cadre of loyal followers. Nevertheless, he probably felt disappointed and resentful at the scant recognition that he received for his wartime efforts. As Tucker concludes, "Whereas Trotsky emerged from the war with much glory and little power, Stalin emerged with little glory and much power. Glory, however, remained his aim."[4]

Stalin's Rise to Supreme Power

Western historians as well as intellectuals in the former Soviet Union are divided about the relationship of Stalinism—the socioeconomic, cultural, and political system that Stalin shaped between 1928 and 1940—to Leninism, the Bolshevik ideology and state that Lenin articulated and built before his death. Some argue that Stalinism grew directly out of Leninism. Others insist that Stalin's actions and policies represented a sharp break from Lenin's. We can certainly ascertain the roots of Stalinism in Lenin's Bolshevism, particularly its reliance on authoritarianism and centralization. Yet Stalinism's evolution from Bolshevism was by no means inevitable. Bolshevism contained several strands of political philosophy and practice, including a moderate, more democratic pattern than the program that Stalin imposed. Therefore, to understand the emergence of Stalinist society, we must examine its context and the forces that led to the triumph of its radical policies.

For Russia and the other lands of the former tsarist empire, the 1920s saw rapid modernization, during which new techniques, ideas, and values challenged and often supplanted traditional ways of life and mores. These dramatic shifts occurred independently of the October Revolution and evolved to some extent beyond the Bolsheviks' control. Socialist principles and ideals, nevertheless, established the parameters within which the transformation of society could unfold. At the same time, Party leaders advanced several conceptions of the socialist future, any one of which the country might have adopted. At first Stalin did not promote a distinctive scheme of his own, and he seemed an unlikely candidate in the struggle for power that followed Lenin's death in 1924. In fact, any contemporary ranking of Communist leaders according to prominence in the Party and public standing would have placed Stalin's name down the list, behind Trotsky, Zinoviev, Kamenev, Alexei Rykov, Bukharin, and Mikhail Tomsky. How then did Stalin emerge as the dominant figure in the Party by the late 1920s?

---

[4]Ibid., p. 209.

Was Stalin Lenin's true heir or, as Trotsky once claimed, the betrayer of Lenin's revolution? Almost two decades ago, historian Stephen Cohen wrote that every great revolution raises a fundamental interpretive question. No issue challenged students of Soviety history more than the nature of the Stalin revolution. Nor was it simply an academic chess match between advocates of Stalinism as the inevitable outgrowth of Bolshevism and those who saw Stalinism as a separate system with unique characteristics. As Cohen argued, the debate also became a political contest, for the "less empathy a historian felt for the revolution and Bolshevism, the less he has seen meaningful distinctions between Bolshevism (Leninism) and Stalinism" (in *Stalinism: Essays in Historical Interpretation,* 1977).

The controversy over Stalinism has taken many forms. In the U.S.S.R. itself, the dispute erupted in the public arena during the 1980s with results few could imagine. Using history as a tool to shake up defenders of the status quo and to stimulate political and economic innovation, Gorbachev sought to detonate the remains of Stalinism by permitting free-wheeling criticism of the Stalin era. Under Gorbachev, writers, journalists, and leading politicians offered a devastating critique of Stalin's collectivization policies. These attacks implied the superiority of moderate socialism like that espoused by Gorbachev over the excesses of socialism. As Thomas Sherlock noted, Gorbachev justified his own "turn to radical reform by comparing it to Lenin's decision to reject the coercive policies of War Communism and to embrace the NEP." For Gorbachev and his allies, the "good" Lenin stood opposite the "bad" Stalin ("Politics and History Under Gorbachev," *Problems of Communism,* May–August, 1988).

But history's didactic potential soon proved to harbor a dangerous mix. Die-hard Party conservatives interpreted attacks on Stalin as a dagger thrust into the heart of the Soviet Union's entire postrevolutionary heritage. And could the new history be reconciled with the standard version of the past: *A Short Course on the History of the Soviet Communist Party,* published under Stalin's watchful eye in 1938 and read by millions, young and old, for fifty years. By 1988 the tug-of-war between Politburo progressives and conservatives over the origins of Stalinism spilled over into newspapers and classrooms. Because politicians could not agree on the U.S.S.R.'s past, educators decided to cancel high-school history examinations in 1988. But, as William Husband observed in a provocative piece on Soviet schools, "canceling exams and authorizing the preparation of new texts proved to be the easiest part" ("Secondary School History Texts in the U.S.S.R.: Revising the Soviet Past, 1985–1989," *Russian Review,* October 1991). From 1989 to 1991, new history textbooks in the U.S.S.R. were shot down almost as fast as they appeared, stunning evidence of the two-edged sword of historical *glasnost'.*

Debates in the West over the origins of Stalinism had fewer public ramifications but proved equally intense for the scholars involved. American political scientist Jerry Hough found the Gorbachev "revolution" a key to understanding the Stalin era, because the 1980s reforms repudiated the anticapitalist core of both Stalinism and its progenitor, Bolshevism. In Hough's view, Gorbachev was mistaken when he glorified Lenin in 1917, for Bolshevism was based on an ideological and emotional aversion to Western market forces that frightened millions of ordinary Russians in the early decades of the century. In 1917 workers had sensed that Lenin offered a "different path of development," one that promised "old communal values and freedom from the insecurities of capitalism." Moreover, Hough postulates a direct Lenin-Stalin connection. Except for the Great Purge of 1937 to 1938, Stalin did exactly what Lenin wanted—he saved his people from capitalist exploitation. Nor could there be any middie ground in the 1920s. Lenin's oppposition shortly before his death to foreign trade intended to save the floundering Soviet economy, coupled with his advocacy of rapid industrialization, meant that there "was no viable alternative to the internal mobilization of 1928–29." Bukharin did not espouse policies intended by Lenin, as some Western scholars asserted. Instead, Stalin proved to be Lenin's spokesman. As for Gorbachev, he set out to dismantle the iron curtains of the Russian Revolution—curtains erected by both Lenin and Stalin—and to reopen Russia to the West (*Russia and the West: Gorbachev and the Politics of Reform,* 1990).

Deep-rooted social trends, not high politics, linked the Lenin and Stalin eras, according to Moshe Lewin. Lewin identified powerful "moving forces" after 1917 that produced "high doses of coercion and destructiveness." For three decades, the peasant way of life and rural culture dominated Soviet society. And by 1921, seven years of war, revolution, and civil war had thrust the peasantry back to a precapitalist, "even pre-petty-capitalist mode." A rare moment in history, this regression was an almost "geological shift of society backward." At the exact moment when Bolshevik leaders viewed themselves as heralds of a grand socialist vision, they in fact could look forward to only a "deadly clash" with a sullen rural mass. The need to construct a socialist economy and a new state amid the rubble of a premodern peasantry hardened by decades of struggle gave Lenin and Stalin a common task. Because they were determined to create order out of chaos, coercive impulses surfaced that produced a brutal despotism, of which Stalinism was the ultimate expression ("Russia/USSR in Historical Motion: An Essay in Interpretation," *Russian Review,* July, 1991).

Yet Catherine Merridale found the origins of Stalinism not in Lenin at all, but in the plight of ordinary people in Russia's "largest village," Moscow. Turmoil bubbled throughout the nation's capital in the 1920s as hundreds of thousands of peasants flooded the city in search of employment. Ten years after the Bolsheviks came to power in 1917, one out of four Muscovite workers had no job. Employees in the private sector still out-earned those in state services, an anomaly hard to reconcile with socialist pledges of egalitarianism and justice. The late 1920s also witnessed a mushrooming of local Party cadres, upwardly mobile workers, and peasants who saw the world as a black-and-white clash of reaction versus progress. The promise of jobs for everyone—a key feature of the 1929 industrialization program—elicited popular support on the streets and among the new urban Communists. As much as any other factor, Merridale concludes, "cadres were the commodity on which the Stalinist system depended" (*Moscow Politics and the Rise of Stalin, 1925–1932,* 1990).

Was Stalin Lenin's legacy? The collapse of the Soviet Union has not ended the debate, either in the West or in Russia. Access to once-closed Party archives makes it possible to explore this issue with greater precision. The opening round in the post-communist era goes to Dmitri Volkogonov, historian, former general in the Soviet army, and the first researcher to see the most secret KGB archives. His biography of the first Soviet leader raises disturbing questions about the Leninist imprint on Russian culture to this day. For years, Volkogonov agonizes, Russians wondered where Stalin acquired the barbarities that he inflicted on his own people, from the concentration camps to the cult of personality. "None of us could begin to imagine they derived from Lenin's lifetime, often on his direct orders." Stalin and his system, Volkogonov asserts, came straight from Lenin, his ideas and practices (*Lenin: A New Biography,* 1994). Whether future revelations will sustain Volkogonov's interpretation remains to be seen.

Part of the explanation lies in his political skill and foresight. Although often depicted as a master organizer and planner, Stalin did not make a particularly capable administrator. His management of the commissariat of nationalities was haphazard, and he ignored or mishandled the running of *Rabkrin* (the Workers' and Peasants' Inspectorate), which audited state operations and verified the execution of government directives, and which Lenin asked him to head in 1919. Moreover, Stalin was far from the hearty, sociable politico. Short and stocky, with a slightly withered left arm, a square, pockmarked face, and narrow green eyes, Stalin was aloof, moody, and impatient. His frequent outbursts of temper and the marked mean streak in his disposition bespoke a volatile personality. Yet the man possessed outstanding political talents, including considerable intelligence, an impressive memory for facts and faces, abundant energy and perseverance, pragmatic decisiveness, and an uncanny ability to identify and to use other people's strengths and to exploit their weaknesses. He was also enormously ambitious and concealed a craving for respect and adulation under a mask of self-effacement. Perhaps, as Robert Tucker suggests, Stalin sought to emulate Lenin as a Communist hero and Ivan the Terrible as a Russian nation-builder.

In his drive for power, Stalin faced several formidable obstacles. As long as Lenin lived, Stalin could not hope to match his brilliance and prestige. He remained a secondary figure in the Soviet government, which frequently was known abroad as the Lenin-Trotsky government. Consequently, during 1921 Stalin shifted his attention to the Party, in which he began to build a broad base of power and influence. Yet at this stage, the Party's relationship to Soviet governing institutions and to the nation was still inchoate. No one knew with certainty whether the path to supreme authority lay through the Party apparatus.

Lenin's first stroke in May 1922 also raised questions about the future leadership of the Party. Lenin had occupied no special position in the organization, exercising control by his prestige and by force of his personality and intellect instead. Nevertheless, Stalin apparently recognized that the Party had come to dominate all aspects of government and society. He shrewdly anticipated that whoever controlled the apparatus would likely emerge as leader regardless of positions, titles, or previous prominence. Using his standing as a senior member of the Party's Organization Bureau, Stalin thus set out to build a political following. Drawing on Party and government contacts made during the civil war, he cultivated a network of officials whom he manipulated through patronage, favoritism, and the dispensation of power, much like the notorious political machine of the American city "boss." Before long, Stalin also proved adept at organizational maneuvering against his rivals, making and breaking tactical alliances with other Communist leaders and, when necessary, using his influence in the Party against them.

Stalin scored his first success at the Tenth Party Congress in March

Lenin and His Successor Stalin made sure that this comradely photo of him with Lenin in 1922 just before the latter's stroke circulated widely after Lenin's death.

1921, during which four of his henchmen—Kliment Voroshilov, Sergo Ordzhonikidze, Valerian Kuibyshev, and Sergei Kirov—won election to the Central Committee. Even better, his ally Viacheslav Molotov was promoted from candidate to full member of the committee and became one of the three secretaries of the Party Secretariat. At the Ninth Congress in 1920, the Secretariat's charter had undergone reorganization. This body was now charged with ensuring the execution of Party policy; with supervising the hierarchy of regional and lower Party officials; and with managing internal Party affairs, including dissemination of information (through the agitational-propaganda section, or agitprop), the women's division, and personnel recruitment, training, and assignments.

Apparently on Lenin's recommendation, Stalin was named general secretary of the Party at the Eleventh Congress in May 1922, an appointment that Lenin soon would regret. By then the Party apparatus had mushroomed into an extensive and intricate web, with almost a thousand people working in the Secretariat and tens of thousands staffing other bodies. Also, new members, with military or administrative experience in the civil war, flooded the Party ranks. These recruits, lacking the sophistication and idealism of many prerevolutionary and 1917 members and accustomed to obeying orders, appreciated Stalin's pragmatism and forcefulness. With their support and through appointing and protecting incoming officials loyal to him, Stalin began to exert control over Party secretaries at republic, district, and lower levels. These individuals had a strong say in the election of delegates to higher Party bodies and to the Party congresses. In 1924, two years after Stalin became general secretary, almost 70 percent of upper-level Party secretaries had held office for less than a year, and many of these novice officials were Stalin's adherents. Controlling selection of delegates to the Party congresses was crucial to Stalin's success: these were the men and women who decided major policy and elected the Central Committee.

In his politicking, Stalin was aided in these early years by his second wife, Nadezhda Alliluyeva, the daughter of well-known Bolsheviks whom Stalin had known for years. (His first wife had died in 1908.) The energetic and outgoing Alliluyeva plunged into Party work at age seventeen after their marriage in 1919. During the 1920s, she increasingly acted the part of the charming and well-informed hostess for Stalin, entertaining and helping him to keep track of Party colleagues.

Following the stroke in March 1923 that in effect removed Lenin from political life, Stalin found himself in the enviable position of being able to play off Politburo factions against one another. He benefited particularly from the hostility that most other leaders felt toward Trotsky, and allied himself loosely at first with Zinoviev and Kamenev. All three resented Trotsky's abilities and position and feared that his prestige in the Party and abroad would make him the logical successor to Lenin. In the summer of 1923, the triumvirate managed to pursue Lenin's NEP policies despite considerable criticism and to run state and Party affairs without major incident. By October 1923, however, Zinoviev had grown alarmed at the rising influence of his junior colleague, Stalin, and tried unsuccessfully to weaken the Secretariat.

Upon Lenin's death in January 1924, a cult honoring him sprang up despite protests by his widow. Streets and localities were given Lenin's name, including the U.S.S.R.'s second largest city, Petrograd, which in 1924 became Leningrad. Parents gave children names like Vladlen, statues of Lenin were erected everywhere, and Lenin's portrait or bust graced every Soviet office as well as many homes. The cult reached its apogee with such oft-repeated sentiments as, "Lenin will always be with us; Lenin lives." His body remained embalmed in an increasingly waxy and glassy state in a handsome modernist mausoleum on Red Square, just outside the Kremlin walls. Over the decades since 1924, millions of

Soviet citizens (and thousands of curious foreign tourists) have stolidly lined up for hours during all kinds of weather for the chance to glimpse the "great Lenin." For some critics of communism, the Lenin cult eerily recalled the veneration of saints' relics so central to Russian Christianity. Although religious undertones pervaded the adulation of Lenin, the idolatry stemmed more from a popular desire for a new "father-tsar" figure, as well as from the Party's need for a unifying political symbol as it extended its control over the vast country. The cult also evolved out of the leader-oriented nature of Russian Marxism as Lenin, with his authority and prestige, had shaped it.

The big loser at this time was Trotsky. Away on a rest cure when Lenin died, the heir apparent made no effort to return to Moscow for the funeral and the subsequent commemorations. He later claimed that Party leaders had deliberately misled him about the date, but he never produced conclusive evidence for this charge. Why he missed this critical occasion to associate himself with Lenin's legacy remains unclear. Stalin, on the other hand, although not playing a major role in the ceremonies attendant on Lenin's death, apparently encouraged the decision to keep Lenin's body on permanent display. He also delivered an important eulogy, later known as the oath speech. In his customary didactic style, Stalin listed six injunctions from Lenin to the Party, ending each with the pledge. "We vow to you, Comrade Lenin, that we shall fulfill your behest with honor!"[5] Stalin took every subsequent opportunity to affirm his loyalty to Lenin's vision.

The general secretary did not know about the damning "Lenin's Testament." Lenin had intended to present its contents in person as part of a broad attack on Stalin at the next Party congress in late March 1923. Lenin's third, incapacitating stroke in early March temporarily saved Stalin from a public airing of Lenin's ire. As we saw in Chapter 5, Trotsky failed to fulfill Lenin's request that he press the campaign against Stalin at the congress.

Lenin's notes focused on the need to preserve Party unity and the dangers the Stalin-Trotsky antipathy posed to such unity. The Bolshevik leader reviewed the strengths and weaknesses of several chief Party figures but focused on what he judged as the two outstanding leaders, Trotsky and Stalin. He characterized the former as possessing "exceptional capabilities" but also as having "too far-reaching self-confidence and excessive absorption in the purely administrative side of things." His first sentence regarding the latter bluntly reflected his disenchantment with Stalin's running of the Party: "Comrade Stalin, having become *gensek* (general secretary), has concentrated boundless power in his hands, and I

---

[5]Robert H. McNeal, *Stalin: Man and Ruler* (New York: New York Univ. Press, 1988), p. 87.

am not sure that he will always manage to use this power with sufficient caution." Lenin made his point even plainer in his postscript, written after Stalin had snapped at Krupskaya, Lenin's wife and helpmeet, on the telephone.

> Stalin is too rude, and this fault . . . becomes intolerable in the office of general secretary. Therefore I propose to the comrades that they devise a way of shifting Stalin from this position and appointing to it another man who . . . falls on the other side of the scale from Comrade Stalin, namely more tolerant, more loyal, more polite, and more considerate of comrades, less capricious, etc.[6]

The danger to Stalin did not disappear with Lenin's death. In May 1924, the Central Committee convened in Moscow to prepare for the upcoming Thirteenth Party Congress, amid whispers that the agenda called for discussion of a secret matter of some urgency. At the committee meeting, Kamenev undertook the delicate and unpleasant task of communicating the special information. Several days earlier, Krupskaya had sent him a document from Lenin, noting that "Vladimir Ilyich expressed the firm desire that after his death these dictated notes of his should be brought to the attention of the next party congress." The day after receiving the material, Kamenev had shown it to Stalin, who as Party general secretary was responsible for congress procedures. On reading it, Stalin burst out, "Lenin shit on himself and he shit on us."

After Kamenev read Lenin's Testament to the Central Committee, "painful embarrassment paralyzed the whole gathering," according to a secretary. "Stalin, who sat on one of the benches of the presidium's rostrum, felt small and miserable. Despite his self-control and forced calm, one could clearly read in his face the fact that his fate was being decided." Indeed, dreadful anxiety must have gripped Stalin. He recognized that he did not control a majority of votes in the Central Committee. On the other hand, he knew that his most important colleagues feared the ascendancy of Trotsky, which would surely follow Stalin's demotion.

In the ensuing discussion, Zinoviev, again the *gensek's* ally, argued for the man of steel,

> Comrades, the last will, every word of Ilyich, is undoubtedly to be regarded by us as law. . . . On one point, however, we are fortunate to be able to say that Ilyich's fears have not been confirmed. I refer to the point concerning our general secretary. You have all been witnesses to our work together in the past

---

[6]Tucker, *Stalin as Revolutionary,* pp. 270–271.

months. Along with me, you have seen to your satisfaction that
Ilyich's fears have not been realized.

Kamenev supported Zinoviev, and they moved to close the discussion,
which passed by a show of hands—a narrow escape for Stalin. But the
question remained of how to transmit the document to the congress, as
Lenin had requested. After some debate, a vote of 30 to 10 decided that
the message should be read aloud in private caucasuses of major regional
delegations, rather than being discussed at the congress or included in its
official proceedings.[7]

At these meetings, Stalin suggested making allowance for the fact
that Lenin was a very sick man when he dictated the notes. Nevertheless,
the general secretary assured the comrades, he would make every effort
to correct the faults described. The guile worked, and Stalin's tactical
offer to resign after the congress was rejected. Although Lenin's Testament was soon known throughout Party ranks and appeared briefly in
the Soviet press in 1927, Stalin would manage to suppress its further publication until his death in 1953. From the grave, Lenin had nearly ended
Stalin's career—but Stalin survived.

Following Stalin's close escape and the burgeoning of the Lenin cult,
the struggle to inherit Lenin's mantle intensified. Polemics broke out in
public speeches and the press over the purity of each leader's Bolshevik
past, particularly regarding the individual's relationship to Lenin. Trotsky was at a disadvantage, his enemies taking care to stress his independent (later distorted as pro-Menshevik) stance among Russian Marxists
and his failure to join the Bolshevik Party until mid-1917. After several
months' silence, Trotsky finally struck back, publishing *Lessons of October*
in November 1924. The essay included a withering attack on Zinoviev
and Kamenev for their opposition to Lenin's decision to launch the October 1917 insurrection. Trotsky's countermove, however, provoked an unpleasant surprise.

With the dispute among the top leaders now in the open, Stalin joined
Zinoviev and Kamenev in the assault on Trotsky's reputation. In late 1924
and early 1925, he added two damning indictments: first, he highlighted a
previously obscure statement made by Trotsky in 1913 that scathingly berated Lenin's policies and the doctrine of Leninism. Also, for the first time,
he spoke of the dangers of Trotskyism, implying that such a position violated Lenin's 1921 stricture against factionalism. To be tainted with anti-
Leninism just as the Lenin cult bloomed severely damaged Trotsky's bid.
By contrast, while downplaying his own deviation from Lenin's views in
March 1917 and over the 1922 Soviet constitution, Stalin touted a number
of instances on which Lenin had turned to him for help and advice. Trot-

---

[7]This account is based on ibid., pp. 292–293, and McNeal, pp. 74–75 and 190–211.

sky's failure to use Lenin's Testament against his rivals, when he so clearly stood on the defensive, remains puzzling. Perhaps he feared that Lenin's critical remarks would do as much political harm to himself as to Stalin. In addition, he made no effort initially to capitalize on the growing anxiety about Stalin's power among other Party leaders, and instead remained aloof and embattled through much of 1925.

Stalin's rise also derived from his success in depicting himself as not only a close colleague and confidant of Lenin but also an unerring interpreter of the Bolshevik leader's doctrine. In the spring of 1924, just as two hundred thousand new recruits joined the Party in honor of Lenin (the so-called Lenin Enrollment), Stalin expounded the principles and practice of Lenin's Bolshevism. First he gave a series of talks at a training institution for Communist cadres, and then he published a pamphlet entitled *Foundations of Leninism*. Rather than contributing ideological views of his own, he systematically elaborated on and codified much of Lenin's thinking, stressing the Bolshevik leader's views on the nature of the proletarian revolution and the subsequent dictatorship of the proletariat. *Foundations of Leninism* served as a useful guidebook for younger Party leaders and initiates and eventually became the second most widely studied publication in the Soviet Union (after the Stalin-sponsored 1938 *Short History of the Communist Party*).

Russia's Socialist Future: The Bolsheviks' Debate

Conflicts over policy issues complicated the political maneuvering among the Party leadership. Top officials and Communist intellectuals gave first priority to the vital question of how best to build socialism in the U.S.S.R. Even during the first years of NEP, all had agreed on the urgency of this aim. Moreover, no one disputed that large-scale industrialization had to precede the birth of a fully socialist society. As Marx had made clear, only highly developed productive forces and a large proletariat could sustain socialism. Most Party leaders acknowledged that the socioeconomic basis of NEP, with its partial industrialization, minority proletariat, and heavy reliance on peasant production, could never provide a stable foundation for a Soviet socialist society. Too, if the Soviet Union wished to model and inspire worldwide socialist revolution, the country had to boast an advanced economy and a proletarian majority. But apart from theory, NEP's nurturing of petty-bourgeois peasants and traders posed a practical and political threat to Communist rule. The Bolsheviks could cement and inflate their power only by basing it on an overwhelming majority of workers, which industrialization would create.

Further, by the mid-1920s, some Party theorists concluded that

NEP's economic benefits were limited. The post-1921 recovery, although encouraging, had depended on the remnants of prerevolutionary capital investment to restore the 1914 level to industrial output. By 1927 this surge had begun to taper off. To lift the economy to the plane needed to support socialism and eventually to furnish the "super-abundance of goods" promised under communism, Party leaders saw that they would have to infuse substantial new capital and equipment.

Finally, imperialist enemies who had almost succeeded in smothering the Soviet infant at birth still surrounded the first socialist society, waiting for another opportunity to stamp out the alien ideology. Only advanced industry fully capable of producing modern weapons could guarantee the security of the Soviet Union and hence protect the prototype and base for international proletarian revolution.

Having agreed on the need to industrialize, the Bolsheviks from 1923 to 1928 debated how best to proceed. As we saw, Lenin originally had expected that workers' revolutions in advanced societies of the West would bring substantial economic assistance to the building of socialism in Russia. By 1923, when this support had not materialized, Lenin began to cast about anxiously for another path. He talked vaguely about basing socialist construction on cooperatives and about the importance of stimulating revolutions in the colonial world, but he failed to find a satisfactory solution. His death in 1924 left the unanswered question to his political heirs.

As one possibility, Lenin and his successors considered drawing on foreign capital to industrialize, as the United States had largely done. Western investors, however, wanted a settlement of tsarist Russia's debts first. Understandably, they also hesitated to help a system outspokenly bent on destroying capitalism throughout the world. Although the Soviet government granted a few concessions to Western entrepreneurs to exploit natural resources in the U.S.S.R., and some international firms invested in the Soviet Union, this aid proved too small to make a decisive difference.

The Soviet leadership also recognized that, in Western industrialization, the capital generated by the exchange of goods between farmers and town dwellers had helped to build factories. Thus they urged heightened trade with the peasantry and the export of the country's agricultural resources, particularly grain, to generate the capital and equipment necessary for industrialization. But they disagreed sharply over how much to pay peasants for their produce, how fast profits from the resale of that produce could be accumulated, and to what degree they ought to link the building of socialism in the Soviet Union with the promotion of proletarian revolution abroad.

These were differences in emphasis rather than antithetical positions. Nevertheless, two fairly distinct points of view emerged. Nikolai Bukharin, a prominent Communist theoretician, led a group that in time became known as the Right Opposition (later the Right Deviation). Its ad-

Communist Theoretician Nikolai Bukharin A young disciple of Lenin, Bukharin became a proponent of gradual industrialization and a leader of the Right Deviation in the 1920s.

herents argued that by applying proper encouragement and controls, the government could push the mixed NEP economy toward higher production and socialism without radically reshaping the system's foundations. Stimulated by new incentives, including the availability of cheap manufactured goods, peasants would produce more and would market their surplus. Through purchase and taxation, the government would accumulate that surplus, which it would then use as capital to build new factories, as food for industrial workers, and as payment to import modern technology from the West. The Right's leaders acknowledged that this process would be slow and gradual. They also believed that, except for purchases abroad, the plan would allow the Soviet Union to fabricate a socialist society largely on its own without depending on external revolutions or foreign capital.

Opponents of the Right quickly pointed out the need for speedy not gradual development, both for ideological and national-security reasons. The threat of a new capitalist attack, groundless but widely rumored in the Soviet press and among the leadership in the summer of 1927, buttressed their argument. These critics also objected to the Right's failure to explain how to make enough cheap manufactured goods available to entice the peasants to produce and sell more. What if the peasants failed to respond as predicted, the Right's foes asked. What if, instead of sending their grain to market, they ate more, stored grain against a day of better prices, and turned the rest into illicit vodka? In 1927, when for various reasons the amount of grain on the market indeed declined, the Right's stance wavered. Even Bukharin began to doubt his policy.

By contrast, the so-called Left Opposition, led by Trotsky and economist Evgeny Preobrazhensky, not only denigrated the Right's views but insisted that only high-tempo industrialization could produce the necessary rapid economic development. The best plan was to force grain sales at low prices and to tax the peasants heavily. This "primitive socialist accumulation" of capital could then be invested in the industrial sector. The Right condemned this scheme as unrealistic, insisting that "you can't build today's factories with tomorrow's bricks." In accordance with his traditional theory of permanent or uninterrupted revolution, Trotsky also maintained that the Communists must simultaneously cultivate industry in the Soviet Union and provoke revolution in Europe and Asia. The Soviet government, he insisted, could build socialism only with assistance from proletarian uprisings abroad.

Until 1928 Stalin refrained from playing a prominent role in the "great debate" about economic policy that raged within the Party. Although he generally supported the Bukharinist line, in late 1925 and again in 1926 he foreshadowed his subsequent policies by holding out hope for a more rapid and radical path of development. As Stalin's main contribution, however, he injected a note of strident nationalism into the discussion. Picking up a casual phrase uttered by Bukharin and turning it directly against Trotsky, Stalin in late 1924 and throughout 1925 developed the doctrine of "socialism in one country." A direct challenge to Trotsky's worldwide revolution argument, this unorthodox thesis stressed the possibility of constructing a viable socialist society in the U.S.S.R. alone.

Stalin based his contrary position on a single quotation from Lenin, taken out of context. In a 1916 article, the Bolshevik leader had speculated that, in exceptional circumstances, a country that passed through a proletarian revolution might build socialism alone, within its own borders, without help from the international socialist revolution. Lenin, however, asserted that *only* an advanced, industrialized country could accomplish this feat. Nevertheless, Stalin applied the idea to the Soviet Union. Naturally, his argument was immensely popular, and it greatly strengthened his position against Trotsky. Stalin in essence assured his fellow citizens, "We, Soviet comrades, by our own effort, sweat, and ingenuity, can build the glorious socialist future in our homeland without having to rely on assistance from foreigners." This appealing nationalistic vision undoubtedly enhanced Stalin's support within the Party and the nation. To this broad slogan Stalin soon added a program of rapid socioeconomic growth, which also won backing among both Communists and the Soviet people.

Early in his struggle with Stalin, Zinoviev, and Kamenev, Trotsky championed a policy issue that weakened him in the long run. After Party leaders squelched opposition to NEP at the Twelfth Party Congress in May 1923, forty-six senior Party members signed a public statement strongly condemning the erosion of democratic practices and the suppression of open discussion in the Party. Trotsky also voiced this critique separately in the summer of 1923 and detailed his argument in a December 5, 1923, letter to a meeting of Moscow Communists. During 1924 and into 1925, Trotsky continued to attack "bureaucratism," by which he meant the increasing manipulation and arbitrary management of Party affairs by secretaries and other Party officials. Yet his actions were largely counterproductive politically. In effect, he castigated the very Party *apparatchiks* (bureaucrats) on whom Party and government operations depended and who increasingly dominated the Party's Central Committee and Congress. Threatened by Trotsky's demands for a thorough house-cleaning and more open management styles, officialdom rallied to Trotsky's opponents and especially to Stalin, to whom growing numbers were beholden for their appointment or advancement.

In the meantime, Stalin steadily multiplied his support in the Party. He encouraged the constant enlargement of the Central Committee, which grew from twenty-seven members in 1922 to forty in 1923 to sixty-three in 1925. Most of the new members were followers of Stalin. In 1925 the general secretary arranged for the elevation to the Politburo of three of his closest supporters—Viacheslav Molotov, Kliment Voroshilov, and Mikhail Kalinin. Emboldened by Trotsky's growing isolation, Stalin engineered his rival's removal as war commissar in January 1925. By fall that year, Zinoviev and Kamenev, now thoroughly alarmed by Stalin's burgeoning power, broke with him politically although they did not yet ally themselves with Trotsky, who maintained his separate struggle against Stalin. With support from Bukharin and his allies, however, Stalin managed to control a majority at the Fourteenth Party Congress in December 1925, during which Kamenev challenged the general secretary's position and role. The attack only fed Stalin's strength in the Central Committee and the Politburo, and he arranged for Kamenev to be demoted to a candidate member of the Politburo. Shortly afterward, the Congress replaced Zinoviev as head of the Leningrad Party organization with Stalin's own man, Sergei Kirov.

During 1926 the political struggle for supreme power increasingly interlaced with the intensifying "great debate" over how to build socialism in the Soviet Union. That summer, Trotsky finally made common cause with the other "outs," Zinoviev and Kamenev, forming the United Opposition. The conflict between Trotsky and Stalin also heated up, centering on the "socialism in one country" question and manifesting itself in sharp policy disputes. In one important case, Stalin insisted that the fledgling Communist party in China align itself with the Chinese nationalist movement, the *Kuomintang*, headed by Chiang Kai-shek. Trotsky urged a more independent and revolutionary course for the Chinese party. Stalin won out, but in 1927 Chiang turned against his Communist supporters and massacred most of the top leadership. The killings decimated the Communist movement in China. Only Mao Zedong and a few others escaped to begin a long, slow rebuilding of the Chinese Communist party. The contest between Stalin and Trotsky grew increasingly personal, as an incident during a Politburo meeting in the summer of 1926 revealed.

When Trotsky dramatically pointed to Stalin during a stormy Politburo session of 1926 . . . and exclaimed: "The first secretary poses his candidature to the post of grave-digger of the Revolution!" Stalin turned pale, rose, first contained himself with difficulty, and then rushed out of the hall, slamming the door. Soon afterwards Piatakov . . . said: "You know I have smelt gunpowder, but I have never seen anything like this! This was worse than anything! And why, why did Lev Davidovich [Trotsky] say this? Stalin will never forgive him until the third and fourth generation."[3]

At the Fifteenth Party Conference in October 1926, the debate over "socialism in one country" climaxed. Stalin stressed that the Soviet people must have assurance that they could complete the task of building socialism themselves. Striking a positive note, he insisted that the nation had the power to achieve independently the promise of Marxism-Leninism—and the time was at hand. He also contended that the Soviet people's success would show everyone else the way to worldwide socialist revolution. By contrast, Stalin argued, Trotsky counseled dependency, under which socialism would develop only through the uncertain intervention of outside proletarian forces. Trotsky's plan was risky, too, for no one could predict if, when, or where other revolutions would break out. Indeed, efforts to stimulate them might even provoke imperialist attacks on the Soviet Union. Stalin offered the more appealing argument, with its patriotic and vaguely Leninist patina. To ensure that Trotsky's views would henceforth be considered anti-Party, Stalin railroaded a conference resolution endorsing "socialism in one country" and another that demanded the restoration of Party unity.

During 1927 the United Opposition steadily lost ground despite last-ditch attempts to carry their message to the public and to win mass support. With limited access to the media and the central Party apparatus, dissenters found themselves outsiders, accused of anti-Leninist views and anti-Communist activity. Under the Leninist conceptualization of the Party, the Opposition had little chance, for only the Party leadership was entitled to define correct doctrine and the limits of debate. By now Stalin and his allies fully controlled the ruling bodies of the Party. Thus in November 1927, Zinoviev and Trotsky, ousted from the Politburo during the last half of 1926, were also expelled from the Central Committee. A few weeks later, in a blatant violation of Party norms and precedent, Stalin in the name of the Central Committee decreed their expulsion from the Party, without holding a vote. A month later the Fifteenth Party Con-

---

[8]Tucker, *Stalin as Revolutionary*, p. 446, citing eyewitness accounts by Trotsky and his wife.

gress confirmed their dismissal and ejected Kamenev and seventy-two other oppositionists as well. Zinoviev and Kamenev recanted their errors and gained readmittance to the Party. Trotsky, however, was exiled to Alma Ata in Central Asia, and many fellow dissenters were sent to various remote parts of the country. In 1929 Trotsky was expelled from the Soviet Union. After brief stays in Turkey and Norway, he settled in Mexico, where a Stalinist agent murdered him in 1940. By the end of 1927, therefore, Stalin and the Rights had routed the Leftists from the Party. In a remarkable turn of events, however, Stalin now appropriated the Left position in the "great debate" and soon thereafter eliminated the Right Deviation, as it was now called.

One incident during 1926 provided a frightening hint of the implications of Stalin's victory. During a dinner of Leningrad officials to celebrate the removal of Zinoviev, the discussion turned to the question of how best to govern the Party without Lenin. Everyone but Stalin spoke up, all agreeing that the soundest solution lay in collective leadership. Having listened in silence, Stalin then rose and walked around the table. "Don't forget we are living in Russia, the land of the tsars," he warned. "The Russian people like to have one man standing at the head of the state. Of course, this man should carry out the will of the collective."[9] No one suspected who Stalin had in mind as that tsar.

As Stalin built his case against members of the Left Opposition in the fall of 1927, he also asked the Cheka's successor, the OGPU, to collect damning information concerning his rivals. He eventually trumpeted charges not just of antiparty activity but also of treason to support his successful drive to expel his opponents from the Party. This use of the secret police foreshadowed the malevolent techniques that Stalin would perfect in the purges of the 1930s.

1928–1929: The Year of the Great Turn

Not long after his triumph over the Left Opposition in late 1927, Stalin engineered a major transformation of Soviet society, a second revolution of sweeping dimensions. Stalin's revolution took place over relatively few years and ranked as the most extensive and fundamental revamping of a whole society in history until the Communist revolution in China in 1949. The "new October" and its aftermath reordered the way of life of some 130 million peasants and reshaped working and living conditions for the remaining 30 million citizens of the Soviet Union. Stalin presided over more loss of life and human suffering than anyone has—including

---

[9]Ibid., p. 312.

Hitler—before or since. Some 10 to 11 million Soviet citizens died in the economic cataclysm, famine, and purges of the late 1920s and 1930s, and another 25 to 30 million were lost to World War II. Yet most people in the United States and throughout the world are only dimly aware of this monumental tragedy.

Ironically, no one is certain exactly what Stalin intended or whether he possessed a clear design for this bold transformation. A secretive person, the Soviet dictator not only left no diaries, letters, or revealing memoranda, but he seldom confided in even close associates. According to biographer Tucker, during the 1920s the Soviet leader gradually developed the concept of another great Communist revolution. He began to implement this scheme only when two circumstances came together: when he felt secure in his control of the Party and government, and when the peasantry began to resist the initial phase of his new policies during 1928 and early 1929.

An altruistic desire to better the Soviet peoples' lot and an ideological commitment to build socialism undoubtedly contributed to Stalin's decision to launch a "second revolution." Yet Russian nationalism also motivated him, as his 1931 speech dismissing complaints about the pace of industrialization demonstrated:

> To slacken the tempo would mean falling behind. And those who fall behind will get beaten. But we do not want to be beaten. No, we refuse to be beaten! One feature of the history of old Russia was the continual beating she suffered because of her backwardness. She was beaten by the Mongol Khans. She was beaten by the Turkish beys. She was beaten by the Swedish feudal lords. She was beaten by the Polish and Lithuanian gentry. She was beaten by the British and French capitalists. She was beaten by the Japanese barons. . . . They beat her because to do so was profitable and could be done with impunity. . . . That is why we must no longer lag behind. . . .
>
> We are fifty or a hundred years behind the advanced countries. We must make good this distance in ten years. Either we do it, or we shall go under.[10]

Ten years and three months later, Hitler's armies would invade the Soviet Union, bent on one more beating.

In 1928 and 1929, Stalin introduced central planning of the entire Soviet economy and approved full-scale industrialization. He also completed socialization of the country's resources by establishing state

---

[10]Joseph V. Stalin, *Works*, vol. 13, *July 1930–January 1934* (Moscow: Foreign Languages Publishing House, 1955), pp. 40–41.

ownership of all industry and trade and collectivizing all agriculture. Earlier, the Soviet leader had begun to eliminate the contradictions inherent in the mixed economy of the 1920s, although he did not officially abandon NEP until the early 1930s. Party policy gradually shut down private trade, curtailing it in 1927 and 1928 and virtually abolishing it by 1930, thus putting an end to the notorious NEPmen. State stores replaced private merchants dispensing all retail goods and services. The government also banned individual peasant farming and ended private use of most land. Ideally, Party theorists wanted to organize agriculture into state enterprises (*sovkhozes*), in which farmers earned wages like factory workers. But mindful of the peasantry's loathing for this plan, Stalin and his advisers instead considered several types of cooperative agricultural production, finally settling on the collective farm. Soviet officials also planned to introduce advanced technology into industry and to mechanize farming with tractors, reapers, and other motorized devices.

The central government of course was to design and oversee the operation and growth of the entire economy. The Party core would set economic goals—above all production quotas—and ensure that workers and farmers achieved the targeted output. Because the Communist leaders had long agreed on the need to industrialize, central planners had begun as early as 1925 to draw up a master national economic plan. By 1927 they had contrived several variants. All of their proposals projected modest rates of growth, in accordance with the gradualist philosophy that dominated the Party as the Left Opposition's power waned. Direct evidence is lacking, but probably during 1927, Stalin probably increasingly worried that slow industrialization would not sustain his grand vision. Apparently, he also began seriously to doubt the government's ability to collect enough grain to invest in capital goods and to import technology needed for rapid industrialization. To overcome the resistance of the Right and to carry the Party with him, Stalin recognized that he had to convey his sense of urgency to Party leaders and members. Thus he warned that Soviet socialism itself confronted a terrible threat. Foreign capitalists, he claimed, were readying a new intervention, and *kulaks* and others at home were preparing to sabotage the economic leap forward.

Providentially, events came to Stalin's aid. In May 1927 the British broke diplomatic relations with the Soviet Union over allegations of Soviet subversion and propaganda, and later that year the French suspended economic negotiations with Moscow. The resulting war scare, although in fact the West had no plans to invade the U.S.S.R., deeply frightened many Soviet citizens. Stalin capitalized on these fears, reiterating the necessity of uniting against the Left and of pushing ahead with industrialization. Moreover, the failure of grain collections in the fall of 1927 gave him grounds to accuse the *kulaks* of undermining the country's security and well-being.

In the spring of 1928, Stalin staged the first of a number of "show trials" that he would repeat over the next decade. The government charged fifty-three engineers from the Shakhty mining district in south Russia with economic "wrecking" (sabotage) of Soviet enterprises at the behest of foreign intelligence agencies and White émigré former owners. Despite obvious signs that some defendants had been physically and psychologically tortured to confess and the flimsy evidence presented, the court found most of the engineers guilty. Five were shot. Stalin used the Shakhty trial to highlight the danger of imperialist subversion and indirectly to discredit the Right leaders, who generally supported the role of non-Party specialists like the Shakhty engineers. Above all, the trial helped him to maintain an atmosphere of crisis and urgency, in which only the sort of bold and revolutionary action that he had in mind could calm the chaos.

The Shakty affair represented only one front in Stalin's widening campaign against Bukharin, Rykov, and other Rightists. The general secretary had turned on the Right almost immediately after he eliminated the Left Opposition at the Fifteenth Party Congress in December 1927. His criticism mounted in January and February 1928 as the state faced a shortfall in grain collections from the autumn 1927 harvest. Stalin insisted that the Right's program of gradually accumulating capital through taxation and the purchase of grain from the peasantry was failing. In part because of crop failures in Ukraine and north Caucasus, in 1927 the state collected only 62 percent of the 1926 acquisitions. Exports of grain languished at less than 10 percent of pre–World War I amounts. These figures not only threatened the push to industrialize but endangered the food supply going to the cities and the Red Army. Apparently, peasants withheld grain from the market because of an earlier government decision to lower its purchase price. The continued gap between that price and the constantly rising prices of manufactured goods that peasants wanted to buy, many of which they could get only on the free or black markets, only worsened the problem. Peasants thus sold commercial crops and livestock, the prices of which had not been lowered, and held back grain in hopes for a higher price. Different procurement policies might have averted the grain collection crisis, but no evidence exists to support Tucker's suggestion that Stalin helped to contrive it.

In any case, an irate Stalin traveled to the Ural region and western Siberia in late January and early February 1928 to try to improve grain procurement. Without consulting the Politburo or the Central Committee, he urged a policy of arbitrary confiscation of grain. He also demanded that local officials arrest hoarders and others who refused to sell to the government. These draconian measures, a virtual return to the grain-requisitioning policies of war communism, yielded some success. The resulting increased procurements may have persuaded Stalin that he was right, that in fact the peasants had been hoarding grain, and that only forcible action would remedy the problem.

The rigorous steps naturally angered *kulaks* as well as middle peasants and soon provoked a storm of criticism from the Right. Even Anastas Mikoyan, one of Stalin's adherents, objected. Stalin temporized, uncertain about how to proceed, or perhaps fearing the Right's ability to arouse broad opposition to his policies. He maintained his claim, however, that the *kulaks* posed a serious menace to the regime. He also argued that as Soviet society advanced toward socialism, the class struggle would intensify. The remnants of capitalism embodied in people like the *kulaks* would put up a last desperate resistance. Bukharin grew so alarmed by what he saw as the dangerous wrongheadedness of Stalin's peasant policy that in July 1928 he secretly contacted Kamenev, then in disgrace.

Stalin nevertheless moved cautiously, acquiescing when in August 1928 the government adopted a Five Year Plan that officials in the *Gosplan* (the State Planning Agency) had drawn up. This comprehensive economic blueprint laid out the development of the economy through 1933, stipulating modest industrial growth and gradual peasant collectivization. By October 19, 1928, however, Stalin felt strong enough to launch his first public attack on the Right Deviation. He renewed his censure at a meeting of the Central Committee in November, denouncing the complete inadequacy of the Right's economic views and demanding acceleration of the drive to industrialize. Thus only a few months after the Left's defeat, Stalin began to support their case for rapid industrialization.

In the fall and winter of 1928–1929, the Party again implemented the harsh policies of the previous year's campaign to increase grain collections. The measures had limited success and only provoked increasing peasant resistance and local violence. The backlash undoubtedly spurred Stalin's efforts to rid himself permanently of the albatross of Rightist moderation. Ridiculing their fears of breaking the Leninist bond with the peasantry as alarmist, Stalin stressed that the only solution lay in quickening the pace.

Stalin also played on latent class hostility among Party members by making *kulaks* the scapegoats. He invoked an earlier formula of Lenin: In the struggle for socialism, there could be no compromise with class enemies. The question centered on who would "get" whom (*kto-kogo* in Russian): "Either we shall pin them, the capitalists, to the ground . . . or they will pin our shoulders to the ground." The Party's duty, Stalin asserted, was to ensure that the proponents of socialism emerged triumphant.

Despite the general secretary's harsh tone, only a few perceptive observers detected the tornado about to rip through Soviet society. The Sixteenth Party Conference in April 1929 endorsed a stepped-up variant of the Five Year Plan but proposed only 15 percent collectivization by 1933. With approval of rapid industrialization in hand, Stalin pushed his campaign against the Right, whose members kept urging more moderate policies. He used his majority in the Politburo to force Bukharin to resign his government posts in April 1929 and to oust him from the Politburo in November. By early 1930, Stalin had removed the remaining Rightists and ruled the Party as its unchallenged *vozhd'*.

The Scourge of Collectivization

Despite its frightful costs, the decision to launch an all-out war on the peasantry is little documented, and its origins remain controversial. One view holds that zealous lower-level officials, intoxicated with the atmosphere of class hatred and high-speed progress stirred up by Stalin and the Party, took it upon themselves to accelerate the pace of collectivization in the last half of 1929. Yet such a major departure in official policy probably could not have occurred without Stalin's encouragement, if not his direct guidance. The shortage of collected grain had compelled the government to introduce rationing in some areas at the end of 1928, extending it to most of the country in February 1929. By summer the recently approved industrialization plan threatened to fall behind its projected rate of investment, and the chronic "goods famine" of the past few years had worsened. Stalin knew that state grain procurements in the fall of 1929 would have to increase substantially if the plan to industrialize were to survive. On July 29, 1929, the state set quotas for compulsory deliveries of grain, not as an emergency measure but as standard practice, a drastic step that Stalin must have sanctioned or even initiated.

Although this action raised collection totals in the fall, Stalin, exasperated by a third year of struggling to accumulate grain, apparently decided to deal with the peasantry once and for all. On June 1, 1929, only about 1 million peasant households, or between 3 and 4 percent of the peasant population, lived on collective farms, up only 1 or 2 percent from the mid-1920s. Between July and late September, without any recorded change in Party policy or public pronouncement, special regional commissions on collectivization oversaw the entry of another 911,000 households into collective farms. In the last quarter of the year, 2.4 million additional families were reportedly collectivized, for a total of 20 percent of the peasantry. (The official figure for 1933 was still 15 percent.) These commissions could not have operated without the approval of Stalin's Secretariat.

Many poorer peasants supported the drive to form collective farms. Because they had little land, livestock, and equipment to donate to the *kolhoz*, they concluded that they had little to lose and might profit by sharing in the contributions of better-off peasants. Middle peasants and more prosperous families adamantly resisted the new arrangements. In many villages their confrontations with the authorities turned violent. Angry peasants chased off, beat, or even murdered Party and Soviet officials. As we have seen, the government sometimes forced peasants to comply. Armed struggled erupted in a few regions. In Dniepropetrovsk province, army units refused to march against insurrectionary peasants. The authorities brought in special secret police troops, and in one village alone, Dmytrivka, one hundred people were arrested. Some protesting peasants were shot and many others sent to the labor camps.[11] In all, several million peasants resisted collectivization; in some areas virtual civil war raged during the last half of 1929.

The question remains as to whether such conflict could have been avoided. From Stalin's point of view, the answer was no. He seemed convinced that the peasantry, led by the class-enemy *kulaks*, deliberately thwarted efforts to obtain the necessary grain surpluses. Therefore, the state had to reorganize the rural population into socioeconomic units that could be corraled under Party control. Two flaws in this argument readily come to mind. Specifically, could the state not have increased the pace of industrialization gradually, as the first version of the Five Year Plan envisioned? Also, could the government not have enticed the peasants to part with their grain by enacting more sensible price and taxation policies, as Bukharin admonished? Coercion bred resistance, which provoked greater force, culminating in civil violence and the virtual breakdown of the agricultural economy. The Right shuddered at the senselessness of the policy, but Stalin ruthlessly determined to carry on.

In his "Year of the Great Turn" article on November 7, 1929, Stalin announced the extensive collectivization in progress but portrayed it as a voluntary movement and a triumphant step on the road to socialism. In a Central Committee meeting that began three days later, Molotov reported the Politburo's decision to scrap the low level of collectivization set in the Five Year Plan. He then urged the committee to endorse mass collectivization over the next five months, before the spring 1930 sowing season. The compliant Party instructed local authorities to proceed immediately. Fearful that failure to meet collectivization goals in their district would leave them open to charges of Right deviationism, these officials acted forcefully, although Moscow did not specify how to establish or structure collective farms. Predictably, the local efforts produced widespread excesses of abuse, the reporting of "paper" *kolkhozes*, and swelling peasant resistance.

In December Stalin publicly called for "liquidation of the *kulaks* as a class," and the repression mounted. But how did he define *kulak*? By earlier Soviet classifications, a *kulak* was a peasant who worked somewhere between twenty-five and forty acres using seasonal hired labor. This description hardly made him a prosperous farmer, much less an agricul-

---

[11]Conquest, p. 155.

tural capitalist. Moreover, even under the early definition, only about 4 percent of the peasantry in the 1920s qualified as *kulaks.* Clearly this small number did not hold sole responsibility for withholding grain from the market or for opposing collectivization. What, then, was the point of Stalin's "dekulakization" campaign? Certainly he sought to rally anti-*kulak* and class-enemy sentiments within the Party behind the cause of all-out collectivization. Stalin's adjutant, Molotov, revealed another purpose when he told a Party meeting in early 1928, "We must deal the *kulak* such a blow that the middle peasant will snap to attention before us."[12]

The push for collectivization during the late summer and fall of 1929 underscored the Party's reason for intimidating the middle peasants. Well-off peasants could not have been the root of the problem. At that time, they were already forbidden to join *kolkhozes,* most had lost their land and property, and many had been arrested and deported. In addition, poor and landless peasants were usually willing to join collective farms, for they had the most to gain from the policy. The main resistance thus came from the middle peasants, who formed the bulk of the farming population.

Consequently, the stepped-up collectivization of January and February 1930, despite the rhetoric of dekulakization, aimed at capturing this middle group by whatever means. The government claimed success, reporting that 14 million households, or about 56 percent of the peasantry, had enrolled in *kolkhozes* by March 1. The sacrifices piled up, however. Between the summer of 1929 and March 1, 1930, the government confiscated the land and property of about 7 million peasants. Authorities sent half of this number to menial jobs in the Urals and Siberia, into exile to remote corners of the Soviet Union, or to the *Gulag* labor camps. Many peasants died resisting arrest or in transit. Thousands more perished in the camps. Between 1928 and 1931, the number of *Gulag* inmates ballooned from 28,000 to 2 million

Local officials supervised the collectivization and the arrests. When force was required, they used first local police and then special troops of the internal affairs commissariat, OGPU squads, and as a last resort the Red Army. Officers, however, were loathe to participate in this suppression, for most of the army's recruits came from peasant families. Some 25,000 young Communist activists supplemented local resources.

By the third week of February 1930, dekulakization and the accelerated collectivization drive had reached a crisis point. In the previous fall, peasants had begun to sell or kill their livestock rather than turn them over to the collective farm. In the succeeding six months, livestock herds of the Soviet Union thus were decimated. By the end of the collectiviza-

---

[12]Tucker, *Stalin in Power*, p. 139.

tion drive in the early 1930s, the country had lost almost half its cattle and horses (essential as power on the farms), two-thirds of its sheep, and almost three-quarters of its pigs. Breeding and raising animals takes time. With the losses World War II would add to these dismal figures, Soviet livestock herds would not recover until the late 1950s. In addition, reports began to flood into Moscow that the turmoil in the countryside threatened the spring sowing. With disaster at hand, Stalin on March 2, 1930, published an article, "Dizzy with Success," in which he heralded the achievements of collectivization. He blamed local officials for excesses and mistakes in implementing the process, however. As a result of his message, local pressure on the peasantry eased, and 8 million households of the fourteen million reportedly collectivized withdrew from *kolkhozes* over the spring and summer of 1930. In a further effort to lure recalcitrant peasants, Stalin also assured those entering collective farms that they could retain a small private plot and a few animals for their own use. At a slowed pace, forcible collectivization continued over the next three years, until a secret order from Stalin ended mass deportations of peasants in 1933.

The collectivization drive burdened Soviet society with enormous costs, including disruption of agricultural production, the destruction of over half the livestock in the country, and the repression of some 15 million people, of whom an estimated 2 million were killed or died en route to or in the *Gulag*. Yet Stalin had achieved his goal of controlling grain production and harnessing the rural population to his economic revolution. By 1933, 65 percent of peasant farming was collectivized, and by 1936, 90 percent.

The collective farm system would last for sixty years. (In the early 1990s, private farming or new agricultural cooperatives began gradually to supplant it.) The standard type of *kolkhoz*, known as an *artel*, was formed by pooling the peasant members' land, larger livestock, and tools. The farmers jointly worked the land and cared for the animals. Each year the *kolkhoz* contracted with state procurement agencies to deliver a certain proportion of the output at fixed, fairly low prices. Of the remaining production, the *kolkhoz* management set a portion aside for seed reserves and for capital improvements. The balance was sold at prices higher than for state agencies, with the proceeds divided among all the collective farmers according to the number of workdays each had accumulated during the year. Farm management allocated workdays according to the skill and difficulty involved in various farm tasks; for example, a day tending the farm's herd of goats might be set at one-half a workday, and driving a combine would count as two-and-a-half workdays. The government permitted each collective farm family to own a homestead, three or four surrounding acres on which to grow vegetables and fruits, a cow, small animals like chickens and ducks, and a few pigs and goats. The family fed itself with the produce from its plot and

"Join a Collective Farm" A Party official backed by portraits of Lenin and Stalin exhorts peasants to enlist in a *kolkhoz* in 1930.

stock and could sell any surplus at free prices in the *kolkhoz* market in the nearest town or city.

To provide technological assistance to a group of collective farms, Stalin set up district machine-tractor stations (MTSes), from which *kolkhozes* could hire agricultural machinery and request agronomic advice. The MTSes also functioned as a means of supervising the collectives. In addition, Party officials worked to have reliable individuals elected chairmen of the farms. These local managers ensured that each *kolkhoz* delivered the contracted grain to the state. In these ways Stalin controlled grain output and used the agricultural surpluses thus acquired to support his drive to industrialize. Yet as we shall see, the collective farm system proved economically inefficient and ultimately drained, not sustained, the Soviet economy.

In the wake of the collectivization program, a devastating famine struck in 1932 and 1933, afflicting most regions of the country but especially Ukraine and the Kuban and lower Volga areas. Although drought and bad weather had cut into grain harvests in 1931 and 1932, collectivization's disruption of agriculture, the peasants' passive resistance to the system, and the Party's mismanagement of *kolkhozes* and grain distribution must bear chief responsibility for the disastrous food shortages of 1932–1933. The unreliability of official Soviet statistics or crop yields and the scant information on which Western estimates are based make it difficult to state how seriously agricultural output declined in 1932.

Whatever the drop, production apparently could no longer feed the population.

Forced to choose, Stalin gave top priority to supplying the Red Army, workers in the industrializing economy, and urban dwellers in key jobs. This decision left peasants scrambling to survive. Historians still debate whether Stalin also deliberately withheld grain from non-Russian groups like the Ukrainians, the Kuban Cossacks, and the Volga Germans. Two cold-blooded policies of Stalin during the famine are not in dispute, however. While hundreds of thousands starved, the Soviet dictator continued to export grain, although in lesser amounts than before. The tonnage traded abroad could have saved countless lives. In addition, Stalin and the Soviet government suppressed news of the famine, and they turned down offers of foreign relief on the falsehood that no problem existed.

Food shortages in the countryside in 1932 and 1933 wrought terrible deprivation and widespread starvation. One survivor reported, "The peasants ate dogs, horses, rotten potatoes, the bark of trees, grass—anything they could find. Incidents of cannibalism were not uncommon."[13] Recent estimates place the death toll at 3 to 4 million in Ukraine and another 1 to 2 million elsewhere—on the heels of some 2 million killed during collectivization.

"Fulfill the Five Year Plan in Four!"

The massive industrial transformation of Soviet society, for which total collectivization provided a base, also accelerated markedly during 1929. The Five Year Plan presented in 1928 contained both a basic and an optimal version, the former projecting substantial but probably feasible targets for economic growth through 1933. The basic design emphasized investment in heavy industry at the expense of agriculture and of light and consumer goods industry. This strategy focused on the rapid build-up of machine tools and other capital goods sectors, which in turn would create the factories to produce both guns (defense matériel) and butter (consumer products) later. As approved by the government in August 1928, the basic plan went into effect on October 1, 1928. Then the Sixteenth Party Conference in April 1929 endorsed the optimal version, but in December 1929 the Politburo raised even these outrageous goals to utterly unrealistic levels.

Why Stalin and his supporters felt compelled to set such arbitrary and unattainable targets is unclear, but these actions nonetheless reflected the 1929–1930 atmosphere of crisis and revolutionary zeal. Stalin

---

13Ibid., p. 192.

"Fulfill the Plan!" Workers display a banner urging their factory to complete the First Five Year Plan in four years.

vilified the Right, already slipping from power, for its shameful timidity, and he used heady figures and visionary goals to whip up enthusiasm and to rally everyone behind the industrialization drive. In June 1930 the Sixteenth Party Congress finally adopted an earlier proposal to fulfill the plan in only four years. On December 31, 1932, the government dramatically declared the goal accomplished, four and one-quarter years after the plan's inception. In the sloganeering of that era, memoirists have left the remarkable image of Soviet schoolchildren marching around their classrooms mindlessly chanting, "Five in four!"

As the push to industrialize proceeded, urban unemployment evaporated and waves of peasants came to work in the newly built factories. This migration to the cities and the rapid mutation of small towns into major urban centers led to housing shortages, overcrowded apartments, and dormitory-style living. Rationing went into effect, and food, clothing, and consumer goods shortages plagued the population. Huge industrial complexes like the iron-steel center at Magnitogorsk in western Siberia and the gigantic hydroelectric dam in the Dnieper River sprouted up. Some projects, such as the canal connecting the White and Baltic seas, exploited *Gulag* labor.

Fruits of Industrialization Soviet workers atop blast furnaces at the huge Magnitogorsk iron-steel complex during the industrialization drive of the 1930s.

Despite the hardships and dislocations, however, many workers, managers, economic officials, and young people wholeheartedly threw themselves into this renewed revolutionary struggle to build socialism. According to a survey recently cited by a Soviet historian, a majority of white-collar employees in 1924 held strongly anticapitalist, nationalistic, and pro-state views. These individuals drew inspiration from the Party's pledge of a bright future. Hard work, low wages, and wretched conditions, they believed, were simply a deposit toward the better life that socialism promised. Stalin's supporters also saw themselves as defending the revolution, the first workers' state, and their homeland against potential aggressors outside and class enemies within. Many undoubtedly thought that they had joined a passionate crusade and shared with fellow workers the comfort of community and the glow of dedication.

Regardless of the authentic idealism and constant pressure from the Party and government, the goals of the First Five Year Plan remained unrealistic. As with the famine denials, disappointment over unmet goals led to lying and self-deception by the Party, flaws that came to characterize the Stalinist system. Because of statistical anomalies, the official figures on the results of the Five Year Plan require careful weighing. Clearly, the Soviet Union did not fulfill the overall goal for industrial output, originally set at an increase of 120 percent and eventually raised to 250 percent. Indeed, the planners eventually dropped this indicator altogether. A 50 percent increase is a more reasonable estimate for what the nation achieved. Output figures for key sectors are shown in millions of tons (see table on page 269).

The country scored the highest successes in oil production and in machine tool manufacturing, but industry failed to meet most other targeted levels. In addition, the plan's outcome revealed serious imbalances in the development of the economy. Agricultural production suffered

First Five Year Plan

	Actual 1927–1928	Basic Variant	Amended Dec. 1929	Actual 1932
Coal	35.4	68	95–105	64
Oil	11.7	19	40–55	21.4
Iron ore	5.7	15	24–32	12.1
Pig iron	3.3	8	15–16	6.2[14]

from the massive disruption of collectivization, and rural artisan industry declined disastrously. Textiles also fared poorly, and the chemical industry showed only feeble growth. The program also created extensive waste as the government commandeered resources and labor power recklessly to compensate for faulty planning and backward technology. Haste, shortages, improvisation, disorganization, and environmental damage marred much of the effort.

At the same time, it is important to recognize that the Five Year Plan, whatever its failures and inefficiencies, accomplished a major aim of Stalin and the Communist Party. At breakneck speed, it built the industrial base for what grew after World War II into the second largest economy in the world. It erected the heavy industry that fended off Hitler's 1941 attack on the U.S.S.R. and that eventually outproduced the Nazi war machine. It advanced the technical modernization of the country and established a scientific and engineering foundation on which the Soviet people constructed an updated economy and pioneered space exploration. The country managed all this in spite of the collapse of the basic assumptions that underlay the plan. Party officials had counted on a rise in agricultural and industrial productivity, yet the former declined because of collectivization and the latter gained only marginally. They had factored in a jump in foreign trade and in world prices for raw materials; instead, a global depression struck. Finally, they had assumed declining defense expenditures. But because of Japan's seizure of Manchuria in 1931 and the rise of the Nazis after 1932, they were forced to divert resources to the military establishment.

In any overall assessment of the push to industrialize, however, it is vital to consider not only achievements but costs. As we saw earlier, collectivization wrought both human and economic catastrophe. The effort took several million lives and spawned untold suffering. It also lowered

---

[14]Based on tables in Alec Nove, *An Economic History of the USSR* (rev. ed., London, 1982), pp. 189–190.

the net worth of the agricultural sector and saddled society and the economy with an inefficient and cumbersome structure. Moreover, although some poor peasants and many urbanites welcomed the changes that industrialization and collectivization promised, almost everyone paid for the process through a decline in their standard of living measured by real income. Alternatives also merit consideration. Some historians argue that had the Party followed Bukharin's policies, Soviet society would have achieved the same gains by the late 1930s, but with far less agony.

Conclusion

The period from the mid-1920s to the early 1930s stands as a revolutionary epoch in Soviet history. It witnessed the rise to supreme power of Joseph Stalin, a second-rank and enigmatic Bolshevik. It also saw the most extensive socioeconomic transformation in human experience. This second revolution included the forcible collectivization of Russia's peasants and an all-out industrialization effort. It rested in part on the hard work and sacrifice of more than 150 million people, but as the Kiev Polytechnical students that we met earlier could not foresee, it also provoked the killing and starvation of millions.

The campaigns of industrialization and collectivization could not have taken place without Stalin in the vanguard. Trotsky and the Left Opposition lacked sufficient backing in the Party and in the country to lead this revolution. Bukharin and the Right opposed the radical, high-tempo plan on political, intellectual, and temperamental grounds and would not have initiated it. Only Stalin possessed the support and the ruthless determination to force such change through against the stubborn resistance of tens of millions of peasants. To some extent, Stalin reacted to circumstances: renewed fears of capitalist attack, a lapse in industrialization efforts, and the sharp drop in grain collections. At the same time, he had a vision of a modernized and powerful socialist system. He dreamed of emulating Lenin's achievement in the October Revolution and paralleling the earlier forcible remakings of Russian society by Ivan the Terrible and Peter the Great.

But Stalin did not act alone. Millions of ordinary Soviet citizens backed his drive to create a beneficent socialist future. Stalin drew extensive support from younger Communists who had joined the Party in the civil war or early 1920s. These officials were less educated, less principled, and more technically oriented than the old Bolsheviks of the prewar and revolutionary eras. Drawn to Stalin's didactic theorizing, strongly nationalist outlook, and authoritarian decisiveness, they also gravitated to his socialist vision. Nevertheless, Stalin's leadership and determination were the sparks that ignited this second revolution.

The revolution had tragic overtones, for an alternative path offered itself: Bukharin's prescription for the future. Bukharin insisted that a gradual approach would earn the country marked economic growth as well as overcome the petty-bourgeois spirit of the peasantry. His plan, he believed, would painlessly but inexorably draw villagers into the net of socialism through cooperative activity in production, marketing, and credit. Bukharin also envisioned not political competition (for he favored the one-party system) but the evolution of a range of voluntary associations and societies to express diverse interests among the population. This array would encourage initiative and responsibility at the local level and could serve as a potent weapon against the overcentralization and bureaucratism already so endemic in the Soviet state. Perhaps Bukharin's program seemed too slow and too utopian, both for the times and for the sentiment of many Communists. We can only speculate what impact it might have had.

Stalin's revolution radically struck at more than the externals of the system. It also dealt a devastating blow to traditional culture and values. Perhaps such a powerful assault was needed to break deep-rooted resistance to change and modernization, but the effort had some unintended and paradoxical consequences. Because Stalin could not entirely crush old ways and attitudes, an altered Soviet citizen emerged from the chaos, a bit disoriented and slightly schizophrenic: socialist and secular, yet individualistic and traditional; urbanized and literate, yet rural and uncritical. The resulting tensions have marked the entire balance of Soviet history.

In Chapter 7, we examine the mobilization of people and resources that fueled Stalin's revolution and the subsequent economic development of the U.S.S.R. We also assess the fundamental political, social, and cultural alterations that accompanied the drive to industrialize.

FURTHER READING

The pertinent chapters of Alec Nove, *An Economic History of the USSR* (London, 1982), and Alexander Ehrlich, *The Soviet Industrialization Debate, 1924–1928,* present the issues and course of Stalin's economic revolution clearly. Moshe Lewin, *Russian Peasants and Soviet Power* (London, 1968), R. W. Davies, *The Socialist Offensive: The Collectivization of Soviet Agriculture, 1929–1930* (Cambridge, Mass., 1980), and Davies, *The Soviet Collective Farm, 1929–1930* (Cambridge, Mass., 1980) focus on the struggle between the state and the peasantry over collectivization. A valuable journalistic account of the upheaval in the countryside is Maurice Hindus, *Red Bread* (rpt., Bloomington, Ind., 1988). The tragic famine of 1932 is described in Robert Conquest, *The Harvest of Sorrow* (New York, 1986).

Stalin's industrial policies are analyzed in Hiroaki Kuromiya, *Stalin's Industrial Revolution: Politics and Workers, 1928–1932* (New York, 1980). An interesting firsthand report on industrialization is John Scott, *Behind the Urals: An American Worker in Russia's City of Steel* (Bloomington, Ind., 1989).

Political history is treated in Robert C. Tucker, *Stalin as Revolutionary, 1879–1929* (New York, 1973) and *Stalin in Power: The Revolution from Above, 1929–1941* (New York, 1990), as well as in Robert H. McNeal, *Stalin: Man and Ruler* (New York, 1988). Other important accounts include Roy Medvedev, *Let History Judge: The Origins and Consequences of Stalinism* (New York, 1989), Merle Fainsod, *Smolensk Under Soviet Rule* (Cambridge, Mass., 1958), based on revealing Soviet archives of that region, and Sheila Fitzpatrick, ed., *Cultural Revolution in Russia, 1928–1931* (Bloomington, Ind., 1977).

Broad judgments of Stalinism's origins appear in Robert C. Tucker, ed., *Stalinism: Essays in Historical Interpretation* (New York, 1977), which contains especially thoughtful evaluations; Theodore von Laue, *Why Lenin? Why Stalin*, 2nd ed. (Philadelphia, 1971); Sheila Fitzpatrick, *The Russian Revolution, 1917–1932* (New York, 1982); Roger Pethybridge, *The Social Prelude to Stalinism* (New York, 1974); and Michael Reiman, *The Birth of Stalinism* (Bloomington, Ind., 1987), a fresh assessment by a Czechoslovak Marxist. Also of interest is Leon Trotsky's summary attack on Stalinism in *The Revolution Betrayed* (Garden City, N.Y., 1937).

7

A VISION DISTORTED
The Turn to Terror

~

For a quarter of a century, from 1928 to 1953, one man dominated the history of the Soviet Union, and, to a considerable extent, the history of the world. Yet despite tidbits about him that have come to light since Mikhail Gorbachev's post-1985 policy of *glasnost'*, Joseph Stalin remains an enigma. Was he the adored leader

> Who broke the chains that bound our feet, now dancing
> Who opened lips that sing a joyous song,
> Who made the mourners charge their tears for laughter
> Brought back the dead to life's rejoicing throng.
> Who is in heart, in every thought and action,
> Most loving, true and wise of Lenin's sons—[1]

Or was he more like Stalin's own self-portrait?

> Everyone knows the indefinable, shattering force of Stalin's logic, the crystal clarity of his intellect, his steel will, devotion to the party, ardent faith in the people and love for the people. His modesty, simplicity, sensitivity to people and mercilessness to enemies are familiar to everyone. His intolerance for sensation for phrase-mongers and chatterboxes, for grumblers and

---

[1] From a late-1930s paean, "The Song of Stalin" in Warren B. Walsh, ed. *Readings in Russian History*, vol. 3, 4th ed. rev. (Syracuse: Syracuse Univ. Press, 1963), p. 761.

alarmists is well known. Stalin is wise, unhurried in the solution of complex political questions.[2]

Perhaps one of his protégés, Nikita Khrushchev, came closest to the mark.

Stalin was a very distrustful man, sickly suspicious. . . . Possessing unlimited power, he indulged in great willfulness and choked a person morally and physically.[3]

Each of these characterizations contains some truth about this complex and disturbed person. At times he made an inspiring leader, instilling a sense of purpose among the Soviet peoples—especially to build the socialist society that would serve as the base for world revolution. In other instances, he proved a tyrant. Delusions and fears arising from Stalin's insecure, paranoid personality drove him to order the persecution, torture, even execution of millions of his fellow citizens. His need for adulation and control pushed him to impose a personal despotism over Soviet society and to nurture a myth of his own infallibility and invincibility. Stalinism, the system that he sculpted, featured not only dictatorial rule and arbitrary repression, but modernizing economic policies, social and cultural transformation, and an ambiguous, state-centered approach to foreign policy.

Foreign Policy Contradictions, 1927–1934

As in other areas of Soviet life, Stalin ultimately directed the course of Soviet diplomacy during the years of industrialization and collectivization. Indeed, the requirements of his "second revolution" shaped Soviet actions in the international arena. For example, it was essential that the Soviet Union avoid war and foreign entanglements while in the throes of sweeping social and economic change and while building an industrial base capable of sustaining a modern military posture. As a result, between 1927 and 1934, Stalin took a cautious and conservative approach to foreign policy. At the same time, however, he ordered the Comintern to pursue tactics of Communist militancy. Conciliatory diplomacy helped to guarantee the short-term security of the Soviet Union. Yet the Comintern's hard line provoked considerable confusion within the Commu-

---

[2]Quoted from *I. V. Stalin: A Short Biography*, in Margaret Ziolkowski, "A Modern Demonology," *The Slavic Review*, 50 (No. 1):61. It is believed that Stalin personally edited and perhaps wrote this biography.

[3]Quoted in Basil Dmytryshyn, *USSR: A Concise History*, 4th ed. (New York: Scribner's, 1984), p. 544.

nist movement (and among foreign observers), and it abetted the Nazis' rise to power in Germany, with dire long-term consequences for the Soviet state.

After sporadic Communist uprisings failed in Germany in 1923, Soviet leaders resigned themselves to the improbability of proletarian revolution anywhere in postwar Europe. That realization, along with their success in allying with defeated Germany through the Treaty of Rapallo in 1922, spurred them to normalize diplomatic and economic ties with the remaining Western countries, as we saw in Chapter 5. In 1925 Japan recognized the U.S.S.R. Of the major world powers, only the United States withheld recognition.

The 1927 rupture of relations with Great Britain and that summer's subsequent war scare did more than agitate the atmosphere of crisis that Stalin needed to add urgency to his planned "new October." The rift also apparently convinced him of the desirability of maintaining peaceable relations with the capitalist West. Although Stalin left no direct record of his foreign policy calculations at this time, we can reasonably infer that, as a convinced Marxist-Leninst, he fretted over the danger of renewed imperialist intervention in the Soviet state. At the same time, he observed the increasing contradictions and strains among the capitalist nations that Lenin had predicted. "Imperialist" rivalries created continuing tensions between Germany and Britain and France in Europe and between Japan and Britain and America in the Far East. To prevent forays against the U.S.S.R., the Soviet dictator called on Communists everywhere to make defending the homeland of socialism their highest priority, and he pursued policies of conciliation toward Japan and the West, seeking to exploit the divisions among the powers.

On the other hand, Stalin believed that the worldwide economic depression that had struck in 1929 had accelerated the deepening crisis of capitalism foreseen by Marx and Lenin and provided a fresh opportunity for sparking proletarian revolution in Europe. The danger, however, was that anti-Leninist evolutionary socialists, organized in most countries into Social Democratic parties, would profit from the death throes of the European bourgeoisie and ascend to power by peaceful and parliamentary means as ruling capitalist governments crumbled. Thus Communist parties faced the urgent task of attacking and weakening their socialist rivals.

Last, the Soviet leader accepted the ideological view developed in the 1920s that fascist movements, like those that first crystallized in Italy and Poland and that later surfaced in Germany and the Balkans, represented the last gasp of capitalism. In an ironic variant of the conservatives' belief in November 1917 that a little dose of Bolshevism would cure the Russian people of radicalism, Stalin concluded that a brief bout of fascism would drive European peoples in flocks to Communism. He clung to this grave misconception into 1934.

The conciliatory side of late 1920s Soviet foreign policy became visible not only in the U.S.S.R.'s relations with nonsocialist states but also increasingly at the level of international cooperation. Lenin had spurned the League of Nations after its founding in 1919. Early 1920s Soviet ideologists had condemned the organization as an imperialist coalition designed to suppress the world's working and colonial peoples and to mastermind new offensives against Soviet Communism. Yet by 1927, it was clearly to Soviet advantage to collaborate with League activities that promoted cooperation and peace. In November 1927, Soviet deputy commissar for foreign affairs Maxim Litvinov presented Soviet proposals for immediate and complete disarmament among all nations to a League-sponsored international conference in Geneva. Litvinov denied any incongruence in his appearance at a League assembly and urged the delegates to take the Soviet propositions seriously.

Although the idea of universal disarmament was fancifully utopian and had little chance of adoption, its espousal promised several benefits for Soviet diplomacy. Advancing the concept put the Soviet Union in a favorable light before world public opinion, for it demonstrated the peace-loving nature of socialism. Moreover, when the capitalists rejected the proposal, Communist propagandists could label Western arms-control talk hypocritical. Of course, any steps taken toward disarmament would also lessen the danger of an attack on the militarily and politically frail U.S.S.R.

Nothing came of the Geneva meetings. Nevertheless, in 1928 and 1929, the Soviet government hastened to ratify the Western-sponsored Kellogg-Briand Pact outlawing war and took the lead in putting the treaty into effect among its neighbors. Pursuing a policy of accommodation and security, Litvinov, who became commissar of foreign affairs in 1930, signed nonaggression pacts with the Baltic states, Poland, Finland, and France during 1931 and 1932. In an important next step, the U.S.S.R. opened diplomatic relations with the United States in November 1933. That year Franklin D. Roosevelt's new administration agreed to a schedule for Soviet repayment of pre-1917 Russian debts to the United States. In return, the Unites States asked for Soviet abandonment of monetary claims based on alleged losses caused by American intervention in Russia in 1918 through 1920. The Soviet government also promised not to conduct seditious propaganda in the United States. Roosevelt hoped that trade with the U.S.S.R. would help lift the American economy out of the Great Depression. For his part, Stalin expected now to expand Soviet exports and to import more and more American technology and specialists. He also undoubtedly hoped that the link with the United States would counterbalance increasingly aggressive Japanese policies in East Asia.

Indeed, in the early to mid-1930s, the most serious threat to the Soviet state came not from the imperialist West, nor even from Nazi Germany, but from martial Japan. After the Japanese occupation of

Manchuria in 1931, tensions mounted along Manchuria's border with the Soviet Union. The fate of the Soviet-controlled Chinese Eastern Railway, which ran from the Trans-Siberian Railroad across northern Manchuria, became a source of contention between Tokyo and Moscow Although Japan's purchase of the railway at a reduced price in 1935 settled matters, border fighting between Japanese forces and the Red Army would break out in 1937–1939.

In China, Stalin followed a complex course. After the disastrous results in 1927 of his urging the Chinese Communists to collaborate with the nationalist Kuomintang, Stalin counseled the Chinese comrades to pursue independent revolutionary activity. They had already begun to do so, and he endorsed efforts by Mao Zedong and other Chinese Communists to set up a rebel base in Kiangsi province in south China. Following the Japanese incursion into Manchuria, Stalin supported but did not press the Chinese Communists' formation of a united front with the Kuomintang against further Japanese expansion. The nationalist leader Chiang Kai-shek resisted this alliance. His onslaughts against the Communists forced them in 1933–1935 to undertake their famous Long March, a six-thousand-mile convoluted odyssey from south China to northwest China to set up a secure base in the Yenan region.

Most of Stalin's policies strengthened the security and international position of the Soviet Union, but in one area they backfired. In Germany, Stalin's obsession with the powerful Social Democratic party, which he saw as the Communists' chief rival for future control of the country, led to consistently wrongheaded choices. Under pressure from the Soviet leader, German Communists attacked the Social Democrats politically and even on occasion cooperated with the rising Nazi party. Perhaps Stalin's ideas made sense at the end of the 1920s; the Nazis did not yet dominate German politics. Moreover, if the German Communists had not combated the government and the moderate socialists, they would have lost their extensive worker support to the Nazis, who strode an ultranationalist and virulently antigovernment line. But after elections in 1932, which revealed the Nazis' growing power, Stalin insisted that the German Communists rebuff Social Democratic overtures to join forces in resisting Hitler. A united left front would have provided at least a temporary majority coalition in German politics. Whether such collaboration could have stopped the Nazi takeover is unknown, but the policy that the Soviet ruler foisted on the German Communists eased the Nazis' seizure of power in early 1933. Hitler soon turned on the German Communists, arresting many and breaking up the movement.

Stalin responded belatedly to Hitler's emergence as leader of an openly anti-Communist Nazi state in Germany, perhaps because the Soviet despot wanted to keep open the possibility of an alliance with Hitler against a Western capitalist offensive. In any case, Stalin before long recognized that a taste of Nazism was not going to provoke an anti-Nazi backlash and a proletarian uprising in Germany. He also realized that Hitler's venomous anti-Communism at home and the führer's dream of absorbing Russia posed an alarming threat to the U.S.S.R.

The Soviet leader began to develop policies aimed against Nazi Germany after Hitler signed a nonaggression pact with Poland in February 1934, an agreement that opened the potential for a joint Polish-German carving up of the Soviet Union. In the winter and spring of 1934, Stalin jettisoned the anti–social democratic line of the Comintern and enjoined the French Communist party to collaborate with socialists and even nonsocialists opposed to fascism. This cooperative policy came to be called the Popular Front. In September the Soviet Union joined the League of Nations and began actively to support "collective security" against fascism. In the summer of 1935, Stalin enlisted in the French security design for Europe by signing a treaty of mutual assistance with France in case of aggression. Further, he agreed to come to the aid of Czechoslovakia if it were attacked, as long as the French also did so. At the Seventh Comintern Congress in July–August 1935, Stalin exhorted all Communist parties to support the policies of the Popular Front and to concentrate their energies against fascism. This last step crystallized the changed course of his foreign policy.

Mobilizing the Arts, Science, and Education

In addition to influencing the Soviet Union's foreign policy, Stalin's sweeping socioeconomic transformation required that the nation's intellectual talents be harnessed to the cause of socialist construction. In an effort parallel to the economic restructuring of the Soviet system, enthusiastic radicals sought to revolutionize thought, attitudes, and behavior. Carefully analyzed by the American historian Sheila Fitzpatrick, the "cultural revolution" lasted from mid-1927 to mid-1931. Like the "great proletarian cultural revolution" in the sixties in China, the movement in the U.S.S.R. reflected a renewal of revolutionary spirit and a zeal to root out bourgeois elements in society. Unlike the Chinese experience, however, the Soviet cultural revolution mainly targeted non-Party citizens and never became a powerful political force. This post-NEP campaign also appears largely a spontaneous, grass-roots affair, which the Party and government capitalized on but did not direct. Worker and student activists in their teens and twenties chiefly spearheaded the movement, along with slightly older Party members either recently enlisted from the lower classes or recruits from the civil war era.

Initially, cultural revolution militants primarily attacked non-Party intelligentsia, particularly educators, writers and artists, and so-called bourgeois specialists in the professions and the state-run economy. The purists objected to the authority and influence that these former class enemies retained. They also criticized the privileged economic position and access to such perquisites as higher education, ration coupons, travel, and elite stores that specialists and pre-1917 intellectuals enjoyed. This phase of the cultural revolution led to a radical (although brief) recasting of Soviet education, the removal of Anatoly Lunacharsky as commissar for education in 1929, the firing of many professors and teachers, the arrest of a hundred staffers in the Soviet Academy of Sciences, and the dismissal of thousands of engineers. As a deplorable by-product of this offensive, the Party staged two more "show" trials, one in 1930 against the alleged Industrial Party (which existed only in the imagination of the secret police) on charges of "wrecking," and another in 1931 of former Mensheviks. The assault on the old intelligentsia raged especially fiercely in the academic and literary communities, as we shall see.

The cultural revolutionists also castigated the bureaucracy and old institutions and values. Ironically, the young zealots adopted several ideas and criticisms voiced by the recently defeated Left Opposition, but they infused them with a fervent vision of a purer, more efficient socialist society based on the latest science and technology and on a true communal spirit. Disgusted by the traditional bureaucratic methods that they observed in many Soviet institutions, the enthusiasts favored the withering away of the state, despite Stalin's 1930 stipulation that this streamlining would have to await the far-off worldwide triumph of socialism. Pressure from these radicals persuaded the Party to "cleanse" the bureaucracy in 1929 and 1930 by firing 164,000 officials.

The cultural revolution trumpeted opportunity and responsibility for its young activists. They demanded, and largely obtained, freer access to higher education. Many gained admittance to universities or received postsecondary training in technical institutes and Party schools. In 1931 the number of workers or workers' children enrolled in universities had tripled from 1928, and hundreds of thousands of proletarians attended other institutions. On graduation, these young people immediately filled engineering, technical, and supervisory jobs opened by the push to industrialize. They soon rose to responsible posts in the Party and state apparatus, forming a new elite that supplanted the old revolutionaries and the pre-1917 intelligentsia and that dominated the post-1945 leadership. As late as June 1978, half the Politburo members had followed this career path.

Because the cultural revolutionists fostered spontaneity, castigated the creeping bureaucratization of Soviet life, and ousted specialists whose talents the modernizing nation needed, Stalin checked their campaign beginning in mid-1931. To ensure full mobilization of the country's human energy and skills in the drive for industrialization, he instead tightened Party control over Soviet cultural life and propounded narrower values and themes.

On one occasion, Stalin had referred to writers as "engineers of human souls." It is not surprising, then, that he turned first to literature to achieve his ends. From April 1928 until April 1932, the Russian Association of Proletarian Writers, RAPP, and its leader, Leopold Averbakh, exercised a virtual dictatorship in the field. They called for novels and stories that focused on industrialization and collectivization and attacked two leading fellow-traveler writers, Boris Pilnyak and Evgeny Zamiatin, in 1929. The former recanted, and the latter emigrated after appealing to Stalin for an exit visa. In 1930 the critic Alexander Voronsky and a group of writers known as *Pereval* came under fire from RAPP for their stories' excessive attention to the individuality of human beings.

In 1932, however, Stalin designated a young protégé, Andrei Zhdanov, to establish closer Party control over literature. Official accusations slammed RAPP's harsh treatment of fellow-traveler writers who produced fiction supportive of industrialization. In fact, the Party probably resented RAPP's autonomous authority in literary matters and found insufficiently ideological its toleration of personalized portrayals of the Stalinist revolution. In any case, the Party dissolved all existing literary organizations and gave the professional Union of Soviet Writers a monopoly in the field that would last into the Gorbachev era.

Between 1932 and 1934, the Party proclaimed a new literary and artistic canon—*socialist realism*—which also would endure for over fifty years. Socialist realism served a mainly inspirational and didactic purpose. Works of art were to uplift people; to inculcate key values of dedication, loyalty, and collectivism; and to portray the glorious socialist future to the masses. Hence, the canon decreed that novelists present positive heroes overcoming harsh backgrounds and complex challenges to accomplish feats associated with the building of socialism. Officially defined as the depiction of "real life in its revolutionary development," in practice the literary guide mandated that writers portray life not as it really was but as it *ought to be* in a socialist society. One socialist realist painting, for example, depicts Stalin—in life shorter than his comrade-in-arms Marshal Voroshilov—as towering over Voroshilov. In the ideal socialist world, the Soviet ruler would be taller. Socialist realism thus had little to do with reality and much to do with the future that Stalin and the Party envisioned.

Of the many novels celebrating industrialization, Valentin Kateyev's *Time Forward* ranks as the most interesting and readable. The book describes the building of the giant iron-steel complex at Magnitogorsk in the Urals. Stressing the frantic tempo of the effort through imaginative literary devices, the story focuses on the attempt of a group of workers to break the world record for pouring concrete. This plot hardly sounds riveting, but in fact Katayev's treatment generates considerable tension. A dramatic rendering of collectivization, Mikhail Sholokov's *Virgin Soil Upturned* portrays disruption and hardship as well as achievement. Because of reordered emphases in history, a number of historical novels also appeared in the 1930s. The best known of these is the unfinished *Peter I* by Alexei Tolstoy, which glorified the reign of Peter the Great, an earlier transformer of Russian society whom Stalin admired.

Socialist realism silenced many talented Soviet writers. Knowing that the Party would never approve their work for publication, they either stopped producing works or wrote "for the drawer"—that is, for family, friends, and the future. Among these stifled artists were the esteemed poets Anna Akhmatova and Osip Mandelshtam, although a poem of Mandelshtam "for the drawer" that bitingly satirized Stalin circulated so widely by word of mouth that he was arrested and eventually sent to the camps, where he died in 1938. Boris Pasternak, refusing to write poetry on demand, immersed himself in translation projects. Vladimir Mayakovsky, the radical herald of revolution in 1917, struggled to accommodate himself to the demanding strictures of RAAP but finally committed suicide in 1930, leaving this poem in his suicide note:

> *Love boat*
> > *Smashed on convention.*
> *I don't owe life a thing*
> > *And there's no point*
> *In counting over*
> > *Mutual hurts*
> > > *harms,*
> > > > *and slights.*[4]

In painting and architecture, criticism of modernism and constructivism had mounted through the 1920s, on the grounds that the masses could not understand symbolic and abstract work. The visual arts hence were failing in their socialist duty to teach and inspire workers and peasants on the road to socialism. By the early 1930s, experimentation ended and socialist realist art predominated. Painting was reduced to technicolored scenes of factories and farms featuring unrealistically healthy and hearty workers and peasants busily engaged in building socialism, or to historical canvases that romanticized pivotal events in Russian or revolutionary history. Of course, artists who portrayed dramatic moments in the October Revolution and the civil war made sure to omit Trotsky and always to place Stalin at Lenin's side. In architecture, elaborate and highly decorated forms replaced the spare functionalism of the 1920s in a monumental style often ridiculed by Western observers as "Stalinist Wedding-Cake."

---

[4]Quoted in Edward J. Brown, *Russian Literature Since the Revolution*, rev. ed. (Cambridge, Mass.: Harvard Univ. Press, 1982), p. 20.

Stalin's Idealized Portrait Faithful to the style of socialist realism, the painter depicts Stalin as the all-wise leader overseeing . . . industrialization and mechanization of agriculture in the 1930s.

In music, a comparable drive for control, simplicity, and accessibility emerged, with formation of the monolithic Union of Soviet Composers and support for tuneful and optimistic compositions. The most renowned Soviet composer, Dmitri Shostakovich, came under attack in early 1936 for "formalism" and for "an intentionally ungainly, muddled flood of sounds" after Stalin attended a performance of his opera *Lady Macbeth of Mtsensk*. Critics had praised the work at its opening only eighteen months earlier. Although Shostakovich and his gifted colleague, Sergei Prokoviev, continued to produce important works into the 1950s and 1960s, Stalin preferred tunes that he could hum and remember.

Overall, socialist realism had a deadening effect on Soviet culture. Although the charge that too often "farm boy meets dairy maid but marries tractor" is overblown, the Party expected happy endings. Most socialist realist art and literature suffered from a tedious, if not downright boring, predictability. Moreover, despite the survival of a few individuals of exceptional talent, a majority of writers and artists who submitted to Party dictates were hacks with little ability, and they produced eminently forgettable works.

Like art, literature, and music, the fields of Marxist philosophy and Party history served as key areas for promoting unqualified support for the Stalinist revolution and for instilling correct values in the increasingly educated Soviet population. Thus these disciplines, too, soon came under rigid Party control and were retooled to convey the new Stalinist orthodoxy. As early as 1930, Stalin intervened in discussions among Soviet philosophers, attacking Abram Deborin, a prominent dialectician of the 1920s, and the early Marxist, Georgy Plekhanov. Stalin made clear that in the future he alone would determine the orthodox interpretation of Marxist philosophy.

In an October 1931 letter to the editors of the journal *Proletarian Revolution,* Stalin advanced his standard into the battlefield of Bolshevik history. He castigated a 1930 article that suggested that Lenin might have misjudged certain factions in the German Marxist movement before World War I. Accusing the hapless author (who was soon arrested and dispatched to a twenty-year Siberian exile) of misinterpreting Lenin and sympathizing with Trotskyism—errors "bordering on crime, on treason to the working class"—Stalin decreed that from now on he would act as the sole arbiter of Party history. He alone would define Leninism and falsification alike. His letter and a subsequent address to the Institute of Red Professors by one of his henchmen set a number of intellectual fields off hunting for Trotskyist heresy and triggered a glorification of Stalin's role in the history of Bolshevism and the country. Possible misjudgments by the future Soviet ruler, such as his failure to attack the Provisional Government in March–April 1917 were expunged from historical accounts, and history was distorted to make Stalin virtually equal to Lenin in the birthpangs and early survival of the Soviet state. This Stalin-centric view of Bolshevik and Soviet history reached its climax in 1938 with publication of the official *Short History of the Communist Party of the Soviet Union,* which soon became the most extensively distributed book in the history of Soviet publishing. Subtle rumors spread that the *vozhd'* himself had not only approved the project but had even drafted part of the manuscript.

In 1934 Stalin broadened his attention to the entire scope of Russian history. A Central Committee edict attacked the dominant historian of the 1920s, Mikhail Pokrovsky, who (luckily for him) had died in 1932. The committee accused Pokrovsky of presenting Russia's past as a series of abstract sociological schemes and for neglecting important individuals and epochs of the prerevolutionary era. In the revisionist history that soon emerged, tsars Ivan the Terrible and Peter the Great were transformed from brutal "feudal despots" into national heroes. Military leaders like General Alexander Suvorov, an antagonist of Napoleon, and key battles such as Peter's defeat of the Swedes at Poltava were lauded as expressions of true Russian valor. The rewritten histories also supplanted earlier condemnation of tsarist imperialism with the argument that the non-Russian peoples' absorption into the Russian Empire was "a lesser evil." After all, inclusion allowed them to come under the influence of the mighty and advanced Russian civilization. Independent judgments about the past disappeared, and omissions, distortions, and unsupported interpretations so corrupted Soviet historical monographs and textbooks from the 1930s to the 1950s and beyond that the Russian-Soviet past became almost unrecognizable.

The biological sciences also suffered under the deadening hand of rigidity. Beginning in the 1930s, Trofim Lysenko, a charlatan agronomist backed by the Party and by Stalin personally, imposed his views, then already discredited among biologists, on Soviet science. According to Lysenko, characteristics developed in a species by changes in its environment could then be transmitted genetically to offspring. As a result of this ideologically driven theory, scientists conducted nonsensical experiments with novel plant hybrids, and the fields of biology and genetics were debased in the Soviet Union for thirty years. The Party imposed inflexible views in several other fields such as linguistics, economics, psychology, and psychiatry while blocking development of the new discipline of sociology. To ensure that research priorities and fund allocations mirrored the regime's requirements, after 1929 the Party took over the most prestigious scholarly institution, the Academy of Sciences, firing some world-renowned researchers and appointing servile professors as ranking academicians.

The Party also dictated the direction of intellectual life by its monopoly on publishing, including the popular media, and by censorship. In the 1960s, one Soviet historian described the four stages of screening that his writing had to pass through in order to get a single word published: (1) approval of his writing plan by the leadership of the sector on the history of the October Revolution, where he worked, and of the Institute of History, the parent body under the U.S.S.R. Academy of Sciences; (2) review and discussion of his draft manuscript by his sector and the Institute; (3) review and approval of the revised manuscript by the state publishing house to which the Institute of History submitted it; and (4) final approval before publication by the censorship agency (*Glavit*).[5] Historical pieces that strayed even microscopically from the Party line were unlikely to survive such vetting.

Stalin also prescribed principles and practices for education. To industrialize and mechanize the nation, the general secretary needed a literate, technically educated population, and after 1930 he reoriented schools and universities toward that goal. The literacy campaign raised the rate from 51 percent in 1926 to 81 percent in 1939, with nearly universal literacy achieved by the 1960s. Nevertheless, many who were classified as literate remained uneducated. In 1939, for example, 78 percent of city dwellers over age ten had only four-year schooling or none at all. Eighty-three percent of trade employees (store workers) had only primary education, and 63 percent of the country's leadership cadres had completed a mere four years of school.

Abandoning the educational experiments of the 1920s and the open enrollments of the cultural revolution, Stalin reinstituted admissions criteria for higher educational institutions. Schools reverted to traditional

---

[5]Discussion with the author, April 1964.

curricula and methods by the mid-1930s, and examinations, discipline in the classroom, and nationally prescribed textbooks were all restored or introduced in elementary and secondary education. The program taught graduates necessary skills, but because classes emphasized rote learning, most students failed to develop analytical and problem-solving abilities.

Stalin also wanted the educational system to produce the "new-type socialist person" that Marxism foresaw emerging in the higher, communist phase of history. Schools and youth organizations like the Octobrists and Pioneers thus indoctrinated young people in socialist values and Bolshevik history, and universities required students to take courses in dialectical and historical materialism (basic Marxism) and in the history of the Communist Party. As higher education spread, it became a major vehicle for upward social mobility, permitting children of workers and peasants to enter the ranks of Party and state officialdom.

Pride, Productivity, and Privilege: Society in the 1930s

Establishing control over Soviet intellectual life and directing it toward the ends of Stalin's second revolution was easy, for the U.S.S.R. had relatively few cultural institutions and educated individuals. Remolding Soviet society as a whole proved considerably harder. The low cultural level and traditional outlook of much of the population, especially the peasant majority, that Lenin had bemoaned continued to retard the pace of modernization in the 1930s. To some extent Stalin's cultural conservatism and patriarchal style reflected that backward-looking mentality, but rural attitudes and entrenched mores also distorted or reshaped his policies in turn. In addition, the most sweeping social changes of the period, industrialization and urbanization, had a life of their own dating back to prerevolutionary times. These movements wrought consequences not always intended by Stalin and his planners. Popular pressure to attain immediate benefits, for example, often intruded on the leadership's long-range agenda. Finally, as recent Western scholarship has demonstrated, the Soviet population sometimes managed to modify Stalinist policies—to act in spite of, not because of, Party decrees and direction.

Overall, however, Stalin and his Party allies set the tone for Soviet development in this period. Workers, peasants, intelligentsia, and state and Party officials at lower levels might evade, fudge, and even marginally alter central directives, but Stalin's determination to force the country down the path of industrialization and modernization prevailed. His unwillingness to entertain dissent or even independent discussion regarding his policies established the rules of the game and largely determined its outcome. Increasingly, the state alone initiated socioeconomic change and dominated all aspects of life.

The continuing industrialization program of the 1930s offers an enlightening example of this process. Under this policy, the Party determined the goals and pace of economic growth while workers, peasants, and bureaucrats effected minor modifications in implementing the plans. When the First Five Year Plan ended, Party leaders and some economic strategists, in a fog of delusive self-congratulation, envisaged another set of exorbitant growth targets for the Second Five Year Plan, which would run from January 1933 through the end of 1937. But 1933 was a difficult year, plagued by famine, a near breakdown of the transportation system, a 14 percent decline in investment, and a sharp drop in the rate of growth of industrial production. The Party hastened to redraft the Second Plan, trimming its goals. Simultaneously, Stalin introduced other, more pragmatic themes: consolidating the economic gains achieved so far, and mastering the skills and techniques required by modern industry. These responses bespoke a more modest and sensible effort than the extravagant aims and frenzied atmosphere of the First Plan.

In the moderated program, Stalin and his advisers emphasized a rapid rise in productivity—that is, an increase in how much each worker produced. This approach had merit, for growth during the period 1928–1932 had depended in large part on a dramatic expansion of the labor force and on mechanization. Now that the U.S.S.R. stood on a firm industrial base, adding workers and machines would augment output only marginally. Productivity increases, though, would quickly and efficiently lead to higher production and sustained growth. Stalin and the planners also raised investment in consumer goods, recognizing that workers would have little incentive to work harder and better if shortages in food, housing, clothing, and other daily necessities persisted. During the course of the Second Five Year Plan, the priorities steadily shifted, however, to stress again producers' goods and heavy industry. This change of focus came about because the growing threat of Nazism demanded a high jump in defense spending and armaments production.

During the First Plan, the Party had used "socialist competition"; that is, bosses encouraged work groups (called brigades) to outdo each other. The strategy yielded little success, and productivity growth between 1928 and 1932 was much lower than planned. Nevertheless, on August 30 and 31, 1935, coal miner Alexei Stakhanov rearranged the work process and drew on auxiliary help from his brigade to extract fourteen times the normal amount of ore in one workday. This feat quickly formed the basis for "Stakhanovism," a Party-sponsored, nationwide push to boost productivity by publicizing, honoring, paying highly, and sometimes instantly promoting outstanding workers who significantly overfulfilled their production norms through technical or organizational innovation. As historian Lewis Siegelbaum concluded, it is unclear whether Stakhanovism

Second Five Year Plan

	Output		
	1932 (actual)	1937 (plan)	1937 (actual)
Producers' goods[a]	23,100	45,528	55,200
Consumers' goods[a]	20,200	47,184	40,300
Coal[b]	64.3	152.5	128.0
Oil[b]	22.3	46.8	28.5
Machine tools[c]	15.0	40.0	45.5
Grain harvest[b]	69.9	104.8	95.0

Source: Table adapted from Alec Nove, *An Economic History of the USSR* (London, 1982), p. 226.
[a]millions of rubles
[b]millions of tons
[c]thousands

raised productivity overall. Yet it doubtless introduced a vital link between the use of correct techniques and substantial material rewards and social prestige. At the same time, managers and workers succeeded in evading certain pressures that Stakhanovism imposed on the productive process, and the movement gradually died out as the 1930s closed. As one lasting effect, Stakhanovism reinforced social differentiation among Soviet workers and further weakened workers' sense of solidarity.

As the figures demonstrate, the Second Five Year Plan achieved only a few of its goals. The continued growth of the Soviet economy shown in part reflected the output and contribution of the factories and industrial base built during the First Plan. But the numbers for expanded output concealed an important factor: the use of forced labor, a work force comprised primarily of peasants deported to remote regions of the country during collectivization and inmates of the *Gulag*'s growing number of "correctional labor" institutions.

The Party might have hit more of its targets but for a marked economic slowdown during 1937. The decline probably derived from the economic impact of Stalin's purges (discussed below), as well as from the shift to defense production as Hitler loomed larger. Between 1933 and 1937, the percentage of the Soviet budget allocated to defense soared from 3.4 to 16.5 and then doubled again between 1937 and 1940. From 1934 to 1939, the size of the armed forces doubled and defense production almost tripled. Preparing the country for war also would undermine the Third Five Year Plan, launched in 1938 but aborted by Hitler's attack on the Soviet Union in June 1941.

Looking at the period 1928–1940, the time span of the industrialization effort, one is struck by how much the Soviet people accomplished, as well as by the price they paid. Soviet industrial growth averaged 12 to 14 percent a year, a record surpassed only by Japan in the 1950s and 1960s. Steel production expanded fourfold, coal five times, and generation of electric power nine times. The plans slighted quality and efficiency and ignored environmental safeguards, but the country laid a solid industrial base that permitted it to withstand and eventually to overcome Nazi aggression in 1941. The First and Second Five Year Plans yielded one remarkable and partly unexpected effect: a dramatic increase in the labor force outside agriculture and a burgeoning of cities. In 1927 and 1928, workers totaled about 11 million, with 15.7 planned for the end of the First Plan. By 1932 the actual number had reached almost 23 million; by 1937, 27 million. The urban population thus far exceeded the expected numbers—38.7 million people in 1932 instead of 32.5 million. Between 1926 and 1939, the proportion of city dwellers climbed from 18 percent to 33 percent of the population. The preponderance of incoming workers and new urbanites were peasant families, a circumstance that produced what historian-sociologist Moshe Lewin called the "ruralization" of Soviet cities. The newcomers brought countrified attitudes and values, and their presence, according to some observers, introduced a rude coarseness that would persist.

The flood of migrants from the countryside, coupled with the First Plan's shortfalls in housing and consumer products, burdened both new and old workers with terrible living conditions. Some laborers ended up living in barracks, dormitories, and other communal accommodations. Most families crowded into one room, sharing a kitchen and bathroom with several other families. Until the end of 1935, when rationing ceased, food shortages continued to plague the cities. Urban dwellers survived on provisions distributed through their factory or other place of work. As agriculture slowly recovered from the ravages of collectivization, food became more plentiful, although many items such as meat, cheese, and eggs could be obtained only at high prices in the collective-farmers' markets.

Working conditions did not fare much better. Because most peasants lacked training or possessed only handicraft skills, they had difficulty adjusting to machine labor and factory discipline. They misused and broke equipment, made mistakes, and wasted materials. Their inability to master tasks often disrupted production. Unaccustomed to the rigors of the factory system, laborers also sometimes failed to arrive at work on time or at all. Frequently they changed jobs, on the average of once in four months at the height of labor turnover in 1932–1933. The Party instituted heavy penalties for absenteeism, including loss of housing (which factories often controlled) and dismissal. In 1938 lateness of even twenty minutes became a criminal offense. To combat job changing, the government

The Struggle to Industrialize As these workers' snacks at the construction site of a massive Dnieper River dam demonstrate, the proletariat sacrificed much in the early 1930s' drive to build heavy industry.

revived the tsarist system of internal passports in 1932. It also required a wage book and then a work book listing a worker's employment record. Peasants were excluded from the passport system until 1974. This restriction enabled the state to control peasant migration to the cities. Industrial plants as well wielded strict discipline, with engineers, foremen, and brigade leaders all determining job assignments and wage rates. As for trade unions, the Party turned them into facilitators of increased output, and they ceased to play any role in defending the interests and rights of the proletariat.

For workers who had a vague notion that socialism meant some kind of social and economic equality, life under industrialization in these years brought a severe shock. In a 1931 speech, Stalin, driven to buttress productivity and hoping to spur workers' efforts through material incentives, decried wage egalitarianism. According to the Soviet leader, the concept of equal pay thoroughly contradicted the socialist phase of history that the Soviet Union had entered, in which individuals would receive reward according to their labor, not according to their needs. The Party set substantial wage differentials, under which skilled workers made up to four times the pay of unskilled workers, technicians and engineers up to eight times, and managers and administrators from twelve to thirty times. Moreover, the vast majority of workers were paid under a progressive piece-rate system—that is, a fixed wage for a minimum amount of output and then increasingly higher wages for additional units produced per hour or day above the minimum. In this system, skilled workers benefited most. The best workers earned other rewards as well, such as housing and living perquisites and special shopping, recreational, and vacation opportunities. Indeed, the Stakhanovite workers mentioned earlier formed a super-elite of the Soviet labor force. Considerable distinctions among levels of workers developed, although the disruption of World War II makes it difficult to determine whether a "labor aristocracy" ever emerged.

Assessing the real income of workers and peasants in the 1930s is also difficult. Data are fragmentary, and it is impossible to measure intangible benefits such as subsidized housing (however inadequate) and recreation, economic security (no unemployment), improved health care, and access to education. Collective farmers also enjoyed the produce and income from their private plots. If one compares the standard of living of unskilled peasants laboring in a factory with conditions they left on the farm, the workers probably had marginally improved their lot. For the labor force as a whole, a rough estimate reveals that the average worker's real income declined by a substantial 20 to 40 percent during the period 1928–1933. This drop derived to some extent from a shortage of necessities but primarily from prices increasing faster than wages. The trend continued but then slowed during the Second Five Year Plan: workers' real incomes climbed somewhat between 1934 and 1938 but probably did not reach the 1928 level. The position of collective farmers who survived dekulakization and famine worsened between 1928 and 1933. Although their lives improved slightly in the next five years, these farmers' average real income before the war probably still measured notably below that of 1928. The conclusion is clear: Stalin's "new October" was made possible by the sacrifices not just of peasants, as foreseen in Evgeny Preobrazhensky's "primitive socialist accumulation" theory, but of workers as well, for whom the October Revolution was ostensibly intended.

Stalin's economic revolution noticeably benefited one group, however: the planners and managers of this vast effort who staffed state factories, government ministries, and supporting Party organizations. A privileged intelligentsia also arose that provided brainpower and manipulated propaganda in support of the push to industrialize. Several factors facilitated the emergence of these elite groups. First, mere generation mattered. Younger individuals born shortly before or around the turn of the century and who embarked on careers following the 1917 revolution began to supplant prewar and revolutionary leaders during the 1930s. In many fields this process was reflected in the replacement or retirement of "bourgeois specialists"; in the Party, fresh activists superseded those "Old Bolsheviks" who were not purged. Nikita Khrushchev—eventually to succeed Stalin—exemplified these rising "new Communists." Born in 1894, Khrushchev in 1935 advanced to leader of the Moscow region Party at the age of forty-one. Three years later he became Party boss of Ukraine. Many new leaders of this sort received engineering or technological training under Party sponsorship and moved rapidly into important administrative posts in the economy and the Party.

Second, Stalin ousted numerous senior personnel from state and Party positions, first in the cultural revolution of 1928–1931 and then during the purges of 1936–1938. By sweeping away most of the revolutionary generation, the Soviet dictator accelerated his protégés' advancement to the topmost levels and opened slots for juniors at lower ranks. These individuals, mostly from humble origins, largely unaware of the Party's democratic past, and dedicated to Stalin's revolution, were inclined to execute the general secretary's policies faithfully.

Third, the new elites were products of the emphasis on education and training that marked the 1920s and early 1930s. The number of students in higher education grew from about 160,000 in 1927–1928 to 470,000 in 1932–1933. By 1938–1939 the total rose to more than 600,000, with almost another million students enrolled in technical training institutes. These graduates moved quickly into responsible jobs in the economy and the Party.

Finally, the privileged groups reflected the special nature of Soviet socialism as it emerged in the 1930s. Owing to the increasingly close marriage of Party and government and of both institutions with economic activity, planners, organizers, managers, engineers, facilitators, administrators, and supervisors formed an interlocking bureaucracy—the Party-state—that ran the country. Party leaders co-opted the most talented executives, and the ablest people shifted easily among managerial, bureaucratic, supervisory, and exhortatory tasks. A young, educated Party member might at first do agitational work in factories or for a local Party committee, a few years later become a district Party secretary, then work as an economic planner or factory manager. In the end, he or she might return to Party work as a republic secretary or as a member of the Party Central Committee secretariat at the all-union level. Conversely, a non-Party graduate of a technical institution might go to work for a factory, advance to a management position, be recruited by the Party, and end up in a government ministry supervising one branch of the economy.

Lacking opinion surveys, we cannot judge the motivations and attitudes of this rising tide. Some undoubtedly were careerists, interested in power, advancement, and privilege alone. Later Soviet novels, plays, and short stories satirize such self-seeking individuals. Others, however, idealistically dedicated themselves to building, if not socialism, at least a more powerful country and a better future. Elite members from worker or peasant backgrounds were more apt to support the unrestrained effort to construct a classless society. Some leaders, especially among the younger generation, were true Marxist-Leninists who, armored with the scientific certainty that the laws of history were inexorably on their side, labored ruthlessly to create their version of a socialist utopia in the Soviet Union and to spread proletarian revolution throughout the world. Still others moved ahead in the system simply to make a living for themselves and their children. Some older, educated elites who survived the disruption of the cultural revolution benefited under Stalinism. Because they were required to work and forbidden to emigrate, they had little choice but to apply their talents within the system. A tiny group of defiant, self-possessed people "dropped out," subsisting in routine jobs and spending most of their time and all of their energy and talent on private pursuits.

A sense of participation, a feeling of contributing to society, provided one incentive for the new elites. The opportunity to share in policy-making or power-broking attracted others. Too, this privileged strata earned substantial pay, their salaries running twelve to fifteen times that of the average worker. Many accumulated far more rubles than they could spend. They purchased household appliances, private cars, and vacations in scenic parts of the U.S.S.R. Some also built country cottages, or *dachas*, on land leased from the state outside their city of residence.

The new elites enjoyed eminent status in Soviet society, and the most outstanding individuals were showered with awards, honors, and prizes. The cream also received a number of perquisites not available to average citizens, such as access to large, convenient apartments, health care at special medical clinics with modern equipment and the best doctors, and the right to shop in special stores that offered a broader selection of higher quality goods than did the state stores. Some of these privileged individuals joined private clubs or recreational organizations. A few at the highest levels were privy to chauffeured state limousines and luxurious vacation retreats. In addition, their children often attended special schools. Although run by the state, the schools offered unusual facilities and top teachers; some emphasized particular disciplines like the arts or a foreign language. Such an institution was commonly referred to as a *blatnaia shkola*, a school where *blat'*, or "pull," would get a child accepted. According to many reports, the new elites also used influence to ensure their children's admission to desirable institutions of higher education, particularly to the most attractive departments of the best universities.

Everything, however—privileges, power, position—depended on doing the job that the Party wanted done, without dissent or protest. The *nomenklatura* system guaranteed that senior Party leaders controlled the appointment of individuals to key posts not only in the Party and the government but in educational, cultural, and all other significant institutions. Individuals who failed to toe the Party line lost a chance at the choicest jobs. Moreover, failure, malfeasance, or the hint of independence could lead to withdrawal of perquisites, loss of position, exile in a remote part of the country, or a term in one of the *Gulag* camps. Because Party policy and decisions, reflecting Stalin's views and whims, often shifted arbitrarily, members of the new elite endured considerable insecurity, even those who survived the purges of 1936 through 1938. Risk and reward alike were high.

Although a number of women qualified as members of the new elites, none held top-ranking positions in the Party or government, and only a handful occupied the highest posts in other fields. Moreover, Stalin's "new October" dictated sharp changes in policies regarding women and family life. Specifically, industrialization and collectivization demanded full female participation in the task of reshaping the economy. Between 1928 and 1940, the number of urban women working full-time outside the home increased from 3 million to 14 million. Women were called on to perform every sort of job, from intricate technical tasks to heavy construction labor. Like male workers, they were exhorted to superhuman efforts in order to surpass production goals. In agriculture, the Party touted tractor-driver heroines as models of achievement for emancipated rural women. In reality, however, most peasant women continued to work at unskilled jobs, and few advanced to technical or management positions on the collective farms.

Recruiting women into expanding industry ended female unemployment, which had skyrocketed in the 1920s. It also permitted some women to develop new skills, to use them in a personally satisfying way, and to assert some financial independence. But the massive entry of women into the labor force also had disadvantages. Growing numbers of women

A Glorified Soviet Woman Farmer Illustrative of the Party's 1930s' idealization of women's economic role, this poster depicts a collective farmer under the slogan, "Shock Work at Harvest Is a Bolshevik Harvest."

struggled under the double burden of a full-time job in the economy and full-time responsibilities as wife, mistress, mother, and homemaker. With rapid expansion of the economy, too, inequalities in pay and power persisted, perhaps even worsening in some areas.

As another consequence of Stalin's "second revolution," the state ignored women's rights in the 1930s, at first brushing them aside to focus on industrialization. Then, when Stalin announced the achievement of socialism in 1936, women theoretically no longer had a platform or a reason to air grievances. According to Marxism-Leninism, the victory of socialism would end the oppression of women as part of its general liberation of the masses. On International Women's Day (March 8) in 1939, Stalin mendaciously concluded: "In every branch of the economy, culture, science, and the arts—everywhere stands emancipated woman alongside man, equal with him, performing great tasks, moving socialism forward."[6] In fact Soviet women were neither emancipated nor equal to men.

During the 1930s, Stalin and the Party buried this reality under a blizzard of slogans, decrees, and awards honoring women workers, dairy maids, wives who supported their Stakhanovite husbands, and Soviet mothers who bore future workers and soldiers for the motherland. Issues such as inadequate day-care facilities, absence of family planning counsel or devices, unequal pay, lack of access to top jobs, and the persistence of traditional views and values about women were simply overlooked. In party committees and state enterprises, the women's sections (*zhensektory*) that replaced the terminated women's departments (*zhenotdely*) concentrated on general political work and agitation and propaganda. Only in Muslim areas did some special efforts to improve conditions for women continue.

On balance, the legal changes of these years also worked to the disadvantage of women. In 1936 abortion was banned on the grounds that the procedure threatened women's health and that terminating pregnancies was unnecessary under a system that supposedly provided care for every woman and child. The ban proved part of a broad drive by the regime to bolster the family and to raise the birthrate. The state exalted children as a blessing and applauded the ever growing numbers of workers who would expand Soviet industry. As the threat of Nazism intensified, the government also added increased staffing for the Red Army as a reason to value children. Mothers were praised, then honored with awards and medals, and finally paid escalating stipends for each child delivered.

---

[6]Quoted in Mary Buckley, *Women and Ideology in the Soviet Union* (Ann Arbor, Mich.: Univ. of Michigan Press, 1989), p. 118.

Stalin supported strengthening family stability, probably because he held traditional views and because he believed that secure families would provide backing for the industrialization campaign. New decrees made divorce harder and much more costly than before. In addition, absent fathers were made more responsible for child support, with stiff fiscal payments of up to one-half of their salary. This last policy benefited women, but the other measures confined their choices and consigned them to traditional roles and unequal status.

In addition to rescinding many women's rights during the decade before World War II, the Party nearly eliminated organized religion in the Soviet Union. First it closed many cathedrals, churches, and mosques. Most tellingly, it imprisoned or executed almost all the top leaders of the Orthodox, Catholic, and Protestant churches. Paradoxically, this sweeping attack on religious institutions had little effect on religious belief. As many as two-thirds of the rural population and one-third of city dwellers apparently retained their faith.

As we saw in Chapter 5, in 1927 the Party had abandoned its support for the breakaway Orthodox organization, the Living Church, when it secured the complete submission to the state of Metropolitan Sergei, the acting head of the traditional Orthodox Church. For a brief period, attacks on religion subsided, but as Stalin launched his "second revolution," the Party renewed the persecution between 1929 and 1932. Stalin's immediate reason for intensifying the antireligious campaign centered on countering the effort begun by an Orthodox bishop in 1928 to extend and expand the church's activity and teachings to children and young people. He sought a broader purpose, however. The Soviet ruler wanted to facilitate the collectivization drive by suppressing a rallying point of peasant resistance the village church and priest in much of the country, and the local mosque and Muslim *mullah* in Soviet Central Asia.

A decree of April 8, 1929, from the Russian Republic had limited religious practice to divine services inside the church. The law strictly prohibited any educational, charitable, or recreational activities of a religious nature. In effect the edict revoked the earlier constitutional protection of the right of religious propaganda. The Party then began to close additional churches and applied new fiscal and legal discrimination against priests and believers. It manipulated surviving congregations by infiltrating Party members and agents of the secret police into their ranks, and it eliminated most of the hierarchical leadership of the churches. Islam came under heavy fire, with prohibitions against women's wearing the veil, against observance of the Muslim holy month, Ramadan, and against believers' making the *hadj*, or pilgrimage to Mecca.

Using as its spearhead the atheistic, "public" organization, the League of the Militant Godless, the Party launched yet another wave of oppression in 1937 and 1938. Although priests had received full citizenship and the right to vote under the 1936 Constitution (see below), the league accused the clergy of influencing local soviet elections. Priests and bishops were arrested and executed, charged during the height of Stalin's purges with anti-Soviet activity and foreign espionage. Accurate figures do not exist, but the number of Orthodox churches apparently shrank from 39,000 in 1925 to fewer than 10,000 in 1939, and the number of mosques declined from more than 20,000 after the revolution to 1,312 by World War II. Even more damaging to the church, the ranks of Orthodox bishops thinned, from 163 in 1930 to fewer than 10 at the end of 1939. Without bishops to consecrate new priests, soon no one would be available to perform the rites of Orthodoxy.

The Orthodox Church resisted the persecution in ingenious ways. It moved to mass confessions when the lack of priests inhibited the hearing of individual confessions, and it secretly conducted baptisms and marriages. When the Party abolished Sunday as a day of rest, parishes held evening worship services. The church also organized covert monasteries disguised as collective farms, and itinerant priests performed the sacraments as they roved from village to village. Orthodox leaders formed "catacomb" churches as well; unregistered, underground congregations concealed from the Party.

The success of these devices and the depth of traditional faith are reflected in the high number of Soviet citizens who remained believers at the end of the 1930s. In fact, the census of 1937 contained the question, "Are you a believer?" The census results so displeased Stalin that he ordered its findings suppressed, perhaps in part because a high proportion of the population answered yes. Providing some substantiation to these rumors, Soviet writers on atheism in late 1937 and 1938 referred to the large numbers of believers as a major reason to intensify the antireligion campaign. Some estimates suggest that by 1940, 80 to 90 million Soviet citizens retained their faith despite two decades of repression and the extensive persecution of the 1930s. Ironically, Stalin would soon be desperately tapping this reservoir of traditional belief and using the remnants of the church hierarchy to support the patriotic effort that World War II would require.

Darkness at Noon: Inspiration, Adulation, and Coercion

The Hungarian ex-Communist Arthur Koestler titled his fascinating novel about the 1930s purges *Darkness at Noon*. The phrase highlights the paradox of Stalin's 1936 proclamation of the brightest moment of Soviet development—the achievement of socialism—at the instant that he launched the show trials and massive arrests that accompanied the purges. A former Marxist dialectician, Koestler saw the ironic contrast between the announced glories of socialist progress and the grim reality of widespread repression under Stalin. Although difficult to rationalize, the coexistence of these antithetical phenomena reflected the essence of Stalinism in the 1930s and confused foreign observers and Soviet citizens alike.

Completion of the First Five Year Plan, Stalin had always maintained, was crucial in building socialism. As we saw earlier, the plan inspired genuine enthusiasm among some Soviet citizens (although not among most peasants). After 1934, as the effort to industrialize began to bear fruit, Stalin sought other ways to evoke support and loyalty. In particular, he wanted to convince the Soviet people of the nation's accomplishments and to deliver some aspects of the good life that the Party had been promising since 1917. To this end, he offered a new constitution that would ensure rights and advantages for citizens. Further, as Stalin pointed out, it would symbolize the Soviet Union's attainment of socialism, the lower phase of the final stage of Marxian historical development. Describing the document as "the most democratic of all the constitutions in the world," he then modestly allowed people to label it the "Stalin Constitution."

Whether the Soviet dictator recognized the obvious incongruence of a constitution guaranteeing individual rights and popular government amid the grim purges is unclear. Probably the two phenomena were entirely separate in his mind. One crystallized, for all to admire, how far he had brought Soviet society. The other comprised a legitimate defense of the state, the Party, and his own idealized self-image against "two-facers" and "enemies of the people" who had determined to denigrate and even destroy the great revolution he had engineered. Perhaps Stalin also believed that by trumpeting the existence of democracy and well-being inside the U.S.S.R., he could divert foreign attention from his systematic elimination of well-known figures in the Party and in Soviet cultural life. In so doing, he could rally Western democratic support for his antifascist foreign policy. He may even have hoped to throw off guard Communist colleagues whom he had marked for purging. For example, in 1935 and early 1936, both Nikolai Bukharin and the writer Maxim Gorky enthused about the democratic and humane course that the constitution apparently symbolized. They seem to have hoped, fleetingly, that Stalin genuinely intended to rein in his dictatorial stampede.

Whatever his motives, from February 1935 Stalin headed a constitutional commission that published a draft on June 12, 1936. Stalin then called for nationwide discussion of the document. Before its ratification on December 5, 1936, some 40 million Soviet citizens guided by local Party leaders pored over the proposed constitution in hundreds of thousands of meetings. They made numerous suggestions for changes, a few of which Stalin adopted. For some, this form of popular plebiscite doubtless was instructive and satisfying. Others grew bewildered as they discussed the constitution's guarantees of freedom while relatives, friends, and neighbors disappeared into the *Gulag*.

In presenting the constitution for ratification, Stalin rejoiced over the U.S.S.R.'s achievement of socialism. Yet he reminded Soviet citizens that the true victory would come only when socialism triumphed on a global scale and when imperialist states no longer threatened the Soviet Union. Similarly, the constitution declared the end of antagonistic classes in the U.S.S.R., but accompanying provisos warned that as long as hostile capitalism encircled the country, the danger of subversion, espionage, and the infiltration of class enemies would persist.

Despite these caveats, the constitution gave full electoral rights to all Soviet citizens over eighteen years old, except for criminals and the insane. This policy eliminated the disfranchisement of certain groups that the 1924 constitution had decreed. Soviet ideologists explained that, with the attainment of socialism, retrograde feudal or bourgeois groups no longer existed. Every four years, everyone would vote directly for deputies to the national legislative body, the Supreme Soviet, and to other soviets at the republic, district, and local level. The overhauled electoral system seemed thoroughly democratic and open. In practice, however, the Party still controlled the process: citizens nominated candidates for election at public meetings in factories, farms, and other organizations, and local Party secretaries made sure that only reliable individuals were put forward. Not all nominees were Party members, but all toed the Party line. As a result, the nominating meetings reached consensus on a single candidate, leaving voters no choice on the ballot. They could cross off the name presented, but to do so they had to enter a booth and line out the Party-approved candidate. Few had such courage, and most elections resulted in at least a 99 percent victory for the single nominee.

The text of the constitution mentioned the Communist Party only once, in Article 126. But the words indicated the extent of the Party's control over the nominating and electoral process and, indeed, over all of Soviet life. The article described the Party as "the vanguard of the working people in their struggle to strengthen and develop the socialist system and . . . the leading core of all organizations of the working people, both public and state."

The Party thus kept a tight rein on all public activity by drawing many able and hardworking people into membership and by directing them under meticulous supervision to carry out the policies formulated at the top by Stalin and his cohorts. In the 1930s, the Party numbered fewer than 4 million people, but its members held all the key jobs. To gain admittance to the Party, an individual had to earn the recommendation or sponsorship of three responsible people and serve a one-year probation. Once accepted, Party members were expected to serve as models of correct behavior, working diligently and setting a high moral standard in their personal life. Constantly subject to scrutiny by Party superiors and colleagues, they were also encouraged to practice self-criticism. As one Party member remarked, "It is smart once in a while to confess in Party meetings little mistakes you have made before some jealous or zealous comrade accuses you of a major error." Party members also faced strict centralized discipline and had to act vigilantly and energetically to carry out Party policies in their institution or enterprise. They were encouraged to exhibit *partiinost'* (Party-mindedness), or putting the Party's interests first.

The constitution did not address the question of why only one political party existed in the Soviet system. However, in 1931 Stalin had explained to American publisher Roy Howard that because parties represented classes and because a socialist society had only a single class—the toiling masses—only one party, the Communists, was needed or made sense. By 1936 Stalin, acknowledging that workers still composed a minority in Soviet society, had the constitution recognize two classes, workers and peasants. Nevertheless, they were deemed "nonantagonistic" classes, a thoroughly un-Marxian concept. He also added a third group, the toiling intelligentsia, not a class but a social stratum. Although the constitution was silent on the issue of who represented these groups, accompanying commentary made clear that the Communist Party fulfilled this role exclusively.

The constitution guaranteed the right to work but noted that "work is a duty and a matter of honor." It also ensured full welfare benefits for Soviet citizens, including medical care and education. Finally, it contained a complete bill of civil rights, promising freedom of speech, press, assembly, and religious worship, as well as full equality for women and nationalities. Ominously, however, it stipulated that citizens were to exercise these rights "in conformity with the interests of the working people and in order to strengthen the socialist system." In practice, Stalin violated every guarantee of the constitution.

The governmental system that the constitution regularized featured a hierarchy of soviets. The national legislative body, the Supreme Soviet, comprised two houses, the Council of the Union (one deputy per 300,000 electors) and the Council of Nationalities (twenty-five deputies per union republic and smaller representation for lesser national minority units). The Supreme Soviet had an impressive 1,400 members and met twice a year for a week to ten days. It simply rubber-stamped legislation presented by the executive branch, the Council of Peoples' Commissars (Council of Ministers after 1946), which in turn received direction from the Party's Central Committee and Politburo. (See chart, p. 209.) The number of republics in the Soviet Union rose to eleven (from the seven set up in 1924) through the splitting of the Transcaucasian Republic into Armenia, Georgia, and Azerbaijan and the addition of Kyrgyzstan and Kazakhstan in Central Asia. This alignment would last until the eve of World War II.

Naming the Constitution of 1936 after Stalin provides only one reflection of the virtual worship of the man that unfolded in the 1930s. Described euphemistically as "the cult of personality" during the de-Stalinization campaign of the 1950s, fawning over Stalin permeated almost every corner of Soviet life. As paeans to the *vozhd'* piled up, Stalin insisted that such fulsome praise was both undeserved and un-Communist. Yet clearly he relished every word and action that confirmed his self-image as the resolute and heroic maker of a new revolution as great as the one that Lenin had led. More chilling, as the public image of the wise, kindly, pipe-puffing father of his people gained strength, Stalin unflinchingly directed the arrest and murder of millions of Soviet citizens. In his personal life, he became increasingly reclusive, withdrawn, and distrustful.

The Stalin cult had begun on his fiftieth birthday in December 1929, shortly after his final triumph over the Right Deviationists and amid the all-out collectivization drive. A ten-day outpouring of encomia and of flattering photographs in the press marked the Soviet ruler's first half-century. Perhaps this panegyric was arranged to steel everybody's resolve in the struggle against the *kulaks* and to celebrate publicly his emergence as undisputed leader of the Party and therefore the nation. In any case, Stalin was feted again at the Sixteenth Party Congress in mid-1930. He failed, however, to cajole the famous author, Maxim Gorky, into writing his biography. Birthday party excesses did not recur until 1933, when Stalin's crony Kliment Voroshilov ended his ceremonial May Day

The Stalin Cult As adulation of Stalin spread, the propaganda machine credited him with every alleged triumph—in this poster, the success of industrialization under the First Five Year Plan.

address in Red Square with the cry, "Long live its [the Party's] leader, the leader of the workers of our country and the whole world, our glorious, valorous Red Army man, fighter for the world proletarian revolution, COMRADE STALIN!"[7] This wording became a standard formula for greetings to Stalin from every kind of domestic and foreign organization, salutations that now were regularly published in the Party and government national newspapers, *Pravda* and *Izvestiia*.

Soon poems, stories, films, music, paintings, and sculpture began to glorify Stalin. The following is by no means the most fawning example of this type of adulation:

Within the walls of the Kremlin there's a fellow
He knows and loves all the land;
Happy and fortunate are you because of him;
He is Stalin and great is his name![8]

In an appellation orgy, mountains, lakes, towns, factories, nurseries, military units, research institutes, and babies were christened or renamed after Stalin. Stalin prizes were created to honor outstanding citizens in a variety of fields. Public receptions and ceremonies played an especially important role in the Stalin cult. At these events, the enigmatically smiling Stalin received the praise and gratitude of his subjects. At one congress of Stakhanovites in 1935, "everyone rose when Stalin appeared, the applause went on for ten or fifteen minutes, and Stalin clapped in response. When, at last, they all sat down, a woman's wild cry went up, 'Glory to Stalin!' Then the 3,000 jumped to their feet again and resumed clapping."[9] Benefiting from the penumbra of the Stalin cult, lesser Communist leaders were also acclaimed, and the Party itself became an object of veneration.

Despite the accolades, Stalinism contained an unintended paradox. Although the Soviet dictator strengthened central authority at the expense of peripheral regions and institutions and sought to quell local independence, his cultural and social policies indirectly promoted non-Russian nationalism. After the forcible absorption of Georgia in 1921, Stalin, emulating Lenin, had spoken as often about the dangers of Great Russian chauvinism as about the threat of local nationalism. But in the 1930s, his emphasis shifted. He beefed up centralized control by Party headquarters in Moscow over every aspect of Soviet life, including

---

[7]Quoted in McNeal, p. 149.

[8]Quoted from the poem "Lullaby" by V. Lebedev-Kumach in McNeal, p. 227.

[9]Tucker, *Stalin in Power*, pp. 331–332, drawing on an eyewitness account by Soviet writer Ilya Ehrenburg.

national minorities, while tightening his grip on the Party through the purges. Stressing the perils of nationalist deviations, he exerted stringent authority over the republics and swept away most of the indigenous 1920s leadership in the non-Russian regions of the union. These areas thus became economic and political vassals of Moscow: their industry and agriculture primarily serving the needs of the central Five Year Plans, and their governments and Parties obsequiously carrying out the directives of the great *vozhd'* in the Kremlin.

The first sign of growing conflict between Stalin's centralism and the national minorities had come during widespread resistance to collectivization in 1929 in Kazakhstan and in Muslim areas of the north Caucasus. As we saw earlier, the Party launched an antireligious campaign that year, partly because it deemed the village church and mosque centers of resistance to the revolutionary reorganization of the countryside. Muslim communities were particularly hard hit; Islam undergirded all their customs, social structure, and daily life, and collectivization thoroughly disrupted their agricultural and nomadic economies. Too, a Party edict replacing Arabic script with Latin letters in their written languages had shattered the continuity of these communities' cultural and educational tradition. Muslims suffered further disruption in 1939 when the Party scrapped the Latin alphabet and imposed Cyrillic characters for Muslim writing.

It is little wonder that extensive and often violent resistance to these policies erupted, including the reemergence of *Basmachi* guerrilla bands in Central Asia. In the fight against collectivization, the Kazakhs killed or sold off 80 percent of their livestock, devastating the pastoral economy there. More than one-third of the Kazakh population was arrested, died by violence and disease, or emigrated across the border to Chinese Turkestan. Central Party authorities closed down local newspapers and journals, locked up thousands of Islamic leaders, and forcibly industrialized and collectivized most of the Muslim areas of the U.S.S.R. In 1933 and 1937, additional Tatar, Azerbaijani, and Central Asian Party officials were purged. By 1938 hardly a single leader from the 1920s remained in place, or even alive, in these regions.

Ukraine, the second largest republic after Russia, with a population of more than 30 million, fared little better. As Khrushchev commented in his de-Stalinization speech of 1956, the Ukrainians survived "only because there were too many of them and there was no place to which to deport them." The imposition of Stalinist centralism particularly seared the Ukrainians because they had enjoyed a privileged status in the family of Soviet socialist states during the 1920s. In those years the Party had permitted, even encouraged, a policy of "Ukrainization," promoting Ukrainian language and culture and assigning Ukrainian Communists to top jobs in the republic.

This policy had generated some friction. On one side, a few Ukrainians protested continuing political and especially economic tutelage from Moscow. On the other side, Stalin criticized Alexander Shumski, the local commissar of education, for pushing Ukrainization too far and for being "against Russian culture and its highest achievement—Leninism." Overall, however, relations between the center and Ukraine remained fairly cordial until Stalin launched the collectivization drive.

As in Central Asia, Ukrainian peasants strenuously opposed Stalin's radical transformation of agriculture. Indeed, many of them had worked before 1917 as independent farmers rather than being tied to a commune. Although evidence is sketchy, considerable violent resistance broke out. To crush the Ukrainians' intractability, Stalin probably starved hundreds of thousands of them in 1932 and 1933, as we saw in Chapter 6. A number of Ukrainian politicians and cultural figures were expelled from the Party in 1933, and in 1937 all but one of the pre-Stalin Communist leaders of Ukraine were ejected. In 1933 Stalin sent Nikita Khrushchev, a young protégé, to Kiev to stamp out any remnants of Ukrainian nationalism and to reinforce the center's tight grip.

A similar pattern developed in Belarus, where in 1933 and 1934 the Party brutally suppressed a budding national consciousness that had emerged in the 1920s. Almost all Belarus's prominent cultural figures and political leaders were eliminated. The Caucasus, too, suffered in the 1930s. The Party accused Azerbaijani Communists of plotting with Turkish imperialists and charged Armenian leaders with scheming to create a greater Armenia independent of Moscow. Lavrenti Beria, a disreputable Georgian sycophant who managed to worm his way into Stalin's confidence, presided over a particularly merciless purge of Caucasian leaders before becoming head of the all-union secret police in 1938.

Jews bore a disproportionate burden during the purges, perhaps because many of them held high positions in Soviet political, professional, and cultural life and thus were cut down when the scythe of Stalin's repression swept through these fields. Possibly Stalin's latent anti-Semitism had already begun to emerge in the 1930s, as biographer Robert Tucker suggests. Jewish culture and religion also fell victim to restrictions on the teaching of Hebrew as well as to closing of synagogues, Yiddish-language newspapers, and theaters.

Stalin's centralizing policies were embodied in the 1936 Constitution, which rescinded the right of the union republics to pass their own legal and judicial codes and instead enhanced the power of the all-union government. Only four commissariats—education, local industry, communal economy, and social security—remained exclusively in the hands of republic officials. The most important commissariats were all-union and run from the Kremlin. The rest were joint bodies, with central and republic branches but with Moscow calling the shots.

The 1930s also saw the elevation of Russian nationalism in history, music, and other fields and the promotion of Russian language and culture in offices, schools, and universities. Yet British historian Geoffrey Hosking has perceptively noted that this phenomenon stemmed more from Sovietization and Moscow's imposition of central control than from deliberate Russification. In fact, by undermining peasant customs, rural social organization, and the Orthodox religion, Stalin did as much damage to traditional Russian society as to non-Russian cultures. What he strove to ensure was identification with and loyalty to the new Soviet system and, above all, to himself.

Further, the Party had a two-thirds Russian majority, a ratio 10 percent higher than the percentage of Russians in the population. After the purges, the number of Russians in non-Russian Party organizations increased substantially. Party and Soviet control thus tended to resemble ethnic Russian domination, especially to the non-Russians. According to Hosking, as Moscow wove its tentacles throughout the vast union, the policies espoused by Lenin and accepted by Stalin in the 1920s fostered the very nationalism that would return to plague and shred the U.S.S.R. in the 1980s. The Party's encouragement of cultural autonomy among non-Russians nurtured the growth of national consciousness and ethnic identity through the use of local languages, the reading of indigenous literature, and the preservation of traditional mores. Moreover, as a result of Stalin's modernization policies promoting literacy, education, and migration to the cities among the rural masses, the burgeoning nationalism in the non-Russian regions spread from the local intelligentsia and urban elite groups to the population at large. Therefore, as Stalin moved toward a monolithic dictatorship and crushed economic and political autonomy among the non-Russians, he also unknowingly sowed the seeds of the dissolution of the Soviet federal system.

The Reign of Terror

The horror of Stalin's purges of the 1930s lies in more than the killings and incarcerations, the individual and familial suffering, and the decimation of an entire stratum of talented and energetic leaders in politics, the economy, the army, and every walk of intellectual life. The repression also spawned a chilling atmosphere of suspicion and fear that permeated a generation of Russians and non-Russians alike. These peoples' hopes for a rewarding and humane way of life shattered, and their children and grandchildren still struggle today to forge a society of integrity, legality, and mutual confidence out of the ruins of Stalinism. The Nazis maintained their Third Reich for barely twelve years and murdered some seven million Jews, Poles, Yugoslavs, and others. The German people recovered from that nightmare quickly. Stalin ruled for twenty-four years, and a modified Stalinist system persisted for another thirty-two. Ten to eleven million Soviet citizens perished in the resistance to collectivization, the famine of 1932–1933, and the purges. The nightmare touched almost every Soviet family, and it will take years more for the country to heal.

Yet no one is entirely sure what provoked this holocaust. Soviet society, changing rapidly during the 1930s, endured manifold tensions and strains, but other societies have modernized without an internal bloodbath. The Soviet system, with its authoritarian streak inherited from Russian political culture and from Lenin, fostered considerable political conflict—between the Party and the people, among rival interest groups, between Russians and non-Russians, and between central officials and local authorities. None of these struggles, however, was irreconcilable or predestined to lead to massive repression and hideous retribution.

One explanation suggests that Stalin, perhaps sensing imminent war with Nazi Germany, determined to rid Soviet society of anyone whose real or potential opposition might weaken the system or whose loyalty might waver under fire. Yet Stalin simultaneously tried again and again to sidestep conflict with Hitler. Further, eliminating the few real subversives hardly required incarcerating millions of people. Among a range of possible reasons for the purges, it seems most probable that the impetus for this terror came initially from Stalin and that he permitted it to continue long after the cleansing served any useful purpose, even by his perverse standards. To be sure, once the search for "enemies of the people" began in earnest, the process snowballed, feeding on a frenzy of denunciations and on vendettas by vengeful or ambitious local authorities Nevertheless, Stalin could have stopped it at any time, as he finally did in 1939.

If Stalin indeed ignited the purges, what motives propelled him? He never explained his policies, and many of the documents that might have shed light on his reasoning were destroyed, either in his lifetime or recently, when Party stalwarts burned or secreted records to prevent their falling into the hands of the new democratic forces in the former Soviet Union. Nevertheless, we can reasonably surmise that several considerations lay behind his actions. As the pattern of his life suggests, Stalin determined to gain absolute control over the Party and the country and to match the glorious accomplishments of his hero, Lenin. He doubtless overrated the strength of his opponents at home and felt paranoid about the menace of enemies abroad. But whatever the reality, he perceived a threat to his position. He probably also shrewdly recognized that arbitrary punishment kept everyone terrified and rendered the population totally dependent on his whim.

Second, he apparently convinced himself that the Party's unity needed strengthening and that deceivers and "two-facers" somehow had infiltrated the ranks. Only by eliminating such real or potential subverters of Party cohesiveness could the nation move forward, especially during risk of war. Finally, as Robert Tucker maintains, Stalin to some extent

New Light on the Issues THE STALINIST HOLOCAUST: VIEWS FROM ABOVE AND BELOW

How shall we judge the lurid crimes of Stalin and Stalinism? How shall we interpret the forced collectivization of the peasants with little regard for the cost in human life, the decapitation of the Red Army, the annihilation of Lenin's original comrades, and the creation of the *Gulag* empire? And what about the Soviet people—could the purges have snowballed to such an extent without popular support? Is it possible that ordinary men and women stood by and condoned the bloodshed? If so, why?

For Robert Tucker, Stalin's principal biographer, the mind and personality of the Kremlin dictator, shaped in part by his sense of historical destiny, provide the keys to the riddle. Stalin's obsession, born of neurosis, to prove himself a revolutionary hero of Lenin-like stature expressed itself in the 1930s as a determination to surpass what all Bolsheviks considered the supreme moment—1917's "Great October Socialist Revolution" under Lenin's leadership. Only a greater triumph, that of building a massive military-national state by Herculean means, in effect a new October in Russian history, could satisfy Stalin's compulsion.

But a second dimension overlay Stalin's craving for fame and glory in the 1930s: the reenactment of an age-old tsarist pattern of state-sponsored revolution designed to shield Russia from a hostile world. Tucker painted Stalin as a reincarnated Ivan Grozny, the sixteenth-century autocrat who bound all classes to the ever-swelling, ever-expanding state. More than that, Stalin fancied himself a modern Ivan out to save his people from treasonable elements who stood in the way of progress. In Ivan's case, the traitors were the *boyars*, the ancient aristocracy; in Stalin's case, they were the Old Bolsheviks who in his mind sabotaged dreams of a modern state. The Great Purge thus combined two critically important characteristics of revolutionary tsarism: an absolute autocracy and a compulsory service-state. Stalin was a Bolshevik of the radical right who looked forward and backward at the same time: forward to a socialist future for the world, backward to Russia's greatness in forging the machinery of empire (*Stalin in Power,* 1990).

The French specialist in Soviet studies Hélène Carrere d'Encausse offered a different linkage between Stalin's personality and Russian history. She viewed Stalin as the latest instance of "Russia's misfortune," the all-too-frequent tendency of its political system to rely on violence. For nearly a millennium, starting in Kievan Rus' where dynastic murder settled questions of inheritance and succession, rulers employed physical destruction to consolidate their power. The centuries-old tradition exploded under the Bolsheviks because of the utopian belief that human beings were the product of their environment and that the average citizen could be remolded at will into *homo sovieticus.* Certainly Lenin had no scruples about using revolutionary terror to squelch opposition to the Bolsheviks' policies. The belief that the ends justified the means reached macabre dimensions when Stalin fashioned a system that made it possible to concoct a scheme of destruction within the framework of the law. A 1935 law extended the death sentence not only to spies and parasites but to all those who might hear of such transgressions, the ultimate definition of guilt by association. Law and terror, so separate in most societies, were joined at the hip in Stalin's Russia, Professor d'Encausse concluded (*The Russian Syndrome,* 1992).

For J. Arch Getty, historian of the purges, this analysis was all too neat. Whereas others saw a well-oiled machine spewing hatred and violence to transform society, Getty perceived a Communist Party riddled with incompetence and sloth and unsure of its policies. While dictatorial—nobody ever claimed that the Bolsheviks were democrats—the Soviet government was not totalitarian, even under Stalin. It resembled a peasant culture trying "clumsily and sometimes half-heartedly to be a modern bureaucracy." Stalin was too busy to nvolve himself day-to-day in the purges. And the violence? It stemmed from the ups-and-downs of a struggle for control between the center and the regions as well as a "quasi-feudal network of politicians accustomed to arresting people." The *Ezhovshchina*—the height of the "cleansing" madness of the 1930s—was not a monolithic terror machine but perhaps its opposite: a radical, "even hysterical reaction to the chaos" at lower levels of the Party and the body politic (*Origins of the Great Purges*, 1985).

American historian Don Rowney discerned something else lurking in the nonelite rungs of Soviet society: millions of young, upwardly mobile men and women whose status on the eve of the purges dic not yet conform to their expectations. Rowney hints at a possible connection between the purges and the social mobility and frustration of skilled workers and Communist Party cadres looking for better jobs. Blocking their advancement was a group of 'fortysomethings," administrators and managers who surged to the fore quickly and urexpectedly as a result of the leadership turnover following the 1917 Revolution. This generation monopolized the top positions and would be "useful for another twenty years." Only by removing these seniors could lower-level functionaries—young, subordinate ex-workers, ex-peasants, and ambitious Communists—find a creative outlet for their energies (*Transition to Technocracy*, 1989).

Sheila Fitzpatrick, an American specialist on Stalinism, sought to square the circle between top-down and bottom-up assessments of the terror. As Fitzpatrick explained, we might best see Stalin's purge as the final chapter in the book of social engineering—a display, admittedly barbaric, of the "revolutionary transformation that had gained ascendancy in 1917" (*The Russian Revolution*, 1982). During the First Five Year Plan, Stalin stressed the importance not only of preparing working-class and Communist specialists but also "of producing leading cadres of the future." Whether on purpose or by accident, these young enthusiasts had scarcely left school when the purges of 1937–1938 "removed almost the entire top stratum of industrial managers and party and government personnel." Virtually without realizing it, these new graduates "stumbled into their places" (*Education and Social Mobility in the Soviet Union, 1921–1934*, 1979).

Is it possible, then, to view the purges as a kind of rough-and-tumble turnover of generations, Soviet-style? We know that until the late 1970s Soviet officialdom rested disproportionately on the so-called Class of '38. According to Fitzpatrick, half of the 1978 Politburo members were upwardly mobile men trained during the First Five Year Plan who replaced victims of the purge in positions of leadership a short time later. Was this pattern, as Fitzpatrick claimed, a "last fulfillment of the promises of the Revolution"? Robert Tucker disagreed. The U.S.S.R. suffered under the "new" Bolsheviks as people of experience and skill sank into oblivion or disappeared into the camps on the eve of World War II. And the beheading of the Red Army left it hopelessly unprepared to defend the country, as Hitler's successful invasion in 1941 would demonstrate. The purge served only one purpose, Tucker concluded: blind loyalty to Stalin. To which we might add—it also inhibited two generations of Soviet leaders from going beyond the person of Stalin himself to explore the social ramifications of the murderous thirties.

lived in a delusional world in which he was compelled to try to reorder the reality around him to match his idealized self-image of heroic accomplishment. Party members and others who questioned or seemed to question his actions and his worth had to be dealt with ruthlessly. Only if *everyone* acknowledged the greatness of Stalin through word and deed—and thought—could Stalin in fact be great. More important, he could then live with himself. Thus, when the upheavals of his "second revolution" caused some to waver, Stalin concluded that spies, enemies masked as genuine Communists, and falsifiers lurked behind a vast conspiracy to deny the magnificent triumphs of *his* October.

Stalin's state of mind and emotional health also may have deteriorated at this crucial time after the tragic death of his young second wife, Nadezhda Alliluyeva. Recollections by their daughter as well as a few other personal accounts from the 1920s and early 1930s indicate that the Soviet leader depended heavily on Alliluyeva psychologically. At a dinner party in November 1932 celebrating the fifteenth anniversary of the October Revolution, Stalin and his wife, who reportedly had been depressed by the excesses and sacrifices connected with the industrialization-collectivization drive, quarreled. She left the party early. It is unclear what happened later that night, but she was found dead from a gunshot wound and reportedly left notes criticizing her husband personally and politically. Probably she committed suicide, or perhaps Stalin accidentally shot her as he struggled to prevent her from taking her own life. In any case, the tragedy haunted Stalin. In the following months, he grew increasingly withdrawn, morose, and sullen. He never again returned to the normal social life with Party comrades that he had enjoyed in the 1920s and over which his wife had presided. To some degree Alliluyeva's death must have contributed to Stalin's profound sense of isolation and his suspicion of being surrounded by untrustworthy people.

The Red Terror of the 1930s differed considerably from the violence of 1919–1921 and from the power struggles of the 1920s. During the civil war, the Party used the secret police and concentration camps primarily against "enemies of the revolution" such as Whites, other socialists, merchants, priests, and those unfortunate intellectuals, workers, and peasants who chose to oppose Soviet rule. It almost never used terror against Bolsheviks. In 1927, although Stalin and his supporters sent some Left Oppositionists to Siberia and expelled Trotsky, they did not execute opponents or incarcerate them in the camps. In fact, Stalin reinstated some of the Left factionalists in their jobs and sometimes in the Party. Similarly, after the 1929 defeat of the Right, Stalin demoted Bukharin, Alexei Rykov, and Mikhail Tomsky but let them continue to serve the Party and the state. Beginning with the *kulaks* in 1929 and continuing into the 1930s, however, Stalin treated opponents, including Party members, whom he now labeled enemies, quite differently. He deported them to the *Gulag*, imprisoned them, or executed them. Where he showed mercy, it was

A Tragic Figure Nadezhda Alliluyeva, far right, accompanies her husband, Stalin, far left, on a walk several years before her death, probably by suicide, in 1932.

brief and soon revoked. Indeed, the terror of the 1930s was far bloodier and more extensive than that of the civil war.

The seeds of opposition to Stalin, real as well as imagined, clearly lay in the struggle to carry out his economic revolution. It was a desperate, stressful time, and as the sacrifices mounted, Stalin refused to waver from the extremist course that he had set and that his cronies supported. Criticism and cries for moderation arose at all levels of society and the Party, including at the top. Local Party officials fumed because Stalin blamed them for the excesses of collectivization in his "Dizzy with Success" speech. Various complaints had found concrete expression in August 1932, when Mikhail Riutin, a Party secretary in one of the districts of Moscow, submitted an appeal to the Central Committee signed by some twenty other Party leaders. The petition protested the growing personal dictatorship of Stalin and denounced his policies as reckless and coercive. Riutin and his supporters were arrested and expelled from the Party but were not executed until later, during the purges. Apparently Stalin sought the death penalty for them in 1932, but the Politburo demurred. Sergei Kirov, the Leningrad Party chief, and several others opposed the idea.

Unable to tolerate criticism, Stalin at this point seems to have convinced himself that disapproval equaled betrayal, and he vowed to exact vengeance on any who withheld wholehearted backing. In the spring of 1933, he ordered a cleansing of Party ranks. As targets, he specified remnants of former oppressing classes who had wormed their way into the Party, double-dealers who subverted Party policy, and "open and hidden violators of the iron discipline of the Party and state . . . who cast doubt on or discredit the Party's decisons and plans. . . ." Tens of thousands were erased from Party rolls.

In ferreting out his opponents, Stalin did not have a master plan or even a consistent approach, as historian J. Arch Getty has shown. Moreover, in the last half of 1933, Stalin seemed prepared to temper his policies and to conciliate his critics. He permitted Grigory Zinoviev and Lev Kamenev, exiled to Siberia in 1932, to return to Moscow. In addition, he appeared to support the counsel of several colleagues, including Kirov, who urged "reconciliation with the people" and restoration of Party unity. Goals for the Second Five Year Plan were relaxed, and Stalin called for consolidating the economy and "making it work."

In this atmosphere of reduced tension, the Seventeenth Congress of the Communist Party opened in Moscow in January 1934 on the tenth anniversary of Stalin's "Oath-to-Lenin" speech (see Chapter 5). Delegates— loyal cronies and forgiven opponents alike—praised Stalin extravagantly. The *vozhd*'s own report to the congess adopted a fairly moderate tone and contained no omen of the firestorm that he would soon unleash against the Party. The congress proved to be the swan song for the prerevolutionary Old Bolsheviks. Twenty-five percent of the nearly 2,000 delegates had joined the Party before 1912, and 80 percent had become members before 1921 (although only 10 percent of all Party members fell into that category). Dubbed at the time "The Congress of Victors" by *Pravda* because of the triumphs of the First Five Year Plan, the Seventeenth Congress turned out to be "The Congess of Victims," for 1,108 of the delegates would be purged during the next four years.

Although we can only speculate, three events at the congress may have inflamed Stalin's suspicions, aroused his jealousy, and pushed him once more toward political retaliation. A group of regional and republic Party secretaries apparently met secretly and decided that, with the crises of industrialization and collectivization ebbing, it was now possible to act on Lenin's 1923 recommendation that the Party move Stalin from the post of general secretary to another position. They allegedly approached Kirov as Stalin's potential successor, news of which undoubtedly reached Stalin's ears. After his address to the congress, Kirov also received a warmer and noisier ovation than had Stalin. Finally, when secret ballots for election to the Party Central Committee were counted, Stalin's name was reportedly crossed off a substantial number of voting cards; the *vozhd'* received one of the highest negative votes, far more than Kirov. He angrily ordered the results doctored to show only three ballots against him.

How deeply this "betrayal" affected Stalin is hard to judge. Scraps of evidence indicate that throughout the remainder of 1934 Stalin and Kirov continued to lock horns over policy—over ration levels in Leningrad, over the role of machine-tractor stations in agriculture, and over the date when Kirov, recently elected a full national Party secretary, should move to Moscow. Perhaps these spats were simply normal disagreements, or perhaps they reflected Stalin's growing fear of Kirov as a rival. In any case, on the evening of December 1, 1934, an assassin killed Kirov in the corridors of the Smolny Institute, Party headquarters in Leningrad. The gunman, a disappointed job-seeker and general misfit, seemed to have acted alone. Nevertheless, persuasive circumstantial evidence shows that the secret police (NKVD) not only permitted him access to Kirov but perhaps urged him to act. Whether Stalin engineered the murder remains unproven, but because the NKVD officers involved had come from Moscow recently and reported to agency chief Genrikh Yagoda, a protégé of Stalin, it is hard to believe that the assassination of the number-two leader of the Party could have been arranged without Stalin's knowledge, even if he did not initiate the plan.

Kirov's murder churned up an atmosphere of tension and vigilance and touched off a series of punitive actions by the state and Party that mark the start of the purges. With curious speed, a decree of December 1 (drawn up only hours after Kirov's death, or already prepared?) called for accelerating the arrest, trial, and execution of terrorists. At first the authorities blamed "White Guard remnants and dissident enemies of the workers" for the murder. Police arrested, tried secretly, and executed more than a hundred "assassins and terrorists" in mid-December. In addition, the NKVD seized and exiled from Leningrad hundreds, perhaps thousands, of individuals, allegedly former members of the bourgeois and professional classes. Waves of arrests also swept across Ukraine and several other regions.

On December 22, however, the investigation took a new turn, with the announcement of links between the Kirov assassin and former Zinoviev oppositionists in the Leningrad Komsomol. Zinoviev and Kamenev were both apprehended, and the controlled press depicted Kirov's murder as one element in a vast conspiracy involving former Left opponents, Trotskyites, and imperialist agents from abroad. Apparently some Party leaders resisted efforts to push the case against Zinoviev and Kamenev to the limit, for at their trial in January 1935 the court acknowledged that the two former leaders of the Left Opposition were unaware of the terrorists' plan to kill Kirov. They received fairly light sentences of ten and five years, respectively. In a separate trial, the presiding judge gave the police officer most negligent in guarding Kirov a conspicuously mild sentence of two years.

Through 1935 and into 1936, direct persecution ceased, although the press continued to call for vigilance. Party members were kept on alert first by a verification of their credentials and then by a requirement that they apply for new Party cards. In a minor ominous note, one of Stalin's oldest and closest comrades, Abel Yenukidze, a longtime Georgian Bolshevik and godfather to Stalin's wife, was callously fired from an important government post and subsequently expelled from the Party.

After some eighteen months of relative calm, the Party suddenly assailed Zinoviev and Kamenev again in mid-summer 1936 and elaborately staged a show trial of the two previously condemned men as well as fourteen others in August. Why Stalin decided to retry his former colleagues is unclear. As Robert McNeal, one of Stalin's biographers, speculates, perhaps sketchy evidence uncovered by the secret police that Trotsky and his supporters in western Europe had tried to use underground contacts inside the U.S.S.R. to resist Stalin convinced the dictator that an extensive conspiracy endangered his life. Or possibly, as Robert Tucker argues, Stalin simply had reached the point at which he saw any criticism as dangerous subversion and decided to eradicate such traitors permanently.

In any case, at the 1936 trial the prosecution charged the accused with organizing and participating in a Trotskyite-Zinovievite terrorist center. According to the indictment, this center killed Kirov, sought to assassinate Stalin and other top Party leaders, and had ties to fascist enemies of the Soviet Union abroad. With only flimsy evidence at hand, the case rested primarily on a series of "confessions," the first extracted from a former police agent and the rest culminating with admissions of guilt by Zinoviev and Kamenev themselves. Throughout the purges, interrogators persuaded people to confess to nonexistent crimes and to denounce others. The authorities achieved their ends through promises of leniency, threats to their victims' families, and the application of psychological and physical pressure ranging from the "conveyor" (hours of ceaseless questioning without sleep or food) to drugging and, occasionally, torture. In a particularly abusive aspect of the process, prosecutors used the "confession" of a trusted colleague to pressure and implicate an accused. Invoking the authority and infallibility of the Party, they convinced others, including Party rank and file and ordinary citizens, of the truth of the charges and of the proliferation of "enemies of the people." In the end, Zinoviev and Kamenev were convicted, sentenced to death, and executed.

Yet Stalin was not satisfied. Testimony at the trial had suggested that leaders of the former Right faction in the Party might also be involved. One of them, Tomsky, subsequently committed suicide. But others mentioned—Yuri Piatakov, a specialist on industry; Rykov; and Bukharin—were still full or candidate members of the Central Committee. To turn on them would imply that no one was safe and that the Party was beginning to devour its own. Apparently, some members of the Central Committee objected to broadening the purge. Stalin, probably annoyed that his secret police head Yagoda had not come up with irrefutable evidence against the Right leaders, replaced him with a rising young ally, Nikolai Yezhov, at the end of September 1936. Yezhov produced results immediately and staged a second show trial of a group of Right leaders in January 1937. The defendants faced accusations of Trotskyism as well as indictments for "wrecking" and sabotage of the economy, a particularly convenient charge because it helped to explain shortages and other failures in industry and agriculture. Two received prison sentences; the others, the death penalty. But the worst was yet to come.

The year 1937 marked the height of the terror, which reached into every corner of the system. The secret police under Stalin's direction executed hundreds of thousands, and several million more died from exhaustion, disease, and malnutrition in the *Gulag*. On February 18, Sergo Ordzhonikidze, a supporter of the executed Rightist Piatakov and one of Stalin's closest collaborators for over twenty years, committed suicide, apparently under pressure from Stalin. During a lengthy Central Committee meeting at the end of February 1937, Stalin reportedly encountered considerable opposition to his demands that Bukharin and Rykov be purged and that the hunt for enemies be broadened and pursued ever more relentlessly. To punctuate his displeasure with that committee meeting, 70 percent of its members were arrested and shot over the next eighteen months. (The percentage ranges even higher if

Forced Labor *Gulag* inmates working to build the White Sea canal in 1934. Camp labor contributed significantly to the industrialization campaign.

one excludes Stalin's fourteen closest henchmen who sat on the committee.)

After March 1937, the terror spread rapidly. Economic administrators and their subordinates, regional Party officials and their staffs accused of negligence or dereliction of duty, and intellectuals charged with allowing Trotskyism to creep into agitational, artistic, and educational work all fell before a rash of denunciations and "confessions." Guilt by association was enough to provoke arrest, imprisonment, and usually sentencing to the camps. In June 1937, Marshal Tukhachevsky, the head of the Red Army, and other senior officers were tried secretly and executed. The purge inexorably trickled down the ranks of the armed forces until 91 of the 101 members of the high command were arrested and most of them shot. These officers included three of five marshals, three of four army commanders, both first-rank fleet commanders, fifty-one of fifty-seven corps commanders, and 80 percent of all colonels.

The purges reached a public climax in March 1938 at a carefully staged trial of Bukharin, Stalin's most formidable Party critic. Before an audience of 350 people—mainly employees of the NKVD plus members of the diplomatic corps, some foreign correspondents, and a few senior Party and government officials—the proceedings took place in the main hall of the House of Trade Unions (formerly the ballroom of the nineteenth-century Nobles' Hall) not far from Red Square. Along with Bukharin, twenty-one prominent Communists were in the dock, including Rykov, a former premier; three eminent Soviet diplomats; five recent commissars of the Soviet government; three important state and Party chiefs from the non-Russian republics; and, ironically, Yagoda, the recently deposed head of the secret police who had supervised the purges of 1936 and 1937. For him the trial scenario, with which he was so familiar, must have had a peculiarly nightmarish quality. Nine of the accused were recent members of the Central Committee of the Communist Party.

Across from the defendants sat the state prosecutor. Andrei Vyshinsky, and his staff. Three military judges presided from a rostrum in the center. At the opposite end of the hall loomed a raised and recessed gallery, where orchestras had once entertained the nobility. Shrouded by a gauze curtain, a hulking mustached man frequently watched the proceedings from this vantage point. Observers identified the figure as Stalin, but they had no way of knowing that a direct connection to his private office in the Kremlin permitted the Soviet dictator to listen to testimory there as well.

Stalin had good reason to follow the progress of the case closely. Doubtless he understood that Bukharin, his most troublesome thorn over the past eight years, would try to turn the trial against him and his policies. Stalin and his NKVD thugs had obtained Bukharin's cooperation, three months after the latter's arrest, only by threatening to harm Bukharin's young wife and small child. For almost nine months, interrogators under Stalin's guidance had shaped and polished Bukharin's "confession." With his family held hostage, Bukharin was not likely to repudiate his statement in court. The danger remained, however, that Bukharin would try indirectly to indict Stalin's policies. Stalin judged the risk worthwhile, for the trial of Bukharin became the capstone of the dictator's effort to discredit Old Bolshevik views forever and to rid the Party permanently of antagonistic elements.

To a few keen observers, the duel between Bukharin and his boss provided a dramatic undercurrent to the proceedings. Entitled "The Case of the Anti-Soviet Bloc of Rights and Trotskyites," the indictment depicted an all-encompassing criminal conspiracy of past, present, and potential oppositionists of every political coloration. These villains, the prosecutor averred, dedicated themselves not only to the customary "wrecking," sabotage, and terrorism but also to treason, dismemberment of the Soviet Union, murder of prominent Communists, and lèse-majesté—attempts to kill the *vozhd'*.

In response to these outlandish charges, Bukharin was precise, logical, and defiant, appearing in the words of an American correspondent "an earnest man completely unafraid but merely trying to get his story straight before the world." Tactically, Bukharin outwitted Stalin by agreeing to the overall charge but denying any knowledge of specific acts—thereby undermining his whole "confession."

> I plead guilty to . . . the sum total of crimes committed by this counterrevolutionary organization, irrespective of whether or not I knew of, whether or not I took a direct part in, any particular act. . . .

Bukharin then denied complicity in a number of specific crimes, such as an attempt to kill Lenin. In a damning aside, which made his confession worthless, he added, "The confession of the accused is a medieval principle of jurisprudence."

In his final statement, the defendant included a strong condemnation of fascism. He managed as well to denounce Stalinism in Aesopian terms.

> For when you ask yourself: "If you must die, what are you dying for?"—an absolutely black vacuity suddenly arises before you with startling vividness. There was nothing to die for, if one wanted to die unrepented. And, on the contrary, everything positive that glistens in the Soviet Union [the vision of socialism] acquired new dimension in a man's mind.

Bukharin's plea was heard on March 12. At 4:30 A.M on March 13, the court sentenced him, Rykov, and thirteen others to die. Firing squads shot them all within forty-eight hours.[10]

With the trial of Yagoda, the terror had reached a point at which even the purgers were being purged. In her moving memoir, *Journey into the Whirlwind*, Evgeniia Ginzburg, a loyal Party official in Kazan and a purge victim, describes her reaction to a fellow inmate's report of a new prisoner in the camp.

> "[He's] a Major Yelshin. He worked in the Kazan NKVD."
> The bread in my hand trembled and dropped to the floor. Major Yelshin! I saw, as if in close-up, the comfortable office with the big window looking out on the Black Lake. I heard the velvety tones of the Major's voice: "Make a clean breast of it . . . . You're just being romantic . . . taken in by those filthy subversives. . . ." It was he who had decided that my crime fell

---

[10]Based on accounts and transcripts in Robert C. Tucker and Stephen F. Cohen, eds., *The Great Purge Trial* (New York: Grosset & Dunlop, 1965); on Stephen F. Cohen, *Bukharin and the Bolshevik Revolution* (New York: Oxford Univ. Press, 1980); and on Fitzroy MacLean, *Escape to Adventure* (Boston: Little, Brown, 1950).

under the article about terrorism that carried the death sentence. It was he who had put me in the fearful category of prisoners sent to solitary confinement. I understood that it was not in his power to have me released if he didn't want to fall foul of the "wheel of history," but all the same, it was up to him whether I got five years or ten: he didn't have to brand me as a terrorist, he could have kept it down to "anti-Soviet agitation," which gave one a better chance to survive. And those sandwiches—could I forget those French rolls with slices of tender, pink, succulent ham that made one's mouth water; how he had put the plate before me, a hungry prisoner from the cellars, and tempted me with the words: "Just sign, and you can eat as much as you like."

"What's the matter? Did you know him? He doesn't seem to have been such a bad fellow. A lot of other NKVD types have been sent here to the mines, but no one seems to have had it in for this one. Anyway, does it matter now? He'll certainly be dead by the night, I can tell only too well. Once their teeth get long and start sticking out of their mouths, it's all over."[11]

As the horror proliferated, Stalin could not possibly have overseen its operations at lower levels and in all regions directly. Instead, as during collectivization, zealous Party and police officials eager to prove their devotion extended and promoted the hunt for "enemies of the people." They were aided by self-serving informers, like the Stalinist child "hero" Pavlik Morozov, who was honored during the collectivization drive for denouncing his parents as shielders of *kulaks*. Yet Stalin provided the impetus from the top, set the tone, and almost daily reviewed lists of victims and "confessions" with his hatchetman Yezhov, indicating who should be arrested, imprisoned, or executed. Most chilling of all, on at least several occasions, Stalin benignly received old comrades pleading for the lives of family or friends. After they left, he invariably summoned Yezhov and ordered the intercessors arrested. He also never hesitated to threaten his associates through their families, purging Lazar Kaganovich's brother and incarcerating Viacheslav Molotov's wife in Central Asia.

During 1938 the witch-hunt slowly slackened, although several members of the Politburo arrested in that year or earlier were executed in 1939 and 1940. In the summer of 1938, Zhdanov and Molotov, two strong supporters of Stalin, criticized NKVD chief Yezhov, and Stalin himself turned against his former triggerman because Yezhov had acted on several matters without informing the Soviet ruler. Although Stalin favored

---

[11] Evgeniia Ginzburg, *Journey into the Whirlwind* (New York: Harcourt, Brace, 1967), pp. 389–390.

Georgy Malenkov to replace Yezhov, the Politburo finally named Beria the new NKVD head in November 1938. Arrested in 1939, Yezhov was shot in February 1940. As a coda to the terror, in 1940 a Stalinist agent assassinated Trotsky, the alleged archfiend behind various plots and conspiracies, at his place of exile in Mexico.

In March 1939 at the Eighteenth Party Congress, only 54 of the 2,059 delegates had attended the previous congress five years earlier. Stalin, although noting the need to maintain vigilance, indirectly assured the new generation of Party leaders that the mass purging had ended. His statement comforted the delegates somewhat, but everyone understood that the justification and apparatus of terror remained in place and that Stalin could apply it selectively and sporadically at will.

As with the escalation of the purges, we can only speculate about why Stalin wound down the terror. With the Nazi threat growing, he may have recognized belatedly that decimating the top military, political, scientific, and intellectual leadership of the country would have detrimental consequences. Perhaps Stalin, now entirely surrounded by reliable yes-men, concluded that he had finally eradicated most of his enemies. Or, he may have decided that the terror had made everyone so beholden to him that his role as supreme leader and Leninist hero was at last secure.

What cost did these manic months exact? The precise number of victims eludes us. However, recent revelations have confirmed longstanding Western suspicions that Stalin suppressed the results of the 1937 Soviet census. Among other information, the census report showed a catastrophic decline in the total population from an expected 180 million to 162 million, a deficit that stemmed from spiraling deathrates and sinking birthrates. Further, the 170 million total reported in the 1939 census was apparently inflated by several million to conceal the losses. In 1989 a Soviet biographer of Stalin, Dmitri Volkogonov, estimated that 4.5 to 5.5 million people were arrested. Eight hundred to nine hundred thousand of these received the death penalty, and many of the rest died en route to or in the *Gulag* during the purges. A controversial 1994 study argues that 2.5 million people were arrested in 1937 and 1938, and that 2 to 3 million died overall during the purges. Whatever the true figures are, the purges stand out as a particularly abhorrent episode in a century marked by evil.

The purges took a heavy toll in other ways as well: destruction of talent, character, and experience; the fostering of psychological insecurity and fear; and the formation of a society based on mistrust. No Soviet citizen after 1937 could feel entirely sure that friend, neighbor, boss, coworker, or even family member might not be informing on them to the Party or secret police. How much all this suspicion and fear weakened Soviet society on the eve of the battle against Hitler is impossible to assess, but the damage was considerable.

Conclusion

Between 1929 and 1939, Stalin led an economic, social, and political revolution that reshaped the lives of more than 150 million people and that transformed Soviet society. Outside sympathizers looked to Stalin's work as the hope of the future. But most Soviet citizens trembled under Stalin's paranoia and despotism.

Stalinism evolved from the interaction of four elements: rapid, forced industrialization and urbanization; the passivity and low cultural level of traditional peasant society; the authoritarian streak inherent in tsarist political culture and in Lenin's Bolshevism, and the mentality and delusions of Stalin himself. Russian society was gradually modernizing, both before the 1917 revolutions and during the 1920s, but Stalin determined to accelerate that process and to impose socioeconomic change by force where necessary. In this sense Stalin's "new October" was indeed a "revolution from above," like that of his hero Peter the Great. Yet its general direction meshed with ongoing changes in both Russian and non-Russian regions of the country. Stalin's revolution quickly elevated the economic strength of the Soviet Union and helped it to survive Hitler's onslaught in 1941 and 1942, but the nation paid a massive toll in human lives and suffering for this accomplishment.

To implement this transformation, Stalin had to rely on the Party-state system that had developed during the 1920s. He had little choice, for at least the rural majority of the Soviet peoples resisted rapid change. Moreover, the peasantry had inadequate training for or experience in self-government (above the level of the *mir*) and were ill equipped to participate in formulating and carrying out social reforms. Despite enthusiasm from some workers and intellectuals, Stalin depended primarily on his own reliable functionaries to overcome backwardness and conservatism.

The magnitude of the economic revolution and the reluctance and low level of skills of much of the populace gradually necessitated draconian methods. This solution dovetailed nearly with the centralizing and authoritarian strands of Leninist doctrine and practice. Party traditions thus blended with the task at hand. Communist cadres were to decide everything, in the words of a slogan of the time.

Yet, having overcome opponents within the Party and having launched the program that would make him the "new Lenin," Stalin suddenly felt himself surrounded by doubters and dissidents. These putative traitors questioned his pace and methods and seemed to threaten the unity of the Communist Party and Stalin's heroic place in history. Determined to eliminate doubters, Stalin initiated a relentless pursuit of "enemies of the people" while encouraging endless praise and adulation of himself. Stalin was not insane, but his warped and suspicious outlook and his unique psychological makeup lay behind the frightful purges of the 1930s and distorted the Soviet system. The U.S.S.R. could have accomplished much in the 1930s without the legacy of terror and mistrust that Stalin imposed on the Soviet people.

The nation had barely begun to settle down from the upheavals of industrialization and collectivization and from the trauma of the purges when a new firestorm broke over the Soviet peoples. Partly because of Stalin's egregious misjudgment of Hitler's intentions, the Nazis would launch a massive onslaught against the U.S.S.R. The origins of that dire conflict, the desperate and finally successful Soviet struggle to survive, and the difficult postwar reconstruction of the country form the core of the next chapter.

FURTHER READING

In addition to the books on Stalin and Stalinism noted after Chapter 6, an older biography by Isaac Deutscher, *Stalin: A Political Biography*, 2nd ed. (New York, 1967), and a study by a Russian historian, Dmitri Volkogonov, *Stalin: Triumph and Tragedy* (New York, 1991), shed light on the 1930s. Issues raised by Stalin's impact are well explored in Chris Ward, *Stalin's Russia* (New York, 1993). Giuseppe Boffa, *The Stalin Phenomenon*, trans. Nicholas Fersen (Ithaca, N.Y., 1992), reviews conflicting views of Stalinism from the standpoint of an Italian Communist journalist with long experience in Moscow.

The purges are treated in Robert Conquest, *The Great Terror*, 2nd ed. (New York, 1993); Robert C. Tucker and Stephen F. Cohen, eds. *The Great Purge Trial* (New York, 1965); Zbigniew Brzezinski, *The Permanent Purge* (Cambridge, Mass., 1956); J. Arch Getty, *Origins of the Great Purges, 1933–1938* (New York, 1985); and Getty and Roberta T. Manning, eds. *Stalinist Terror: New Perspectives* (New York, 1993).

The terror's instrument is described in Simon Wolin and Robert M. Slusser, eds., *The Soviet Secret Police* (Westport, Conn. 1975), and Amy Knight, *The KGB* (Boston, 1980).

Revealing memoirs and personal accounts appear in Evgeniia Ginzburg, *Journey into the Whirlwind* (New York, 1975); Alexander Solzhenitsyn, *The Gulag Archipelago, 1918–1956*, 3 vols. (New York, 1973–1979); Alexander Barmine, *One Who Survived* (New York, 1945); Victor Serge, *Memoirs of a Revolutionary, 1901–1941* (New York, 1963); Anton Antonov-Ovseenko, *The Time of Stalin* (New York, 1981); and the insightful view of a Finnish observer, Arvo Tuominen, *The Bells of the Kremlin: An Experience in Communism* (New York, 1983).

Three novels that capture the atmosphere of the 1930s include Arthur Koestler, *Darkness at Noon* (New York, 1970); Anatoli Rybakov, *Children of the Arbat* (Boston, 1988); and Alexander Solzhenitsyn, *One Day in the Life of Ivan Denisovich* (New York, 1963), and *First Circle* (New York, 1968).

Various aspects of Soviet society are dealt with in Loren Graham, *Science in Russia and the Soviet Union* (New York, 1992); David Joravsky, *Soviet Marxism and Natural Science, 1917–1932* (New York, 1961); Kendall Bailes, *Technology and Society Under Lenin and Stalin* (Princeton, N.J., 1973); William C. Fletcher, *A Study in Survival: The Church in Russia, 1917–1943* (London, 1965); Harold Berman, *Justice in the USSR*, rev. ed. (Cambridge, Mass., 1963); John Erickson, *The Soviet High Command, 1918–1941* (New York, 1962); Mary Buckley, *Women and Ideology in the Soviet Union* (Ann Arbor, Mich., 1989); Wendy Goldman, *Women, the State, and Revolution: Soviet Family Policy and Social Life, 1917–1936* (New York, 1993); Leonard Schapiro, *The Communist Party of the Soviet Union*, rev. ed. (New York, 1970); Lewis Siegelbaum, *Stakhanovism and the Politics of Productivity in the USSR* (New York, 1985); Joseph Berliner, *Soviet Industry from Stalin to Gorbachev* (Ithaca, N.Y., 1988); William G. Rosenberg and Lewis Siegelbaum, eds., *Social Dimensions of Soviet Industrialization* (Bloomington, Ind., 1993); and Vera S. Dunham, *In Stalin's Time: Middleclass Values in Soviet Fiction* (Cambridge, 1976).

DISASTER, VICTORY, AND A NEW EMPIRE

~

As was his custom, Stalin retired late on Saturday night, June 21, 1941. That evening, he had attended meetings in his Kremlin office to review recent reports of an imminent German invasion of the Soviet Union. Reluctantly he had yielded to his advisers' pleas to alert all Soviet forces, but he had added a warning that troops not be "provoked" into conflict. The Soviet ruler was then driven to his *dacha* outside Moscow and soon fell fast asleep.

Ordinarily no one dared disturb Stalin until he appeared at midmorning. But at 4 A.M., just as the midsummer's eve dawn broke, a bodyguard called Stalin urgently to the phone. The sleepy dictator found General Grigory Zhukov, the Red Army's chief of staff, on the other end of the line. Zhukov blurted out that enemy planes were bombing Kiev, Minsk, and other Soviet cities. Stalin made no reply. The agitated Zhukov asked, "Did you understand me, Comrade Stalin?" Still no response came, but Zhukov heard heavy breathing. When the chief of staff pressed Stalin again, the Soviet leader ordered an emergency meeting in the Kremlin within the hour.

Zhukov, Commissar for Defense Semyon Timoshenko, and members of the Politburo quickly assembled in their leader's office to hear Stalin express incredulity at Hitler's gall. At first he wanted to contact the German ambassador, perhaps hoping to salvage some diplomatic solution, but Commissar for Foreign Affairs Viacheslav Molotov reported that the German ambassador had just delivered a message that amounted to a declaration of war. Clearly, the attack was no mistake.

Pale and shaken, Stalin lapsed into a long silence. Finally, General Zhukov urged him to engage the Red Army. Stalin assented, but still hoping that Hitler's generals and not the Führer had provoked the bombing, he approved this limited directive:

> . . . [T]roops will attack enemy forces and liquidate them in the areas where they have violated the Soviet frontier [but] unless given special authorization ground troops will not cross the frontier.

Far from likely to cross the frontier, the Red Army, taken by surprise, was everywhere in disorderly and hasty retreat. Stalin's order suggests his desperate delusion that Hitler would not attack.

News of relentless German advances and the destruction of Soviet war planes and air fields poured in. Stalin, apparently unwilling to be linked with the mounting disaster, designated Molotov to break the news to the Soviet people. Shortly after noon on June 22, 1941, on a nationwide radio broadcast, Molotov haltingly intoned,

> Citizens, men and women of the Soviet Union! . . . This morning at four o'clock, without any claims having been presented to the Soviet Union, . . . German troops attacked our country. . . .[1]

The war between the U.S.S.R. and Nazi Germany had begun, a brutal struggle that would last almost four years and that ranks as the most extensive, destructive conflict in human history. The war cost 30 million lives and reduced large sections of each country into rubble. The losses and suffering often proved unnecessary, as when more than half a million soldiers and civilians perished in the battle for Berlin long after Nazi Germany had any chance of prevailing. The Soviet peoples' remarkable, albeit costly, victory determined the outcome of World War II in Europe. By their sacrifice, the Soviet Union emerged as one of two superpowers that would dominate the postwar order and shape world history over the next fifty years.

Stalin's misguided diplomacy of the late 1930s, designed to avert conflict with Hitler, in fact permitted the Nazi leader to concentrate all his forces against the U.S.S.R. in 1941, as the Führer sought to fulfill his dream of establishing German hegemony over the "inferior" Slavs. But for Hitler's blunders, the Nazis might have subjugated the Soviet Union within six months. Given a reprieve, however, the Soviet government and citizenry rallied; by 1943 they had turned back the German invaders, and in 1944 and 1945 Soviet forces inflicted a crushing defeat on Hitler. The fortitude and patriotism of the population, as well as Stalin's ability to use Soviet socialism's centralized party-state system to marshall the country's resources, contributed to this surprising victory. The U.S.S.R.'s eventual triumph notwithstanding, the war demolished the Soviet home-

---

[1]This account is based on Anthony Read and David Fisher, *The Deadly Embrace* (New York: Norton, 1988), pp. 633–642, and Robert C. Tucker, *Stalin in Power: The Revolution from Above, 1928–1941* (New York: Norton, 1990), p. 265.

front, tallying huge losses of life and property and uprooting and redistributing much of the population. Yet despite a slight relaxation of controls during wartime, Stalin reimposed strict orthodoxy and economic sacrifice on the Soviet peoples in 1946. Ideological warfare broke out with the U.S.S.R.'s wartime allies, and the Party repressed dissent and innovation at home. In an ironic twist, World War II thus vindicated and then hardened the essence of Soviet socialism.

Stalin's Grand Delusion

The Soviet leader's refusal in the spring of 1941 to believe that Hitler would assault the Soviet Union burdened millions of Soviet citizens with grievous, needless hardship. This miscalculation grew out of Stalin's faulty assessment of Hitler's intentions, his mistrust of the British, and his inability to admit that the great *vozhd'* might have made a mistake. Stalin and his collaborators had worried about Hitler's intentions as early as 1934, when Nazi Germany made a pact with the U.S.S.R.'s perpetual enemy Poland. Moreover, the Soviet dictator possessed a copy of *Mein Kampf*, Hitler's political and ideological blueprint for world conquest, and had even underlined the passages in which the author announced his determination to destroy Russia. Nevertheless, Stalin somehow convinced himself that he could avert or indefinitely postpone Hitler's offensive.

The Soviet leader's strategy toward Hitler in the 1930s unfolded through two stages: encouraging European resistance to fascism, and then, when that plan failed, striking a bargain with the German dictator. At first Stalin hoped that a united front against the Nazis and Fascists would catalyze a major struggle between the Western democracies and the dictatorships of Italy and Germany. The U.S.S.R. could then join or abstain from such a conflict depending on Soviet interests. From 1936 to 1938, Stalin sent aid to the Spanish republican government as it struggled to quell a rightist revolt supported by arms, advisers, and funds from Hitler and Mussolini. However, in 1938 Hitler gobbled up Austria and threatened Czechoslovakia. Stalin undoubtedly began to harbor doubts about the efficacy of his antifascist policy.

Moreover, in the Far East the military-dominated Japanese government, emboldened by its conquest of most of north China in 1937, exerted pressure along the Soviet-Manchurian border. Over the next two years, clashes and several pitched battles broke out in the region. Although Soviet forces rebuffed the Japanese probes, Stalin and his advisers grew concerned at the prospect of getting pinned between Japanese expansionism to the east and German aggression from the west.

This dual threat could not have come at a worse time. The Soviet economy was sputtering, rearmament had barely begun, and the purges had decimated the military leadership. Dismayed at the democracies' craven behavior in the 1938 Czechoslovakia crisis, Stalin moved to secure his western border. The Soviet Union had earlier forged a treaty with Czechoslovakia in which it promised military assistance on the condition that France also honor its commitment to defend that smaller nation against aggression. Yet the Soviet government's resolve was never tested, for the French reneged on their vow. Under any circumstances, it is highly unlikely that Stalin would have come to the Czechoslovaks' aid. To do so, the weakened Red Army would have had to cross a reluctant Romania. The U.S.S.R. ignored Romania's offer to discuss the passage of Soviet troops and planes into central Europe, and no evidence has ever surfaced of Soviet preparations to assist Czechoslovakia.

The Anglo-French sacrifice of Czechoslovakia to Hitler at the infamous Munich Conference of September 1938 apparently marked a turning point in Stalin's thinking. The Soviet dictator now saw no reason to ally with France and Great Britain. He had always distrusted capitalists, and he had no wish to be drawn "into conflicts by warmongers who are used to having others pull chestnuts out of the fire for them." In the end, Stalin decided to strike a deal with Hitler. Perhaps the Soviet dictator deemed it safer to bargain with a fellow realist than to count on the ideologically unreliable democracies.

Although he did not publicly abandon the possibility of an anti-Hitler coalition with the West, Stalin began pursuing a pact with Hitler in the fall of 1938. Indirect overtures to Hitler, of which early versions dated back to 1934, grew more vigorous during negotiations for commercial and economic agreements between Germany and the U.S.S.R. after Munich. Stalin also gave the Nazis discreet diplomatic assurances that he would downplay propaganda attacks on fascism and that the Soviet regime harbored no ideological bias against improved relations with Hitlerite Germany.

At the Eighteenth Party Congress on March 10, 1939, Stalin signaled his readiness to reach an accommodation with Hitler when he declared that the Soviet Union would not be dragged into the brewing imperialist war or provoked into a conflict with Germany. The Soviet Union, he asserted, would maintain its peaceful policy and was prepared to conduct straightforward relations with any country that did not violate Soviet interests. Two months later, the Soviet leader fired his long-time commissar for foreign affairs, Maxim Litvinov, who had strongly advocated collective security with the democracies against Nazism. Molotov, one of Stalin's closest collaborators, replaced Litvinov at the post. Hitler noted these developments but still made no response.

To maintain pressure on Hitler, Stalin began negotiations in the spring of 1939 with the French and British, who in April had guaranteed Poland's independence. Yet the negotiations proceeded dilatorily, partly because effective Soviet military assistance against Germany hinged on

Polish cooperation: the Red Army would have to cross Poland to confront Germany, a prospect that the Poles viewed with trepidation. In the meantime, Hitler stepped up political and diplomatic pressure on Poland. Nevertheless, the Führer's generals warned him to neutralize either the Allies or the Soviet Union before launching major military operations. Otherwise, Nazi Germany could become mired—possibly buried—in a disastrous, two-front war.

In July Hitler made his first positive response to Stalin's overtures and authorized political talks with Soviet representatives. The Germans then hinted that if the Soviet government signed a nonaggression treaty, the U.S.S.R. might acquire territory and influence in eastern Poland and the Baltic states. Stalin responded favorably, and in August 1939, the Soviet dictator and Hitler's foreign minister, Joachim Ribbentrop, announced to a stunned world an agreement between Europe's two sworn enemies, Bolshevik-hating Nazi Germany and fascist-baiting Communist Russia. The Soviet-German Nonaggression Pact provided that neither side would join in an attack on the other. An accompanying secret protocol promised Stalin a third of Poland; spheres of influence over Latvia, Estonia, and Finland; and a claim to Bessarabia, a province of Romania bordering on the Soviet Union. (Russia had acquired Bessarabia in the nineteenth century, but Romania had annexed it in 1918.) A month later, Stalin traded some Polish territory for Soviet hegemony over Lithuania.

With his flank secure, Hitler launched the German army into Poland on September 1, 1939, igniting World War II. Communists throughout the world recoiled from Stalin's "pact with the devil," and thousands resigned from the party in protest. Inside the Soviet Union, the deal left many people stunned and puzzled. How could their leader forge a friendship with their well-remembered enemy from World War I and with the detestable fascists? No one knew about the secret protocol, which was neither acknowledged nor published in the U.S.S.R. until fifty years later.

According to Khrushchev's memoirs, Stalin boasted to his colleagues after signing the pact that he knew what Hitler was up to: "He thinks he's outsmarted me, but actually it's I who have tricked him!" In retrospect, such vainglory seems tragic indeed. Stalin thought that he had averted a Nazi assault on the Soviet Union. Perhaps he also calculated that if the Allies belied their earlier behavior and stood by Poland, Germany would be drawn into a long, draining war with the West. Stalin might not have been so sanguine had he known that only two weeks earlier, Hitler had railed,

Everything I am doing is directed against Russia. If the West is too obtuse to grasp this, then I shall be forced to come to terms with the Russians and turn against the West first. After that I will direct my entire strength against the USSR. I need the Ukraine, so that nobody can starve us out again, as they did in the last war.[2]

To be sure, as Stalin intended, his pact with Hitler temporarily kept the Soviet Union out of war and won valuable time for the U.S.S.R. to continue defense preparations. Stalin also gained additional territory as a buffer between the Soviet Union and Nazi Germany, although he would soon squander this advantage. But the Soviet dictator paid an enormous price for these benefits. For one thing, he gave Hitler a free hand in Poland and supplied the Nazi war machine with raw materials for the next twenty-two months, under supplemental Nazi-Soviet commercial agreements. He also permitted Hitler to concentrate the might of the *Wehrmacht* (the German armed forces) against the French and British the following spring. Thus, when Hitler refocused his efforts on *Lebensraum* (space for expansion) to the east, the Red Army had to face the battle-tested, expert German troops alone.

In Stalin's defense, he hardly expected the war in Western Europe to end so quickly. Moreover, he chose to ally himself with Hitler in part because he did not trust the capitalist democracies to fight. He feared that the West would abandon the Soviet Union to the German advance, and given the democracies' record to that point, Stalin had valid concerns. Nevertheless, the Soviet dictator's miscalculations hardly excuse his failure to understand Hitler's determination to carry out the agenda of *Mein Kampf:* that Germany would some day conquer European Russia. Stalin should have realized that the best way to prevent Hitler from carrying out that design was to join forces with the Führer's enemies in the West.

The false harmony between Germany and the Soviet Union that followed the signing of the nonaggression pact lasted for some time. Because of the rapidity of the German advance across Poland, Stalin had to accelerate Soviet occupation of eastern Poland. Nevertheless, he insisted publicly that his September 1939 incursion had no connection with Germany's aggression against Poland. Instead, he claimed, the Soviet government was responding to the desires of Ukrainians and Belarusans living in eastern Poland to be reunited with their Soviet brethren. The occupying Communist authorities quickly sovietized the newly acquired territories, deporting 1.25 million Poles and others to Siberia and Soviet Central Asia. Some Poles were not that "lucky." In the Katyn Forest in eastern Poland, Soviet secret police executioners shot 4,443 captured Polish officers and dumped their bodies into a mass grave. Another sixteen thousand Polish soldiers were executed at other sites, all on the orders of

---

[2]Quoted in Read and Fisher, pp. 183–184.

Stalin and three Politburo colleagues, according to documents that the Russian government would deliver to the Polish government in 1992. During World War II, the Nazis also committed terrible atrocities in this region, killing hundreds of thousands of Jews and executing more than a hundred thousand Soviet prisoners of war.

Further, Stalin moved immediately to exercise his authority in the Baltic region. In late September and early October 1939, he imposed mutual-assistance pacts on the reluctant governments of Estonia, Latvia, and Lithuania. The accords provided for Soviet bases and troops on Baltic territory for "defensive" purposes. In early summer 1940, as Hitler waged his campaign in Western Europe, Stalin completed his absorption of the Baltic states. He forced the election of pro-Soviet national assemblies, which duly voted to have their countries join the Soviet Union as its latest constituent republics. Soviet institutions were introduced, and potential oppositionists were incarcerated, executed, or shipped to the *Gulag*. More than one hundred thousand Baltic peoples thus fell victim to Soviet repression.

Next it was Bessarabia's turn. In June 1940, Stalin determined to annex both Bessarabia and the neighboring Romanian territory of Bukovina. When Germany protested, he settled for taking northern Bukovina as well as Bessarabia (see map, page 334), territory that became the Moldavian Republic of the U.S.S.R. (In 1990 this republic would declare its independence as the state of Moldova.) But the Soviet ruler's pushiness in the Balkans irritated Hitler, and Stalin's success in biting off a Romanian morsel whetted the appetites of Hungary and Bulgaria. Eager to protect Romania for its rich Ploesti oil fields, Hitler intervened to settle the claims against it. He failed to consult Stalin, who fumed at the slight.

Finland became another source of friction between the two unlikely allies. Although the secret protocol had allocated Finland to the Soviet sphere of influence, Hitler strove to protect German interests there. As he saw it, an uncooperative Finland might threaten German access to important mineral deposits in Scandinavia. To Hitler's annoyance, Stalin acted to extend his sway over Finland within weeks of signing the pact. In early October 1939, the Soviet leader offered the Finns the same sort of mutual-assistance agreement that he imposed on the Baltic states. Stalin also renewed earlier demands that Finland cede to the Soviet Union the Karelia territory north of Leningrad as well as lease the U.S.S.R. a base at Hanko, at the entrance to the Gulf of Finland. The independent Finns, possessing a small but well-trained army and extensive fortifications along the Soviet border, refused to knuckle under, and Stalin launched the Red Army against them on November 30, 1939.

The Finns fought courageously, yet Soviet forces eventually prevailed despite amateur generalship and shoddy tactics. Stalin permitted the Finnish government to sign fairly lenient peace terms in March 1940, perhaps because the British threatened to aid the Finns and the Soviet leader did not wish to become entangled in Hitler's war with the West. The Finns yielded the territorial concessions that Stalin had initially demanded and paid reparations; nevertheless, they retained their independence. Hitler maintained strict neutrality during the conflict, but in September 1940, he suggested a high-level meeting to review the status of Finland and other issues of discord between the Soviet Union and Nazi Germany.

This summit, conducted in Berlin on November 12–13, 1940, by Molotov and Ribbentrop, with Hitler's occasional participation, was merely a charade to the Nazi leader. The previous July, shortly after defeating France, Hitler had announced to senior German officers and Nazi officials a tentative decision to move against the Soviet Union in the spring of 1941. Planning for this invasion lagged as the Führer preoccupied himself with seeking ways to force the British to surrender. By the time Molotov arrived in Berlin, however, preparations for an attack on the U.S.S.R., which Hitler would approve formally in December 1940, were well advanced. To avoid alarming Stalin, Hitler pretended to take the discussions with Molotov seriously. Privately, however, he felt outrage over the demands that Stalin had sent with Molotov: a Soviet sphere of influence in Bulgaria, bases on or near the Turkish Straits, and an end to Nazi interference in Finland. The talks ended inconclusively, and from that point Hitler turned a deaf ear to Soviet efforts to pursue the issues raised in Berlin.

By early spring 1941, intelligence reports of Hitler's planned invasion poured into Moscow, both from Soviet sources abroad and from the British and Americans. Stalin's spy in Japan even conveyed the date and battle order of the attack. Why Stalin steadfastly refused to believe this information remains bewildering. His faith that Hitler would not back out of their deal while Germany was still fighting Britain apparently dominated his thinking. In addition, the ever wary Soviet leader may have deceived himself that the British were planting false and provocative reports to drag him into their war with Hitler. Finally, Stalin's deluded sense of his own grandeur may have prevented his facing the fact: he had badly misread Hitler's intentions.

In retrospect, the two dictators approached their alliance from opposite perspectives. In Stalin's view, the bargain offered advantages for both sides. As he saw it, making the effort to overcome minor differences was worthwhile. The deal provided for a sensible division of Eurasia between two pragmatic leaders for whom self-interest outweighed ideology. The Soviet ruler, although disheartened by France's collapse—which dashed his hopes for a protracted war between the fascists and the capitalists—clung to his belief that Hitler also valued the pact. Even after the Soviet Union had finally defeated Germany, Stalin would remain puzzled by Hitler's actions. On several occasions, he would remark to his daughter, "Ekh, together with the Germans we would have been invincible."

Hitler, for his part, approached the treaty in an entirely different spirit. He perceived it as a temporary device to give him a free hand in the West and to bolster the Germany economy until he could grasp Russia's riches for the Greater Reich. The ideologically driven Nazi dictator had long determined to subjugate the lowly Slavs and to wipe out the Bolsheviks. Hitler had no intention of sharing dominion over Eurasia with Stalin or with anyone else.

Operation Barbarossa

Although Stalin counted on his pact with Hitler to forestall a Nazi attack, in the fall of 1939 he was sufficiently wary to accelerate the Soviet defense build-up begun in 1937 and 1938. After the Finnish war, the Soviet leader approved further expansion and rigorous retraining and reequipment of the armed forces. By the spring of 1941, more than 5 million men and women swelled the ranks of the armed forces, streams of tanks and aircraft rolled off the production lines, and a few experienced officers were returned to active duty from the *Gulag*. Stalin bragged that any attacker would need at least a 2-to-1 advantage to overcome Soviet might.

Despite the *vozhd's* optimism, he himself held chief responsibility for major deficiencies in the U.S.S.R.'s readiness for war. Like Hitler, Stalin took a personal hand in military policy and even decided on the design and procurement of some new weapons and munitions, many of which proved mistakes. He also interfered in the strategic deployment of Soviet forces. Instead of basing the nation's westward defense on a line of redoubts along the country's 1939 frontier with Lithuania, Poland, and Romania, the Soviet leader ordered these fortifications abandoned or destroyed and a second set built farther west, on the 1940 borders. The U.S.S.R. had barely begun constructing the new defense line when in late 1940 Stalin reappraised the situation and commanded his main forces, including munitions stocks and other supplies, to entrench as far forward as possible. He had determined never to yield "one inch" of even newly acquired Soviet territory. He also unrealistically believed that in the event of war, Soviet armies would immediately take the offensive and carry the battle into the enemy's homeland. Despite repeated warnings of Hitler's impending assault, Stalin refused to put the armed forces on defensive alert, and the Nazi invaders caught Soviet units completely off guard. Stalin's mistakes would cost millions of Soviet lives, waste billions of rubles in lost equipment and destruction, and put the entire nation at risk.

Hitler's war plan—code-named Operation Barbarossa after the popular name of a medieval Holy Roman Emperor who led a crusade to the east—provided for a surprise attack on the U.S.S.R. on May 15, 1941. Instead, the invasion took place nearly six weeks later. Until recently, many historians attributed this delay to a subsidiary German campaign in the Balkans in the spring of 1941. In 1940 and 1941, Hitler's ally, the Italian dictator Benito Mussolini, became entangled with a tough Greek army, which the British soon backed with troops and supplies. The Führer was compelled to rescue the Italians by sending German troops into Yugoslavia and Greece in April–May 1941. This diversion, however, did not significantly set back Operation Barbarossa. The German high command rerouted most of the troops and resources funneled off in the Balkan campaign to the eastern front. Not Mussolini's distress but a late spring in Eastern Europe forced Hitler to postpone the invasion. Swollen streams and rivers and fields of mud stymied the tanks, mechanized vehicles, and trucks on which the Nazis' *blitzkreig* tactics depended.

Despite meticulous and extensive preparations for Barbarossa, a lack of clear goals and miscalculation of the depth of Soviet human and material resources undercut German planning. Specifically, Hitler and his generals failed to define either the immediate or the long-range objectives of their offensive. Did they seek primarily to destroy the Red Army and the Soviet state? Or did they aim to occupy and exploit most of European Russia on a line running from Archangel to the Volga River and down to Astrakhan (see map, p. 334), regardless of whether the Soviet government and its forces retired to Siberia and tried to fight on from there? In the first assault, should German forces seek to seize Leningrad and Moscow, so as to break the enemy's will to resist? Or should the campaign target Ukraine and the Caucasus, with their rich supply of food, oil, and minerals? The Nazis' failure to select among these goals led to indecision at crucial junctures in the offensive and forced them to shift resources from one front to another. The hesitations and deviations of its foe helped the U.S.S.R. to survive the 1941 onslaught and eventually to mount a counteroffensive.

In addition, Hitler failed to consider that the war might drag on longer than the planned six to ten weeks. A handful of alarmed officers noted the long-run Soviet advantage in manpower and natural resources, but the Führer ignored their warnings. Scorning the Slavs as inferior and dismissing Communist Russia as a house of cards that would collapse at the first push, the German leader grievously underestimated the resiliency of Soviet society and the patriotism of the Soviet peoples once roused.

On June 22, 1941, supported by some Romanian units, the *Wehrmacht*'s 3.4 million soldiers, 3,350 tanks, and 2,000 warplanes—the largest invasion force in history—overwhelmed surprised Soviet troops along an 800-mile front stretching from the Baltic to the Black seas. Within hours, Nazi aviators destroyed a majority of front-line Soviet planes, many of them on the ground. Soviet units fell back in confusion or were surrounded and captured. One prong of the German attack

The Nazi Army on the Move A mechanized German unit speeds through a Soviet village in the opening phase of June 1941's Operation Barbarossa.

pushed along the Baltic coast toward Leningrad; a second moved north of the Pripet Marshes on the road to Smolensk and Moscow; a third struck north of the Black Sea into Ukraine. (See the map, World War II: The Eastern Front, 1939–1945). In six weeks, the Germans advanced 300 to 400 miles into the Soviet Union, slaughtering and capturing almost 1 million Soviet troops.

A confused and shaken Stalin met regularly with his colleagues but took no public steps in the first ten days of the war. Scattered memoir accounts indicate that he mainly reacted to suggestions. To provide unified command of the armed forces, a new institution—the *Stavka*—was established. Stalin's long-time close associate, Lazar Kaganovich, headed the Commission on Evacuation, responsible for withdrawing people, factories, and goods eastward ahead of the German advance. The State Defense Committee (GKO) was created to coordinate the entire war effort. Functioning as an inner Politburo, the GKO undertook all key wartime decisions and issued decrees and resolutions that carried the force of law. Originally, the committee consisted of five members: Stalin as chair, Molotov, Lavrenti Beria, Kliment Voroshilov, and Georgy Malenkov, a rising Party star favored by Stalin. Later, Party specialists on economic affairs joined these policymakers, and another Party general, Nikolai Bulganin, replaced Voroshilov. Because the Soviet dictator also chaired the *Stavka* and the chief government executive

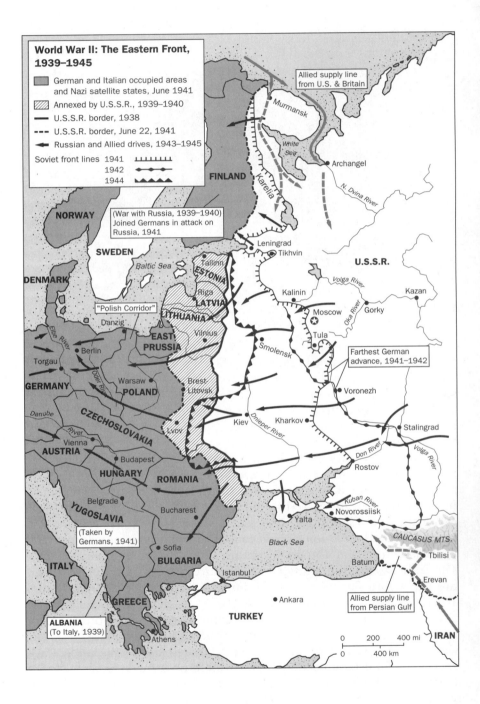

World War II: The Eastern Front, 1939–1945

German and Italian occupied areas and Nazi satellite states, June 1941

Annexed by U.S.S.R., 1939–1940

—— U.S.S.R. border, 1938

- - - U.S.S.R. border, June 22, 1941

◄— Russian and Allied drives, 1943–1945

Soviet front lines 1941
1942
1944

Allied supply line from U.S. & Britain

Murmansk

White Sea

Archangel

N. Dvina River

Karelia

FINLAND

NORWAY

(War with Russia, 1939–1940) Joined Germans in attack on Russia, 1941

SWEDEN

Leningrad
Tikhvin

U.S.S.R.

DENMARK

Baltic Sea

Tallinn
ESTONIA

Kalinin

Volga River

Kazan

Riga
LATVIA

Moscow

Oka River

Gorky

"Polish Corridor"

Danzig

LITHUANIA

Vilnius

Tula

EAST PRUSSIA

Smolensk

Farthest German advance, 1941–1942

Berlin

Elbe River

Oder River

Torgau

Warsaw

Brest
Litovsk

Voronezh

GERMANY

POLAND

CZECHOSLOVAKIA

Danube

Kiev

Dnieper River

Kharkov

Stalingrad

Lvov

River

Vienna

AUSTRIA

Budapest

HUNGARY

ROMANIA

Don River

Volga River

Rostov

Belgrade

Bucharest

Kuban River

Novorossiisk

YUGOSLAVIA

(Taken by Germans, 1941)

Yalta

CAUCASUS MTS.

Sofia

Black Sea

Tbilisi

ITALY

BULGARIA

Batum

Istanbul

Erevan

GREECE

Ankara

TURKEY

Allied supply line from Persian Gulf

ALBANIA
(To Italy, 1939)

Athens

0   200   400 mi

0   400 km

IRAN

body, the Council of People's Commissars, as well as continuing as general secretary of the Party, he held all the system's reins of power in his hands and wielded more personal authority than even Hitler. Thus, both the successes and failures of the war effort can largely be laid at Stalin's door.

Soviet wartime leaders faced the immediate task of rallying the population behind the nation's defense. Because Party propaganda during the preceding months had downplayed the Nazi threat, the German attack left most people shocked and perplexed. The invasion triggered fear and pessimism among some, who rushed to empty their bank accounts and hoard food. A larger number, however, hastened to express support for the government and army and derision toward the Germans Tens of thousands volunteered for the army or for work in defense industries. Tragically, some of these patriotic citizens were enrolled in a hastily formed people's militia. Ill-trained and ill-equipped, they perished while defending key cities like Kiev and Leningrad.

As news of front-line defeats and massive withdrawals trickled home, the morale of the populace plummeted. Stalin and his colleagues invoked the honor of the homeland and traditional Russian nationalism to rekindle public dedication. On July 3, 1941, in an unusual nationwide radio talk, Stalin addressed the Soviet peoples not only as "comrades and citizens" but as "brothers and sisters." Speaking slowly, he stressed the gravity of the union's plight and tried to whip up his subjects' patriotism.

The theme of nationalism, especially the Russian variety, had emerged as far back as 1934, when Stalin criticized Soviet textbooks. Nationalism had also welled up in Soviet propaganda on the eve of the war, and became the dominant focus of wartime discourse and ideology. As one example, on the November 1941 anniversary of the Bolshevik Revolution, Stalin delivered a speech to military units marching directly from Red Square to the front. The Soviet leader sent the troops west with tributes to past Russian achievements, evoking the names of glorious Russian heroes such as Alexander Nevsky and Peter the Great, as well as the famous military commanders of the Napoleonic era. In the fall of 1941, Party propagandists dubbed the conflict the "Great Patriotic War." By contrast, references to socialism and to the worldwide proletarian revolution dwindled during the war years.

Stalin also enlisted the Orthodox Church in his effort to stiffen his peoples' resistance. Within hours of learning of the German attack, the acting head of the church, Metropolitan Sergei, issued a proclamation strongly condemning the invasion and appealing for all-out defense of the Soviet state despite the regime's depredations against religion in the 1930s. Church officials collected funds for the war effort, cared for children orphaned in the struggle, and regularly issued encyclicals supporting the government's wartime policies. In return, Stalin made peace with the church, reaching an informal concordat in 1943 that permitted thousands of churches to reopen. He also allowed an increase in the number of bishops and priests, reestablishment of a central church administration, and the election of Sergei as patriarch. Although the Party would renew its campaign against religion in the late 1950s, the terms of coexistence between church and state that Stalin approved during the war would persist to the end of the Soviet period in 1991. As reward for political subservience, including support for postwar propaganda efforts, the government permitted the religious establishments in the Soviet Union (except for Judaism) to exist and to hold religious observances, although it still prohibited proselytizing and religious education.

Yet the greatest irony of the war is not that Stalin and the Communist Party had to call on the heroes and churches of the despised tsarist past for help. Rather, the unifying struggle for survival and the ultimate triumph served to legitimize Communist rule, the socialist system, and Stalin's tyranny. What had been built at staggering cost in the preceding two decades proved capable of turning back the ferocious onslaught of the most advanced nation in Europe. Both Stalin and the Party would emerge from the war as victors, their dominance assured.

To maintain Soviet cohesion and dedication, Stalin did not rely solely on emotional appeals to patriotism. He unflinchingly used coercion against his own subjects when he suspected disaffection or slackening of support. Even in the first days of the war, Stalin dismissed or shot officers whom he considered responsible for Soviet defeats. Further, he made clear that soldiers who surrendered to the Germans would be treated as traitors. In September 1941, he introduced special secret police units into the Red Army with instructions to machine-gun troops fleeing the front lines. The Soviet dictator maintained these strict policies throughout the war and even into the postwar period, when he sent numerous Soviet citizens and prisoners of war repatriated from Eastern Europe and Germany straight to the *Gulag*.

Stalin dealt equally harshly with civilians on the home front. In his July 3, 1941, speech he promised that "all who by their panic-mongering and cowardice hinder the work of defense, no matter who they may be, must be immediately hauled before the military courts." He was as good as his word: on September 21, 1941, he ordered the Leningrad command to shoot on sight captured Soviet civilians whom the Germans were using to urge the surrender of the city.

Finally, to ensure maximum war production, the Soviet ruler placed workers in key defense industries and on the railways under military discipline. For absenteeism or substandard performance on the job, tens of thousands of laborers were shot or sent to the camps.

Stalin singled out several non-Russian minority groups for especially brutal treatment. As the Germans advanced in 1941, he ordered almost 1 million Soviet citizens of German descent forcibly removed from Ukraine and areas along the Volga River. Catherine the Great had settled Germans there at the end of the eighteenth century, and they had served as productive and useful citizens ever since. No evidence existed that the Russian Germans sympathized or intended to collaborate with the advancing *Wehrmacht*, but they had resisted collectivization. Stalin, ever suspicious, scattered these peoples throughout Soviet Central Asia.

In late 1943 and early 1944, with the *Wehrmacht* finally in retreat, the Soviet dictator uprooted several non-Russian nationalities on the flimsiest of treason charges: Tatars who had lived in the Crimea for five centuries; Kalmyks from north of the Caspian Sea; Chechen-Ingush, Balkars, and Karachai from the north Caucasus. Ironically, recent accounts reveal that these peoples were shipped to Siberia and Central Asia in trains acquired through the American Lend-Lease aid program to the U.S.S.R. Almost one-third of the deportees perished. After 1957 the government would revoke the accusation of Nazi collusion and, in the late 1980s, would restore these peoples' rights, although without returning all their lands. Despite only a few cases of collaboration between the *Wehrmacht* and persons living in the Caucasus, Stalin apparently wanted mainly to punish the exiled groups for earlier resistance to Soviet rule and to eliminate them as a potential source of unrest after the war.

More threatening to Soviet survival than possible subversives in the Crimea and the Caucasus, many Ukrainian, Belarusan, and Baltic citizens greeted the advancing Nazi armies as liberators in 1941. Moreover, although most Soviet soldiers taken prisoner were captured involuntarily, some quickly surrendered and others deserted. Those who looked to Nazi rule as an alternative preferable to Stalinism expected that the Germans would end the detested collectivization system, curtail repression, and restore religious and other local traditions. The Nazi leaders, however, soon squandered this opportunity to undermine Soviet resistance. As another sign of disaffection with Communist rule, the German army persuaded some Red Army prisoners of war and people from the occupied territories to perform auxiliary service for the *Wehrmacht*. In addition to several Russian formations, these so-called *Osttruppen* (East troops) included Cossack, Muslim, and other non-Russian brigades, a few of which stood in combat alongside the Germans.

German military officials also encouraged a captured Soviet general, Andrei Vlasov, to develop an anti-Stalin movement and army to be used in the struggle on the eastern front. Why Vlasov cooperated with the Nazis is unclear. Perhaps he was repelled by the Red Army's lack of preparation for the German offensive and the inadequacies that hamstrung the war effort during its first year. In any case, in 1943 and 1944, Vlasov formed what became known as the Movement for the Liberation of the Peoples of Russia. He espoused a vague program that emphasized Russian nationalism, although later he would urge self-determination for non-Russian peoples. The liberation movement also stressed civil liberties, social welfare, the right to private property, and a future Russia "without Bolsheviks or exploiters."

Vlasov elicited some support among anti-Communist Russians in German hands and among the populace of German-occupied Soviet territory. Yet Hitler, because of his racist views, adamantly opposed arming the Slavic peoples and consistently vetoed the *Wehrmacht*'s efforts to promote Vlasov and his movement. In the fall of 1944, Heinrich Himmler, Hitler's secret police chief, finally managed to arm two divisions of ragtag Russians for Vlasov behind Hitler's back, in a desperate attempt to bolster declining German fortunes. Involved only briefly in the fighting, the Vlasovites were soon either captured by the advancing Red Army or interned by the Americans, who repatriated them to the Soviet authorities. As might be expected, many of the soldiers were sent to the *Gulag;* their leaders were secretly tried for treason in the summer of 1946 and hanged. The Nazis never gave Vlasov an opportunity to build sufficient support, but one wonders whether in different circumstances a popular anti-Stalinist organization might not have emerged in the occupied territories. On the other hand, only tens of thousands cooperated with Vlasov and the Germans, as against the tens of millions who staunchly defended Mother Russia and the Soviet homeland.

In the end, German racism and shortsightedness precluded a broad anti-Soviet movement. Throughout the conquered lands, German policy rarely veered from repression, persecution, and exploitation, although competing agencies and fiefdoms within the Nazi hierarchy and German government debated the policy, and a sprinkling of farseeing military authorities objected. The perverse tone had been set before the invasion when Hitler, fearing that his military professionals would prove too soft on the *Untermenschen* (subhuman) Slavs, hectored his leading generals on March 30, 1941.

> The war against Russia will be such that it cannot be conducted in a knightly fashion; the struggle is one of ideologies and racial differences and will have to be conducted with unprecedented, unmerciful, and unrelenting harshness. . . . The [Soviet] commissars are the bearers of ideologies directly opposed to National Socialism. Therefore the commissars will be liquidated. German soldiers guilty of breaking international law . . . will be excused.[3]

Many officers and Hitler's civilian minions in the occupied territories faithfully carried out this brutal policy, executing not only Communists and, of course, Jews but other local leaders as well. No one tried to estab-

---

[3]Quoted in John Keegan, *The Second World War* (New York: Viking Penguin, 1989), p. 186.

lish self-government or to win over the conquered population. To ensure food and manufactured goods for the *Wehrmacht* and the home front, the German occupiers retained centralized control of industry and the collective-farm system. Citizens in occupied territories received minimal rations, and many were pressed into service, either as auxiliaries in the Germany army (almost 1 million by 1944) or as forced laborers in factories back in Germany (about 3 million by the end of the war). The Nazis treated Soviet Jews and POWs especially brutally. Of approximately 5.7 million Red Army soldiers taken prisoner throughout the war, 3.3 million or 57 percent died of starvation, unbearable conditions, and cruel treatment.

As news of the Germans' handling of civilians and prisoners spread, Soviet soldiers fought with increased tenacity and ferocity. Some individuals in the occupied regions joined anti-German partisan detachments. Before 1941, Stalin had discouraged plans for partisan warfare, fearing that he could not control such units. By 1942, however, spontaneous bands had sprung up in response to the Nazis' atrocities, and the Soviet government began to support them. The partisans made a small but useful contribution to Red Army victories in 1943 and 1944 by cutting German lines of supply and communication and harassing rear echelons. Overall the Nazis' vicious policies in Russia thus only steeled the Soviet peoples' resolve to repel the invaders. This major political blunder cost Hitler the chance to undercut Soviet resistance.

From Disaster to Triumph

During the summer of 1941, many observers and perhaps some Soviet leaders questioned whether the Soviet Union could hold out against the Germans. Post-1991 charges suggest that Stalin sought to negotiate a separate peace with Hitler and supposedly offered to give up the Baltic region, Moldavia, the Crimea, and large parts of Ukraine and Belarus. Clearly, these serious accusations need fuller investigation. In any case, those in the Kremlin must have considered ways to avert total defeat during the darkest days of 1941 and 1942. Churchill supplied moral support by allying Britain with the U.S.S.R. soon after the Nazi attack, but he could pledge only limited material assistance. The United States, not yet embroiled in the war, sympathized with the Soviet Union's plight and proffered Lend-Lease aid in September 1941, but the support did not begin to arrive in quantity until late 1942.

Three factors saved the Soviet Union in 1941: the dogged resistance of the Red Army despite horrendous losses, the rapid mobilization of the country for an all-out effort that the bulk of the population fully supported, and the errors of Hitler and his compliant generals. The early winter also helped Soviet survival, but contrary to widely held belief, stubborn defense and Soviet reserve forces—not Generals Mud, Snow, and Ice—defeated the Germans at the gates of Moscow.

By the end of July, the three parallel Nazi drives toward Leningrad, Moscow, and Kiev had all made remarkable progress (see map, p. 334), but German forces needed to catch their breath, refit, and await needed supplies. Nevertheless, the commander of Army Group Center informed Hitler that his forces would be ready in about a week to resume the advance on Moscow and that he expected to capture the capital by mid-September. If ordered forward in early August, the optimistic general undoubtedly could have met this goal. Hitler hesitated, however. At one point, the führer decided to make Leningrad and the Baltic his highest priority; then he reversed himself and targeted the riches of the Ukraine. Army Group Center thus sat virtually motionless for almost a month. When Hitler finally assented to the move on Moscow on September 5, the window of good campaigning weather had narrowed, and Stalin and General Zhukov had garnered precious weeks in which to strengthen the capital's defenses. If the Germans had taken Moscow in the fall of 1941, the war might have ended then or the following year. Hitler's midsummer irresolution proved a fatal misstep for the Reich.

But Stalin also made mistakes. In late July, with German units already at the Dnieper River, Zhukov urged the evacuation of the Ukrainian capital Kiev in order to prepare a more solid defense farther east. When Stalin called this recommendation "rubbish," Zhukov resigned his post as chief of staff, although he continued to oversee the defense of Moscow. The German advance continued, but on September 11, Stalin refused a plea from the Kiev defenders to be allowed to withdraw. A week later, the Germans encircled and captured the city. The Red Army lost half a million men and huge quantities of equipment; the fall of Kiev remains the most ghastly defeat of the war and perhaps in all military history. Stalin was clearly to blame.

In the Baltic region, the Nazi armies crept toward Leningrad, at first expecting to take the city by September. But the Finns, who had entered the war against the Soviet Union several weeks after Operation Barbarossa began, refused to advance on Leningrad from the north and instead held their line on the 1939 frontier. After some initial confusion at the local level, Zhukov, Molotov, and Malenkov—all dispatched in haste from Moscow—reorganized Leningrad's defenses by drawing on the volunteer labor of almost 1 million city residents. Hitler decided that, rather than seizing Leningrad and having to feed its inhabitants over the winter, German forces would invest the city and starve it into submission. Stalin bears some responsibility for this disaster as well. Despite warnings from the front, he delayed evacuating the city. As a result, only about a half-million of its more than 3 million inhabitants and a negligible amount of equipment and supplies were withdrawn before the German siege began

Water of Life Desperate Leningrad citizens struggle to draw water from the city's frozen canals in the icy winter of 1941 to 1942 as the German siege tightens.

in mid-September. Moreover, in order to guarantee supplies for Moscow, Stalin blocked efforts by GKO member Anastas Mikoyan to send extra food to the city. Local authorities also share the blame, for they failed to prepare for the siege and mishandled food shipments in the first months of entrapment.

Supplies to Leningrad diminished to a trickle during the fall and winter of 1941–1942. The first provisions arrived by boat across Lake Ladoga (see map, p. 334). In January 1942, after the lake froze, trucks carried staples across the icy "Road of Life," as Leningraders dubbed it. The city's inhabitants resisted bravely but suffered horribly. More than 1 million people died from starvation, cold, and disease. At times lacking heat, water, or transport, Leningrad essentially stopped functioning. Desperate citizens ate pets, pigeons, rodents, even human flesh. A doctor remembers being called to an apartment in January 1942.

My eyes met a frightful sight. A half-dark room. Frost on the walls. On the floor a frozen puddle. On a chair the corpse of a fourteen-year-old boy. In a child's cradle the second corpse of a tiny child. On the bed the dead mistress of the flat. . . . Beside her, rubbing the dead women's breast with a towel, stood her oldest daughter Mikki. But life had gone, and it could not be brought back. In one day Mikki lost her mother, her son, and her brother, all dead of hunger and cold. At the door, hardly able to stand from weakness, was her neighbor, Lizurova, looking without comprehension upon the scene. On the next day she died, too.[4]

Leningrad never surrendered. After two and one-half years of agony, the siege was lifted. Only 639,000 people remained in the city. Although soon rebuilt, Leningrad would not regain its prewar population until 1959 and would never recover its status as the virtual equal of Moscow in economic strength, culture, and scientific activity.

At the core of the U.S.S.R., the Germans launched their assault on Moscow, code-named Operation Typhoon, in late September. In the first ten days, the Germans surged forward, inflicting heavy losses on the Russians scrambling from their path. Soldiers on both sides must have recognized the pivotal role of this battle. Fighting was fierce, as this account by a German survivor makes clear:

> When they [a German company] had advanced about 300 yards, the hidden Russians suddenly opened fire. . . . Within minutes German and Russian soldiers were locked in deadly, hand-to-hand combat. Bullets, rifle butts, hand grenades, bayonets, daggers, broken tree limbs, even fists, became the weapons of the desperately struggling men. Some sank silently to the ground, as if felled by a terrific unseen force. Others staggered and lurched about, screeching in terror and pain. One young German soldier sagged limply against a tree, reluctant to fall, unable to stand. His helmet and weapons were gone; part of his tunic was sheared off. Blood trickled down his blond hair; he stared in disbelief at the gory stump that had once been his right arm.[5]

In mid-October 1941, fall rains and muddy terrain slowed the Nazi offensive. By November a harsh, early winter descended. The frozen ground allowed tanks and other vehicles to move forward again, but in other ways the cold stymied the *Wehrmacht.* Believing that the Russian campaign would end by fall, the German High Command had failed to order winter clothing and supplies until the end of August. Most of these items would not arrive until after the Battle of Moscow. German soldiers suffered terribly in the cold, and trucks and Panzer tanks froze. Nevertheless, the Germans slogged ahead and reached the outskirts of Moscow, some twenty-five miles away, in early December.

As the initial German advance neared Moscow, what had begun as

---

[4]Quoted in Harrison Salisbury, *The 900 Days: The Siege of Leningrad* (New York: Da Capo, 1958), p. 491.

[5]Quoted in Alfred W. Turney, *Disaster at Moscow: Von Bock's Campaigns, 1941–42* (Albuquerque: Univ. of New Mexico Press, 1970), p. 97.

an orderly, government-directed evacuation of the diplomatic corps, key ministries, and officials to the central Volga town of Kuibyshev (now returned to its ancient name, Samara) turned into panic. Rumors that the Germans were about to enter the city terrified tens of thousands of citizens not authorized to leave. By bus, train, car, and on foot, they escaped with as many of their belongings as they could carry. Disorders broke out in the city, looters rampaged through stores, and the city's defense threatened to collapse. Stalin and his Party colleagues countered with aggressive action. The Soviet dictator publicly announced his determination to stand by the capital and ordered the police and NKVD to shoot looters and fleeing citizens. The Moscow panic marked the one time during the war when Soviet morale cracked, if only momentarily.

As the pitiless weather and staunch Red Army resistance slowed the German offensive, Zhukov threw fresh, well-trained troops from Siberia and the Soviet Far East into the battle. After signing an April 1941 neutrality pact with Japan and receiving reliable reports that Japan planned to expand into Southeast Asia instead of Soviet territory, Stalin concluded that he could safely transfer these forces to European Russia. Almost a hundred thousand experienced troops, accustomed to winter fighting, flooded Moscow during November and December. With their help, the Red Army mounted a brief counteroffensive that rolled the German lines back some sixty miles from the capital.

The city and the country had been saved, but at a staggering cost. In the first six months of the war the Red Army had lost almost 3 million soldiers, dead, wounded, or captured; twelve thousand tanks; most of its air force; and huge quantities of artillery and other equipment. Because the Germans had seized rich, productive areas that housed many armaments factories, Soviet leaders had to scramble to replace essential personnel and matériel. Yet equally ominous dangers lay ahead.

Both sides planned offensives for the second year of the war. Heartened by their success in driving the Germans back on the central front and by the recapture of Rostov-on-Don in late 1941, Stalin and the *Stavka* planners launched a general attack in late winter. Because of stiff German resistance and feeble Soviet execution, however, the effort fizzled, with heavy Soviet losses. Hitler, concerned about Germany's need for additional resources in a protracted war, focused the *Wehrmacht*'s main 1942 offensive in south Russia. He envisioned cutting the Soviet nation in two by crossing the Volga River and capturing the Caucasus, with its agricultural and petroleum resources. But again, as in the summer of 1941, Hitler vacillated: although German forces reached the north Caucasus, the *Wehrmacht* increasingly committed to the easterly direction of the offensive, which targeted the key Volga city of Stalingrad (see map, p. 334).

Despite its vulnerable location on the western, exposed bank of the river, Stalin determined to defend the city, partly because of its name and partly because of its importance as a provincial center and transportation

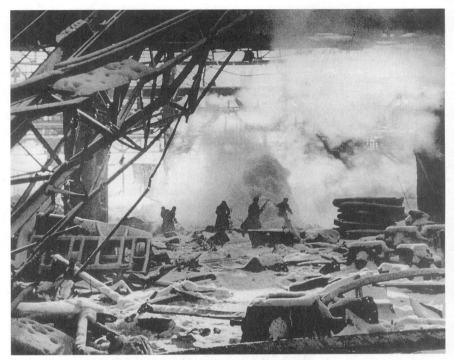

Fierce Fighting at Stalingrad In fall 1942 Red Army soldiers fire on advancing Germans inside the "Red October" factory during the Battle of Stalingrad.

hub. Soviet armies fought desperately in and around Stalingrad from late summer 1942 until early February 1943. German forces penetrated deep into the city in fearsome house-to-house, hand-to-hand fighting but could not dislodge the Soviet defenders. This vivid memoir, by a Red Army noncommissioned officer trapped in a grain elevator, reveals the Soviet soldiers' resolve:

> The explosions were shattering the concrete; the grain was in flames. We could not see one another for dust and smoke, but we cheered one another with shouts. . . . On the west side of the elevator the Germans managed to enter the building, but we immediately turned our guns on the parts they had occupied. Fighting flared up inside the building. We sensed and heard the enemy soldiers' breath and footsteps, but we could not see them in the smoke. We fired at sounds. . . .[6]

---

[6]Quoted in Alan Clark, *Barbarossa: The Russian- German Conflict, 1941–45* (New York: Quill, 1985), p. 231.

In November 1942, the Red Army launched a full-fledged counterattack on the *Wehrmacht*'s exposed northern and southern flanks and before long trapped the entire German Sixth Army in a pocket west of the city. Tragically for the Reich's soldiers, Hitler refused to let the surrounded army fight its way out and delayed a German attempt to break through to the encircled units from the west. As the Red Army squeezed the pocket ever tighter, the physical and psychological despair of the trapped men deepened, as this final letter home from one German soldier reflects:

> ... Well, now you know that I shall never return. Break it to our
> parents gently. I am deeply shaken and doubt everything. I used
> to be strong and full of faith; now I am small and without faith. I
> will never know many of the things that happen here; but the
> little that I have taken part in is already so much that it chokes
> me. No one can tell me any longer that the men died with the
> words "Deutschland" or "Heil Hitler" on their lips. There is
> plenty of dying, no question of that. But the last word is
> "mother" or the name of someone dear, or just a cry for help.[7]

When the remnants of the Sixth Army—only 110,000 men of an original 400,000—finally surrendered on February 2, 1943, their defeat marked a decisive turning point. Heavy fighting lay ahead, but the Germans had lost the strategic initiative. The extensive resources of the Soviet Union now began to unfold against them. Further, at the high-water mark of their advance, the Germans were a distant 1,200 miles from Berlin, manning a front almost 1,200 miles long from Finland in the north to Turkey in the south. Logistics and reinforcements faltered.

After the disaster at Stalingrad, the *Wehrmacht* was forced to withdraw from the north Caucasus, and during the spring of 1943, the Red Army drove them back in the south. Through July and August, the Germans massed much of their remaining strength for the Battle of Kursk, one of the most dramatic struggles in modern warfare. Almost three thousand German tanks maneuvered and cannonaded against nearly four thousand Soviet tanks in this epic clash. Neither side won a definitive victory, but the Germans exhausted their tank reserves. Never again would they match growing Soviet tank superiority or mount a major offensive. By September 1943, the Red Army had pushed the Germans back to the line of the Dnieper River, and in early 1944 Soviet forces recovered almost all the territory in the south that Germany had overrun since June 1941.

---

[7]Quoted in *Last Letters from Stalingrad,* int. by S. L. A. Marshall (New York: Morrow, 1962), p. 50.

In 1944 languishing Leningrad was also finally relieved, and Soviet forces rebuffed Finland and reestablished the 1940 frontier. They then occupied Germany's allies, Romania and Bulgaria; reconquered Estonia and Latvia; liberated Belarus; and moved into Poland. The last action led to another tragedy and a fresh example of Stalin's cruelty. As the Red Army approached the Polish capital of Warsaw in early August 1944, the Polish underground boldly rose up against the city's German occupiers. The rebel leaders believed that advancing Soviet troops would pin down the *Wehrmacht*. Yet the Red Army halted just short of Warsaw and left the Polish resistance to battle the Germans alone. Soviet authorities declared that their armies needed to rest and wait for supply trains. After over two months of desperate fighting, the Nazis killed, wounded, or imprisoned almost three hundred thousand Poles and destroyed the city's center. There is little doubt that Stalin stood aside and let the Nazis wipe out the Polish underground movement because it was non-Communist. In his view, the insurgents posed a threat to the domination of postwar Poland by puppet Polish Communists following the Red Army.

By early 1945, Soviet forces had crossed into central Europe and eastern Germany, and the Allies had advanced on Germany from the west. In a despair bordering on madness, Hitler and his subalterns fought on, costing the Red Army three hundred thousand more casualties in the final two-week Battle of Berlin. The Germans surrendered on May 9, 1945, and Stalin, fulfilling an earlier promise to Roosevelt and Churchill, entered the war against Japan on August 9. Soviet troops defeated Japanese forces in Manchuria within two weeks. This Asian victory at last ended Soviet military participation in World War II.

"All for the Front!"

How did the Soviet system and society withstand the shock of total war? The answer lies above all in the toughness and determination of the Soviet peoples. If they had not fought so valiantly and endured such pitiful living conditions, the country's vast resources and its centralized structure would not have had a chance to take effect. Soviet citizens pushed back the Germans primarily to defend their homeland and families, although barbaric German occupation policies further stiffened their resolve. Moreover, they resisted the onslaught in spite of the country's inadequate preparedness and their own astonishment at the attack. To be sure, Stalin's Five Year Plans had built a base of heavy industry that could produce either "guns or butter." But in keeping with Stalin's emphasis on offensive military action, the Kremlin had made almost no emergency preparations and had stockpiled little food or matériel. In addition, although some capital investment in the 1930s had built plants in the Urals and Siberia, most industrial development had unfolded in European Russia. Few, if any, enterprises had prepared a blueprint to move operations east, out of harm's way, in the event of war. Similarly, the government had made no provisions to evacuate people and to provide for refugees.

As a result, evacuees and the threat of industrial collapse haunted the home front in the first weeks of the war. Those fleeing the German advance clogged roads and railway lines. Stalin ordered a "scorched earth" policy, which burdened those left behind but at least delivered few resources to the Nazi occupiers. Industrial and agricultural production plummeted as the *Wehrmacht* seized factories and fields and disrupted supply lines. By November 1941, the Germans occupied areas that contained 40 percent of the U.S.S.R.'s prewar population (78 million people); one-third of all prewar mining and manufacturing output, including more than half of such key metals and minerals as coal, iron, steel, and aluminum; 40 percent of the country's railways; and 45 percent of its livestock and grain. These losses dealt a devastating blow to the Soviet economy. The nation would not recover its prewar industrial level until 1949, its grain output until the mid-1950s, and its livestock production until the early 1960s.

Nevertheless, Soviet officials managed to evacuate to the Urals, western Siberia, and Central Asia more than 6 million workers and 1,500 factories, several of which were back in production within three or four months. In addition, some farmers and herds walked east away from the war, for rail transport was reserved for workers and factories. By harvesting crops early, harried farmers succeeded in salvaging some of the 1941 output.

To maintain armaments production, the GKO controlled allocations of key materials, its authority superseding that of *Gosplan* and state ministries. A comprehensive manpower act was instituted in February 1942. The government enforced strict labor discipline, meting out severe penalties for lateness, absenteeism, and unauthorized job changing. To replace heavy personnel losses, the Red Army, which grew to 11.6 million soldiers, conscripted 8 million men during the war. The government, however, failed to weigh the country's overall human-resources needs carefully. As one example, the army drafted highly skilled workers or allowed them to volunteer; by 1943 it had to return many of these individuals to the workbench—their experience and abilities in the factory proved more essential than their gallantry at the front.

Because the economy had stood at nominal full employment before the war, the extra labor power needed for war production came mainly from longer working hours and the recruitment of additional peasants and women, as well as youngsters and pensioners, into the work force. After the war, the newly employed peasants remained in the cities, swelling the urban population from about 35 percent in 1939 to 50 percent in 1959. Wartime recruitment accelerated women's participation in the paid labor force as well. Their percentage of total public-sector em-

The Horror of Recognition Surviving villagers search for loved ones among the bodies of civilians slain by invading Germans.

ployment rose from 38 percent in 1940 to 55 percent in 1945 and remained high afterward. Women not only worked in the fields and factories; they also grieved.

> . . . That was the day I received notification that my husband had been killed in action. I cried all night, remembering every single day of the war—the fear and horror of seeing enemy planes bombing our village in November 1942, the endless days in the fields from sunrise to sundown with no rest at all, and the nagging fear for the four little children I had been left with. But while I cried, my hands kept knitting the woolen socks—I had already made umpteen pairs and sent them to our soldiers. . . . Early in the morning I gave the children their breakfast and covering my head with a black shawl I went out to the field. The villagers didn't see me cry. It was a routine workday. . . . [8]

Many Soviet women also performed bravely and effectively in the armed forces, in more than auxiliary and noncombatant roles. A number

---

[8]Quoted in *Russian at War, 1941–45,* int. by V. Karpov (New York: Vendome, 1987), p. 62.

Women Warriors Three Soviet female fighter pilots prepare for their next mission against the Germans.

were decorated for valor in front-line or partisan fighting. Among many noted women warriors, a squadron of pilots on the southern front stood out. Known as the Night Witches, they harassed the German lines and shot down *Luftwaffe* fighter planes in aerial combat. Less glamorous but just as courageous, women infantry soldiers displayed skill and grit fighting alongside men.

> When the war started a group of girls at our factory, including myself, enlisted. . . . I was wounded in a battle when the odds were heavily against us. Both legs and my hipbone were shattered. But I managed to crawl to the forest where I lay semi-conscious on the snow all night. In the morning I was found by some partisans. . . . When I was evacuated to Moscow, both my legs had to be amputated. . . .
>
> As soon as I was discharged from hospital, I went back to my factory. It wasn't at all easy to stand a shift with my artificial limbs, but the thought that it was no easier where the fighting was kept me going.[9]

---

[9]Ibid., p. 79.

The U.S.S.R. in wartime scored an impressive record in armaments production. Although the output of weapons and munitions had grown by 1940 to two and one-half times the 1937 level, between 1940 and the peak of the war effort in 1944, armaments production quadrupled again. At its height, Soviet *monthly* output stood at 3,400 aircraft, nearly 1,800 tanks and armored vehicles, 11,000 guns and mortars, 200,000 rifles, and 19 million shells, mines, and bombs.[10] Soviet leaders achieved such astounding production primarily by depleting the civilian economy, which fell to less than half its prewar level in 1942. Agricultural production, too, had sunk to only 40 percent of its 1940 capacity by 1942. Yet these sectors had to sustain 60 percent of the prewar population. By the end of 1942, a debilitating shortage of goods, services, and food for civilians threatened military output. Greater attention to and investment in civilian production gradually redressed the imbalance, but because of the need during 1943 to rebuild and support the lands retaken from the Germans, the economy did not return to an even keel until 1944.

Indeed, despite its notable war production, the Soviet Union would emerge from the war with only one-quarter to one-third the economic base of the United States. The postwar replacement cost of the total material losses caused by wartime destruction has been estimated at seven years' worth of earnings of the 1945 labor force. Moreover, the war further widened the gap in living conditions between the countryside and the city, a problem that would not be addressed until the late 1950s under Khrushchev.

Food shortages presented a major threat to the entire war effort. Despite the catastrophic losses of some of the best land and livestock to the Germans, the wartime leadership initially gave agriculture low priority. The Red Army requisitioned tractors, trucks, and horses from the farms and left cows and people to pull plows, tillers, and reapers. The commandeered agricultural equipment was not replaced until 1944 and 1945. In 1943 available food per person dwindled to only one-half the 1940 level. Despite rationing, many Soviet citizens suffered from hunger and malnutrition, and some starved to death, even outside Leningrad. Arrangements for feeding evacuees often proved inadequate, and several eyewitness accounts describe bodies piled alongside railroad stations in Siberia and Central Asia. In addition, hundreds of thousands of forced laborers in the *Gulag* succumbed to starvation and overwork as their rations were cut back.

As the food crisis worsened, the GKO decided to retain centralized control of food supplies for the army but to decentralize food production

---

[10]These and most statistics in this section from John Barker and Mark Harrison, *The Soviet Home Front, 1941–1945* (London and New York: Longman, 1991), p. 183 and *passim.*

and distribution for the civilian population. Factories, institutes, and other economic units were now encouraged to grow produce on any available piece of land. Families were urged to till garden plots; many also supplemented their official rations by buying or bartering for scarce items in the collective-farm free markets. Almost all wartime memoirs dwell on the amount of time and effort that the Soviet peoples put into sustaining a minimum diet.

Allied aid, primarily American Lend-Lease supplies, bolstered the Soviet war effort in several ways. Totaling about $11 billion, the bulk of this assistance arrived between mid-1943 and the end of 1944. Lend-Lease deliveries included thousands of aircraft, tanks, trucks, and jeeps; 1.3 million tons of machinery and industrial equipment; 6 million tons of steel, other metals, and chemicals; 4 million tons of foodstuffs; 2,000 engines and railway cars; and 15 million pairs of army boots. The aid arrived too late to help the Soviet forces check and repulse the German advance in 1942 and 1943. However, it did contribute to the Red Army's recovery of the U.S.S.R.'s western territories and its subsequent drive into east central Europe and Germany in 1944 and 1945. Although only a small proportion of the total, foodstuffs arrived at a time when Soviet rations had shrunk to a perilous level. Despite Soviet attempts during the Cold War to denigrate the value of Lend-Lease aid, in 1943 and 1944 this assistance arguably amounted to between 20 and 25 percent of Soviet net national product. In addition, Lend-Lease freed one in seven Soviet workers for war tasks. The program also benefited the economy at its lowest point and noticeably subsidized the postwar reconstruction of the U.S.S.R.

The war strengthened Stalin's and the Party's dominant role. The GKO, which included representatives of the Party, the military, and the secret police, decided policy and executed it through special plenipotentiaries, usually Party members. The GKO also used regular Party and state channels to implement its decrees. Despite some confusion and friction with local authorities, Soviet wartime leaders achieved total mobilization and accomplished tasks necessary to win the war, although not always efficiently. The war underscored the power of the military and the secret police as well. The former had extensive authority over areas near the front lines, over the western territories when they were first recovered, and in the occupied lands in Eastern Europe and Germany. The army also benefited from the prestige and prominence that victory bestowed. The influence of Beria and the NKVD expanded primarily because of the significant role that *Gulag* prisoners played in the wartime economy, particularly in construction projects and in the extraction of timber and minerals. Yet neither Red Army generals nor the shadowy heads of the security apparatus could match the power and glory that attached to Stalin, "the great architect of victory." His cult burgeoned during the war and into the postwar period.

The war altered Soviet society in other important ways. Because many lower-level Communists were killed, the Party's profile changed. In 1946 two-thirds of Party members were under thirty-five years old. The proportion of peasants and workers had dropped; almost half the membership now came from "the working intelligentsia"—that is, from urban professional, service, or bureaucratic strata. Some evidence suggests that these younger, "citified" cadres would form a core of support for Khrushchev's policy changes of the 1950s.

The wartime alliance with the Western democracies also fostered the freest intellectual atmosphere that the U.S.S.R. had known since the 1920s. A few Soviet writers and professionals traveled to the West or met foreigners visiting the Soviet Union. As long as they expressed unrestrained support for the war, writers, artists, and performers could treat subjects and themes outside the canon of socialist realism. This respite from Stalinist conformism would not last, but undoubtedly seeds of future change took root during the hiatus.

Patriotism, sacrifice, and hatred of the enemy suffused wartime popular culture. In posters, cartoons, and films, the despicable fascists were limned as rodent-like creatures skulking in dark corners. Various media harped on German atrocities, and in a widely printed and broadcast poem, Alexei Surkov railed

My house has been defiled by the Prussians,
Their drunken laughter dims my reason.
And with these hands of mine
I want to strangle every one of them.[11]

At the same time, artists venerated the motherland, *rodina*. An immensely popular heroine, Zoya Kosmodemyanskaya, was enshrined in drama, poetry, photo, statue, and children's tale for her role as a young partisan captured and tortured by the invaders. The protagonist of a prewar ballad, "Katyusha," took new form as a Soviet rocket launcher wiping out regiments of Germans.

Radio played a crucial role in knitting together the scattered elements of the population. Radio Moscow read nine thousand letters exchanged between soldiers in combat and their families, strengthening the bonds and dedication between the front line and the home front. Broadcasts stressed the whole range of national culture, from classical music to plays and stories to jazz and popular songs. Entertainers performed not only over the airwaves but in person at army bases and naval and air stations. Filmmakers produced powerful documentaries of the battles of Moscow

---

[11]Quoted in Richard Stites, *Russian Popular Culture: Entertainment and Society Since 1900* (Cambridge and New York: Cambridge Univ. Press, 1992), p. 100.

and Stalingrad and feature films that dehumanized the enemy and exalted the simple virtues and courage of the Soviet soldier.

In addition to its impact on culture, the war reinforced significant demographic and social changes that had begun in the 1930s. The population shifts of the prewar years continued as refugees, soldiers, war workers, deportees, and many others moved around and across the country. This upheaval loosened traditional social ties and forced many people to adjust to new jobs and strange circumstances. As the populations of the Urals region, Siberia, and Soviet Central Asia mushroomed, these areas amassed economic strength and political importance. The astounding loss of at least 27 million people combined with the low wartime birthrate also created a population deficit that the country would not close until 1956. Moreover, the striking imbalance that arose between men and women—88 men for every 100 women—deprived numerous Soviet women of marriage prospects in the three decades after the war. At the same time, this ratio encouraged independence among many women, and the female percentage of the work force continued to rise.

Non-Russians, especially Ukrainians, Belarusans, some peoples of the Caucasus, and Jews, suffered disproportionately during the war. Many minorities lived on the western and southern borders of the Soviet Union and thus bore the brunt of the German attack. These people also fell victim to Stalin's persecutions and deportations. Such tribulations alienated some non-Russians from Soviet rule and fueled the smoldering fires of local nationalism.

Nevertheless, for most citizens, victory over the Nazis strengthened both personal self-esteem and identification with the Soviet system. They had bonded in a common struggle against a clearly identifiable foe, and many individuals took pride in their contribution to the ultimate triumph. A cult of the Great Patriotic War emerged, nurtured partly by the Party and partly by veterans and other survivors determined to memorialize their sacrifice.

The Grand Alliance

The truism that "war and politics make strange bedfellows" aptly fits World War II. Despite the Soviet Union's frosty if not hostile relationship with the Western democracies through the 1920s and 1930s, once Operation Barbarossa began, compelling self-interest on both sides bound the Soviet homeland of socialism and the capitalist West closely together. For the sake of survival, Stalin proved quite willing to set aside Marxist postulates in order to elicit and augment Western support. Indeed, from the beginning, his primary concern focused on not just material help but direct military assistance. During the dire first months of the Soviet-

Only recently have historians probed the social dimension of war, either as a springboard for understanding political and economic change or as a subject in its own right. In writing about the impact of World War I on Russia's industrial economy, for example, Norman Stone portrayed the conflict as "a crisis of growth, a modernization crisis in thin disguise." At first imperceptibly, but soon with relentless force, the Great War (1914–1918) thrust Russia into circumstances that required public planning, organization, and—especially—technical competence. And although the tsarist regime ultimately failed to cope with the demands of modern war, the response of the educated public to the problems engendered by the struggle—from public health care to refugee assistance to hospital management—revealed society's potential for development (*The Eastern Front, 1914–1917,* 1975).

Just as World War I challenged the viability of the tsarist system, World War II tested the staying power of Soviet society. Until a decade ago, partly because most Soviet archives for the period were closed, Western specialists had written little on the domestic history of the U.S.S.R.'s struggle against Hitler. In 1985 a major work appeared, based on papers presented at a Louisiana State University symposium by scholars from Europe and the United States. Examining how the Great Patriotic War affected Soviet life, *The Impact of World War II on the Soviet Union* (Susan Linz, ed.) concluded that in spite of its incredible economic and human costs, and the near collapse of the system, the war in fact strengthened Soviet institutions. James Millar, a contributor to the volume, underscored that paradox, noting that the Stalinist regime, itself the nightmarish product of the 1930s, proved well suited to extreme wartime circumstances. Millar's point is well taken: Soviet administrative patterns in the 1940s echoed those from the Bolshevik past. The "personalization of power" and its "accountability" under excruciating stress mirrored prewar Soviet practices. In that respect, the war "proved the workability and reliability of [Soviet] political and economic institutions" ("Impact and Aftermath of World War II," in Linz).

But questions remain, prompted by two studies that dispute the extent of totalitarian controls in the wartime Soviet Union. In *Bread of Affliction* (1990), William Moskoff shows that Moscow had to fight two wars, one against the Nazis and one against hunger. Unable to do both, Kremlin leaders, deliberately and early on, handed over responsibility for the civilian food supply to local authorities and individual citizens. Almost immediately, a variety of ingenious makeshift operations sprang up, united only by everyone's grim determination to avoid death by starvation. Villagers and townspeople adapted "quickly and efficiently" to the food crisis through networks of private plots, farmers' markets, and factory farms. Officials ignored widespread profiteering by energetic peasant entrepreneurs who hiked prices on foods in short supply. Not since the NEP two decades earlier had Soviet authorities granted so much license to the private sector and with such startling results. The resurgence of free markets sparked a massive redistribution of money as urban dwellers flocked to the suburbs or to the countryside to buy food. Some results were almost comical: excluded from the wartime food rationing system, cash-rich peasants, with no goods to purchase, now bought savings bonds issued by the government to defeat Germany. In the end, as Moskoff says, the Soviet people survived in large measure "not because of the system, but in spite of it."

John Barber and Mark Harrison concur with this assessment, noting the limits to wartime centralization and a concurrent process of decentralization that forced millions of workers to become wholly self-sufficient. Munitions factories "learned" to manufacture their own instruments and machine tools because the overloaded system of centralized distribution of equipment collapsed under transport shortages. Steel-works spawned their own sideline production of tools, metals, and electric power. And workers developed a self-reliance without which "the industrial economy and its human agents could not have weathered the storms of 1941–1942."

As for the peasants, Barber and Harrison echo Moskoff. Throughout the war, sur-vival on collective farms depended on the private plot. Far from being a secondary source of income, as politically correct Party officials tried to maintain, peasant gar-dens, minuscule as they were, became the "main source of subsistence." Even hard-working collective farmers—those who overfulfilled state work norms by 200 percent—derived a whopping two-thirds of their income from private plots. Along the way, individual peasants grew wealthy. Hundreds bought bonds for sums as high as 100,000 rubles and, in one instance, for 400,000 rubles.

A third group, the cultural intelligentsia, also profited from the wartime relaxation of ideological controls. Closely monitored by the Party in the 1930s, artists, writers, and scientists now experienced, in the words of Soviet novelist Boris Pasternak, a "breath of fresh air" as opportunities exploded for consultation and propaganda work. Scientists assumed key government posts at the newly created State Defense Com-mittee or at Gosplan. Not surprisingly, by 1945 many academic and cultural leaders savored the hope that postwar society would look dramatically different from the So-viet Union a decade earlier (*The Soviet Home Front, 1941–45*, 1991).

The widespread desire for enhanced freedom in peacetime soon foundered on the shoals of Stalin's draconian postwar policies. Historian Sheila Fitzpatrick explored the theme of a return to "normalcy" that never occurred and suggested that the sup-pressed urge for reform contributed to social changes that followed Stalin's death in 1953. To be sure, as Fitzpatrick noted, the reimposition of state controls from 1945 to 1953 had deep roots in the Party's political culture. For this generation of Soviet leaders, "normalcy" meant the 1930s and campaigns of industrialization and collec-tivization, not the 1920s and the cultural and economic pluralism of the NEP. Then, too, such rulers believed that the wartime acquisition of new territories such as the Western Ukraine peopled by non-Russians fiercely resistant to communism required enforced orthodoxy. Yet the most pressing argument against relaxation of state con-trols may have been the war's impact on Soviet citizens' attitudes and values. Soviet leaders from Stalin down understood all too well that peasants now talked of a "post-war abolition of the *kolkhoz*," and intellectuals, of a cultural thaw. Inside the frame-work of Stalinist centralization, society and behavior had been reshaped by wartime, and the Party elite recognized that they had to smother these dangerous tendencies at all costs ("Postwar Soviet Society: The Return to Normalcy," in *World War II*, Lloyd Lee, ed., 1991).

For years scholarly attention centered on how victory over the Nazis reinforced the Soviet system and its claims to legitimacy. We are only beginning to examine the other side of the coin: the liberating effects of World War II and their meaning for sub-sequent generations.

German war, Stalin implored Churchill either to open military operations against the Germans somewhere in Europe (a "second front") or to send British troops to the U.S.S.R. via Iran or North Russia. For their part, Churchill and Roosevelt recognized that if the Soviet Union fell, Britain and the democratic cause might also ultimately succumb to the Nazis. They agreed to ignore Communist Russia's ideology and provide as much assistance as they could spare.

After the Nazis attacked, the U.S.S.R. and Britain signed a mutual-assistance pact in July 1941. The United States, not yet engaged in the war but already backing Britain, agreed in September to provide Lend-Lease aid to the Soviet Union as well. When Hitler declared war on the United States following Pearl Harbor, the United States joined Britain and the Soviet Union in a tripartite alignment known as the Grand Alliance. In January 1942, this anti-Nazi coalition settled its war aims when Stalin reluctantly agreed to the Atlantic Charter, a vague affirmation of basic freedoms drawn up by Roosevelt and Churchill in August 1941.

Despite the larger considerations of survival, which held the alliance together until victory, suspicion and friction marred Soviet-Western wartime cooperation. Initially troubles arose over military and strategic issues and then increasingly over territorial and political questions. The second front remained one bone of contention between the Soviet Union and its allies. In May 1942, Soviet foreign minister Molotov returned from a visit to Washington with the erroneous impression that the democracies intended to invade Europe that year. Instead, November 1942 saw British-American landings in North Africa. The dismayed Stalin and his colleagues knew that Soviet lives still constituted the main expenditure in the war, with 193 German divisions on the eastern front versus 4 in North Africa.

In early 1943, the western Allies tentatively agreed to invade France at the end of that summer. Yet the British objected that the democracies had insufficient forces for this operation, so the Allies landed in Sicily and Italy instead, much to Soviet disgust. Finally, at the Teheran Conference in November 1943, Churchill and Roosevelt personally promised Stalin an invasion of France the following spring. By the time Allied forces landed in Normandy on June 6, 1944, however, the Red Army had almost completely ousted the Nazis from Soviet territory. Although the invasion tied up one-third of the *Wehrmacht* on the Western Front, the Red Army faced eleven more months of tough fighting.

In 1942 and 1943 political issues came to the fore in discussions among the alliance members as they looked ahead to the postwar world. The three reached surprising agreement on the need for an international body—a United Nations—to serve as a successor to the League of Nations. However, each also conceived the UN as a mechanism for extending their power over the postwar world. The Soviet Union, Britain, and the United States became the original permanent members of the UN's executive organ, the Security Council. China and France soon gained seats on the council, which had veto power over all important decisions.

At first, the question of Germany's future evoked more confusion than disagreement, largely because conflicting views on how to treat Germany abounded, even among policymakers within each alliance nation. Should Germany not only be disarmed but deindustrialized as well? Should it be decentralized, perhaps even partitioned? Stalin at the outset seems to have favored dismemberment, although he finally accepted the idea of a demilitarized unitary German state. Undoubtedly Stalin recognized that if Germany were divided, its richer, more industrialized western regions would accrue to the West and Soviet influence would cover only the poorer eastern lands. At the Teheran Conference in November 1943, Stalin, Churchill, and Roosevelt agreed to control Germany jointly and to establish an advisory commission to determine postwar policy toward the aggressor nation.

The issue of how to treat postwar Eastern Europe grew especially pressing in 1944 as the Red Army began to occupy countries there. At a meeting in Moscow in October 1944, Churchill informally broached the idea of dividing the Balkans into western and Soviet spheres of influence, but this proposal never bore fruit. After the Nazis had seized Poland and Czechoslovakia in 1939, the British had supported formation of governments-in-exile for these countries and housed them in London. Stalin was reluctant to see these non-Communist administrations dominate postwar Czechoslovakia and Poland. He himself was grooming Polish and Czech Communists in Moscow to rule these countries after the Nazis were ousted. To worsen matters, in April 1943, the Germans discovered the mass grave of Polish officers in the Katyn Forest and soon charged Soviet security forces with the murders. Soviet denials and Stalin's refusal to assist the Polish underground's 1944 uprising in Warsaw embittered relations between the Polish government-in-exile and Moscow.

Stalin also insisted that to ensure the U.S.S.R.'s security, the Soviet government should wield dominant influence in Eastern Europe after the war. The Western leaders acknowledged Soviet interests there and reluctantly acquiesced in Soviet annexation of the Baltic states, a part of eastern Poland, and Bessarabia, although the United States officially continued to recognize the prewar independence of the Baltic nations. Poland received compensation for territorial losses in the east with land in the west usurped from Germany (see the map, U.S.S.R. Gains in Europe from World War II).

Lengthy negotiations over future political arrangements in Eastern Europe culminated in an apparent victory for the Western allies at the Yalta Conference in February 1945. In this historic meeting, Stalin agreed to allow free elections in Poland and by implication elsewhere in the east. Soon, however, Stalinist operatives forced a Communist-dominated government on Romania, and elections in Poland were postponed. The Red

Army occupied all the Eastern and Central European countries except Austria, which the victorious powers had agreed to hold jointly, and Yugoslavia, which local Communist partisans had largely liberated on their own. This military presence, along with support from the Kremlin, provided powerful if indirect backing for local Communists as they moved to subvert democratic elections and coalition governments throughout Eastern Europe. Why Stalin agreed to free elections at Yalta and then undermined the process remains unclear. Perhaps zealous Soviet and Eastern European Communists, eager to spread the socialist revolution, convinced Stalin that he could control a buffer zone to his east only if Communist governments held sway there.

Also at Yalta, the Soviet, American, British, and Free French governments agreed on joint control of and common policy toward Germany, although each power was to manage a separate zone of occupation. All four powers were to administer Berlin, even though it fell into the Soviet occupation zone. Germany was to pay substantial reparations, half of which were to go to the Soviet Union to compensate for its preponderant losses. Discussion of Germany's fate continued at the Potsdam Conference in July 1945, held after Germany's defeat. On this occasion Stalin met with a changed Western leadership. Harry S. Truman had succeeded

The Big Three at Yalta Prime Minister Churchill of Great Britain, President Roosevelt of the United States, and Soviet leader Stalin during their February 1945 meeting at Yalta in the U.S.S.R. to plan the postwar world.

to the American presidency after Roosevelt's death, and Clement Attlee, leader of Britain's Labour party, replaced Churchill in midconference following the prime minister's defeat in postwar elections. The victorious powers agreed that the Soviet government could transfer factories, equipment, and goods from its zone of occupation in eastern Germany to the U.S.S.R. as part of German reparation payments. Western observers soon concluded that the Soviet Union was taking advantage of this accord to plunder East Germany, and disputes erupted. Irreconcilable disputes over the treatment of Germany would contribute to the outbreak of the Cold War, discussed below.

Military developments in the Pacific at first forestalled Soviet-Western friction in the Far East. At the Yalta Conference, Roosevelt obtained Stalin's commitment to join the war against Japan three months after Germany's surrender. In return the Soviet Union received the southern half of Sakhalin Island and the Kuril Islands (see map, p. 358), as well as promises of future remuneration. The Soviet Union fulfilled its end of the bargain and attacked Japan. Its quick victory over Japanese forces in Manchuria and the United States' use of atomic bombs on Japan in August 1945 hastened the Japanese surrender and averted Soviet participation in any final assault on the home Japanese islands. Truman thus felt justified in excluding the Soviet Union from the occupation or management of postwar Japan. This cold shoulder undoubtedly heightened Stalin's suspicions concerning the West's postwar intentions. Finally, for military reasons, the U.S.S.R. and the United States agreed to divide Korea into two zones of occupation, which soon would become separate, antagonistic states and serve as another ongoing source of tension between the West and the Soviet Union.

Stalinism Renewed

The Soviet peoples who survived World War II emerged flushed with optimism and high expectations. For four decades, they had prevailed over war, revolution, and civil strife; collectivization and industrialization; the purges; and the struggle with fascism. Physically and emotionally exhausted, they looked forward to a respite and reward for their heroism and suffering. Stalin soon wrecked these dreams. In a speech on February 9, 1946, he told a stunned populace that, surrounded by a threatening world, they once again would have to make sacrifices and redouble their effort to build industry and strengthen the country's economy. Moreover, it soon became clear that along with a vigorous round of forced industrialization, the Soviet peoples would have to weather a return to Stalinist control and Communist orthodoxy in intellectual life.

Stalin faced two urgent problems at home in 1945. First, he had to restore the country physically and economically. One in seven people had died in the war, and hundreds of thousands more suffered severe physical or psychological wounds. Millions had lost their homes, and several million in the Baltic area, eastern Poland, and Bessarabia had to be reincorporated into the Soviet state. Soviet losses ranked five times greater than those of Germany and seventy times those of the United States.

In addition, Soviet industry faced a wrenching reconversion. Agriculture and the civilian economy, slighted during the war, showed weak performances. To spur recovery, Stalin counted on reparations from Germany and Japan, the labor of German prisoners of war and of *Gulag* inmates, and in the late 1940s, some matériel obtained from Eastern European satellite states. For a time, Stalin apparently hoped for assistance from the United States, but he soon dismissed this possibility as unlikely. The Soviet Union also received limited but useful aid from the United Nations Relief and Rehabilitation Administration. Clearly, however, the burden of reconstruction would fall most heavily on the Soviet peoples.

Recovery proceeded apace under the Fourth Five Year Plan, adopted in 1946, and by 1950 the U.S.S.R. had met ambitious goals in heavy industry. The Union logged less progress in agriculture and consumer goods production. Housing remained a major irritant for the Soviet population. Not only had many homes and apartment buildings been destroyed in the war, but the rural population continued to throng to the cities. Many urban dwellers lived in shanties and dormitories or endured overcrowding in decrepit apartments. In some cases, six to twelve people jammed into one room, with three or four families sharing a squalid kitchen and bathroom.

Food shortages persisted, in part because a drought struck southern Russia in 1946. As in 1932 and 1933, famine ravaged a number of areas. Rationing remained in effect until 1947, and food prices soared. Clothing and consumer goods also were in short supply. Instead of the more comfortable life that they had expected, Soviet citizens subsisted on a standard of living that ranked lower even than that of their former enemies in Germany and Eastern Europe.

Collective farms suffered from a shortage of labor and machinery and from artificially low prices set by the government. Farmers not only earned minimal incomes, but the government reduced their private plots and raised their taxes. A 1947 currency devaluation, ostensibly aimed at speculators and black marketeers, hit hardest those industrious collective-farm families who had accumulated rubles during the war by selling surplus produce at high prices on the open market. The deplorable conditions in the countryside only accelerated the flight to the already teeming cities.

Stalin took several measures to solve his second postwar domestic problem: reestablishment of tight control over Soviet society. Named "Generalissimo" in the glow of victory, Stalin remained the indisputable dictator. But he also continued to feel insecure, and he suspected that not everyone appreciated his contribution to socialism and the U.S.S.R. Indeed, with age—he was sixty-five at the end of the war—his secretiveness and paranoia intensified. It is intriguing to imagine Stalin as a "prisoner of the Politburo" or as struggling to control ideological "hardliners" at home and revolutionary adventurists abroad, as some historians have suggested. Nevertheless, it is more likely that he dominated by playing ambitious subordinates off against each other.

The State Defense Committee dissolved after the war, but some of the loose organizational methods used in prosecuting the war persisted. Overlapping of Party and state functions continued, with responsibility for particular issues or areas of governance delegated to *ad hoc* committees or to one of Stalin's lieutenants. The Politburo and the Central Committee met sporadically, and a Party congress would not be convened until seven years after the war, in 1952. This informality and flexibility facilitated the Soviet leader's continuing despotism. Stalin also demoted war hero Marshal Zhukov, posting him to command the Odessa Military District, and reestablished the authority of Party secretaries in army units. In addition, the Soviet leader reimposed rigid control over the Baltic region and western Ukraine, where guerrilla bands tenaciously fought Soviet rule for several years after the war.

Stalin likewise grew concerned about the subversive impact of Western ideas to which Soviet citizens had been exposed during the war. He first took stern measures against some 2 million prisoners of war, forced laborers, and displaced persons. Many of these Soviet citizens were loath to return to Stalin's Russia. Yet hoping to preserve the wartime coalition, the Western governments forcibly repatriated them in 1946 and 1947 in return for British prisoners liberated by the Red Army. Some returnees were shot on arrival; others faced interrogation and imprisonment. The majority ended up in forced labor camps. Stalin also reimposed strict censorship and cut off all contacts between the Soviet Union and Europe, prompting Winston Churchill's famous image of an "iron curtain" descending across the continent.

The Soviet dictator turned to Andrei Zhdanov to whip the intellectuals back into line. Stalin had earlier trusted Zhdanov to take over leadership of the Leningrad Party organization after Sergei Kirov's 1934 assassination. Zhdanov's role in the defense of Leningrad during the war had earned him a reputation for heroism and steadfastness that he perhaps did not entirely deserve. After the war, Zhdanov emerged as Stalin's "expert" in ideological affairs. In the immediate postwar months, Zhdanov made public remarks that suggested he favored continued liberalization of intellectual life. Why he suddenly changed direction is not clear. Perhaps Zhdanov took up the theme of ideological purification at Stalin's behest. Perhaps he advanced this campaign, with Stalin's support, as a way of undercutting his major Party rival Malenkov, who was accused of neglecting ideology in favor of economic and personnel affairs during the war. In any case, the drive to restore "correct" views in Soviet cultural life began in late spring 1946 at about the same time that Malenkov was demoted.

The first attacks of what came to be known as the *Zhdanovshchina* fell on certain hapless Ukrainians who were charged in June 1946 with excessive nationalism in several literary and historical works. In August, Party ideologues accused two Leningrad journals of kowtowing to foreign influences. Party cultural commissars then castigated two internationally known writers, the satirist Mikhail Zoshchenko and the lyrical poet Anna Akhmatova, for purveying anti-Soviet and "personal" themes in their works. The crusade soon spread to other arts. The Party press indicted the world-famous film director Sergei Eisenstein for an unflattering portrayal of Ivan the Terrible, one of Stalin's heroes. Guardians of cultural propriety also held that the music of such renowned composers as Dmitri Shostakovich and Sergei Prokoviev was "formalistic" and prone to Western bourgeois influences. In 1947 Stalin attacked Georgy Alexandrov, a prominent ideologist and the dean of Soviet philosophers, for overestimating the impact of Western ideas on Marxism. The Soviet dictator also criticized leading economist Evgeny Varga, who had argued that because capitalism seemed unlikely to collapse, the U.S.S.R. should make some accommodation with the West. Soviet propagandists boasted of Russian preeminence in scientific invention. Party hacks credited Russian scientists and engineers with discovering everything from the steam engine to the radio and airplane.

During the winter of 1947–1948, Zhdanov's star began to wane, possibly because Stalin grew to resent his prominence. Or perhaps his adversary, Malenkov, with support from Beria, succeeded in sabotaging him politically. Zhdanov's sudden death in August 1948 probably stemmed from natural causes, although rumors later circulated that he was murdered. The campaign for ideological orthodoxy ground on, however, and spread to other fields in 1948 and 1949. Its most shameful aspects included the final victory in the biological sciences of Trofim Lysenko. (His crackpot theories about the inheritability of acquired characteristics are discussed in Chapter 7.) Although not a Party member, Lysenko had become acquainted with Stalin and had won the generalissimo's complete support. His toadies were installed after the war in key positions in biology and agronomy. The triumph of this charlatan led to the dismissal of world-renowned Soviet scientists and set back by several decades the country's research and training—and its credible reputation—in the biological and agricultural sciences.

The reemergence of open anti-Semitism for the first time since tsarist days marked a final, particularly abhorrent stage in the reimposition of Stalinism. During the war, Soviet Jews had suffered overwhelming misery. The Nazis had rounded up and shot some locally, as in the infamous killings in the Babi Yar ravine near Kiev, and had sent others to forced labor or extermination camps. The prewar population of 4.8 million Jews shrank by at least 2.5 million from 1941 to 1945. The Soviet government supported the creation of the state of Israel in 1947 and 1948, primarily as a way to weaken British influence in the Middle East. Yet Stalin undoubtedly began to have second thoughts when many Soviet Jews embraced this new homeland and Zionist sentiments spread among some Jewish circles in the U.S.S.R. Attacks on "rootless or bourgeois cosmopolitanism" (a euphemism for pro-Israel or pro-Western sentiment) cropped up in mid-1948. Jewish cultural institutions were closed, and prominent Jewish intellectuals came under fire. Although some Soviet Jews escaped harassment, many Jewish professionals lost their jobs, withered in prison, or were ordered to the camps. These unfortunates included even the Jewish wife of Molotov, Stalin's oldest and most loyal comrade. In addition, twenty-four Jewish leaders were secretly tried and executed in 1952, for allegedly plotting to establish a separate Jewish state in the Crimea.

After Zhdanov's death in 1948, a purge of government and Party officials in Leningrad and of others closely associated with Zhdanov swept the country. Hundreds, perhaps thousands, were put to death or sent to the *Gulag* in what came to be known as the Leningrad Affair. Evidently Malenkov, working with Beria, carried out this "cleansing" of his rival's supporters. Stalin's involvement, if any, in suggesting, initiating, or directing the affair remains unclear. In any case, this purge reminded everyone in the government and Party of the insecurity of their positions. It may even have portended a major Party purge that Stalin apparently was planning in 1952, just before his death.

The Cold War Ignites, 1946–1950

Debate over who deserves the blame for the Cold War has raged for forty years. Most Western scholars posit that the Soviet Union's expansionist policies and refusal to cooperate with its former partners caused the break. "Revisionists," however, contend that U.S. foreign policy sought American dominance in Europe and the rest of the world. This ambition to surround the socialist countries and to ensure Western control of vital resources and trade routes was the culprit, they argue. In the face of this American-led "imperialism," the Soviet Union understandably took steps to safeguard its security and its economic independence.

As with so many controversial issues, both positions contain elements of truth. Stalin did desire Soviet domination of Eastern Europe and hoped to see socialist revolution spread across the globe. And given the fate of the Eastern European peoples who fell under Soviet control, Western leaders had ample reason to resist what they saw as a Soviet propensity to expand wherever the opportunity arose. On the other hand, Stalin and his advisers were justifiably concerned by Allied efforts to establish pro-

Western governments in Eastern Europe and Germany. The U.S.S.R. also had cause to object to the West's building bases and "areas of strength" around the Soviet perimeter as part of the policy of containment that the United States officially adopted in 1947. Consequently, it is fruitless to attempt to assess blame for the Cold War. The breakdown of joint policy and action, the mutual recriminations, and the growing hostility between the Soviet Union and the West had deep roots in ideological mistrust. Each side believed the other to be intrinsically committed to worldwide hegemony. Marxism-Leninism taught that as the capitalist system neared its death throes, the capitalists would do everything possible to crush socialism and thus stave off their inevitable demise. To Stalin, Western efforts to "encircle" the Soviet Union must have confirmed this postulate. Conversely, American and Western leaders believed that the Communists were committed to destroying capitalism and to carrying out a world revolution. In the West's view, only vigorous counteraction and countervailing force would check the U.S.S.R.'s drive for global domination.

In conversations with foreigners and in his few public statements soon after the war, Stalin asserted that because of the urgent need to rebuild his shattered nation, he hoped to continue cooperative or at least unhostile relations with the West. Undoubtedly he worried about the United States' economic power and its monopoly on nuclear weapons. Whether he genuinely feared that the "imperialists," led by the United States, would launch an assault on a weakened Soviet state is unclear. In any case, his postwar foreign policy initially reflected a strong desire to avoid armed conflict with the West. At the same time, the Soviet leader sought to maximize Soviet security by acquiring as much territory along Soviet borders and as many resources as possible.

Despite Stalin's desire to maintain nonantagonistic relations with the West, two serious issues put the victors at loggerheads between 1946 and 1947. Stalin saw Eastern Europe as crucial to his country's security. At first he had no particular interest in what form of government prevailed in Eastern European countries, as long as these states were not inimical toward the Soviet Union. When it seemed that the upstart regimes there might either prove unreliable on this score or, worse, might fall under Western influence, the Soviet dictator brought them to heel in the only way he knew: he sovietized them. This move expanded the socialist bloc and benefitted the U.S.S.R. politically and ideologically, but revolutionary expansion was not Stalin's chief goal. His discouragement of a Communist uprising in Greece, his refusal to countenance independent socialism in Yugoslavia, and his lukewarm support for Mao's revolution in China all suggest otherwise.

In addition to ensuring his nation's security, the Soviet leader strove to acquire the economic resources essential to rebuild his country. Pushed by his advisers and perhaps by power-hungry Eastern European Communists, Stalin sought to dominate not only the politics but the economies of

Eastern Europe. He also labored to prevent their reintegration into the Western European capitalist network. The importance of Germany's factories and equipment to the economic reconstruction of the U.S.S.R. apparently led Stalin to endorse his subordinates' decision to take more reparations from eastern Germany than the Allies had agreed to and than the West was willing to tolerate. Resistance in London and Washington to Moscow's efforts to extract the maximum resources from the Red Army's zone of occupation in Germany perhaps convinced the Soviet leader that the capitalist powers intended to rob him of the fruits of victory.

The U.S. decision in June 1947 to extend massive economic aid to Europe catalyzed Stalin's anxiety about Western policy toward Germany and Eastern Europe. When Secretary of State George Marshall first proposed the assistance program that came to bear his name, the Soviet ruler did not reject it outright, perhaps hoping that part of the American largesse would funnel to the U.S.S.R. and the nations of Eastern Europe. In fact, coalition governments in Poland and Czechoslovakia welcomed the Marshall Plan. But another concern lay behind the overriding U.S. purpose of stabilizing the war-ravaged economies and fractured societies of Western Europe, particularly in France and Italy with their strong Communist Parties. American statesmen also saw that the plan, if broadened to include all of Europe, would help to enfold the German and Eastern European economies into the Western system.

By midsummer 1947, Stalin persuaded himself that the Marshall Plan was primarily directed at undermining Soviet domination of Eastern Europe and luring a united Germany to the Western side. He abandoned his earlier quest for amicable relations and initiated a confrontational policy, first forbidding Czechoslovakia and Poland to participate in the plan, then convening a conference of European Communist parties in September 1947. At this gathering, he established a permanent organization, the Cominform, to oppose the Marshall Plan and to block American imperialism in Europe. His chief ideologist Zhdanov declared at the conference that the world had split into two estranged and incompatible domains, the "peace-loving" socialist camp and the "warmongering" imperialist camp. Stalin blocked adoption of the Marshall Plan in Eastern Europe, but those economies languished while West European recipients of American aid prospered. In retrospect, the Soviet-Western division over the Marshall Plan clearly marks the start of the Cold War.[12]

The case of Finland supports this analysis of Stalin's postwar diplomatic course. The Finns were prepared to subordinate their foreign pol-

---

[12]This analysis is based on Scott D. Parrish, "The Turn Toward Confrontation: The Soviet Reaction to the Marshall Plan, 1947," Cold War International History Project, Working Paper #9, March 1994.

icy to Soviet interests and thereby ensure Soviet security in that quarter. They also agreed to provide substantial economic assistance on terms favorable to the Kremlin. The Soviet ruler thus made no effort to sovietize Finland and instead permitted it to remain independent, democratic, and capitalist. To be sure, he may also have worried that subjugating Finland would provoke the very conflict with the West that he wanted to avert. Yet if Finland had tied itself to the West or in any other way had threatened Soviet security interests, it is hard to believe that Stalin would have spared this neighbor, no matter what the risks.

Other issues, although less important to Stalin, intensified the West's suspicion of Soviet policy. Allied leaders grew alarmed by Greek Communists' efforts to overthrow the Athens government and saw the move as part of a pattern of Soviet expansionism. They were unaware that the Yugoslav leader Tito, not Stalin, was in fact the chief supporter of the Greek Communist rebellion (which the Greek government finally suppressed with British and American assistance). Stalin's diplomatic pressure on Turkey to cede to the Soviet Union bases on or near the Turkish Straits (an idea that Molotov had first broached to Hitler in November 1940) and abortive Soviet efforts to annex a slice of northern Iran further upset democratic statesmen. In the spring of 1947, President Truman announced that the United States would provide economic and military support to Greece and Turkey and to any other country threatened by communism. This principle soon became known as the Truman Doctrine and formed the basis of American containment policy.

By the end of 1947, Stalin moved vigorously to rebuff what he saw as capitalist efforts to encircle the Soviet state. With the Cominform in place, he cemented Soviet control over Eastern Europe. Early 1948 saw a Communist coup in Czechoslovakia that overthrew the last independent coalition government in Eastern Europe. The West expressed outrage but could do little else. Military intervention was out of the question, for while the Red Army exerted a powerful presence in the region, the Western countries had all demobilized.

Just when Soviet hegemony over Eastern Europe seemed complete, however, a quarrel broke out in the spring of 1948 between Stalin and Tito, the head of Communist Yugoslavia. The Yugoslav Communists, who had made their own revolution during the war, held independent ideas about how to build socialism and about how they should relate to other Balkan states. Tito envisioned himself as dominating the Balkan peninsula and controlling Communist Bulgaria. Annoyed by the Yugoslav leader's pretensions and angered by his resistance to Soviet domination, Stalin expelled Yugoslavia from the Cominform in June 1948. Stalin reportedly bragged that he would wiggle his little finger and that would be the end of Tito. But Tito stubbornly opposed Soviet subversion and pressure, and Stalin apparently decided that occupying Yugoslavia would be too costly and might risk war with the West.

Stalin also provoked a major showdown with the West over Germany. In addition to ongoing Western complaints over Soviet "plundering" of eastern Germany, disagreements arose over de-Nazification, the reestablishment of political parties, and economic relations among the four occupation zones. Britain and the United States began to coordinate activities in their two zones and indicated that they would welcome joint action with the French zone. Alarmed that this policy represented a first step to a reunified West Germany that might later menace the Soviet Union, Stalin blocked land access to Berlin in June 1948. Stalin may have wanted to force the Western powers out of Berlin, or perhaps he simply hoped to extract concessions from them that would prevent the formation of a separate West Germany. The Western authorities rejected a show of force and instead launched a round-the-clock airlift of supplies to their sectors of the old capital. After eleven months, Stalin called off the blockade, but Berlin remained a thorn in East-West relations. By the end of 1948, the de facto division of Germany had taken place. Before long, two separate German states emerged, the German Democratic Republic (East Germany) under Soviet domination and the Federal Republic of Germany (West Germany) allied with the West.

The Cold War grew chillier in 1949. The Western powers banded together in a mutual-assistance alliance known as the North Atlantic Treaty Organization (NATO). The Soviet Union responded in 1955 by creating an eastern alliance system, the Warsaw Pact (see the map, The Cold War, 1950). In September 1949, in part owing to data transmitted by Western pro-Communists Klaus Fuchs and Ethel and Julius Rosenberg, the Soviet Union tested its first atomic bomb, opening four decades of nuclear rivalry between the superpowers. At the end of 1949, Mao and his comrades brought communism to China, defeating Chiang Kai-shek and the Nationalists in a civil war that had raged periodically since 1927 and intensively since 1947. Even though Stalin had given little support to the Chinese Communists and had until late 1949 maintained ties to their opponents, Americans saw Mao's victory as greatly enlarging communism's reach and another step in a Soviet plan for world domination. U.S. policymakers felt vindicated in this view when Mao and Stalin signed a mutual-assistance treaty in February 1950.

In June 1950, the Cold War turned hot as North Korea invaded South Korea. American forces under UN sponsorship rushed to the defense of the south. U.S. leaders believed that Moscow had instigated the attack, but early 1990s evidence from Soviet archives indicates instead that Stalin acquiesced in the invasion and supplied equipment, arms, and high-level military advisers only after persistent North Korean appeals for Soviet assistance. He apparently feared that withholding support would drive the North Koreans into the arms of the Chinese. When the North Korean armies faced defeat, the Soviet leader sent air-defense forces, including a few Soviet pilots, and supported the Chinese Commu-

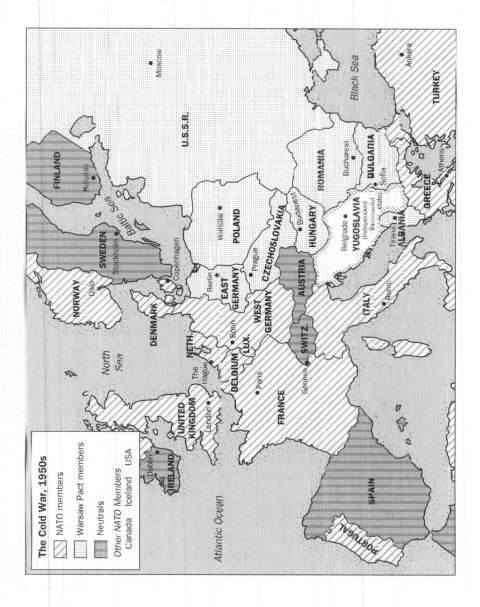

The Cold War, 1950s

NATO members

Warsaw Pact members

Neutrals

Other NATO Members
Canada   Iceland   USA

nists' decision to intervene. Stalin may have hoped to get the Americans and Chinese tangled in a long ground war in Asia, but Mao's armies withdrew after the two antagonists reached a military stalemate.

Stalin's postwar foreign policy achieved some goals important to the Soviet Union. Except for Greece and Finland, the entire tier of Eastern European states became Communist, although Yugoslavia (and later tiny Albania) rejected Soviet direction and dominance. These countries served as political and military satellites of the Soviet Union and were controlled economically through the regionwide Council on Mutual Economic Assistance. East Germany was incorporated into the Soviet bloc, and Communist states were established in North Korea and China. On the other hand, Soviet policies in Eastern Europe and Germany and the invasion of South Korea provoked a strong reaction from the Western powers and led to their rearmament and formation of NATO. Moreover, after the establishment of West Germany, the Soviet Union's faint hope of extending its influence into Germany as a whole evaporated. The position of Communist parties in France and Italy weakened as well. Stalin had strengthened Soviet security in some ways, but the balance sheet showed decidedly mixed results.

Conclusion

The Soviet peoples' feat in vanquishing the Nazi armies perhaps stands as the decisive event of the twentieth century. If Hitler had subjugated and exploited Russia, the course of World War II and the history of the past five decades would have taken quite a different road. Soviet survival allowed the U.S.S.R. to emerge as a superpower whose rivalry with the United States would dominate world affairs until 1989.

Stalin's consternation on the night of June 22, 1941, stemmed from his misplaced trust in the bargain that he had struck with Hitler in August 1939. Eager to avoid war and suspicious of the West, the Soviet ruler gave Hitler a free hand in Poland and permitted the Führer to hurl the full might of the *Wehrmacht* against the Low Countries and France the following spring. Stalin thought that his deal with Hitler safeguarded Soviet security; in fact, because of the collapse of the French army, the pact gravely endangered the Soviet system.

Soviet society barely survived Operation Barbarossa. But for Hitler's strategic hesitations, the war might have ended in 1941. Contrarily, Stalin's blunders almost led to total defeat, yet his leadership helped to save the U.S.S.R. from total ruin. The majority of the population rallied to his nationalistic and religious appeals and valiantly defended the homeland. The Soviet system, with its centralized control, command economy, and rigid coercion, proved effective, if not efficient, in meeting the demands of all-out war. After a precipitous decline occasioned by the initial losses and German seizure of the western lands, industrial production began to recover in 1943, and munitions output far outstripped that of Nazi Germany by 1944. Overemphasis on war work nearly desolated food production and the civilian economy, but this imbalance was partially righted before the end of the war.

Like the 1930s industrialization drive, the conflict traumatized Soviet society. Millions were evacuated or fled the western regions before the advancing Germans. Some 60 million Soviet citizens fell under Nazi occupation. At least 2 million Jews, several million captured Red Army soldiers, and untold other millions perished at the hands of the Nazis. In addition to Stalin's deportation of almost 3 million non-Russians to Siberia and Soviet Central Asia, the non-Russian peoples, many of whom lived on the country's frontiers, endured disproportionate losses. On the other hand, many individuals advanced during or after the war into better positions, replacing Party, government, and professional leaders lost to the war effort. Women assumed new responsibilities at home, on the farm, and in military service; they also entered the paid labor force in greater numbers than before. Peasants flocked to the cities and often stayed there, as conditions of life in the countryside grew more wretched.

The war both validated and indicted the Soviet system. Just as in the industrialization drive, Stalinism crafted a victory but at an astounding cost. If we add the war dead of at least 27 million to some 10 million who died during collectivization, the famine of 1932–1933, and the purges, almost one in five Soviet citizens perished in seventeen years of Stalin's despotic rule, a genocidal record unparalleled in history. These losses are analogous to most of the population of the eastern seaboard of the United States being wiped out during the Depression, New Deal, and World War II.

And for what purpose? The Soviet people took pride in their achievement and gloried in the postwar emergence of the Soviet Union as a superpower. Until the late 1980s, that sense of accomplishment helped to justify the hard life and repression that they continued to endure. Yet one of the most ironic cruelties of the war was how little the Soviet peoples benefited from their triumph. Renewed industrialization and the reimposition of Stalinism required yet additional sacrifice and a return to a closed, repressive society. Moreover, Stalin's policies, while only partly responsible for the Cold War, nevertheless injected new insecurity and tension into Soviet life and into the country's relations with the outside world. The Soviet people had won a remarkable victory, but their effort went unrewarded. For the survivors, life ground on virtually unchanged, and the socialist vision of 1917 still hovered far from their grasp.

FURTHER READING

No general comprehensive history of the U.S.S.R. in World War II exists. Military history is treated in Alan Clark, *Barbarossa: The Russian-German Conflict, 1941–1945* (rpt. New York, 1985); Albert Seaton, *The Russo-German War, 1941–1945* (London, 1971); and John Erickson's two detailed volumes, *The Road to Stalingrad* (New York, 1975) and *The Road to Berlin* (Boulder, Colo., 1984). Monographs on aspects of the military struggle include Harrison Salisbury, *The 900 Days: The Siege of Leningrad* (New York, 1958); John Armstrong, *Soviet Partisans in World War II* (Madison, Wisc., 1964); Catherine Andreyev, *Vlasov and the Russian Liberation Movement* (Cambridge, 1987); Seweryn Bialer, ed., *Stalin and His Generals: Soviet Military Memoirs of World War II* (New York, 1969); and Alexander Dallin, *German Rule in Russia, 1941–1944* (rpt. New York, 1980). Konstantin Simonov, a Soviet author/journalist, wrote a heroic novel about the Battle of Stalingrad, *Days and Nights* (New York, 1945).

An excellent treatment of domestic events is John Barker and Mark Harrison, *The Soviet Home Front, 1941–1945* (London and New York, 1991). Useful earlier accounts include Alexander Werth's journalistic eyewitness story, *Russia at War, 1941–1945* (rpt., New York, 1984) and S. J. Linz, ed., *The Impact of World War II on the Soviet Union* (Totowa, N.J., 1985). A revealing monograph is William Moskoff, *The Bread of Affliction: The Food Supply in the U.S.S.R. During World War II* (New York, 1990).

Prewar diplomatic history is treated in Anthony Read and David Fisher, *The Deadly Embrace* (New York, 1988), which focuses on the 1939 Nazi-Soviet pact, and in the last chapters of Robert C. Tucker, *Stalin in Power: The Revolution from Above, 1928–1941* (New York, 1990). A recent collaboration on wartime diplomacy among British, American, and Russian historians is David Reynolds, Warren F. Kimball, and Alexander O. Chubarian, *Allies at War* (New York, 1994). For postwar foreign policy, see Marshal Shulman, *Stalin's Foreign Policy Reappraised* (rpt., Boulder, Colo., 1985); William Taubman, *Stalin's American Policy* (New York, 1982); Melvyn P. Leffler, *A Preponderance of Power: National Security, the Truman Administration, and the Cold War* (Stanford, Calif., 1992); and Scott D. Parrish, "The Turn Toward Confrontation: The Soviet Reaction to the Marshall Plan, 1947," Cold War International History Project, Working Paper #9, Woodrow Wilson Center, Washington, D.C.

On political issues, consult Werner Hahn, *Postwar Soviet Politics* (Ithaca, N.Y., 1982), and William McCagg, *Stalin Embattled, 1943–1948* (Detroit, 1978), which argue in different ways that Stalin struggled with contending political forces at home and in Eastern Europe. On specific issues, see Robert Conquest, *The Nation Killers: Soviet Deportation of Nationalities* (New York, 1970), and David Joravsky, *The Lysenko Affair* (Cambridge, Mass., 1970).

9

A VISION REFURBISHED
The Khrushchev Era
~

Nikita Khrushchev, the new leader of the U.S.S.R., was nearing the end of his famous speech to the February 1956 Twentieth Party Congress, "On the Crimes of the Stalin Era." According to a political fable widely told in the Soviet Union in the late 1950s, as Khrushchev castigated Stalin for his abuse of power, a voice in the back of the hall bellowed. "Comrade Khrushchev, what were you, a high Party official, doing when Stalin was committing all these crimes?"

Khrushchev halted his presentation, peered out at the 1,500 assembled Party stalwarts, and demanded, "Who made that remark?" Silence reigned in the audience. The Soviet leader pulled out his pocket watch and placed it pointedly on the rostrum. "I will give the comrade who asked that question exactly one minute to stand and be identified," he announced. Still no response came from the hall. The seconds ticked by. No one stirred, no hand was raised, no individual stood up. Khrushchev snapped his watch shut and returned it to his pocket. "Now I am quite happy to answer that question," he said. "When Stalin was committing his crimes, I was doing the same thing that the comrade questioner has been doing for the past minute."

This anecdote strikingly illustrates the danger that Khrushchev and his colleagues faced in denouncing the Soviet dictator after his death. Because, having survived, they all must have supported Stalin loyally, embarrassing questions haunted Khrushchev's listeners and other Soviet citizens: Were current Party leaders not also involved in the dictator's transgressions? Should not *all* Party and government officials involved in the repressions be brought to account? Did Stalin's ability to commit such outrages not reveal a fundamental flaw in the Party and the Soviet socialist system? Khrushchev's implication that he and others sought only to save their skins hardly provided a satisfying answer. In Party meetings called to discuss Khrushchev's speech, many participants raised these questions. Some went to jail for their pains. Others were expelled from the Party or transferred to undesirable jobs.

Khrushchev's attack on Stalin proved the most audacious of several reforms that the new leader sought to implement. Condemning Stalin personally permitted Khrushchev to adjust the system without uprooting it. To alleviate the mounting inefficiency and rigidity of late Stalinism, Khrushchev encouraged limited innovation and flexible problem solving in a serious effort to improve industry, agriculture, and consumer services and to better Soviet citizens' lives. The new Soviet leader also recognized the suicidal dangers of nuclear confrontation with the United States and pursued accommodating and interactive foreign policies, albeit inconsistently. But although he largely eliminated Stalinism's paralyzing terror, Khrushchev did nothing to dismantle the elitist and statist framework of Soviet society. Moreover, most of his reforms foundered on Party conservatism and bureaucratic intransigence. After ten years, those who preferred old ways ousted Khrushchev from power and returned the Soviet ship of state to its traditional course.

Some historians and Khrushchev supporters have cast him as a David defying the Goliath of Stalinism and as a populist determined to make socialism work for the common people. In this interpretation, his policies reflected deep-seated reformist currents swirling within the Communist Party and presaged the changes that Mikhail Gorbachev would attempt thirty years later. His defenders also argue that although most of Khrushchev's reforms failed, he created an atmosphere of hope and pragmatism that inspired a generation of Soviet students and intellectuals who would become the driving force behind Gorbachev's later efforts. Khrushchev's detractors, in contrast, portray him as a bumbling, self-important meddler who tinkered thoughtlessly with Soviet society—a disruptive buffoon who achieved little. To those holding this view, he careened from one policy to another, but in the end Stalinist authoritarianism and inefficiency prevailed. The fairest assessment lies between these extremes. Khrushchev scored some successes, but he failed to overcome the irrationality, bureaucratization, and arbitrariness that hampered Soviet socialism.

Khrushchev contrasted sharply with his predecessors. Lenin had been cosmopolitan, theoretical, single-minded, and masterful. Stalin proved parochial, pragmatic, despotic, and unfathomable. Khrushchev, for his part, nurtured a deep loyalty to socialism and the Soviet future. Forthright in his personal and public dealings, he committed himself to helping the Soviet people. Yet Soviet intellectuals ridiculed his boorishness and impetuosity, and Party colleagues resented his growing self-righteousness and insensitivity. Because he failed to deliver the better life that he had promised, the Soviet people finally scorned him.

The Rise of Khrushchev and De-Stalinization

By the early 1950s, Stalin's faltering regime had pushed the Soviet Union close to ruin. During his last years, the aged dictator grew increasingly delusional and paranoid. He surrounded himself with a personal secretariat, and ignoring established procedures and organizations, he set and executed policy through individual senior Party members. He worked strange hours. Rising at noon, he reached his Kremlin office in early afternoon and stayed there until midnight or later. Often he telephoned top Soviet officials and sometimes foreign ambassadors late in the evening, forcing these unfortunates to adjust their work schedules accordingly.

By 1950 postwar reconstruction had returned industry nearly to its prewar level of output, but agriculture and the economy's consumer goods sector still lagged. Even industry would soon need massive infusions of capital, for the war had left plants and equipment worn and outdated. Numerous collective farmers struggled at a subsistence level, while workers suffered from intolerable housing, inadequate wages, and inescapable shortages of crucial goods. Most Soviet administrators, fearful of incurring their quixotic leader's ire, hesitated to address mounting economic problems. Memories of the recent *Zhdanovshchina* paralyzed intellectual and cultural life as well. Finally, Stalin had unsettled foreign relations by breaking with the U.S.S.R.'s wartime allies. Despite Soviet domination of Eastern Europe, the country appeared chronically beleaguered and isolated. The Stalinist system, succumbing to inertia, stagnated.

In late 1949 Stalin promoted Nikita Khrushchev, assigning him to the Party Secretariat and making him head of the Moscow region Party organization. Outwardly Stalin wanted his energetic appointee to reorganize the Party's operations and to untangle the intractable problems in agriculture. Yet Stalin's actions at that time—including Khrushchev's posting—often seemed aimed at controlling potential rivals or stifling threats from within the party system. Perhaps Stalin thought that Khrushchev's advancement would keep his other lieutenants from acquiring too much power and prestige. Indeed, the Soviet dictator soon balanced Khrushchev's rise to the Party's top ranks by permitting Georgy Malenkov to deliver the chief report to the October 1952 Nineteenth Party Congress (the first since 1939, although Party rules required one at least every five years). In another example of Stalin's paranoia, he apparently grew annoyed at the acclaim given a 1947 economic overview of socialism authored by Nikolai Voznesensky, the supervisor of the wartime Soviet economy and its reconstruction. Stalin countered with his own *The Economic Problems of Socialism*, a murky treatise that became the official bible of economic policy. In 1949 and 1950, as a follow-on to the Leningrad Affair (Chapter 8), the aging tyrant arranged the purging and execution of Voznesensky, then regarded as the number two Soviet leader. Ever suspicious, even of long-time comrades and close collaborators, Stalin used the Nineteenth Party Congress to dilute the power of senior Party leaders. He increased the ranks of the Central Committee by almost 50 percent and expanded the Party Presidium (formerly the Politburo), possibly to prepare for a new purge aimed at top officials.

Soon after the Party Congress, the bizarre "Doctors' Plot" unfolded. In November 1952, the secret police arrested nine prominent physicians attached to the special Kremlin clinic that treated high Party and state personnel. In January 1953, the Soviet press charged the doctors with treason, claiming they acted as agents of American and British intelligence, murdered several Party leaders (including Andrei Zhdanov), and conspired to mistreat and eliminate current top officials. Because seven of the doctors were Jewish, the case patently renewed the anti-Semitic campaign of 1948 and 1949. The *Pravda* article on the putative plot also criticized the state security agencies for laxness in the affair, an ominous sign for secret police boss Lavrenti Beria. Malenkov, an ally of Beria, must have felt uneasy as well, not to mention Lazar Kaganovich, who was Jewish, and Viacheslav Molotov, whose Jewish wife had already been arrested. We will never know the denouement of the drama or the fate that awaited top Party leaders: Stalin suffered a stroke on March 1 and died on March 5, 1953.

Because his close associates apparently had much to gain by Stalin's timely death, it is tempting to speculate that they may have helped him on his way to the hereafter. A few anomalies clutter the circumstances of his last hours, but Stalin probably died naturally, as announced. To be sure, he passed away at a most advantageous moment for his colleagues. Many Soviet citizens, on the other hand, had revered Stalin as the builder of socialism and their wartime leader, and hundreds of thousands grieved openly at his funeral. Because of insufficient crowd control at the scene, almost two hundred people were trampled to death, ironically becoming the last of Stalin's many millions of victims.

Stalin's death posed both immediate and long-range challenges for his successors. Having lived under coercion for so long, they worried that his passing would instigate popular upheavals. The announcement of his death included a call for vigilance against foreign and domestic enemies and warned against disorder and panic. Relieved when no protests or riots broke out, Stalin's lieutenants publicly proclaimed their adherence to the Leninist principle of "collective leadership." In private, however, they vied for dominance, setting aside the looming problems that the dead dictator had bequeathed them. Perhaps fearing Malenkov's emergence as Stalin's replacement, other senior Presidium members prevented his adding the position of premier to his post as top Party secretary. This accretion would have placed Malenkov, in emulation of Stalin, as head of both the government and the Communist Party. Instead, Malenkov was named premier, and Khrushchev was appointed acting first secretary of the Party.

The top jobs settled, the Presidium members now turned to the most pressing political issue: what to do about their colleague Beria. Reprieved from almost certain disgrace by Stalin's death, Beria had fortified his position by importing secret police troops and weapons into Moscow to provide security for the funeral. Afterward he took advantage of his colleagues' fear of popular unrest to justify keeping these units in the capital. The other leaders worried, however, not just about the armed force that Beria commanded but about the information that the secret police had collected on each of them over the years. They also fretted about Beria's ability to fabricate provocations and "cases" against them. All of them, including Beria's erstwhile ally Malenkov, understood that neither their own position nor the system's stability would be secure until Beria had been removed and the secret police curtailed. After careful preparation, including replacing Beria's Kremlin guards with army troops, they convened a special Presidium meeting on June 28, 1953. Khrushchev's account undoubtedly inflates his role, but it captures the drama of the moment.

> And so I came to the session. Everyone took their seats, but Beria was not there. Well, I thought, he has found out. It will cost us our heads. No one knows where we will be tomorrow. But then he showed up carrying a briefcase. My first thought was "What does he have there?" I also had something in store for such a contingency.... [Here Khrushchev slapped the right pocket of his jacket.]
>
> Beria sat down and asked, "Well, what's on the agenda for today? Why are we holding this surprise meeting?" I nudged Malenkov with my foot and whispered, "Open the meeting and give me the floor." He turned pale. I looked at him and saw that he was unable to open his mouth. Then I jumped to my feet and said: "There is one question on the agenda. The anti-Party, divisive activity of imperialist agent Beria. There is a proposal to expel him from the Presidium, from the Central Committee, to expel him from the party, and to try him in a military court. Who is in favor?" I was the first to raise my hand. All the others followed suit. Beria turned green and reached for his briefcase. But I knocked the briefcase away with my hand and picked it up. "You're joking," I said. "Don't try it." I myself pressed the button. Two officers from Moskalenko's military garrison ran into the room (I had arranged this with them beforehand). I gave them the order: "Take this skunk, this traitor to the Motherland, away to the proper place."[1]

---

[1]Khrushchev's story as reported by one of his aides, Fedor Burlatskii, "A Political Portrait of Khrushchev," in Donald J. Raleigh, ed., *Soviet Historians and Perestroika: The First Phase* (Armonk/London: Sharpe, 1989), pp. 232–233.

Beria's chief subordinates were soon seized as well, and the security apparatus was curbed and put under direct Party control. The Presidium members accused Beria of trying to take over the Party and government, of being an imperialist spy, and of abandoning East Germany in favor of a unified, bourgeois German state. In December Beria was secretly tried and executed. Malenkov and Khrushchev had collaborated to oust Beria, but by the end of 1953 they emerged as rival candidates to succeed Stalin.

How had Khrushchev managed to become a chief contender for supreme power? Short, rotund, and homely, he hardly affected a commanding presence. Yet this incisive description by a personal secretary sums up the essence of the man:

> . . . [H]e looked very strong, lively, and cheerful to the point of naughtiness. His broad face, his double chins, his enormous bald head, his large turned-up nose, and protruding ears could belong to any peasant from a central Russian village. The impression of being a man of the common people was

Khrushchev Shocks the UN Soviet leader Nikita Khrushchev pounded the podium during a September 1960 speech at the United Nations to underscore his assertion of the U.S.S.R.'s rights as a world power.

strengthened by his stout plump figure and his long hands that were almost continuously gesticulating. And only his eyes, his tiny, shrewd, gray-blue eyes that variously radiated kindness, imperiousness, and anger. only his eyes, I repeat, showed him to be a thoroughly political man who had gone through fire and water and was capable of making the most abrupt changes.[2]

The uneducated, prolix, and rambling Khrushchev was not a spellbinding orator, and his official reports and short articles revealed a prosaic style. Nevertheless, his organizational skill and enthusiasm for the Party and the cause of socialism propelled him to the seat of power.

Born in 1894 in Kursk region in south central Russia, near the northeast border of Ukraine, Khrushchev received only primary schooling before his father moved to the Donbass mining region to work in the coal pits. The son soon joined him and became a machinist and fitter in the mines. Radicalized by Marxist literature as a teenager, Khrushchev enthusiastically participated in strikes before and during World War I. In early 1917, he won election to his enterprise's factory committee and by the end of the year had joined the Bolshevik Party and enlisted in the Red Guards to fight the Cossack general Kaledin. In 1918 he was drafted as a political worker in the Red Army, and he fought in Russia's civil war for two years before entering regular Party work.

Khrushchev rose rapidly in Party ranks. He was recruited in 1928 to the Secretariat of the Central Committee of the Ukrainian Communist Party, which then was courting *apparatchiks* with proletarian backgrounds. From 1929 to 1931, the Party sent him to the Industrial Academy in Moscow, an institution that trained higher Party workers. It is unclear, however, whether his assignment was to acquire a good education or to root out anti-Stalinists in the staff and student body. He accomplished the latter task but left without completing the academic program.

As he ascended the Party hierarchy, Khrushchev embodied a new generation of Party leaders. Too young to participate in the pre-1917 Bolshevik movement or the October Revolution itself, these new cadres had been steeled in the cauldron of civil war and thrust into full-time, professional Party work. Usually given technical training by the Party, the rising specialists had proved invaluable in the struggle for industrialization and collectivization. They had endorsed the precepts and methods of Stalinism and advanced rapidly as the Soviet dictator decimated an older generation of Bolsheviks.

Khrushchev clearly benefited from the removal first of Left Oppositionists, then of Right Deviationists. At age thirty-seven, he gained the important post of district Party secretary in the Moscow region on the

---

[2]Ibid., p. 231.

recommendation of Politburo member Kaganovich, who had appreciated Khrushchev's work in Ukraine. From the Party's viewpoint, he compiled an impressive record in Moscow; he helped to expand the city's industrial base and oversaw completion of the first lines of the famous Moscow Metro (built in part with prison labor). With the purges clearing the way, he emerged in January 1938 as first secretary of the Moscow region and candidate member of the Politburo. Loyal to Stalin, he sometimes dined with the dictator, who perhaps considered the hard-working, ebullient, and somewhat sycophantic Khrushchev as part court buffoon and part protégé.

Khrushchev's 1930s assignment in Moscow, although crucial to his ascent to power, also marks a dark spot in his career. He survived the purges, perhaps because of his close relationship with Stalin, and acquiesced in the terrible cleansing of 1937. Evidence is lacking that he engaged in denunciations of colleagues, but he made no effort to defend condemned Moscow Party comrades, and he even signed some orders of incarceration. When he later reviled Stalin's crimes, he hardly did so with "clean hands." The purges gave Khrushchev's career yet another boost in mid-1938. That year, he rushed off to Ukraine to become head of that republic's Party and to restore order after the top Ukrainian Communists had been shot. Executions stopped, but arrests persisted.

Khrushchev's career during and soon after World War II also included brutal actions. He supervised the incorporation of eastern Poland into the U.S.S.R. in the wake of the Soviet-German Pact of August 1939, a process marked by grim repressions and the shipping of hundreds of thousands to the *Gulag*. Recognizing his disciple's important work as senior political commissar with the Red Army on the southern front, Stalin assigned him in February 1944 to rebuild Ukraine. Khrushchev was also charged with reincorporating the region into the Stalinist system, a task that included suppressing anti-Soviet and nationalist guerrilla forces who roamed the forests and marshes of Ukraine for several years after the war ended.

For unclear reasons, the future Soviet leader's ascent suffered a setback in early 1947. Stalin sent Kaganovich, Khrushchev's former patron, to Ukraine to supervise the ideological cleansing of Ukrainian nationalists, and Khrushchev was demoted. Whatever Khrushchev's sins, Stalin apparently forgave him, returning him to Moscow in 1949. The next year, he successfully amalgamated small collective farms with larger and stronger ones, a step that for a time boosted agricultural output. Nevertheless, Khrushchev may have been on Stalin's 1952–1953 purge list, for the dictator severely condemned and then blocked Khrushchev's 1951 scheme to build agricultural cities, or *agrogorods*, as centers for clusters of collective farms. This project, which would have required huge capital investment, exemplifies Khrushchev's penchant for grandiose but unrealistic plans, a trait that would land him in trouble later.

After Stalin's death and Khrushchev's election as Party first secretary, he labored to undermine his rival Malenkov's position. Taking advantage of his control of Party affairs and appointments, Khrushchev named his own people to the central apparatus and to district and regional posts. He also campaigned to insert his supporters into the Central Committee at its next election. Khrushchev defended the military against cuts that Malenkov wanted in order to free funds for consumer goods production. He also appeared to side with those advocating continued emphasis on heavy industry against Malenkov's proposed shift to light industry. In addition, Khrushchev subtly blamed the continuing agricultural crisis on Malenkov. (At the Nineteenth Party Congress in 1952, Malenkov had ill-advisedly declared the Soviet Union's grain problem solved.) Finally, Khrushchev played his trump card. Most Party officials, eager to eradicate the insecurity and random terror of the Stalin era, recalled with distaste Malenkov's collusion with Beria in the Leningrad Affair only a few years before. Khrushchev, not linked to any particular purge, played on their doubts about Malenkov while taking credit for the release of high Party officials from the camps. Malenkov lost ground, and in February 1955, Khrushchev engineered his rival's demotion from premier to minister of electric power stations, although Malenkov remained on the Presidium.

Once they had resolved the problems of stability, political security, and rivalry for Stalin's mantle, Khrushchev and his colleagues confronted the dilemma of buttressing the economy and making the system responsive to consumer needs without compromising the principles and structure of Soviet socialism. They also turned to easing the Cold War tensions generated in the last years of Stalin's reign. Because domestic issues had implications for Soviet foreign policy as well, let us examine them first.

After Stalin's death, and even more following Beria's execution, tens of thousands of appeals for the release of political prisoners and requests for information about the fate of relatives and friends deluged central Party headquarters in Moscow In 1953 and 1954, prisoners in a number of camps revolted. Some seized control of camps, forcing the administration to dispatch military units to suppress the uprising. In 1953 the new leaders acceded to these pressures by granting amnesty to several thousand relatives, friends, and individuals with skills useful to the state. As the clamor for release of political prisoners mounted in 1954 and 1955, the Party chiefs freed an additional twenty thousand camp internees, including many former Party members. The latter's demand to have their names cleared forced Khrushchev and his comrades to face the scope and illegality of the purges squarely.

Most top Party leaders acknowledged the urgency of eliminating arbitrary terror from the system. They also recognized the need for economic and social reforms and for changes in foreign policy. Khrushchev shrewdly linked these issues upon assuming the mantle of power. Personal and political security, he saw, would lead to initiative and efficiency, and a retreat from hard-line policies abroad might release defense funds to spur economic productivity. Yet attacking Stalin's legacy entailed risk. Not only were the Soviet and foreign Communist parties filled with lifelong Stalinists who might resist a frontal assault on their recent patron, but criticism of Stalinism could backfire into condemnation of the Party itself and its methods.

Of the top Party leaders, only Khrushchev had the audacity to manage the debunking of Stalin. While investigating Beria's activities and the status of camp prisoners, Presidium members had collected damning information on the purges. However, they haggled over whether to report this data to the forthcoming Twentieth Party Congress. Even after the congress convened, the issue remained unresolved, although Anastas Mikoyan injected mild criticism of Stalin into a speech. At the last minute, Khrushchev threw together an account of some of Stalin's transgressions, to be presented to the congress. His comrades assented on one condition: the evidence would be read in a closed session without discussion. Nevertheless, everyone recognized that Khrushchev's speech, delivered to an audience of more than a thousand people including observers from foreign Communist parties, could hardly be kept "secret." Moreover, copies of the text were soon made available to regional Party secretaries charged with briefing the rank-and-file membership on this issue. Before long, even the U.S. State Department released a copy, apparently acquired from Eastern European sources. Inside the U.S.S.R., however, the speech would not be published until 1989.

On February 24, 1956, Khrushchev delivered the historic address, which revealed a good deal but withheld the whole truth. After acknowledging Stalin's important role in the Party before 1934 and his achievement in industrializing the country, Khrushchev focused on the dictator's misdeeds and mistakes: illegal purging of Stalin's own close supporters; failure to prepare the country for Hitler's 1941 attack; numerous wartime blunders; unjustified deportation of non-Russian nationalities in 1943 and 1944; and the counterproductive ousting of Tito from the socialist camp. But Khrushchev avoided issues that bore directly on the contemporary structure of Soviet society or that cast doubt on existing Party policies. He omitted the horrors of forced collectivization of 1929 to 1931, for example, as well as the managed famine in 1932 and 1933 and the repression of intellectuals and Jews after World War II.

Aware of the risk in denigrating Stalin, Khrushchev nevertheless foresaw substantial gains from doing so. He wanted to preempt embarrassing questions and pointed accusations, as he admitted in his memoirs: "It's inevitable that people will find out what happened; if they start asking us about it after we've kept silent, they'll be sitting in judgment over us. I don't want that to happen. I don't want to accept responsibility in that way. I'd rather we raised the matter ourselves."[3] In addition, he probably hoped to discredit political opponents, such as Malenkov and Molotov, more intimately tied to Stalin than Khrushchev. Generally, too, he sought to restore legality and security, promote initiative and responsibility, rattle the entrenched bureaucracy, and open closed doors in foreign policy.

Khrushchev cleverly blamed the crimes of the Stalin era on the mistakes and personality defects of Stalin himself. He tried to distance the Party and the system from these evils by claiming that the dictator's narcissism and suspiciousness were at fault. As he put it, "the cult of personality" had distorted Party, government, and public activity in the Soviet Union. Khrushchev gave this chilling description of working with the dictator:

> Stalin was a very distrustful man, sickly suspicious. . . . He could look at a man and say: "Why are your eyes so shifty today?" or "Why are you turning so much today and avoiding to look me directly in the eyes?" The sickly suspicion created in him a general distrust even toward eminent party workers whom he had known for years. Everywhere and in everything he saw "enemies," "two-facers," and "spies." Possessing unlimited power, he indulged in great willfulness and choked a person morally and physically.[4]

As part of the de-Stalinization effort, top Party leaders slashed the authority and jurisdiction of the secret police. Tight Party control now muzzled the security apparatus. The prosecutorial and law enforcement functions usurped by the security organs in the purges and under Beria were restored to the prosecutor general of the Soviet Union, his subordinate institutions, and the courts. In addition, in 1956 hundreds of thousands of additional inmates were released from the *Gulag*, along with the bulk of the remaining political prisoners in 1957.

Dampening the Cold War

Khrushchev proved as innovative in foreign policy as in domestic affairs. In Stalin's last months, the dictator seemed to recognize the link between his confrontational foreign policy and the West's intensifying military stance. As a result, he had urged moderation on Western European Com-

---

[3]N. S. Khrushchev, *Khrushchev Remembers* (Boston: Little, Brown, 1970), p. 349.

[4]Translated in Basil Dmytryshyn, *USSR: A Concise History*, 4th ed. (New York: Scribner's, 1984), p. 544.

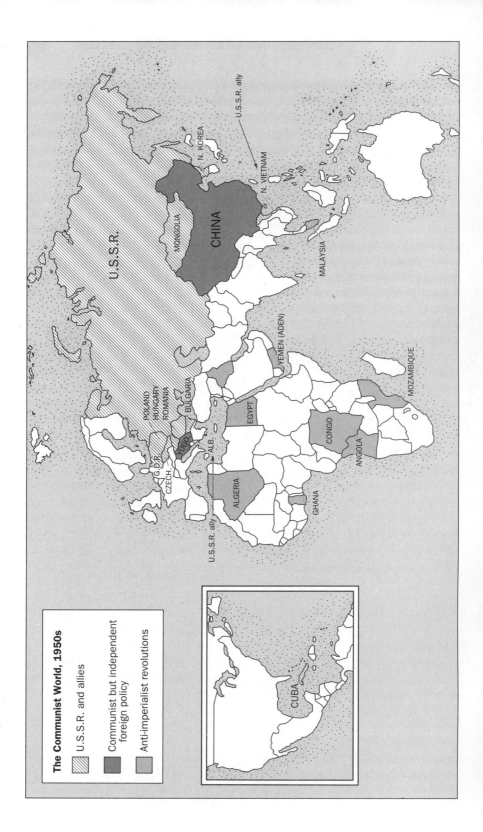

The Communist World, 1950s

U.S.S.R. and allies

Communist but independent foreign policy

Anti-imperialist revolutions

U.S.S.R.

MONGOLIA

CHINA

N. KOREA

N. VIETNAM

U.S.S.R. ally

MALAYSIA

POLAND

HUNGARY

ROMANIA

BULGARIA

G.D.R.

CZECH.

YUGO.

ALB.

YEMEN (ADEN)

EGYPT

CONGO

ANGOLA

MOZAMBIQUE

GHANA

ALGERIA

U.S.S.R. ally

CUBA

munist parties and counseled the Chinese and the North Koreans to seek an armistice in the Korean War. Whether Stalin intended to follow these tactical shifts with a major realignment of Soviet foreign policy is uncertain. (See the map, The Communist World, 1950s.)

Eager to avoid crises abroad during the interregnum and fearful that the "imperialists" might twist to their advantage the least sign of disunity or hesitation, Stalin's successors followed an accommodating line toward the West. In Korea they pushed for the armistice finally agreed to in July 1953. They also endorsed a 1954 cease-fire in the civil war that had erupted in Vietnam after World War II. They even acquiesced in a partition of Vietnam between forces of the Communist revolutionary leader Ho Chi Minh and French-backed conservative elements in the south. In Austria they accepted a peace treaty that provided for the withdrawal of occupation forces—Soviet and Western—in exchange for an Austrian pledge of neutrality.

The German question, however, remained unresolved. East Germany was then stumbling toward socialism and required costly Soviet subsidies. East Germany's stability wavered further when more than a hundred thousand citizens fled to the West in early 1953 and riots erupted in June that year. The post-Stalin leaders also took alarm at the incoming Eisenhower administration's campaign promises to "roll back communism" in Europe. In response, they tried to block Western plans to integrate West Germany into European defense programs. Beria opposed further expensive support to East Germany and instead pressed for a unified, neutralized Germany. Molotov and Khrushchev overruled him, but his colleagues used Beria's willingness to abandon East Germany as one ground for arresting him in July 1953.

Malenkov supported conciliation with the West as a way to elicit concessions, but at first his was a minority view. Khrushchev began to emerge in 1954 and 1955 as the chief architect of Soviet foreign policy. The first secretary rejected the Stalinist worldview of two implacably hostile camps—socialist and imperialist—between which other nations had to choose. He argued that world affairs were shaped not simply by class struggle but by the national interest of individual states as well. True, the Soviet Union needed nuclear armaments to deter Western aggression. However, in Khrushchev's view, the socialist motherland could best advance its interests by stressing its peace-loving nature and by arousing "progressive forces" in the West and throughout the world. This approach, he hoped, would force the imperialists to recognize legitimate Soviet interests.[5]

---

[5]Summary of Khrushchev's outlook based on James Richter, *Khrushchev's Double Bind: International Pressures and Domestic Coalition Politics* (Baltimore: Johns Hopkins Univ. Press, 1994).

Khrushchev also advocated reversing the U.S.S.R.'s isolation by reaching out to nonsocialist nations and peoples, particularly in the developing countries of Asia, Africa, and Latin America, where anti-imperialist revolutions brewed. Hence he traveled with colleague Nikolai Bulganin to India, Burma, and Afghanistan in late 1955 and promoted Czechoslovakia's sale of arms to Egypt in August 1955.

Finally, Khrushchev sought to improve relations within the socialist sphere. In September 1954, he visited China and agreed to provide Mao with economic aid, technical advisers, and assistance in developing nuclear energy and weapons. In June 1955, he journeyed to Belgrade in hopes of repairing the 1948 rupture in Soviet-Yugoslav relations. Although he met a chilly reception, he did restore scientific, economic, and cultural ties between the two countries.

All of Khrushchev's measures, however, lacked a firm doctrinal foundation. Soviet foreign policy still rested on the Leninist thesis that although imperialist and socialist systems could coexist peacefully for a time, their competition would lead inexorably to what Lenin called "a frightful collision"—a war from which socialism would emerge triumphant on a world scale. Yet after the Soviet Union acquired the atomic bomb in 1949 and Soviet scientists developed a hydrogen bomb in 1955, Party leaders could hardly look with equanimity on Lenin's promised showdown between imperialism and socialism. Waged with nuclear weapons, the predicted confrontation would annihilate both opponents.

Consequently, in a major foreign policy address to the Twentieth Party Congress in February 1956, Khrushchev amended Leninism by espousing the doctrine of "the noninevitability of war." Khrushchev explained that Lenin had rightly postulated the victory of socialism. But in the mid-twentieth century, this conquest did not require an armed clash. Instead, socialism could prevail by nonmilitary means, including political, economic, and ideological struggle. As a corollary, Khrushchev added that socialism's rise in individual countries did not have to follow a single formula of proletarian revolution. It could proceed through diverse channels, including nonviolent, even parliamentary, means. Moreover, Marxism-Leninism did not prescribe a blueprint for building socialism; each socialist state had to blaze its own trail in accordance with its unique circumstances.

Khrushchev's new foreign policy approach chalked up some successes in 1956 and 1957 but suffered setbacks as well. Specifically, the Western powers pressed ahead with the rearmament of the Federal Republic of Germany (West Germany). They also integrated the FRG into NATO, a threatening development for Soviet security. Because Molotov not only failed to obstruct these moves but also adamantly opposed full normalization of relations with Yugoslavia, Khrushchev fired the longtime head of Soviet diplomacy in June 1956. Molotov would remain a member of the Presidium, however. Later in the year, the Yugoslav leader Tito visited Moscow, and ties between the Soviet Union and Yugoslavia were fully restored. Nevertheless, Yugoslavia continued to pursue an independent foreign policy and to craft its own version of socialism.

Khrushchev's new national security policy also yielded mixed results. In February 1955, he became commander-in-chief of the armed forces and appointed World War II hero Marshal Zhukov minister of defense. He then promoted the build-up of Soviet nuclear forces and unilaterally cut the armed services by 640,000 personnel in July 1955 and by an additional 1.2 million men in May 1956. To supplement the deterrent effect of the U.S.S.R.'s nuclear arsenal, he supported Soviet peace campaigns around the world and supplied aid to anti-Western governments in the Third World. Yet Soviet backing and the support of global "progressive circles" failed to prevent an attack on Egypt by France, Great Britain, and Israel in November 1956. Both the Soviet Union and the United States intervened in the dispute. Although Khrushchev claimed that his threats resolved the crisis, in fact American pressure on its Western allies led to their withdrawal from Egypt. When the U.S. government refused to assist Gamal Abdul Nasser in his lofty project to tame the Upper Nile River with the Aswan Dam, Khrushchev came to the Egyptian leader's rescue. The Soviet Union became the chief supplier of aid and arms to Egypt in the late 1950s.

In the fall of 1956, political activists in Poland and Hungary, emboldened by Khrushchev's attack on Stalin and his toleration of hybrid socialism, challenged Soviet hegemony in Eastern Europe. Polish workers rioted in Poznan in June 1956. Polish Communists, fed up with rule by ineffective and corrupt home-grown Stalinists, set up a reform government that ended or moderated hard-line social and economic policies. The Polish leaders defied Khrushchev in a tense October meeting, warning that if Moscow tried to reimpose strict conformity on Poland, the Polish people—down to the last man, woman, and child—would fight. Khrushchev backed down.

Hungarian intellectuals also agitated for change in 1956. They found a sympathetic hearing among reform-minded Communists and democratic leaders from the presocialist era. But antisocialist and anti-Soviet sentiments among Catholics and nationalists created a volatile political brew. Old-line Party leaders lost control of the situation, and on October 23 antigovernment riots broke out in Budapest and other cities. Hoping to see locals quell the disorders and temper the movement for reform, Soviet leaders waited. Orthodox Hungarian Communists and the Soviet ambassador, Yuri Andropov (later to head the Soviet secret police and, briefly, the Soviet regime), pressured Moscow for armed assistance to put down the uprising, which they labeled counterrevolutionary. Hungarian reformers formed a new government and struggled to control developments, but dissatisfied rebels continued to attack security forces and

Party institutions and personnel. Revolutionary groups called for the removal of Soviet troops in Hungary and the withdrawal of Hungary from the Warsaw Pact. Moscow sent two Presidium members to Budapest on October 24 to study the situation. Based on their reports, the Presidium offered concessions to the Hungarian reformers and seemed prepared to negotiate on October 30.

On the following day, however, strident demands for intervention from Andropov persuaded Soviet leaders to authorize Marshal Zhukov to plan military action against the Hungarian revolution. Khrushchev reportedly opposed the use of force at first. But when the reform government declared an independent foreign policy in early November, he and other Presidium members determined to act lest Hungary's intended defection unravel the entire Warsaw Pact. It is unclear how much they also feared Hungarian reformism's impact on political and social stability at home. On November 4, sixty thousand Soviet troops moved into Hungary and bloodily suppressed the revolution. Soviet forces suffered more than six hundred dead; Hungarian casualties totaled more than four thousand dead and wounded. The Soviet authorities installed a subservient orthodox regime under Janos Kadar. Subsequent reprisals saw some three hundred revolutionaries executed and more than ten thousand imprisoned. In addition, thousands of Hungarians fled their homeland.

Caught by surprise and embroiled in the crisis over Egypt, the Western powers reacted slowly to the thwarted Hungarian uprising. They judged direct support to the revolutionaries too risky and instead settled for aiding Hungarian refugees. In the United Nations, they condemned Soviet intervention. Many socialists around the world, shocked at the spectacle of Soviet tanks and troops gunning down workers and students in the streets of Budapest, left the communist movement. Inside the Soviet Union, information on what actually happened in Hungary spread quickly by word of mouth, supplanting official accounts of quelling a counterrevolution. Protests erupted and hard questions cropped up in Party meetings.

The Cultural "Thaw"

Suppression of the Hungarian revolt accelerated some Soviet intellectuals' disenchantment with the regime. Yet even before Khrushchev had launched his de-Stalinization program in February 1956, intellectuals had begun to shake off the shackles of Stalinist orthodoxy. As early as two months after the dictator's death, poet Olga Berggolts asserted her right to compose lyrical but not socially useful poems, and a film criticism article deplored the artificial heroes of Soviet movies and scripts that subordinated human love to production quotas. In November 1953, the renowned composer Aram Khachaturian published an article attacking Party interference in music and demanding, "Let the individual artist be trusted more fully and not be constantly supervised and suspected." Edited by the poet Alexander Tvardovsky, the journal *Novy mir* (*New World*) championed the cause of cultural freedom and began to publish stories emphasizing the writer's personal point of view. In early 1954, Ilya Ehrenburg, a war correspondent, journalist, and author, published his novel *The Thaw*. Although not outstanding even by contemporary standards, the work caught the imagination of Soviet readers who soon baptized this entire period the "thaw." Instead of depicting a "positive hero" who overcomes all obstacles for the good of socialist society, Ehrenburg focused on a narrow-minded bureaucrat who wounds and alienates people in his zeal to meet production goals. The minor characters display admirable human qualities, and the author ends with the sanguine view that after a long, frozen winter (read Stalinism), a spring thaw lay at hand. Other works, such as Vera Panova's novel *Seasons of the Year* (1953) and Leonid Sorin's play *The Guests* (1954), attacked the ostentatious lifestyle of Party bureaucrats and the morally corrupting inheritance of Stalinism.

Conservatives in the cultural bureaucracy fought back in 1954. Gaining control of the powerful Union of Soviet Writers, they expelled some of its more independent members, replaced with Party hacks the editors of several liberal journals, including *Novy mir*, and condemned the brash critics of socialist realism. Nevertheless, through 1955 some journalists and artists continued to portray defects and absurdities in Soviet life.

Following Khrushchev's "secret" speech at the Twentieth Party Congress, intellectual ferment bubbled still more furiously. A few young scholars and students formed groups to identify vestiges of Stalinism in the system and to promote democratic socialism. Scientists dared to criticize charlatanism in genetics, and for a time Trofim Lysenko lost his dominating position, only to be befriended by Khrushchev and reinstated. Historians began to correct the distortions proselytized by Stalin and even to reevaluate the Party's role in the 1917 revolution. Some writers demanded the investigation and punishment of cultural bureaucrats who had persecuted artists in the Stalin era. Little was done in this area, although the Stalinist lackey and former head of the Writers' Union, Alexander Fadeyev, committed suicide.

The year 1956 also saw a spate of creative activity in literature, the theater, and the movies. Vladimir Dudintsev's novel *Not By Bread Alone* scathingly blasted bureaucratic obscurantism and corruption by describing the inability of a talented individual to get his bosses to adopt and apply his useful invention. The young poet Yevgeny Yevtushenko drew crowds to his readings of poems that challenged established verities.

They skillfully tried to distract him
from the aching questions "how come?"
Diligently critics expounded
on the absence of conflict to him.
Someone assured him ponderously
that the road was smooth and exact,
though a string of contradictions
might have led to disbelief.

. . . .

Year by year now things are getting harder
The lie and the twists cannot conceal
what was created by the people,
in the name of truth, and not of the lie.[6]

Also in 1956, the novel *Dr. Zhivago*, written by well-known translator, poet, and author Boris Pasternak, won wide recognition among intellectuals. The masterpiece presented a personal and at times critical interpretation of the 1917 revolution and the early years of Soviet rule. Although Soviet editors rejected the manuscript, Pasternak agreed to let an Italian firm issue the book, a development that Party officials tried desperately to prevent. In 1958 Pasternak won the Nobel Prize for literature, but Soviet authorities forced him to turn it down. Expelled from the Writers' Union and harassed by Soviet officialdom, Pasternak died in 1960, a hero to those struggling against the reimposition of orthodoxy. Despite the official rejection of *Dr. Zhivago*, new plays and films also abandoned socialist realism. They focused instead on everyday problems of personal life and portrayed rounded characters rather than the cardboard-cutout stereotypes of Stalinist productions.

As a first step toward opening the closed society that Stalin had scrupulously isolated from the outside world, Khrushchev permitted selected Soviet scientists, artists, performers, and sports teams to travel abroad, even to nonsocialist countries and to the West. Tours by violinist David Oistrakh and the Bolshoi Ballet earned enthusiastic receptions and enhanced the image of Soviet society in the outside world. In return, beginning in 1956, Soviet authorities invited Westerners to the Soviet Union. By 1959 cultural, educational, and scientific exchanges with the West and other countries had proliferated. Soviet participation in the 1952 and 1956 summer Olympics marked the beginning of appearances by state-

---

[6]From the 1955 poem, "In a red woolen cap . . . ," written when Yevtushenko was twenty-two, in Yevgeny Yevtushenko, *The Collected Poems, 1952–1990*, Albert C. Todd, ed. (New York: Henry Holt, 1991), pp. 28–29.

Soviet Athletes Shine at the Olympics During the 1952 Olympic games in Helsinki, Finland, Soviet discus thrower Nina Romaschkova sets a world record of 168.7 feet.

subsidized Soviet athletes in international sporting events. Soviet citizens, who adored sports viewing and participation as a recreational outlet, applauded the appearance of Western athletes in the U.S.S.R.

In the spring of 1957, Party conservatives took alarm at the efflorescence in cultural life and the arts and persuaded Khrushchev to dress down a group of leading writers in May. He warned the cowed assemblage that if artists and authors strayed beyond acceptable boundaries, he would not hesitate to rein them in. For a time this tongue-lashing by the Soviet leader quieted the cultural restiveness. Nevertheless, Khrushchev himself remained ambivalent concerning the function of artists and other intellectuals in the Soviet socialist system. He was shrewd enough to recognize that a complex industrial society depended heavily on their talent and skills. He also knew that his hopes for improving the Soviet economy and raising the standard of living rested on input from scientists, engineers, and technicians. To encourage fresh ideas and initiatives, the Soviet leader realized he would have to grant leeway to the intelligentsia.

Khrushchev therefore advocated the establishment of scientific institutes and research centers and promoted the growth of special scientific cities such as Novosibirsk, in which a large proportion of the population were scientists and other intellectuals. He also invited non-Party specialists to attend high-level meetings, including on occasion assemblies of the Presidium and the Central Committee. He valued the contribution of scientific and technical experts in the making of public policy, while keeping decision-making authority in the hands of the Party. Yet typical of many uneducated people, Khrushchev never really trusted or liked intellectuals. He knew that they mocked his lower-class ways behind his back, and he resented their superior air and the incomprehensibility of some of their artistic works.

For their part, some members of the cultural intelligentsia determined to use de-Stalinization as a pathway to creative freedom. However, they failed to perceive the limits to Khrushchev's attack on his predecessor. A few artists and authors, especially among the younger generation who had felt little of the Stalinist grip, expected a complete relaxation of Party controls. When this easing did not happen, they grew disenchanted with the system. Some became dissidents, as we shall see in Chapter 10.

Thus the "thaw" saw Party watchdogs tolerating some fresh approaches but also setting vague limits on what they deemed acceptable. Intellectuals straining for creative independence finally burst these constraints in 1962, when artists broke new ground in several fields. The popularity of blossoming poets like Yevtushenko and Andrei Vosnesensky found confirmation in growing audiences. Winning further notice, Yevtushenko published a bold new poem, "Stalin's Heirs," in the Party newspaper *Pravda* in October 1962. The piece called for incessant vigilance against the recrudescence of Stalinism. In the hitherto tightly restricted fields of painting and sculpture, a February article in the government newspaper *Izvestiia* defended modern, even abstract, art. In literature, a coterie of fledgling reformers seized control of the Moscow branch of the Writers' Union in April. And the November issue of *Novy mir* carried Alexander Solzhenitsyn's *One Day in the Life of Ivan Denisovich*, a harrowing tale of prison camp experience that Khrushchev had personally approved for publication.

Alarmed conservatives readied a counterattack. Pointing to popular unrest sparked by high food prices in the summer of 1962 and to the Soviet setback in the Cuban missile crisis, they argued that ideological tolerance had gone too far. But to win their case, they realized that they would have to provoke Khrushchev himself. Knowing his views on modern art, they cleverly arranged for a semiprivate showing of abstract art to augment a display of standard Soviet painting in Moscow's Manezh exhibition hall. Gladdened by the apparent acceptance of their works, the modernists were stunned when two days later Khrushchev, four other Presidium members, and several key figures in the Party Secretariat suddenly arrived to view their paintings. Those who had mousetrapped the Soviet leader could not have been more pleased with the results. Much of what Khrushchev said is unprintable, but loosely translated, his impression of the first picture was, "I would say that this is just a mess." It reminded him of another still life full of "messy yellow lines which looked, if you excuse me, as though some child had done his business on the canvas when his mother was away and then spread it around with his hands." After muttering asides castigating modernist music, jazz, and contemporary dancing, Khrushchev berated the artists as "jackasses, parasites, and pederasts." He hinted ominously that he would be glad either to strip their government subsidies or to ship them all off to the "free" world, where they could practice their nonsense at will. The Soviet leader avowed, "Art should ennoble the individual and arouse him to action," and delivered an angry warning to the artists.

> You've gone out of your minds, and now you want to deflect us
> from the proper course. No, you won't get away with it. . . .
> Gentlemen, we are declaring war on you.[7]

The cultural militants capitalized on Khrushchev's revulsion and launched an energetic campaign to restore the socialist realist canon and to outlaw experimentation. Leading artistic liberals responded by appealing directly to Khrushchev, who agreed to a meeting on December 17, 1962, with four hundred prominent intellectuals. His ideological spokesman, Leonid Ilychev, condemned abstract humanism and reminded the audience that art must above all inculcate the values of socialism and "Party-mindedness." By early 1963, the battle spread to literature, and Khrushchev's scolding grew more acrid. Nevertheless, in early summer the campaign's violence abated, perhaps because European Communist leaders had expressed dismay at the attacks on prominent Soviet literati and artists. Khrushchev needed the European Communists' support in maneuvers he was preparing against the Chinese. Although the authorities refused to award the 1964 Lenin Prize in literature to Solzhenitsyn's novel, the artistic scene remained calm until after Khrushchev's ouster in October 1964.

Sparking the Economy:
Khrushchev Under Fire

Khrushchev's political position weakened as unease grew over the softening of cultural and ideological controls. The Eastern European setbacks to his foreign policies and de-Stalinization agenda worsened matters. Yet

---

[7]Quoted in Priscilla Johnson, *Khrushchev and the Arts: The Politics of Soviet Culture* (Cambridge, Mass.: M.I.T. Press, 1965), pp. 101–105.

Breaking New Ground Early settlers on the "Virgin Lands" in Kazakhstan pitch tents preparatory to cultivating the new acreage.

opposition to his dominance crystallized over another issue, his management and reorganization of the Soviet economy. At first Khrushchev's plans garnered considerable support among Party leaders. In fact, the early success of agricultural reforms that he had initiated in 1953 through 1955 abetted his climb to power. In a blunt, incisive report to the Party Central Committee in September 1953, Khrushchev had deplored the sorry state of agriculture. Noting its low productivity and faltering livestock growth, he decried the inadequate investment levels and miserable standard of peasant income. Over the next several years, he effectively addressed some of these shortcomings. He provided funds for the collective farms to buy machinery and fertilizer and to erect new buildings. In addition, he reduced the heavy tax on produce from collective farmers' private plots. Finally, he raised the prices that the government paid for required crop deliveries, and he pressured peasants to devote more work time to the collective farm. The process of amalgamating collective farms continued, and their numbers dropped from 125,000 in 1950 to 69,100 in 1958. Two decades later, in the 1970s, the total would shrink to 36,000.

At the same time, Khrushchev knew that postwar population growth was swiftly outpacing agriculture output. He hit upon a daring and ambitious scheme to expand the acreage under cultivation. During a crash campaign started in February 1954, in which he enlisted not only Party *apparatchiks*, farm managers, and agronomists but also workers, students, and other young enthusiasts, Khrushchev ordered the tilling of millions of acres of "virgin lands" in Kazakhstan and southwestern Siberia. Undeterred by critics' warnings of the region's uncertain rainfall, and the threat that overcultivation would exhaust the shallow soil, he poured money, people, and agricultural machinery into the project. At first 31 million acres came under the plow; cultivation soon mushroomed to 86 million acres, a vast area equal to the total tilled land of Canada. Almost three hundred thousand people were moved to these territories, many of them subjected to the hardships of frontier life. Fortunately for Khrushchev, abundant rain fell during the first and third years of the project. Yields from the new acreage helped to boost Soviet grain output from 82.5 million to 125 million tons between 1953 and 1956.[8]

In a second pet scheme, Khrushchev campaigned to expand the growing of feed corn, or maize, throughout the country. His constant hectoring on this issue earned him the nickname Comrade Corn. Making more fodder available to livestock, he argued, would put more meat on each citizen's table. Initial achievements of the virgin lands and maize schemes emboldened the ever optimistic Khrushchev to declare a rejuvenation of Soviet agriculture. Its output, he boasted, would soon surpass that of even the United States. His colleagues were understandably skeptical.

Khrushchev also determined to confront the inefficiency and capital shortages plaguing industry. Poor quality and faulty planning, as well as a lack of incentives to try new technology and methods, also dragged down the rate of growth. In addition, consumers endured insufficient housing, shoddy products, limited choice of goods, and long waiting lines for desirable items. As we saw earlier, during the succession struggle Malenkov had favored emphasizing consumer goods and light industry, whereas Khrushchev backed the traditional focus on heavy and defense industry. Once in power, however, Khrushchev acknowledged the need for better housing, higher wages, and heightened production of consumer goods. By cutting nonnuclear defense outlays and reducing the number of military personnel, he hoped to free funds for industrial investment and to alleviate a grave labor shortage. Khrushchev also encouraged restructuring wages to motivate quality performance. He tried to streamline the planning process and to stimulate input, responsibility, and efficiency at the enterprise level, but the massive bureaucracy frustrated his efforts.

The Soviet ruler launched the first of several radical reorganizations in February 1957. He abolished most central economic organs and transferred management of the economy to 107 regional economic councils called *sovnarkhozy*. A *sovnarkhoz* was established for each of the smaller

---

[8]Alec Nove, *Economic History of the USSR*, rev. ed. (London: Allen & Unwin, 1982), pp. 332–333.

New Light on the Issues KHRUSHCHEV REVISITED

"The past is not dead," William Faulkner once said. "It's not even past." In 1995 Americans were reminded of Faulkner's admonition as a rancorous public dispute erupted over their own past—the U.S. government's decision to drop an atomic bomb on Hiroshima in August 1945. Critics objected that the text accompanying a planned exhibit at the Smithsonian Museum about the Enola Gay, the B-29 plane that carried the bomb to Japan, denigrated the American war effort by painting the United States as the aggressor and the Japanese as helpless victims in World War II. Faced with a political firestorm of the first order, the exhibit was canceled, a poignant reminder that perceptions of the past are also battlegrounds of the present.

Contests over historical memory, often for avowed political purposes, are a subtext of Soviet history. An outstanding example of such historiographic gyration developed in the 1980s as conservatives and reformers battled over the nature of the Khrushchev era. Two early Soviet studies of the Khrushchev years—the first in 1977 by the brothers Roy and Zhores Medvedev (*Khrushchev: The Years in Power*), followed in 1982 by Roy Medvedev's seminal biography, *Khrushchev*—came to light in the West but not in the Soviet Union. Even the fallen leader's memoirs, published in 1971 shortly before his death, were for Western eyes only; Soviet readers had to content themselves with underground (*samizdat*) copies, circulated hand to hand.

But the possibility of change in the Soviet Union and the coming to power of Gorbachev sparked widespread interest in Khrushchev both at home and abroad. And the reason was clear: the explicit use of historical images as a lever for institutional renovation soon led to the partial resurrection of Khrushchev as a symbol of reform. Thomas Sherlock discerned three "intertwined calculations" behind Gorbachev's readiness to "re-image" the past. First, the Soviet leader concluded that "current dysfunctions" facing the nation could not be remedied until people recovered the truth about their past. The loss of collective memory and its replacement with false historical narratives undermined the "health and coherence" of Soviet socialism. Second, remnants of the Soviet bureaucracy, which Khrushchev had sought to dislodge, still stood in the way of even modest change. Too many bureaucrats from Moscow on down had a stake in the maintenance of the rigidly controlled economic mechanism. Finally, Soviet reformers, led by Gorbachev, embraced Khrushchev because, except for Bukharin in the 1920s, he was the only credible reformer in Soviet history ("Politics and History Under Gorbachev," *Problems of Communism,* May–August 1988).

Of course, reform opponents did not remain silent as the historical debate unfolded. After all, as David Nordlander showed, conservatives could and did argue that Khrushchev's unbecoming demise only "demonstrated the futility" of revisionist change in the U.S.S.R. They harped on Khrushchev's impetuous methods and his failure to elevate living standards after the initial burst of the 1950s. This backlash forced progressives to unveil a nuanced portrait that depicted Khrushchev's shortcomings as well as his virtues. While acknowledging the Soviet reformer's policy zig-zags and his overbearing personality, they treated his record as a cautionary tale that revealed not only the need for well-planned improvements in the Soviet system but the urgency of mobilizing society to push through reform. In the end, Khrushchev's decision to launch de-Stalinization, praised by Gorbachev as an act of singular courage, was interpreted as the 1950s' most lasting political legacy. Gorbachev's supporters saw the Khrushchev era as a "catalyst for the political maturation of a new epoch," and they believed that his fundamental impulses, however flawed in certain respects, provided the crucial underpinning for *glasnost'* and *perestroika* ("Khrushchev's Image in the Light of *Glasnost* and *Perestroika*," *Russian Review,* April 1993).

Western interpretations of the Khrushchev years also focused on the heritage of de-Stalinization, but few more tellingly than British historian Donald Filtzer. In two closely reasoned studies, Filtzer discerned parallels between Khrushchev and Gorbachev that explained the dilemma facing both leaders. From 1956 onward, de-Stalinization had one overriding purpose to which "all others were subordinate": to motivate workers to produce more without endangering the property and power arrangements that sustained the Party elite. This policy required persuading workers to abandon a "complex network of shop-floor practices" dating back to the 1930s that protected individuals against a seemingly omnipotent state. In this maneuver, workers had one major trump card: chronic labor shortages that compelled factory managers to accommodate employees' demands in order to avoid massive job turnover. Soviet industrial bosses were pressured to accept slower production tempos, the ignoring of quality controls and a benign neglect of draconian labor laws that prohibited worker tardiness and absenteeism.

According to Filtzer, Khrushchev's failed economic policies underscored the "abortive character" of de-Stalinization. Not that innovations weren't tried. Khrushchev sought to stimulate output through higher wages, bonuses, repeal of the 1940 Law criminalizing absenteeism and a green light for trade unions to veto management decisions to fire workers or raise output quotas. Nonetheless, workers still clung to their autonomous "security blankets" against state power. Moreover, unions never gained the authority to bargain collectively or to become independent of management and the economic bureaucracy. Recognizing this fatal flaw, workers relapsed into a state of general apathy best characterized by the humorous saying—"we pretend to work and they pretend to pay us." Khrushchev's key failure was his inability to alter the inner core of Soviet officialdom, a near impossibility given that too many bureaucrats were mortally threatened by fundamental economic reform (*Soviet Workers and De-Stalinization*, 1992).

Faced with the same problem in 1985, Gorbachev went much farther than his frustrated predecessor. Like Khrushchev, Gorbachev realized that the system had reached a dead end: economic growth had stopped and popular morale had sagged to an all-time low. Like Khrushchev, too, Gorbachev perceived that to move ahead the regime had to enhance output without "jeopardizing" the institutional controls that kept the Party in power. In pursuit of this objective, he sought to "restructure the labor process" in order to overcome the worker's ability to brake production and lower productivity. *Perestroika* addressed this need partly through orthodox labor policies—wage restructuring—and partly through management innovations. In theory, factory managers could fire unproductive employees in order to meet profit criteria and could manage their wage funds to provide incentives for increased output. Labor support for this carrot-stick package soon flagged, however. Workers feared the immediacy of unemployment before the long-term benefits of an improved economy and a higher standard of living kicked into place. Gorbachev's decision to shift toward a free-market system signaled the failure of his earlier efforts to restructure the economy while preserving the Party's domination of Soviet society (*Soviet Workers and the Collapse of Perestroika*, 1994).

What happened next is, as they say, history. Were conservatives right when they claimed, first after 1956 and again in the 1980s, that true reform would sweep away the system and everyone with it? In considering the Khrushchev legacy, we face one of the great ironies of our times. If left untouched, the Soviet economy was fated to remain in never-ending crisis, but any meaningful reform would lead to its undoing.

republics, and the Russian, Ukrainian, Uzbek, and Kazakh republics were divided into councils. The novel arrangement aimed to break the bureaucracy's stranglehold on the economy and to bolster local Party leaders' participation in and supervision over decision making and production. Khrushchev also hoped to encourage regional managers and planners, who had hands-on experience and local knowledge, to improve economic efficiency. As we will see, the *sovnarkhozy* offered advantages as well as many drawbacks, but their immediate impact was political. Khrushchev had attacked the vested interest of many top leaders whose careers and political support rested on the centralized economic apparatus that had burgeoned since the end of World War II.

Khrushchev's critics found other reasons besides the economy to criticize their new leader's performance. Some disliked his elevation of the Party and its apparatus above all other institutions and personnel. Others feared that peaceful coexistence really meant knuckling under to the imperialists and relinquishing hopes for world revolution. Still others fretted about the dangers of the cultural thaw. Unfortunately for the Soviet leader's opponents, they failed to develop a common, coherent platform. All that united them was their dislike of Khrushchev, as Molotov would point out in his memoirs.

Taking advantage of Khrushchev's absence on a state visit to Finland in mid-June 1957, four old-line Stalinists—Molotov, Malenkov, Kaganovich, and Voroshilov—persuaded Bulganin and three junior Presidium members to join them in ousting Khrushchev as first secretary of the Party. They apparently intended to offer him the post of minister of agriculture instead. Although only three members voted for Khrushchev in the Presidium meeting assembled to determine his fate, his opponents had no way to enforce their action. Since Beria's execution, Khrushchev underlings had controlled the security forces, including the Moscow secret police. Moreover, according to Party rules, the first secretary was elected by the Central Committee, which thus qualified as the only body that had the authority to fire Khrushchev, as he argued upon his return. Fortunately for the first secretary, several key Central Committee members were already in Moscow. With their help and that of Minister of Defense Marshal Zhukov, who reportedly flew several committee members to the capital on military transports, he forced the Presidium to convene a Central Committee meeting. The week-long session resounded with acrimonious exchanges between pro- and anti-Khrushchev speakers. In the end Khrushchev won handily, and the Central Committee confirmed him in office.

Khrushchev survived this attempt to depose him partly because a near majority of committee members had been appointed since Stalin's death. Many of these members were beholden to the first secretary. His opponents had fewer clients, and most younger Party leaders did not relish working under the Old Guard who sought to remove Khrushchev.

Khrushchev's policies also appealed to that group. He had built up and defended the Party managers against the economic bureaucracy that his critics represented. In addition, many Central Committee members were regional Party secretaries who had assumed responsibility and status in the *sovnarkhoz* reform that the anti-Khrushchev forces wanted to overturn. Finally, few Party members wanted a return to Stalinism, the direction that Molotov and his supporters seemed to favor.

To Khrushchev's credit, he did not treat his defeated critics in the harsh manner that many of them yearned to restore. Eschewing the firing squad and the *Gulag*, Khrushchev labeled his opponents the "anti-Party group" and had them expelled from the Presidium and the Central Committee. He let them retain their status and privileges, however, and assigned them to minor jobs in the vast Soviet bureaucracy. Molotov became Soviet ambassador to Mongolia, then Soviet representative to the International Atomic Energy Agency in Vienna. Malenkov was named manager of a power plant in Kazakhstan. Kaganovich was appointed head of a cement factory in the Urals. Dmitry Shepilov, a candidate member of the Presidium who had supported the conspirators, became a researcher at an institute of the Academy of Sciences. Voroshilov and Bulganin, who recanted, were permitted to linger on until demoted to minor posts a year or two later.

Khrushchev then expanded the Presidium from eleven to fifteen members and replaced his opponents with his own loyalists, including Marshal Zhukov, who moved from candidate to full member. In October 1957, however, Khrushchev fired the marshal, resentful of Zhukov's widespread popularity in the Party and among the public. The Soviet leader also disliked Zhukov's attempts to weaken Party control over the military and to block proposed budget cuts for conventional weapons. Zhukov undoubtedly wondered what sort of gratitude this treatment reflected for his support of Khrushchev against the anti-Party group.

From Showdowns to Détente

Khrushchev's unquestioned supremacy found confirmation in March 1958, when he became prime minister and head of the State Defense Council while continuing as Party first secretary. With a renewed mandate, he pressed ahead with domestic reforms and bold initiatives in foreign policy. The Soviet leader needed successes abroad to divert resources from defense to the civilian economy and to compensate for mounting failures at home. Yet with a few exceptions, his diplomatic endeavors brought setback and even humiliation.

On the bright side, the Soviet Union achieved dramatic milestones in launching the first space satellite, *Sputnik*, in October 1957, and in orbiting the first man in space, Yuri Gagarin, in 1961. These feats fostered pride among the Soviet leadership and people and enhanced Soviet prestige in the Third World, but they provoked concern in the United States and sparked a determination to catch up. Khrushchev also expanded relations with Africa and strengthened ties with India and Indonesia. In 1961 he established a beachhead in Latin America when Fidel Castro, the leader of a 1959 revolution in Cuba, declared himself a Marxist-Leninist. Finally, Soviet ideologists developed a doctrine of national liberation that encouraged socialists in the Third World to collaborate with nationalists seeking to overthrow imperialist rule or reactionary governments. This new doctrine pledged Soviet aid to "national liberation movements" to enable former colonial countries to pass directly from feudalism to socialism, thereby skipping capitalism. Limited support to revolutionaries in Algeria and Vietnam put this theory into practice.

Behind the iron curtain, however, Soviet relations with Yugoslavia, Albania, Romania, and China worsened. Khrushchev, alarmed by Tito's independence and Yugoslavia's dominance in the Balkans, canceled Soviet credits to Yugoslavia in May 1958. Albania, ruled by an unreconstructed Stalinist, voiced increasing criticism of its Soviet big brother. Despite Khrushchev's efforts in 1959 to mend relations, Albania rejected Soviet tutelage and sided with China in the escalating dispute between the two socialist giants. Although Romanian Communist leaders maintained a harsh, Stalin-style regime at home, they evolved an autonomous foreign policy. To Soviet annoyance, in 1963 they declared neutrality in the friction between the Soviet Union and Communist China.

Many factors contributed to the mounting Sino-Soviet tension. On the personal level, Chinese dictator Mao Zedong resented Stalin's stinginess toward the Chinese Communists from 1944 to 1949, the crucial period of their revolutionary struggle. Mao's irritation intensified when Stalin offered limited aid to the new Chinese Communist government in 1950 and required repayment with interest. The Soviet dictator's refusal to treat Mao as an equal when the Chinese head of state visited Moscow in December 1949 still rankled as well. Likewise, Mao grew annoyed when Khrushchev failed to consult him about de-Stalinization and peaceful coexistence, policies that Mao believed took too soft a line in international affairs. After Stalin's death, Mao saw himself as the world's chief Marxist theoretician and senior Communist leader, yet Khrushchev treated him as a junior ally. The Soviet leader's brash, informal style offended Mao also, and the Chinese took umbrage at the high-handed manners and methods of Soviet advisers and technical personnel in China.

Fundamental territorial and political-ideological issues widened the Sino-Soviet split. Since the seventeenth century, when Russian expansion eastward had reached the border of the Chinese Empire, disputes had cropped up over the boundaries of the interlying regions. According to the Chinese, from the 1880s to the 1940s, Russian and Soviet leaders had exploited China's weakness to extract unfair territorial concessions from China. Soviet officials argued that their position in the Far East was historically justified and that since 1949 they had tried to make border adjustments that would satisfy the Chinese. Such quarrels began to erode the already cooling friendship in the late 1950s, and Khrushchev made little effort to resolve them.

Political rivalry soured relations between the two states as well. Soviet rulers assumed that they would head the international socialist movement, given their revolutionary seniority and power. Chinese leaders, citing China's glorious past and its huge population, rejected the Russians' self-proclaimed role. They accused the Soviet leaders of mismanaging the affairs of the socialist bloc. In Africa and Asia, China and the U.S.S.R. competed for influence. As examples, the Soviet Union supported the North Vietnamese against the Chinese, while the Chinese backed Pakistan against the Soviet Union's friend India. China's invasions of Indian border regions in August 1959 and October–November 1962 presented Khrushchev with a vexing dilemma. Although he was wooing the Indians, he risked losing face with the world socialist movement if he criticized China. In 1959 the Soviet Union declared neutrality but indirectly decried the Chinese action. In 1962 Khrushchev supported India. The Chinese soon withdrew from much of the territory that they had seized, yet the Sino-Soviet contest for predominance in Asia persisted.

On the ideological front, the Chinese leaders charged Khrushchev and his colleagues with "revisionism." As the Chinese saw it, Soviet leaders had violated Marxist-Leninist doctrine by downplaying the need for revolution in achieving socialism's worldwide victory. Mao and Chinese ideologues cursed the tenet of peaceful coexistence as appeasement of the imperialists. Moreover, they condemned Soviet timidity in providing insufficient aid to anticolonial forces. They also criticized "national liberation" theory for endorsing alliances with bourgeois nationalists. The Chinese urged that aid go only to true revolutionary elements—peasants and workers.

On the practical side, China was particularly incensed by what it deemed inadequate Soviet support in a 1958 crisis. That year, Communist Chinese forces shelled Quemoy and Matsu, islands off mainland China that Chiang Kai-shek's Nationalist government on Taiwan controlled. To block a possible Chinese invasion of the islands or of Taiwan itself, the United States inserted its Seventh Fleet in the straits between Taiwan and mainland China. In China's view, Soviet leaders failed to protest the U.S. action with enough alacrity.

For their part, Soviet leaders accused the Chinese adventurists of risking nuclear war. An apocryphal story that circulated widely in Moscow in the early 1960s appalled Soviet listeners. The tale recounted Mao's response to warnings about the horrors of a global thermonuclear conflict: "Yes, such a war might kill 200 million Chinese, 200 million Russians, and 200 million Americans, but there would still be 600 million Chinese left."

Khrushchev could not stem the deterioration of Sino-Soviet relations, and in July 1960 the Soviet Union recalled its specialists from China and sent home Chinese students studying in the U.S.S.R. The Chinese particularly resented Khrushchev's efforts to dissuade them from building their own nuclear arsenal and fumed when he cut off scientific and technical assistance for this purpose. Although the two sides papered over their wrangling at a December 1960 meeting of the world's Communist parties, the Chinese increasingly assailed Khrushchev's policies toward the West in 1962 and 1963. In the latter year, both sides made their mutual recriminations public. Relations unraveled further in 1964 as Khrushchev sought to organize a meeting of international socialist parties to condemn the Chinese.

In contrast to the East, Soviet-Western relations from 1958 to 1964 saw highs of tentative cooperation and lows of tense confrontation. The powers remained troubled by Germany, especially the status of Berlin. Negotiations had proceeded desultorily in the mid-1950s, but no one could agree on either reunification terms or a final peace treaty. In November 1958, Khrushchev suddenly threatened to sign a unilateral peace treaty with the German Democratic Republic (East Germany) and to give the G.D.R. jurisdiction over access routes to the Western sectors of Berlin. Only if the Western powers agreed within six months to withdraw their occupation forces from Berlin and recognize the city as an independent entity would the Soviet leader put aside the treaty.

Several factors appear to have pushed Khrushchev to issue this unexpected ultimatum. During the mid-1950s, the West had steadily nurtured NATO, particularly its nuclear capability, whereas Khrushchev, trying to funnel money into the civilian economy, had cut Soviet troop strength. Even after ejecting the anti-Party group and firing Zhukov, the Soviet leader ran into sharp criticism for his military reductions. His strategy of building nuclear muscle to compel the West to accept the Soviet position in Germany and Eastern Europe also generated skepticism. He apparently hoped that pressure on Berlin would force the West to grant de facto recognition to the German Democratic Republic. Such a concession would validate his approach and strengthen his authority to plunge ahead with his domestic reforms. Khrushchev may also have wanted to impress his critics at home and in the world socialist movement, particularly after his futile protests over the American intervention in Lebanon in the summer of 1958. Perhaps Khrushchev decided to take a rigid stand on Germany so as to undercut censure from the U.S.S.R.'s largest Marxist neighbor. The Chinese had berated the idea of peaceful coexistence to socialist leaders around the globe. Indeed, they seemed to have elicited some backing from the East Germans, who in August 1958 endorsed

Mao's aggressive posturing over Taiwan more enthusiastically than Soviet leaders had.

Unfortunately for all these calculations, the Soviet leader had not thought through his tactics on Berlin carefully, and the ploy failed. The United States rejected Khrushchev's ultimatum and insisted that the Soviet Union live up to the four-power agreements on Berlin. The Americans further informed the U.S.S.R. that they would take strong action, as in the blockade of 1948 and 1949, to maintain the Western presence in Berlin. The Eisenhower administration refused to meet Khrushchev's demand for a summit conference on Berlin, urging that foreign ministers address the question first. In March 1959, when British prime minister Harold Macmillan promised Khrushchev to arrange a summit meeting, the Soviet leader finally dropped his ultimatum. Later that year, Khrushchev visited the United States. In his talks with Eisenhower, the Soviet leader mistakenly inferred that the White House would soon revisit Berlin's tenuous status.

From the first failed showdown over Berlin, Khrushchev soon achieved a pinnacle of conciliation with the United States. His growing confidence in the Soviet economy's ability to catch up with U.S. production (a hope soon to be dashed) and in the prospects for socialism's expansion in the Third World propelled the Soviet leader in this direction. Perhaps he had also become convinced that socialism could defeat capitalism by peaceful means, that Soviet prosperity would win over the uncommitted. This sanguine outlook lay behind Khrushchev's remark to an American audience in 1959, "We will bury you." Misinterpreted by some as a threat of world conquest, the statement actually reflected the Soviet leader's optimism about the ultimate nonviolent triumph of socialism.

In June 1959, Khrushchev stopped helping China to develop nuclear weapons. Scattered evidence suggests that he hoped to trade this gesture for Western restraint in rearming West Germany and for steps toward recognition of East Germany. In September 1959, Khrushchev was cordially received on his visit to the United States. This symbol of friendlier relations with the U.S.S.R.'s chief antagonist boosted his political position at home and enhanced his stature as a world leader. Khrushchev soon expanded cultural relations with the West, and in January 1960, he unilaterally reduced Soviet troop strength. Hoping that his new tactic of conciliation would elicit major concessions from the West, Khrushchev looked forward in the spring of 1960 to a long-delayed summit and to an exchange visit by Eisenhower to the Soviet Union in the summer. These expectations collapsed when Soviet air defenses shot down an American U-2 spy plane in May. The revelation of the U.S. transgression and Eisenhower's reluctant assumption of responsibility for the espionage mission strengthened the hand of Khrushchev's hard-line critics. The Soviet leader was forced to pull out of the summit talks in Paris and to cancel Eisenhower's visit to Moscow.

The new administration of President John F. Kennedy had hardly taken office in early 1961 before it launched a rapid build-up of nuclear weapons, widening the already considerable gap between the two super-powers' nuclear inventory. Kennedy's supporters also introduced a novel strategic doctrine of flexible response to replace the previous threat of massive retaliation, which, given the potential mutual destruction of nuclear war, had never seemed credible. Under flexible response, American forces were prepared to fight conventional wars when appropriate. The United States soon applied the new tenet by stepping up aid in 1962 to the anti-Communist forces in the Vietnamese civil war.

The U.S. nuclear build-up and the flexible response doctrine undermined Khrushchev's strategy of using nuclear strength to force the West to the bargaining table while reducing conventional forces. To see what Kennedy had in mind and to pursue the understanding about Germany that Khrushchev thought that he had reached with Eisenhower, the Soviet leader met with the U.S. president in Vienna in June 1961. Rumors that Khrushchev expected to push the younger, inexperienced Kennedy around remain unsubstantiated.

When Kennedy showed no interest in resolving the German question, Khrushchev decided to dramatize it once more. The continued flight of talented East Germans to the West, many of them through Berlin, added urgency to the issue. The Soviet leader again threatened unilateral action if the West did not accept East German jurisdiction and urged the NATO powers to make some concession. In July Kennedy agreed to negotiations but concurrently called up American military reserves and reinforced the Berlin garrison. Khrushchev pushed back: in August he agreed to East German leaders' plans to insulate the German Democratic Republic from West Germany by erecting a barrier between the two states. In Berlin, this obstacle took the form of a twelve-foot-high concrete wall. The United States denounced the construction of the Berlin Wall. (In 1963 President Kennedy flew to the divided city and proclaimed publicly in Boston-accented but crowd-pleasing German, "Ich bin ein Berliner!" ["I am a Berliner!"].) The Western powers reaffirmed their resolve to remain in Berlin. Both sides, however, managed to avoid a direct confrontation. Alarmed that the West might try to dismantle the Berlin Wall, Khrushchev in September agreed to open talks and in October quietly dropped his ultimatum. Negotiations dragged on into the spring of 1962, with no resolution. The uncertain status quo would persist until 1972.

The Berlin Wall crisis amounted to a serious setback for the Soviet leader. His critics slammed Khrushchev for nudging the nation to the brink of war over a relatively unimportant issue and then slinking away without a single concession. The Berlin Wall also damaged the Soviet image throughout the world. Under pressure from his colleagues,

A Tense Confrontation American tanks oppose Soviet tanks 2¢0 yards up the street at a checkpoint on the border between West and East Berlin in October 1961.

Khrushchev finally shifted resources to defense spending. He thus had to weaken his domestic program at a critical moment.

The Soviet leader worried about the fiscal pressures from defense competition with the United States and growing American nuclear superiority. In the spring of 1962, he dreamed up yet another bold initiative. His action would lead to the gravest episode of his rule: the Cuban missile crisis. Indeed, the incident would become the most dramatic moment of the forty years of superpower rivalry. In the fall of 1961, the Kennedy administration revealed that the United States had amassed a huge lead in the nuclear race. A year later, this "gap" amounted to a U.S. stockpile of almost 350 intercontinental and submarine-launched missiles, against some 20 Soviet long-range missiles. Khrushchev may have feared that the United States would take advantage of its lopsided superiority to launch a first-strike preventive war against the Soviet Union. He also knew that closing the gap would require his country to invest enormous expenditures over many years.

To the U.S.S.R.'s advantage, the Soviet regime had recently acquired a strategically placed client state, Cuba. Cuban leader Fidel Castro, rebuffed by the United States, had turned to Moscow for help in building a socialist society. In April 1961, the Kennedy administration had half-heartedly supported an ill-conceived invasion of Cuba by a group of refugees from Castro's despotism. The Cuban army had easily turned back the attackers at the Bay of Pigs. Nevertheless, anti-Communist "hawks" in the United States continued to call for decisive action against Castro's socialism. Khrushchev may have worried that American troops would soon descend on the island in force.

In April 1962, Khrushchev was struck by an observation of his defense minister, Marshal Rodion Malinovsky. As Malinovsky noted, American intermediate-range missiles recently placed in Turkey could strike Moscow in ten minutes. The idea occurred to Khrushchev that he could use Cuba to put the United States under a comparable threat. Moreover, placing medium-range Soviet missiles in Cuba would with one stroke eliminate the American nuclear advantage. Perhaps a military foothold near the United States would also discourage an American first strike or an attempt to use nuclear blackmail against the U.S.S.R. Such a move would prove far cheaper than trying to match the U.S. nuclear build-up. Khrushchev received Castro's permission to emplace the missiles and reassured himself that the Americans would not discover the weapons. On June 10, 1962, he gave the go-ahead for the project. Soviet military authorities hoped to have forty missiles operational by November or early December, a plan that would have threatened the entire southeastern United States. Khrushchev and his military advisers knew that American reconnaissance planes regularly flew over Cuba; how then could they have expected to keep their activities secret? Possibly Khrushchev believed that if the United States spotted the missiles, he could use the partially deployed weapons as a bargaining chip to squeeze concessions from the Kennedy administration.

When American intelligence discovered the missiles, President Kennedy and his advisers spent several days absorbed in somber discussion. On October 22, 1962, they ordered a blockade of Cuba to prevent further Soviet warhead shipments to the island. Kennedy also demanded that the Soviet government withdraw the missiles already in place. The tense showdown threatened war. If the Soviet Union refused to back down, the United States would have to invade Cuba to remove the missiles. In that event, devastating exchanges between the superpowers could hardly have been averted, especially because the Soviet commander in Cuba may have been authorized to use tactical nuclear weapons.

At first, Soviet ships continued steaming toward the American naval forces stationed off Cuba. At the last minute, however, they either turned back, or if they had no military cargo, they submitted to being stopped and searched. After a frightening few days, an exchange of letters and indirect messages communicated Khrushchev's willingness to pull the missiles from Cuba in exchange for an American pledge not to invade the island. The United States had no plans to attack Cuba, so Kennedy agreed. This face-saving device permitted Khrushchev to claim that he had thwarted the aggressive designs of American imperialism. Kennedy

Soviet Missiles in Cuba A U.S. satellite photograph taken in October 1962 showing a nearly completed Cuban launching site for Soviet missiles targeted on the U.S. 90 miles away.

also informally assented to a Soviet request to remove American missiles in Turkey; these weapons were being phased out anyway as submarine-launched warheads took over their functions. Castro, whom Khrushchev had not deigned to consult during the crisis, quietly fumed but could do nothing, for Cuba remained utterly dependent on Soviet economic subsidies. Khrushchev's backdown in the Cuban missile crisis damaged his authority at home and would provide his opponents with further ammunition when they decided two years later to unseat him.

To recoup his position, Khrushchev switched tactics, seeking accommodation with the West as a way of eliciting concessions from that quarter. In 1963 he scored some success when the Soviet Union, the United States, and Great Britain signed a treaty banning all but underground tests of nuclear devices. The Soviet and American governments also agreed to establish a "hot line" of direct communications between Moscow and Washington. These steps down the road of peaceful coexistence evoked only derision from the Chinese. Moreover, the continuing U.S. military build-up in Vietnam, as well as the unrelenting American development of advanced nuclear weapons, weakened Khrushchev's claim that he had established a favorable relationship with America. Yet a few hints suggest that Khrushchev was considering new conciliatory gestures toward West Germany in the fall of 1964, just before his ouster.

Plenty and Paradox: Life in the Khrushchev Years

Khrushchev was neither a doctrinaire ideologue nor a brilliant theorist. Nevertheless, he believed firmly in socialism's promise of a better life and in the ability of material incentives to elicit public effort toward that goal. In his view, the Party should direct this effort, without resorting to random terror. In his optimistic moments, Khrushchev concluded that the Soviet people could build a fully communist society "in the main" within twenty years.

Many of Khrushchev's domestic policies reflected these convictions. After coming to power, he strove to remove arbitrary restrictions on social and public life and to establish "socialist legality"—that is, to ensure the rule of law and justice in everyday life, except in unusual circumstances. As long as people acted within the bounds of socialist and Leninist norms and did not engage in anti-Party or anti-Soviet actions, they need not fear capricious and illicit punishment from the regime. At times Khrushchev narrowed these limits. In the 1960s, for example, he made certain economic crimes liable to the death penalty and enacted laws prohibiting "parasitism," loosely defined as not working to contribute to society. But for the most part, Soviet citizens knew for the first time in years exactly what legal sanctions and rights applied to them. Khrushchev's revised law codes embodied this refreshing approach. He also reined in the secret police and increased responsibility and accountability for prosecutorial and judicial institutions. Finally, he summed up his public policies and philosophy in a new Party program, approved at the Twenty-second Party Congress in 1961. Jettisoning earlier rhetoric about class struggle and the dictatorship of the proletariat, the program called for collaborative efforts to achieve socialism by 1980 in a "state of all the people." The plan broke with Stalinism by urging that public organs replace state institutions in some areas.

At the same congress, Khrushchev reinvigorated the de-Stalinization campaign by revealing even more transgressions of the dictator. He had Stalin's body removed from Lenin's mausoleum in Red Square to a grave between the mausoleum and the Kremlin wall and changed the name Stalingrad to Volgograd. That switch set off pervasive retitling of places and institutions that bore the former leader's name. Khrushchev also advanced plans to draw up a new constitution to replace the 1936 document. The project would not reach fruition, however, until the late 1970s.

In several ways, Khrushchev tried to put into practice his ideal of involving citizens in public life. Crisscrossing the country, he harangued his people to labor harder. He encouraged non-Party activism, inviting average citizens as well as specialists to get involved at the grass-roots level in improving social and economic life. He also worked to broaden citizen participation in local and district soviets and to improve the effectiveness of these organs. He established "comrades' courts," in which ordinary citizens judged minor offenders. Last, he urged city police to patrol with citizen assistants, known as *druzhiny* (after guards of the early Kievan princes). In the early 1960s, one often saw these individuals, dressed in mufti but wearing a red armband, striding the streets of Moscow. Their apparent chief task: helping police pick up drunks to be carted off to the "drying-out tanks."

Khrushchev encouraged public criticism of bureaucratic errors and inaction—within limits. On the other hand, he bristled at personal criticism and brooked no generalized attacks on the Party or the system. Nor did he suggest citizen participation at the higher levels of policy formulation and decision making. Instead, he invigorated the Party's role in running the country. The new Party program called for the withering away of the state as some of its functions were transferred to citizen groups, yet the Party continued to dominate public life. Party membership ballooned by more than 50 percent during the Khrushchevian decade, and the educational level of Party members rose. Furthermore, Party stalwarts were urged to pursue training and to achieve high levels of specialization.

The quality of life for Soviet citizens improved considerably in the first years of Khrushchev's rule. Reversing Stalin's bias against the peasantry, the new leader raised rural standards. He granted peasants internal passports, documents held by everyone else as identification. The passports permitted rural dwellers to travel around the country, to change residence, and to register legally with the police. Khrushchev also included peasants in the U.S.S.R.'s disability and pension system for the first time. Last, he enhanced peasant income through agricultural policy changes noted earlier, although in the final years of his administration, he began to discriminate against the collective farmers' private plots.

Workers also fared well in the Khrushchev era. The Soviet leader made inroads on the housing shortage that rapid urbanization and the wholesale destruction of World War II had spawned. In July 1957, he gave new construction high priority. Six months later, he promised "every family an apartment, not a room, but an apartment." Between 1959 and 1965, 84 million families moved to new apartments, and erection of residential housing doubled. Although not everyone benefited, millions of Soviet citizens no longer had to crowd into one room and to share a kitchen and bath. Having waited years, sometimes decades, they gloried in their own dwellings, despite the shaky quality of the massive complexes and the lack of nearby shops and amenities. By increasing investment in light industry, the Soviet leader also provided a range of consumer goods, although they were cheaply made and often in short supply. He doubled the minimum wage and, through raises and a complicated restructuring of the pay system, lifted average earnings by 50 percent. He narrowed the income gap between rich and poor and more than doubled pensions paid to the elderly. As a result, Khrushchev reduced the number of Soviet citizens living in poverty from 100 million to 30 million. He shortened the work week to 42 hours as well, and he relaxed the draconian laws on labor discipline inherited from Stalinist times.

Educational opportunities continued to expand at various levels. Basic four-year primary education extended to almost all areas, including remote rural regions, and the country inched toward universal seven-year education. The number of students in specialized technical and university education tripled between 1950–1951 and 1964–1965. The Party's adult political-education program mushroomed from 6.2 million enrollees (15 percent non-Party) in 1957–1958 to 36 million (78 percent non-Party) in 1964.

At the same time, in another grandiose but doomed project, Khrushchev attempted to redirect the focus of secondary education from liberal learning to polytechnical skills. In 1958 new decrees required students in their last two years of high school to spend time at productive labor, either in special facilities set up at their school or on a factory production line. The reform also proposed establishment of boarding schools, from which Soviet students would make occasional weekend visits home. Khrushchev justified the polytechnical reform on the ground that Soviet youth needed familiarity with work experience. In his view, too many students graduated with only book learning. Not only had they no practical training, they even harbored a distaste for labor. The Soviet leader wanted to use polytechnical education to shunt young people into the factories, both to reduce elitism and to compensate for a mounting labor shortage stemming from wartime birth deficits.

To promote the idea of boarding schools, Khrushchev and his educational backers touted the program's benefits for less-well-off families and for working couples who lacked time to supervise their children. The schools also aimed to provide superior academic and civic training for students. Yet Soviet parents, who had no desire to hand their children over to the schools, objected. In light of their resistance—and the program's exorbitant cost—few boarding schools were set up, and the notion faded away.

Polytechnical education fared almost as badly. Struggling to meet production quotas, factory managers were loath to devote resources and time on inexperienced and resistant apprentices. Under pressure, some plants complied with the concept, and a few pilot schools received funds to acquire machines for a "production corner." But school administrators, teachers, factory directors, and most parents, who wanted their children to go on to university or at least to achieve white-collar careers, resisted the reform. The plan was quietly shelved in the mid-1960s.

In several areas, Khrushchev worsened the conditions of Soviet life. Although we cover developments among non-Russian nationalities in detail in Chapters 10 and 11, we should note here that Russian domination of these groups intensified during the Khrushchev years. The ruler himself had little to say on this issue, but one of the charges that he and his colleagues leveled against Beria in 1953 was that the secret police chief had stirred up "bourgeois nationalism" in the Caucasus. After Beria's execution, central authorities exerted tight control over the non-Russian republics. In Ukraine, for example, Moscow squelched efforts to enlarge the study of Ukrainian literature and history and reprimanded and demoted several Ukrainian politicians for nationalist leanings. Perhaps in compensation, Khrushchev decided in 1954 to transfer the Crimean peninsula from the jurisdiction of the Russian to the Ukrainian Republic on the occasion of the three hundredth anniversary of the first Ukrainian treaty with tsarist Russia. The inhabitants of the Crimea, a majority of whom were Russian after Stalin's expulsion of the Crimean Tatars from the peninsula, were neither consulted nor pleased by the change.

Khrushchev also cracked down on organized religion, possibly convinced by Party ideologists that these institutions threatened to undercut his efforts to shore up socialism. In 1959 he launched a repressive campaign against the Orthodox church and other faiths that prevailed until his overthrow in 1964. The government forced the closure of almost six thousand Orthodox houses of worship (40 percent of those existing), as well as some seventy to ninety monasteries. Bishops and parish clergy were harassed or dismissed, and some were jailed Individual believers faced antireligious propaganda and heavy social pressure, including visits by proselytizing "scientific atheists" to their homes and mockery of their children at school, and some went to prison. In July 1961, Party authorities forced a compliant Patriarch Alexei and his bishops to accept revised decrees that weakened their authority over church administration. The new regulations transferred control of each parish from the local priest to a three-member executive board representing the community. Despite the harassment, many in the church, including bishops, priests, and believers, resisted passively and in some cases continued their religious practice covertly. Khrushchev's vendetta failed to lessen the role of the church in Soviet life or to diminish the number of believers, and the program would be abandoned immediately after his ouster.

In the Khrushchev years, degradation of the environment that had begun during Stalin's industrialization drive also continued apace. Women's increasing significance in the work force and in society marked this era as well. Finally, as literacy mushroomed and the number of city dwellers approached half the population, a "low" or popular culture in books, films, music, and entertainment spread through urban society. Yet because these trends reached full flower under Khrushchev's successors, they are treated at length in Chapters 10 and 11.

Economic Desperation

In the late 1950s, Khrushchev had boasted about the progress of the Soviet economy. An abundant harvest in the fall of 1958 made him even more confident that the U.S.S.R. would soon match the United States in milk, butter, and meat production. During 1958 the inveterate reorganizer scrapped the machine tractor stations (MTS) that supplied equipment to the collective farms. Enacted hastily and without sufficient funding, the reversal placed a heavy burden on individual *kolkhozes*, which had to drain their capital reserves to pay for the machinery transferred from the MTSes. In addition, the farms lacked the technicians needed to service and repair their newly acquired equipment. The resultant upheaval worsened a decline in agricultural growth that began in 1959.

Discarding the Sixth Five Year Plan, Khrushchev in early 1959 had the specially convened Twenty-first Party Congress approve a new seven-year plan that set ambitious production targets. The plan, however, reduced capital investment in agriculture by almost half, a change that would have deleterious effects. As the agricultural sector continued to falter in 1960, the Soviet leader resorted to exhortations and further organizational tinkering. He promoted unrealistic competition in meat production that led to the premature slaughtering of herds, and he journeyed about the countryside badgering officials and farmers to plant corn and to cultivate fallow land. In 1961 Khrushchev restricted production on the peasants' private plots, complaining that they were not spending enough time on collective farm work. Finally, he repeatedly reorganized agricultural administration. At one point he even attempted to close the vast central offices of the Ministry of Agriculture and move all its operations and bureaucrats out to farm country.

None of these impulsive measures worked. Worse, between 1958 and 1962, urban population shot up by 16 percent while agricultural output increased only 6.6 percent. Demand for food and consumer goods heightened. To dampen the clamor for products and to bring prices in line with manufacturing costs, Khrushchev raised prices on meat and butter on June 1, 1962. Widespread protests ensued. One such outburst in the city of Novocherkassk led to a riot in which soldiers fired on demonstrators and killed a number of unarmed persons. In the early 1960s, too, erosion and insufficient rainfall plagued the virgin lands, and production there plummeted. In 1963 a poor harvest compelled Khrushchev to import grain from abroad, a humiliating setback that prompted a witty saying:

"Comrade, have you heard that the latest miracle of Soviet science is to sow wheat in Ukraine and harvest it in Canada?" Grasping at another panacea, Khrushchev in 1964 launched a campaign to jump-start the chemical industry, in part to provide fertilizer to rescue Soviet agriculture.

Khrushchev compiled an equally weak record in industry. Three factors slowed the rate of industrial growth from 1962 to 1964. Inherent conditions, such as the complexity of managing an expanding economy and a systemic lack of incentives to innovation and efficiency, continued to brake output. In addition, developments abroad forced an estimated 30 percent expansion of the Soviet military budget in 1961 and smaller but still substantial increases in the following two years. Despite Khrushchev's efforts to maintain the U.S.S.R.'s global position while reducing conventional forces, he felt obliged to react to the U.S. nuclear build-up and the Berlin and Cuba crises in 1961 and 1962. The growing need to reinforce Far Eastern defenses against a possible Chinese threat also impelled him to strengthen the military budget. This diversion of funds squeezed other sectors and exacerbated the shortage of capital funds crucial for investment. Finally, the *sovnarkhozy* established in 1957, although they initially elicited some local initiative and decentralized problem solving, increasingly encouraged regional collusion at the expense of the broad interests of the national economy.

Yet instead of attacking the core problems, Khrushchev once again resorted to slapdash rearrangement. In late 1962 he divided Party units at all but the local level into industrial and agricultural sectors, and in early 1963 he reduced the number and enlarged the geographic jurisdictions of the regional economic councils. Separating Party oversight of agriculture and industry generated confusion and did little to improve economic performance. More important, this radical reorganization had major political consequences for its architect.

Khrushchev's Downfall

Not long after his colleagues unseated Khrushchev in 1964, an Olympic year, this joke circulated in Moscow: "Comrade, have you heard that Nikita Sergeevich won an Olympic gold medal— for the longest fall from the highest place!" The reasons for Khrushchev's downfall are clear. More obscure is why he failed to foresee or prevent the plot against him. Probably his son Sergei came closest to the mark when he noted that after almost ten years of wielding nearly absolute power, the Soviet leader had become used to obedience and adulation and had surrounded himself with yes-men and flatterers. Khrushchev thus neglected the political consensus-building that had brought him to high office and dismissed the possibility of opposition. In 1964, after perfunctory investigation, he discounted two warnings of a plot against him.

Several factors of fairly equal weight caused Khrushchev's ruin. Failures in his domestic and foreign policy eroded his credibility and authority with both his Party comrades and the Soviet people. He had promised his fellow citizens better living conditions at home and a secure and esteemed position for the Soviet Union abroad. Instead, peasant income, after shooting up in the late 1950s, dropped in the 1960s. Workers' incomes improved slightly, but their expectations had risen even more in response to the Soviet leader's bombastic promises. Shortages and inadequate consumer services persisted. People concluded resignedly that although their children might see a life of comfort and ease, they themselves would not. Internationally, despite successes in space exploration, Soviet prestige suffered when Khrushchev backed down before the West in Berlin and Cuba. The American nuclear build-up; continuing tension with Yugoslavia, Romania, and Albania; and the deepening rift with China all worsened the problem. Although Khrushchev had made gains in the Third World, Party leaders as well as the average citizen recoiled at the costs of Soviet aid there. The waning of Khrushchev's popularity among the populace gave conspirators a green light.

If Khrushchev's reforms had rejuvenated the economy, his critics might have overlooked the disruption and confusion that his frenetic policy shifts caused. But in the face of failure, Party and government officials at many levels finally found his ceaseless tinkering intolerable. Relentless change upset familiar patterns of administration and career advancement almost as much as Stalin's unbridled terror had. Bureaucrats had no idea what to expect next, a most unsettling prospect in a system run and supported by officialdom. Khrushchev's division of the Party into industrial and agricultural sectors and his enlargement of the *sovnarkhozy* proved particularly damaging in this regard. The programs added or broadened some fiefdoms for Party secretaries and economic administrators, but it removed others, creating uncertainty and insecurity.

Even more upsetting, the Soviet leader attempted to initiate a regularized turnover of Party personnel by establishing term limits for most offices. According to updated Party rules that Khrushchev proposed in 1961, Presidium members would serve only three terms (except in special cases, which seemed to mean Khrushchev himself). Even secretaries of basic Party organizations would serve only two terms. The restrictions would impose on all Party central and executive committees turnover rates from one-quarter at the national level to one-third and one-half at regional and local levels. Because such policies would have deprived participants of a lifelong career of Party service, incumbents objected and Khrushchev could not sell his program to the Party. Nevertheless, he determined to carry out his own version of turnover. Between 1957 and 1964, he dropped seven members of the Presidium, all former supporters. He also replaced two-thirds of Party regional secretaries in the same period.

Khrushchev's proposals and his high-handed personnel actions stirred hostility against him among virtually all elements of the Party bureaucracy. By 1964 he had alienated every important constituency in the Soviet system: military leaders who despised his inconsistent handling of the defense budget, his interference in strategic policy, and his arrogant treatment of Marshal Zhukov and other top officers; the economic bureaucracy that he had consistently criticized and reshaped; ideological conservatives and proponents of artistic freedom alike, frustrated by his contradictory behavior in 1962 and 1963; top Party leaders whom he hectored and insulted; and key Party officials at every level, shaken by his constant changes.

Khrushchev's style and attitude also helped to do him in. As early as 1957, he began announcing decisions and policies before the Presidium and the Central Committee could discuss and approve them. By the late 1960s, he was regularly ignoring or overriding the views and advice of his senior comrades. In their opinion, his unpredictability and brashness undercut sensible policy and at times even endangered Party interests and Soviet state security. Colleagues deeply resented the cavalier and capricious way in which Khrushchev increasingly treated them.

Preliminary discussions among Khrushchev's senior critics began as early as 1963 but accelerated in the spring of 1964. His enemies spread damaging information about a trip to West Germany by Khrushchev's son-in-law, journalist Alexei Adzhubei. They also covertly encouraged disapproval of the Soviet leader's trip to Egypt, where he awarded Nasser the Soviet Union's highest decoration despite objections from Presidium members. Several Party leaders, including Leonid Brezhnev, who would succeed Khrushchev as Party first secretary, organized the opposition. Recalled from vacation on October 12, 1964, Khrushchev returned to Moscow with his sole supporter, Mikoyan, to find that the Presidium had decided to "retire" him for reasons of health. Their real motives included a long list of grievances presented to a plenary meeting of the Central Committee the following day. The collaborators charged him with "hasty decision making and hare-brained scheming," abuse of power, ignoring the Presidium, mismanagement of industry, arbitrary policies in agriculture and foreign trade, damaging the Party by ill-considered organizational changes, worsening relations with China, and offending foreign Communists and other leaders by tactless remarks and behavior. After some protestations, Khrushchev acquiesced in the Presidium's decision. Later, in retirement, he would comment philosophically,

Perhaps the most important thing I did was just this—that they were able to get rid of me simply by voting, whereas Stalin would have had them all arrested.[9]

---

[9]Quoted in Roy Medvedev, *Khrushchev* (Oxford: Oxford Univ. Press, 1982), p. 245.

Conclusion

The Khrushchev era marked a turning point in Soviet history. In his "secret" speech to the Twentieth Party Congress, Stalin's successor boldly attacked the worst features of the dead dictator's legacy and initiated the painful process of confronting the nightmare of Stalinism. Khrushchev then undertook reforms aimed at advancing Soviet society toward Great October's socialist vision. For several reasons, his policies largely failed. In part the new Soviet leader proved unable to articulate and pursue clear goals. He sensed the problems in Soviet life but grasped at solutions haphazardly. Instead of issuing orderly correctives, he jumped from one impulsive change to another. His slapdash measures and frenzied reorganizations undercut his good intentions.

More important, his ideological commitment to Soviet socialism and his training in high Stalinism drove him to act only within the constraints of the command economy and personalized authoritarian structure established in the 1930s. Like tsarist reformers Catherine the Great and Alexander II and like Mikhail Gorbachev in the 1980s, the Soviet leader sought to modernize and improve the regime without altering its basic structure or principles. The ineffectiveness of Khrushchev's policies indicated that the Soviet Union could not attain the ideal of communism within the framework of the existing system. Minor modifications would never yield the economic efficiency and the individual creativity required to achieve the productive, fair society of Nikita Khrushchev's dreams.

Nevertheless, Khrushchev's abortive effort in part laid the groundwork for Gorbachev's more sweeping reforms of the 1980s. By attacking the worst features of Stalinism and espousing socialist legality, he largely eliminated random terror from the Soviet experience. Future generations would feel free to at least consider new methods and goals without fearing for their lives. Although his policies proved inconsistent, Khrushchev widened the permitted range of intellectual and artistic activity and opened Soviet society to outside ideas, norms, and influences. He encouraged the use of specialists and those with training and talent in solving economic, social, and other public policy problems. This practice, continued by his successors, formed the fertile soil from which, two decades later, the critical activity known as *glasnost'*, or "openness," would flower. Moreover, the spirit of change and hope that the Soviet leader generated, particularly in 1959–1961, fired the imagination of a new generation then coming of age. Many of these young people, including Gorbachev, would become reformers after 1985. Some, disillusioned by the gap between Khrushchev's rhetoric and Soviet reality, became dissidents in the 1960s and 1970s.

In world affairs, the Soviet leader strove both to enhance the U.S.S.R.'s power and influence and to ease tension between the superpowers, often incompatible aims. Nevertheless, he opened the door to détente in Soviet-American relations when he rejected war as the inevitable outcome of the struggle between socialism and imperialism. He was convinced that in long-term, peaceful competition, socialism would win through its example, not its military might. Although Khrushchev had a role in fueling the nuclear arms race, in part he was reacting to American advances in technology and numbers. After the near-disasters of Berlin and Cuba, he took steps to defuse the Soviet-American rivalry by installing the hot line and signing a partial test-ban agreement, and he laid the groundwork for future arms-control negotiations. Subsequent superpower relations saw many ups and downs, but after 1964 both sides sought to coexist under the umbrella of nuclear deterrence.

Khrushchev's social policies proved less dramatic than his achievements abroad, but they enhanced the lives of Soviet citizens. Although he failed to bring them the good life that he had promised, he raised the standard of living and the prospects of farmers, and he rationalized the wages and improved the housing of urban dwellers. He also broadened the pension system and supported the continuing expansion of education opportunities for all, including rural children. He released millions from the *Gulag* and established the rule of socialist law and a degree of personal security, and he encouraged citizens to participate in public life, although not in decision making. His populist instincts led him to favor government of and for the people, but his Leninist creed and Party upbringing ruled out government by the people.

Khrushchev's failures were manifold, as his successors delighted in pointing out. Despite his remodeling, the system remained inefficient and cumbersome. People's expectations outran any modest gains that Khrushchev engineered, and the U.S.S.R. fell farther behind the West militarily and technologically. Dishonest about his past under Stalin and increasingly vain and vulnerable to flattery, the Soviet leader developed a personal style that exasperated his colleagues and provoked popular ridicule. His posturing overshadowed his passion for rekindling the torch of socialism. Nevertheless, Khrushchev was not afraid to act as his convictions and experience impelled him. He courageously cast light on the Stalinist holocaust, and he wisely pulled back from nuclear war in 1962. His successors would have far less to be proud of.

FURTHER READING

No definitive biography of Khrushchev exists although Professor William Taubman of Amherst College is preparing one. The best introduction to the era is Martin McCauley, ed., *Khrushchev and Khrushchevism* (Bloomington, Ind., 1987), a collection of generally thoughtful articles that emphasizes domestic developments. S. Cohen, A. Rabinowitch, and R. Sharlet, eds., *The Soviet Union Since Stalin* (Bloomington, Ind., 1980), contains many articles that throw light on the Khrushchev years. The Russian Marxist historian Roy

Medvedev presents an interesting analysis in his *Khrushchev* (Oxford, 1982). Full treatment of Khrushchev's foreign policy is found in James Richter, *Khrushchev's Double Bind: International Pressures and Domestic Coalition Politics* (Baltimore, 1994). Both the two volumes of Khrushchev's memoirs, *Khrushchev Remembers* (Boston, 1970 and 1974), and his son's account, Sergei Khrushchev, *Khrushchev on Khrushchev* (Boston, 1990), provide inside if partisan insights and information. Khrushchev's "secret" speech appears in N. S. Khrushchev, *Crimes of the Stalin Era* (New York, 1962). Of a number of older biographies and symposia, Abram Brumberg, ed., *Russia Under Khrushchev* (New York, 1962), remains useful.

Specialized studies of politics include George Breslauer, *Khrushchev and Brezhnev as Leaders* (Boston, 1982); Carl Linden, *Khrushchev and the Soviet Leadership, 1957–1964* (Baltimore, 1967); and Barbara Chotiner, *Khrushchev's Party Reform* (Westport, Conn., 1984). George Feifer, *Justice in Moscow* (New York, 1964), provides interesting firsthand material on legal affairs and society.

For cultural history, good introductions are Deming Brown, *Soviet Russian Literature Since Stalin* (New York, 1978); George Gibian, *Interval of Freedom: Soviet Literature During the Thaw, 1954–1957* (Minneapolis, 1960); and Priscilla Johnson, *Khrushchev and the Arts: The Politics of Soviet Culture* (Cambridge, Mass., 1965).

Foreign policy is treated in the pertinent chapters of the general history, Adam Ulam, *Expansion and Coexistence* (New York, 1968), and in these specialized studies: Graham Allison, *Essence of Decision: Explaining the Cuban Missile Crisis* (Boston, 1971); J. M. MacIntosh, *Strategy and Tactics of Soviet Foreign Policy* (London, 1963); Herbert Ellison, ed., *The Sino-Soviet Conflict* (Seattle, 1982); David Floyd, *Mao versus Khrushchev: A Short History of the Sino-Soviet Conflict* (New York, 1964); F. Fejto, *A History of the People's Democracies: Eastern Europe Since Stalin*, 2nd ed. (London, 1974); Zbigniew Brzezinski, *The Soviet Bloc: Unity and Conflict*, rev. ed. (New York, 1961); Paul Zinner, *Revolution in Hungary* (New York, 1962); and Michael R. Beschloss, *The Crisis Years: Kennedy and Khrushchev, 1960–1963* (New York, 1991).

Recent accounts of the Cuban missile crisis that draw on new information and recollections of participants on all sides include Robert A. Divine, ed., *The Cuban Missile Crisis*, 2nd ed. (New York, 1988); James G. Blight, *On the Brink: Americans and Soviets Reexamine the Cuban Missile Crisis*, 2nd ed. (New York, 1990); Dino A. Brugioni, *Eyeball to Eyeball: The Inside Story of the Cuban Missile Crisis* (New York, 1993); and James G. Blight, B. J. Allyn, and D. A. Welch, *Cuba on the Brink: Castro, the Missile Crisis, and the Soviet Collapse* (New York, 1993).

10

A VISION FADING
Stagnation and Transformation Under Brezhnev
~

It was February 10, 1966. The small hall was hot and crowded. Some 150 spectators, almost all men, filled the main courtroom of the out-of-the-way Moscow Province Court. Each person attending had had to show a special invitation card, which security agents had checked at the entrance to the building and then again at the chamber door. The authorities had barred foreign journalists, even from Communist newspapers. Guards had drawn the window shades. Flickering fluorescent bulbs cast a dim light on the yellow walls and the two defendants, the writers Andrei Sinyavsky and Yuli Daniel. Sinyavsky, slight with a straggly red beard, looked the part of a Russian intellectual. Daniel, the taller of the two, wore a cowboy shirt and a faded jacket.

Shortly after 10 A.M., the court clerk proclaimed the traditional "The court is in session." The Russian words, translated, also mean "The Trial Begins," ironically the title of a Sinyavsky novel that constituted part of the evidence against him. The imposing presiding judge, Leonid Smirnov, entered, accompanied by two lay assistants. The clerk read the indictment charging the defendants with publishing anti-Soviet works abroad in violation of Article 70 of the Criminal Code. The law prohibited the production or dissemination of "slanderous inventions defamatory to the Soviet political and social system." The offensive material by Sinyavsky, published under the pseudonym Abram Tertz, included two novels and a trenchant critique of Soviet literature. The indictment singled out a novel and several short stories by Daniel.

A pretrial article published in *Izvestiia* had accused the defendants of "hatred for our system, vile mockery of everything dear to our Motherland and people. . . . They like nothing in our country, nothing is holy for them either in its present or in its past. They wish to slander and curse everything that is dear to Soviet man." The prosecution followed this line of argument. Daniel protested,

> I've always thought and I continue to think that my books were not anti-Soviet and that I put no anti-Soviet meaning into them, since I did not criticize or make fun of the basic principles of our life.

After four days, the trial ended in convictions. The judge sentenced Sinyavsky to seven years at hard labor and Daniel to five. Despite objections within the Soviet Union and appeals for clemency from abroad, the authorities refused to pardon the two writers. However, Sinyavsky and Daniel were eventually permitted to emigrate to Western Europe, after they had served most of their sentences.

Several notable features distinguished the trial. Despite five months' interrogation, both men denied their guilt, and no "confessions" were extorted in the manner of the show trials of the 1930s. The authors' writings contained harsh criticism of the Soviet system, but each avowed his dedication to socialism. The trial also marked the first time that a Soviet regime had publicly indicted and convicted authors exclusively for what they had *written*, for their ideas. Earlier, officialdom had harassed and censored writers and artists or purged them secretly. Finally, the trial revealed the determination of Nikita Krushchev's successors to reimpose Stalinist controls over artistic and cultural life, a policy that soon brought them into protracted confrontation with a core of resilient intellectuals.[1]

Soviet and Western historians have labeled Leonid Brezhnev's predominance from 1964 to 1982 "the era of stagnation." At first the new leadership garnered backing by ending the confusion and false promises of the Khrushchev era. Into the mid-1970s, most Soviet citizens remained quiescent under the Brezhnev regime because their living standards gradually improved. But by the end of that decade, economic progress slackened and grumbling intensified. Inefficiency and corruption spread, and the ideal socialist society envisioned in 1917 stayed maddeningly out of reach. Brezhnevian policies emphasized stability and conformity. Indeed, on the surface Soviet society appeared unchanged. Nevertheless, beneath the sluggish exterior, generational and attitudinal alterations that budded during the 1950s and 1960s now ripened. Subterranean pressure for cataclysmic transformation of the Soviet system mounted and would climax in the years after 1985.

---

[1]This account is based on Max Hayward, trans. and ed., *On Trial* (New York: Harper & Row, 1966), passim.

The Political Process: "Trust in Cadres"

The small group of Party leaders who ousted Khrushchev moved immediately to shore up their position and to banish their predecessor's ghost. Like Stalin's successors, they urged calm and stressed the collective nature of their leadership. They ensured a smooth transfer of power by parceling out key jobs among the chief conspirators. Leonid Brezhnev became head Party secretary; Alexei Kosygin, premier; and Nikolai Podgorny, head of state a year later.

Although Khrushchev's replacements permitted him to keep a residence in Moscow and a *dacha* outside the city, they treated him as an "unperson," expunging his name from public discourse and printed materials. For they still feared his impetuosity. On one occasion, the supplanters nearly panicked when they thought that he wanted to "crash" a Red Square reception for Soviet cosmonauts. They harassed the former premier and his family in petty ways, especially after he arranged in the late 1960s to have his memoirs published in the West. Even in death, Khrushchev worried them; the leadership took elaborate precautions to prevent a popular demonstration at his funeral in 1971 and closed his grave site to the public. They need not have fretted; most Soviet citizens had little love for the stout ex-leader. In their eyes, he had promised much and delivered little.

The new guard promptly abrogated many of Khrushchev's "harebrained schemes." They canceled his reorganizations of economic and agricultural administration: traditional economic ministries and *Gosplan* soon replaced the *sovnarkhozy* and the Ministry of Agriculture was restored to its central place. Regional agricultural associations ended, along with efforts to organize agricultural activity by kinds of product. They also discarded Trofim Lysenko's fraudulent doctrines, as well as Khrushchev's antireligion campaign.

The rulers hastened to reassure lower-level Party leaders and the rank-and-file members that their jobs remained secure. Although they did not repudiate the anti-Stalin declarations of the Twentieth and Twenty-second Party congresses, they pursued a moderate ideological course. They slowed the pace of de-Stalinization while vetoing efforts to rehabilitate the tarnished dictator. They also revoked the Party's division into industrial and agricultural departments and dropped term limits for Party officials. These latter moves especially pleased Party *apparatchiks*.

Brezhnev later codified the revamped policy as "trust in cadres," or reliance on the Party bureaucracy. The arbitrary transfers and firings of Khrushchev's day ended, and Party officials could now count on careers of steady advancement and increasing privilege. The new atmosphere produced political stability but led to "localism," the advancement of regional interests by Party authorities who collaborated with state administrators at the same level. As a corollary, corruption spread, particularly the misuse of state and Party funds for personal interests. The emphasis on stability and "trust in cadres" also fostered petty despotism, for "little Stalins" had time to cultivate power and political machines in their bailiwicks. These grasping officials subsisted not only on graft but on favoritism and deception about the true state of affairs in their districts. Last, special privileges for Party officials that had originated in the Stalin and Khrushchev eras expanded to include high incomes, preferred housing, exclusive stores and medical clinics, elaborate *dachas* and vacation retreats, chauffeured limousines, and bribed access to the best schools and universities. What the Yugoslav Marxist Milovan Djilas called "the new class" dominated Soviet society. Ordinary people suffered under this elite's bureaucratic indifference and arrogance and naturally resented the new class and its superior ways.

Brezhnev was ideally suited to lead this bureaucratic counterreform. Conservative and cautious, he avoided rocking the boat. Instead, he strove to build consensus among Party policymakers and conformity among the populace. Born in 1906 in south Russia, the son of a metalworker, Brezhnev embodied the upward mobility of the Stalinist epoch and the growing professionalization of the Party brass. He acquired a technical education, working briefly as a metallurgical engineer, and entered full-time Party work in the mid-1930s, at age thirty. After serving as a political commissar with the Red Army during World War II, he became a Party official in the Dnieper region and in Moldavia (now Moldova) until 1952, when he came to Moscow as a Khrushchev protégé. From 1954 to 1956, he supervised the "virgin lands" scheme in Kazakhstan. Brezhnev then returned to Moscow, joining the Presidium (formerly the Politburo) in 1957 and serving as head of state from 1960 to 1964.

The butt of Soviet jokes for his stolidity and later senility, Brezhnev is revealed in his diary (published in 1994) as dull, petty, and provincial. Hardly mentioning major policy or dramatic world events, he instead noted his daily meals, weight changes, and hunting triumphs. A typical entry reads,

> Was home at the dacha. Had lunch—borscht with fresh cabbage. Rested in the yard, finished reading material. Watched hockey game . . . [later] evening news. Had dinner, went to bed.

Russian historian Dmitry Volkogonov comments poignantly about the diary, "When I read this, I was sorry for Brezhnev, but I was sorrier for the great nation he led."[2] The pedestrian qualities reflected in his diary,

---

[2]Quoted in *Newsweek*, June 6, 1994, p. 41.

along with his easygoing manner, assisted Brezhnev's rise in a Party bureaucracy inherently resistant to innovation or brilliance. The new Soviet ruler, always careful to cultivate friends and avoid making enemies, threatened no one. Like the boss of an American city political machine, he espoused no particular policy line, and he proved adept at reconciling conflicting interests. Working easily with fellow oligarchs, he made an ideal candidate for Party chief.

Indeed, in the first eight or nine years after Khruschev's downfall, Brezhnev seemed merely a member of the collective leadership. As head of the Party, however, he clearly ranked as *primus inter pares*—first among equals. Like Stalin and Khrushchev, Brezhnev used control of the Party apparatus to build a strong support network and to accumulate personal power. In 1973, after eight years during which Politburo members had been listed in the press in alphabetical order, Brezhnev's name appeared first. In 1976 the delegates to the Twenty-fifth Party Congress hailed him as the Party's "universally acclaimed leader" and *vozhd'*. That same year, Brezhnev made himself a marshal of the Red Army, and grandiloquent praise exaggerating his wartime exploits began to proliferate in the press. In 1977 he added the duties of head of state to his leadership of the Party, and in 1980, on Kosygin's death, he became premier as well Awards and honors were heaped on him, including a Lenin Prize for literature for his ghost-written memoirs. On his seventy-fifth birthday in 1981, the fulsome adulation approached a new "cult of personality."

Brezhnev ultimately amassed more medals and orders than Stalin and Khrushchev combined, and more military distinctions than World War II hero Marshal Zhukov. His health, however, began to fail in the mid-1970s, and for the last five or six years of his regime, he delegated much of the work of ruling to close subordinates. After a severe stroke in 1976, his speech grew slurred and his gait laborious.

This politically skillful but increasingly pompous man based his staying power on a simple formula, sometimes described as an unwritten "social contract." Brezhnev made an implicit bargain with the Soviet people: he would guarantee them stability, secure and undemanding jobs, and a slowly improving standard of living; in return, they would acquiesce to his authoritarian, oligarchic rule. The vast majority of Soviet citizens accepted this arrangement.

Brezhnev promised gradually increasing material benefits, but he dropped Khrushchev's idea of a "transition to communism" and made no predictions about when the Soviet Union would attain full socialism. Instead, he claimed that the U.S.S.R. had achieved "developed socialism," which implied an efficient, technologically advanced, productive society, although he never defined the term precisely. In 1977 Brezhnev proudly superintended the ratification of a new (and final) Soviet Constitution. The document, which made only minor changes to the 1936

Constitution, primarily updated and clarified legal provisions and reaffirmed the leading role of the Party.

Under Brezhnev, the Politburo continued to make all major policy decisions. (The name Presidium was dropped in 1966.) We do not know exactly how this body operated, but Brezhnev probably acted as an "honest broker." Although the Soviet system was hardly pluralistic, officials with common concerns could articulate views and influence policy through the Party hierarchy and Politburo. Brezhnev's role was to mediate policy disagreements and jurisdictional conflicts among Politburo members who represented noteworthy interest groups. When a problem arose—for example, a dispute between security forces and the scientific establishment over the extent of contact with the West—Brezhnev would suggest a compromise, which would satisfy all parties.

With its emphasis on stability, the entrenched leadership resisted change or innovation. Politburo members' average age reached the lower seventies in 1981, and new members joined infrequently. The Politburo thus acted as a conservative and ponderous committee running a complex, huge, and shifting society. Rather than establishing goals or advancing a special agenda, Brezhnev supported general desiderata of enhanced Soviet military power and economic performance.

The Politburo and the Party controlled not only the political process, the economy, and social and intellectual life but the KGB (secret police) and military establishment as well. As in the past, Party and other important officials were appointed through *nomenklatura*. Under this system, the Party secretariat at each level, from all-Union to district, assigned members to key jobs in the Party and other organizations. To make the Party more effective and efficient, Brezhnev encouraged training and reeducation for top officials. He also urged them to introduce sophisticated managerial techniques adapted from the West. Yet his "trust in cadres" policy undercut these efforts to upgrade the organization. Although he called for discipline and accountability from Party officials, he also assured them that they would not face arbitrary transfer, dismissal, or reprimand, as under Khrushchev. Thus he had little leverage for removing passive or corrupt Party bureaucrats, and in the 1960s and 1970s, Party secretariats experienced a low rate of turnover.

Brezhnev appears to have been aware of—but unable to resolve—two other problems in the Party. Membership had exploded by about 70 percent under Khrushchev. The ranks continued to swell in the Brezhnev era, but more slowly. By 1982 Party rolls showed about 17 million members, or a little more than 10 percent of the adult population. Size put the Party's essential nature in question. If Party leaders kept recruiting talented people, membership would expand considerably, for the number of well-educated people holding responsible jobs had mushroomed. Yet an influx of newcomers—however talented—would undermine the Party's status as an elite, vanguard group and would dilute the percentage of workers in the organization. This quandary remained unresolved, as the weight of urban, educated Party members grew. In the early 1980s, more than 40 percent of Party men over thirty years old possessed a higher education.

On occasion Brezhnev lamented the absence of new blood in the Party leadership, but in practice he ignored the generational gap dividing the institution. His age group, formed largely in the Stalinist years of collectivization, industrialization, purges, and war, composed a small minority in the Party, although they occupied all the top posts. By 1980 almost three-quarters of Party members had joined the Party after Stalin's death. Their outlook and experiences differed markedly from those of the ruling gerontocracy. The generational split was mirrored among the overall population, in which young people tended to criticize Brezhnevian conservatism and to yearn for reform.

Détente and Its Downfall

Besides assuring the Party bureaucracy that their careers were safe, Brezhnev and his fellow Politburo members faced several immediate foreign policy challenges on assuming power. They had no quarrel with Khrushchev's strategic or diplomatic objectives but regarded his behavior abroad as brash and counterproductive. The new leaders postponed a December 1964 meeting of international Communist parties that Khrushchev had planned as a forum for denouncing the Chinese. They also ended the shrill polemics against Mao Zedong and his supporters that had cropped up in the Party and international socialist press. In March 1965, they organized a smaller conference of sixteen Communist parties. The Chinese, however, refused to accept Soviet resolutions proclaiming the unity of the world movement. In particular, they deplored the U.S.S.R.'s inadequate support of the North Vietnamese struggle with American imperialism.

Despite this setback, Brezhnev and his comrades continued to seek resolution of the dispute. But Mao's launching of the Great Proletarian Cultural Revolution in 1966 radicalized politics inside China and isolated moderate leaders who favored reconciliation with the U.S.S.R. In addition, the Chinese grumbled at the Soviet government's mediation of a brief war between India and Pakistan. They did not welcome strengthened Soviet influence in India or a weakening of their client, Pakistan. Tensions heightened as both sides pressed claims to territory along the Yalu River, which separated the Soviet Far East from Chinese Manchuria. In March 1969, armed conflict erupted when Red Army units contested Chinese forces for control of Damansky Island, a strategic point in the channel. Both sides suffered a few casualties.

Later in 1969, Moscow managed to set up an international socialist conference (boycotted by Mao and several Asian parties), at which Brezhnev garnered only lukewarm support for his condemnation of the Chinese. At the same time, Soviet and Chinese leaders vied for control of Communist parties in Africa and for the support of socialist regimes in Romania and Yugoslavia. In the fall of 1969, as the political turmoil in China subsided, Soviet leaders renewed efforts to settle the quarrel. Talks between the two governments muted the dispute during the early 1970s. Sino-Soviet relations deteriorated late in the decade, however, after Vietnam, a Soviet client, occupied Cambodia and repulsed a Chinese attack across its borders. The Soviet Union's invasion of Afghanistan in 1979 worsened matters. Restored relations between the two socialist giants would have to await Mikhail Gorbachev's coming to power in 1985.

Khrushchev's successors also decided to suspend his efforts to promote closer ties with West Germany. After some floundering, they chose instead to fold the issue of West Germany into a pan-European policy. This orientation aimed to check German rearmament and to obtain Western recognition of the Soviet position in Central and Eastern Europe. In 1966 Brezhnev called for a Europeanwide security summit, an idea that the West accepted after some hesitation. Events in the Middle East, Southeast Asia, and Eastern Europe, however, combined to delay convocation of the conference for five years.

Brezhnev and his associates continued Khrushchev's forward policy in the Third World, increasing aid to friendly states and extending military and political influence there. In 1966 this approach seemed to have scored another success when a pro-Soviet government came to power in Syria. Yet as the Arab states increased pressure on Israel, war broke out in June 1967. Despite superior numbers, the Arabs suffered a crushing defeat after only six days. Israel occupied the Golan Heights on the Syrian border, the west bank of the Jordan River, the Gaza Strip, and the Sinai Desert along the Egyptian border. The humiliation of its client states Egypt and Syria and the expense of replacing heavy losses of arms and equipment drastically set back Soviet policy in the Middle East.

In Southeast Asia, the massive American intervention in the Vietnamese civil war had failed by 1967–1968 to overcome the Communist rebellion in the south or to defeat the North Vietnamese forces of Ho Chi Minh. Many Americans believed that Soviet aid to the Vietnamese Communists had frustrated the American effort. Under newly elected President Richard Nixon, the U.S. government sought in 1969 to end the war in Vietnam and solicited Soviet cooperation. First, however, the two powers had to overcome a chill in their relations caused by an earlier event: Soviet armed intervention in Czechoslovakia in August 1968.

The crisis in Czechoslovakia unfolded slowly. Khrushchev's successors maintained his policy of granting a modicum of autonomy to the Eastern European states. They tolerated Romania's somewhat independent foreign policy and assented to economic reforms advanced in Hun-

gary. Not surprisingly, first intellectuals and then reform-minded socialists in Czechoslovakia began to discuss liberalizing their system in 1967.
A Slovak Communist, Alexander Dubcek, took the lead in criticizing the
existing hard-line leadership, and in January 1968 he became head of the
Czechoslovak party. Mounting discussion of how to create "socialism
with a human face" included consideration of a free press, other civil liberties, and the participation of nonparty individuals and groups in social
and political life. At first Soviet leaders expressed polite interest in the reform movement in Czechoslovakia, dubbed "the Prague spring" of 1968.
But when the reformers moved from talking to enacting changes, Brezhnev and his advisers snapped to attention. In mid-July a meeting of Soviet and Eastern European leaders warned Dubcek and his supporters
not to push matters too far. During the next month, Soviet officials met
separately with the Czechoslovaks and with other rulers behind the iron
curtain.

Politburo members worried that the Prague spring's reforms would
lead to a weakening of Warsaw Pact defenses and to increasing Western
infiltration and influence in Czechoslovakia. They also wrung their

Czechoslovak Defiance During the August 1968 Soviet-led invasion of Czechoslovakia,
an angry citizen shakes a bloodstained Czechoslovak flag at a Red Army tank crew
entering Prague.

hands at the thought of such radical ideas as a free press and a Communist Party's sharing governance with nonparty groups spreading to East Germany and Poland. Apparently not satisfied with Dubcek's response, and pressed by conservative Czechoslovak and Eastern European Communists and by their own military and KGB advisers, the Politburo approved armed intervention during a three-day meeting, August 15–17. Soviet and Warsaw Pact (except Romanian) troops crossed the Czechoslovak border on the night of August 20–21. The stunned Czechoslovaks staggered under the massive force. Individuals bravely defied their conquerors, however. Some strode in front of Soviet tanks unarmed but waving their national flag; others brandished anti-Soviet banners in the streets of Prague. One hundred Czechoslovaks were killed and 335 severely wounded. The Czechoslovak president, war hero General Ludvik Svoboda, flew to Moscow and won release of Dubcek and other captured reformist leaders. Yet Soviet authorities had overestimated the extent of antireform sentiment in Czechoslovakia and failed to create a shadow government to legitimize the intervention and to assume power afterward. They had to negotiate at first with Dubcek and his supporters, and only six months later did they succeed in installing a puppet government under a reliable conservative.

After the invasion, Brezhnev declared that socialist countries had a duty to interfere in societies that threatened to "damag[e] either socialism in their own countries or the fundamental interests" of the socialist cause. This precept, which became known as the Brezhnev doctrine, earned the Soviet leader international scorn. The Romanians had declined to participate in the invasion, and the Yugoslav and Italian Communist leaders condemned the intervention, as did the Western countries and their outspoken press. The brutal suppression of the Czechoslovaks' modest reform effort seriously undercut Soviet prestige worldwide and set back the détente between the Soviet Union and the West that had taken shape since 1963. The debacle also ignited protests among Soviet students and intellectuals and fueled the growing dissident movement in the U.S.S.R.

After the furor over Czechoslovakia died down, the Soviet Union and the West resumed talks begun before August 1968 on arms control and on convening a pan-European security conference. Brezhnev and his supporters retained Khrushchev's strategic and defense policies, adding only a build-up of conventional forces to the continued amassing of nuclear might. Although Soviet policymakers eschewed the word *deterrence*, in practice they accepted the principle. They maintained enough retaliatory nuclear capability to discourage a first strike from the West. Nervous about Western technological advances, however, they urged making the U.S.S.R.'s arsenal numerically superior to that of the United States. Should deterrence fail, they argued, Soviet ground forces would have to ready themselves to wage an offensive war in Western Europe. The Soviet leaders also strengthened naval forces, and their warships soon dotted the Indian Ocean and the Mediterranean Sea.

Naturally, all this military buttressing required funds. After strategists adopted the doctrine of mutual deterrence in the mid-1960s, the Brezhnev Politburo sought ways to reduce the defense burden on the economy. This concern led to the first round of Strategic Arms Limitations Talks (SALT I) between the Soviet Union and the United States during 1969–1972. Both sides agreed to curtail antiballistic missile (ABM) systems, a field in which Soviet military planners feared a developing U.S. technological lead. Brezhnev and President Nixon signed the ABM limitation treaty in Moscow in May 1972, together with the SALT I accords. The latter agreements set maximum numbers of nuclear weapons in the three basic categories of submarine-launched and intercontinental ground-launched missiles (SLBMs and ICBMs) and devices carried by bombers.

The SALT I pact did not reduce armaments; it permitted the superpowers to accumulate the weapons that they already had planned and to upgrade missiles within certain categories. Nevertheless, the accord capped the amassing of weapons and set a precedent for further negotiations. In November 1974, Brezhnev and American president Gerald Ford, meeting in Vladivostok, agreed on principles for a future arms-control treaty, designated SALT II. This pact was completed in 1979 but not ratified, although both countries informally abided by its provisions. Progress in arms control would halt at the end of the 1970s as détente dissipated.

In Western Europe, Brezhnev chalked up several successes in the 1970s. Finally recognizing the division of Germany as a *fait accompli* and yielding to the Western powers' determination to remain in Berlin, Soviet leaders agreed to a peace treaty with West Germany and to revised arrangements safeguarding the status of West Berlin in 1970 and 1971. These accords paved the way for convocation of a European security conference in Helsinki, Finland, in the summer of 1975. There, Soviet, Eastern and Western European, and American leaders agreed to guarantee the postwar borders between Poland and East Germany and between Poland and the Soviet Union, as well as other boundaries in the region (see map, p. 358). Negotiations also approved articles designed to expand trade and cultural contacts and to protect human rights across Europe, including the Soviet Union. The Helsinki Accords and the earlier admission to the UN of both East and West Germany completed the process of legitimizing the postwar order and achieved a long-desired Soviet goal of gaining international recognition for East Germany. Finally, the NATO allies and Warsaw Pact members began negotiations to reduce conventional weapons and troops stationed on each side of the iron curtain that bisected Europe, talks that would drag on fruitlessly for years.

President Nixon's decision in 1970 to reestablish American relations with China, cut off in 1949, put pressure on the Soviet leaders to bolster détente with the West. A Sino-American alliance against the U.S.S.R. was unlikely. Nevertheless, any cooperation between their chief socialist rival and their major capitalist opponent was bound to alarm the Kremlin, especially given that about one-third of the Red Army's forces and hardware were deployed in the Soviet Far East against China.

Brezhnev also needed to broaden economic and technological relations with the United States so as to upgrade the Soviet economy and to fund the defense expansion. At the time of the ABM treaty in May 1972, the Soviet leader signed several agreements on technical and scientific cooperation with the United States, and further joint measures were approved in 1974. Two years earlier, President Nixon had granted the U.S.S.R. most-favored-nation trade status and proferred new credits in return for Soviet promises to negotiate a final settlement of the World War II Lend-Lease account. Nixon also facilitated Soviet grain purchases after the disastrous crop of 1972. Conservative U.S. congressmen, however, passed the Jackson-Vanik amendment, which approved expanded trade only on the condition that the Soviet government ease restrictions on Jewish emigration. Annoyed by this seeming intrusion into their affairs, the U.S.S.R. canceled the commercial agreement in early 1975, and trade languished. After an initial drop, the number of Jews leaving the Soviet Union fluctuated in the 1970s and then diminished to a trickle in the early 1980s.

From its high-water mark in the Helsinki agreements of 1975, détente unraveled over the trade issue and other irritants. First, despite the SALT I treaty and progress toward SALT II, both sides despised the other's armaments policy. The United States feared Soviet preponderance in heavy missiles with large warheads that threatened U.S. missile sites. It also objected to Soviet deployment of intermediate-range missiles, SS-20s, that could reach targets in both Asia and Europe. To counter the former threat, American strategists increased the range and accuracy of U.S. submarine-launched missiles and expanded the number of missiles that carried multiple warheads. Against the new SS-20s, the United States placed their own shorter-range Pershing and cruise missiles in Europe and aimed them at the western regions of the Soviet Union. By the end of Brezhnev's rule, arms control was in abeyance, and both superpowers had locked horns in the dangerous contest. Détente seemed doomed indeed.

Jimmy Carter, the U.S. president elected in 1976, provided a second irritant in American-Soviet relations. In accordance with his personal principles, and sensitive to the intensifying public criticism of Soviet actions, Carter condemned Brezhnev's repression of intellectual and religious dissidents. He demanded that the Soviet government cease its human rights violations, which blatantly reneged on the Helsinki Accords. He also pressed for free emigration for Soviet Jews. Brezhnev and his advisers found these *demarches* offensive and snapped that the United States had no business nosing into Soviet domestic policies. The running battle over human rights, which did much to eviscerate détente, would not find resolution until Gorbachev's accession to power in 1985.

Finally, Brezhnev's efforts to expand Soviet influence in the Third World also weakened the East-West thaw. The Soviet Union possessed certain advantages in competing with the United States in Asia, Africa, and Latin America. Soviet propagandists, pointing to their country's success in industrialization and its military might, urged Third World leaders to look to the Soviet socialist example. The U.S.S.R. extended military and economic assistance aimed at luring "friendly" countries to embrace socialism and to support the Soviet Union on the world stage. Soviet leaders also capitalized on anti-imperialist and anti-Western sentiment in the Third World. In some countries, local Marxist-Leninist parties or anti-imperialist national liberation movements promoted Soviet interests. The Soviet government even sponsored cultural and educational exchanges and arranged for thousands of Third World students to study at Moscow's Patrice Lumumba University, named after a martyred hero of the anti-Western revolution in Africa. (See the map, Soviet-U.S. Rivalry, 1945–1989.)

To be sure, Soviet efforts in the developing countries fell flat at times. Some Third World leaders feared Soviet military dominance and resented the high-handed methods and arrogant attitudes of Soviet advisers and technical experts. Others pointed to the U.S.S.R's intervention in Hungary in 1956 and in Czechoslovakia in 1968. Judging Soviet socialism too authoritarian, they moved to protect the freedoms for which many Third World peoples struggled.

In Asia, Africa, and Latin America, the U.S.S.R.'s agenda yielded mixed success. In the Middle East, the Egyptian government, anticommunist and annoyed by Soviet meddling and dictation, terminated Soviet aid and expelled Soviet advisers in 1972. The following year, the Arabs attacked Israel and ultimately suffered another humiliating defeat. The Soviet government also saw its influence in the Middle East fade as the Nixon, Ford, and Carter administrations dominated a post-1973 peace process that excluded the Soviet Union. U.S. efforts culminated in the Egyptian-Israeli peace accords signed at Camp David in 1979. A war between Iran and Iraq that broke out in 1980 further confounded the Soviet government. Iraq was its client state; Iran, a potentially disruptive neighbor. Unsure of whom to support, Soviet leaders tried to stay neutral during the conflict.

Vacuums of power in Africa generated considerable tension between

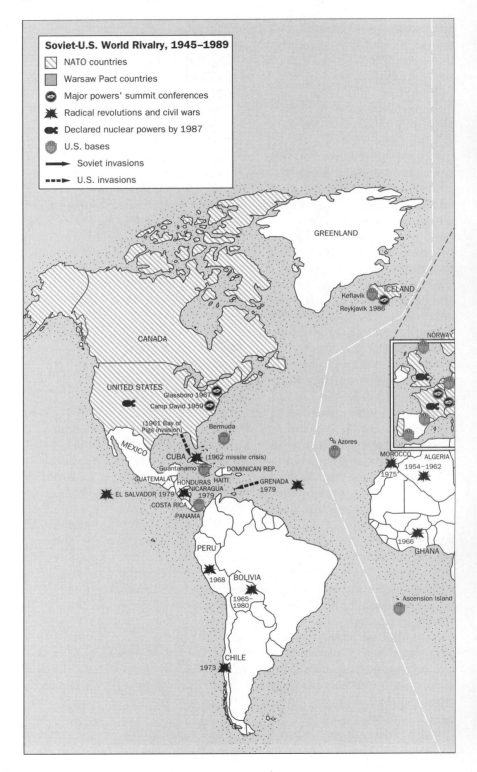

Soviet-U.S. World Rivalry, 1945–1989

- NATO countries
- Warsaw Pact countries
- Major powers' summit conferences
- Radical revolutions and civil wars
- Declared nuclear powers by 1987
- U.S. bases
- Soviet invasions
- U.S. invasions

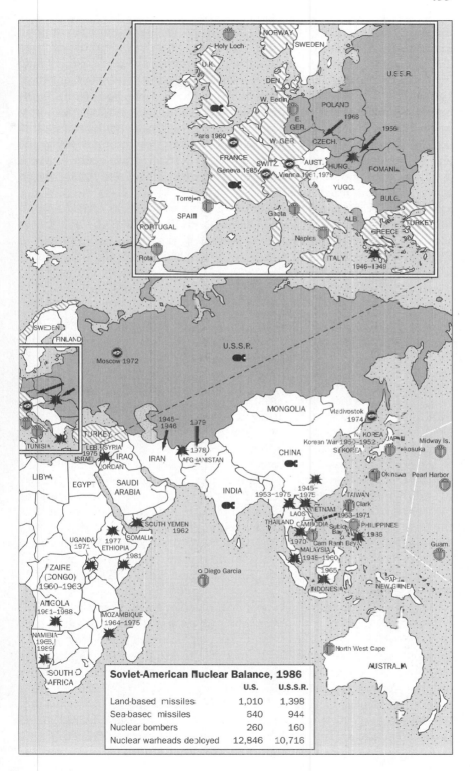

Soviet-American Nuclear Balance, 1986		
	U.S.	U.S.S.R.
Land-based missiles	1,010	1,398
Sea-based missiles	640	944
Nuclear bombers	260	160
Nuclear warheads deployed	12,846	10,716

the superpowers. After Marxist leaders failed to set up a pro-Soviet state in the former Belgian Congo (now Zaire) in the 1960s, Marxist governments came to power in Angola and in Ethiopia in the 1970s. Using Cuban proxies, the Soviet government provided military and technical aid to these regimes. For a time, the U.S.S.R. also enjoyed strong influence in Somalia, stirring Western fears of Soviet domination of the northeastern Horn of Africa. This area lay dangerously close to Saudi Arabia and the Persian Gulf, the chief sources of Western oil imports. Yet by the end of the Brezhnev era, Soviet influence in Africa would begin to wane, as Ethiopia and Somalia pursued independent policies and most African governments shunned socialism.

In Latin America, the hope of using Cuba as a base to spread revolution throughout the Western hemisphere heartened ideologues in Moscow. A radical regime under Salvador Allende came to power in Chile in the late 1960s; a Marxist revolutionary group, the Sandinistas, seized control in Nicaragua in 1980; and a revolutionary struggle persisted in El Salvador. On the other hand, the effort of Ché Guevara, a Cuban apostle of radical socialism, to raise a peasant revolution in Bolivia fizzled with his capture and execution. An American-supported military coup toppled the Allende regime in 1973, and the Sandinistas lost popular support owing to their own mismanagement and a U.S.-sponsored embargo. Maintaining a socialist toehold in Cuba proved costly as well. Hampered by its weak, sugar-dependent economy, an American embargo, and Castro's maladministration, Cuba devoured hundreds of millions of dollars annually in Soviet subsidies. By the early 1980s, chances for the spread of socialism and the extension of Soviet influence in Latin America looked bleak.

In Vietnam, Soviet ties strengthened at China's expense after Ho Chi Minh's defeat of South Vietnam and its ally, the United States. In the rest of Asia, however, Brezhnev could point to little progress in advancing the cause of socialism. Relations with Japan remained strained because of the U.S.S.R.'s refusal to discuss returning the southernmost Kuril Islands, and Japan cultivated closer ties with the United States. The Southeast Asian governments stayed firmly anticommunist after 1965, and India pursued a democratic and independent course while still accepting substantial Soviet aid.

Brezhnev's biggest foreign policy blunder in Asia came at the end of 1979, when he sent Soviet forces into Afghanistan. After a revolutionary upheaval there (not instigated by the Soviet Union), a weak Marxist government came to power in Kabul in 1978. Its socialist, antireligious policies and repressive methods soon provoked widespread resistance among Afghanistan's 15 million Muslims. By fall 1979, the fledgling regime had begun to totter. Soviet leaders dreaded the collapse of a neighboring socialist government. Worst of all, they feared—erroneously, according to available evidence—that an anti-Soviet Islamic regime linked to the United States and China would replace the revolutionary government. Such a development might have a long-range unsettling effect on Muslims in the U.S.S.R. Moreover, an Afghan administration friendly to the Soviet Union's two chief rivals would threaten security on the nation's southern border.

On December 12, 1979, the Politburo decided to intervene. Two weeks later, Red Army forces advanced southward. Soviet leaders expected to crush the Afghan insurrection and to set up a viable puppet government within weeks. But the Afghan people, historically known as tough fighters, retreated to the mountains and organized a fierce resistance. To strengthen their position, the Muslim partisans obtained logistical and political support from Pakistan, China, and the United States. More than 3 million Afghan citizens fled their country, and the Soviet government eventually had to send in almost a hundred thousand troops. Soviet forces would wage a tiresome war for eight years—with shocking casualties on both sides and widespread devastation—but without dislodging their foe. The United States' role in prolonging the bloody struggle by arming and aiding Afghan resistance fighters remains controversial.

The invasion of Afghanistan severely damaged the Soviet Union's reputation throughout the Islamic world. As a sign of U.S. displeasure, President Carter imposed a grain embargo against the U.S.S.R. Ironically, the embargo primarily hurt American wheat growers when the Soviet Union bought its grain elsewhere. The United States also boycotted the 1980 Olympics in Moscow and suspended ratification of the SALT II treaty. These measures only aggravated an American disillusionment with détente that had gathered momentum in the late 1970s. U.S. leaders and the public had assumed that détente meant not only an easing of tension but also fruitful cooperation. They were first irritated and then outraged by the Soviet nuclear build-up and by the U.S.S.R.'s intrusions in

Death to the Invader! An Afghan rebel fighter's visage reflects the fierce determination that sparked his people's eight-year resistance to Soviet efforts to impose atheistic Marxism on Islamic Afghanistan.

Africa and Latin America. Afghanistan provided the last straw. Soviet leaders, for their part, could not understand the American attitude, especially what they saw as Carter's "hot-and-cold" policies toward the U.S.S.R. They had never conceived détente as a cessation of superpower competition in the world arena. They still expected to stir up trouble for imperialists wherever they could. For them, détente signified merely reducing tensions where possible and striking deals of mutual self-interest—not generating friendly, open relations forever.

At an ebb in 1980, détente suffered a near-fatal blow with Ronald Reagan's election that November. The incoming president had made a campaign promise to wage unremitting battle against what he later called the Soviet "evil empire." His administration immediately accelerated the military build-up Carter had begun and condemned Soviet activities in the Third World. Startling developments in Poland only worsened matters. In the summer of 1980, an independent workers' movement, Solidarity, arose spontaneously in Poland as a protest against economic inequities and the Communist regime's mismanagement and corruption. Workers' opposing a Marxist-Leninist government that claimed to represent their interests portended the later disintegration of Eastern European socialism in 1989. Before long, more than 10 million Poles had joined Solidarity. The government began to weaken, and the economy neared collapse. Heady with success, Solidarity radicals in the fall of 1981 discussed new demands for a share in economic and political decision making. Despite stern warnings from Moscow, Polish leaders appeared ready to abandon one-party rule.

In December 1981, General Wojciech Jaruzelski seized power in Poland, imposed martial law, and arrested key figures in the Solidarity movement. Soviet leaders thus escaped the need to intervene and avoided the civil strife and world condemnation that would have erupted had they meddled. Although Jaruzelski later insisted that he acted independently to save Poland from Soviet invasion, he undoubtedly received strong hints from Moscow that if Poland did not halt its slide toward pluralism, the Kremlin would invoke the Brezhnev doctrine and provide military "assistance." The West protested Jaruzelski's action vociferously but could do nothing as Poland once more bowed to authoritarianism.

By the time of his death in 1982, Brezhnev's foreign policy lay in shambles. He had achieved nuclear parity with the United States and had elevated the Soviet Union's presence throughout the world. But with détente comatose and the Soviet Union bogged down in a wasting war in Afghanistan, his successors also had to face an unwinnable arms race with the United States. Moreover, NATO missiles in Europe, the unresolved dispute with China, expensive but unproductive forays into the Third World, and shaky control over an increasingly restive Eastern Europe—all compounded the headaches that Brezhnev bequeathed to his heirs.

An Economy Falters

Throughout his almost two decades in office, Brezhnev struggled to rejuvenate the Soviet economy. As in foreign policy, he made some gains, but overall his policies failed. He maintained economic growth for a time, but the rate eventually dwindled toward zero. He built the Soviet economy into the second largest in the world, but its inefficiencies multiplied and a fifth of the GNP was devoted to military production. As he toiled to shore it up, the economy fell farther behind those of the United States, Western Europe, and Japan. He improved his subjects' standard of living but not fast enough to keep pace with their rising expectations. Compared to people in other advanced industrial societies, Soviet citizens lived spartan lives. Increasingly, they became aware of the disparity.

Brezhnev concentrated on several key issues in his drive to upgrade the Soviet economy. As under Khrushchev, agriculture remained a particularly irksome problem. Despite investment, a rise in acreage under cultivation, seed innovations, and added fertilizer, crop yields responded listlessly. Output grew only modestly and lagged behind consumer demand. The slow growth hampered Brezhnev's other economic measures. In poor harvest years, he was forced to purchase grain with precious foreign exchange better used to acquire advanced technology. Worse, he had to scramble to maintain the modest rise in living standards that he had promised the Soviet people and that provided vital motivation for Soviet workers.

Brezhnev and his colleagues resorted to an array of measures to boost agriculture. Besides suspending Khrushchev's restrictions on private plots, they established a guaranteed annual income for collective farmers. In 1965 they raised procurement prices for livestock without increasing retail prices, with further hikes in 1970 and after. These price boosts improved meat production but drained the national budget; livestock subsidies totaled 23 billion rubles by 1979. To eliminate marginal or impoverished *kolkhozes,* Brezhnev and his colleagues continued to amalgamate collective farms and to convert collectives into state farms. They pushed investment in agriculture from 19 percent of total investment in 1961–1965 to 26 percent in 1971–1975.

None of these antidotes had much effect, owing to intrinsic and intractable problems plaguing Soviet agriculture. First, the unreliable climate has always handicapped food production. Because the Russian lands lie so far north, the growing season on much of the arable acreage is short. Rainfall passes from west to east, making the amount reaching east central Russia, west Siberia, and Kazakhstan unpredictable. Drought and bad weather frequently damage harvests. No commissar can control these natural conditions.

Second, Brezhnev, like Stalin and Khrushchev, had committed himself to maintaining agriculture's organization into collective and state farms. Ideology forbade private land ownership and private agricultural production, except for collective farmers' household plots. Yet socialized farms provided little incentive to produce, for farmers neither controlled nor profited directly from the crops or the animals that they tended. Indeed, productivity on individual household plots far exceeded that of collectives. In 1977 these tiny plots, although composing only about 2 percent of total agricultural acreage, produced 27 percent of all output, including half the vegetables and potatoes and 34 percent of all livestock products.

Besides climatic and ideological restraints, a cultural bias worked against agricultural abundance. The old quandary, "How're you gonna keep 'em down on the farm?" fit Soviet society as it modernized after World War II. Ambitious and talented people fled rural society for the bright lights and opportunities of the city. The spread of primary education to the villages accelerated this flight, as many skilled young people opted to leave. The pattern of male emigration set in the nineteenth century persisted, whereas traditional family values and patriarchal attitudes kept many women at home and undereducated. In the 1970s, the labor force on most farms consisted of two-thirds women, who had more interest in tending to their families and private plots than in performing compulsory work for the collective or state farm. The remaining third of farm laborers were aged or unproductive men and older teenagers.

Last, despite sporadic efforts to decentralize decision making, ponderous central control hamstrung the agricultural system. Officials made ill-considered decisions about crop selection and work schedules and falsified output figures. When one Soviet observer asked an agricultural planner why dairy farming was practiced in regions clearly unsuited to milk production, the official replied, "Economic indices, profitability, and law of cost don't mean anything here. There is not enough milk; it must be produced everywhere, in the largest amount possible, and at any price."[3]

Brezhnev also focused his economic policies on the administration of industry. After abolishing Khrushchev's regional economic councils, the new Soviet leader recentralized economic management in Moscow and restored the authority of Gosplan. Yet he also espoused devolution of economic decision making to the individual factory. Named after their original proponent, economist Evsei Liberman, these new policies held local enterprise managers accountable for meeting profit criteria and achieving sales quotas, to prevent unsold goods from accumulating in

---

[3]Quoted in Roy D. Laird, "The Political Economy of Soviet Agriculture Under Brezhnev," in Donald R. Kelley, ed., *Soviet Politics in the Brezhnev Era* (New York: Praeger, 1980), p. 66.

factory storehouses. The Liberman reforms also gave factory administrators limited control over production decisions and over wage and bonus funds. In certain cases, managers could reassign or even fire surplus or unproductive workers.

The Liberman reforms sparked lively discussion among Soviet intellectuals, most of whom supported the policies, and they foreshadowed economic changes that would come two decades later under Gorbachev. Although they bolstered productivity in some cases, the conservative reaction after the crushing of the "Prague spring" weakened their backers. In addition, many central planners and administrators feared the impact of decentralization on their careers. They opposed Liberman liberalism and persisted in meddling in economic decisions at regional and local levels. Factory managers, besides trying to cut costs and turn a profit, still had to meet the output targets set by the annual and five-year plans. The latter criteria, they soon came to understand, took priority over profits. Finally, because local factory administrators lacked control over inputs into the productive process, such as delivery of raw materials and availability of skilled labor, they often had to resort to costly measures to meet their demanding output goals. Most enterprises eventually used *tolkachi*, or "expediters"—roving managerial assistants who made deals with other factories and organizations—to ensure timely delivery of materials and to recruit able workers.

As the initial benefits of the Liberman reforms began to fade in the early 1970s, the Brezhnev regime introduced another administrative change: networking related production enterprises plus affiliated supply units and research institutes into "territorial production associations." These organizations endured into the early 1980s and may have facilitated planning and administration. They failed to reverse the faltering economy, however.

Brezhnev also put great stock in technological upgrading and scientific management of the economy, a movement soon dubbed the "scientific-technical revolution." He computerized and streamlined some central-planning procedures. He encouraged introduction of automation and other advanced productive processes, and he urged Soviet administrators to apply proven Western management and accounting techniques. In the early 1970s, Brezhnev contracted with the Italian automobile company Fiat to build a state-of-the-art plant. When completed, it was turned over to Soviet workers and management and soon became the largest producer of vehicles in the U.S.S.R. Yet few other Soviet factories copied its techniques, and the Soviet Union still trailed far behind the West in technological innovation. As long as meeting gross output targets remained the chief indicator of plan fulfillment, Soviet managers resisted introducing expensive and initially disruptive techniques.

Impeded by inherent agricultural problems, erosion of the Liberman reforms, and limited application of the "scientific-technical revolution," the Soviet economy's growth rate slowed during the Brezhnev era. The mounting defense burden contributed to the decline, as did the inefficiencies resulting from planning based on fixed prices that ignored production costs. The lethargic performance of Soviet workers completed the nightmare.

Industrial growth alone had slipped from 5 and 6 percent in the 1950s to 4 and 3 percent in the 1960s. In the 1970s, it sank to 2 and 1 percent, finally reaching zero in the early 1980s. Other factors interacted with these negative trends to engineer economic crisis. Annual growth of the Soviet population and raised expectations elevated consumer demand and put the entire system under stress. Brezhnev's costly foreign policy and the arms race added to the strain, so much so that the leadership had to freeze defense budgets in the late 1970s. In 1971 the Twenty-fourth Party Congress decided to raise investment in the consumer sector. The policy increased the number of available goods in the mid-1970s, but demand soon outpaced supply again. Party leaders recognized that failure to meet rising consumer desires could mean serious consequences for the regime's political stability.

The widening gap between personal incomes and available goods and services catalyzed recurring shortages, frustration, corruption, and rising free prices in collective-farm markets. It also nurtured a system of semilegal and black-market operations known as the "second economy," which may have accounted for as much as a fourth of economic activity in Brezhnev's Soviet Union. Those active in this underground realm moonlighted in afterwork jobs, often providing repair and consumer services for rubles or goods and bribing or bartering with shopkeepers for scarce products and decent-quality items. They filched desirable materials, produce, or goods from factories and stores, and sold or traded them at exorbitant prices. Some daring entrepreneurs used government equipment, including automobiles, for private purposes and organized clandestine workshops to produce consumer items for private profit. They oiled their way with cash into spacious apartments, finer restaurants, prime vacation spots, and elite schools and universities. Many institutions and factories resorted to the "second economy" to meet their plant quotas. Most citizens yielded to the seduction of this shadowy underworld as well. This seedy aspect of Soviet society prompted growing cynicism and alienation, as this widely circulated joke shows:

> "I think," Ivan comments to Sasha, "that we have the richest country in the world."
> "Why?" asks Sasha.
> "Because for nearly sixty years everyone has been stealing from the state and there's still something left to steal."

In one area, space exploration, the Soviet economy chalked up consistent successes during the Brezhnev era. Although marred by a few accidents and setbacks (hidden until Gorbachev's *glasnost'* of the late 1980s), the space program produced a string of spectacular flights and a manned orbiting space station that inspired pride in Soviet hearts. Soviet scientists and cosmonauts made key contributions, particularly in their prolonged, weightless sojourns in the outer atmosphere.

External trade also burgeoned, with major gains in exchanges with the West. The Soviet economy moved far from its autarchic position under Stalin and insinuated itself into the world economy. Yet much of its commercial progress came from arms sales to the Third World and from "colonial" trade—shipping raw materials such as oil, natural gas, and timber in return for Western technology and products. Despite the size of the economy and some achievements, Brezhnev would leave a massive economic quagmire to his successors.

The Changing Soviet Citizen

Soviet adults of the Brezhnev years differed markedly from preceding generations. For the first time since the founding of the Kievan state a millennium earlier, they were not predominantly peasants, with traditional rural attitudes and values. Almost two out of three persons now lived in cities. Indeed, location partly determined prestige and status. Those living in Moscow or Leningrad, for example, enjoyed the highest standing. An individual holding a residence permit for either of these cities became a sought-after marriage partner. Dwelling in a remaining major city of the Russian Republic or in another republic capital earned one the next most preferred status. Residence in smaller cities and towns ranked somewhat lower; country living, lowest of all.

Citizens had better education and more skills than ever before. In 1981 over 10 percent of the employed Soviet population possessed a higher education, compared to 3 percent in 1959; more than 70 percent had completed secondary school, against 40 percent in 1959.[4] Most adults held jobs requiring more stringent qualifications than those at which their parents had worked, and they wanted their children to enjoy even better positions.

Brezhnev's subjects also knew more about the outside world than any previous generation had. They drew not only on widely distributed Soviet publications but on broadcasts by the BBC and the Voice of America and on word-of-mouth information spread by returning Soviet travelers Soviet visitors to the West and Western cultural and educational exchanges in the U.S.S.R. provided Soviet intellectuals insights into external events and trends. Often hazy on details, a majority of citizens in the

---

[4]Basile Kerblay, *Modern Soviet Society* (New York: Random House, 1983), p. 128.

U.S.S.R. nevertheless knew that their standard of living ranked below that of the capitalist West. Most galling, they realized that even their socialist comrades in Eastern Europe were better off than they. Many intellectuals also envied the freedom of expression that their compatriots in the West enjoyed.

Equally important, people under the age of fifty recalled World War II only dimly, and those under forty-five had had no direct experience with Stalinism. An aging leadership groomed in the Stalin era thus ruled a predominantly post-Stalin population. The younger and older generations possessed not only different life histories but increasingly divergent attitudes and outlooks. Old-timers felt comfortable with Brezhnev's conservatism, whereas youths and young adults privately expressed a desire for change.

Like Khrushchev, his successors sought to tap the talents and ideas of the increasingly educated citizenry. Although they did not forge a participatory system, they maintained a quasilegal society, without open terror. People felt free to make suggestions and recommend minor innovations, particularly in the workplace. The Brezhnev regime did not tolerate criticism of the system's essentials and kept a tight check on the media, on access to economic advancement, and on the right to travel and correspond outside the country. Nevertheless, as long as individuals refrained from anti-Soviet and anti-Party positions and left political authority to the officials, they could expect the government to respect their ideas, and they could contribute to institutional and social life. Senior specialists, in particular, could offer data and advice to Party and government leaders. Because of its reliance on legal norms and its emphasis on stability, the Brezhnevian system, although hardly a civic society, attracted the support of some citizens. Inadvertently, the encouragement of expertise input may also have stimulated the educated stratum's desire for change.

As ideology eroded and the vision of a future communist society faded, pragmatism predominated. What counted was what worked. The search for effective solutions led to subconscious, sometimes open, questioning of traditional methods. Simultaneously, as the economy faltered, as foreign and defense policy grew more costly and unwieldy and as social problems deepened, thoughtful individuals concluded that the system itself needed change.

In one area, the Brezhnev regime reluctantly permitted a spontaneous citizens' movement to emerge. The drive to industrialize from the 1880s into the 1960s had proceeded apace without regard to its despoiling of the environment. Industrialization polluted air and water and wasted natural resources. As early as 1957, a major nuclear disaster struck at a plutonium plant near Chelyabinsk in the Ural Mountains. Nuclear wastes exploded, releasing a radioactive cloud over a large area.

The accident caused radiation sickness in hundreds of people and forced the resettlement of more than ten thousand citizens. The government suppressed news of the tragedy. In the late 1960s, an accident at a biological weapons factory in the Urals blanketed the region with fatal germs, and an unknown number of people died. This disaster was also kept secret. When alarming rumors later spread in the West, the Soviet government denied them.

Concurrently, scientists and local citizens discovered that pulp and chemical factories had polluted Lake Baikal in Siberia, the world's deepest lake and the habitat of unique plants and fish. Distraught observers gained the attention of several prominent Soviet writers and soon mounted a widespread, well-publicized campaign to clean up the lake. The regime tolerated this effort, although the bureaucrats and economic administrators in charge of the offending factories resisted it for fifteen years. Only in the Gorbachev era would the pollution of Lake Baikal finally stop. A cadre of journalists, scientists, writers, and local citizens launched a similar campaign to block a proposed diversion of water from Siberian rivers to Central Asia. The group had little success at first. Under Gorbachev, however, the diversion scheme would be dropped. Such efforts showed intellectuals and other citizens that they could influence policy in areas of minor importance to the leadership. Emboldened, they considered change in more sensitive spheres.

Not all the shifting attitudes and values of the Brezhnev era had positive effects. Many Soviet citizens felt apathetic about environmental, social, and moral issues. They submitted to authoritarian, bureaucratic governance, grumbling about it but doing nothing. With their personal and consumerist values, they supported the "second economy" and the slack atmosphere of most workplaces. Used to petty corruption and bribery, they had grown cynical and present-oriented. A few expressed the hope that their children would see the fruits of socialism, but the average person simply lived from day to day. Disillusioned by Khrushchev's failed promises, most Soviet citizens had little respect for the system, its leaders, or the bureaucrats who ran their lives. Some had taken pride in the Soviet victory in World War II and their country's postwar growth, but most concerned themselves more with family, friends, and personal pursuits such as hobbies, sports, reading, music, and for city dwellers, excursions into the countryside.

Burgeoning social problems only heightened the overall sense of alienation. Although drugs circulated primarily in the southern regions of the U.S.S.R. and there on a limited basis, alcoholism pervaded Soviet life. Over 10 percent of adults were alcoholics, and the U.S.S.R. registered the highest death rate from alcohol poisoning in the world. Drunks committed a majority of crimes, including murder, rape, assault, and robbery. Alcohol fostered wife and child abuse, and drinking became the single

Assessments of the Brezhnev years have taken on added significance as scholars
seek to explain what followed. For instance, how do we account for the torrent of reformism under Gorbachev if, as some Western writers claimed in the early 1980s, the
Soviet system was incapable of major change? How can we explain the rise of someone like Gorbachev himself: a university-trained lawyer with a professional spouse and
a daughter and son-in-law turned medical doctors? Or, still later, how must we understand the implosion of the empire in 1990–1991 except as society's liberation from
the state despite the best intentions of top-down renovators such as Gorbachev?

Major studies of Soviet politics on the eve of the Gorbachev era emphasized the
stability and coherence of the system. In the early 1980s, Robert Daniels, a historian
of Russian life, wrote that "all of the competing interests in the Soviet system are
parts of one vast bureaucratic structure, subject to the dictates of Communist Party
leadership" (*Russia: The Roots of Confrontation,* 1983). Daniels's skepticism toward
the idea of impending change found support in Seweryn Bialer's *The Soviet Paradox:
External Expansion, Internal Decline* (1986). Although Bialer saw a "crisis of effectiveness" in the U.S.S.R. by 1986, he discounted any likelihood of social or political
disintegration. Quite the contrary: he theorized that the sources of stability ran wide
and deep, including a high-profile coercive apparatus and an economy strong enough
to appease the needs of key players (such as the military-industrial complex) but corrupt enough to satisfy the material aspirations of ordinary citizens. Above all Bialer
found an odd overlap of class origins of upper and lower strata. As one consequence
of the 1930s purges, he explained, the Soviet leadership became "peasantized" as
new men from the rural classes were placed in positions of power. Forty years later,
many of them still held those positions. Thus, Bialer asserted, "the Soviet Union is
one of the few societies where the cultures of the mass and elite are almost insepara-
ble."

These studies focused on the state as the engine of Soviet life. To the extent that
a crisis loomed, such historians placed it within the system itself, a kind of arte-
riosclerosis of a once mighty and vibrant body politic. Bialer's thesis represented the
dominant view: for decades the political heights commanded the socioeconomic base.
In other words, politics determined society rather than the other way around, as Marx
had averred. Virtually no one at the dawn of *perestroika* and *glasnost* considered the
possibility of a movement from below, or of a society increasingly independent of the
state's values, even under Brezhnev.

Yet precisely that possibility burst into view by the end of the 1980s. Best articulated by Moshe Lewin in *The Gorbachev Phenomenon* (1988), a fresh interpretation of
the evolution of Soviet society emerged. This view characterized Brezhnev's Russia as
an urban culture brimming with people in search of personal freedom and self-reliance.
While Brezhnev slept, unofficial and informal social networks proliferated to safeguard
individual rights against an overweening government. As one example, dozens if not
hundreds of environmentally conscious groups coalesced to express "horror and disgust at the ecological disasters of the state's relentless focus on massive industrial
projects." The state may have been stagnant, Lewin closed, but society definitely was
not.

Whereas Lewin cast his net over the whole society, Richard Stites scrutinized
one of its little-studied components, mass culture (*Soviet Popular Culture,* 1992).
Much of that culture reflected a traditional bent, he noted—war novels, cheap movies,
nostalgia for yesteryear—yet other areas, such as jazz and disco music, revealed a

Western, innovative direction. Even under Brezhnev, Soviet hippies "appeared wearing jeans, bell bottoms, peace medalions [and] mini-skirts." Culture wars broke out between the purveyors of official entertainment and the rockers, a clash that recapitulated similar Western conflicts of the 1950s. Out of an urban milieu—some of it right under Brezhnev's nose—emerged elements not tied to the establishment, notably a younger generation seeking comfort in the "exotic appeals of the outside world," Stites concluded.

The mania of Soviet youth for rock music provided the theme of *Red and Hot* (1983) by S. Frederick Starr. Almost without warning, Moscow and Leningrad were "hit by the sounds of the Beatles, the Rolling Stones, Stevie Wonder and the Shadows." The reaction of outraged officials was predictable: "Ban it!" But as often happens when the custodians of approved taste try to stamp out popular appetites, censorship failed miserably. By 1980 the gerontocracy in the Kremlin looked out at the first "twentysomethings" in Soviet history that "fully shared" the pop culture of America and Europe.

In a later essay, Starr offered a tantalizing explanation of the dissonance and crosscurrents swirling across the Brezhnevian landscape of the 1970s ("The Road to Reform," in *Chronicle of a Revolution,* Abraham Brumberg, ed., 1990). To be sure, he argued, the system was top heavy, yet it was not frozen. The "quixotic" Brezhnev resembled Nicholas I (1825–1855), the outwardly reactionary tsar who behind the scenes presided over "a series of experimental reforms which paved the way for gigantic changes following his death." Thus, while tenaciously clinging to the command-administrative system, Brezhnev quietly encouraged subordinates to decentralize decision making to individual factories and promoted "the ideal of local management as a counterweight to centralized ministerial rule." Amazingly, Starr concluded, after a decade in office, Brezhnev in 1977 flirted with the notion of multicandidate elections to Party offices. His idea foreshadowed Gorbachev's move twelve years later.

Revisionist views of Brezhnev help to clarify the interaction of state and society as a foundation of Soviet history. They also raise important questions not only about the 1970s but the entire sweep of the post-Stalinist decades. We ask again: what source underlay the crisis threatening the Soviet system on the eve of the Gorbachev era? Was it the basic institutions of the party-state and the command economy, or the evolution of a society struggling to break free of state tutelage? The question looms larger than any one chapter on twentieth-century Russia, for the answer hinges on a conception of history in general. Which is more fundamental in human development, politics or society? Which better explains the Soviet experience, a totalitarian model that takes Leninist politics at its word, or one that treats Communist Russia as a variant of universal modernity, however deformed? Is it insightful or naive to see Soviet social movements as evidence of an incipient "pluralism" somehow analogous to the evolution of other industrialized countries free of a formalized ideology? As the Gorbachev years unfolded, the debate between these two schools intensified.

most-cited reason for divorce. Drunkenness led to absenteeism as well as poor performance and job accidents. Alcoholism had posed a serious problem in tsarist times, but the Bolsheviks had failed to address it. After 1917 Soviet officials refused to recognize alcoholism as a disease, and because state revenues depended in part on the sale of vodka, the regime made no effort to curtail drinking. The government would not confront the epidemic until the Gorbachev era.

Public health also declined under Brezhnev. Particularly striking, life expectancy for men dropped, while the infant mortality rate climbed. Alcoholism probably contributed to both trends, causing premature death among males and multiplying the number of alcoholic mothers. The declining percentage of the Soviet budget allocated to health care and the failure to keep up with new medical techniques and equipment also played a role.

The Brezhnev era witnessed jumps in crime, poverty, and divorce as well. Theft of state property, violence, and juvenile delinquency (called hooliganism) all skyrocketed in the 1970s and 1980s. Because Soviet ideology argued that crime sprang from antisocial attitudes and behavior inculcated in the bourgeois era, officials concealed crime statistics and failed to attack the socioeconomic roots of lawlessness. Yet some Soviet sociologists admitted that more than sixty years after the socialist revolution, the state had not yet created the "new socialist person" and could not reasonably blame its predicament on "bourgeois remnants" of the past. Poverty and crime undoubtedly had links, but Soviet ideology also stipulated that want could not exist under socialism. Data are sketchy, but some observers estimate that as much as one-fifth of the Soviet population in the 1970s lived at a minimal subsistence level, despite improvements in income, housing, food, and clothing since Stalin's day.

Rising divorce rates in these years in part reflected the shifting status of women, who shared in the social and attitudinal changes under Brezhnev. Women increasingly made independent choices about marriage, divorce, family size, and career. More women than ever lived in cities in the 1970s. Better educated than before, they also enjoyed a higher standard of living. Although time narrowed the gap in numbers between men and women caused by the decimations of World War II, women still constituted almost 54 percent of the population by the late 1970s. For rural women as well, life improved in the Brezhnev years. Whereas only 21 percent of peasant women had completed high school in 1959, that figure had climbed to 48 percent by 1970. Urban women still obtained more education, however; 75 percent possessed a high school diploma in 1970. Women in the countryside enjoyed better clothing, housing, and food than their rural forebears, but lived not nearly as comfortably as female city dwellers.

Under Brezhnev, women's participation in the work force continued to surge. In the 1980s, almost 100 percent of non-Asian women of working age were either students or jobholders, compared to about 75 percent in 1939. Women made up 51 percent of employed citizens. In some fields, women predominated, accounting for the following shares of all employees:

Retailing—83 percent
Health care and other social services—82 percent
Physicians—80 percent
Educators—75 percent
Agriculture—70 percent
Engineers—50 percent

Yet most positions in these specialities (including medicine) paid little, and many afforded low status. Moreover, the top jobs—heads of hospitals and research labs, school principals, department store managers—

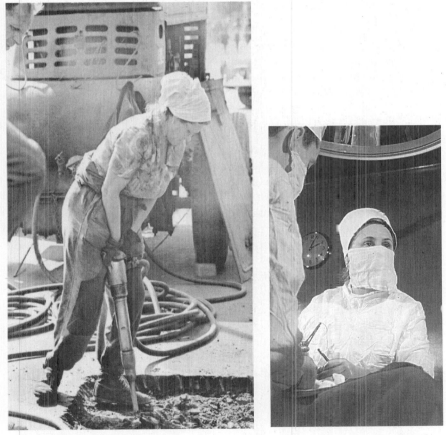

Soviet Women at Work A capable construction worker and a skilled surgeon reflect the diversity of women's roles in the U S S.R.'s labor force.

were usually filled by men. To illustrate, although women were well represented in higher educational posts, a mere 1.5 percent of the members of the country's most prestigious scholarly body, the Academy of Sciences, was female. Few women headed state or collective farms, and a slim 1 percent of tractor drivers were women. Overall, women earned only 73 percent of the average male wage. Some women rose to manage factories, institutes, and other Soviet organizations, but very few held senior positions in the economic and political power structure. Only one-quarter of Party members and 4 percent of Central Committee members were female. For a time in the 1970s, the top-ranking woman in the Soviet government was a deputy minister of higher education.

The underrepresentation of women in significant jobs partly reflected traditional patriarchal beliefs about women's roles and work. It also stemmed from the onerous "double burden" that women still bore: combining full-time employment with up to thirty hours a week of domestic responsibilities, including shopping, cooking, cleaning, washing, and caring for children. As one working mother expressed her plight,

> You fly out of work round the shops, buy as much food as you
> can so you won't have to go again tomorrow, get home from the
> shops as fast as you can. At home you've got to cook supper and
> prepare tomorrow's lunch, your daughter's coming out with all
> kinds of questions which you haven't got time to answer. . . .
> You go on putting up with it all and taking your "patience" out
> on your husband or your child.[5]

Soviet husbands, with few exceptions, offered little assistance at home. Rural women shouldered a "triple burden": laboring on the collective farm, tending the family's private plot, and running a home.

In numerous respects, women continued to suffer from manifestations of long-term oppression: alcoholic and often abusive husbands; the absence of sex education, contraceptive devices, and decent gynecological services; crowded and humiliating conditions at abortion clinics; inadequate child-care facilities; shortages of household products and consumer services; discrimination against single parenthood; and dangerous working conditions in the textile and construction industries. (A 1981 law finally forbade employment of women in more than four hundred hazardous jobs.)

Policy changes during the Brezhnev epoch had contradictory impacts on women's lives. In 1955 under Khrushchev, Stalin's 1936 prohibition of abortion was repealed. By the late 1970s, the number of abortions annually approached two times the number of live births. Be-

---

[5]Quoted in Linda Edmondson, ed., *Women and Society in the Soviet Union* (Cambridge: Cambridge Univ. Press, 1992), p. 196.

cause of inadequate understanding of contraception and the shortage and poor quality of birth-control devices, many Soviet women had three to five abortions, some as many as a dozen. Although access to abortion permitted women some control over reproduction and family size, many found the experience painful and upsetting and would have preferred to rely on modern contraceptive techniques. In 1958 divorce was also made easier, and the rate climbed until almost half of Soviet marriages failed in the 1980s. Women, increasingly unwilling to stay in abusive or unsatisfactory marriages, initiated 70 percent of all divorces. The state also took measures to facilitate paternity suits and to force extramarital fathers and divorced husbands to accept financial responsibility for their children.

On the other hand, in the mid-1970s, the Brezhnev regime launched a pronatalist campaign that glorified family stability, denounced divorce, and reinforced stereotypical attitudes about women's nurturing role. As one leading educator, Vera Khripkova, argued, "I am convinced that if we succeed in instilling femininity and gentleness in girls from an early age, if we can raise boys to be genuine knights, then society will benefit and the family will grow stronger."[6] The Soviet media urged early marriage and lauded the virtues of family life. In 1981 the government increased maternity benefits; women were entitled to eighteen months of partially paid leave before and after childbirth and three years' unpaid leave for child rearing without losing their positions and seniority. Soviet leaders apparently pursued profamily policies for two reasons: (1) to support and advance their general goal of stability in Soviet society and (2) to raise the birthrate among the non-Asian population, an issue examined below. These initiatives cast women in a traditional role and exalted their maternal function at the expense of their social, economic and political emancipation. Positive role models, such as the Soviet cosmonaut Valentina Tereshkova, shone, but the government persecuted active feminists. As one example, the regime harassed and finally forced into exile Tatiana Mamonova, the editor of *Women and Russia: An Almanac*, a short-lived underground journal espousing women's rights.

Non-Russians: The Struggle for Identity

The Brezhnev years saw a marked shift in the composition of the Soviet population. Overall, the proportion of Slavs declined, and the percentage of Central Asians rose. The change derived from differential fertility rates, as the following table reflects:

---

[6]Quoted in Susan Bridger, *Women in the Soviet Countryside* (Cambridge: Cambridge Univ. Press, 1987), p. 224.

Annual Rate of Population Growth (Percent)		
	1959–1970	*1970–1979*
Russians	1.1	0.7
Ukrainians	0.8	0.4
Belarusians	1.2	0.5
Uzbeks	3.9	3.4
Kazakhs	3.1	2.4
Tadzhiks	3.9	3.4
Turkmen	3.9	3.2
Kyrgyz	3.7	3.1

Although rates of increase for Central Asians slipped marginally through 1979, their lead over the Slavs widened. Between 1959 and 1979, the Central Asians grew from about 6 percent of the total population to 10 percent.[7] The proliferating Azerbaijani and Tatar peoples boosted the percentage of non-Russians further and also added to the total number of Muslims living in the U.S.S.R. As it became clear that the Slavic (and Baltic) peoples' population would soon level off, Soviet demographers and officials took alarm. By the end of the century, they warned, one-third of youngsters entering the work force and the army would be non-Russians, many of whom would speak and read Russian poorly. Moreover, the emerging generation of laborers would live predominantly in Soviet Central Asia and the Caucasus, far from the existing manufacturing centers. Analysts also feared that demographic change would erode the Slavs' domination of political and economic life, a concern that prompted the pronatalist policies described earlier.

Nevertheless, in their overall nationality policy, Stalin's successors loosened the monolithic centralization and toned down the Great Russian patriotism associated with Stalinism. The Party program adopted in 1961 reaffirmed the ambivalent goals of Lenin's policy on minorities, calling for both the flourishing of ethnic culture and the gradual merging of all national groups into a common Soviet identity. After coming to power, Brezhnev reassured non-Russians that neither the Party nor the state would force convergence. By the 1970s, discussion of a single, unified ethnicity and references to Russians as the "elder brothers" of the Soviet peoples disappeared. Taking advantage of the regime's policy of benign tolerance, minority groups gained some autonomy and reinvigorated their national consciousness in the Brezhnev era.

---

[7]Figures from Ralph S. Clem, "The Ethnic Factor in Contemporary Soviet Society," in M. P. Sacks and J. G. Pankhurst, eds., *Understanding Soviet Society* (Boston: Unwin Hyman, 1988), pp. 4–5.

Indigenous Culture Preserved An Islamic wedding ceremony in the Soviet Central Asian republic of Uzbekistan reflects the Communist government's policy of tolerating local traditions.

Besides state policy, urbanization, higher education, and access to information encouraged nationalism and fired aspirations for self-government among the non-Russian peoples. Although these developments exerted less impact on the traditional and still heavily rural Central Asian communities, they affected all ethnic groups to some degree. In the non-Russian regions, these modernizations exposed people to their national traditions, history, and culture. Educated city dwellers, to a far greater extent than illiterate peasants, shared knowledge about and belief in their group's unique identity and past. National consciousness awakened or intensified, and in some areas, intellectuals formed study circles or community associations focused on national themes.

Study of indigenous language and literature also enlivened nationalist sentiments in this period. Although most non-Russians learned Russian, some fluently, the dominant languages of each republic flourished. Literary works and historical treatises were increasingly published in the native language, and folk tales, songs, and ethnic performances blossomed. In an especially interesting case, the Estonians used their long tradition of mass choral singing to foster national solidarity, group cohesion, and emotional patriotism. At one songfest in the 1980s, almost a third of the Estonian population participated. In 1978 a government proposal to make Russian as well as Georgian an official language of the

Georgian Republic provoked street protests and demonstrations in Soviet Georgia until the idea was dropped.

Resentment over perceived economic exploitation by the central government also propelled the rise of nationalism. Whether and how much Moscow drained the economies of the non-Russian regions is a highly controversial and probably insoluble question, but almost all the ethnic groups believed that the central government was taking advantage of them. The Baltic peoples, more developed economically and better off than the rest of the country, nevertheless complained about Russian exploitation. Even many Central Asians, who had benefited from Soviet aid and investment, viewed themselves as colonial victims of the commissars in Moscow. Ukrainian nationalist Ivan Dzyuba argued in his underground publication *Internationalism or Russification?* that Russians were profiting from the Ukrainian economy as well as forcing Russian culture on the Ukrainian people. Indeed, not only intellectual nationalists such as Dzyuba but orthodox national Party leaders as well clamored for ever larger funds and investment for their regions. Petr Shelest, the leading Ukrainian Communist in the 1960s, decried the government's policy of investing heavily in Siberia. Ukraine, he argued, could guarantee higher returns for the national economy. Local non-Russian Communist leaders labored to retain resources in their region and to build up local economies. Tension between Moscow and the non-Russian areas over the dispersal of economic benefits thus heightened local nationalism and led Brezhnev and his colleagues to espouse an overarching Soviet patriotism.

The minorities' resentment of the center's tight political control and of the Slavs' domination of top posts added fuel to the fire. In 1981 only a handful of the Red Army's generals and colonels came from non-Russian lands. Less than 20 percent of the Party Central Committee were non-Slavs, although the latter made up more than 25 percent of the population. Only one in ten Party secretaries was non-Slav, and the Politburo contained only token non-Slav representatives. This imbalance provoked underground mutterings about a return to Slavic or Russian imperialism reminiscent of tsarist times.

Although Soviet leaders relied on indirect rule through local elites in the republics and regions, wherever possible they sought to reinforce their control by putting Slavs second in command to local officials. Thus the Party first secretary would be a native; the second secretary, a Slav. This approach was thought to promote stability and continuity, but when combined with "trust in cadres," it led to entrenched cliques running their areas as fiefdoms and facilitated corruption and petty tyranny. Moscow found it difficult to hold local leaders accountable, to get accurate information from them, or finally to oust them. The regional satrapies, clinging to their desire for autonomy, nursed their resentment of interference from a central government dominated by Slavs.

Friction between Moscow and the republics erupted twice during the

Brezhnev era. In 1972, amid charges of widespread and blatant corruption, the central Party purged Georgian Communist leaders, who had held power for nineteen years. The new Georgian first secretary was Edvard Shevardnadze, later Gorbachev's foreign minister and after 1992 head of an independent Georgia. In Ukraine, local boss Shelest, in office for nine years, was also ejected in 1972, on the ground that he had encouraged Ukrainian nationalism. In fact, he had increased the size of the Ukrainian Party by 50 percent and, as we saw, had championed Ukraine's economic rights.

In the Baltic provinces, the Moldavian Republic, eastern Ukraine, and Kazakhstan, local nationalities had further cause to complain. In the several decades since World War II, large numbers of Russians had moved to these regions, mostly as factory or agricultural workers. In Latvia and Kazakhstan, as a result, Russians totaled nearly 50 percent of the population by the early 1980s. These substantial Russian minorities competed with the indigenous population for jobs, housing, and services. Policy disputes also erupted over whether schooling should be conducted in Russian or the local language and whether resources should go to Russian or non-Russian cultural activities. These clashes further stoked the fires of local nationalism.

Religion: Conformity, Revival, Opposition

Whereas the Brezhnev government had a clear plan for maintaining its grasp on political power throughout the U.S.S.R., it exhibited confused policies toward the Soviet Union's various religious groups. The situation of the Jews presented an endemic problem. Wartime losses reduced their number from almost 5 million to less than 2.5 million. Jews lacked their own territory, except for the remote and underdeveloped autonomous region of Biro-Bidjan in the Soviet Far East. Those practicing Judaism faced governmental persecution. The dearth of synagogues, pressures against rabbinical training, and obstacles to obtaining religious materials and preparing kosher food only worsened matters for them. At the same time, Jews were strongly represented in higher education, science, the professions, and cultural life. In the 1970s, however, as the number of university-trained people soared and the competition for better-paying jobs intensified, so did discrimination against Jews in employment and university admissions. Some thought that universities applied quotas to Jewish student applicants and faculty positions, a throwback to tsarist practice. As a result, numerous Jews decided to emigrate to Israel, the United States, and Western Europe.

The Brezhnev regime waffled on the emigration issue. At times, as in the early 1970s and again in 1979, it permitted tens of thousands of Jews to leave. The government apparently had decided that it made sense to rid the country of dissatisfied citizens and potential troublemakers. In other years, however, Soviet officials grew resentful of U.S. pressure for unrestricted emigration and worried over the loss of educated and skilled citizens. The government then reduced the outflow of Jews to a trickle. As more and more Jews sought to escape the Soviet Union, and as public criticism of constraint mounted in the West, the emigration question took on political overtones. Jews who applied to emigrate often found themselves dismissed from their jobs, evicted from their apartments, and subjected to petty harassment. Those whose applications were delayed or denied became known as "refuseniks," and many joined the strengthening dissident movement.

As for the chief religions in the U.S.S.R., their history contains a startling paradox. Religious belief and practice endured despite seventy years of Marxist-Leninist atheism, antireligion propaganda, officially sponsored persecution, and powerful pressures for modernization and secularization. Some evidence even suggests that under Brezhnev a considerable religious upsurge took place, and more than 100 million people counted themselves as believers in Christianity or Islam by the early 1980s.

The Brezhnev Politburo soon abandoned Khrushchev's virulent, ineffective campaign against religion, yet the government allowed only a small number of churches to reopen. The majority of the hierarchy and clergy of the chief religions, cowed by the Khrushchevian whirlwind, continued to accept Party and state domination. Orthodox Patriarch Alexei, who had acquiesced in the 1961 decree undercutting the authority of priests in their own parishes, died in 1971. After thirteen months of preparation and arm-twisting, the government permitted convocation of a church council, at which critics of church-state relations had no voice and a compliant new patriarch, Pimen, was elected. To bolster Pimen's standing, the authorities approved a limited printing of Bibles and continuation of the official Orthodox *Journal of the Moscow Patriarchate*. They also encouraged church officials to form ties with world religious institutions, such as the World Council of Churches. Orthodox dignitaries, impressive in their full beards, tall hats, and black robes, dutifully testified abroad that the practice of religion was freely permitted in the Soviet Union. They lent support as well to Soviet peace and disarmament campaigns at international gatherings. Nevertheless, by the early 1970s, newly formed religious groups condemned state interference in spiritual life and called for revived, independent churches. Both the conformist hierarchs of the various churches and the Soviet authorities hastened to suppress this opposition.

The dissenting movement in Russian Orthodoxy arose in part as a rejection of the church leadership's timidity in the face of Khrushchev's repressive policies. It also represented a quest for new spiritual and intellectual guideposts, as individuals grew disillusioned with Marxism-

Leninism. This disenchantment emerged among both churchmen and laity. In 1964 and 1965 two courageous priests, fathers Nikolai Eshliman and Gleb Yakunin, published letters demanding respect for the Soviet Constitution's guarantee of the church's right to freedom from state interference. Archbishop Hermogen and several bishops then took up their argument and appealed to then Patriarch Alexei for convocation of a church council to reconsider the 1961 reform. Alexei responded by removing the priests from their parishes and forcing Hermogen's retirement to a monastery. Criticism persisted, however, as outspoken priests such as Vsevolod Shpiller and Dmitri Dudko reaffirmed the right to freedom of worship to the crowds that thronged their services. Dissenters within the church smuggled underground materials to the West, where agitation about the infringement of believers' rights put Soviet spokesmen on the defensive

The religious opposition also found support outside the church. As we shall see, a wide range of critics of the Soviet regime emerged in the late 1960s and 1970s. Two currents among the dissident movement took up the cause of freedom of religion. Intellectuals and writers who had become devout adherents to the Orthodox faith comprised one wave. These critics struggled as lay persons to return the church to its pure Slavic nature undefiled by Soviet distortions. The reformers included scientist Lev Regelson and writers Anatoli Levitin and Alexander Solzhenitsyn; authorities forced the two authors into exile abroad in 1974, and they arrested and tried Regelson in 1980. Although lay Orthodox dissenters voiced a range of theological and political points of view, they represented a new generation of highly educated and articulate believers who wanted to energize the church. Most Orthodox intellectuals were also Russophiles, although their politics ranged from liberal to reactionary. Dissenting churchmen received additional backing from secular defenders of human rights, the predominant group within the dissident movement as a whole. These supporters argued for freedom of religion in general, assisted individual religious oppositionists, and in 1976 helped to form the interdenominational Committee for the Defense of Believers' Rights.

Orthodox dissent found further expression through the ongoing activities of unregistered or underground parishes, whose members recognized neither a church hierarchy nor the Soviet authorities. In Soviet Central Asia, a thin layer of official clergy and a small number of acknowledged mosques masked a widespread, hidden practice of Islam. Thousands of illegal mosques and mullahs operated on behalf of some 40 million believers. In west Ukraine the Uniate church, banned by Stalin in 1946, similarly survived underground until restored to legality in the Gorbachev era. It had close links with growing Ukrainian nationalism. Meanwhile, in Lithuania, local Party bosses and church prelates looked the other way while oppositionists published the quarterly

Chronicle of the Lithuanian Catholic Church, which reported abuses and backed religious rights. These critics also supported Lithuanian nationalism. Thus proponents of freedom stymied government efforts to suppress religious opposition through political control of the official religious institutions and through arrests and persecution. Defenders of religious liberty formed part of a spreading network of regime critics, a web that included non-Russian nationalists and dissident intellectuals as well.

The Dissident Movement

During the twenty-year stretch from the mid-1960s to the mid-1980s, a courageous group of Russian and non-Russian intellectuals struggled to defend their creative and civil rights. The dissident movement arose partly out of frustration with the oscillations of cultural and intellectual policy that followed de-Stalinization and the initial thaw in the mid-1950s. A decade later, whiplashed by alternating government repression and toleration, a dedicated core gathered to plead the cause of human rights in the U.S.S.R. The rising level of sophistication and expectations along with increased contact with Western ideas and individual Western artists, scientists, and scholars after 1958 intensified the climate of dissent. Brezhnev's armed intervention in Czechoslovakia in August 1968 galvanized the fledgling movement.

Although the secret police had harassed a few cultural figures in the early 1960s, the arrest and trial of Sinyavsky and Daniel in late 1965–early 1966 marked the dramatic start of a long clash between the regime and its intellectual critics. The trial and convictions ignited a furor among the educated elite, evoked public protests, and prompted formation of the first informal groups committed to protecting the right of free expression. Concurrently, the government acted to suppress nationalism in Ukraine, arresting twenty Ukrainian intellectuals in late 1965. Sixty-two prominent writers petitioned the Twenty-third Party Congress, which met in spring 1966, for artistic freedom. The Congress ignored them, and in a separate speech, Brezhnev threw down the guantlet.

> Unfortunately, one also encounters those tradesmen in the arts who, instead of helping the people, select as their specialty the denigration of our system and slanders against our heroic people. . . . The Soviet people cannot overlook the disgraceful activity of such individuals. They treat them as they deserve.[8]

---

[8]Leo Gruliow, ed., *Current Soviet Policies,* vol. 5, p. 23.

Writers in the Dock Dissident authors Sinyavsky and Daniel at their 1966 trial for purveying anti-Soviet views in their works.

Most 1960s dissidents still believed in socialism and made their case on moral and cultural, not political, grounds. They wanted the system to observe the guarantees of the UN charter and the Soviet Constitution and to live up to the democratic promises of socialism. In short, they sought to reform the regime, not to overthrow it. After the Sinyavsky-Daniel trial, as the government tightened cultural controls, intellectuals increasingly resorted to *samizdat*, or self-publication. In manuscript form, they circulated stories, articles, poems, and plays that the censors would not permit in the government press. In some cases, writers sent works abroad for publication, a move that infuriated Brezhnev's cultural commissars.

In the late 1960s, the opposition organized into committees for the defense of human rights, and the renowned physicist Andrei Sakharov joined the movement. Sakharov had withdrawn from work on nuclear weapons after growing disenchanted with the regime's goals and foreign policy. In 1975, after the Soviet government approved the Helsinki Accords, a clause of which guaranteed civil liberties to citizens of the signatory countries, the dissidents set up Helsinki Watch committees to document and publicize regime infringements on human rights. An underground journal, *The Chronicle of Current Events*, regularly denounced state abuse of civil freedoms.

The human rights activists also took up the cause of religious dissenters, as we have seen, and of nationalist oppositionists. *The Ukrainian Herald*, an illegal publication similar to *The Chronicle*, soon emerged in

Ukraine. Human rights advocates protested the persecution of Ukrainian nationalists Ivan Dzyuba and Viacheslav Chernovil, along with Georgian writer Zviad Gamsakhurdia (who would rule Georgia autocratically for a brief period in 1991–1992). Former Soviet general Peter Grigorenko supported the efforts of the Crimean Tatar community, exiled to Central Asia in 1944, to return to their homeland on the Crimean peninsula. Finally, in the 1970s the dissident movement defended the right of Soviet Jews to emigrate. Prominent refuseniks such as Yuri Orlov and Anatoli Shcharansky cooperated with human rights leaders to advance this freedom.

The government countered the campaign for human rights with a harsh program of harassment. It expelled dissidents from jobs and housing, arrested them, exiled them at home and abroad, imprisoned them, and confined them in mental hospitals. Solzhenitsyn was forced from the Writers' Union in 1969 and forbidden to accept the Nobel Prize in literature in 1971. Three years later, after he published abroad *The Gulag Archipelago,* a monumental condemnation of the labor camps, the regime deported him. Other talented writers who chose or were compelled to leave included Joseph Brodsky, Vasily Aksyonov, and Vladimir Voinovich. Among others who emigrated because they could not pursue their artistic goals were ballet stars Natalia Makarova and Mikhail Baryshnikov, musician Mstislav Rostropovich, film director Andrei Tarkovsky, and chess champion Boris Spassky. Sakharov was exiled to Gorky in 1980 to stifle his contacts with Western scientists and journalists.

The invasion of Czechoslovakia disillusioned a number of dissidents toward the prospect of reforming Soviet socialism. During the 1970s, an array of nonsocialist ideologies emerged among the oppositionists, ranging from the conservative religious Slavophilism of Solzhenitsyn to the democratic liberalism of Sakharov. Many writers and artists renounced politics altogether and articulated various forms of individual expression. The censors let most of these works pass, for they contained no explicitly anti-Soviet material, although their themes were a far cry from socialist realism.

Dissidents never numbered more than a couple of thousand people. Like their precursors, the radical intelligentsia of the nineteenth century, they had little contact with the masses, most of whom swallowed the Party line, which claimed that the dissidents were unpatriotic malcontents or hirelings of Western intelligence agencies. The oppositionists thus posed no threat to the government's grip on power and served more as annoyances than serious competitors to the Party's monopoly on "truth." Although an irritant in Soviet-Western relations, the dissidents had little effect on the government's foreign, domestic, or cultural policies. Even though their valor and principles evoked widespread admiration in the West, it would be a mistake to overestimate their significance. It would also be wrong to dismiss them. They kept alive traditional and modern values that the regime sought to obliterate, and they served as a conscience for other educated Soviet citizens. Oppositionists reminded their compatriots and the outside world that the Russian and other national traditions contained worthy ideals and goals. These precepts, they argued, differed markedly from the norms and outlook of the oppressive Soviet system under Brezhnev. Perhaps most important, the movement symbolized the hope that alternatives to "developed socialism" existed and might one day emerge among the Soviet peoples.

"Village Writers" and Valor: Literature and Popular Culture in the Brezhnev Era

Like religion, literature and popular culture were also renewed with fresh currents in the Brezhnev era. Some writers reacted to the years of stagnation by avoiding standard Soviet literary themes of industrialization, modernization, and Party-mindedness in favor of stories of traditional rural life. Others, although careful not to criticize the system itself, portrayed the seamier aspects of daily urban existence. Popular audiences lapped up romantic tales, World War II sagas, thrillers, and films. Comedians and balladeers gathered enthusiastic followings with satiric commentary on the foibles of Soviet society. By the early 1980s, rock groups had emerged as the young generation's bulwark against established, Party-endorsed values and mores.

FoLowing in the footsteps of such nineteenth-century authors as Ivan Turgenev, a group dubbed the "village writers" emerged in the late 1960s and early 1970s. Although these literati focused on rural society and traditions and criticized the impact of industrialization, urbanization, and consumerism on Soviet society, they hardly romanticized life in the countryside. They took care to point out the persistence of rural destitution, pettiness, ignorance, and superstition. However, they stressed the strength and integrity of individual villagers and the noxious effects of external bureaucratic interference in village life. They praised the simplicity, harmony, and wisdom of time-honored values and beliefs. One of the first stories in this genre, *Matryona's House* by Solzhenitsyn, emphasized virtues drawn from Russia's spiritual heritage. Valentin Rasputin in *The Last Days* and *Farewell to Matyora* illustrated the lack of contact and understanding between city dwellers and villagers and the harmful effects of industrial progress on a way of life deeply rooted in Russia's past. Most village writers' works treated the Russian tradition. Central Asian storyteller Chinghiz Aitmatov, however, dealt with rural mores in Kyrgyzstan and Kazakhstan, and Fasil Iskander set his stories in the Caucasus.

Other writers concentrated on Soviet urban society. A few novels, like Vitaly Syomin's *Seven in a Single House*, depicted the life of workers, usually in a stark, critical manner. Yuri Trifonov, one of the best authors of the period, portrayed upper-middle-class intellectuals. With superb characterizations, Trifonov's *House on the Embankment* revealed these individuals as shallow and opportunistic—posturing souls devoid of ideals or integrity. A talented group of women writers, including Galina Serebryakova and Tatiana Tolstaya, treated the isolation and struggles of women in Soviet society. Natalia Baranskaya in *A Week Like Any Other* convincingly demonstrated the hectic odium of daily life in the city and the impossible burdens placed on Soviet women.

A few writers turned to historical themes. Anatoly Kuznetsov set his *Babi Yar* in World War II, whereas writer-singer Bulat Okudzhava revisited the Decembrists to create an allegory of the censorship, bureaucratic spying, and cruelty that he deplored in the Soviet system. Solzhenitsyn wrote powerful indictments of the atomization of Soviet society in *First Circle* and *Cancer Ward* but had to publish them abroad. Lydia Chukhovskaya's *Deserted House* movingly detailed the devastating impact of the arrest of a loved one, and Vasily Grossman's *Everything Flows* and *Life and Fate* revealed anew the horror of denunciations and imprisonment.

For reasons not entirely clear, Party watchdogs permitted publication of Mikhail Bulgakov's long-suppressed 1920s masterpiece *The Master and Margarita,* a wildly imaginative satire of the Soviet ruling class and the greedy public. The innovative Taganka Theater under its able director Yuri Lyubimov even received permission to stage Bulgakov's novel in the late 1970s. Numerous talented writers and artists, nevertheless, left the Soviet Union to pursue careers in the West.

Although many of the above works were widely read, television, films, and popular music reached a much larger audience. By the early 1980s, almost 90 percent of Soviet families owned a television set, which they watched regularly. Programmers for the government monopoly supplied a strong dose of "high culture"—opera, ballet, plays, and lectures on a range of serious topics—but viewers preferred movies and pop concerts. Soviet fans also enjoyed watching sports. Large crowds jammed stadiums to cheer soccer and ice hockey matches, and millions followed the fortunes of Soviet athletes in the summer and winter Olympic games. The government also employed Soviet athletic groups and stars to enhance the nation's prestige abroad.

Science-fiction fantasies and spy and detective adventures proved the most popular films in movie houses and on television. Audiences also favored romantic or nostalgic stories about daily life and foreign, especially American, films. During the 1950s, Tarzan movies had been avidly attended, especially by youth, and Soviet audiences had devoured American musicals. In the 1960s and 1970s, Westerns had particular appeal. World War II served as the most common cinematic topic by far. Although most war films paraded clichés and Soviet patriotism, several outstanding movies dealt sensitively with the impact of war on individual lives and probed themes of love, duty, and loss. *Ballad of a Soldier* (1959), *The Cranes Are Flying* (1957), and *The Fate of a Man* (1965) were immensely popular and well received by Western critics. Heralded filmmaker Andrei Tarkovsky produced such daring and poignant movies as *Andrei Rublev* and *My Name Is Ivan*. Yet it was *Moscow Does Not Believe in Tears* (1980) that became the most widely watched film of the post-Stalin years. The Academy Award–winning movie portrays three young girls' struggle to find careers, love, and happiness in contemporary urban society. It also faithfully delineates the details of daily existence and spotlights seedier sides of Moscow life. The ending, however, strikes an optimistic note, as the heroine becomes a factory manager and finds a stalwart lover. Soviet audiences appreciated the film's honest depiction of reality and embraced its populist sentimentality.

Popular literature included Russian classics from the nineteenth century and translated Western favorites, especially works by Jules Verne, Arthur Conan Doyle, John Steinbeck, and "frontier" authors Jack London and James Fenimore Cooper. American science-fiction writer Mitchell Wilson, although little known in the United States, also generated enthusiasm. As with films, science-fiction and detective stories had wide appeal. Although Cold War thrillers exploring the machinations of the CIA abounded, books by Yulian Semenov achieved the biggest sales over the last twenty years of the Soviet period. Semenov chose various milieus for

A Dazzling Feat Soviet citizens of all ages loved the acrobatic skill and glamorous productions of national and regional circus troupes.

his crime novels, but his most famous, *Seventeen Moments of Spring*, dealt with a Soviet agent in Nazi Germany, a society that he depicted in chilling detail. Semenov had a knack for blending conformist Soviet mores and attitudes with exotic ideas and allusions. His technique put his readers on familiar ground while titillating them.

The U.S.S.R. also boasted two popular entertainment forms less familiar in Western mass culture: the circus and comedic acting. With its glitzy productions, daring acts, talented and stylish performers, and hilarious clowns, the Soviet circus appealed to young and old alike. Troupes played small towns and rural regions as well as the big cities. The great comedian, Arkady Raikan, used monologues and skits to blend biting social commentary with a sympathetic understanding of human foibles. Raikan invented this credible dialogue between two sloppy drunks:

Do you respect me?
Yes. Do you respect me?
I respect you.
Then we're both respectable people.[9]

Finally, popular music reached millions, although young people enjoyed it most. Scoffed at by intellectuals, sentimental songs consistently won the favor of most Soviet citizens. Everyone knew and enjoyed the catchy "Evenings Outside Moscow," for example, with its tale of romantic love set in a nostalgic rural atmosphere. Patriotic songs also proved popular, despite rather saccharine lyrics.

Where does the motherland begin?
With the pictures in your schoolbook
With comrades good and true
Living in the courtyard.
. . . with that song our mother sang us
. . . the old bench at the gate
That birch tree in the field . . . [10]

Young Soviet citizens craved Western clothing, particularly blue jeans and sweatshirts, and they adored Western music. Jazz, the forbidden fruit of the 1950s and the icon of the modish Soviet youth known as *stilyagi* (tight skirts for girls, modified zoot suits for boys), finally gained acceptance in the Brezhnev era. Soviet musicians became adept in arranging and playing varieties of jazz. By then, however, young people

---

[9]Quoted in Richard Stites, *Russian Popular Culture: Entertainment and Society since 1900* (Cambridge: Cambridge Univ. Press, 1992), p. 138.

[10]Ibid., p. 155.

had moved on to rock and roll, which the authorities tried in vain to control. By the 1980s, Soviet rock groups—some of them even heavy-metal bands—performed openly and regularly.

A unique and powerfully influential form of mass entertainment emerged with the poetic songs of guitarist/singers or bards. These artists' works circulated widely through illegal recordings and tapes known as *magnitizdat*. Alexander Galich, Vladimir Vysotsky, and Bulat Okudzhava led the way in combining protest verse with melodies that plucked at the heartstrings of the Russian soul. Vysotsky, a talented stage and film actor, sang of the marginal and the disappointed in Soviet life and railed against privilege, hypocrisy, and degradation in Soviet society. Okudzhava, also a well-known author, satirized the falseness and pomposity of Soviet bureaucracy and custom. These bards used common language drawn from the army, the forced labor camps, and the street. Their songs, despite efforts to suppress them, reached millions of Soviet citizens. Indeed, Vysotsky's funeral in 1980 drew the largest spontaneous public demonstration of the whole period.

Conclusion

When Leonid Brezhnev died in 1982, his passing evoked only indifference. One Moscow wag, after hearing that the Soviet leader was dead, inquired, "How could they tell?" Almost no one nurtured Brezhnev's legacy, and few mourned him. His hounding of independent spirits such as Sinyavsky and Daniel had alienated many intellectuals and helped to spawn and shape the dissident movement. Yet the citizenry for their part showed little interest in promoting human rights and instead passively accepted their lot. A few regime supporters noted that Brezhnev had overseen a rapid expansion of Soviet military power, the growth of Soviet influence in the Third World, and at least until the mid-1970s, a gradual but steady improvement in the average person's standard of living. The Soviet economy ranked second only to that of the United States; incomes had doubled since 1960; almost every family had its own apartment, refrigerator, and television; and individuals possessed more education than the previous generation had. Many people seemed content with these improvements and willing to tolerate a continuation of the Soviet order. All appeared "normal" and "in order," to use two favorite Russian expressions.

Yet just when the system seemed stable and enduring, currents of transformation bubbled beneath the surface. No one foresaw the collapse that these changes signaled, although the contradictions in the "era of stability" should have provided a few clues to the fate of Soviet socialism. In politics, the leadership stressed its collective nature, yet by the early 1970s a single figure, Brezhnev, dominated. The Politburo chieftains castigated Khrushchev and reversed many of his reforms; at the same time, they continued most of his basic policies. The rulers maintained an oligarchic dictatorship over the Party and country but increasingly had to rely on specialists, technicians, and local authorities to keep the cumbersome system going. Brezhnev and his cronies lauded Soviet patriotism and urged the gradual "growing together" of Russians and non-Russians, yet anti-Russian and nationalist feeling accelerated among the minorities, and a populist, nostalgic chauvinism spread among many Great Russians. The leadership pursued a foreign policy based on military power, control of Eastern Europe, and the promotion of the Soviet position in the world. These policies, however, yielded a reactive Western military build-up, the downfall of détente, repression in Czechoslovakia and Poland, a continuing rift with China, and only a few tenuous toeholds in the Third World.

In economic policy, the regime looked to the "scientific-technological revolution" to solve deficiencies in planning and production, but the nation fell farther behind the West, especially in applied research and technological innovation. Although the economy continued to expand, its rate of growth and its ability to meet defense and consumer demands slipped. Investment in agriculture rose and crop yields improved, yet food shortages persisted and dependence on grain imports grew. Rising population and expectations outpaced a slightly improving standard of living up to the mid-1970s. The slipshod quality and unavailability of many products limited consumer choice and frustration festered. Foreign trade mushroomed, yet the Soviet economy remained largely "colonial," exporting raw materials such as oil and timber in exchange for technology and finished goods.

In cultural and social life, the leadership and the policies of most institutions remained outdated and Stalinist, despite the emergence of a forward-looking, post-Stalin generation. The regime clung to patriarchal and exclusive attitudes and methods of control, squelching dissent and creativity. The population, however, had become urban, educated, and sophisticated. The ideology trumpeted unrealistic and jejune goals, while the people pursued private, materialistic ends. Authorities promulgated atheism, but religious belief persisted and even spread. Treatment of women changed hardly at all, despite their increasingly important role in society. Soviet practices continued to degrade the environment; simultaneously, defenders of the country's resources and beauty arose and influenced public policy. The aging oligarchs mandated a dull cultural uniformity, while vitality and creativity sparkled in underground art and literature. The leadership dropped the pretense that the just, equitable, and humane society envisaged in 1917 lay just around the corner, but no one provided an alternate vision. Soviet society, operating on inertia, was dangerously adrift.

FURTHER READING

No up-to-date biography of Brezhnev exists. An earlier, journalistic account is John Dornberg, *Brezhnev* (New York, 1974). Useful interpretations of his rule appear in Breslauer and in Cohen, Sharlet, and Rabinowitch, both named in Chapter 9's Further Reading list, and in S. Bialer, ed., *Stalin's Successors: Leadership, Stability, and Change in the Soviet Union* (New York, 1981).

For insights into Soviet society and life in the Brezhnev era, see an anecdotal but often revealing account by the longtime *New York Times* correspondent in Moscow, Hedrick Smith, *The Russians* (New York, 1976); Basile Kerblay, *Modern Soviet Society* (New York, 1983); Gail Lapidus, *Women in Soviet Society* (Berkeley, Calif., 1978); Robert Edelman, *Serious Fun: A History of Spectator Sports in the U.S.S.R.* (New York, 1993); and James Millar, ed., *Politics, Work, and Daily Life in the USSR: A Survey of Former Soviet Citizens* (New York, 1987).

For ideology and cultural life, consult Boris Kagarlitsky, *The Thinking Reed* (New York, 1988); John Dunlop, *The Faces of Contemporary Russian Nationalism* (Princeton, N.J., 1983); Stephen Cohen, ed., *An End to Silence: Uncensored Opinion in the Soviet Union* (New York, 1982); and Geoffrey Hosking, *Beyond Socialist Realism: Soviet Fiction Since Ivan Denisovich* (New York, 1980).

The arms race and efforts at arms control are covered in David Holloway, *The Soviet Union and the Arms Race* (New Haven, Conn., 1983); John Newhouse, *Cold Dawn: The Story of SALT* (New York, 1973); Andrew Cockburn, *The Threat: Inside the Soviet Military Machine* (New York, 1983); and Raymond Garthoff, *Détente and Confrontation: Soviet-American Relations from Nixon to Reagan* (Washington, 1985), a general history that emphasizes arms control issues.

Other books on foreign policy include R. Edmonds, *Soviet Foreign Policy: The Brezhnev Years* (New York, 1983); Jiri Valenta, *Soviet Intervention in Czechoslovakia, 1968* (Baltimore, 1979); Bruce D. Porter, *The Soviet Union in Third World Conflicts* (Cambridge, 1984); Thomas Hammond, *Red Flag Over Afghanistan* (Boulder, Colo., 1984); and H. Bradsher, *Afghanistan and the Soviet Union* (Durham, N.C., 1983).

11

A Vision Revived
and Abandoned
The Gorbachev Reform Era

~

Soviet citizens who rose early on August 19, 1991, were startled to hear their radio newscaster announce that eight leaders of the Soviet government had formed the State Committee on the Emergency Situation to address crisis in the nation. President Mikhail Gorbachev, the announcer said, had fallen ill. In fact, the Soviet leader felt fine, but supporters of the Emergency Committee had placed him under house arrest at his vacation retreat in the Crimea the previous evening when he refused to sanction its formation. The committee members, all conservatives and all Gorbachev appointees, included the vice president, the premier, the minister of defense, the head of the KGB, and the minister of the interior.

Early that morning, the leaders of this coup attempt had deployed hundreds of tanks along Moscow's main thoroughfares. But it soon became clear that the soldiers had no stomach for firing on civilians. One tank commander even switched sides to defend the White House, government headquarters of the Russian Republic. Russian president Boris Yeltsin, who had left his *dacha* outside Moscow early that morning just before the coup plotters' agents arrived to arrest him, dramatized this turnaround by climbing atop a tank and loudly condemning the coup attempt as illegal. His defiance and the coup leaders' ineptitude at a televised press conference that evening galvanized opposition. By nightfall, more than fifty thousand citizens had gathered around the White House, erecting makeshift barricades and forming a human wall against would-be attackers.

The crisis was by no means over, however. For one thing, not everyone sided with Yeltsin. Moreover, a special commando force stood ready to storm the White House under cover of darkness. But once again, Yeltsin supporters persuaded the troops not to attack. Leningrad's liberal mayor,

Anatoly Sobchak, also persuaded the commandant of the Leningrad military district not to use force on coup opponents demonstrating in the city center. By Tuesday the crowd clamoring at the White House swelled to almost a hundred thousand. Yelena Bonner, widow of recently deceased human rights champion Andrei Sakharov, drew warm applause when she vowed to the assembled Yeltsin defenders, "[The coup leaders] think they can direct and order us, feed us or not. . . . But we will show them, prove to them, that we are people, **people,** and not just cattle." Popular poet Yevgeny Yevtushenko thrilled the crowd with such lyrical lines as these:

> *This August day shall be glorified in*
> > *songs and ballads.*
> > *Today we are a nation—*
> > > *no longer fools,*
> > > > *happy to be fooled.*

Sadly, that night the crew of a withdrawing armored car panicked and inadvertently killed three young protesters. These three men, along with one person shot in Lithuania, became the only casualties of the crisis.

By August 21, the coup had failed owing to Yeltsin's courageous opposition, the *putschists'* blunders, the military's reluctance to fire on civilians, and popular resistance in Moscow and other key centers. Two conspirators committed suicide; the rest were arrested. Later, they were

Yeltsin Denounces the Plotters On August 23, after the attempted coup had failed, Boris Yeltsin, head of the Russian republic, who led the resistance to the *putsch,* addresses a crowd of Muscovites in front of the statue of Feliks Dzerzhinsky, first leader of the Soviet secret police.

released on bail. Gorbachev, freed on August 22, flew back to Moscow to retake the reins of government.[1]

The coup's collapse sparked profound changes that within months would lead to the shocking fragmentation of the Soviet Union into fifteen independent states. Gorbachev fell from power in December, and Yeltsin emerged as a forceful new leader of Russia. Only half a decade earlier, Gorbachev had taken the helm of a seemingly mighty and united country and had vowed to make it a shining example of a harmonious, just, socialist society. What had gone wrong?

When he came to power in 1985, Mikhail Gorbachev, a relatively young, little-known Party leader, repudiated many of Brezhnev's policies and replaced most of his appointees. Profoundly disturbed by the deficiencies of the system that he had inherited, the new leader confidently launched *perestroika*, an effort to restructure the Soviet economy to make it efficient and competitive with the West and Japan. Gorbachev also fostered *glasnost'*, or open discussion of Soviet problems and freedom of creative and intellectual activity, albeit within broad limits. Encouraging citizens to participate in social and public life, he urged the democratization of Soviet institutions as well while retaining the dominant role of the Party. Too late, however, did he recognize the intensity of the non-Russians' demands for autonomy and national self-assertion. Gorbachev set in motion changes that he could not control and whose consequences he did not foresee. Events soon outpaced him, and Soviet society began to fly apart. Caught between those who wanted to slow or reverse the pace of change and those who sought full democracy and private enterprise, Gorbachev waffled and then stood helpless as the U.S.S.R. and its socialist system collapsed. Yet despite the disasters at home, this relatively young visionary revolutionized world affairs by ending the Cold War, substantially cutting nuclear and conventional armaments, and acquiescing in the Eastern Europeans' throwing off of socialism. His efforts initiated an era of Soviet-American cooperation that ultimately enhanced the prospects for world peace.

Gorbachev's Rise to Power

The new Soviet leader did not launch his administration with such bold objectives and sweeping changes in mind. Initially, Gorbachev hoped for no more than to revive the economy and to rejuvenate the system, as

---

[1]This account of the coup is based on James H. Billington, *Russia Transformed: Breakthrough to Hope* (New York: Free Press, 1992), part two; *Newsweek*, special issue, "The Second Russian Revolution," September 2, 1991; and Robert Cullen, "Report from Moscow: The Coup." *The New Yorker*, November 4, 1991, pp. 54–88.

Khrushchev and the tsarist reformer Alexander II had attempted before him. In short, he wanted to modify, not recast, Soviet society. But he soon was drawn into undertaking more and more changes, a pattern that produced a more radical cumulative impact than he had intended. As one example, to make *perestroika* effective, he introduced *glasnost'*, which encouraged criticism and new ideas. But *glasnost'* soon snowballed into doubts about the political system and then to distrust in socialism itself. Beginning in 1988, Gorbachev began to define his vision more precisely: a humane, just, and democratic society but one still socialist, Party led and Russian dominated. Yet the rush of events and his own miscalculations deprived him of reaching this goal.

Neither did Gorbachev develop his program single-handedly. He engaged talented advisers and supporters at home and enlisted the cooperation of major leaders abroad. He also proved able to mobilize and direct two powerful currents surging through society. As we saw in Chapter 10, in the 1980s Soviet citizens had become predominantly urban, well educated, and increasingly critical of the relative hardship of their circumstances. The more restive among them had already begun agitating for a more participatory and effective system than the mediocrity that the Brezhnev years had offered. Gorbachev believed that he had only to unleash and encourage such critics and to direct their reformist impulses at particular targets. In his view, they would then arouse their fellow citizens. The new Soviet leader led the reform charge, but he also benefited from the strong impulse for change already coursing through the upper echelons of Soviet society.

At the same time, Gorbachev unwittingly tapped a broader and deep-seated vein of popular revulsion against the corruption and inefficiency of the Brezhnev system. By the early 1980s, people who had less education and sophistication than the intellectual elites had begun to detect deceitfulness in their leaders. Increasingly, the promise that life would improve struck them as a fraud. They began to see socialism as a hollow vision that would never find fulfillment, and more and more their "bosses" seemed to bask in privilege and affluence while they stooped daily to bribery, petty immorality, and inconvenience just to live modestly. Many people equated the rottenness at the heart of the system—which Gorbachev, too, wished to eradicate—with the Party, which he wanted to preserve. In the beginning, however, Gorbachev drew strength from the moral repugnance and economic resentment gnawing at Soviet citizenry.

These trends undergirded Gorbachev's reform program. Yet his own intellect, inclination, energy, and talents also contributed to the breadth and forcefulness of the changes of the last half of the 1980s. As a young man, Gorbachev had absorbed the Khrushchev years' optimism and desire for improvement, and he came to power determined to reinstitute a major overhaul of the Soviet system. Born in 1931 in southeastern Russia of peasant parents, Gorbachev had firsthand knowledge of deformities in Soviet life. During the 1930s, one grandfather was exiled to Siberia and another imprisoned, facts that Gorbachev would not reveal until 1990. Ambitious and forceful, the young Russian walked miles each week to attend secondary school. His excellent grades there, his role as a Komsomol leader, and his peasant background helped him to win admission to prestigious Moscow State University in 1950.

As a law student, Gorbachev became acquainted with Western political writings. Although he joined the Party, the young activist also displayed a wide-ranging curiosity and considerable intellectual independence, according to contemporaries. He met and married fellow student Raisa Titorenko, a philosophy major familiar with Western literature. Highly intelligent, cultivated, and ambitious, she made a perfect match for Gorbachev and advised him at every stage of his career. In his last two years at the university, Gorbachev shared in the excitement and intellectual awakening induced by the thaw that followed Stalin's death in 1953.

After graduating in 1955, the future Soviet leader returned to his home region as a Komsomol administrator in the provincial city of Stavropol. Advancing rapidly, he won promotion to Party work in 1960 and the following year attended the Twenty-second Party Congress, at which Khrushchev expanded the de-Stalinization campaign begun in 1956. By 1966 Gorbachev served as first secretary of the Stavropol city Party committee. He became first secretary of the region in 1970 and, at age forty, was elected to the Party's Central Committee in 1971. As rising stars in the Party, he and Raisa were also permitted to join Soviet delegations that visited France and Italy in the 1960s. This firsthand look at the West may have raised questions in Gorbachev's mind about his own country's inefficiency and backwardness. Buoyed by agricultural successes that he oversaw and well acquainted with such national leaders as Alexei Kosygin and Yuri Andropov, who regularly visited a mineral-water spa in Gorbachev's region, Gorbachev ascended to Party secretary for agriculture in 1978. Two years later, he joined the Politburo, its youngest member by far. Ultimately, he would become a national leader even though he had little experience in industry (Stavropol lay in a primarily agricultural region) or contact with the Soviet Union's non-Russian minorities. Nevertheless, he knew Party politics thoroughly and, later, he felt confident that by effectively employing that instrument, he could improve Soviet life.

During his early career, however, Gorbachev had to weather a stormy period in the top leadership. In the late 1970s, as Brezhnev's frail health eroded his grip on power, his would-be successors began to jockey for position. Pitted against each other were two sharply contrasting personalities: Konstantin Chernenko, an undistinguished Party hack but Brezhnev's hand-picked successor, and Andropov, an austere, intelligent, and complex senior leader. After long experience in the Central Committee secretariat, Andropov had served for over a decade as head of the KGB. In the months before Brezhnev's death, Andropov's agents brought corruption charges against several Brezhnev devotees and close associates of his daughter. To further bolster his position as Brezhnev's health declined, the secret police chief also urged efforts to overcome the U.S.S.R.'s economic crisis. Backed by the army, Andropov became the country's leader in November 1982 and promptly began to crack down on worker malingering and absenteeism. He also sustained the anticorruption drive and experimented selectively with economic decentralization.

Yet Andropov left a legacy of contradiction. On one hand, he identified a few key problems, initiated steps to correct them, and replaced Party "deadwood" with reform-minded technocrats. On the other hand, he reduced Jewish emigration to a trickle; clamped down on culture, the arts, and the media; and pursued a hard line in foreign policy. By February 1983, longstanding health problems had forced Andropov onto kidney dialysis, and a few months later he was hospitalized in a clinic outside Moscow. In his absence, his protégé and supporter Gorbachev directed the Party secretariat and frequently served as courier and intermediary between the ailing Andropov and the anxious Politburo.

Nevertheless, when Andropov died in February 1984, Chernenko, not Gorbachev, succeeded him. This decision came because most Politburo members were conservative Brezhnev appointees. Perhaps the Party hierarchs also recognized that Chernenko, in his midseventies and in failing health, would function mainly as a transitional leader. Chernenko adhered to Andropov's policies except in the arena of foreign policy, where he initiated resumption of arms-control negotiations with the United States. Last appearing in public in December 1984, Chernenko died in early March 1985 after ruling a little over a year.

With Chernenko's death, the Politburo split evenly between older Brezhnevites and younger supporters of Gorbachev. The latter's chief rivals each had handicaps, however, ranging from reputations for unseemly behavior to accusations of corruption. Perhaps to ensure cohesion at the top, Andrei Gromyko, the most senior of the Old Guard and a loyal Party stalwart since the 1930s, nominated the fifty-four-year-old Gorbachev as the new head of the Party. The Central Committee endorsed Gorbachev on March 11, 1985. For the first time since Lenin, a well-educated, cultivated, and resolute leader stood at the helm of the Soviet Union. Gorbachev, determined to transform the economy, virtually burst with energy and ideas. It remained to be seen whether he could look beyond his Party upbringing and orientation and whether he would overcome popular lethargy and the opposition of a massive bureaucracy.

Groping for a Formula, 1985–1987

Few Soviet observers and no Western experts expected that Gorbachev would prove more than another Khrushchev, a tinkering reformer destined to fail. Outsiders pronounced the deadening hand of Soviet ideology and practice immutable and predicted that the system, although faltering, would keep stumbling ahead. Awed by the pervasiveness of Party and police controls and the weight of Soviet military power, they deemed profound change unlikely. The wellspring and instigators of radical reform were not yet rippling the surface of Soviet life.

Yet change was stirring. 'Objective circumstances," one of Lenin's favorite phrases, demanded it These conditions included the disintegrating economy; the alienation and passivity of the people; the replacement of ideology by cynicism and petty immorality the unbearable defense burden created by military and political competition with the West and with China; the demoralizing war in Afghanistan; and the example of Poland, where popular revulsion against a corrupt and moribund regime had nearly overthrown socialism. In addition, reform ideas, preserved quietly since the Khrushchev era, had resurfaced under Andropov, who formed expert committees to study the U.S.S.R.'s problems and who tolerated the circulation of blunt critiques by leading intellectuals. Two such documents had proved especially powerful: a 1983 analysis of Soviet socioeconomic problems known as the Novosibirsky Report by the sociologist Tatyana Zaslavskaya, and a 1984 withering dissection of the economic malaise of the country by economist Abel Aganbegyan. Both barrages had put the onus for economic stagnation on the system.

In December 1984, Gorbachev gave a speech that he probably hoped would influence like-minded Party leaders and boost his chances of succeeding Chernenko. The address hinted at key parts of his later reform program. Deploring the state of the economy and praising the effectiveness of decentralized management, he espoused greater self-government and improved living standards for the population and urged openness and socialist democracy. He repeated most of these themes throughout the following year, yet in all these pronouncements, his goals and methods remained vague. Gorbachev grasped the need for a major overhaul of the system, but in these early months, he strained to decide precisely how to proceed. Initially, this indecision hampered his reform program.

Gorbachev first set out to establish control over the Party apparatus, which he expected to wield as his main agent of change. He immediately elevated key Andropov supporters to the Politburo. (These men, although considered reformers at the time, later became conservative opponents of Gorbachev.) The new Party leader also surrounded himself with reformist advisers and, through 1985 and early 1986, arranged the retirements of important Brezhnevite Politburo members. Promoting Gromyko to head of state, Gorbachev replaced him at the Foreign Ministry with the Georgian reformer Edvard Shevardnadze, whom he also added to the Politburo and who would become a close confidant. Gorbachev brought in new members of the Party secretariat as well, including Yeltsin, Lev Zaikov, and Alexandra Biryukova, the first woman to serve at the center of power since 1961. At the Twenty-seventh Party Congress in March 1986, he helped to maneuver a turnover of almost half the members of the Central Committee. Finally, during his first year in office, he began the complex process of replacing Party officials at the republican, provincial, and district levels. (Because conservatives had a hand in selecting appointees, however, not all these newcomers would turn out to support Gorbachev's program.)

Gorbachev and his advisers focused first on the floundering economy. They recognized its poor performance, especially compared with the flourishing systems of the United States, Western Europe, and Japan. Only radical changes, they believed, could preserve the Soviet Union's security and superpower status and raise its peoples' standard of living. The determined Soviet leader saw three key economic difficulties: inefficiency, backwardness, and low morale. To his colleagues and in some public speeches, he pointed out the system's wastefulness and the decline in growth and productivity that came just as demands on the economy intensified. Gorbachev also acknowledged that Soviet technology and techniques lagged behind the times. Soviet products were costly and shoddy and the Soviet quality of life clearly inferior to that of the West and Japan. Not only was the U.S.S.R. falling behind its chief competitors; it threatened to sink into the second tier of the world's countries. Last, Gorbachev attacked the widespread apathy, sloth, corruption, cynicism, and alienation that he observed seeping into the fabric of Soviet society— symptoms summarized as a collapse of civic virtue. Perhaps he took to heart a Soviet joke of the 1980s: a patient insists to the nurse that he must see the eye-ear doctor. Despite the nurse's explanation that the clinic employs eye specialists and ear-nose-and-throat doctors but no eye-ear physicians, the patient remains adamant. To the nurse's exasperated question, "But why do you demand the services of an eye-ear doctor?" the patient replies, "Because all around me I keep hearing one thing but seeing quite another."

For Gorbachev, all the deficiencies that he discerned taken together— and he saw them as mutually reinforcing—impaired the U.S.S.R.'s military and political power. Worse, they threatened to prevent Soviet socialism from achieving its goals. The new leader insisted that a reformed Soviet Union could build a thriving, technologically advanced economy; a rational, humane system; and a peaceful, mutually beneficial relationship with the rest of the world. When the U.S.S.R. reached these targets, he believed, Soviet society would stand as a shining paragon of modern socialism and soon win over the majority of the globe's nations to the socialist cause.

Yet with the caution bred by his success in the Party bureaucracy, Gorbachev at first proposed only modest changes in the economy. His pleas to "accelerate" industrial activity amounted chiefly to exhortations to managers to cut costs and use raw materials more wisely. He also urged workers to labor harder and argued for linking pay and other rewards to performance. Finally, he provided emergency funds to upgrade the Soviet machine-tool industry, which he hoped would supply advanced technology to other industrial sectors.

On the recommendation of conservative Politburo member Yegor Ligachev, the new Soviet ruler also launched an ill-planned antialcohol campaign in the spring of 1985. He aimed to raise labor productivity by reducing absenteeism, accidents, and incompetence caused by drunkenness and to ameliorate the mounting social and criminal problems that alcoholism provoked. Instead of stressing education, treatment, and social pressure, however, Gorbachev's program sought to curtail the availability of alcohol. The plan reduced the places and times allotted for its sale, cut back the production of vodka, and banned alcoholic drinks at official receptions. These measures only inconvenienced and irritated the population while doing little to stop drinking. Citizens rushed to ferment their own vodka, a process that requires sugar, and depleted the country's supply of the precious commodity. Sugar soon had to be rationed. Black-market peddling of vodka mushroomed, while state revenues, one-fifth of which came from vodka sales, shrank. Worst of all, some unfortunates died or suffered disabling damage from drinking antifreeze and other deadly vodka substitutes. The antialcohol campaign would be quietly abandoned in 1989.

As 1985 wore on, Gorbachev began to talk more about fundamental change, not only in the system but in attitudes and behavior. Although he had used the word *perestroika*, or restructuring, all along, he now began to spell out his program. The main task was to restructure not only the economy but all other facets of public life: "social relations, the political system, the spiritual and ideological sphere, and the style and work methods of the Party and all our cadres."[2] This sweeping vision reflected his growing realization that saving the economy went hand in hand with healing the other ills plaguing Soviet life. In this way, *perestroika* came to describe the totality of Gorbachev's reform effort, although it primarily focused on economic restructuring.

Gorbachev's initial changes proved modest, but his leadership style marked a sharp break with the behavior of most post-Leninist officials

---

[2]Quoted in Robert G. Kaiser, *Why Gorbachev Happened* (New York: Simon & Schuster, 1991), p. 132.

and foreshadowed the more radical reforms that he would introduce in 1986 and 1987. Only two months after assuming office, he visited Leningrad. Soviet citizens were surprised to view their leader on television, mingling with crowds in offices, factories, and streets. Previous Party chiefs had been seen "with the people" mainly in artificial, staged settings, yet here was Gorbachev listening to complaints, joking and arguing with everyday citizens, and obviously enjoying himself. Moreover, whereas wives of Soviet leaders had remained almost invisible in the past, the attractive, well-dressed Raisa accompanied Gorbachev everywhere. (At first, Raisa captivated the public, but eventually most Soviet citizens came to resent her smart Western clothes, her involvement in politics, and what some considered her haughty demeanor.) To everyone's amazement, Gorbachev delivered an unscripted speech in Leningrad, in which he spoke honestly and directly about problems of daily life and pleaded for his listeners' participation and support. Later, he would not only formally encourage openness, or *glasnost'*, about issues of concern, past and present, but also propose democratizing the nation's economic, social, and lower-level political life, a radical concept.

An Unprecedented Gripe Session Reformer Mikhail Gorbachev accompanied by his wife Raisa mingles with a crowd of citizens to hear popular complaints.

Although the phrase did not come into use until 1987, Gorbachev also introduced "new thinking" in foreign policy almost immediately on taking office. He aimed primarily to reduce the huge outlays for defense, which consumed up to 25 percent of GNP. He also sought to avoid a space-weapons race with the United States, which President Ronald Reagan's announcement of the Strategic Defense Initiative (SDI) in 1983 seemed to presage. Further, he wanted to foster a calm international climate while pursuing his storm of internal reforms. In March 1985, he expressed his hope for a summit meeting with Reagan, and in April he announced a unilateral suspension for seven months (later extended) of Soviet deployment of SS-20 missiles in Europe. During the next few months, Gorbachev added a proposal to cut strategic weapons by 50 percent and declared a moratorium on underground testing of nuclear arms. Having made successful visits to Canada (1983) and Britain (1984) before assuming power, Gorbachev flew to France in the fall of 1985. There he gave an unprecedented interview to French television and held an open press conference with international journalists. During both events, he acquitted himself ably.

Meeting Reagan in Geneva in November 1985, Gorbachev achieved exactly what he intended: he convinced the deeply anti-Soviet American president of the genuineness of the new direction of Soviet foreign policy, and he drew the U.S. government into an ongoing dialogue on arms limitation and other issues hampering Soviet-American relations. The Geneva summit produced no concrete agreements, but the five hours of private talks between the superpower leaders marked the beginning of the Cold War's resolution and paved the way for an unprecedented era of cooperation and mutual trust. Gorbachev's success in winning over the champion of conservative forces in the West, who had characterized the Soviet Union as an "evil empire" as recently as 1984, also induced fruitful arms-control negotiations.

During 1985 Gorbachev began to talk not only about preventing nuclear war but also about broad international cooperation on such global issues as the environment, disease, and developing nations. The Twenty-seventh Party Congress in March 1986 supported these positions as well as an earlier appeal by Gorbachev for all nations to eliminate nuclear weapons by the year 2000. In addition, the congress approved Gorbachev's new strategic policy, dubbed "reasonable sufficiency." According to this doctrine, the Soviet Union would abandon offensive plans and would retain only enough nuclear and conventional forces to protect the country from attack. Over the next few years, despite considerable opposition from senior military figures, Gorbachev announced substantial unilateral cuts in Soviet military force levels and in various weapons categories. To his dismay, however, these savings proved more limited than he had hoped and did little to revive the economy.

During 1985 Gorbachev also signed trade and educational exchange agreements with China and declared his interest in normalizing Sino-Soviet relations. The Chinese leadership responded coolly. Before a rapprochement with the U.S.S.R. could occur, they explained, the Soviet Union would have to withdraw from Afghanistan, persuade its client state Vietnam to end its occupation of Kampuchea (Cambodia), and slash Soviet troop deployments along China's borders. Gorbachev would manage to satisfy all of these demanding ultimatums within three years.

In October 1986, a second summit meeting held in the Icelandic capital of Reykjavik strengthened the renaissance of détente in Soviet-American relations. The Soviet and American leaders again cordially exchanged views. They also came close to an agreement on the elimination of all nuclear weapons on both sides, much to the consternation of their military advisers. Because Reagan rejected a Soviet proposal to limit SDI to laboratory research, Gorbachev refused to sign agreements on other issues. He nevertheless advanced anew his idea of cutting nuclear arsenals in half and seemed willing to consider an American proposal to eliminate all intermediate-range missiles in Europe. Thus the two leaders built the foundation for further progress, and Gorbachev reaffirmed his desire to pursue arms control.

On April 26, 1986, Gorbachev's reform program suffered a major setback when the worst disaster of the nuclear age struck at Chernobyl', in northern Ukraine. An accidental explosion at an old-style nuclear reactor, triggered by a combination of human error and faulty design, scattered radioactive material across the region and nearby Byelorussia (now Belarus). Considerable traces reached as far as Western Europe. The official death toll came to thirty-eight, but recent evidence suggests that more than 100,000 people later died or suffered severe harm from radiation, including thousands of inadequately protected clean-up workers. The fallout devastated hundreds of square miles and rendered large areas uninhabitable.

Swedish air monitors and newspapers first reported that something was amiss. Local Soviet officials, then republican and central government bureaucrats, tried to cover up or minimize the havoc. When the Gorbachev regime remained silent, wild rumors abounded. Finally the Soviet government provided a scant, unsatisfactory account of what had happened. On May 14, almost three weeks after the accident, Gorbachev defensively discussed the problem in a televised address. His stock with his own population and in the West plummeted. Many Soviet citizens and outside observers criticized the secrecy, the ineptitude, and the confusion surrounding the tragedy and concluded that, despite *perestroika,* the same old repressive system still held sway.

Chernobyl' nevertheless yielded some positive consequences. The incident's economic losses, running into billions of rubles, persuaded reformers to press for more radical changes in the economy in 1987. The terror at Chernobyl' also spurred international efforts to impose stricter safety standards on the development of nuclear energy. Moreover, Gorbachev used the accident to bolster his campaign for limitations on nuclear arms. Finally, although it is unclear whether the impetus came from Gorbachev and his advisers or from scientists and other members of the intelligentsia, official information policy changed. Frank discussion of issues was encouraged, and *glasnost'*, more a slogan than a reality in the first year of Gorbachev's leadership, expanded to include the press, the arts, and history. The regime now actively sought to dispel public mistrust of official pronouncements, a longstanding attitude that the handling of the Chernobyl' disaster had pushed to the brink. All the same, in Ukraine, the disaster stirred resentment against the central government and fueled developing nationalism.

Yet even before the Chernobyl' catastrophe forced candor on the government, Gorbachev had started to encourage freedom of expression in cultural life. In May 1986, a slate of reformers ousted the Party Old Guard from the top positions in the Soviet film industry, and the new leaders called for release of all previously censored films. In June Gorbachev urged the cadres in the Central Committee to stop dictating to intellectuals and instead to enlist their support. At a meeting with leading writers, he asked for their backing. That summer, the press began to publish accounts of the radiation dangers resulting from Chernobyl', and within a few months the government welcomed international assistance in treating victims of the disaster. The media, breaking a traditional Soviet taboo, began to report transportation accidents. Moreover, Alexander Yakovlev, Gorbachev's adviser on ideology and culture, helped to arrange for independent, proreform editors to take over several journals in Moscow. These publications included *Novy mir*, which soon began to print works banned in the Brezhnev era; *Ogonyok*, which became a daring proponent of openness and change; and *Moscow News*, originally published in several foreign languages for tourists. The last journal expanded into investigative reporting and sought out radical pieces by controversial writers. As one example, it ran a shocking exposé of malnutrition among Central Asian children.

In December 1986, Gorbachev escalated his effort to win the backing of the Soviet intelligentsia. He personally telephoned nuclear scientist and prominent dissident Andrei Sakharov at his place of internal exile in Gorky and invited him to return to Moscow to resume his normal work and life. Gorbachev thus conceded the error on the part of the Party and the government in condemning and illegally sequestering the scientist. His action called into question other steps taken against dissidents during the Brezhnev years and earlier.

Also in late 1986, *Repentance*, an allegorical film by Georgian director Tengiz Abuladze, was released. The work, made in 1984 but then banned, scored an instant hit and illustrated how far *glasnost'* had advanced. In abstract, surrealistic fashion, the movie depicts the degradation and havoc visited on a family by a cruel, delusionary tyrant. A damning indictment of Stalin's despotism, the film wrenchingly portrays the futility of resistance, the baseness of acquiescence, and the persistence of evil. *Repentance*'s modern technique and brutal candor created a sensation. The film also paved the way for further historical revelations about the horrors of Stalinism.

As with so many of his achievements, Gorbachev expanded and intensified *glasnost'* not because of adherence to an abstract principle such as freedom of speech but for pragmatic reasons. By the summer of 1986, he had seen that hidebound opponents of his reform effort possessed far more power than he had expected. He knew that he would have to use public discussion to put pressure on or oust traditionalists. He also hoped to persuade talented individuals to devise solutions for the problems that *glasnost'* revealed. Finally, he yearned to energize the bulk of the population to work harder and contribute to the reform effort. As he put it in a speech delivered in September 1986, "We want our people . . . to say what they think. When we come to know how things really are— when we stop telling each other niceties and begin to discuss things in a businesslike and open way . . . then we will undoubtedly find answers to all our questions."[3] *Glasnost'* did not yet mean complete freedom of expression, however. Criticism still had serious limits: challenges to socialism, to the basic principles of the Soviet system, and to Gorbachev were forbidden.

Despite his successes abroad in 1985 and 1986 and manifestations of *glasnost'* in late 1986, Gorbachev's reform record, after almost two years in office, was not impressive. Although the Twenty-seventh Party Congress in February 1986 had supported some of his ideas, the economic acceleration that Gorbachev had sought did not materialize. After a slight upturn, the economy again fell back in early 1987. Moreover, despite personnel changes, resistance to reform within the Party and the state bureaucracies had stiffened. Gorbachev would have to resort to drastic measures.

The Apogee of Reform, 1987–1989

Gorbachev understood that improving the economy was an essential precondition for reviving the Soviet system. In 1987 he moved beyond cosmetic economic reforms and introduced "market socialism." This policy sought to temper state ownership of major industries (reminiscent of the "commanding heights of industry" of the NEP period) with economic decentralization, limited privatization, and a simulated market. Gorbachev wanted first to minimize the suffocating blanket of regulations through

---

[3]Quoted in ibid., p. 141.

which planners and administrators micromanaged the economy. However, he faced a formidable challenge in trying to replace a bureaucratic mechanism with one driven in part by incentives and supply and demand. A vast network of officials, 25 to 30 million strong, controlled several hundred thousand industrial, agricultural, and trade enterprises, setting prices on every item produced and issuing millions of orders and prohibitions annually. Only a few participants in this colossal bureaucracy were eager to revolutionize the system; most had a vested interest in keeping it unchanged.

In a January 1987 meeting of the Central Committee, Gorbachev outlined his second-phase economic reforms, only to encounter intense resistance. At a follow-up session in June 1987, he won grudging assent to proceed. By the end of the year, he had launched most of his new package. The program retained central planning, and most industries remained state-owned; thus the U.S.S.R. did not embrace capitalism, as some accounts in the Western media suggested. Instead, Gorbachev and his advisers initiated five key economic changes. Most important, they tried to decentralize day-to-day decision making and to move factories and other economic units such as retail organizations toward self-sufficiency and profitability. Put very simply, the plan required each factory's managers to decide for themselves what to manufacture, how to produce it most efficiently, and where and how to sell it. Each production unit would make contracts with other entities, including the state, for sales and for acquisition of the necessary machinery and raw materials. Each unit could also set wages and hire and fire workers, but workers received the right to participate in selecting their bosses. Most enterprises would no longer enjoy state subsidies and would have to be "self-financing"; that is, businesses would have to earn a profit. The majority of these changes were embodied in the Law on State Enterprises, which went into effect on January 1, 1988.

To supplement such decentralization, the reformers sought to encourage competition in wholesale transactions. For some products, they established free bidding on contracts for purchases and sales in the hope that this procedure would force economic units to make cost-efficient decisions. Because expensive and shoddy materials would find no purchasers, the reformers reasoned, this shift would generate both lower costs and higher quality.

Gorbachev also fostered cooperatively owned private businesses in retail services like restaurants and repair shops and in light industry such as clothing and household supplies. To prevent skilled managers from leaving existing enterprises, though, the program specified that people already employed could not form cooperatives. Cooperatives could own property (except land), and members divided profits among themselves. The new organizations could set their own prices, which usually ranged higher than those established by the state. Cooperatives mushroomed in 1987 and 1988. Despite heavy state taxation, many of them stacked up impressive profits because they offered goods and services either unavailable in state shops or of better quality than the state could supply.

In addition, Gorbachev promoted foreign trade and outside investment in the U.S.S.R. He hoped to acquire high-technology products from abroad such as computers and communications equipment and to upgrade Soviet technology and methods through exposure to advanced techniques from Japan and the West. Ending the previous state monopoly on foreign trade, he permitted economic units to make their own arrangements with foreign suppliers and purchasers. He also encouraged joint ventures with foreign companies.

Finally, Gorbachev introduced limited reforms in agriculture. The most important of these allowed families or other small groups to lease part of their collective- or state-farm land and to work it independently. The farm would contract with them for part of what they produced, and they were free to sell the remainder on the open market. Yet the leasing program made little headway, owing to farm managers' resistance and farmers' reluctance to risk bad weather, low prices, and a possible governmental change of heart.

This package of economic reforms saw uneven implementation, but most changes were well established by 1989. As we shall see, however, the results overall were disappointing. Only cooperatives demonstrated success, growing from 13,921 with 155,880 employees on January 1, 1988, to 245,300 with more than 6 million employees on January 1, 1991. By this latter date, they accounted for 21 percent of consumer-goods production and 38 percent of retail services.

In 1987 Gorbachev also turned his attention to democratization. Yet just as *perestroika* did not imply complete rejection of socialism, nor *glasnost'* untrammeled freedom of opinion, so democratization did not signify a fully representative system. But Gorbachev's changes revamped the political structure and substantially enhanced popular participation in government. Although earlier he had talked vaguely about reviving "socialist democracy," Gorbachev decided in 1987 to install direct democratic practices. As he saw it, democratization would dislodge old-fashioned or corrupt bureaucrats, especially those who hobbled his reform program. He also hoped that it would unlock popular energy and initiative and give citizens a stake in the system. As Gorbachev pithily put it, "A house can be put in order only by a person who feels that he owns the house." As a by-product of democratization, Gorbachev wanted to infuse his peoples with a renewed sense of purpose and direction, attitudes that Stalin had crushed and that Soviet society had lacked since the heady days of the revolution and the difficult building of Soviet power.

To democratize the workplace, reformers demanded that directors and managers be held accountable for labor policies and production failures and that employees elect them directly or through councils. Gorbachev urged workers to insist on full and honest reports from their bosses and to replace inefficient or corrupt managers. This plan was implemented in some factories and other organizations, but in most institutions, party or state officials still appointed executives and managers or manipulated the elections.

Focusing on the political structure, Gorbachev argued at the January 1987 Central Committee meeting that electoral democratization was essential to the success of his reform program. He received a lukewarm response but pressed his case at the June Central Committee meeting that year. The committee reluctantly agreed to hold a special Party Conference the following year to decide the issue. Gorbachev then tried multicandidate voting in local Soviet elections in fall 1987. After lengthy, heated debate at the conference, he won approval for permitting (but not requiring) more than one candidate in elections to Party and governmental bodies, for limiting officials to two five-year terms, and for creating a new system of soviets. The last change aimed to replace the primarily symbolic, rubber-stamp Supreme Soviets with active, popular assemblies chosen in broadened, two-tier elections at the republican and national levels. Through direct elections and associations, citizens were to choose a Congress of People's Deputies, which would then select a full-time, working legislature still known as a Supreme Soviet. The revised legislative structure, embodied in changes to the Constitution, won approval on December 1, 1988. A constitutional review commission, akin to the U.S. Supreme Court, was established as well.

In March 1989, the first nationwide democratic elections in more than seventy years (since the voting for the abortive Constituent Assembly in 1917) produced an 89.8 percent electoral turnout and attention-getting results. In some instances, Party stalwarts, in time-honored fashion, manipulated nominating meetings so that only one candidate appeared on the ballot. Yet in 75 percent of the districts, two or more candidates won nomination. Instead of the traditional electoral method of a single, Party-designated nominee, citizens could choose among candidates with differing views. In a surprising number of cases, prominent Party and state officials lost, including the first secretary of the Leningrad Party committee and several government ministers. Voters elected two-thirds of the 2,250 members of the new national Congress of People's Deputies. One-third were appointed by various organizations, including the Party, trade unions, and scientific groups. The congress in turn chose a Supreme Soviet of 542 deputies, which elected Gorbachev as its chairman. He thus became president of the Soviet Union as well as head of the Party. Gorbachev clearly intended to use the Supreme Soviet as a tool, independent of the Party, to further his reform program.

The March 1989 elections saw a major breakthrough toward a

democratic system. Nevertheless, the outcome was hardly representative. Establishment institutions chose one-third of the deputies. At the national level, officials constituted 65 percent of the deputies; workers and collective farmers, only 23 percent. Although five religious leaders and several prominent members of the scientific and cultural intelligentsia, including Sakharov, emerged as deputies, Party members made up 87.6 percent of those elected. Women captured only 17 percent of the seats. Minorities also felt underrepresented, and their dissatisfaction intensified nationalist stirrings in the non-Russian regions.

Despite this weighting toward the existing power structure, the Congress and the Supreme Soviet soon reflected the increasingly acrimonious nationwide debate over Gorbachev's reform program. Television coverage of sessions of the national Congress of People's Deputies and of the Supreme Soviet offered Soviet citizens unheard of exposure to conflicting opinions over state policy and the amazing spectacle of the Supreme Soviet's rejecting one-third of the government's nominees as ministers. In late 1989, democratization advanced another step when the Congress of People's Deputies eliminated nominating meetings for most of the country. The congress also approved direct elections to republican Supreme Soviets everywhere except in the Russian Republic, which retained its Congress of People's Deputies. As we shall see in Chapter 12, this holdover would create political gridlock after 1991.

At the grass-roots level, democratization capitalized on informal associations that had emerged in the 1970s and early 1980s. At first these groups had operated in such politically "safe" areas as environmental protection, historic preservation, and veterans' rights. Stimulated by *glasnost'*, they ballooned after 1986 and embraced a range of issues: children's and women's rights, promotion of national cultures, critiques of socialism, memorialization of the victims of Stalin's oppression, and many others. Reactionary bodies also sprang up: *Pamyat' (Memory)*, for example, promoted Russian chauvinism and attacked "Jewish-Masonic conspirators" for undermining traditional ways. By 1990 tens of thousands of organizations had registered with the government.

Also that year, the Soviet political scene saw the emergence of more than twenty political parties, though none of them represented a broad constituency or clear program. Ambitions and petty quarrels led to splits and constant reorganizations. The instability in turn yielded chaotic, unpredictable voting in the Congress of People's Deputies and the Supreme Soviet, with neither the government nor its opponents able to control a dominant bloc of deputies. Gorbachev, still based in the Communist Party, failed to build a political coalition in support of *perestroika* and soon found his program under attack from both the left and right.

His radical critics included Sakharov, who warned against a possible Gorbachev dictatorship, and Yeltsin, who demanded an end to Party privileges and to the Party's dominance of social and political institutions. Yeltsin, a year younger than Gorbachev and the son of a worker, had grown up in the Urals near Sverdlovsk (now returned to its pre-Soviet name, Ekaterinburg). A talented student, he graduated from the local technical institute and worked as a construction engineer for over a decade before entering full-time Party work in his mid-thirties. He rose to head the Party in Sverdlovsk and was promoted to Moscow Party chief in 1985 and then to membership in the Politburo. Some observers mistakenly thought that Yeltsin was Gorbachev's disciple. In fact, he proved an independent and somewhat quixotic politician.

In Moscow Yeltsin soon earned a reputation as a maverick by railing against the failures of the city administration. He traveled throughout the capital to meet residents and hear their complaints directly. He urged broader and more rapid reform and emerged as a populist critic of the establishment, especially Party *apparatchiks* who stood in the way of change. Yet Yeltsin, a disorganized administrator stymied by the overall floundering economy, failed to improve conditions substantially in Moscow. Dismayed that opponents of change seemed to be gaining the upper hand, he chafed at Gorbachev's reluctance to stand up to them. Yeltsin wrote to the Party leader on September 12, 1987, bemoaning the slow pace of reform and the high-handed, obstructionist behavior of Ligachev, Gorbachev's deputy for the Party's routine affairs. Yeltsin concluded by asking to be relieved of his Party responsibilities. Gorbachev suggested that they discuss Yeltsin's criticisms in mid-November after the extensive celebrations of the seventieth anniversary of the Bolshevik revolution.

But in late October, Yeltsin unexpectedly aired his complaints at a meeting of the Central Committee, again castigating Ligachev and, indirectly, Gorbachev. Yeltsin's denunciation of the Party and of Gorbachev was unprecedented. Gorbachev's response, however, smacked of the old methods of Party centralism. At a special meeting of the Moscow Party Committee two weeks later, the Soviet leader blasted Yeltsin and oversaw the latter's removal as head of the Moscow Party. Soon, however, Gorbachev gave Yeltsin a ministerial-rank job in the Soviet government. Yeltsin emerged the top vote-getter in the March 1989 Congress elections, and Gorbachev then supported his election to the Supreme Soviet as well. There the stubborn reformer ultimately headed the opposition.

Gorbachev's treatment of Yeltsin in the fall of 1987 illustrated the dilemma that increasingly burdened the Soviet leader. To appease Party traditionalists, whom he still hoped to win over to reform, he concluded that he had to sacrifice Yeltsin. Yet by retaining the Moscow leader in the government, Gorbachev sought to convince the radicals that he still supported reform. This compromise marked the beginning of Gorbachev's attempts to satisfy both liberal and conservative elements in the Party and the country, a tightrope act that he could not sustain.

Although officials at first suppressed Yeltsin's October denunciation of the Party and its leadership, news soon leaked out. Spontaneous pro-Yeltsin rallies convened, and letters of protest flooded newspapers and Party headquarters. Reformers rallied to his support. Concurrently, Gorbachev grappled with pressure from conservative forces led by Ligachev and Viktor Chebrikov, head of the KGB. In March 1988, a letter to a conservative newspaper from Leningrad educator Nina Andreeva sharply attacked the very bases of reform. The missive blamed *perestroika* and *glasnost'* for undercutting moral values and socialist tradition and argued that reforms promoted instability and insecurity among the bulk of the population. Radical reformers feared that Andreeva's obviously Party-sponsored condemnation of current policy signaled the triumph of conservative elements. A rejoinder to her criticism did not appear for three weeks. Worse, at the special Party conference in June, conservatives muscled a strong showing. It seemed that *perestroika* might suffer a reversal.

In addition to a reactionary backlash, the Soviet leader saw his popular support melt away throughout 1989. Democratization proved a mixed blessing for Gorbachev. As he intended, it energized the nation, and the elections and legislative bodies introduced in 1989 initially sparked widespread interest and support. But when reform institutions were revealed as a conglomeration of quarreling politicians unable to effect practical improvements, fascination with democracy turned to disgust and cynicism. Domination of the new power structure by familiar Communist faces stirred disillusionment as well. In the public's view, the government had provided a captivating facade, but the same old bosses still ran the show. Because of the deteriorating economy, Soviet citizens' lives had turned harsher than ever. As a moonlighting taxi driver bitterly protested to American journalist Hedrick Smith,

> People see how the *verkhushka* [the elite] live—not one *dacha*, but two! All kinds of medicines. We can't get such medicines. But *they* get them from you in the West. Why don't they get them for everyone. . . . My kitchen is only six feet by six feet. . . . It's like a closet. But *they*—they get three- and four-room apartments with kitchens three times the size of mine. These bureaucrats "sit" on our backs. . . . We have to get rid of these high mucky-muck bureaucrats.[4]

By the end of 1989, Gorbachev, still betting on the Party, had little prospect of rallying the electorate to his support.

Most important, the deepening of *glasnost'* from 1987 to 1989 eroded any legitimacy and moral authority that the Party and the ideology of socialism still retained. Gorbachev supported this deepening despite resis-

---

[4]Quoted in Hedrick Smith, *The New Russians* (New York: Avon, 1991), pp. 201–202.

tance by Ligachev and other conservatives. But he either failed to foresee, or failed to understand, that mounting criticism of past abuses and present privilege, designed to eliminate outdated ways and stimulate problem solving, might also spawn a broad rejection of the overall system, including its current leader. Gorbachev himself had led the attack on the Party's recent record. During his first year in office, he had denigrated the "stagnation," bombast, and graft of the Brezhnev era. By 1988 he reversed the naming of places and institutions after Brezhnev. Rehabilitating Khrushchev, a "nonperson" since 1964, the new Soviet leader endorsed Khrushchev's reform efforts. In January 1987, Gorbachev declared that "the people need the whole truth. . . . Openness, criticism and self-criticism, and control exercised by the masses are guarantees of the healthy development of Soviet society." Heeding reformist historian Yuri Afanasyev's call for truthful history and revamped textbooks, Gorbachev promised in February 1987 to fill in the "blank spots" in Soviet history.

That summer, *glasnost'* journals published details about collectivization and the purges, and the rehabilitation of Stalin's victims continued. Author Mikhail Shatrov outpaced the historians with searching plays about the early days of Soviet rule. In fall 1987, existing textbooks and history curricula were scrapped, and leading historians established a commission to set new guidelines for Soviet history. Nevertheless, some topics, such as the 1917 revolutions and the 1930s industrialization, and certain figures, like Bukharin and Trotsky, remained off limits.

Historians and other intellectuals eagerly anticipated a speech that Gorbachev had announced for early November 1987, the seventieth anniversary of the Bolshevik Revolution. Yet Gorbachev's review of the past disappointed many liberals. Clearly a compromise crafted by the Politburo, his cautious text praised Lenin and even the early Stalin while condemning Trotsky. Gorbachev described high-tempo industrialization as expeditious but admitted to errors in collectivization. Further, he conceded that Stalinist methods had led to excessive centralization, bureaucratism, and a rigid command-administrative system that ignored the needs of the people and that had led to mass repressions of "many thousands." (The true figure was many millions, as Gorbachev well knew.) Nevertheless, radicals found solace in Gorbachev's conclusion, which announced establishment of a Central Committee commission on history and encouraged extended "truthful analysis" of the past.

New revelations soon followed. In February 1988, Bukharin was rehabilitated, and in 1989 the first dispassionate treatment of Trotsky appeared. In May 1988, the journal *Novy mir* published Vasily Seliunin's article, "Roots," which linked Stalinist terror directly to Lenin and accused the father of Bolshevism of crushing the people's free spirit. Mass graves of tens of thousands executed by the secret police in the 1930s were discovered and publicized. In 1989, partly in connection with the fiftieth anniversary of the prewar Nazi-Soviet pact, the protocol that

A Polish Victim of Stalin's Secret Police   A Red Cross doctor examines the body of a Polish officer shot by the NKVD in 1940 in Katyn, a site discovered by the Germans during their retreat from Russia in 1944.

divided Eastern Europe between the two states was discussed in a television session of the Congress of Peoples' Deputies and finally published. And Khrushchev's "secret" speech to the Twentieth Party Congress in 1956 was finally printed.

Glasnost' spread beyond history. In the arts, works written but unpublished under Brezhnev were released. Long-banned books, including Boris Pasternak's *Doctor Zhivago* and George Orwell's *Animal Farm,* a biting satire of the Stalin era, appeared, along with previously prohibited poems by Anna Akhmatova and Alexander Tvardovsky. Journals took on new life, printing works far removed from the dreary tenets of socialist realism, including a spate of moving fiction and poetry by women writers. Expatriated authors such as Vladimir Nabokov and Alexander Solzhenitsyn saw their works issued in the Soviet Union for the first time. Abstract and expressionist paintings by foreign, émigré, and Soviet artists were widely shown, and religious art, long banned, enjoyed a renaissance. Plays and films that criticized the bureaucracy and that portrayed the problems of daily life won wide attendance and ardent discussion.

The media, although mindful of the limits of the relaxed information policy, began offering frank treatments of previously suppressed social problems, including drug abuse, prostitution, crime, suicide, rising infant mortality, wife abuse, and unequal pay and growing unemployment for women. Investigative journalists ferreted out corruption, bureaucratic arrogance, and economic discrimination, and particularly reviled elite privileges. Blunt debates about industrial and agricultural failures replaced glowing reports of Five Year Plan triumphs. Even the KGB invited journalists to visit and ask questions. Iconoclastic television programs like "View" in Moscow and "600 Seconds" in Leningrad attracted millions of viewers, and sales of *glasnost'* journals such as *Ogonyok* skyrocketed. The deluge of information overwhelmed many citizens, who complained that they lacked the time to keep up with all the latest revelations.

Finally, *glasnost'* stimulated widespread public discourse on environmental, preservationist, and ethical issues. Publications and organizations advocated the restoration and protection of historical buildings and the conservation of wildlife and natural areas. Ecologists grew particularly active, and their vocal opposition helped to block schemes to divert the headwaters of some Siberian rivers into Central Asia and to dam the Gulf of Finland near Leningrad. With a few exceptions, authorities tolerated public demonstrations and meetings, including rallies to support the building of a memorial to Stalin's victims. Nostalgic interest in the Romanov family, tsarist memorabilia, and the prerevolutionary nobility sprang up. Many Orthodox churches and monasteries reopened, and the ranks of religious believers swelled. In December 1989, on the occasion of a visit to the Pope in Rome, Gorbachev legalized the Ukrainian Catholic, or Uniate, Church, which Stalin had banned almost fifty years earlier.

An interesting corollary of *glasnost'* came with Gorbachev's decision to reverse his predecessors' emigration policy. He permitted Volga Germans to leave for West Germany, and he gradually allowed unrestricted emigration for Soviet Jews. Some seventy thousand Jews departed for Israel and the United States in 1989. This new openness salved a major sore point in Soviet-American relations.

The legally trained Gorbachev also sought to establish the rule of law in Soviet society. Almost all remaining political prisoners were released. Conditions in prisons and correctional labor camps improved, and the KGB came under tight control. In addition, Gorbachev encouraged the prosecution of corruption cases and the drafting of a modernized and more humane code of criminal law. He backed formation of a committee on constitutional oversight and supported measures designed to ensure the independence of the courts. Finally, he made clear that he aspired to a system in which "everything not specifically prohibited is allowed."

Democratization and *glasnost'* exerted a powerful impact on the non-Russian minorities, as we will see below. By burnishing the image of the Soviet Union abroad, the reforms also contributed to Gorbachev's 1987–1989 string of triumphs in foreign relations. At first Gorbachev's successes in international affairs delighted Soviet citizens, who felt his moves deterred the threat of war. They also welcomed the government's lightening of Soviet burdens on behalf of client states and in the Third World, and the expansion of travel and other contacts with foreign cultures. But when conditions at home began to deteriorate and the Soviet "empire" in Eastern Europe broke up, many people turned critical. They groused that Gorbachev had neglected his people to reap personal glory in the West, and they accused him of endangering Soviet security by relinquishing the country's buffer region.

Continued cutbacks in nuclear arms did little to assuage these fears. In December 1987, Gorbachev met President Reagan in Washington to sign a historic treaty eliminating an entire class of weapons. The two leaders agreed to ban all land-based missiles with a range of 300 to 3,400 miles and to verify the missiles' destruction through on-site inspections of each other's facilities. In late spring 1988, Reagan visited Moscow. Although this summit produced few concrete agreements, the two leaders made progress on a formula for cutting strategic warheads by 50 percent, and they pledged to nurture the superpowers' growing rapprochement. In late 1988, Gorbachev delivered an address to the United Nations General Assembly that, remarkably, contained no Marxist formulations or socialist dogma. Instead, the Soviet leader espoused universal human values and pledged full Soviet cooperation in tackling transnational concerns about the environment, health, and poverty. He also announced a unilateral troop cut of half a million Soviet personnel and soon would press for further reductions of Warsaw Pact and NATO forces.

As for "regional issues," or Third World points of contention between the United States and the U.S.S.R., Gorbachev dropped the rhetoric of national liberation and renounced any Soviet expansionist intentions in Asia, Africa, and Latin America. In late 1986, the Politburo had deemed the war in Afghanistan unwinnable and began planning the withdrawal of Soviet forces, which Gorbachev announced in April 1988. After reviewing the loss of fifteen thousand soldiers there, annual expenditures of 5 billion rubles, and the war's unpopularity at home and in the Muslim world, the Soviet leaders apparently concluded that the manifold costs of battling the Afghan guerrillas had risen to an unacceptable level. Following agreements with the United States and Pakistan to cut off aid to the combatants in Afghanistan, the Red Army completed its withdrawal on schedule on February 15, 1989. Gorbachev also counseled Marxist forces in Angola and the Sandinistas in Nicaragua to settle matters with their foes, and he reduced Soviet support for Cuba. He backed efforts to end the Iran-Iraq war, and he urged the Vietnamese to withdraw from Cambodia, which they agreed to do in 1989. Last, he signaled his intent to reduce Soviet troop deployments in Mongolia and along China's northern border.

Now that Gorbachev had met China's prerequisites for improved relations, he visited that country in May 1989 to seek normalization of Sino-Soviet ties. His stay in Beijing was complicated by swelling Chinese student protests (which led to the bloody crackdown in Beijing's Tienanman Square a month later), and negotiations over border issues dragged on. Yet his trip helped to inaugurate an era of closer relations between the two socialist giants.

In the most startling development of these years, however, the U.S.S.R. relaxed its grip on Eastern Europe. As early as his first year in power, Gorbachev had indicated that he expected the Soviet bloc countries to pursue their own *perestroika* and to seek local solutions to their problems. But Eastern Europeans only slowly recognized that the Brezhnev doctrine was dead. Could they trust that Gorbachev would not intervene in their affairs, no matter how much they deviated from Soviet and socialist orthodoxy? As in 1980 and 1981, the Poles asserted their rights first. Since the suppression of Solidarity in December 1981, Wojciech Jaruzelski had fought vainly to win popular support and to improve the dismal conditions of life in Poland. Harassed by widespread strikes in 1988, Polish Communists finally turned back the clock eight years and in early 1989 began talks with the opposition—former Solidarity spokesmen, prominent intellectuals, and Catholic leaders. These negotiations led to semifree elections in the spring of 1989 and a parliament in which the Communists formed a minority. In August 1989, Gorbachev advised the Polish Communist leadership to join a Solidarity-led government, a signal that Moscow would not impose its will in Eastern Europe even if nonsocialist governments came to power. Poland set off on an independent course, dismantling much of its socialist system and pursuing a pan-European foreign policy

Before long the rest of the eastern bloc fragmented. A massive flight of talented East Germans to the West and peaceful weekly vigils and demonstrations by hundreds of thousands of people in key East German cities brought the collapse of that government in November 1989. Even the Berlin Wall crumbled under jackhammers, symbolizing the end of East-West confrontation in Central Europe. In early December, determined Czechoslovak students protesting police repression led a "velvet" revolution that brought a non-Communist government to power headed by playwright and prominent dissident Vaclav Havel. Hungary had begun to move to a multiparty system and away from socialism, and Bulgaria, long a fortress of orthodoxy, installed a new, reformist government. The collapse of communism catalyzed violence only in Romania, as the hard-line regime of Nicolai Ceausescu tried unsuccessfully to cling to power in bloody confrontations in late December 1989.

Gorbachev's "new thinking" in foreign policy had transformed the shape and tenor of world affairs, and for that he won the Nobel Peace Prize in 1990. His efforts to craft a safe, stable world had stemmed partly from personal conviction. Perhaps more important, however, he needed to reduce Soviet commitments abroad, to curtail the nuclear arms race, and to ensure calm on his borders so as to concentrate on rejuvenating his own society. His critics argued that his successes had cost the Soviet state a sharp reduction in prestige and power, especially in Eastern Europe, and had enticed the advance of Western influence across Germany to the Polish border. On the other hand, as Gorbachev pointed out, the security of the country and the welfare of its people had grown stronger with the Cold War's end and with the U.S.S.R.'s cooperative participation in world affairs.

During the apogee of the reform effort, the first ominous signs emerged of a trend that ultimately propelled Gorbachev's downfall. As early as December 1986, combined political-ethnic riots broke out in Kazakhstan after Gorbachev fired Dinuakhmed Kunaev, the long-time, unscrupulous Party boss in that republic, and replaced him with a Russian. Kunaev's henchmen apparently instigated street protests to decry Gorbachev's failure to appoint a Kazakh as Party chief, but local Kazakh youths magnified the uprising into a violent anti-Russian outburst. Gorbachev, to his detriment, ignored the incident's nationalist overtones and omitted ethnic concerns in the broadened reform program that he introduced in 1987.

A second warning sign appeared in February 1988, when turmoil erupted in Nagorno-Karabakh (see the map, Nationalism in the U.S.S.R., 1987–1991), an enclave with a majority Armenian population inside the Azerbaijan Republic. Stalin had allotted Nagorno-Karabakh to Azerbaijan in 1923 during formation of the federal Soviet Union. As nationalist sentiment, encouraged by *glasnost'*, intensified after 1985, Armenians inside the region publicly agitated for transfer of sovereignty over Nagorno-Karabakh to Armenia. Nationalists in Azerbaijan tried to tighten their control over the region and tolerated a violent pogrom against Armenian residents of Sumgait, an industrial city in Azerbaijan. By the time Moscow sent in the army to restore order, dozens of people had been killed in rioting in Sumgait and Nagorno-Karabakh. In Armenia hundreds of thousands demonstrated daily in support of their brethren in Nagorno-Karabakh, and sporadic fighting broke out along the Armenian-Azerbaijan border. Gorbachev sent senior officials to try to mediate the confrontation but refused to endorse the shift of Nagorno-Karabakh to Armenian jurisdiction. Dismayed by the outburst of ethnic violence, he appeared not fully to understand its origins and seemed unable to set a long-term course of action. He made vague promises to consider nationality demands in developing *perestroika* and to include such issues in the summer 1988 Party Conference, but no clear policy emerged.

Separatist movements accelerated in 1989. Nationalists in the Baltic republics began to press openly for autonomy. In the Soviet Georgian capital Tbilisi, Red Army units bloodily suppressed nationalist demonstrations in April 1989, using gas and beating some protesters to death with shovels. Early that summer, ethnic violence between Uzbeks and a

Nationalism in the U.S.S.R., 1987–1991

◿ Areas of growing nationalist activity

▨ Areas of nationalist conflict

Turkish minority group, the Meskhetians, erupted in the Central Asian region of Ferghana.

Unable either to ignore or to resolve these outbreaks, Gorbachev grew increasingly frustrated. He also faced tough political challenges in Moscow in the summer and fall of 1989. On one hand, conservatives continued to block implementation of *perestroika*; on the other, radicals pressured him to go further. Gorbachev's control over the process that he had launched with such high hopes three years earlier rapidly unraveled. His leadership and the Soviet system together approached a final crisis.

Gorbachev Eclipsed, 1990–1991

Several forces spelled the doom of Soviet socialism and of Gorbachev: the failure of economic reform; *glasnost*'s revelations about the past, which discredited the Party, the Soviet system, and Marxism-Leninism; and the power of non-Russian nationalism. These factors lay largely outside Gorbachev's direct control, yet his own training as a Party leader also imprisoned him and limited his ability to consider solutions outside the Party aegis to the U.S.S.R.'s problems. As his measures faltered and the system began to unravel, Gorbachev appeared much like a cork tossed on the mighty waves of change that he had impelled.

The poor performance of the economy in 1988–1989 and its collapse in 1990–1991 undercut the viability of the old system and gravely damaged Gorbachev's ability to govern. Although figures for these years are incomplete, it appears that economic growth reached only about 2 to 3 percent in 1987–1988, fell flat in 1989, and registered a *decline* of 8 percent and 20 percent, respectively, in 1990 and 1991. The picture for consumers played out even worse than these bleak figures suggest. Disorganized reform efforts disrupted consumer production and distribution and led to unpredictable and inexplicable shortages. In mid-1989, for example, soap and related products simply became unavailable in many Soviet cities, and in August 1990, it was impossible to buy a light bulb anywhere in Leningrad or Moscow. During 1990 the government introduced rationing of meat and sugar in many cities, reviving memories of Stalinist and wartime privation. Inflation escalated, hitting 8 percent *a month* in 1990 and making life precarious for retired people and others on fixed incomes.

As the overall standard of living slumped, individuals on the lowest rungs of the socioeconomic ladder slipped into dire poverty. Begging and homelessness, seldom visible in prereform days, made ugly appearances. One destitute woman told American journalist David Remnick that she and thousands like her lived in parks in the summer and in train stations and airports in the winter: "Sometimes I get five rubles a day scrubbing the floors on the trains after they pull into Moscow," she reported. "Right now I'm broke, and everything I have is what you see—the coat and the clothes I'm wearing."[5] Even those with jobs possessed little.

In July 1989, miners in Siberia struck, demanding not just better working conditions but a steady supply of basic consumer items—soap,

---

[5]Quoted in David Remnick, *Lenin's Tomb* (New York: Random House, 1993), p. 200.

Please Help Us! *Glasnost'* permitted homeless people, suffering under the economic dislocations caused by Gorbachev's reforms, to camp out in Moscow near Red Square and St. Basil's cathedral.

toothpaste, sausage, shoes, tea, and underwear. When Remnick visited one of the mining villages, he found polluted air and water; primitive housing; filthy, undernourished children; and only canned tomatoes, oatmeal, and rotting cabbages in the grocery store. Valentina Alisovna, a member of the mine's Party committee, tearfully explained,

> We live like pigs, I'm sorry to say it, but it's true. The mine is a century behind the times. When we go home we can t count on electricity. The water goes out on us. I'm no capitalist, but it's obvious this system has done nothing for us.[6]

Why did Gorbachev's reforms fail to save the Soviet economy? One broad answer lies in its unresponsive and inefficient structure and its socialist principles that precluded competition. In the face of these handicaps, no amount of tinkering could have salvaged it. In fact, the half-measures of 1987 to 1989 that permitted a little privatization through cooperatives and a bit of marketization through bidding on enterprise contracts incorporated some of the worst evils of both socialism and

---

[6]Quoted in ibid., p. 228.

capitalism. Restricted to a small economic sector and hampered by high taxes and intrusive government regulations, cooperatives could make only a tiny dent in pent-up consumer demand. For industrial enterprises, state orders were supposed to make up no more than 50 to 60 percent of total production, with the rest allotted to freely negotiated contracts. Yet in practice, state orders remained at a whopping 80 to 90 percent. Thus, just as before, enterprises served to fulfill the demands of central planners and ministerial bureaucrats. Moreover, because economic officials provided subsidies to forestall the collapse of key industries under their control, local managers had little incentive to cut costs and to achieve profitability. And as inflation shot up, so did workers' wages, a hedge by authorities striving to avert labor strife and political protest. Consequently, workers had no reason to labor harder or more efficiently.

During 1990, as the crisis deepened, experts propounded various radical reform plans. The best known of these theorists was economist Stanislav Shatalin, who in September 1990 proposed all-out privatization, an open market, and the complete freeing of prices within five hundred days. Yet Gorbachev had always remained committed to socialist tenets and feared the political fallout of the runaway inflation that would surely follow the end of price control. At first he endorsed the Shatalin plan, but then he backed off. In early 1991, he finally promulgated a compromise that did little. Whatever policy the Soviet leadership may have settled on, however, abandoning a command-administrative system for a market-based, private-enterprise economy would have entailed chaos and widespread hardship. Perhaps aware of this hard fact, Gorbachev throughout 1990 and 1991 hesitated to act boldly, terrified of fueling his growing unpopularity. Yet as conditions worsened, people blamed first *perestroika* and then more directly its architect, who had promised so much and delivered so little. By the spring of 1991, Gorbachev's approval rating among the Soviet population had sunk to 20 percent.

Few of Gorbachev's critics acknowledged the enormity of the task at hand. The chances of transforming a complex and entrenched system within a few years were slight indeed. Nevertheless, Gorbachev compounded the difficulties by failing to develop a clear plan and by making strategic errors. For one thing, the reformers gave agriculture low priority, even though observers pointed out that a boost in agricultural productivity would provide goods to meet consumer needs, would assist industry by raising rural demand, and would generate savings that could be invested in new industry. The Chinese experience, in which the freeing of agriculture had stimulated an economic boom, underscored the appropriateness of this approach. But because privatizing agriculture, the only way to rejuvenate the farming sector quickly, struck at the heart of socialist dogma, Gorbachev seems never to have considered this option. As a result, agriculture lagged—and still does—putting the brakes on the entire economy. Similarly, the rapid freeing of prices, foreign economists noted, would encourage decentralized managers to make sensible decisions about production costs, sales, and profits. But Gorbachev also rebuffed this step as too direct a path to a market economy and as an almost certain trigger of political unrest.

Aside from these errors in strategy, attitudes in Soviet society blocked radical economic reform. Bureaucratic inertia and resistance eviscerated even the partial reforms of 1987–1989. Not only central planners but local administrators and producers as well had grown used to operating in the old ways. Some were simply incapable of change. Others actively opposed *perestroika* for fear of losing their positions of power and influence. Popular caution as well thwarted change. After years of moderate work loads and a modest but assured livelihood, many Soviet citizens wanted no part of the demands and risks that *perestroika* entailed. Working hard and efficiently did not seem to promise much of a reward when there was little to buy or do. Moreover, numerous people worried that reform would bring higher prices and unemployment. Women, especially, knew that they would be the first to see their wages slashed or their jobs snatched.

The idea of rough equality, deeply ingrained in Russian peasant culture and part of the socialist myth inculcated in Soviet citizens for seventy years, also worked against economic reform. People did not care about "keeping up with the Ivanovs," but they *did* want to make sure that the Ivanovs did not get ahead of them. Most citizens deeply resented those individuals, viewed as profiteers, who benefited financially under *perestroika,* and they became convinced that "the Mafia" controlled free market goods and services. Early on, Gorbachev had forewarned that *perestroika* required not just economic restructuring but a new outlook and behavior as well. He made little headway on the first prerequisite and almost none on the latter.

Further, the surge of non-Russian nationalism hamstrung the Soviet economy. As Moscow's authority weakened and power devolved first to the republics and then to smaller regional entities, national decision making and the countrywide market sputtered. Factories often failed to obtain supplies from or deliver goods to other republics, as each national group tried to maximize its advantage. Economic integration eroded, production fell, and imbalances widened. Jurisdictional disputes erupted as central authorities, republican officials, and local administrators fought over who controlled raw materials, factories, shops, and other assets.

Constrained by the blinders of his Party upbringing, Gorbachev could not grasp the extent to which the socialist ethic was disappearing among Soviet citizens. This erosion of faith had begun at the Twentieth Party Congress in 1956 with the obvious question, "What kind of Party and system was it that had permitted the crimes of Stalin to occur?" *Glasnost'* stepped up this questioning of old verities. As the oppressions and mistakes of the past came to light, blame inevitably fell on the Party, which for all those years had stood as the self-proclaimed "guiding force." And because the Leninist version of socialism had placed the Party in that role and had set the tone for a nationalized economy that had failed, the system as a whole came under fire. Rejecting the Soviet socialist experience, however, did not mean that people embraced capitalism. In fact, most citizens feared that the alternative market system would bring the evils that Soviet propaganda had long told them scourged the West: exploitation, joblessness, crime, and poverty. Disoriented, they had lost their old faith but still struggled to find a new one.

Individuals fumed not just about past deceits and deprivations. They also objected to the continued privilege that the Party elite enjoyed. Yeltsin's popularity stemmed in part from his early and persistent attack on Party perks. The 1917 revolution to some extent had represented a revolt against privilege. Although not consciously harking back to that assault on the upper crust, Soviet citizens in the 1980s and 1990s utterly abhorred the unchecked power and preferred position of Party leaders. As reformer-sociologist Yuri Levada summarized the results of his poll-taking in the late 1980s, "The main form of [popular] consciousness is a wild hostility toward the *apparat*, which they [the masses] feel fills its pockets, takes bribes, enjoys privileges."[7] Gorbachev, nurtured by the Party and profiting from the system, understandably failed to grasp the sweeping and unrelenting scope of this loathing. At the personal level, he could not comprehend the people's hatred of Raisa's elegant clothes and of his own fancy *dachas*. In the national political struggle, Gorbachev clung far too long to his belief in the Party and in socialism. Given his background, career, and position, perhaps it was impossible for him to push for a complete reversal of the old order and for creation of a fully democratic, free-enterprise system.

Yeltsin, on the other hand, began urging market reforms and abandonment of the Party's leading role as early as 1989, and he dramatically resigned from the Party in 1990 to fight for political pluralism. Battling dwindling popularity, Gorbachev reluctantly abandoned his defense of a one-party system in February 1990. The following month, he instructed the Congress of Deputies to abrogate Article 6 of the Soviet Constitution, which enshrined the Party's leading role in society. Despite this grudging concession, Gorbachev continued to insist that although other parties were acceptable, the Communist Party should continue to lead society and state. Yet the Party itself suffered from weaknesses and divisions between conservatives and reformers. Democratization inside the Party proceeded sluggishly, and Party ranks thinned; 4 million members, al-

---

[7]Smith, op. cit., p. 91.

most 20 percent of the membership, resigned during 1990 and 1991. The Party's youth branch, the Komsomol, unable to attract recruits, ceased to exist in 1991. Gorbachev therefore could not count on Party backing; in fact, many Party leaders conspired against him.

Aware of his fading support in the Party and among the populace, Gorbachev managed in 1990 and 1991 to expand his powers as chief executive. During 1989 and early 1990, liberals had pushed for direct election of the Soviet president. Gorbachev resisted this effort, accurately sensing that he might lose in such a contest. In a March 1990 compromise, he at last called for selection of a president by the Congress of Deputies, with the proviso that all future presidents be chosen by nationwide popular vote. The Congress elected Gorbachev the Soviet president, by 71 percent of the deputies' votes. This outcome reflected not popular support but the conviction of the deputies, most of whom were conservative members of the Party establishment, that they had no other choice. Despite warnings from Sakharov and others of the dangers of dictatorship, Gorbachev also won expanded presidential powers to rule by decree and to suspend the legislature in an emergency. In practice he used his new authority sparingly. Some critics believe that he should have forced through radical economic reforms by decree. But still hoping to save some vestiges of the socialist system, he hung back.

Struggling at home, Gorbachev nevertheless continued to chalk up successes abroad. In mid-1990 he visited the United States, where the Bush administration and the press and public warmly welcomed him. In June 1991, Gorbachev and Bush signed a new strategic arms reduction treaty (START I) that cut long-range weapons substantially. Negotiations to implement its provisions continued into the mid-1990s. After initial reluctance, the Soviet leader agreed in late 1990 to West Germany's absorbing East Germany, as well as the unified Germany's joining NATO. In return, German chancellor Helmut Kohl promised economic aid and assistance in relocating to the U.S.S.R. the Red Army units previously stationed in East Germany. These troops all returned home by September 1994. In 1991 Gorbachev also approved the phased withdrawal of Soviet forces from Hungary and Poland. Reflecting the end of East-West confrontation, the Warsaw Pact dissolved. Finally, Gorbachev supported American and UN policy in the 1990–1991 Persian Gulf War. Only in the U.S.S.R.'s relations with Japan was Gorbachev foiled. He could not find a way to return the Kuril Islands to Japanese sovereignty without enraging Russian nationalists at home

Unfortunately for Gorbachev, these foreign policy achievements not only failed to help him domestically but probably intensified right-wing opposition to him. Conservatives accused him of giving away Germany as well as Eastern Europe and of dangerously weakening the U.S.S.R.'s security. They also heaped scorn on his failed economic program and urged a return to state administration of the economy. Pleading for

Down with Gorbachev! Soviet citizens, disappointed in the outcome of *perestroika*, demonstrate for Yeltsin and against Gorbachev, with placards demanding the Soviet leader resign.

resurrection of Party dominance in the state, they cried for reestablishment of law and order. More and more isolated, Gorbachev suffered attacks from the left as well. Liberals accused him of balancing in the center and demanded further democratization and prompt institution of a full market economy. The citizenry grew increasingly cynical and disillusioned, spurning left and right politicians alike. People expressed special bitterness over the skyrocketing crime rate and the accelerating drop in living standards. A 1990 poll showed that 45 percent of the populace believed that their legislative deputies had forgotten the people's interests, and only 14 percent had confidence in the country's governing institutions.

With the nation in despair, the economy careening downhill, and the leadership locking horns, the sense of crisis sharpened. A revolt of the non-Russian minorities against the centralized Soviet state delivered the fatal blow. First stirring in the late 1980s, these forces had escalated out of control by the summer of 1991. Perhaps if the Soviet leader had acted promptly to satisfy the nationalists' initial, moderate demands, he might have held the federal state together, at least for a time. But after several years of gathering momentum, the nationalist tide proved unstoppable, and the non-Russians on all sides clamored for full independence. The sources of their discontent had long roots in centuries of Russian domination; in accumulating resentment of political centralization and economic

exploitation during the Soviet period; and, ironically, in Lenin's nationality policy, which had promoted local culture and pride.

But it took Gorbachev's reform program to uncork the bottle of nationalist discontent. *Glasnost'* fostered the airing of past grievances and
criticism of current circumstances. Democratization then encouraged accountability, popular representation, and greater self-government, all of
which non-Russians used to press for autonomy. In retrospect, the surprise is not that the Soviet Union disintegrated so quickly but that it had
held together for so long.

As we have seen, nationalist unrest first flared in Kazakhstan and in
Nagorno-Karabakh. Yet the main impetus for the assertion of minority
rights came from the Baltic republics, whose Western-oriented peoples
had endured Soviet domination only since 1940, after twenty years of independence. Initial protests broke out on anniversaries connected to Soviet annexation of the region. Taking advantage of *glasnost'*s penchant for
historical revelations, Latvians demonstrated in June 1987, recalling bitterly the tens of thousands of their fellow citizens deported to the *Gulag*
in the summer of 1940 following Soviet occupation of the country. In August 1987, the Baltic peoples held anti-Soviet commemorative meetings
on the anniversary of the Nazi-Soviet pact, which had denominated the

The Baltic Region Erupts Demonstrators in Lithuania protesting Soviet rule in August
1989, the 50th anniversary of the Nazi-Soviet pact that gave Stalin control over the
Baltic area.

area as a Soviet sphere of influence. In August 1988, Estonians published the secret protocol of the pact. By the fall of that year, an active nationalist "popular front"—a broad coalition of citizens of varying classes and political views—arose in Lithuania, where it took the name *Sajudis*. Other fronts sprang up in Estonia and Latvia, and in 1989 similar organizations emerged in the Caucasian republics and Moldova.

The popular fronts generally supported *perestroika* but also pressed for nationalist rights, such as permission to fly traditional flags, to celebrate religious and national holidays, and to expand use of the local language. The Baltic peoples also protested the environmental blight that had accompanied Soviet rule and demanded an end to Russian immigration. Since 1940 ethnic Russians had become a substantial minority in Estonia and almost half the population in Latvia. Meanwhile, Communist leaders in the Baltic republics pressed Moscow for greater political autonomy and for increased control over their own economies, noting that the republics administered less than 10 percent of the industries on their territories. They bridled, too, over the insufficient representation the Soviet Congress of Deputies and Supreme Soviet relegated to the non-Russian areas. Gorbachev agreed only to discuss possible economic decentralization, which accorded with the current phase of his economic reforms.

Politically astute overall, the Soviet leader nevertheless responded reluctantly to non-Russians' demands. Gorbachev appeared to cling to the Soviet myth that socialism had solved the nationality problem and that all peoples of the Soviet Union had learned to live together in harmony. His lack of exposure to minority issues in his early political career may also have contributed to his allotting these matters low priority.

During sessions of the Congress of People's Deputies and of the Supreme Soviet in 1989, representatives from the offended Baltic republics adopted an increasingly independent stance. In August that year, the fortieth anniversary of the Nazi-Soviet pact, more than 1 million Balts joined hands in a human chain that stretched across the three countries to demonstrate their desire for independence. In December 1989, the Lithuanian Communist Party broke from the centralized Communist Party of the Soviet Union in an effort to retain influence in the burgeoning nationalist movement. The other Baltic parties soon followed suit. However, in elections to republic supreme soviets in February and March 1990, non-Communist nationalist forces emerged triumphant, with *Sajudis* obtaining 90 out of 141 seats in Lithuania.

During 1989 and 1990, nationalist sentiment welled up also in the Caucasus, Ukraine, and Moldova. Negotiations to find a compromise resolution to the Nagorno-Karabakh dilemma hit a dead end, and during much of 1989 Moscow ruled the area through virtual martial law. Relations between Armenia and Azerbaijan continued to deteriorate, as more than a hundred thousand Muslims left Armenian territory and almost two hundred thousand Armenians fled Azerbaijan. Although the Moscow government and outside agencies provided substantial aid to these refugees, as well as to earlier victims of a December 1988 earthquake in Armenia, no one could ease the disruption and rancor. In January 1990, violent disorders against Armenians erupted in Baku, the capital of Azerbaijan, requiring Red Army intervention. Hostility between the two peoples and republics ground on through 1990 and 1991, despite efforts by Baltic leaders to mediate.

In Georgia, anti-Soviet nationalist forces raged after the brutal suppression of the April 1989 demonstrations. In delayed republican elections in October 1990, the Georgian equivalent of the Baltic popular fronts, "the Round Table for a Free Georgia," won 54 percent of the seats and began to agitate for full independence. The situation grew complicated when protests flared over Georgian rule of two minorities living within the republic: the South Ossetians and the Abkhaz. Some members of these groups appealed to Moscow for protection while others sought autonomy within a Georgian state. In March 1991, the Georgians demanded full independence and elected separatist and former dissident writer Zviad Gamsakhurdia president of the self-proclaimed state.

In Ukraine, *Rukh*, an organization originally founded to promote Ukrainian culture, elected a number of nationalist deputies to the spring 1990 republican supreme soviet. Joining several deputies who supported environmental issues in reaction to the Chernobyl' disaster, the *Rukh* faction took an increasingly nationalist line in 1990 and 1991 under the leadership of Leonid Kravchuk, a veteran old-line Communist politician. Pressure to make Ukrainian the official language mounted, and in July 1990 Ukrainian leaders declared that their laws would take precedence over Soviet or all-Union legislation. In Moldova, formerly Bessarabia and annexed by Stalin in 1940, a strong anti-Soviet movement also emerged in 1989–1991. Although a few Moldovans dreamed of reuniting with Romania, whose culture and language many of them shared, most nationalists favored an independent state. The issue was clouded, however, by the presence of a large Russian and Ukrainian community living at the mouth of the Dniester River, which insisted on autonomy, or even their own minirepublic.

Even in Russia, nationalist sentiment spread. In 1990 a separate Russian Communist Party was set up for the first time, and other all-Union organizations began to establish distinct Russian branches. In the spring 1990 elections to the Russian supreme soviet, both Russian nationalists and radical critics of Gorbachev did well. The deputies chose Yeltsin to head the soviet, and the following year Russian Republic citizens elected him president with 57.3 percent of the vote. He had become the most popular politician in the country, far outshining Gorbachev.

Unable to keep pace with events, Gorbachev protested futilely when a majority of republican soviets declared that their laws would take

precedence over those of the Soviet state. He consistently mishandled negotiations with the Baltic republics, in the vanguard of the independence
movement. In the first act of open defiance of the Soviet Union, the
Lithuanian soviet on March 11, 1990, voted in principle for independence. Only a declaration, this step could have formed the basis for
drawn-out, friendly negotiations. But Gorbachev castigated the Lithuanian leaders and imposed an economic embargo on the republic. Later that
year, thanks to the intercession of various intermediaries, the Lithuanians
agreed to suspend their mandate, and talks with Moscow commenced.
But in January 1991, conservatives in the Soviet government and bureaucracy organized a direct attack on the Baltic nationalists. Soviet security
units tried to seize communications facilities in Vilna, the Lithuanian capital, by force. The fighting left 13 dead and 112 injured and stoked the
fires of nationalism not only in the Baltic area but throughout the non-
Russian regions of the country. Gorbachev claimed that local commanders acted without authorization, but even if he did not know about this
action, he tolerated a growing hard line in the Baltic region and failed to
shoulder the blame for the use of force. His mishandling of the incident
seriously marred his tenure of power and made it almost impossible for
him to achieve a compromise settlement with any of the non-Russian nationalists.

Except for agreeing to economic decentralization, Gorbachev made
no concession to the nationalities during 1989 and into early 1990, although he finally acknowledged that their demands constituted a major
issue for his regime. In the spring of 1990, he called for a new federal constitution, and at the Twenty-eighth (and last) Party Congress in July 1990,
he asserted that the U.S.S.R. needed an entirely new structure. In March
1991, a presidential commission proposed guidelines for "a union of sovereign states." The draft contained nary a word about socialism and prescribed that membership in the union be voluntary. The central
government would take responsibility for foreign policy, defense, law
enforcement, and some all-Union fiscal matters; everything else would be
run jointly, although it was unclear just how members would make decisions. Put to a popular vote, the principle of a new constitution won
strong support, but six republics (the Baltics, Georgia, Moldova, and Armenia) declined to participate in the referendum.

Further negotiations between Gorbachev and the heads of the nine
republics that did take part produced a more detailed treaty for a "Union
of Soviet Sovereign Republics" on July 24, with its signing set for the following month. Although a notable effort, this compromise probably
came too late. Earlier that year, Lithuania and Georgia had declared their
independence, and several Western countries had moved to support
them. Russia and Ukraine, the two biggest republics in the proposed
union, had stipulated that they wanted virtually exclusive control over
their own resources and economies. Under these conditions, what would

undergird the rewritten union? Too, Gorbachev evidently saw himself as head of the new state, a prospect that pleased almost no one.

Despite his popularity abroad, Gorbachev's status at home had sunk to a low ebb by 1991. In December 1990, his colleague Shevardnadze had resigned from the government, warning of a possible dictatorship from the right unless Gorbachev could establish democracy firmly and broaden economic reform. In late 1990–early 1991, Gorbachev's rejection of the Shatalin plan, his dismissal of liberals from the government, and the use of force in Vilna struck many as efforts to appease conservative forces in the Party and country. Yet by April 1991, he again advocated stronger reforms, and in June he rebuffed a conservative attempt to undercut him. Gorbachev struggled to maintain a centrist position, but the center was fast disappearing as radicals and conservatives alike grew disenchanted and the populace disdainful. As the beleaguered president sought to modify the Soviet Union's federal structure, conservatives added to previous accusations that he had weakened the Party and "lost" Eastern Europe. He was now wrecking the state itself, they barked, destroying the unity that had earned power and pride for over seventy years. Ignoring the uncertain political climate and rumors of a right-wing plot to seize power, Gorbachev left for his usual end-of-summer vacation in the Crimea shortly after the new union treaty was accepted. He planned to return only for the formal signing on August 20. But a treacherous core of conservatives in the government, most of whom Gorbachev himself had appointed, had determined to stop the treaty. On August 19, they launched their doomed coup and thereby sealed the fate of both the Soviet Union and Gorbachev.

Conclusion

More than any other person, Gorbachev shaped the history of the late twentieth century. He is both a heroic and a tragic figure: heroic because he tried to improve his society and the world; tragic because his upbringing and career blinded him to the changes that his fellow citizens most desired. Because his reform efforts often yielded unintended consequences, in the end the innovative forces that he himself had unleashed flung him aside.

When he came to power in 1985, Gorbachev knew generally that all was not right in the Soviet Union. He could have followed Brezhnev's example and papered over the severe problems. But influenced in youth by the brief euphoria that Khrushchev's reforms had aroused, he determined to try to right things. As he told his wife Raisa, "Our country cannot go on living like this. I have to make the changes."

Applying his intelligence and zeal, Gorbachev first tackled the faltering economy, hoping that discipline, sobriety, rationality, and

Could the Soviet Union have saved itself, or was it doomed? The question arises from
the spectacular way in which the U.S.S.R. fragmented in 1991, in contrast to the fate
of earlier empires. The Ottoman empire expired in bits and pieces over many decades.
The British empire also declined slowly, at times voluntarily, as London realized that
the costs of sustaining the colonies outweighed the benefits. A protracted and savage
European war sealed the demise of the Hapsburg empire. The Soviet empire, on the
other hand, imploded in peacetime, from a self-inflicted wound (the abortive August
coup of 1991), flying apart into fifteen new nations. A supposed industrial giant, possessed of advanced scientific technology and bristling with weapons, went. . . poof!

The rapid dissolution of the Soviet system baffled historians, intelligence analysts, and pundits alike. Understandably, during much of the Gorbachev era Western
specialists focused on the new Soviet leader's sweeping agenda of political and economic transformation. The sudden, almost pathetic irrelevance of Gorbachev, the "author" of *perestroika* and *glasnost'*, stunned not only the Kremlin leader but all those
from U.S. president George Bush down whose image of the U.S.S.R. as a salvageable
entity hinged on his being in power. As the salvage operation broke down, curiosity
about Gorbachev's prospects transmuted to postmortems on his failure.

Two of the liveliest accounts of Gorbachev's rule came from Robert Kaiser, acclaimed journalist, and Seweryn Bialer, Soviet specialist at Columbia University.
Kaiser and Bialer agreed on much. Both argued that although no life-threatening crisis
loomed when the last Soviet leader came to power in 1985, Soviet society had severe
problems. The new ruler, with a small group of visionaries, set out to fix the ailing system. Both Kaiser and Bialer emphasized the haphazard nature of Gorbachev's policies
in determining the final outcome, above all his decision to undertake political and economic reforms simultaneously. Both authors pictured Gorbachev as a tragically flawed
figure, a centrist-turned-radical who at critical moments drew back in horror from the
chaos he had helped to unleash. For Kaiser, that moment came in January 1991,
when Gorbachev crushed Lithuanian demands for independence (*Why Gorbachev Happened,* 1991). For Bialer, the Lithuanian crackdown, although a major milepost on the
road to Soviet implosion, chiefly reflected Gorbachev's inability to control Party opposition to more radical change. Gorbachev failed not because he lacked a goal or strategy but because he stuck too closely to the sacred Leninist tradition of "democratic
centralism" ("The Death of Soviet Communism," *Foreign Affairs,* Winter 1991/92).

But what if contingency, policy, and personality proved necessary but insufficient
to explain the outcome? Why, we might ask, did Gorbachev proclaim that the Soviet
engine needed a complete overhaul seventy long years after the "Great October"?
What if the Soviet Union's demise had roots stretching as far back as its creation in
1917?

Several retrospective accounts pointed to the long-standing demands of non-
Russian nationalities for independence as the central reason for the Soviet Union's
downfall. For Harvard University historian Roman Szporluk, communist leaders simply
extended the Russian empire and used socialism as a mask for Russian domination.
The Marxist experiment in Moscow did not herald a new civilization, as Soviet leaders
boasted, but represented an old imperialism masquerading under new management
("After Empire, What?," *Daedalus,* Summer 1994). French specialist Hélène Carrere
d'Encausse concurred, noting that Gorbachev indeed omitted the national question
from his original agenda and subsequently failed to grasp its potential explosiveness.
No matter, she concluded: no amount of tactical flexibility at the center could have

corralled this centrifugal force. The officially trumpeted *homo sovieticus* was a myth. As these scholars argued, communism evaporated because of the fatal gap between ethnic policy and practice, between cultural recognition for non-Russian communities and a lack of outlets for their political expression. "National feeling toppled communism into the history of dead utopias," d'Encausse concluded (*The End of the Soviet Empire*, 1992).

An ideology-based explanation of Soviet communism's imminent failure emerged as early as 1990, still at the height of the "Gorby Cult" in the West. That year, *Daedalus* published "To the Stalin Museum," authored by the anonymous Z, later identified as Martin Malia, Russian historian at the University of California, Berkeley. Malia, who insisted on secrecy on the grounds that use of his name might lead the KGB to his sources, denied that the imperatives of economic and social development sooner or later would transform the Soviet Union into a modern society. He concluded instead that the Soviet experiment was doomed because of its utopianism, its unique attempt in the twentieth century to implement "full non-capitalism" in the name of equality. That effort produced a "surreal" world in which power and ideology substituted for property, prices, the market, and civil society. The system could command, as it did at its height under Stalin, but it could not over time allocate human and material resources in an increasingly complex world. Nor could Soviet socialism learn from its mistakes. A party-state (partocracy) rewrote the laws of history to suit its own purposes and drove society into a cul-de-sac from which there was no escape short of a collective nervous breakdown. In this analysis, the Soviet Union was an instance of perverse modernity, of a mad-hatter's tea party lasting seven decades ("To the Stalin Museum," *Daedalus*, January 1990).

The end of the world's first socialist state will inspire as much intense scrutiny as its beginning. Reflections will center not only on what transpired, but on how historians make sense of it. Access to archives once closed to outside view will facilitate fresh analyses. Even a brief review of the first round of Western historiography on this topic reveals the need to expand our analytical framework from the quantitative to the qualitative, from models of society based only on what is measurable to what is less measurable but no less important. Gale Stokes, historian of Eastern Europe, concludes that "studies that do not adequately take into account such intangibles as ethical values, religion, and national sentiment" are flawed ("The Lessons of 1989," *Problems of Communism*, September–October 1991). Gorbachev was not alone in overlooking the corrosive force of nationalism; with few exceptions, many in the West also ignored its impact or vaunted claims of proletarian internationalism until those claims evaporated.

John Lukacs has suggested that although we live forward, we can think only backward (*The End of the Twentieth Century*, 1993). The Gorbachev era, so unforeseen both at its outset and in its extraordinary denouement, serves as a double reminder: first, of the danger of reducing reality to an underlying principle, any principle; second, of the likelihood that the only safe conclusion we can venture about the future is that it will surprise us.

"acceleration" would revive it. He also recognized that the Brezhnevian norms of mediocrity and passivity were wasting the talents of an increasingly educated and sophisticated populace. Thus he sought to enlist the Soviet peoples in his crusade by encouraging their creativity and openness and by granting them say in the running of their own institutions and society. When the economy responded only minimally to his early cures, Gorbachev decided to initiate more sweeping changes and to deepen *glasnost'* and democratization.

To facilitate his reform program, the Soviet leader needed to reduce the burden of the arms race with the United States. At the same time, he genuinely believed in international cooperation and helped to reverse forty years of superpower rivalry and confrontation. He made unilateral concessions that opened the door to substantial reductions in nuclear weapons; he ended Soviet interference in the Third World; he patched up relations with China; and he acquiesced in the demise of socialism in Eastern Europe.

Yet economic revival at home eluded him, and his standing among the Soviet people began to slide. Moreover, he had believed from the start that he could revitalize the Soviet system without felling two of its pillars—socialism and the leading role of the Party. Indeed, he sought to use a refurbished Party as his instrument of change. Although he agreed in 1987 and 1988 to a limited market, he continued to oppose private ownership and free prices. He remained a dedicated Leninist seeking a better, but nonetheless *socialist*, society. As he once concluded, "Should I denounce whole generations as if they had lived in vain? No, I think we will never agree to trample underfoot that which we, our fathers and grandfathers have been doing for decades."

As he struggled to promote change without losing control, Gorbachev failed to see that the citizenry blamed the Party for past excesses and current deficiencies and had determined to throw off its yoke. The Soviet people were also fed up with the broken promises and hypocritical cant of socialism. Although hardly fans of capitalism, they wanted no more of the old faith. Still trying to balance between reforming radicals and the conservative elite, Gorbachev maneuvered desperately through 1990 and 1991 to hold the middle ground.

The final blow to Gorbachev's hopes came with the unstoppable surge of anti-Soviet sentiment among first the non-Russian minorities and then the Russians themselves. Gorbachev, still mesmerized by the Soviet ideal of ethnic harmony and common socialist interests, realized far too late that *glasnost'* and democratization had released pent-up, uncontainable forces of anticentrist sentiment and national pride. Giving ground grudgingly, he missed the chance to satisfy the aspirations of the republics and only angered conservative leaders. When bumbling right-wingers, whom he himself had brought into the government, attempted to seize power and restore the earlier ways, the reformers, inspired by

Yeltsin, defied the old guard and the coup collapsed. This event marked the end of the Soviet state and of Gorbachev's hold on power.

Gorbachev had wrought remarkable change, far more daring than anyone could have imagined in 1985. Future generations will undoubtedly laud his achievements in opening the door to fundamental reform in the U.S.S.R. and Eastern Europe and in ending the Cold War. Yet he failed on his own terms. He set out to reform the Union's socialist economy. Meeting opposition, he used *glasnost'* to scatter foes of reform. Ironically, *glasnost's* revelations about the Soviet past undermined the very legitimacy of the system and led to the collapse of the ideals Gorbachev embraced. Perhaps his successors in Russia and the other former republics may yet find a way to salvage the vision of socialism that Gorbachev so hoped to resurrect. However, as the nascent states struggle to fashion independent nations from the wreckage of the Soviet Union, they face formidable problems of economic regeneration, political stability, and cultural resurrection, as we see in Chapter 12.

FURTHER READING

It is too soon for a comprehensive scholarly biography of Gorbachev, but his own account of the beginnings of reform is useful: Mikhai S. Gorbachev, *Perestroika: New Thinking for Our Country and the World* (New York, 1988). Although written before Gorbachev's failure, Moshe Lewin's *The Gorbachev Phenomenon* (Berkeley, Calif., 1988) offers helpful insights. The best short general account of the whole period is Stephen White, *Gorbachev and After*, 3rd ed. (Cambridge and New York, 1992). Of several books analyzing the demise of Soviet socialism, the most intriguing is Loren Graham, *The Ghost of the Executed Engineer: Technology and the Fall of the Soviet Union* (Cambridge, Mass., 1993), which focuses on an individual in an earlier period but tells volumes about why the system failed.

Several sound journalistic and personal accounts of the downward path of the U.S.S.R. exist: Robert G. Kaiser, *Why Gorbachev Happened* (New York, 1991); David Remnick, *Lenin's Tomb: The End of the Soviet Empire* (New York, 1993); Hedrick Smith, *The New Russians* (New York, 1991); and William and Jane Taubman, *Moscow Spring* (New York, 1989).

An excellent analysis of the precollapse Gorbachev era is Geoffrey Hosking, *The Awakening of the Soviet Union* (Cambridge, Mass., 1990). Helpful on economic reform are Robert W. Campbell, *The Socialist Economies in Transition* (Bloomington, Ind., 1991); Padma Desai, *Perestroika in Perspective: The Design and Dilemma of Soviet Reform* (Princeton, N.J., 1989); and Marshall Goldman, *What Went Wrong with Perestroika* (New York, 1992).

Helpful articles on various aspects of the Gorbachev years are found in Seweryn Bialer, ed., *Politics, Society, and Nationality Inside Gorbachev's Russia* (Boulder, Colo., 1989). Political and social issues are treated in Yeltsin's autobiography, Boris Yeltsin, *Against the Grain* (New York, 1990). Other noteworthy sources include Linda J. Cook, *The Soviet Social Contract and Why It Failed* (Cambridge, Mass., 1993); T. Anthony Jones, *Perestroika: Gorbachev's Social Revolution* (Westview, Conn., 1990); Gail Lapidus, *State and Society in the Soviet Union* (Boulder, Colo., 1989); Stephen Kotkin, *Steeltown USSR: Soviet Society in the Gorbachev Era* (Berkeley, Calif., 1991); Mary Buckley, ed., *Perestroika and Soviet Women* (Cambridge, 1992); Francine Du Plessix Gray, *Soviet Women: Walking the Tightrope* (New York, 1990), and R. W. Davies, *Soviet History in the Gorbachev Revolution* (Bloomington, Ind., 1989).

Nationality issues are treated in Ronald Suny, *The Revenge of the Past: Nationalism, Revolution, and the Collapse of the Soviet Union* (Stanford, Calif., 1994); Gail Lapidus and Victor Zaslavsky, eds., *From Union to Commonwealth: Nationalism and Separatism in the Soviet Republics* (Cambridge, 1992); Anatol Lieven, *The Baltic Revolution* (New Haven, Conn., 1993); John B. Dunlop, *The Rise of Russia and the Fall of the Soviet Empire* (Princeton, N.J., 1993); Michael Rywkin, *Moscow's Lost Empire* (Armonk, N.Y., 1993); and Boris Rumer, *Soviet Central Asia: A Tragic Experiment* (Boston, 1989).

Important works on the environment are Murray Feshbach and Albert Friendly, Jr., *Ecocide in the USSR* (New York, 1993), and Zhores A. Medvedev, *The Legacy of Chernobyl* (New York, 1992).

IN SEARCH OF NEW VISIONS
The Post-Soviet States

~

Just after daybreak on October 4, 1993, the first shells from Russian army tanks stationed across the street crashed into the upper floors of the White House, the seat of Russia's parliament, the Supreme Soviet. Flames spurted from windows, and the building's pale facade blackened. Defenders within the White House fired back with rifles and small automatic weapons. Some nearby Moscow residents leaned out their apartment windows to watch; others paused on their way to work to stare. As the fighting intensified, several bystanders were killed or wounded. They were among the 146 fatalities in Moscow on October 3–4.

The assault on the White House marked the culmination of a political and constitutional crisis that had paralyzed Russian politics during the preceding year and a half. Ex-Communists, nationalists, conservatives, and even a few moderates in the Supreme Soviet had steadily opposed Russian president Boris Yeltsin's rule and blocked liberal reforms. Because the Soviet deputies had been chosen before the 1991 collapse of the U.S.S.R. by only partly democratic procedures, Yeltsin had insisted that the legislature did not accurately reflect the voters' wishes. In September 1993, the Russian president had struck back by dissolving the Supreme Soviet and seeking new legislative elections for December. In the ensuing altercation over the legality of Yeltsin's action, two hundred Soviet deputies and almost a thousand extremist hangers-on staged a sit-in at the White House. Yeltsin cut off utilities to the building but allowed Soviet supporters to supply blankets, lamps, food, and small arms and ammunition to the resisters. He also swore not to resort to violence.

The standoff dragged on for ten days. Soviet negotiators agreed to a phased disarming of the White House defenders, but the opposition leaders inside the building rejected this compromise. On Sunday, October 3, a work holiday, agitators and militants thronged the streets of the capital, and angry Soviet supporters massed at several city squares. That afternoon, one group broke through the police lines surrounding the White House and clustered around two speakers: Soviet chairman Ruslan Khasbulatov and vice president Alexander Rutskoi, leaders of the resistance to Yeltsin.

The two oppositionists' faces showed the strain from the long siege. Having deluded themselves that the people of Moscow backed the Soviet, they now urged the throng to seize city hall and the main television station. Fighting broke out at both sites, with casualties on each side, but the Soviet's supporters failed to capture the media facility. When word of the attempted takeover reached Yeltsin at his country *dacha*, he hastened to Moscow in the early evening. Not until midnight, however, did Russian army units reinforce the police and interior ministry troops and secure the television station. It is unclear whether army leaders were waiting to see how the tide of battle would turn, or whether they simply needed time to mobilize and coordinate the forces required.

The next day, October 4, military detachments easily overwhelmed the White House resisters. The government imposed a curfew, banned extremist parties, censored the media for several days, and arrested Rutskoi and other oppositionist leaders. (A new parliament amnestied them in late February 1994.) Yeltsin set new parliamentary elections for De-

Aftermath of the Assault on Russia's White House Government soldiers patrol near the blackened ruin of the White House in Moscow following its capture by Yeltsin loyalists on October 4, 1993.

cember 12 and approved half a million dollars to restore the damaged White House as offices for the Russian government.

Yet although the anti-Yeltsin forces had suffered a setback, their loss proved temporary. Yeltsin's use of violence appalled most citizens, and his standing among the population began to decline. The October shootout at the White House highlighted the tortuous path of change that the Russian people had walked since the failed right-wing *putsch* of August 1991. Within only two years, Yeltsin had sought to move his country from membership in the Soviet empire to viable independence as a nation state, from a planned economy to a private-enterprise, free-market system, and from Communist authoritarianism to democracy. This threefold transition marked one of the most sweeping upheavals in recent history, and it is hardly surprising that the process wrought hardship, turmoil, and violence. In 1994 old patterns of power and control reasserted themselves, and Yeltsin and his supporters confronted major obstacles to completing the reforms.

The Disintegration of the Soviet Union

Yeltsin's critics have argued that he failed to take advantage of the surge of democratic sentiment that followed the failed August 1991 coup to install a new legislature and constitution in Russia. If he had done so, they maintain, he could have averted the bloody showdown in October 1993. But in the fall of 1991, Yeltsin, as president of Russia, a union republic within the collapsing Soviet federation, had to concentrate on delineating Russia's future role as an independent nation. Moreover, he faced a dilemma. He wanted to assert Russia's separateness from the Soviet system and government. Yet he also sought to preserve Russia's predominant position in whatever new relationships emerged among the former components of the Soviet Union.

Ironically, the August 1991 coup, designed in part to halt the weakening of the centralized U.S.S.R., hastened the Union's dissolution and the demise of Mikhail Gorbachev's federal government altogether. After the coup's collapse, Gorbachev had resumed his position as head of the Soviet state, but it was a hollow vindication. Yeltsin, more popular than ever after his defiance of the *putschists*, overshadowed the Soviet president. All the while, the republics' drive for independence accelerated, and regional and local authorities increasingly ignored Moscow.

During and immediately after the coup attempt, Estonia, Latvia, Ukraine, Belarus (formerly Byelorussia), Moldova (formerly Moldavia), and Azerbaijan declared their independence; Lithuania and Georgia had announced their secession earlier. The fate of the U.S.S.R. now hinged on Russia's reaction. On August 21, Yeltsin had taken a step toward independence by decreeing that the Russian Republic owned all economic

enterprises and resources on its territory. A day later, the Russian
Supreme Soviet approved his proposal to replace the Soviet Russian flag
of a yellow hammer and sickle on a red background with the pre-1917
Russian flag of white, blue, and red horizontal stripes, minus the tsarist
double-headed eagle. The new flags soon blossomed all over Moscow.
In a further assertion of anticommunism and Russian nationalism, the
residents of Leningrad narrowly approved the reversion of their city's
name to its original St. Petersburg. Drawing on his high popularity after
the coup, Yeltsin soon demonstrated that Russia was moving toward independence. Yet, because he wanted to preserve Russia's influence over
the affairs of the former union, he also argued against full sovereignty
for the other republics, especially Ukraine. The Russian president hoped
to form a confederation with solid economic ties and common foreign
and defense policies among the republics. Understandably, non-Russian
leaders feared that the largest member, Russia, would dominate such a
structure.

Hoping to stave off the complete disintegration of the U.S.S.R., Gorbachev in early September persuaded the All-Union Congress of People's
Deputies to adopt his proposal for a radically altered central administration of the country. The plan stipulated a state council consisting of Gorbachev and the republics' leaders that would exercise executive authority
over federal issues, coordinate domestic and foreign policy, and rule on
requests for independence from the republics. It also specified a new bi-
cameral legislature, with deputies selected by the republics, and a federal
economic council. A desperate attempt to salvage a remnant of centralized government, the plan never came to fruition. The state council approved independence for the three Baltic republics on September 6 but
could agree on little else. The other republics largely disregarded the new
structure, and the old central administration, unable to enforce its policies or collect taxes, gradually ceased to function, although it did not formally dissolve.

During the fall of 1991, as the politicians in Moscow struggled to find
a new basis of association among the constituent parts of the fragmenting
U.S.S.R., Yeltsin and Gorbachev frequently cooperated. The Ukrainians,
however, dealt a death blow to any hope that the old union, even in the
loose form established in September, could survive. In a referendum on
December 1, voters in Ukraine overwhelmingly approved independence
and chose Leonid Kravchuk as president. The longtime Communist *appa-
ratchik* had converted to Ukrainian nationalism in 1990. On December 8,
without informing Gorbachev, Yeltsin met the Ukrainian and Belarusan
leaders at Minsk, the capital of Belarus, to create a new entity, the Commonwealth of Independent States (CIS). The presidents of the three
Slavic republics declared the Union of Soviet Socialist Republics terminated. They also recognized the existing borders of each other's republics
and agreed on a common currency, on joint control of nuclear weapons,

and on a single economic zone. Details would be worked out later, they decided. On December 21, the remaining republics adhered to the CIS, except Georgia embroiled in civil strife, and the Baltic states already pursuing a separate path. All parties agreed to take responsibility for the international treaties and obligations of the former U.S.S.R. On December 25, 1991, Gorbachev resigned as Soviet president, and the Russian flag rose over the Kremlin. The Soviet Union, formed almost seventy years earlier, officially dissolved. As a private citizen, Gorbachev would travel widely abroad but carry almost no political influence inside Russia.

The new commonwealth encountered roadblocks from the start. To avert charges of Russian domination, its founders established the CIS Secretariat in Minsk, but the republics' representatives could agree in detail on only a few peripheral issues. Disputes over economic cooperation, minority rights control of military forces, and territory plagued the new entity. Fearing Russian subjection, Azerbaijan withdrew from the group. During 1992 each successor nation acted independently in foreign affairs, and the major global powers recognized the new states. The United Nations admitted all of them, with Russia assuming the Soviet Union's permanent Security Council seat. A CIS summit meeting on January 22, 1993, failed to resolve basic disagreements and postponed approval of a draft treaty of confederation. By mid-1993 the CIS appeared moribund.

In late 1993, however, Russia breathed life into the organization as a way of enhancing Russian influence in the other successor nations. In conjunction with bilateral agreements with Russia (discussed below), Georgia joined the CIS, and Azerbaijan gained readmittance. The Russian government pushed for economic cooperation among the commonwealth members, and talks on a range of multilateral issues resumed. Peacekeeping forces nominally under the CIS banner but controlled by Russia, were deployed to Tadzhikistan, where civil war raged. By mid-1994 the CIS paradoxically served both Russia's and the other states' purposes. For the latter, it offered members a forum for interaction on joint problems and a shield against their absorption by Russia. For Moscow, the organization provided a screen for the promotion of Russian interests in the other post-Soviet states.

Russia, the "Near-Abroad," and the World

Apart from the CIS framework, Russia pursued active bilateral relations with the other successor nations, dubbed in Moscow the "near-abroad." Yeltsin's policy interwove nationalist, political/strategic, and economic strands. The welfare of some 26 million Russians living in the other post-Soviet states soon became a contentious issue. Because expatriate Russians feared economic and political discrimination and resented suddenly imposed requirements to use local languages, some 2 to 3 million of them returned to Russia in 1992–1994. This influx burdened local and Moscow authorities with demands for jobs, housing, and social services. Other Russians living in non-Russian successor states sought to organize politically in their localities and looked to Moscow for support. Lithuania, with a Russian minority of only 10 percent, secured the withdrawal of Russian (formerly Soviet) troops on its territory by providing procedures for Russian residents to acquire citizenship. Difficulties arose, however, in Latvia, with its Russian minority of almost 40 percent, and in Estonia, where a third of the population is Russian. The Russian government protested to the UN and the European Union that these states' laws made it difficult for Russians who moved to the region after World War II to become citizens. In 1993 Yeltsin deliberately slowed the withdrawal of Russian troops from the troublesome Baltic states and demanded protection for the rights of their Russian minorities. Nevertheless, as promised earlier, he pulled Russian troops from Latvia and Estonia on August 31, 1994, coincident with the return to Russia of the last Russian (former Soviet) forces in Germany.

In Moldova, Yeltsin resisted nationalist pressure in Moscow to come to the aid of local Russians and Ukrainian inhabitants who organized the so-called Dniester Republic. In Ukraine, where almost 12 million Russians live, both Yeltsin and Ukrainian president Kravchuk sought to prevent ethnic tension. Russia urged the Ukrainian government to grant maximum autonomy to the Crimea, which Nikita Khrushchev had transferred from Russia to Ukraine in 1954 but which housed a predominantly Russian population. In February 1994, Crimean voters elected a pro-Russian president. A Crimean effort to rejoin Russia would arouse nationalist passions in both Russia and Ukraine and seriously endanger relations between the two countries. In Central Asia, Kazakhstan president Nursultan Nazarbayev cooperated with Yeltsin to control friction arising from the presence of 2 million Russians living in that state.

Yeltsin's nationalist critics insisted that he had done too little to defend the rights of Russians in the near-abroad, and a few extremists exhorted Moscow to incorporate areas with large Russian minorities into Russia. Although the Russian president pursued a fairly moderate line, in mid-1994 this issue remained a potential flash point in Russia's relations with its near neighbors.

Besides concern with the welfare of expatriate Russians, Yeltsin and his foreign minister Andrei Kozyrev affirmed a general Russian protectorate over the states of the former Soviet Union during 1993 and 1994. The two men shunted aside U.S. efforts to act as peacekeeper and mediator in the region. Indeed, Yeltsin campaigned to block the extension of NATO membership to the East European states bordering on the old U.S.S.R. The Russian leader also proclaimed Russia's responsibility for the security of the successor nations' southern borders with Turkey, Iran, Afghanistan, and China. Accordingly, he negotiated agreements with

Georgia, Tadzhikistan, and Turkmenistan for military bases and the stationing of Russian troops along those countries' borders.

During 1993 the Russian government established a dominant political presence in Georgia, Azerbaijan, and Tadzhikistan. Yeltsin claimed a prerogative to oversee affairs in these troubled regions of the former U.S.S.R., a sort of Monroe Doctrine for the Caucasus and Central Asia. As evidence of this policy, Russian military units intervened in fighting between the Georgian government and a separatist minority in Abkhazia. Outraged Georgians charged that the Russian forces supported the breakaway Abkhazis. Russian leaders insisted that they were only protecting the lives and property of Russians living in the region. In mid-1993, when it seemed that armed supporters of deposed Georgian president Zviad Gamsakhurdia might overthrow the government of Edvard Shevardnadze, Gorbachev's former foreign minister, Russian troops interceded and helped defeat the rebels. (Gamsakhurdia subsequently committed suicide.) His country ravaged by civil war and its economy bankrupt, Shevardnadze had no choice but to reverse his previous anti-Russian stance. In early 1994, he signed a series of accords providing for Russian economic assistance and the stationing of Russian troops in Georgia. For the near future, Georgia's well-being will depend on Russian largesse.

The Human Cost of Ethnic Strife In 1991 a mother and daughter mourn the destruction of their home in the bitter war between Azerbaijan and Armenia over Nagorno-Karabakh.

As for Azerbaijan, war with Armenia still raged over Nagorno-Karabakh, and the Azerbaijan government depended heavily on Russian economic and military assistance. In Tadzhikistan, a civil struggle persisted between the country's ex-Communist authoritarian government and democratic and Islamic opponents. This unrest compelled the government to accept substantial economic aid from Russia, Russian troops stationed on its soil, and near-satellite status in Russia's sphere of influence.

Economic and fiscal control provided a final weapon in Moscow's bid to establish hegemony over the other CIS states. During 1994, Belarus and Azerbaijan moved closer to Russia economically, although some critics in Moscow argued that sponsoring such weak economies only undermined Russia's own recovery. Except for Turkmenistan, blessed with abundant petroleum resources, the remaining CIS members relied to varying degrees on Russian-supplied oil and natural gas and on the Russian market for export of their products. Moreover, Russian subsidies and credits virtually supported the economies of the three Caucasus states and of Tadzhikistan in 1993 and 1994. Ukraine and Moldova also depended heavily on Russian loans and indirect support.

Does Russia intend to incorporate former Soviet republics? At the end of 1994, only Belarus seemed a possible candidate for union with Russia. These Slavic neighbors share a closely related linguistic and cultural heritage, and Belarus lacks an ardent nationalist movement and historic experience with independence. Further, merging with Russia may be the only way for Belarus to salvage its collapsing economy. Most of the remaining states, although bowing to growing Russian influence, seem committed to preserving their cultural and constitutional separateness. Tadzhikistan, Azerbaijan, and Georgia will have to live with Russia's tutelage for a time but seem unlikely to surrender their nominal independence.

In relations with Europe and the United States, the Yeltsin government proved a cooperative partner through 1992 and much of 1993, but then began to assert a more independent role. As Yugoslavia split apart and Serbs, Croats, and Bosnian Muslims battled for control of the central region of Bosnia-Herzegovina, Russia resisted American pressure for stronger action against Serb aggression. Russian nationalists saw the Serbs as brother Slavs for whom Russia had gone to war in 1914, and they loudly objected to Western intervention in the Yugoslav civil war. In February 1994, Russia finally brokered a compromise with the Bosnian Serbs that led to the despatch of Russian peacekeepers to Bosnia in return for a Serb withdrawal from the capital of Sarajevo. Russia also insisted on modification of previously agreed reductions in NATO-Russian weapons. The shift permitted the Russian army to deploy more tanks and other forces in the Caucasus and Central Asia. Finally, although Yeltsin continued to oppose admission of the Baltic and Eastern European states to NATO, he cooperated in promulgation of the American-sponsored alternative, "Partnerships for Peace," a halfway step toward NATO membership. In June 1994, Yeltsin urged that NATO grant Russia "special" status. Nevertheless, he signed on to the Partnership program.

Despite these signs of obstinacy in Russia's foreign policy, overall Yeltsin and Kozyrev pursued close ties to the West from 1992 through 1994. Ignoring cries from communist and nationalist critics that Russia had become a lapdog of the capitalist world, the Russian leaders made substantial progress in mutual reductions of nuclear weapons, in obtaining Western aid and technical assistance, and in scientific and cultural cooperation with the West. Under the START I treaty signed in July 1991, the U.S.S.R. had accepted a reduction from 10,841 warheads and bombs to around 8,040, and the U.S. arsenal shrank from 12,081 to 10,395 weapons. Although these cuts were moderate, the treaty featured detailed procedures for mutual on-site verification of the reductions. After the dissolution of the Soviet Union, presidents Yeltsin and Bush agreed in principle in February 1992 to seek lower levels of nuclear armaments. They subsequently approved START II negotiations (confirmed by President Clinton in April 1993) designed to leave each side with three thousand or fewer warheads by the year 2003. Overriding objections from Russian military specialists and nationalist politicians, Yeltsin agreed that the American nuclear force could contain a substantial proportion of submarine-launched missiles on virtually undetectable submarines while Russia would give up its heavy intercontinental ballistic missiles. In January 1994, during a visit by the American president to Moscow, Clinton and Yeltsin agreed to retarget their nations' missiles away from each other, an important step toward curtailing the risk of accidental nuclear war.

During that same visit, the American and Russian presidents met with Ukrainian president Kravchuk. The three leaders pledged to cooperate in dismantling Ukraine's nuclear weapons. The American and Russian governments provided guarantees of Ukraine's territorial integrity and security in exchange for Ukrainian surrender of its 176 former Soviet missiles and 1,600 nuclear warheads. The United States also agreed to provide financial and technical assistance for scrapping the weapons after their transfer to appropriate facilities in Russia, and the Russian government promised to pay Ukraine for the nuclear fuel salvaged. In return for Ukrainian fulfillment of this agreement, the United States separately pledged $700 million to Ukraine in 1994.

Although skeptics argued that chauvinist sentiment and political gridlock might prevent Ukraine from fulfilling its obligations, responsible Ukrainian leaders confirmed their commitment to the agreement. The country's desperate need for financial assistance from Russia and the West provided the best guarantee of the treaty's implementation. In earlier negotiations, Kazakhstan and Belarus had also agreed to surrender their small number of former Soviet nuclear weapons. Thus, in late 1994, nuclear conflict in the former Soviet Union seemed unlikely, even though complex logistical problems and the difficulty of recruiting enough skilled technicians had slowed the dismantling process.

Yeltsin made Western aid a second urgent objective of Russian foreign policy. To assuage nationalist misgivings, he insisted that Russia would not be dictated to by the Western powers or by the International Monetary Fund, but would design and implement its own reform program. He further asserted that outside help would play only a supplementary role; Russia, he argued, had to solve its own economic problems and would not grow addicted to Western handouts. By the end of 1992, the Group of Seven industrialized countries (Canada, the United States, Great Britain, Germany, France, Italy, and Japan) had set aside $24 billion in aid to Russia and some $20 billion for the other post-Soviet states. Only a small portion of this assistance was delivered, however, because of delays in setting specific aid targets. In addition, much of the help was channeled through the International Monetary Fund, which required the Russian government to meet strict budgetary and fiscal requirements before receiving the funds.

Besides multilateral assistance, most Western countries offered direct support to Russia, the two largest donors being the United States and Germany. During several summit meetings with Yeltsin in 1993 and 1994, President Clinton proposed several billion dollars in American assistance, most of it earmarked for specific needs such as housing for demobilized troops, support for entrepreneurs, and equipment and technical assistance urgently needed by the Russian oil industry. Despite problems in delivering aid to Russia, Russian sources confirmed the importance of Western help as emergency relief, as a stimulus to privatization, and as financial stabilization.

At the same time, many observers argued that private investment would help Russia even more in its transition to a market economy. In June 1992, President Bush had granted Russia most-favored-nation status and signed several significant commercial agreements designed to encourage American investment in Russia. By mid-1994, however, the results proved meager. The Russian government failed to regularize property and contract laws and to adhere to consistent taxation policies. Thus most American and other foreign investors hesitated to plunge into the Russian market. For each minor success, such as McDonald's, multinational firms like Weyerhaeuser wood-products company suffered major losses. In October 1993, more than 11,000 Russian-foreign joint ventures had registered with the government, but their capital assets totaled less than $500 million. Nevertheless, the future holds promise as outside investors contemplate ways to meet the pent-up demand of 150 million Russian consumers and to take advantage of highly educated, relatively low-paid Russian workers.

Yeltsin also sought commercial agreements with the European

Moscow Welcomes Fast Food Muscovites crowd around the first McDonald's in Russia just after its opening in early 1990.

Union. Although trade with Western Europe revived in 1993, Western concerns over alleged Russian "dumping" (selling abroad at artificially low prices) and the poor quality of Russian goods prevented spectacular increases. From 1992 to 1994, virulent nationalist opposition to Yeltsin's proposal for a compromise with Japan on the long-disputed issue of the Kuril Islands blocked progress in Russian-Japanese commercial and political relations. On the other hand, Russia's ties with Israel warmed during the same period, as some 410,000 Soviet Jews departed for Israel between 1989 and 1992 and as the emigrés' lot in their new homeland began to brighten.

As a final strand in his policy toward the West, President Yeltsin signed a number of cultural, educational, and scientific accords with Western European countries and the United States. For example, the Russian and American space programs agreed to exchange personnel and to cooperate in developing a space station. In early 1994, a Soviet cosmonaut joined U.S. colleagues on a space shuttle flight, and two American astronauts began training for participation in a future Russian space voyage.

In Asia, the Yeltsin regime improved relations with its looming neighbor, China. In September 1994, during the first visit to Moscow of a top Chinese leader since Mao's journey in 1949, the Russian president signed agreements with China's head of state, Jiang Zemin, to retarget nuclear missiles away from each other's country, to reduce forces on each side of the Sino-Russian frontier, and to improve economic ties. Despite the cordiality of the meeting, disputes concerning borders and trade persist.

Too Much Shock, Too Little Therapy?

The post-1993 assertiveness of Yeltsin's foreign policy alarmed some American pundits and former Cold War "hawks." Yet Western leaders and most specialists on Russia focused on the struggling Russian economy. After 1991 President Yeltsin had sought to transform Russia's inherited, centrally planned and administered economy to a system based on private ownership and free markets. Although post-Communist governments had launched similar efforts in Eastern European countries after 1989, their experience proved only marginally relevant to the much larger Russian economy that had operated in the Soviet style for more than sixty years. Almost everyone in Russia, including conservatives, nationalists, and ex-Communists critical of Yeltsin, agreed on the need to change, but sharp differences of opinion on the methods and pace of change soon emerged.

Young Russian economists—supported by such Western consultants as Harvard specialist Jeffrey Sachs, who had earlier advised the Polish government—urged so-called "shock therapy," or rapid, concurrent adoption of free prices, private ownership, tight control of the money supply, higher taxes, and restricted government spending. The shock therapists acknowledged that such an overnight transformation would spur chaos and disruption at first but insisted that the short-term pain would be less severe than the drawn-out woes that would accompany gradual reform. They also admitted that their plan would force inefficient factories to close, would create unemployment, and would permit temporary profiteering. Still, they maintained, only brisk, radical reform could produce a stable, efficient economy in the long run.

Their opponents favored a phased introduction of markets and freeing of prices, with the state continuing to manage some sectors of the economy. They wanted to cushion the shock of the changeover by providing subsidies to struggling farms and factories, by controlling wages and prices on essential consumer items, and by increasing government expenditures for social welfare.

At first the proponents of quick reform had the upper hand. In October 1991, President Yeltsin approved an economic platform modeled on the abortive "five-hundred days" Shatalin plan of the year before (see Chapter 11). Late that year, he installed thirty-four-year-old economist Yegor Gaidar to oversee the administering of "shock therapy" to the Russian economy. The Gaidar team benefitted from the advantages of

Russia's size and resources. With the collapse of the Soviet Union in late 1991, the Russian Republic emerged as the largest, most important successor state. Russia accounts for 51 percent of the former U.S.S.R.'s population, 76 percent of its territory, and 61 percent of its gross national product. The immense state sits on about 90 percent of the Soviet Union's oil and 75 percent of its natural gas, and it mines 55 percent of its coal. Russia also possesses extensive timber and other natural resources, central fiscal institutions, and a foreign trade surplus.

At the same time, the reformers confronted formidable problems. In late 1991, the Russian economy neared total collapse. Some Western observers doubted that Russians could survive the winter without suffering starvation, mass unemployment, and rioting. Moreover, the sins of the old Soviet system burdened the economy. The breakdown of the former command-administrative structure before substitute market institutions and mechanisms could be installed had already dragged production down. In 1991 Soviet output fell 17 percent. In 1992 Russia alone suffered a further drop in production of about 20 percent and additional declines of some 15 percent each year in 1993 and 1994. These official figures for the latter two years probably understated output, however, for new private producers reported less than they actually manufactured to avoid taxes. Indeed, some economists estimated a 15 to 20 percent rise in production in 1994. Runaway inflation, huge budget deficits, devolution of economic activity to regions, disruption of interrepublican commerce upon the Soviet Union's break-up, and a plunge in foreign trade—all exacerbated the economic disaster facing the reformers.

The Gaidar team acted promptly and vigorously. They eliminated almost all price controls in January–February 1992. A range of domestic and imported goods appeared at once in stores and kiosks, although at high prices. Prices jumped three- and fourfold, but by mid-1994 the monthly inflation rate had stabilized between 4 and 5 percent. Although prices escalated in fall 1994, the government set a target of reducing the monthly inflation rate to 1 to 2 percent by the end of 1995. Service industries sprang up, and some enterprises successfully converted to market competition. Days lost to strikes in 1992 declined to one-sixth the 1991 level. Production of household goods rebounded, and some local economies, such as that in the city of Nizhny-Novgorod, blossomed. Grain harvests stabilized at below Soviet levels. Yet because less grain was needed to feed reduced livestock herds, Russia cut imports of foreign grain to almost zero by 1994. Finally, the reform government reduced budget deficits and rebuilt Russia's foreign exchange reserves.

The reformers' most significant and lasting success, however, lay in privatizing the economy. Before January 1, 1992, no more than a few hundred enterprises in Russia had shifted to private ownership. By fall 1994, almost 95 percent of small-scale businesses, including trade outlets, restaurants, and service institutions, and nearly 70 percent of large factories had passed into private hands. To accomplish this remarkable transformation, the government distributed privatization vouchers to 95 percent of the population and registered more than three hundred investment funds to channel the vouchers into purchases of state assets. After July 1, 1994, privatization continued on the basis of money bids for enterprises. Because privatization changed both property relationships and attitudes, this program should exert a longlasting, fundamental impact on Russian society. Now that many Russians own a stake in the economic system, reversing the marketization under way appears highly unlikely. On the other hand, privatization of agriculture lagged far behind as conservatives blocked needed reform. In 1994 conversion to private or jointly owned farms accelerated, but the government and parliament struggled to enact a land law that would guarantee private farmers' rights. Because the government needed the political support of agrarian interests, it continued subsidies to inefficient state and collective farms. As a result, agricultural output and productivity remained dismal.

Despite their achievements, the Gaidar team suffered a number of setbacks. Trying to transform the entrenched, inefficient Soviet system proved far more difficult than anyone had imagined. Imbalances, inequities, and breakdowns plagued the process. Stringent International Monetary Fund stipulations and bureaucratic ineptitude in donor countries and Russia choked foreign aid to a trickle. Lack of laws protecting property rights and contracts, the declining value of the ruble, and political instability frightened off foreign investors. President Yeltsin, who probably never fully understood the complexity of the proposed changes, blew hot and cold on the reforms. The interaction of political opposition and skeptical popular attitudes emerged, however, as the chief obstacle to change.

During 1992 and 1993, the power struggle between Yeltsin versus conservatives and ex-Communists in the government and in the Supreme Soviet intensified and climaxed in the violent confrontation at the White House. As part of that contest, Yeltsin's opponents strove to weaken or block Gaidar's policies. With an ally as director of the central bank, they forced the government to raise pensions and wages and to maintain subsidies to most large state enterprises and farms. They demanded distribution of grants and loans to regions within Russia and to weak republics in the CIS as well. Finally, they opposed the reformers' efforts to slash military expenditures. Their actions stimulated inflation and ran the budget deeply into the red. To cover subsidies and deficits, the state bank issued millions of rubles, and the reformers lost control of the money supply. As a result, the Gaidar government failed to maintain tight fiscal management of the economy or to stabilize the currency. In an effort to placate the opposition, Yeltsin dismissed Gaidar in December 1992 but insisted that the reforms go forward. Gaidar returned to the cabinet in September 1993 but was dropped again in January 1994.

The Struggle to Survive An elderly Russian pensioner tries to barter her old sweater for one fish in January 1992 just after the government's economic reform freed retail prices.

The economy's uneven performance and the public's complaints strengthened the critics' case that the reformers had gone too far, too fast. Most Russians, disillusioned with *perestroika*, had looked to the post-1991 Yeltsin-Gaidar program as the vehicle to deliver the better life that their leaders had promised since 1985. When some citizens continued to suffer, many people turned against reform. Prices soared, wages and pensions slumped, and fear of unemployment dogged people's daily lives. A minority profited in the new economic milieu. For many, however, incomes and living standards dropped, and the gap between rich and poor widened. Pensioners, veterans, laid-off state employees, and single parents felt the pinch particularly.

To survive, many individuals worked at more than one job, and families cultivated garden plots outside the cities or at their *dachas*. Just getting by became a preoccupation for millions of Russian citizens. As a machinist in an aircraft factory commented in early 1994, "In the past I took life for granted and wouldn't think about what to do or how to live. Now we have to think about it all the time, just to scrape by." People stood stoically along shopping thoroughfares or alleys outside markets, proffering passersby for sale or barter a pair of shoes, a worn photograph, a tattered party dress, or some other personal possession. Youngsters and seedy-looking characters sold vodka and pornographic magazines on street corners. Nearby kiosks peddled whiskey, electronic equipment, and perfumes at prices few could afford. As maintenance of apartment houses virtually ceased, tenants endured crumbling walls, blown lights, and irregular utilities. Break-ins and burglaries became common, and soaring crime rates made many citizens afraid to walk the streets.

Popular dissatisfaction with the results of reform sank the reformist parties in new elections, and a conservative parliament took power in January 1994. Despite President Yeltsin's public assurances that economic change would continue, he proceeded hesitantly and relied heavily on his new prime minister, Viktor Chernomyrdin, a former Soviet industrial boss. Balancing conservative and reformer interests, Chernomyrdin managed to stabilize the economy and received a $1.5 billion International Monetary Fund loan in April 1994 as a reward. Government statistics in July showed that the average standard of living also had increased by almost 10 percent over the previous year. Such data did little to assuage the fears of the small but growing ranks of unemployed or the estimated one-fifth of the population living below the poverty line. Yet other Russians continued to invest in new enterprises and even in financially unsound "pyramid" schemes, despite the collapse in August 1994 of the popular joint-stock venture MMM. Its president escaped jail by winning a legislative by-election and obtaining parliamentary immunity, all the while promising his bamboozled shareholders that MMM would some day make good on their securities. In late September, the value of the ruble collapsed. Government intervention partially restored it, but the crisis triggered the firing of the cabinet's economic ministers and weakened Chernomyrdin's position. With a new head of the central bank and the former privatization chief as economic tsar, Yeltsin renewed his pledge to maintain a reform course and to stick to a sensible budget in 1995.

Although economic improvement appeared evident at the end of 1994, particularly in major cities, inequities between the prospering, often younger, generation and the struggling, often older, poor persisted. Disparities between urban centers and the rest of Russia also continued. The economy remained fragile, but blessed with vast natural resources and an educated work force, Russia could look forward to substantial outside help once it attained economic and political stability and once secure conditions for foreign investment were in place. The four-to-five year transition period will undoubtedly be difficult, but the nation should emerge in the twenty-first century with a healthy economy and a rising standard of living.

Who's on Top?

The bitter power struggle that raged through 1992–1993 between democratic elements led by Yeltsin and the government's conservative and nationalist opponents had close links to the battle over economic reform. Yeltsin emerged from the failed 1991 coup a Russian national hero. He undoubtedly counted on his popularity and the broad support he received from the Soviet at that time to bolster his government in the months ahead. Instead, while he occupied himself in fall 1991 with leading Russia out of the Union to independence and membership in the CIS, his foes in parliament multiplied and gathered strength among the electorate. Although Yeltsin installed the reformist Gaidar cabinet and launched radical economic changes in early 1992, criticism mounted from ex-Communists ("reds") who yearned for the old days when they ran the country. Attacks also came from nationalists ("browns") who mourned the loss of empire, and from conservatives who philosophically opposed democracy and free enterprise.

In the face of this opposition, the existing constitutional/political structure proved increasingly unworkable. As we saw in Chapter 11, when other republics adopted electoral and legislative reforms in 1990, the Russian Republic retained its Congress of Peoples' Deputies. This body of 1,041 members had been appointed and elected in March 1989 and contained a plurality, if not majority, of old-line Communists and other traditionalists. The Russian Congress in turn chose the Russian Supreme Soviet of 248 members, which also had a hefty bloc of conservatives. Under the much-amended Soviet-era Constitution, the president had considerable executive authority and could introduce some measures by decree, but his "red-brown" opponents fought him at every turn.

The conflict climaxed during the Seventh and Eighth Congresses of People's Deputies in December 1992 and March 1993, respectively. Yeltsin narrowly survived impeachment efforts and won marginal support for continued reform. Political quarreling continued, however, and after complicated legal maneuvering, the two sides agreed to a political referendum to be held April 25, 1993. This plebiscite asked voters whether they supported Yeltsin, whether they endorsed his economic program, and whether they favored early elections for the president and the legislature. The conservatives, led by Alexander Rutskoi, an Afghan veteran and Russia's vice president, and by parliamentary speaker Ruslan Khasbulatov, calculated that popular disgust with the economy would translate into a rejection of Yeltsin's leadership. But the public was fed up as well with legislative squabbling, and neither conservative spokesman appealed to the bulk of the citizenry. Further, many still regarded Yeltsin as a down-to-earth, genuinely Russian leader who had the best interest of the people at heart.

To his critics' dismay, the president emerged triumphant from the referendum. Almost two-thirds of the electorate voted. Fifty-eight percent expressed confidence in the president, and an amazing 53 percent backed his economic policy despite its paltry results to date. In a rebuff to Yeltsin's legislative opponents, 43 percent voted for new Soviet elections and only 32 percent for new presidential elections. Yeltsin won handily in Moscow and St. Petersburg, in north Russia, and in the Russian Far

East but failed to obtain majority support in some south central Russian regions and in the republic's non-Russian territories.

Nevertheless, he moved quickly to exploit his victory, organizing a seven-hundred-member constitutional convention in early June over the objections of his opponents. Yeltsin presented a draft constitution that provided for a strong presidency on the model of France's Fifth Republic. The document also gave considerable power to regional authorities, on whom he had to rely in organizing the convention. His critics countered with a proposed constitution that gave the legislature the dominant role. As refining of the constitutional drafts proceeded, the two sides bickered over how the constitution should be ratified.

A second issue plagued President Yeltsin during 1992 and 1993: relations between the central government in Moscow and local and regional authorities throughout the federated Russian Republic. This same problem had spelled the doom of the U.S.S.R. Anti-Russian feeling on the part of the almost 30 million non-Russians living in the new state heightened the struggle for power between Moscow and the periphery. Yet overwhelmingly Russian areas, such as Siberia and the St. Petersburg region, also pressed for full autonomy and local control.

The most difficult ethnic issues arose among peoples in autonomous republics of the former Soviet Union, particularly the Tatars living along the central Volga River; the Chechen, Ingush, and Ossetian groups of the north Caucasus; the Bashkirs of the lower Volga area; the Finns living in the Komi and Karelian regions of north Russia; and the Yakuts and other indigenous peoples residing in eastern Siberia. (See the map, The Post-Soviet States.) Only the Tatars, some two million strong, and the Chechens moved toward complete rejection of Russian rule, but they and the other non-Russian enclaves were islands in a Russian sea, which made secession from the new Russian state virtually impossible. Moreover, whereas ethnic Russians had composed only 50.7 percent of the Soviet population, they made up 82.6 percent of the new Russia's citizenry.

By largely acceding to pressure for local home rule, Yeltsin's government avoided ethnic violence except in the North Caucasus. There, a complicated struggle over land and indigenous rights among Ingush, Chechens, Ossetians, and Russian Cossacks led to rioting and pillaging in the fall of 1992. The outburst left several hundred people dead and buildings and fields ravaged before three thousand Russian army troops restored order. In 1993 local chieftains reaffirmed an earlier assertion of independence for the Chechen region. After clumsy Russian attempts to subvert the breakaway government failed, Defense Minister Pavel Grachev and hard-line advisers to Yeltsin persuaded the president to assault the Chechen rebels in December 1994. After a bungled offensive that caused several thousand civilian and military casualties, Russian troops finally occupied the Chechen capital, Grozny, in January 1995. Rebels vowed to wage a guerrilla resistance in nearby mountains, and

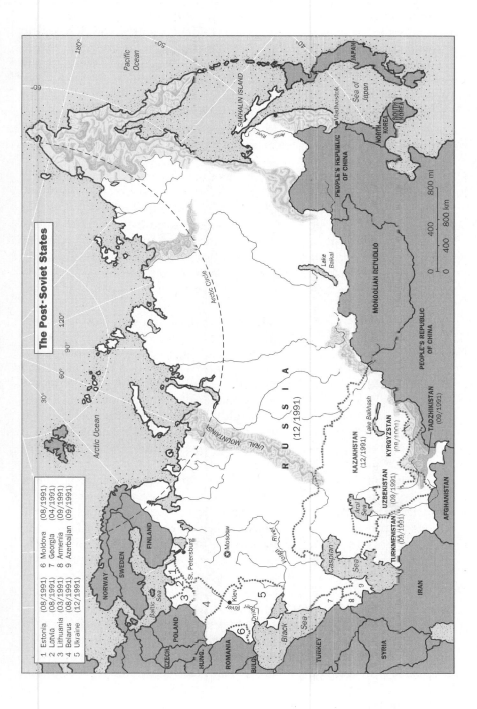

The Post-Soviet States

1	Estonia	(08/1991)	6	Moldova	(08/1991)
2	Latvia	(08/1991)	7	Georgia	(04/1991)
3	Lithuania	(03/1991)	8	Armenia	(09/1991)
4	Belarus	(08/1991)	9	Azerbaijan	(09/1991)
5	Ukraine	(12/1991)			

the Russian government's arrogant statements and its mishandling of the situation severely damaged the Yeltsin regime's credibility. Only a few nationalists in Moscow supported the president. Centrist and democratic elements expressed outrage, and critics abroad, from the Western powers to Islamic states, roundly condemned Russia's brutal use of force. To little avail Yeltsin insisted that he had been forced to act to hold the Russian Republic together. Leaders of Russia's autonomous Muslim areas of Tatarstan and Bashkortostan and of the Central Asian Islamic states expressed sympathy for the Chechens, and many Russian and Western commentators questioned Yeltsin's commitment to ethnic rights and democratic processes.

Areas with a predominantly Russian population also sought greater independence from Moscow. Taking advantage of the contest preoccupying the presidency and the legislature, local authorities obtained financial allocations from each side and resisted efforts from the capital to control regional appointments and policies. In addition, the central government found it increasingly difficult to collect taxes from the new republic's 89 regions and districts. Local officials understandably tried to send as little revenue as possible to Moscow and to spend public funds in their own areas.

In the regions, however, executive-legislative tension parallel to that in Moscow often hamstrung city, district, and area governments. Mayors battled city councils, and governors clashed with district and provincial soviets. Some observers opined that by 1994 executives had gained the upper hand. Moreover, the reform process, treated by the Western media as primarily a Moscow-centered or national phenomenon, in fact proceeded apace in some localities while meeting substantial obstacles in others. Much of the fate of democratization and marketization rested in the hands of the regions and remained largely outside the control of the president or the parliament.

As the political struggle in Moscow heated up in fall 1993, Yeltsin maneuvered to garner support in the regions. He proposed a Federation Council made up of senior local executives and legislators chosen by the regions, which would wield considerable constitutional and administrative power. When many likely council members wavered during the showdown at the White House on October 3–4, however, Yeltsin revised the council idea. The constitution adopted in December 1993 provided for an upper house of the new legislature, the Council of the Federation, with 178 members, two elected in each region or district. In January 1994, federation deputies chose a moderate Yeltsin supporter as their speaker. Except for continuing unrest in Chechnya, regional and ethnic issues remained quiescent through 1994. Nevertheless, the government's need to increase tax revenues and to create legal and constitutional safeguards for minorities' rights remained major challenges for Yeltsin and the Federation Council.

During 1993, despite the ups and downs of the political struggle, Yeltsin pushed ahead with economic reform. Over the summer, opposition leaders attacked the privatization program, leveled corruption charges against key Yeltsin appointees, and proposed an inflationary budget that doubled the annual deficit. In September the Soviet started drafting a law imposing criminal penalties on cabinet officers who failed to execute parliamentary decisions. At last, the president concluded that the political stalemate threatened to deflect economic reform. On September 21, 1993, he dissolved the Soviet and set new elections for December, a step that brought the long political clash between the president and the parliament to its dramatic climax at the White House. Yeltsin also pledged to hold presidential elections in June 1994, two years before his term would expire. Later, he reneged on this promise. He apparently decided to see what sort of new legislature emerged from the December elections before committing himself to an early presidential contest.

After squelching the October 3–4 uprising, Yeltsin announced that the electorate would vote on the new constitution in December, concurrent with the election of deputies to a new legislature. To no one's surprise, the proposed constitution released a few weeks later provided for a strong executive. Under its terms, the president names the prime minister and the cabinet, federal judges and prosecutors, and the chairman of the central bank. The president also has the power to call new elections if the parliament refuses approval of his ministers three times or consistently rejects budgets or other key government proposals. Yeltsin made clear that he gave high priority to getting the constitution approved. Despite considerable grumbling from an array of politicians, as well as popular apathy, 55 percent of the electorate voted, 58 percent of whom approved Russia's constitution. (See the figure, Party Representation in Russia's Duma.)

Pro-Yeltsin candidates fared poorly, however, in the legislative contests. Western and Russian observers urged the president to form his own party and campaign vigorously for it. Yet Yeltsin chose to remain above the fray, perhaps because he saw the constitutional referendum as more important than the legislative voting. The party closest to the president, *Russia's Choice*, led by *Gaidar*, entered the race a considerable favorite but emerged with only 15 percent of the vote and 70 of the 444 seats in the State Duma, or lower house.

The misnamed *Liberal Democratic Party* representing extreme nationalist viewpoints did surprisingly well, garnering 23 percent of the vote and 64 seats in the Duma. Liberal Democratic leader *Vladimir Zhirinovsky* proved a flamboyant demagogue who won voters' attention in dynamic television appearances. Calling for law and order, Zhirinovsky tossed out slogans that tapped into national pride, such as "Raise Russia from Her Knees!" His idiosyncratic and rude behavior when the Duma convened

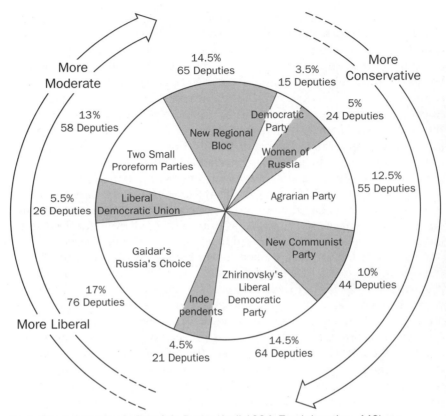

Party Representation in Russia's Duma (April 1994: Total deputies, 449)

in January 1994, however, cost him any chance of playing an influential role there. Nonetheless, he vowed to run for president in June 1996.

Neo-Communists won 48 seats; the conservative Agrarian party, 33 seats. These deputies, together with the Zhirinovsky bloc, could have mustered a controlling plurality in the Duma, but during 1994 parties and individuals pursued disparate interests and personal agendas. Yeltsin's adversaries forced through an amnesty of the August 1991 and October 1993 rebels but proved unable to derail new reform measures. The disunity of the government's opponents, plus the determination of Prime Minister Chernomyrdin and the Duma speaker, Ivan Rybkin, to pursue constructive legislative work, contributed to relative political calm during the year. Further, Women of Russia, an independent party that won twenty-three seats, and many of the more than one hundred nonparty deputies eschew political confrontation and cooperated with the government and the Duma leaders on some issues. Finally, Yeltsin did not hesitate to introduce a few measures by fiat over Duma objections, a right that the constitution now accorded him.

In October, after the ruble's collapse, the government survived a no-confidence motion in the Duma, in part because the deputies did not want to risk the president's proroguing the parliament and calling new elections. At the end of 1994, all sides in the political fray sought to position themselves for parliamentary elections scheduled in late 1995 and for the June 1996 presidential contest. Yet the democrats, who controlled about 125 Duma seats, remained as divided as the opposition, and Gaidar's efforts to form an electoral bloc with several other reform parties had yet to bear fruit. Political apathy had spread through all elements of the citizenry as well. As an additional factor, the propertied elements from whom the democrats and reformers needed to draw political support had only just begun to consolidate their position and views. Unless the economy produces benefits for the bulk of the population during 1995, voters may give the Yeltsinites short shrift in the forthcoming elections.

Worsening Social Problems

The government's electoral defeat in December 1993 and its tenuous political situation in 1994 stemmed not just from the country's economic malaise. Voters also protested the deepening social and environmental crisis in Russia. After 1991 conditions of daily life continued to deteriorate, and health hazards multiplied. Public-interest defenders of the environment, having scored some successes under *perestroika*, had entered the post-Soviet period full of hope. However, neither they nor the Yeltsin government commanded the resources to address the environmental ruin left by five decades of heedless Soviet industrialization. Some harmful practices ceased, but enforcing environmental safeguards or remedying previous damage received low priority as Russia struggled toward a free-enterprise system. Moreover, the nation needed to earn foreign exchange by exporting natural resources, such as timber, petroleum, gold, and other minerals. Expensive, less wasteful extractive procedures and long-term conservation measures were luxuries it could ill afford.

Most experts predict that it will take twenty to thirty years for the former Soviet republics to recover from severe air, water, and land pollution inflicted during the era of high-tempo industrialization. Worst of all, many citizens continue to suffer from environmentally related illnesses, including respiratory diseases, cancer, and slow poisoning by toxic chemicals, which have contributed to a rise in the death rate in recent years. Updated estimates put the number of radiation-induced deaths caused by the Chernobyl' disaster in the tens of thousands. Despite the shortage of funds to clean up and preserve the environment, citizen activists remain determined to protect Russia's resources and natural beauty.

The state of public health also worried many Russians. By the end of the Soviet period, the rise in infant mortality had signaled a catastrophe in the health-care system, which the government had steadily under-funded from the 1960s on. The dissolution of the Soviet Union only wors-ened matters, as equipment, medicines, and other supplies grew scarce and costly. In addition, the government could provide few rubles to maintain existing health facilities or to build new ones. As medical pro-fessionals struggled to supply health services and to support their fami-lies, many of them understandably engaged in private, fee-for-service treatment. Emergence of this type of practice, although it had always ex-isted on a small scale, angered many citizens, who deemed it another ex-ample of the inequalities that came with the transition to a free-enterprise economy.

The near collapse of the health-care system, a dramatic decline in public-health standards and nutrition, and despair among the population created a demographic crisis in Russia in the early 1990s. Infant mortality continued to rise as prenatal care and well-baby services virtually disap-peared. Pediatricians reported that as many as a third of newborns were sickly. Lack of immunization and outbreaks of diphtheria likewise threatened the health of infants. The birthrate plunged from 1.7 percent in 1987 to .9 percent in 1993. The number of children born to each woman dropped to slightly more than 1.3, well below the level needed to replace the population. In 1993, 216 abortions took place for every 100 live births. Clearly, Russian women did not want to bear children in the conditions of the early 1990s.

Also reflective of the desperate times, death rates increased sharply, dropping life expectancy for men to 59 years and creating an annual pop-ulation loss (deaths over births) of almost 800,000 in 1993. No industrial-ized country has ever experienced such a calamity in peacetime. Rising rates of alcoholism, of industrial accidents (often caused by intoxicated workers), and of suicides contributed to the surge in deaths, but general social conditions and psychological attitudes were also to blame. Al-though immigration reduced the net loss of population, Russia, whose citizenry numbered 150 million in 1991, could have as few as 141 million inhabitants by the year 2005.

Alcoholism aggravated Russia's other social ills in the 1990s. The rate of hard-liquor consumption rose steadily after Gorbachev's antialcohol campaign ended in 1987, and in 1993 Russia ranked first in the world in per-capita drinking. Drunkenness pushed up divorce and crime rates, both of which climbed relentlessly between 1990 and 1993, and added to the swarms of the homeless and destitute in Russian cities. Violent crimes mushroomed, especially assaults, burglaries, muggings, rape, and murder. Juvenile delinquency and the spread of street gangs widened the incidence of crime and further terrorized Russian citizens. Strong-arm ex-tortion squads representing the "Mafia" (local gangs) pressured not only kiosk tenders and street-corner vendors but bankers and major entrepreneurs for "kickbacks" and "protection money." Bribery became common as underpaid civil servants accepted payoffs to provide normal governmental services. In an upsurge of racism, many ethnic Russians blamed the crime, drugs, and prostitution on Tatars or people from "the south" (Caucasians and Central Asians). Despite a sweeping anticrime decree of June 1994 and some apparent leveling off of the crime rate, long-term improvement hinged on reform of the police and the judiciary, both inveterate holdovers from the Soviet era.

After 1991 deteriorating social and economic conditions plagued women particularly. Burgeoning crime and alcoholism brought danger into their lives. In the shrinking job market, they were often the first to be laid off and had the most difficulty finding entry or replacement positions. Women's wages, averaging about three-quarters of men's salaries before 1991, declined to about 60 percent of male compensation by 1993. A small percentage of women resorted to prostitution to survive or to supplement meager incomes. At home, falling family income, rising prices, and the closing of many day-care centers made it a struggle just to fulfill the traditional tasks of raising children and managing the household. Finally, economic stringency blocked improvement of health, contraceptive, gynecological, and abortion services for women, urgent needs identified under *glasnost'*. Poorer women in particular suffered when government clinics began charging for previously free abortions.

Women made some progress, however. Informal feminist groups, restored *zhensovety* (governmental women's councils), and women-only associations connected to nationalist movements sprang up after August 1991 to articulate women's concerns. In February 1994, a group of women active in public affairs organized the Liberal Women's Foundation to assist women in professional, business, and political activity. That August several women organized the first ever center for victims of sexual abuse in Moscow. The political party Women of Russia won 23 Duma seats and 8 percent of the vote in the December 1993 elections. Its predominantly ex-Communist leadership espoused politically conservative and Russian nationalist views, but its platform tempered an emphasis on traditional family values with calls for equal economic opportunity and expanded social and welfare services for women. The party played a constructive role in the 1994 parliament, giving Russian women a viable political voice for the first time in their history.

Values, Religion, and Culture in Russia

Under *perestroika* and increasingly after 1991, a marked generation gap split Russia. The conflict centered on attitudes toward the West and toward economic reform, as well as other issues. Despite post-Soviet hardships, many young people saw freedom of expression and a more representative government as major achievements of the 1980s and looked to the future with high hopes. They rejected the Soviet past and the experiences of the older generation and even derided the cult of World War II, much to the indignation of veterans of that conflict. Young people welcomed Western values and culture, and some went to extremes to mimic Western dress, style, and behavior. Many supported the move to a market economy, which, they were convinced, would soon offer them tempting opportunities and benefits. They felt empowered to make choices about their careers and lives. Attracted to politics in 1992, youngsters nevertheless grew increasingly apolitical during 1993 and 1994. An August 1994 poll found only 4 percent still interested in public affairs, whereas the great majority gave high priority to making money and acquiring material possessions.

Most people over thirty-five years old, on the other hand, felt profoundly disoriented. *Glasnost'* had discredited the values on which they had been raised, and they could discern only greed and moral laxity as post-1991 norms. Some mourned the old days and yearned for a firm hand to quiet the chaos, but the great majority of Russian citizens felt baffled over what to believe. Disillusioned with the old regime and disgusted by the Party, they nevertheless quailed at the uncertainties and inequalities that transition brought. At first many had placed their hopes in democracy, but as the Yeltsin government struggled with the economic crisis and squabbled with the Soviet, faith in the new political system eroded. A December 1993 poll showed little popular interest in political and ideological issues. Instead, respondents gave top priority to "stabilizing the economy" and ridding Russia of "organized crime and corruption." Aware of the unemployment, homelessness, and crime that irked capitalist America, and steeped in Russian and socialist convictions that no one should get too far ahead of the pack, many Russians demurred from embracing Western free-enterprise values and methods. Liberals talked wistfully about the advantages, however vaguely understood, of Sweden's socialist "middle way." Conservatives looked to the Chinese model of political authoritarianism, socialist welfare, and controlled marketization. No one knew what course would best suit Russia.

Many Russians also suffered a loss of national pride and self-esteem. Whatever the faults of the old order, the Soviet Union had stood as a world power. Now, with the empire disintegrated, the economy in shambles, and the military hobbled, some Russians found it painful to accept their nation's diminished stature. Extremists blamed the CIA, a Jewish conspiracy, or Western schemers variously or together for Russia's downfall. Anti-Semitism, which had persisted throughout Soviet rule, emerged more openly after August 1991, but mostly among the older generation. Chauvinists dreamed of restoring a greater Russia. Traditionalist romantics such as Alexander Solzhenitsyn, who returned to live in Russia in May 1994, saw salvation in a Slavic brotherhood of Russia, Ukraine, and Belarus.

Some Russians turned to religion to guide them through their difficulties. Yet they found no simple answers there. The Russian Orthodox Church had emerged from the last stages of *perestroika* apparently much strengthened. In 1988 celebrations of the millennium of Kievan Rus's conversion to Christianity brought the church worldwide attention and support, including promises by Gorbachev to respect the church's independence. In June 1990, a month after the death of Patriarch Pimen, a council of clergy and laity elected a new patriarch, Alexei II, formerly metropolitan of Estonia. In October 1990, Russia's Supreme Soviet adopted a freedom-of-conscience law that regularized the church's position. This legislation made the church a juridical entity and gave it rights to own property, to proselytize and conduct educational activity, and to organize independent parishes.

Although many churches reopened and nominal church membership soared after 1991, with 60 million Russians identifying themselves as Orthodox believers in a 1993 poll, regular attendance at church services remained low. Older women made up the majority of worshipers. The several-hour duration of the mass, the custom of standing throughout the service, and the unintelligibility of Church Slavonic, the language of the liturgy—all discouraged young Russians, brought up in a secularized society, from finding a fresh orientation in Orthodoxy. Moreover, indecisive leadership and internal quarrels weakened the Orthodox Church's ability to reshape doctrines and practices to appeal to the younger generation. Patriarch Alexei II, although conciliatory and moderate, could not

Blessing St. Basil's Cathedral As part of the post-1991 resurgence of the Orthodox Church, Patriarch Alexei II sanctifies St. Basil's cathedral in Red Square for its reopening after 70 years of Soviet atheism.

control divisive reformist-conservative disputes within the church hierarchy and among Orthodox laity. Democratic critics even accused the patriarch and a number of metropolitans and bishops of the past collaboration with the KGB. Investigatory commissions set up by the Supreme Soviet and by the church itself failed to clear up these charges. At the same time, chauvinist circles attacked the church hierarchy for inadequately defending the pre-1917 values of "true" Russian culture and Orthodox belief.

Orthodox leaders encountered other obstacles as well. The Russian Orthodox Church Outside Russia, based in the United States, had not recognized the patriarchs of the Soviet era on the ground that they had betrayed the church to the atheistic Communists. In the 1990s, this group set up its own parishes in Russia, as did the True Orthodox or Catacomb Church, which had repudiated patriarchal authority after Metropolitan Sergei's 1927 submission to the Soviet regime. These challengers competed with the established church for believers and financial support. Further, the reestablished Uniate (Eastern Rite Catholic) church reclaimed many buildings and parishes in western Ukraine, which the Russian Orthodox Church had acquired after Stalin had banned the Uniates in the 1940s. To make matters worse, the Orthodox Church in Ukraine split into pro-Russian and pro-Ukrainian factions after Ukraine gained its independence.

Finally, the beleaguered Russian Orthodox leadership faced substantial incursion by non-Orthodox Christians from the West. Ignoring pleas from Alexei II, Pope John Paul II approved establishment of Roman Catholic parishes in Russia. More upsetting to the hierarchy, evangelical Protestants and special sects like Mormons and Jehovah's Witnesses from the United States and Western Europe swarmed across Russia. By 1994 the Russian Orthodox Church had failed to ease the spiritual crisis in Russia. Never renowned for its resiliency or its social gospel, it seemed incapable of overcoming decades of subservience to the Communist government or countering the legions of energetic competition.

The late 1980s and early 1990s also saw ferment in the field of education. Reformers attacked the previous rigid, ideology-oriented system and demanded new subjects and innovative methods. A July 1992 law on education gave parents the right to choose among state, municipal, private, and religious schools or to elect home schooling, with minimum tuition guaranteed for any option. All schools were granted self-government and freedom to determine their own curriculum and methods. By the 1993–1994 school year, many state schools offered a range of elective subjects but required competitive admission to the last two years of secondary instruction. In some cases, schools also required students to pay for the last year of precollege education. Nevertheless, schools struggled with shortages of money, facilities, textbooks, and supplies. As an additional burden, the Russian Ministry of Education had to finance special-education programs and textbooks in Russian for the 8.5 million children attending Russian-language schools in Ukraine, Kazakhstan, Belarus, and other successor states.

Lack of funding also hampered universities and research institutes. Some resorted to paid contract work or to attracting private tuition students. By 1994, 10 percent of university students paid full tuition and fees, and competition remained keen for admission to the most desirable institutions, such as the Russian Academy of Economics or the new Russian State Humanities University. Other postsecondary schools sought to establish ties abroad, and some scientists and scholars emigrated to Europe, Asia, and the Americas. Russian education at all levels remained in considerable turmoil. In most other post-Soviet countries, educational authorities wrestled not only with similar problems but also with expanding instruction in the national language, as each new state required.

In post-1991 Russia, cultural icons labored to adjust to both diminished status and financial stringency. True, the intelligentsia traditionally opposed tsarism, and prominent artists, writers, and intellectuals had participated in Khrushchev's thaw, in the dissident movement in Brezhnev's time, and in Gorbachev's *glasnost'*. But most highly educated and talented Soviet citizens had in fact prospered under Communist rule. Privately, they railed against the system and dreamed of superior alternatives, but in daily life a great many accepted the prestige and material rewards that the regime lavished on them to ensure their cooperation. After the system's collapse, the intelligentsia lost their privileged standing and were forced to jockey for position and economic benefit with everyone else. They particularly resented the new entrepreneurs and "fast-ruble" businessmen whose wealth permitted them to live ostentatiously and to exert political pressure on the government. Some intellectuals recognized that they had to descend from their ivory tower and plunge into political and social life, but others grew bewildered and isolated as their standard of living declined.

Cultural institutions also searched for their place in modern Russian society. Formerly well supported by the state and operating under close centralized control, arts organizations suddenly confronted slashed budgets and the need to finance and manage themselves. Such worldrenowned groups as the Bolshoi and Kirov opera and ballet companies met the challenge by reorganizing and earning hard currency on foreign tours. Yet even they had difficulty maintaining their facilities and keeping key performers from emigrating to the West. Internal dissension plagued the Bolshoi company as well. Although state subsidies fell from 3 to 4 percent of the total Soviet budget to less than 1 percent of the new Russian budget, some regional arts and performance organizations survived by winning support from local governmental authorities and by unearthing private sponsorship.

Overall, however, the postcoup period looked bleak for the arts in Russia. The end of Communism did not generate the burst of cultural creativity that some Western observers had expected, and individuals and organizations groped for new directions and new sources of inspiration. Indeed, Russian artistic life seemed crushed by the dual burdens of its Soviet past and the onrush of commercial Western culture. A few artists in dance, in theater, and in visual arts innovated. Others elaborated on Western avant-garde developments. Good literature, quality drama, and challenging art appeared, but the cultural scene as a whole remained barren. Artists, writers, and performers, like everyone else, struggled to support themselves. No longer assured sales, audiences, or salaries, they had to improvise to survive. Supplies, equipment, and facilities were expensive and private patronage rare.

The film industry sank into the doldrums. The largest studio, Mosfilm, which once released sixty movies a year, planned on producing only a dozen or so in 1994. Faced with outrageous costs and moviegoers unable to pay inflated ticket prices, filmmakers resorted to working on advertising commercials or cooperating with foreign producers, primarily on documentaries or television serials. The few Russian-language films made ran the risk of being "pirated" on television or in videocassettes. In any case, many viewers considered them too gloomy and preferred Grade B thrillers and "sexploitation" films imported from the West.

Even with Russian government subsidies, newspapers and journals floundered, and many ceased publishing. Some private magazines, newspapers, and TV stations flourished, but most barely subsisted as costs skyrocketed and support dwindled. Low-quality American TV dramas and sitcoms, videos, and films flooded Russian living rooms and theaters. The serial "Santa Barbara" and Mexican soap operas provided widely watched fare in 1993 and 1994. Western rock music still strongly influenced popular culture, and Western clothing and styles remained in vogue. Signs and billboards advertising Western products lined St. Petersburg's Nevsky Prospekt and Moscow's Red Square, although a government decree declared that only words transliterated into Russian be used. The adulation of the West among young people juxtaposed with the sense of inferiority and wounded pride felt by many Russians warned of a future nationalist reaction, particularly if the democratic market system should fail. Outsiders can only hope that artists will become economically self-supporting and throw off the blanket of Western commercialism to reassert Russia's unique cultural tradition in new and vibrant forms.

Soviet Successor States in Europe

The fifteen countries that emerged from the wreckage of the U.S.S.R. encountered unique circumstances as well as common problems. Every state wrestled with two major economic challenges: (1) how to reorient economies that had derived 30 to 60 percent of their value from free trade with other republics in the U.S.S.R. and (2) how far and how quickly to move from a centrally planned to a market system. Except for the Baltic states, most proceeded even more slowly than did Russia toward a free-enterprise economy. Every country, except perhaps Turkmenistan, which benefited from substantial natural gas revenues, faced considerable economic hardship. Almost all the new states grappled with the difficulties of establishing their own monetary, fiscal, and banking systems.

Politically, each new state experienced conflict between democratic reformers and former Communist leaders turned nationalists. In many cases an unstable coalition of these antagonists ran the government. Efforts to install democracy made the most progress, however unevenly, in Russia, the Baltic states, and Kyrgyzstan. Harsh dictatorships held sway in Uzbekistan, Turkmenistan, and Georgia, and authoritarian neo-Communist cliques dominated Ukraine, Belarus, and Kazakhstan. Civil war plagued Tadzhikistan, Azerbaijan, and Georgia. Internal ethnic conflicts or border disputes rent several of these states. In foreign policy, each country defined itself first in terms of its relationship with Russia, the giant among them.

The second richest and second most populous successor state, Ukraine, traveled a rocky road after its citizens voted for independence in December 1991. Compared to other European nations, Ukraine ranked between France and Germany in size and economic potential. With a population of about 52 million (including 11 million Russians and 500,000 Jews), Ukraine possessed almost two-thirds of the U.S.S.R.'s coal reserves and more than a third of Soviet iron and steel output. It also produced 30 to 40 percent of total Soviet agricultural goods. Yet its economy floundered as the political leadership stalemated over economic reform. By mid-1994, production dwindled to two-thirds of preindependence levels, near-hyperinflation raged, and the government had privatized only 5 percent of the economy.

Although almost all Ukrainians supported full independence, the Russified eastern half of the country, which contained much of the industry and the bulk of the Russian population, proved less nationalistic than the more rural western half where the Uniate Church predominated. Nationalist politicians ran the Ukrainian government and parliament but disagreed on basic issues of economic change, democratic reform, and foreign policy. Confronting the daunting task of creating a state and administration from scratch, President Kravchuk promised change. Unfortunately, he failed to implement a coherent program or to win over reformers and moderate nationalists, who suspected him of authoritarian ambitions. *Rukh*, the Ukrainian nationalist movement that had led the drive to independence, split into two factions. A majority reluctantly supported Kravchuk because of his promise to build Ukrainian statehood, and a minority urged democratic reforms and marketization. An

"It's 10:00 P.M.," the TV screen blinked. "Do you know who's running Russia?" The newspaper cartoon epitomized both the turbulence of the postcommunist world and the perplexed reaction of many Americans to it. Should we be bullish or bearish about Russia's future? Does a foundation, a historical heritage, exist for Russia's 1990s romance with the market, and for the democracy that we hope is associated with it? Or are such hopes futile, wistful at best, because, as some in the West believe, Russia has no democratic roots to nurture the latest experiment? These questions have ramifications far transcending the concerns of academic or journalistic Moscow watchers. For Russia's future—how things turn out in the world's largest state—will profoundly influence the international scene and global progress well into the next century. Like it or not, we must recognize that our destiny is linked to Russia's.

Decidedly bullish, S. Frederick Starr in *Prospects for Stable Democracy in Russia* (1992) traces a long history of private initiative and civic virtue from tsars to commissars. Although Russia suffered for centuries under autocracy, its rulers in fact had little control over people's daily lives, according to Starr. By 1914 individual initiative flowed throughout a rapidly marketizing economy, political parties had coalesced in less than a decade in the State Duma, and Russian statesmen and jurists "conceived their country's further evolution within the ideologically diverse spectrum of European development as a whole."

The strands of individualism persisted even after the triumph of Soviet power, Starr avers. Consequently, in a brutal effort in the late 1920s and 1930s to stamp out "bourgeois" and democratic remnants in Russian society, Stalin applied massive force against a recalcitrant people. By the 1980s, an entire underground economy coexisted with the sclerotic state-run sector. Thousands of voluntary associations mushroomed across the U.S.S.R., with interests ranging from ecology to rock music to historic preservation. Gorbachev's reforms ran aground in part because society had outgrown the suffocating collectivism of the state. The impetus for change now came from the bottom up rather than the top down. Thus, Starr concludes, the present government can draw from a deep reservoir of past activities and values that support a modern civic culture.

Not so, rejoin two other prominent scholars, one Russian, the other American. Yuri Afanasyev, historian of medieval Muscovy, paints a gloomy portrait of the coming decade (*Foreign Affairs,* March/April 1994). What's wrong, according to Afanasyev? Almost everything, he argues, as Russia's fabled troika hurtles headlong into the dark night of the apocalypse. The *nomenklatura* enrich themselves through their former connections; ultranationalists and former communists storm the ramparts of the Duma; and relations between Russia and the other post-Soviet states strain under Moscow's self-proclaimed guardianship of the latter's Russian-speaking populations. Like every good historian, Afanasyev's analysis of the present is rooted in an appreciation of the past, in this case a variant of earlier liberal pessimism concerning Russian character and its destiny. Indeed, Afanasyev's vision of the future perfectly parallels the past. As in centuries gone by, Russians—faced with an influx of alien (read Western) institutions and practices—have turned inward, rejecting the path toward a modern polity. "The state reigns supreme and the people . . . still have not shown the political will to take a more direct road to democracy."

Stephen Cohen, biographer of Nikolai Bukharin, quite agrees. Writing in *The Nation* (October 1994), Cohen spins a horror tale of a deeply divided society composed of a few rich and many poor. Most Russians, Cohen is convinced, have grown disgusted with market reforms, which they blame for escalating crime, soaring unemployment, and plummeting health care. Cohen puts little faith in Boris Yeltsin, who may yet postpone the 1996 presidential elections. In any case, Cohen adds, the Russian president rules with an illegal "authoritarian Constitution." The likely outcome? Probably something resembling Spain under Franco—in short, a semimilitary state led by Yeltsin or a general.

What can a student of Russian affairs conclude? Surely both of these points of view cannot be right. Is there a middle ground, one balanced between the two extremes of modern civic society and military state? Some observers—in particular two seasoned scholars, Daniel Yergin and Thane Gustafson—have tried to break the deadlock. Yes, the authors of *Russia 2010* (1993) say, Russia appears chaotic and unpredictable. Three epic changes are advancing simultaneously: a transition from dictatorship to democracy, a move from a command economy to a free market, and a devolution from empire to nation-state. Echoing Afanasyev and Cohen, Yergin and Gustafson acknowledge that failure may well be in the cards, and that Russia could revert to authoritarianism or a new Time of Troubles. "No other modern society has gone through such high inflation and depression, the ravages of living standards, the destruction of its political system or the collapse of its official ideology."

Yet, Yergin and Gustafson continue, signs of a brighter future exist. Blessed with extensive natural resources, a well-educated citizenry, and strong integrative forces such as language, a shared past, and sense of national identity, Russia might make a miraculous recovery and develop a prosperous, democratic, and stable society. Echoing Starr, the authors of *Russia 2010* see little alternative to democracy, Russian style. The army is badly divided and demoralized, as are extremists in the parliament. Crime, although significant and growing, reflects underlying and transitory weaknesses of early capitalism more than the disintegration of society. Privatization of medium- and small-sized businesses has forged ahead, and the opposition to Yeltsin has moved from the streets to the floor of the Duma. Slowly but surely, according to Yergin and Gustafson, Russia's likely future comes into view—a more or less "normal" country pulling back from the extremes of left *and* right.

The twentieth century closes in much the same way that it began: with revolution in Russia, the Eurasian heartland. Our historiographical survey ends with the same question that we posed in the opening chapter: "Whither Russia?"

What do you think?

outdated, Soviet-era constitution prescribed no clear delineation of executive and legislative authority. Quarrelling over the spoils of the old order and struggling for advantage in the new system created gridlock, with neither the president, the cabinet, nor parliament free to act decisively.

Parliamentary elections in the second quarter of 1994 returned a plurality of former Communists and minority fractions of nationalists and reformers but did not furnish any political tendency with a clear mandate. Yet, to many observers' surprise, the two-stage presidential elections of June–July 1994 not only drew a whopping two-thirds of the electorate but led at last to the breaking of the political-economic impasse in Ukraine. Russian-speaking Leonid Kuchma, former head of a huge missile plant in Dniepropetrovsk, defeated Ukraine's first president, Leonid Kravchuk, thanks to heavy voter turnout in Russian-oriented eastern Ukraine and last-minute support from some reformers and ex-Communists.

Prompted by the disastrous state of the economy and contingent offers of Western aid, Kuchma, who had served as prime minister under Kravchuk from 1992 to 1993, soon fulfilled his campaign pledges of economic reform and improved relations with Russia. In early October, he decreed new foreign trade, investment, budget, and price policies and promised to override parliamentary opposition to industrial and agricultural privatization. The International Monetary Fund speedily anointed this boldness with $365 million in support. In November 1994, President Kuchma arrived in Washington with the Ukrainian parliament's recent ratification of the Nuclear Nonproliferation Treaty and was rewarded with further guarantees of Ukraine's sovereignty and security and with an extra $200 million in U.S. assistance beyond the $700 million allotted in January 1994. Additional help from Western Europe and Japan had earlier been promised. Both multilateral aid agencies and the American government made clear that further funds would be promptly provided as soon as the reforms evidenced notable economic progress and as long as Ukraine continued to dismantle its nuclear missiles, as former president Kravchuk had agreed to do in January 1994.

In addition, with Western support, Kuchma took initial steps to defuse tensions in the Crimea, where the pro-Russian president was embroiled in an unproductive power struggle with his local parliament, and to advance détente with Russia. Negotiations with Moscow resumed on final disposition of the former Soviet Black Sea fleet. Originally destined to be split between Russia and Ukraine, the latter had agreed in principle in 1993 to sell its half to Russia. By 1994 Ukraine had begun to operate its own navy; the value of the aging ships in the fleet seemed marginal; and the Ukrainian side appeared mainly interested in leasing to Russia at a steep price the fleet's naval base at Sebastopol. Talks with Russia also began on reducing the some $3 billion that Ukraine owed Russia for past deliveries of oil and natural gas. In addition, both sides presented preliminary proposals for swapping Russian equity in the pipelines that deliver petroleum products across Ukraine to Europe for future energy deliveries to Ukraine. By autumn 1994, Ukrainian prospects definitely appeared brighter, although most observers predicted a lengthy period of further sacrifice and slow recuperation.

In cultural matters, the first three years of Ukrainian independence witnessed government promotion of Ukrainian history, literature, and culture and demands that the Ukrainian language be used in business, government, and education. Russian and Jewish minorities resisted these policies, hoping to retain schools and organizations advancing their own culture and language. They delayed implementation of mandatory instruction in Ukrainian in higher educational institutions, but the drive for Ukrainization of all institutions continued. Disturbing rumors of anti-Jewish pogroms in spring 1989 ended, but many Jews, apprehensive about traditional Ukrainian anti-Semitism, emigrated to Israel or to Russia. Nevertheless, most Ukrainians eschewed discrimination against ethnic minorities in the new state, and Ukraine was spared outbreaks of racial violence.

Belarus, Ukraine's Slavic neighbor to the north, also elected a new president in mid-1994 and wrestled with an old-style, nearly bankrupt economy. Formerly the Byelorussian Republic of the Soviet Union, Belarus possessed no history as an independent state. Its reformist movement, the Belarusan Popular Front, founded in June 1989, was spawned by resentment of Moscow's mishandling of the Chernobyl' cleanup in Belarus and by anger over the 1988 discovery of the graves of 250,000 KGB victims at Kurapaty. Initially, the front did not seek independence, and in the Soviet-wide referendum of April 1991 (see Chapter 11), 80 percent of Belarusan voters favored maintenance of the U.S.S.R. Belarus's Communist leaders supported the failed coup of August 1991. They finally declared independence in part because Ukraine's vote for secession forced their hand and in part because they saw a quick transition to separate status as the only way for the Communist Party to retain power in Belarus.

Remembering the Chernobyl' disaster (which contaminated 23 percent of Belarus), postindependence leaders, with wide popular support, declared the country a nonnuclear state. They transferred Belarus's small nuclear arsenal to Russia for dismantling and ratified the Nuclear Nonproliferation Treaty. The new nation also maintained cordial relations with its neighbors, Poland and the Baltic states, and sought closer ties with Western Europe and the United States.

At home in Belarus, the postindependence political and economic system remained in a Soviet mold. Former Communists dominated the cabinet and the parliament. Deputies to the latter, still called the Supreme Soviet, had been chosen in the Soviet era. The leadership circumvented a reformist referendum for new elections, and in January 1994 the old-line prime minister engineered the removal of the Soviet's moderate head.

Based on a population of almost 11 million, the predominantly agricultural economy tumbled after 1991. The government took few steps toward privatization or marketization. By 1994 inflation reached 50 percent a month, and Belarus owed huge energy bills to Russia. A negotiated economic and monetary union with Russia languished because of doubts on both sides about how it would affect each economy.

In this bleak situation, Belarus held its first presidential election in July 1994. Alexander Lukashenko, a thirty-nine-year-old former collective-farm boss, waged a dynamic, populist campaign. He railed against corruption, promised a better life, and leaned toward union with Russia. Rejecting the old-guard prime minister, 80 percent of the voters supported Lukashenko. Despite the economic conservatism and pro-Moscow stance of his platform, the incoming president soon declared his support for Belarusan independence and cautiously initiated modest steps toward economic renovation. Although many Russians and Belarusans favor integration of the two states, Russian leaders would need to count the costs of Western disapproval and of absorbing a much weaker economy. Lukashenko and his advisers, on the other hand, fear domination by the larger state and remain skeptical of Russia's democratic and free market leanings. Thus, at the end of 1994, the rejoining of these two Slavic neighbors seemed unlikely. Down the road, however, Belarus may find it beneficial, for economic and security reasons, to enter a federated relationship with Russia.

In sharp contrast to Belarus and Ukraine, the new Baltic nations made substantial economic and political progress, albeit at an uneven pace, after declaring independence. Lithuania, with a population of 3.8 million and small minorities of Poles, Russians, and Belarusans, witnessed the slowest economic transformation and the widest political swings of the three states. Its predominantly agricultural economy continued to depend heavily on trade with former Soviet states, and its overall output dropped between 1991 and 1994. By contrast, Latvia's and Estonia's commerce eastward declined to levels of 60 percent and 20 percent, respectively. Lithuania also attracted less foreign investment and had stormier relations with its nationals living abroad than Latvia and Estonia.

Politically, former Lithuanian Communists, who had separated from the Soviet Party in 1989 and formed the Democratic Labor party after 1991, handily defeated the conservative nationalists of *Sajudis* in free elections held in late October 1992. Their platform of social justice and economic betterment also urged realistic relations with Russia while avowing their full commitment to Lithuanian independence.

For several reasons, Lithuania had markedly better relations with Russia than did Latvia and Estonia. First, it could export agricultural products and hydroelectric and nuclear power to Russia in return for manufactured goods. In addition, many Russians living in Lithuania obtained Lithuanian citizenship, which neutralized a potential source of friction. Lithuania also cooperated in transit and economic arrangements for the Russian region of Kaliningrad, the northern part of formerly German East Prussia. Kaliningrad was cut off by Lithuanian territory from its mother country (see map, p. 529). Finally, Lithuania, alone among the Baltic states, facilitated the withdrawal of Russian forces from the area by offering to pay part of the costs of resettling the troops in Russia.

Latvia and Estonia followed similar patterns of development after 1991. More industrialized than Lithuania, both states staggered under severe economic problems. Efforts to reorient their trade to Scandinavia and Western Europe finally began to pay off in 1993, as each country's currency became internationally convertible. Assistance from international, Western, and emigré sources pushed Latvia and Estonia along the road to economic recovery. By 1994 Latvia had not quite overcome the precipitous post-1991 drop in production, whereas Estonia was projecting economic growth of 6 percent for the year and had privatized 90 percent of its economy. The rapid economic changes in Estonia, although successful, undermined the popularity of its reformist government, and most observers predicted that conservative forces would prevail in early 1995 elections. Bickering among ardent nationalists, democratic reformers, and former Communists plagued the politics of all three states. In Latvia a small neo-Nazi movement emerged.

The biggest problem confronting Latvia and Estonia, however, centered on the fate of their large Russian minorities. The issue strongly influenced the two states' relations with Russia and the evacuation of Russian troops from the Baltic area. Latvia, with almost 40 percent of its 2.7 million people Russian and Ukrainian, and Estonia where Russians made up one-third of the population of 1.6 million, both initially asserted that only people who resided, or whose parents resided, in Latvia and Estonia before 1940 qualified as citizens of the new states. Further, each government tied naturalization to competence in the extremely difficult indigenous languages. Because only citizens were allowed to vote in post-1991 elections, most Russian residents were disfranchised. These and other restrictions on the rights of the Russians in the two states provoked a dispute with Russia. The Russian government appealed to the United Nations and to the Conference on Security and Cooperation in Europe to protect its minorities in the Baltic states.

Two other issues clouded relations between Latvia and Estonia and Russia. Estonia, especially, pressed for restoration of borders agreed to by the Soviet Union in the 1920–1921 period, when Lenin's government had recognized the independence of the interwar Baltic states. Russia favored a frontier less generous to Estonia than the one Stalin had arbitrarily established during his 1940 annexation of the Baltic countries and that the Soviet government had specified when it rerecognized Baltic independence in 1991. The area in dispute, although small, carried symbolic significance for each side. Latvian and Estonian relations with Russia were further complicated by economic questions related to new commercial arrangements, reparations for property seized and environmental damage caused during Soviet rule, and compensation for withdrawing Russian troops.

In negotiating these matters, both sides tried to use Russian troops in the region as bargaining chips. In 1992 Yeltsin promised to complete the evacuation of former Soviet forces by the end of 1994, and in 1993 he withdrew Russian units from Lithuania. On several occasions, however, the Russian president announced a suspension of troop withdrawals until Latvia and Estonia provided satisfactory guarantees of the rights of their Russian minorities. In January 1994, during President Clinton's visit to Moscow, Yeltsin agreed to evacuate the remaining 25,000 Russian forces in Latvia and Estonia during 1994 in return for an American commitment to cooperate with the Baltic nations in developing safeguards for minority rights. Despite some last-minute bluster, Yeltsin withdrew his troops as promised by August 31, 1994. In return, Estonia and Latvia softened citizenship requirements for ethnic Russians, and Latvia permitted Russia to retain a base there. Although at the end of 1994 the three Baltic states clearly relied for their security on support from the West and correct, if not friendly, relations with Russia, their future as independent and prosperous countries looked bright.

Moldova, formerly the Moldavian Republic of the U.S.S.R., has a population of 4.4 million. At one time, Moldova had formed part of the province of Bessarabia. Annexed by Russian tsars in the nineteenth century, it was absorbed by Romania in 1918 and reacquired by Stalin in 1940. Even before Moldova declared independence in late August 1991, its ethnic Romanians (64 percent of the population) had formed the nationalist Popular Front, gained control of the local government, and decreed that Romanian become the official language by 1994. Russians and Ukrainians living on the eastern border of the republic in a region known as Transdniestria resisted these policies, foreseeing loss of their privileged status and cultural heritage. Backed by elements of the former Soviet Fourteenth Army stationed there, this group proclaimed the autonomous Trans-Dniester Republic. Fighting between the separatists and Moldovan units broke out in March 1992, putting the survival of Moldova at risk. Presidents Yeltsin of Russia and Kravchuk of Ukraine pursued a conciliatory policy and helped to avert civil war and outside intervention.

To address the concerns of the Transdniestrian Russians and other minorities, who together make up one-third of Moldova's population, a moderate government formed in August 1992 offered them full cultural autonomy and equal citizenship. Many non-Romanians accepted integration into the new state, although some Russians pressed for legalization of Russian as an official second language. The government further tempered minority fears by declaring its opposition to unification with Romania. It also promised no future change in Moldova's status without full consultation with nationality groups.

Economic decline and political stalemate among nationalists, reformers, and ex-Communists spawned new parliamentary elections in Moldova in February 1994. A divided Popular Front fared poorly, winning, with another nationalist party, only 17 percent of the vote. The Agrarian Democratic party, conservative in economic policy but favoring autonomy for the minorities and greater participation in the CIS, garnered almost 50 percent of the seats in the legislature and dominated the new government. In July the parliament approved a new constitution that provided substantial self-rule to Transdniestria and other nationality areas. A month later, Russia's minister of defense announced that he was downgrading the Fourteenth Army to an operational group. Shortly afterward, Russia and Moldova agreed that Russian troops would withdraw from Transdniestria within three years in return for political autonomy for the region. For the first time since its birth, Moldova seemed well on the way to solving its ethnic problems

Despite close historical, cultural, and linguistic ties to Romania, in March 1994 the majority of Moldova's population overwhelmingly approved a referendum reaffirming Moldova's independence. Although nationalists in Romania continued to agitate for Romania's reabsorption of Moldova, other Romanians disdained Moldova for alleged cultural and economic backwardness. Relations between the two states proved prickly in 1994. For the near future, it seems likely that Moldova will continue as an independent state, enjoying economic ties with Russia and the CIS and advancing cautiously toward economic reform and political stability.

Post-Soviet States in the Caucasus and Central Asia

Most nations formed from the non-European splinters of the former U.S.S.R. encountered more severe problems than those facing their neighbors to the west. With a long history of imperial subjugation and ethnic strife, the three republics of the Caucasus region ran into especially daunting challenges in their second experience with statehood. (They had achieved brief independence in 1918–1921.) Georgia's 5.5 million citizens, who, with the Baltic peoples, had propelled the drive for independence from the U.S.S.R. in 1989–1990, elected dissident writer Zviad Gamsakhurdia president in May 1991. Georgia operated as an independent state well before the late-1991 formal dissolution of the Soviet Union. The new nation refused to join the CIS in December 1991.

Gamasakhurdia proved ruthless and dictatorial, and his policies split the nationalist movement and the country within his first six months in office. In addition, two significant minorities within Georgia—the South Ossetians and the Abkhazis—strongly resisted the imposition of centralized Georgian rule.

By fall 1991, popular protests against the president and ethnic clashes in Ossetia and Abkhazia had torn the country apart. After a bloody civil war that dragged on from December 1991 to March 1992, moderate forces triumphed and invited Edvard Shevardnadze, a former Soviet foreign minister and Gorbachev ally, to replace the ousted Gamsakhurdia.

Relations with Russia remained tense, however. Georgia charged Moscow with interfering in Georgian affairs by supporting the Ossetians and Abkhazis. Russia retorted that its troops had intervened only to protect Russian lives and property. In fall 1993, with the government about to topple under domestic opponents and the Abkhazian rebels, Russian forces threw their support to Shevardnadze. In return, they demanded Georgian agreement to join the CIS and to permit Russian bases and the stationing of Russian troops in Georgia. The bitterness, destruction, and terror of the civil strife forced many Russians to flee Georgia, disrupted the society, and ruined the economy. Now dependent on Russia, Georgia will need years to recover.

Armenia, the smallest non-Baltic successor state, contained only 3.3 million people. Nevertheless, it relished bright prospects on gaining independence. The republic boasted a well-educated, hard-working population, a fairly prosperous economy, and the support of millions of Armenians in the Middle East, Europe, and the Americas. Yet liberation from Soviet rule brought only hardship and despair as the nation became consumed by the Nagorno-Karabakh dispute with Azerbaijan. As we saw in Chapter 11, the conflict over this mountainous enclave had erupted in 1988. It remained unresolved in 1994. The undeclared war between Armenia and Azerbaijan has cost thousands of lives, created hundreds of thousands of refugees, and demolished the economies of both states.

Bordered on the south by its longstanding enemy Turkey and by Muslim Iran, landlocked Armenia traditionally depended on trade from Russia across Georgia and Azerbaijan. When the latter state blockaded Armenia, severing energy and other supplies, and unrest and sabotage disrupted the transit of goods through Georgia, Armenians suffered bitter winters with almost no fuel, electricity, or heat. Production fell drastically, and Armenia became dependent on subsidies from abroad and from Russia, which could ill afford them. Despite popular protests against democratically elected President Levon Ter-Petrosyan, his government survived and directed Armenian forces to major military victories. In 1994 Armenia controlled most of Nagorno-Karabakh and a substantial swath of Azerbaijan itself. Yet the country was exhausted and the economy expiring.

Azerbaijan's stormy existence as an independent state also had close links with the Nagorno-Karabakh quarrel. A strong popular-front movement, like those in the Baltic states, developed in 1989 among the republic's 7 million people. In early 1990, however, after a massacre of Armenians in the capital of Baku, Red Army troops intervened. This action strengthened the position of ex-Communists, who formed the first independent government in September 1991. In spring 1992, the oppositionist Azerbaijan People's Front came to power in democratic elections. Rejecting both Islamic fundamentalism and neo-Communist authoritarianism, the new administration strove to find a balance among contending factions in the People's Front and to assuage demands for greater autonomy from the regions of Legizstan and Nakhichevan. It failed, however, to introduce promised economic and political reforms. Discontent mounted, and as the Armenians gained military victories, many Azerbaijan nationalists turned against the government. Civil strife engulfed the area in the summer of 1993.

Former Soviet Politburo member Geidar Aliyev assumed authority in Azerbaijan, vowing to restore order and to revive the war effort against Armenia. Heavily dependent on Russian economic assistance and military support, the new president took Azerbaijan back into the CIS. His armies had little success on the battlefield, however. In addition, conditions for the flood of war refugees worsened, and the economy floundered. Aliyev resorted to authoritarian measures to quell mounting political unrest. Despite nationalist charges that he had turned the country into a Russian satellite state, Aliyev clung to power. He worked out a major contract for conducting oil exploration and upgrading the petroleum industry with a Western consortium headed by British Petroleum, although Russian pressure forced Azerbaijan to give the Russian oil giant Lukoil a share of the deal. Buoyed by material assistance from Turkey and Russia, Azerbaijan struggled in 1994 to restore its economy and maintain political stability.

The five Central Asian post-Soviet states encountered problems not unlike those that plagued the new nations of the Caucasus. At the same time, they confronted unique challenges. Among the 50 million Muslims of the region, Islam flourished and national cultures blossomed after 1991. To be sure, Islam had its strongest influence in Tadzhikistan and among the rural populations of each society. Nevertheless, throughout the region thousands of mosques and hundreds of religious schools opened, millions of copies of the Koran provided by Saudi Arabia were distributed, and tens of thousands of Central Asians made the *hadj* to Mecca for the first time, the pilgrimages financed by the Saudi government. On the other hand, protagonists of Islam acknowledged that it would take years to convert the secular outlook of most Central Asians, developed under Soviet rule and nurtured by increasing educational opportunities.

Islamic fundamentalism, at least in its Iranian guise, appeared to have little impact on these former Soviet states. Central Asian Islamic leaders, who are Sunni Muslims, had no close theological ties with Shi'ite Iran. Many also scorned the authoritarian system of the ayatollahs. Instead, numerous Central Asian Muslims looked to Turkey or Pakistan as possible models while welcoming assistance from Arab countries, Malaysia, and Indonesia. At the same time, most leaders recognized that, to survive, the new states would have to recreate mutually beneficial relations with Russia and establish contact with China and the West.

All the Central Asian nations hastened to develop national cultures and literatures, and each instituted obligatory use of indigenous languages at varying paces. These countries also abrogated Stalin's edict that their languages be written in the Cyrillic alphabet. The Tadzhik language (related to Persian) returned to Arabic script, and the other languages, all Turkic, shifted to the Latin alphabet used in modern Turkey. Lack of textbooks written in the indigenous languages hindered educational change and progress. Cultural leaders of every nation bridled at the postindependence incursion of Western culture.

The five nations, except Kyrgyzstan, maintained a conservative, authoritarian political culture. Social structure, especially outside the urban areas, remained traditional and patriarchal, and the position of women worsened following the end of Soviet rule. Economically, all the states except Turkmenistan suffered as customary links with the large Soviet economy dissolved and leaders sought new markets for major export products such as cotton, vegetables, and fruit.

The Central Asian heads of state met in January 1993 to form a loose economic union and to plan for regional cooperation. In July 1994, the presidents of Kazakhstan, Kyrgyzstan, and Uzbekistan agreed to additional economic links and pledged close cultural, technical, and political cooperation. Kazakh leader Nursultan Nazarbayev pointedly contrasted this progress to the slow pace of integration under the CIS.

Indeed, Nazarbayev, a reformed Communist, emerged after 1991 as the region's dominant figure. He wholeheartedly backed Yeltsin against the August *putschists* and was instrumental in founding the CIS. Nazarbayev endorsed nuclear disarmament as well and signed the Nuclear Nonproliferation Treaty. In return, President Clinton invited him to Washington in February 1994 and tripled American aid to Kazakhstan from $91 to $311 million. After his country of 17 million inhabitants declared its independence, Nazarbayev promised economic and political reforms. Despite a halting start, his government moved toward a market system and in April 1994 undertook a sweeping privatization program. Kazakhstan also actively encouraged foreign investment in 1993 and 1994 and initiated development of its potential petroleum deposits.

Frustrated by alleged obstructionism in the old parliament, Nazarbayev called new elections in March 1994. The voting produced a

A Central Asian Dynamo On the right, President Nursultan Nazarbayev of the new state of Kazakhstan, who has emerged as a major post-Soviet leader, is given red carpet treatment by Turkey's President Turgut Ozal as Nazarbayev arrives in Ankara for a state visit in September 1991.

comfortable majority of his supporters in the new legislature. Although some outside observers reported electoral irregularities, others concluded that the elections proceeded fairly. In October 1994, Nazarbayev complained of sluggish economic progress and fired his cabinet, but no political crisis erupted.

Confronted with a delicate balance between the state's 6 million Russian residents and its 7 million Kazakhs, Nazarbayev acted prudently to protect the Russian minority from attacks by extreme nationalists. In addition, he and Yeltsin promised to respect the borders between their countries. Interestingly, demands to annex to Russia northwestern areas of Kazakhstan, where many Russians live, came not from the region's Russian residents, but from nationalist hotheads in Russia like Zhirinovsky, who was born in the Kazakh capital Alma-Ata, now Almaty. Although the president has at times harassed the political opposition and squelched media criticism, Kazakhstan's chances of emerging as a partially democratic, prosperous society seemed hopeful at the end of 1994.

Uzbekistan's 20 million inhabitants made it slightly larger in population than Kazakhstan, but the country logged little progress after independence. Its president, Islam Karimov, established dictatorial rule, suppressing opposition political groups and locking up dissidents. The Uzbek leader also strongly supported the conservative side, which included local Uzbeks, in the civil war in Tadzhikistan, discussed below. Heavily dependent on cotton, the economy tottered. In response, Karimov promised sweeping economic changes in February 1994, but by the end of the year, the results proved meager.

Turkmenistan, replete with petroleum reserves and possessing a tiny population of 3.5 million, fared well economically, arranging to sell its natural gas directly to Turkey via a new pipeline to be built across Transcaspia. The country established cordial relations with its impressive neighbor Iran but appeared not to fall under Iranian influence. Turkmenistan's president, Saparmurad Niyazov, ruled with an iron hand and encouraged a minicult of personality around him. In 1994 chances for either economic or political reform appeared slim.

Kyrgyzstan, with an agricultural and nomadic economy and population of 4.3 million, is the poorest and most isolated of the Central Asian states. Nevertheless, its leader, Askar Akayev, a former prominent scientist, established democratic rule as early as October 1990 and turned back a right-wing coup attempt at the time of the August 1991 *putsch* in Moscow. After independence and his election as president, he continued to lead an open, representative society, although he supported curbs on the press in 1994. That same year, Akayev sought to whip up political enthusiasm by holding referenda on his presidency (overwhelmingly approved) and on replacing the old Soviet-style parliament with a new streamlined legislature (also endorsed). Most of the population remained apolitical, however. Although Kyrgyzstan developed its own stable currency and kept inflation low, production lagged, and with few resources, the economic future seemed bleak in 1994. Some citizens, with traditional ties to China, hoped that the last big Communist nation would come to their assistance, but in fact international and Western aid furnished the country's chief support.

The last Central Asian country, Tadzhikistan, endured almost continuous political turmoil in its first eighteen months of independence. A protracted and inconclusive struggle between old-line Communists and a coalition of reformers, Islamic nationalists, and regional chieftains finally erupted into civil war in May 1992. Not until early 1993 was order restored, in part through political mediation by Russia, Uzbekistan, Kazakhstan, and Kyrgyzstan. These states sponsored mainly Russian peacekeeping forces. Russia furnished emergency economic assistance as well, and provided subsidies that accounted for two-thirds of Tadzhikistan's budget. Russian troops also propped up the conservative government and took responsibility for patrolling the border between the new state and Afghanistan. In mid-1994, as a result of mediation efforts by the

UN, Pakistan, and Iran, the Tadzhik government of Imamali Rakhmonov and opposition leaders agreed on a cease-fire. In November 1994 elections, a new constitution was adopted and Rakhmonov was chosen president. Peace and stability seemed secured for the moment, but President Rakhmonov's rule boded ill for economic reform or progress toward democracy in Tadzhikistan.

Given that the five new states in former Soviet Central Asia border on Iran, Afghanistan, and China, their future will continue to interest Russia and the Western powers. These fledgling states will need both multilateral and bilateral technical and economic assistance to develop into stable, modern nations.

Conclusion

As the Soviet Union fell apart, doomsayers predicted domestic chaos and international tension. Neither came to pass. Indeed, the transition to independent states and to new social, political, and economic arrangements proved smoother overall for the former Soviet peoples than even optimists would have dared imagine. Most beneficial of all, the Soviet Union did not go the way of Yugoslavia. With the exception of the Nagorno-Karabakh conflict and sporadic civil war in Georgia and Tadzhikistan, the demise of Soviet Communism produced little violence. Moreover, in the Caucasus, Central Asia, and Moldova, political and ethnic strife did not evoke outside intervention nor spill over into neighboring states. Although the problem remains of how best to protect minority rights in the new nations, most leaders of the successor states have individually and collectively shown restraint and caution in relations among themselves and in addressing flash points in their neighbors' bailiwicks.

After Ukraine's overwhelming vote for full independence dashed Yeltsin's lingering hopes to salvage a union from the wreckage of the U.S.S.R., the Russian president and Nazarbayev promoted the Commonwealth of Independent States. Dominated by Russia, the CIS provides a forum for collaboration but seems unlikely to evolve into a working confederation. The increasing dependence on Russia of Georgia, Azerbaijan, and Tadzhikistan reflects the Russian government's determination to fulfill its self-proclaimed role as guardian of the region.

In 1991 concerns about instability and about the fate of Soviet arms worried Western leaders. When the former scenario did not come to pass, efforts turned to reducing and dismantling nuclear weapons and to encouraging progress toward democracy and economic recovery. Belarus and Kazakhstan shortly agreed to abide by previous arms-control arrangements and to transfer their former Soviet missiles to Russia for disarming, but Ukraine hesitated. Finally, in early 1994, President Kravchuk pledged to surrender Ukraine's nuclear weapons in return for security guarantees and economic aid. In Russia and other successor countries, substantial Western assistance, although in process, awaits legal, institutional, and fiscal reforms before it can be fully delivered.

In the words of Serge Schmemann, *New York Times* correspondent in Moscow, Russia in 1994 appeared to be "messy but working." Although many citizens expressed nostalgia for past stability and anxiety about the future, they endured new deprivations stoically and hoped for a better life. Few seem interested in a return to Communist triumphalism and Soviet mediocrity. Nevertheless, conservative nationalism emerged as a significant political force during 1993. Despite the quelling of the October *putsch* by Yeltsin's opponents, nationalists and ex-Communists made gains in the December parliamentary elections. Yeltsin's position weakened, and the pace of economic reform slowed. The government pressed ahead with privatization, however. Foreign investment picked up, and Yeltsin pledged a renewed commitment to economic reform in October 1994. Signs of recovery emerged, despite a widening gap between rich and poor. The determination by younger people to forge ahead boded well for the survival of democracy and a free-market system.

Among the predicaments that all successor nations grappled with, struggles for power between central governments and local power centers ranked high. The issue of the rights of Russians in other states remained volatile, and diverse ethnic tensions plagued several post-Soviet nations. Yet, compared to what might have happened, the death of Soviet socialism and the emergence from the ashes of a new order in one-sixth of the globe has progressed equably and peacefully overall. The peoples of that huge area now hold in their hands the opportunity to develop their own visions of social progress and economic betterment.

FURTHER READING

The brief period between August 1991 and the end of 1994 saw a number of books published that attempted to react to the onrushing events but few that provided historical perspective and analysis. Of several journalistic accounts, the most interesting is Jonathan Steele, *Eternal Russia: Yeltsin, Gorbachev, and the Mirage of Democracy* (Cambridge, Mass., 1994). Although the tone is understandably self-exculpatory, and at times emotional and almost self-pitying, the Russian president's memoir of these years, Boris Yeltsin, *The Struggle for Russia* (New York, 1994), sheds light on the two coup attempts and on the January 1992 decision to launch economic reform.

Two broad-ranging and helpful collections of articles are Gail W. Lapidus, ed., *The New Russia* (Boulder, Colo., 1994), which focuses on politics, the economy, and foreign policy, and James R. Millar and Sharon L. Wolchik, eds., *The Social Legacy of Communism* (Cambridge, 1994), which emphasizes social, work, and ethnic issues. Karen Dashiwa and Bruce Parrott, *Russia and the New States of Eurasia: The Politics of Upheaval* (Cambridge, 1994), and Daniel Yergin and Thane Gustafson, *Russia 2010 and What It Means for the*

World (New York, 1993), both assess the changes and indicate future directions. On politics, see Michael McFaul and Sergei Markov, *The Troubled Birth of Russian Democracy* (Stanford, Calif., 1993).

Books on nationality issues and on the environment cited in Chapter 11's Further Reading list also treat early post-1991 developments in those fields. In addition, see the provocative short treatment of economic reform, Walter Adams and James W. Brock, *Adam Smith Goes to Moscow: A Dialogue on Radical Reform* (Princeton, N.J., 1993), and a thorough review of the new Islamic states by a Pakistani journalist, Ahmed Rashid, *The Resurgence of Central Asia: Islam or Nationalism?* (Atlantic Highlands, 1994). Also helpful is Ali Bantiazizi and Myron Wiener, eds., *New Geopolitics of Central Asia* (Bloomington, Ind., 1994).

Controversial and often challenging reflections about the collapse of Soviet communism by prominent scholars in Soviet and Russian studies appear in *The New York Review of Books*, September 15, 1994, and *The Times Literary Supplement*, November 6, 1992.

EPILOGUE WHAT WENT WRONG?

I first met Arkady S. in 1985. He had survived the siege of his native city Odessa at the start of World War II. The Nazis killed his parents, and he nearly starved to death in the famine of 1946. Yet he had moderately prospered under Soviet rule, and although he was unhappy about conditions during *perestroika* and in the early 1990s after Odessa became part of an independent Ukraine, he remained optimistic. In fall 1994, he and his wife and son suddenly decided to emigrate to the United States. The move proved wrenching. His son told me that the first time the family shopped at an American supermarket, his father began to cry. 'Why was life at home not better; why did my hard work amount to nothing?" Arkady blurted out. "What went wrong?"

Justifiably, many other former Soviet citizens have asked the same questions. The demise of Soviet Communism also confounded and grievously disappointed Westerners who saw the U.S.S.R. as the chief bulwark against fascism, as well as Third World intellectuals and leaders who believed that the Soviet example pointed the way to their own salvation. Finally, socialists everywhere who cherished the conviction that Marxism's promise would come to fruition in Soviet society lamented the system's collapse. The Soviet peoples' tragic experience dominated much of twentieth-century world history, and the U.S.S.R.'s breakup has now ushered in a unique historical era. Unlike one of Aesop's fables, the Soviet story contains no shining moral. Yet we may face the next century more clearheadedly if we understand and learn from the Soviet experiment. Why did the bright vision of 1917 remain unfulfilled? Why did the revolutionary dream of a just, humane, and equitable society turn into a nightmare of authoritarianism, repression, and insecurity? Can anything be salvaged from Soviet Communism's rubble?

Perhaps the promise itself was utopian and unrealizable. The central socialist aim of a life of freedom, security, and fairness remains a powerful beacon for everyone. But Soviet methods of substituting state ownership for private control of the economy, government planning for the free play of market forces, and social benefits for income incentives produced an inefficient and increasingly laggard system. The Soviet performance makes clear that to achieve the socialist ideal, other means will have to be found.

Bolshevism acted as another force pushing Soviet socialism off course. Partly because of Lenin's personality and partly thanks to the milieu of conflict with tsarist liberal, and socialist foes in which the Party was nurtured, Bolshevism emerged in 1917 as an exclusionary, hard-nosed doctrine and organization. Its leaders disdained accommodation and easily resorted to coercion and then violence when others, including the masses, blocked their self-chosen path. They also rejected the outside world and tended toward Russocentrism, despite Lenin's warnings. As a result, the Bolsheviks built a fatally flawed, centralized, Moscow-dominated system. In the process, they largely trampled on non-Russians' economic and political rights while granting them a cultural autonomy that contained the seeds of future nationalisms. In short, although Leninism may not have directly spawned Stalinism, its genes appeared throughout the body politic that the ruthless Georgian erected in the 1930s. Stalin found much in the Leninist tradition on which to draw, and the persistence until 1989 of a one-party, nonparticipatory, elite political system was a direct legacy of Bolshevism's founder.

Yet ineffective methods and an authoritarian organization cannot wholly explain the fate of Soviet socialism. Even with finely tuned instruments and a flexible party, Russian socialists would probably still have failed to reshape the mass of peasants peaceably and democratically. Their overwhelming numbers and tradition-bound outlook obstructed the road to modernization. As Lenin noted just before his death, the rural population's limited economic and social development and their cultural backwardness provided formidable barriers to progress.

Nevertheless, beyond this inherent liability from Russia's past, the "objective circumstances" (as Lenin liked to label them) in which the Bolsheviks and their successors labored to transform the Soviet peoples proved monumentally unpropitious. The October Revolution erupted in a demoralized and defeated society heavily damaged by World War I. The Soviet leaders took their first halting steps as defenders of a beleaguered armed camp against domestic opponents and foreign interventionists. They survived but were left with a devastated economy, a shell-shocked society, and a sullen and exhausted population, hardly ideal building blocks for a new order. Then, when outside help might have boosted their all-out industrialization drive, the Great Depression struck. This global catastrophe drove grain prices down, curtailed foreign trade, and forced the Soviet modernizers to soldier on alone. Just as they detected some signs of progress, the fury of Hitler's armies burst over the country, destroying human and material resources and setting the U.S.S.R. back years. Finally, the last forty years of Soviet development took place under the psychological threat of the Cold War and the economic burden of the Soviet-American arms race. External pressures and internal conditions alike hampered Soviet socialism at almost every point in its evolution.

Yet it is fair to ask: once Stalin died, could not effective methods, more open policies, and the rising educational level of the Soviet population have furnished the basis for a sensible campaign to grasp the vision of 1917? Indeed, two able leaders appeared. Both recognized the flawed nature of what his nation had so far accomplished. Both urged and even implemented some changes. Yet Khrushchev and Gorbachev came little closer to the goal than had Lenin and Stalin. Their efforts ended in mild reaction, in Khrushchev's case, and in the system's downfall under Gorbachev.

Where did they go astray? Apart from personality weaknesses, the two men failed for parallel reasons. Both were committed to communist values. Ideologically, neither Khrushchev nor Gorbachev could bring themselves to scrap the collective-farm system and liberate Soviet agriculture. Yet such a change was virtually a prerequisite to reforming other sectors and to genuine economic improvement. Moreover, both clung to a faith in central planning and government control, even while they encouraged some tinkering with the economy. Khrushchev certainly and Gorbachev largely rejected the centrality of the market and private trade and ownership to economic growth and efficiency.

Besides their commitment to Soviet socialist principles, Khrushchev and Gorbachev both relied on the Party and faced an entrenched *nomenklatura* system that neither succeeded in reshaping. At the very end, Gorbachev abandoned the Party's political monopoly, but he never fully shed his Party skin. Last, neither leader understood the intensity and potential subversiveness of non-Russians' yearnings for control over their economic and political lives. For Khrushchev, this failing mattered little because he maintained centralized rule from Moscow. For Gorbachev, however, his ignoring non-Russians' aspirations proved fatal once *glasnost'* and democratization unleashed their passions and their powers to organize.

Amid this dismal saga, bright spots occasionally shine through. The world is richer for the achievements of Soviet artists, writers, musicians, actors, balladeers, scientists, and cosmonauts. However costly the process, an industrial economy arose. Soviet educators vanquished illiteracy, and the population reached educational levels equal to that of other industrialized societies. Despite persecution, the Orthodox faith persisted, providing comfort to millions. Untold talented and humane individuals in Russia and the other former Soviet territories continue to struggle for a better life, although through non-Soviet institutions and by non-socialist means. In their quest, some may remember the quenched vision of 1917. With ingenuity and dedication, they may yet recapture some part of that dream, finding new paths and fresh structures to create a happy, just, and secure life.

APPENDIX A   ABBREVIATIONS KEY

ABM   Antiballistic missile system

A.M.O. Commune   Automotive Workers of Moscow Commune; well-known experiment in communal living established in the 1920s–1930s

CIS   Commonwealth of Independent States; association formed in December 1991 to replace U.S.S.R.

F.R.G.   Federal Republic of Germany

G.D.R.   German Democratic Republic

GKO   State Defense Committee; established during World War II to coordinate the entire war effort

Gulag   System of correctional-labor and concentration camps run by secret police

ICBM   Intercontinental ballistic missile

IMF   International Monetary Fund

KD (Kadet)   Constitutional Democratic party; liberal political group in Russia, 1905–1918

KGB   Committee of State Security; name of secret police organization after 1953

LEF   *Left Front of Art*; revolutionary modernist cultural movement and journal founded in 1920s by Vladimir Mayakovsky

Left SR   Radical wing of Socialist Revolutionary party that split off in the fall of 1917

MMM   Russian joint-stock venture; collapsed in August 1994

MRC   Military Revolutionary Committee; formed in October 1917 by Mensheviks; charged with defending Petrograd; used by Trotsky as a tool in Bolsheviks' takeover

MTS   Machine-tractor station; station set up by Stalin from which *kolkhozes* could hire agricultural machinery and request agronomic advice

NATO   North Atlantic Treaty Organization; Western mutual-assistance alliance forged in 1949

NEP   New Economic Policy; 1921 retreat from socialism and end of "war communism"; featured free trade and some privatization to alleviate economic problems

NKVD	People's Commissariat of Internal Affairs; controlled secret police, 1933–1953
OGPU	*Cheka's* successor as secret police organization, 1921–1933
RAPP	Russian Association of Proletarian Writers; literary watchdog during First Five Year Plan; called for literature that focused on industrialization and collectivization
RSDLP	Russian Social Democratic Labor party; the first Marxist party, founded in 1898; split into Mensheviks and Bolsheviks after 1906
SALT	Strategic Arms Limitations Talks
SDI	Strategic Defense Initiative; U.S. president Ronald Reagan's proposed program of space-based defense
SLBM	Submarine-launched ballistic missile
SR	Socialist Revolutionary party; chief rival of Russian Marxist party at turn of the century; members active in 1917 Revolution and in Provisional Government
START	Strategic Arms Reduction Talks
U.S.S.R.	Union of Soviet Socialist Republics

APPENDIX B   RUSSIAN AND SOVIET LEADERS

LAST TSARS OF THE RUSSIAN EMPIRE
Alexander I 1801–1825
Nicholas I 1825–1855
Alexander II 1855–1881
Alexander III 1881–1894
Nicholas II 1894–1917
   wife Alexandra
   heir Alexis

IMPORTANT TSARIST PRIME MINISTERS
Sergei Witte 1905–1906
Peter Stolypin 1906–1911

EARLY MARXIST LEADERS
George Plekhanov
Vladimir Lenin (Ulianov) *(later a Bolshevik)*
   wife Nadezhda Krupskaya
Leon Trotsky (Bronstein) *(later a Bolshevik)*
Alexandra Kollontai *(later a Bolshevik)*
Fedor Dan *(later a Menshevik)*
Pavel Axelrod *(later a Menshevik)*
Victor Chernov *(later a Socialist Revolutionary)*

KEY NON-MARXISTS IN THE 1917 REVOLUTION AND THE 1918–1921 CIVIL WAR
Georgy Lvov, first prime minister, Provisional Government
Alexander Kerensky, chief leader, Provisional Government
Paul Miliukov, Kadet leader, foreign minister, Provisional
   Government
General Lars Kornilov, leader of abortive putsch, August 1917
Admiral Alexander Kolchak, White leader in Siberia
General Anton Denikin, White leader in south Russia
General Nikolai Iudenich, White leader in northwest Russia
General Peter Vrangel, White leader in Crimea

MAJOR RUSSIAN POETS OF THE 1920S AND 1930S
Anna Akhmatova
Alexander Blok
Sergei Esenin

Osip Mandelshtam
Vladimir Mayakovsky
Boris Pasternak

KEY BOLSHEVIKS OF THE 1920S
Vladimir Lenin
Joseph Stalin

Left Opposition
Leon Trotsky
Leo Kamenev
Grigory Zinoviev
Evgeny Preobrazhensky

Right Deviation
Nikolai Bukharin
Alexei Rykov
Mikhail Tomsky

LEADERS OF THE SOVIET UNION
(ALSO HEADS OF COMMUNIST PARTY)
Vladimir Lenin 1917–1924
Joseph Stalin 1924–1953
Georgy Malenkov 1953
Nikita Khrushchev 1953–1964
Leonid Brezhnev 1964–1982
Yury Andropov 1982–1984
Konstantin Chernenko 1984–1985
Mikhail Gorbachev 1985–1991

IMPORTANT POST-SOVIET LEADERS
Boris Yeltsin, president, Russian Republic
Yegor Gaidar, chief economic reformer, Russian Republic
Victor Chernomyrdin, prime minister, Russian Republic

Leonid Kravchuk, president, Ukrainian Republic, 1991–1994
Leonid Kuchma, president, Ukrainian Republic, 1994–

Nursultan Nazarbayev, president, Kazakhstan, 1991–
Edvard Shevardnadze, president, Georgian Republic, 1992–
Gedar Aliyev, president, Azerbaijan Republic, 1993–

APPENDIX C   CHRONOLOGY

NINETEENTH CENTURY

1855	Alexander II becomes tsar
1861	Private serfs emancipated
1864–1871	Era of "Great Reforms"
1870	Lenin born
1876	University courses for women established
1877–1878	Russo-Turkish War
Mid-1878	Congress of Berlin
1879	Stalin born
March 1881	Alexander II assassinated; Alexander III becomes tsar
1891–1894	Franco-Russian alliance formed
1894	Alexander III dies; Nicholas II succeeds him
1895	Russian Women's Philanthropic Society established
May 27, 1896	Nicholas II coronated
1898	First Marxist party, RSDLP, founded

TWENTIETH CENTURY

1900–1914	"Silver Age" of the arts
July 1903	Second Congress of RSDLP (in Europe)
January 1904	Russo-Japanese War begins
1904–1906	Revolution of 1905

1905

January 22	Bloody Sunday
June	*Potemkin* mutiny
September	Russo-Japanese War ends; Treaty of Portsmouth signed
October 30	Nicholas II issues October Manifesto
December	Armed uprising of Moscow Soviet suppressed

1906–1914

May 1906	Fundamental Laws adopted; First Duma opens

1906–1910	"Stolypin reforms" in agriculture
1907	Triple Entente formed
February–June 1907	Second Duma
July 1907	Stolypin changes electoral law
1908	Founding of Ballet Russe; Bosnian crisis; First All-Russian Women's Congress
1909	*Vekhi* published
September 1911	Stolypin assassinated
1912	Stalin co-opted to Bolshevik Party Central; Stalin aids Lenin on nationality policy
August 1914	World War I begins

1917

March 8–12	February Revolution in Petrograd (February 23–27, old calendar)
March 12	Provisional Government formed; Soviet elected
March 15	Nicholas II abdicates; Order Number 1 issued
April 16–17	Lenin returns and issues April Theses
Early May	Provisional Government faces first crisis; moderate socialists join cabinet
June	First All-Russian Congress of Soviets
July 16–18	"July Days"
August	"Kornilov Affair"
September	Bolsheviks win majorities in Petrograd and Moscow soviets
October 23	Bolshevik leaders vote for insurrection
November 4–5	Trotsky's Military Revolutionary Committee asserts control over most of Petrograd garrison
November 7–8	Bolshevik or October Revolution (October 25–26, old calendar)
November 8	Second All-Russian Congress of Soviets gathers; Lenin forms Soviet government, issues decrees on peace and land rights
Late November	Elections to Constituent Assembly
December	Armistice with Germany and Austria-Hungary set; Finland asserts independence; anti-Bolshevik Volunteer Army formed; *Cheka* established

1918

January	Soviet government disbands Constituent Assembly; decrees separation of church and state; issues Declaration of Rights of Toiling and Exploited Peoples; Ukrainian *Rada* declares independence
March	Treaty of Brest-Litovsk
March–June	British and American troops move into north Russia
May	Caucasian states declare independence; Czechoslovak Corps seizes Trans-Siberian Railroad; anti-Bolshevik governments form in Urals and Siberia; Lenin abandons economic policy of state capitalism, institutes centralized control, and launches "war communism"
July	Adoption of first Soviet Constitution; Left SR uprisings; fall of Baku Commune; movement of U.S. and Japanese troops into Vladivostok
August	Assassination attempt on Lenin; Whites' seizing of Kazan; White victories in south Russia
September	Red and White Terrors clash
November	Coup makes Kolchak head of Siberian government; World War I ends

1919

	Baltic states establish independence; civil war erupts in Ukraine and Crimea.
February	U.S. troops withdraw from north Russia
March	French-led intervention at Odessa; Bullitt peace mission to Russia; founding of Comintern; establishing of Politburo by Eighth Party Congress
April	Kolchak offensive threatens Moscow
June	Kolchak advance checked
July	Versailles peace treaties (Russia excluded)
October	White armies under Denikin threaten Moscow
November	White armies under Iudenich threaten Petrograd

December	Denikin turned back, Kolchak defeated

1920

January	U.S. troops withdraw from Siberia
March	Ninth Party Congress creates *nomenklatura* system, expands Secretariat; Democratic Centralists and Workers' Opposition emerge
March–April	Bolsheviks establish Soviet rule in Azerbaijan
April–October	Soviet-Polish War
June–November	White forces in Crimea under Vrangel defeated
September	Congress of Toiling Peoples of the East
November–December	Bolsheviks establish Soviet rule in Armenia
1920–1924	*Basmachi* revolt in Central Asia

1921

February	Red Army invades Georgia; establishes Soviet rule
March	Treaty of Riga (formal peace with Poland); Kronstadt Revolt; Tenth Party Congress's approval of NEP and endorsement of resolution "On Party Unity"
1921–1922	Widespread famine; help from ARA; birth of literacy campaign; activity by *zhenotdels*

1922

April	Stalin becomes general secretary of Party; Treaty of Rapallo between Soviet Russia and Germany signed
May	Lenin's first stroke; Soviet government's arrest of Patriarch Tikhon and support of "Living Church"
December	Soviet Union formed in practice; Lenin drafts less Russocentric nationality policy, draws up "Testament"
Early 1920s	Western powers (except United States) recognize Soviet Russia; Party tolerates experimentation in culture but increases its control and censorship

1923

March	Lenin's third, incapacitating stroke
March–April	Twelfth Party Congress, at which Trotsky fails to press Lenin's attack on Stalin
July	Constitution of U.S.S.R. approved
1923–1925	Triumvirate of Stalin, Zinoviev, Kamenev runs Party and state

1924

January	Formal ratification of Constitution of U.S.S.R.; death of Lenin; birth of Lenin cult
May	Thirteenth Party Congress, at which Stalin survives discussion of Lenin's "Testament"
November	Trotsky publicly attacks Zinoviev and Kamenev
January 1925	Trotsky dismissed as minister of war
1925–1927	Debate over how to industrialize; development of Stalin's theme of "socialism in one country"
Mid-1926–1927	United Opposition of Trotsky, Zinoviev, and Kamenev versus Stalin and Rightists

1927

July	Acting head of Orthodox church Sergei agrees to complete submission of church to government
Summer	"War scare" after breaking relations with Britain
Fall	Insufficient grain collected from peasants
November	Soviet Union proposes universal disarmament
December	Fifteenth Party Congress confirms Stalin's expulsion of Zinoviev and Trotsky from Party

1928

January–February	Stalin travels to Urals and Siberia, where he urges forcible grain collection
May	Trial of "Shakhty" engineers
August	Industrialization launched through moderate-growth variant of First Five Year Plan
October	Public attacks on Right Deviation begin
1928–1931	Cultural revolution

1929

April	High-growth variant of Five Year Plan incorporated
July	State sets compulsory grain deliveries, accelerates collectivization
November	Stalin's article, "Year of the Great Turn," written; Bukharin ousted from Politburo, Rights beaten
December	All-out collectivization and "liquidation of kulaks as a class" approved; Stalin cult begins on his fiftieth birthday
1929–1930	Party dominates Academy of Sciences
1929–1932	Party conducts campaign against religion
March 1930	Collectivization drive briefly halted after *Pravda* article "Dizzy with Success"
March 1931	Stalin delivers his "beating" speech
1931–1932	Nonaggression pacts with Poland, France signed; tension with Japan mounts after its occupation of Manchuria; Stalin forces German Communists to attack German Social Democrats

1932

	Party-controlled Union of Soviet Writers created; artistic doctrine of "socialist realism" asserted; internal passports instituted; appeal for moderation from Riutin and other Party secretaries circulated
November	Stalin's wife, Alliliuyeva, dies
December	First Five Year Plan completed in four years
1932–1933	Famine strikes Ukraine and south Russia
Early 1930s	Non-Russian minorities persecuted
Early 1933	Nazis come to power in Germany
November 1933	United States recognizes Soviet Union
1933–1937	Second Five Year Plan

1934

	Soviet policy of collective security begins; Popular Fronts against Fascism form; U.S.S.R. joins League of Nations; Stalin sets Party line in history

	January	Seventeenth Party Congress, at which Kirov is acclaimed
	December	Kirov assassinated
1935		First trial of Zinoviev and Kamenev, charged with conspiracy in Kirov's murder; treaty of mutual assistance with France; beginning of Stakhanovite movement
1936		
	August	Second trial of Zinoviev and Kamenev
	September	Yezhov appointed head of NKVD
	December	"New" Stalin Constitution adopted
	1936–1938	Soviet Union sends aid to Loyalists in Spanish Civil War
1937		
	January	Trial of Right politicians
	Summer	Height of purges known as *Yezhovshchina*
	1937–1938	Armed clashes with Japanese forces on eastern borders
1938		
	January	Khrushchev becomes first Party secretary for Moscow region
	March	Trial of Bukharin, Rykov, and twenty others
	September	Munich Conference, at which Britain and France abandon Czechoslovakia to Hitler
	November	Yezhov fired, replaced by Beria
	1938–1941	Third Five Year Plan, aborted by World War II
1939		
	March	Eighteenth Party Congress, at which Stalin signals his readiness to deal with Hitler
	May	Molotov replaces Litvinov as foreign minister
	August	German-Soviet Nonaggression Pact
	September	World War II opens with German attack on Poland; Soviet forces occupy eastern Poland
	November	U.S.S.R. attacks Finland

1940

March	Finns defeated, yield territory but retain independence
June	Germany defeats France; Hitler eager to attack U.S.S.R.
June–July	Stalin incorporates Baltic states, Bessarabia, northern Bukovina into U.S.S.R.
August	Stalinist agent murders Trotsky in exile in Mexico
November	Molotov visits Berlin for fruitless talks
December	Hitler approves final plans for U.S.S.R. invasion

1941

April	Soviet-Japanese neutrality pact made; Stalin ignores warnings of imminent Nazi attack
June 22	Operation Barbarossa (German invasion)
June 30	GKO formed to direct Soviet war effort
July	Anglo-Soviet alliance forged against Hitler-Mussolini
August	Hitler's indecision delays drive to Moscow
September	Disastrous Soviet defeat at Kiev; beginning of siege of Leningrad
October	Operation Typhoon (German attack on Moscow)
December	Red Army stops Germans on outskirts of Moscow
1941–1944	Stalin deports Volga Germans, Chechens, and other minorities whom he deems unreliable to Central Asia and Siberia

1942

January	Grand Alliance of U.S.S.R., Britain, and United States formed; Stalin adheres to Atlantic Charter
September	Germans assault Stalingrad

1943

January–February	Germans defeated at Stalingrad
April	Germans discover NKVD massacre at Katyn Forest

July–August	Tank battle at Kursk
November	Teheran Conference
1943–1945	U.S. Lend-Lease supplies aid Soviet war effort; captured Soviet general Vlasov forms anti-Communist movement and army under Nazis' aegis

1944

January	Siege of Leningrad lifted
June	D-Day; U.S.-British forces establish second front in France
August–October	Abortive Warsaw uprising

1945

February	Yalta Conference
April–May	Battle of Berlin
May 9	Germany surrenders; war in Europe ends
July	Potsdam Conference
August	U.S.S.R. enters war against Japan
September	Japan surrenders
February 1946	In speech to public Stalin calls for renewed sacrifices
1946–1950	Fourth Five Year Plan
1946–1948	*Zhdanovshchina* cultural purge with antisemitic overtones

1947

March	Truman Doctrine enunciated
June	Marshall Plan
September	Cominform organized under Soviet auspices

1948

February	Communist takeover of Czechoslovakia
Spring	Soviet-Yugoslavia split
June	Berlin blockade

1949

September	Soviet Union explodes its first atomic bomb
December	Communists under Mao take power in China

1950

February	Sino-Soviet alliance
June	Beginning of Korean War
1951–1955	Fifth Five Year Plan
November 1952	Nineteenth Party Congress

1953

January	"Doctors' plot" announced
March 5	Stalin dies
June	Beria arrested
July	Long-term armistice reached in Korean War
September	Khrushchev named Party first secretary
Mid–1953	*Gulag* prisoners revolt
1953–1954	First political prisoners released

1954

1954–1956	"Thaw" in arts and culture
	Khrushchev transfers Crimea to Ukrainian Republic, begins "virgin lands" project

1955

Soviet Union explodes hydrogen bomb; peace treaty with Austria signed, Soviet occupation ended; Warsaw Pact formed; Soviet government repeals 1936 ban on abortion; Khrushchev visits Yugoslavia and Asia; Gorbachev graduates from Moscow State University

1956

February	Khrushchev delivers "secret" speech to Twentieth Party Congress on crimes of Stalin, prepares foreign-policy report enunciating doctrine of "noninevitability of war"
October	Polish reformers defy Khrushchev
October 23–November 4	Hungarian revolt
1956–1959	U.S.S.R. opens to foreign contacts

1957

February	Khrushchev establishes regional economic councils (*sovnarkhozy*)

June	Khrushchev's political foes fail to oust him
October	Soviet Union launches *Sputnik,* world's first space satellite
1958–1960	Abortive reform of Soviet education

1958

March	Khrushchev becomes prime minister as well as Party first secretary
October	Khrushchev makes first attempt to force Allies to hand over Berlin to the East Germans

1959

1959–1964	Khrushchev wages campaign against religion
1959–1966	Khrushchev introduces new Seven Year Plan
Late 1950s	Rift with Communist China grows
	Albania rejects Moscow's tutelage; Khrushchev visits the United States

1960

	Soviet Union downs U.S. U-2 spy plane; Soviet-U.S. summit canceled

1961

April	Soviet Union sends first man into space, Yuri Gagarin
June–August	Berlin crisis leads to erection of Berlin Wall
November	Twenty-Second Party Congress decides to remove Stalin's body from Lenin's tomb

1962

June	Riots break out in Novocherkassk over high food prices
October	Cuban missile crisis
November	Khrushchev divides Party units into industrial and agricultural sections

1963

	United States and Soviet Union agree on partial ban of nuclear weapons tests, establish "hot line" between Washington and Moscow
November 1964	Khrushchev deposed by other Party leaders
1965	End of Khrushchev's reorganizations and

	antireligious campaign; new policy of "trust in cadres"; first public demands for religious freedom
1965–1966	Liberman economic reforms initiated
1966	Sinyavsky-Daniel trial takes place; U.S.S.R. proposes Europewide security meeting
1966–1968	Chinese Cultural Revolution
1967	U.S.S.R.'s Arab clients lose war with Israel
1968	Dissident journal *Chronicle of Current Events* appears; divorce laws eased
August	U.S.S.R.–East European allies invade Czechoslovakia
September	Brezhnev Doctrine announced
Late 1960s	Agitation to clean up Lake Baikal begins
1970–1971	U.S.S.R.-West agree on Berlin and Soviet peace treaty with Germany
1972	U.S.S.R. and United States sign ABM and SALT I treaties; Party leaders in Ukraine and Georgia fired
1973	Brezhnev's name listed first among Party elite
1974	Solzhenitsyn forced into exile
August 1975	Helsinki Accords signed
1976	Brezhnev suffers stroke but still rules; dissidents form "Helsinki Watch" committees to monitor human-rights violations in U.S.S.R.; U.S. president Carter criticizes U.S.S.R.'s human-rights record
1977	Revised Constitution approved
1978	Marxist revolution in Afghanistan; Soviet influence in Ethiopia, Somalia, Angola; street protests in Tbilisi to uphold Georgian language
1979	SALT II signed but not ratified
December	U.S.S.R. invades Afghanistan

1980		U.S. boycotts Olympics, embargoes Soviet grain; Solidarity movement in Poland forms; Sakharov put under house arrest in Gorky; Gorbachev promoted to Politburo
1981		U.S. Reagan administration urges crusade against "evil empire" of U.S.S.R.; Polish general Jaruzelski crushes Solidarity
1982		Brezhnev dies; Andropov succeeds him
	February 1983	Andropov's health worsens
	February 1984	Andropov dies; Chernenko succeeds him
1985		
	March	Chernenko dies; Gorbachev succeeds him
	June	Antialcohol campaign begins
	November	First Gorbachev-Reagan summit meets, Geneva
1986		First reforms of *perestroika;* "new thinking" introduced in foreign policy
	April	Nuclear disaster at Chernobyl'
	Summer	Beginning of *glasnost'*
	October	Second summit, Reykjavik, Iceland
	December	Sakharov returns to Moscow on Gorbachev's invitation; ethnic riots erupt in Kazakhstan
1987		
	February	Gorbachev calls for filling in "blank spots" in Soviet history
	June	Special Party Conference reluctantly approves Gorbachev's reform policies; Latvians protest on anniversary of their incorporation into U.S.S.R.
	August	Widespread protests break out in Baltic states on anniversary of Nazi-Soviet pact
	November	Yeltsin fired as Moscow Party chief
	December	U.S.S.R. and United States agree on banning intermediate-range nuclear missiles

Late 1987	Gorbachev launches "market socialism" and urges democratization of Soviet institutions
1987–1988	Informal citizens' groups proliferate

1988 Celebrations of millennium of Christianity in Russia

January	Law on State Enterprises
February	Bukharin rehabilitated; ethnic conflict erupts in Nagorno-Karabakh
March	Conservatives sponsor anti-*perestroika* letter by Nina Andreeva
April	Gorbachev announces Soviet intention to withdraw troops from Afghanistan
November	First national movement, *Sajudis,* forms in Lithuania
December	New legislative system of Congress of People's Deputies approved; Gorbachev gives major non-Marxist speech to UN

1989 Jewish emigration freely permitted; popular fronts form in Baltic republics, Moldova, Caucasian republics; recurrent demonstrations erupt in Baltic region; Khrushchev's "secret" speech and secret protocol to Nazi-Soviet pact published

February	U.S.S.R. withdraws last troops from Afghanistan
March	First nationwide free elections since 1917 to choose Congresses of People's Deputies
April	Bloody suppression of riots in Tbilisi fires Georgian nationalism
May	Gorbachev's visit to Beijing; semifree elections in Poland
July	Miners strike in Siberia
August	Non-Communist government takes power in Poland
November	East Germany collapses; Berlin Wall dismantled
December	"Velvet" revolution in Czechoslovakia; bloody overthrow of Ceausescu in Romania

1990   Gorbachev wins Nobel Peace Prize;
                                    Gorbachev agrees to German reunificiation;
                                    Rukh emerges as powerful nationalist
                                    movement in Ukraine

        February   Nationalists win control of Supreme Soviets
                                    in Baltic states

        March   Lithuanians assert independence in principle;
                                    end of Communist Party monopoly
                                    approved; Congress of People's Deputies
                                    elects Gorbachev as president of U.S.S.R.

        June   New patriarch Alexei II elected
        September   Shatalin proposes radical economic reform

1991
        January   Soviet units attack nationalists in Vilna
        March   Georgians demand independence; Gorbachev
                                    proposes "union of Soviet states"

        April   Yeltsin elected president of Russian Republic
                                    of U.S.S.R.

        June   START I accords signed
        August 19–21   Moscow coup fails
        August 22   Russian Republic approves new flag
        August–September   Estonia, Latvia, Ukraine, Belarus, Moldova,
                                    and Azerbaijan declare independence

        September   Gorbachev sets up state council of leaders of
                                    republics

        December 1   Ukrainians vote overwhelmingly for indepen-
                                    dence

        December 8   Ukraine, Belarus, and Russia form CIS
        December 25   Gorbachev resigns, U.S.S.R. dissolves, Russia
                                    becomes independent

1992
        January   Gaidar introduces radical economic "shock
                                    therapy" in Russia

        March   Civil war in Georgia culminates in overturn
                                    of Gamsakhurdia and coming to power of
                                    Shevardnadze; Russians in Moldova form
                                    breakaway republic of "Trans-Dniestria"

        May   Civil war erupts in Tadzhikistan

October	Former Communists win elections in Lithuania

1993

January	Leaders of Central Asian states agree in principle on loose union
April	Yeltsin wins referendum on his policies
September	Yeltsin dissolves Russian Supreme Soviet
October 3–4	Yeltsin attacks White House and arrests political foes rebelling within
December	Russian voters elect new legislature Duma, and approve new Constitution; Yeltsin appoints Victor Chernomyrdin new prime minister

1994

January	Russia and United States agree to retarget missiles away from each other; Ukraine agrees to give up its nuclear arsenal
February	Russia sends peacekeepers to Bosnia; Kazakhstan president Nazarbayev visits United States, receives U.S. aid
March	Elections held in Kazakhstan
May	Solzhenitsyn returns to Russia
June	Yeltsin agrees to join NATO's "Partnership for Peace" program
July	New presidents elected in Ukraine, Belarus; new constitution approved in Moldova
September	Chinese head of state visits Moscow
November	President Kuchma of Ukraine visits United States, receives further U.S. aid; elections held in Takzhikistan
December	Yeltsin orders army to attack rebellious region of Chechnya

PHOTOGRAPH CREDITS

Introduction p. 7, Culver Pictures, Inc.; p. 14, United Nations.

Chapter 1 p. 23, Paul Grabbe Archives; p. 26, Victoria & Albert Museum; p. 38, The Granger Collection; p. 43, Private Collection. Photo courtesy of Endeavour Group UK; p. 50, Stock Montage, Inc.; p. 53, Stock Montage, Inc.

Chapter 2 p. 65, Sovfoto; p. 71, David King Collection; p. 73, Museum of Modern Art/Film Still Archive; p. 81, David King Collection, London; p. 84, State Archive of Film and Photographic Documents, St. Petersburg. Photo courtesy of Endeavour Group UK; p. 95, Culver Pictures, Inc.

Chapter 3 p. 109, David King Collection, London; p. 112, David King Collection; p. 117, Hulton Deutsch Collection Limited; p. 123, David King Collection; p. 134, UPI/Bettmann; p. 137, David King Collection.

Chapter 4 p. 155, State Archive of Film and Photographic Documents, St. Petersburg. Photo courtesy of Endeavour Group UK; p. 162, Sovfoto; p. 164, Rodney Sprigg. Collection/Hoover Institution Archives; p. 180, F. Sokolov. Collection/Hoover Institution Archives; p. 186, Sovfoto; p. 187, Sovfoto.

Chapter 5 p. 200, David King Collection, London; p. 214, The Bettmann Archive; p. 216, Novosti from Sovfoto; p. 220, ITAR-TASS/Sovfoto; p. 225, Poster Collection. Collection/Hoover Institution Archives; p. 228, Novosti from Sovfoto.

Chapter 6 p. 237, Stock Montage, Inc.; p. 245, The Bettmann Archive; p. 252, ITAR-TASS/Sovfoto; p. 265, Novosti Photo Library, London; p. 267, Novosti Photo Library, London; p. 268, Slava Katamidze Collection. Photo courtesy of Endeavour Group UK.

Chapter 7 p. 282, Leo Poliakov, from *Russia: A Portrait*. By permission of Farrar, Straus & Giroux; p. 289, David King Collection, London; p. 293, Poster Collection. Collection/Hoover Institution Archives; p. 300, *History Today Magazine*; p. 309, RIA-Novosti/Sovfoto; p. 314, David King Collection, London.

Chapter 8 p. 333, Ullstein Bilderdienst; p. 341, Vladimir Nikitin Collection, St. Petersburg. Photo courtesy of Endeavour Group UK; p. 344, David King Collection, London; p. 348 ITAR-TASS/Sovfoto; p. 349, UPI/Bettmann; p. 359, UPI/Bettmann

Chapter 9   p. 378, UPI/Bettmann Newsphotos; p. 391, UPI/Bettmann; p. 394, Novosti Photo Library, London; p. 405, UPI/Bettmann; p. 407, UPI/ Bettmann.

Chapter 10   p. 427, AP/Wide World Photos; p. 435, Steve McCurry/ Magnum Photos; p. 437 (left), from *Russia: A Portrait*, by Leo Poliakov. Reproduced by permission of Farrar, Straus & Giroux; p. 437 (right), John Launois/Black Star; p. 451, Sovfoto; p. 451, ITAR-TASS/Sovfoto; p. 466, Pace/Black Star.

Chapter 11   p. 468, Novosti Photo Library, London; p. 476, Novosti/Sygma; p. 488, Sygma; p. 495, Pascal le Segretain/Sygma; p. 500, Reuters/Bettmann; p. 501, Reuters/Bettmann.

Chapter 12   p. 512, Robert Wallis/SABA; p. 517, ITAR-TASS/Sovfoto; p. 521, Reuters/Bettmann; p. 525, Reuters/Bettmann, p. 537, ITAR-TASS/ Sovfoto; p. 553, Reuters/Bettmann.

GLOSSARY

agrogorods Khrushchev's 1951 planned agricultural cities consisting of clusters of collective farms; blocked by Stalin

aktivisti activists in the Stalinist collectivization drive

apparatchiks Party bureaucrats

artel standard form of *kolkhoz* in which peasant members' land, large livestock, and tools were pooled, and in which farmers jointly worked the land and cared for animals

ataman a Cossack military leader

barin noble serf-owner

Basmachi armed bands of Muslim resisters who fought Soviet rule with guerrilla warfare from 1918–mid-1920s

blatnaia shkola a school where influence got one's child admitted

Bolshevik member of Lenin's radical wing of the Russian Marxist party

boyars traditional noble families, fifteenth through seventeenth centuries, who resisted centralized rule by tsars

Bund organization founded in 1897 by Jews in Russia to protect Jewish autonomy

Cheka Extraordinary Commission to Combat Counterrevolution, Sabotage, and Speculation; Soviet secret police formed by Bolsheviks in 1917

Comintern Communist International, 1919–1943; Moscow-dominated organization to encourage and guide pro-Leninist Communist parties around the world

dacha country cottages owned by elite members of Soviet society

Dashnaks Armenian nationalists

Dashnaktsutiun Armenian Revolutionary Federation; nationalist organization founded in 1890 in the Caucasus

détente reduction in tensions between the U.S.S.R. and the United States, 1960s–1970s

druzhiny citizen assistants to city police; established by Khrushchev in early 1960s

duma Russian semi-representative legislature, 1906–1917; revived in December 1993 as national legislative assembly for democratic Russia

frontoviki Russian soldiers evacuated from World War I front lines for retraining, recuperation, or rest; often radical element in Russian cities during 1917 Revolution

gensek general secretary of Soviet Communist party

glasnost'   openness; Gorbachev's policy of open discussion of problems and freedom of creative and intellectual activity, within limits

Gosplan   State Planning Agency

hadj   Muslim ritual pilgrimage to Mecca

Izvestiia   literally, news; name of official Soviet government newspaper

kolkhozes   collective farms established by Stalin

Komsomol   Communist League of Youth; organization in which youths from age seventeen to early thirties could serve as adjuncts of the Party

kulaks   Party's epithet for avaricious and well-to-do villagers

Kuomintang   Chinese nationalist movement; headed by Chiang Kai-shek

lebensraum   living space; Hitler's goal of expanding to the east

likbezy   tutorials or circles to spread literacy

lubki   small prints depicting folk or religious themes, collected by peasants

lubochnaia   short literary works recounting religious or folk themes or romance and adventure; popular among peasants around the turn of the century

magnitizdat   illegal artistic recordings and tapes

Mein Kampf   *My Struggle*; book written by Hitler while in prison that outlined his views and plans, including conquest of Soviet Union

Menshevik   member of moderate wing of the Russian Marxist party; members active in 1917 Revolution and in Provisional Government

mir   village commune; also means *peace* and *world* in Russian

Mir iskusstva   The World of Art; 1898–1910 cultural movement that melded artistic, written and visual interests and modes

Mussavat   Azerbaijani national movement

muzhik   peasant

narod   the Russian people as a whole

nomenklatura   system by which Party members were matched to key jobs in the Party, government, and other institutions of Soviet society

Novyi mir   *New World*; journal founded in 1950s championing cultural freedom and writers' personal points of view

Ogonyok   *Little Flame;* Soviet journal that propounded *glasnost'* after 1987

Okhrana   tsarist special or secret police to monitor antigovernment or dissident activity

Orgburo   Organization Bureau of the Bolshevik (later Communist) Party; handled party administration

Osttruppen   East troops (German); non-Russian brigades from German-occupied territories used by Hitler's forces

Pamyat' Memory; 1980s and 1990s organization promoting Russian chauvinism and attacking "Jewish-Masonic conspirators"

partiinost' Party-mindedness, putting the Party's interests first

perestroika restructuring; Gorbachev's overall reform effort but primarily his reorganizing the economy

Politburo Political Bureau of the Bolshevik (later Communist) party; set party policy

Pravda *Truth;* name of official Bolshevik (later Communist) newspaper

Proletkult Association for Proletarian Culture and Education; group that sponsored workshops for proletarian writers, palaces of culture, and workers' clubs, 1918 through early 1920s

putsch attempted *coup*

rabfaks schools for workers sponsored by universities

Rabkrin Workers' and Peasants' Inspectorate; organization that audited state operations and verified execution of governmental directives; headed by Stalin in 1919

Rabotnitsa *Woman Worker;* special publication for women produced by Bolsheviks

Rada Ukrainian Central Council; formed in March 1917; initially focused on cultural and educational issues; later urged independence for Ukraine and formed separate government in 1918 and 1919

refuseniks Jews in the U.S.S.R. whose applications for emigration were delayed or denied

Rukh Ukrainian national cultural movement that grew increasingly nationalist in the early 1990s

Sajudis Lithuanian nationalist coalition formed in the late 1980s

samizdat literally, self-publication; circulation by hand of Soviet writers' non–Party line manuscripts, 1960s–1980s

Secretariat executive and administrative central body of Bolshevik (later Communist) party

sosloviia nineteenth-century population categories, comparable to premodern European estates

soviet council of elected representatives; militant organization established by Russian workers in 1905; revived in 1917 and became constitutional structure of Communist state after 1917

sovkhozes state farms favored by the Party as socialist "land factories," in which farmers are paid wages

sovnarkhozy regional economic councils established in 1957 by Khrushchev to strengthen local involvement in decision making

Sovnarkom Council of People's Commissars; cabinet formed by Lenin in November 1917 to direct new government based on soviets executive body of Soviet government in 1920s and 1930s until replaced by Council of Ministers

Sputnik   first space satellite; launched by Soviet Union in October 1957

Stavka   general headquarters of the Russian and Soviet armed forces in World Wars I and II

stilyagi   1950s youngsters who defied Soviet authorities with garish clothing and outrageous behavior

terem   special living quarters in which upper-class Russian women were segregated until the eighteenth century

tolkachi   expediters used by Soviet factory administrators to ensure timely delivery of materials and hiring of able workers

untermenschen   subhumans (German), Nazi epithet for Slavs

Vekhi   *Signposts;* 1909 collection of articles refuting the political and ideological assumptions of the radical intelligentsia; published by Christian philosophers, liberals, and former Marxists

verkhushka   members of the elite

Vikzhel   trade union of railway workers who demanded in November 1917 that Lenin's new government be transformed into an all-socialist organization

v narod   going to the people; late nineteenth-century rural reform movement led by students and intellectuals

volost   peasants' local administrative unit, late nineteenth century

vozhd'   leader

Wehrmacht   war machine; German armed forces

zemskii nachalnik   rural position of land captain, installed in 1889 to oversee peasant affairs at the district level

zemstvos   local self-governing bodies after 1860s to supervise health, education, and welfare

Zhdanovshchina   drive led by Andrei Zhdanov to restore "correct" views in Soviet cultural life, 1946–1948

zhenotdels   commissions on women's affairs attached to Party bodies at all levels

zhensektory   women's sections within Party structure that replaced terminated women's departments (*zhenotdels*)

zhensovety   governmental women's councils restored by feminist groups in early 1990s

Zionism   Europewide movement to establish a Jewish homeland in Palestine

INDEX